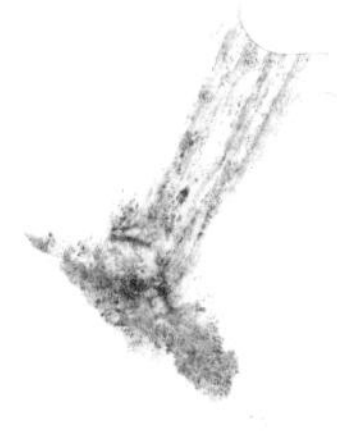

Winds from the North

Winds from the North

Tewa Origins and Historical Anthropology

Scott G. Ortman

THE UNIVERSITY OF UTAH PRESS
Salt Lake City

The Defiance House Man colophon is a registered trademark of the University of Utah Press. It is based upon a four-foot-tall, Ancient Puebloan pictograph (late PIII) near Glen Canyon, Utah.

Library of Congress Cataloging-in-Publication Data
Ortman, Scott G., 1970-
Winds from the north : Tewa origins and historical anthropology / Scott G. Ortman.
p. cm.
Includes bibliographical references and index.
ISBN 978-1-60781-172-5 (cloth : alk. paper)
ISBN 978-1-64769-028-1 (pbk: alk. paper)
ISBN 978-1-60781-992-9 (ebook)

1. Tewa Indians—Origin. 2. Tewa Indians—Migrations. 3. Tewa Indians—Antiquities. 4. Tewa language—History. 5. Mesa Verde National Park (Colo.)—Antiquities. I. Title.
E99.T35O75 2012
978.9004'97494—dc23

2011038061

Printed and bound in the United States.

For Tito,
who laid down my road.

Contents

Foreword

Owéy hae ba ho?, p'ingpiye de thaa waeng....
Long ago, far to the north they lived....

So begins the traditional Tewa story of emergence. It is not just a story describing emergence and migration, but a story that fills the Tewa world with meaning; meaning that is as relevant today as it was centuries ago. Just as this story provided guidance and a sense of history in the far past, so it does today. Weathering the ages, this story is a road sign for the path that stretches unabated into the future.

Non-Tewa scholars have previously minimized the importance of language and cultural traditions that carry on today as a source for understanding the past. To these scholars, the emergence story was considered a myth transfigured by generations of retelling and thus of little value. It was assumed that modern cultures and traditions could provide little guidance to understanding the past. Scott Ortman, on the other hand, has made Tewa culture and language an important cornerstone of his study of Tewa ethnogenesis and the connections of Tewa people to the Mesa Verde region. While looking at classic archaeological evidence, Ortman hunts for unique language metaphors pinpointing possible relationships. He has even assisted with the resurrection of morphology as a tool for looking at genetic relationships between groups of people. Through detailed charts and striking maps, Ortman painstakingly shows the migration of people. Altogether, Ortman constructs a mountain of evidence to prove what Tewa people have known for generations.

This does not in any way discredit the incredible volume of work that Ortman has invested in this book. In fact, the unique melding of Tewa language and culture to archaeological evidence has provided a fresh and more holistic view of the Tewa past. It is a view that simultaneously has value to Tewa people, archaeologists, and anthropologists. When Tewa language, history, and cosmology can be matched to archaeological evidence, the picture of the past becomes even clearer. Suddenly, the vibrant voices of Tewa today can be heard echoing into the past atop rubble mounds in southwestern Colorado. No longer are those voices the visceral experiences of only Tewa people, but they are also given credence in the outside world. Like the Tewa story of emergence, this book provides many road signs for greater understanding along the path that leads into the future.

Porter Swentzell
Santa Clara Pueblo, New Mexico

Acknowledgments

The seeds of this book were first planted in 1993, when I was a research intern at the Crow Canyon Archaeological Center. Between then and now, many people have helped it grow. Bill Lipe played a formative role by encouraging me to ask "why" questions the first summer we worked together, by engaging with my early analyses of metaphor in language and material culture, and most recently, by introducing me to the literature on Tewayó. Bruce Bradley also deserves special mention for inspiring me to investigate links between P'oseyemu and the Mesa Verde migration many years ago. Betsy Brandt deserves many thanks for introducing me to cognitive and historical linguistics, and for her long-term support of my work in this area. Kurt Anschuetz and Dick Ford have also been extremely generous with their time, knowledge, and relationships with Tewa community leaders. I could never have learned Tewa Basin archaeology as quickly or as well without their help. Finally, I might never have taken the first steps in this journey if Tito Naranjo had not encouraged me to pursue the work I felt was most important with an open, sensitive, and respectful heart.

Many others have contributed to my work in substantial ways. George Cowgill helped me get comfortable with quantitative methods and taught me to generalize my specific ideas into methods that could be applied more broadly; Mark Varien taught me how to develop arguments that link archaeological evidence to research questions; Jane Buikstra and Chris Stojanowski introduced me to the method and theory of biodistance analysis; Rich Wilshusen encouraged me to think big and push the envelope; and Keith Kintigh provided a terrific role model and sage advice. Finally, Michelle Hegmon, my graduate advisor at Arizona State University, helped me formulate a coherent way of studying a massive and complex problem, and helped me present my ideas in ways that I hope will resonate with others.

Over the years, many teachers, fellow students, and peers have helped me define and refine the ideas and arguments presented in this book. The list includes Miguel Aguilera, Wes Bernardini, Bob Bolin, Andrew Duff, Sam Duwe, Sev Fowles, Brandon Gabler, Donna Glowacki, Colin Greer, Jeremy Kulisheck, Stephanie Kulow, Cathryn Meeghan, Andrea Parkes, Matt Peeples, Jim Potter, and Ian Robertson. Much of the material presented here was also first tested out on groups of adult participants in Crow Canyon programs. Their feedback on my work has played a larger role than these people will ever know.

A number of researchers helped me compile the archaeological data examined in this study. Mike Adler, Kurt Anschuetz, Jon Driver, Andrew Duff, Brandon Gabler, Brett Hill, John Kantner, Tim Kohler, and Sam Ruscavage-Barz all graciously shared published and unpublished data. In addition, Scott Geister provided data from the New Mexico Cultural Resource Information System; Steve Shackley and Fumi Arakawa assisted with obsidian sourcing; Lou Haecker, Diane Bird, and Minnie Murray provided access to unpublished reports at the Laboratory of Anthropology; and Thomas Ireland, Brad Vierra, and Kurt Anschuetz provided copies of CRM reports from the Tewa Basin. I also thank Tom Windes for directing me to the Tsama Pueblo collection, and Dave Phillips of the Maxwell Museum for allowing Crow Canyon to work with it. Sara Davis, Dona Daugherty, Jamie Merewether, Jonathan Till, Fumi Arakawa, and Ben Bellorado helped me analyze this collection, and Dean Wilson trained all of us in the identification of Northern Rio Grande pottery.

Several individuals assisted in various ways with the linguistic analyses. Andrew Jones and Jackie Dooley at the University of California, Irvine, Karen Carver at the University of Utah, and Sheila Goff and Ellen Zazzarino at the Denver Public Library assisted with archival research. Betsy Brandt and Laurel Watkins provided Kiowa-Tanoan language data from their personal files, obscure references from their personal libraries, and invaluable feedback on the linguistic analyses. Finally, Tessie Naranjo and Porter Swentzell deserve many thanks for checking my analyses of Tewa words and phrases, for helping me learn proper pronunciation, and for supporting my efforts to integrate archaeology and language.

A large number of researchers assisted me in compiling the craniometric database. Nancy Akins, Lane Beck, Cindy Bradley, Cory Breternitz, Jim Cheverud, Debra Martin, John McClelland, Will Pestle, Michael Schillaci, Linda Smith, Maria Smith, and Dave Weaver all graciously shared unpublished data. In addition, Chuck Adams, Diane Bird, Linda Cordell, Shamsi Daneshvari, Ed Evans, Dennis Gilpin, Winston Hurst, Bill Lipe, Khaleel Saba, Kate Spielmann, Christy Turner, Cheryl Weber, David Wilcox, and Richard Wilshusen all provided help with archival searches.

I thank the administration of Crow Canyon Archaeological Center, especially Ricky Lightfoot, Melinda Burdette, Debbie Fish, Dan Mooney, Gayle Prior, and Mark Varien, for allowing me to take several leaves of absence to pursue the Ph.D. from which this book derives. My doctoral studies were also supported by Arizona State University, the National Science Foundation (DDIG-0753828), and the Robert and Florence Lister Fellowship. The dissertation was written while I was a Dissertation Completion Fellow of the American Council of Learned Societies and the Andrew W. Mellon Foundation. During this period Jane Dillard graciously provided a quiet place for me to write.

I completed the process of turning the dissertation into a book as an Omidyar Fellow at the Santa Fe Institute, and the Lightfoot Fellow at Crow Canyon. I wish to thank both institutions for giving me the freedom and resources to complete this project. It is important to emphasize that, in addition to slight reorganization and expansion, this book corrects a number of minor errors in the dissertation and thus supersedes it.

In addition to my Ph.D. committee at Arizona State University, Nancy Akins, Eric Blinman, Jane Buikstra, Tim Kohler, R. G. Matson, Bill Merrill, Michael Schillaci, Stephen Shennan, Steven Simms, Rich Wilshusen, and Laurel Watkins have all provided many helpful comments on earlier versions of this work. I also wish to thank Reba Rauch, Don and Catherine Fowler, and the University of Utah Press staff for all their help in shepherding a lengthy and complex manuscript through to publication.

Finally, and most importantly, I thank my mom and dad, wife Gigi, and sons Ian and Ben. I can never fully repay them for their patience and understanding, and could not have completed this project without their love and support.

The Puzzle of Tewa Origins

This book addresses a widespread but underappreciated pattern in human diversity. The human species exhibits biological variation that could only have developed through reduced gene flow between, and independent evolution within, localized mating networks in the past. Most human languages also group into families that imply the spread and diversification of speech communities over time. However, despite these clear indications that descent from common ancestors has been a regular feature of human history, it has often proved difficult to trace the cultural dimension of this process using archaeological evidence. Archaeologists have had great success tracing descent with modification in local archaeological sequences, but attempts to link these sequences, or to relate them to speech communities or biological lineages, have often led to extended and inconclusive debates. Thus, the Indo-European language tree can be laid over the archaeological record of agricultural expansion or the spread of horses and wheels (Anthony 2007; Mallory 1989; Renfrew 1987); debate continues on the relationships between Fremont, Pueblo, and Numic peoples (Madsen and Rhode 1994; Simms 2008); different analyses of the same data lead to opposing conclusions on the cultural phylogeny of Austronesian-speaking settlers in New Guinea (Shennan and Collard 2005; Welsch and Terrell 1992); and the archaeological record does not clearly indicate when and from where Uto-Aztecan languages entered central Mexico (Beekman and Christenson 2003; Cowgill 1992; Dakin and Wichman 2000; Fowler 1983; Hill 2001; Kaufman 2001).

A notorious example of this phenomenon from the U.S. Southwest concerns the relationship between the contemporary Rio Grande Pueblos and earlier peoples of the Mesa Verde region. At AD 1200 the Mesa Verde region of southwestern Colorado and southeastern Utah was the most densely populated portion of the Pueblo world (Hill et al. 2010), but by shortly after AD 1280, this entire population had either died or permanently moved away. The population of the Northern Rio Grande region in north-central New Mexico increased dramatically as the population of the Mesa Verde region declined (Cordell 1979; Cordell et al. 2007; Habicht-Mauche 1993; Kidder 1924), and the linguistic diversity of the present-day Rio Grande Pueblos suggests that they do derive from several, historically distinct groups (Davis 1959, 1979; Reed 1949). Yet Mesa Verde material culture did not reappear in the Northern Rio Grande or anywhere else these people might have moved to (Boyer et al. 2010; Ford et al. 1972; Lakatos 2007; Lipe 2010; Varien 2010), so even though it is generally accepted that the present-day Pueblo Indians are among the descendants of Mesa Verde people, there is no consensus on precisely how, or if, Rio Grande Pueblo groups are related to earlier, Mesa Verde region groups.

In this study I investigate how this particular situation came about by examining the origins of the largest Pueblo group of the Northern Rio Grande. Archaeologists agree that the Tewa people have lived in that portion of the Northern Rio Grande region known as the Tewa Basin from at least the late AD 1200s (Anschuetz 2005; Boyer et al. 2010; Ford et al. 1972; Fowles 2004b; Kohler and Root 2004b; Snead et al. 2004). There is, however, a striking lack of consensus on how this ethnic group formed: some view it as the result of mass migration from the Mesa Verde region (Jeançon 1923; Reed 1949); others view it as resulting from the amalgamation of several groups with distinct prior histories (Cordell 1979; Kidder 1924; Habicht-Mauche 1993); and still others view the Tewa people as descendants of the earliest Pueblo people to inhabit the Northern Rio Grande (Boyer et al. 2010; Steen 1977; Wendorf 1953; Wendorf and Reed 1955). Debate on Tewa origins has persisted for nearly a century, but as of yet no model that accounts for the full range of available evidence has been presented in the literature. I will build such a model here by tracing the biological, linguistic, and cultural heritage of the Tewa people, paying special attention to possible connections with the Mesa Verde region and other areas of the San Juan drainage.

Characteristics of the Mesa Verde and Northern Rio Grande archaeological records suggest that the fate of Mesa Verde people may have been distinct from the fate of their culture—and perhaps also their language. This, in turn, raises the possibility that the genes, language, and culture of the Tewa people also derive from different sources. These are not implausible suggestions, as anthropologists have long acknowledged that the genes, languages, and cultures of ethnic groups need not evolve as packages (Barth 1969; Hill 1996; Moore 1994; Terrell 2001); however, these possibilities do pose a methodological challenge. Many studies have sought to trace the histories of ethnic groups by correlating patterns of genetic, linguistic, and cultural variation in a region (e.g., Ammerman and Cavalli-Sforza 1984; Bellwood and Renfrew 2003; Cavalli-Sforza et al. 1994; Ford et al. 1972; Madsen and Rhode 1994; Ross 1998; Rouse 1986). This approach is not appropriate for this study because it assumes genes, language, and culture have evolved as a package in bounded social groups, when in fact this is an empirical question to be answered for this particular case. How, then, can one trace the genetic, linguistic, and cultural heritage of ethnic groups without assuming that they have followed parallel patterns of descent?

In this book I suggest that the answer is to employ methods that tie past populations and protolanguages directly to the archaeological record. Rather

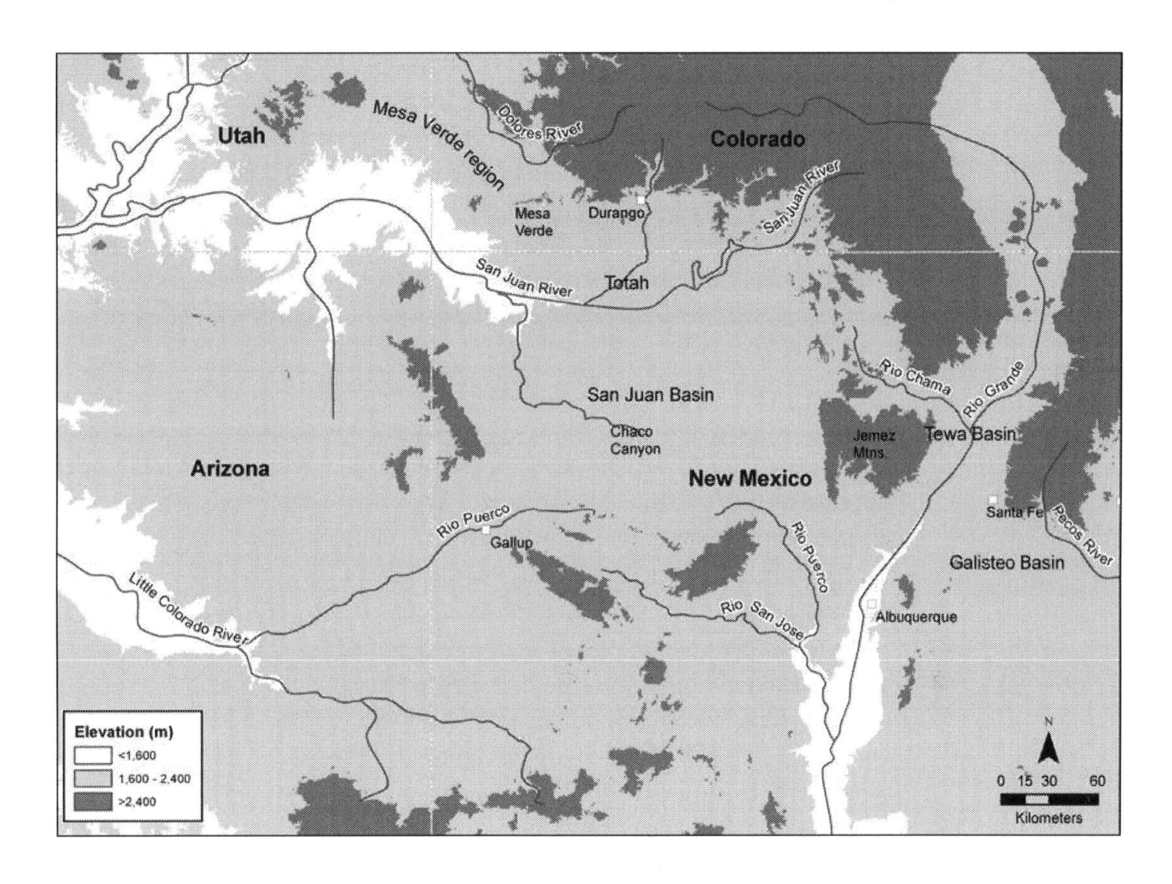

FIGURE 1.1. The Eastern Pueblo area.

than correlating independently derived patterns of genetic, linguistic, and cultural variation, I focus on areas where human biology and language intersect the archaeological record directly. Such methods allow one to tie down genetic, linguistic, and cultural reconstructions to specific times and places without assuming that they have evolved in parallel. As a result, one can evaluate a much wider range of models than is possible using the pattern-matching approach. This is not to suggest that genes, language, and culture do not each exhibit descent with modification, or that they cannot evolve as packages under certain circumstances. It is merely to emphasize that in order to make sense of cases like Tewa origins, it is necessary to employ methods that allow the genes, language, and culture of ethnic groups to derive from different sources.

The U.S. Southwest represents one of the world's great natural laboratories for anthropological research, and as a result, many aspects of Pueblo Indian history are well known. Thus, the first order of business for this study is to illustrate that despite intensive, long-term research, a consensus on Tewa origins remains elusive. To establish this fact, and to demonstrate the need for a study such as this, the following pages introduce the geographical and culture-historical context of Tewa origins, review the range of positions that researchers have taken on this issue, and suggest some of the reasons why the literature on Tewa origins has become so tangled.

The Geographic and Culture-Historical Context

The geographic focus of this study is the Eastern Pueblo region, which I define as encompassing the drainages of the San Juan and Rio Grande rivers in the U.S. Southwest (Figure 1.1). Both rivers originate in the Rocky Mountains of southern Colorado but drain opposite sides of the Continental Divide, which runs between them. The San Juan runs west for several hundred miles — and nearly through the "Four Corners," where Colorado, Utah, Arizona, and New Mexico meet — before merging with the Colorado River beneath present-day Lake Powell. From there the Colorado flows southwest through the Grand Canyon in Arizona and south along the border between California and Arizona before emptying into the Gulf of California and the Pacific Ocean. The Rio Grande flows south through New Mexico to El Paso, Texas, and then southeast along the international border between the United States and Mexico before emptying into the Gulf of Mexico and the Atlantic Ocean.

At present, there are six Tewa-speaking pueblos in a portion of the upper Rio Grande drainage known as the Tewa Basin, a Y-shaped trough bounded by the Santa Fe divide on the south, the Jemez Mountains on the west, the Sangre de Cristo Mountains on the east, and the Rio Chama and its tributaries in the north (Anschuetz 2005). Numerous ancestral Tewa sites occur throughout this area, indicating that Tewa-speaking peoples have occupied this region for many centuries (Harrington 1916; also see Chapter 8). At the time of Spanish contact additional Tewa-speaking villages were located in the Galisteo Basin southeast of Santa Fe, but these villages did not weather colonization as well as their northern cousins, and the last remnants of the Southern Tewa population left the Galisteo Basin for other Pueblo villages in 1794 (Harrington 1916:483–485; Schroeder 1979). A final Tewa-speaking village, on Hopi First Mesa in northern Arizona, formed as a result of migration from the Tewa Basin in AD 1696. Because the largest prehispanic Tewa populations were located in the Tewa Basin, and most present-day Tewas live there today, this study focuses on the origins of Northern Tewa communities.

The temporal focus of this study begins at AD 1150, shortly after the collapse of the regional system centered on Chaco Canyon, in the San Juan geologic basin of northwest New Mexico (Lekson 2006; Mills 2002). At this time most of the population of the Eastern Pueblo region resided in the San Juan drainage and in the San Juan Basin (Adler 1996). There were several centers of population, including the flanks of the Chuska Mountains, which run along the Arizona–New Mexico border; the Totah District in northwestern New Mexico, where several major northern tributaries flow into the San Juan; and the area in southwest Colorado and southeast Utah known as the Mesa Verde region, defined by Mesa Verde proper to the east, the Mancos and San Juan rivers to the south, and the Colorado and Dolores rivers to the north.[1]

Over the next 250 years the San Juan drainage was completely depopulated, and a new population center developed in the Rio Grande drainage. By AD 1400

TABLE 1.1. Correlation of archaeological periods considered in this study

SAN JUAN DRAINAGE	RIO GRANDE DRAINAGE
Pueblo II (AD 920–1140)	Developmental (AD 900–1200)
Pueblo III (AD 1140–1280)	Coalition (AD 1200–1350)
Unoccupied	Classic (AD 1350–1540)

the Pueblo settlements and peoples that would be encountered by Spanish explorers 150 years later were essentially in place. This study examines the nature of the relationship between these two developments. As such, it encompasses the Pueblo III period (AD 1140–1280) in the San Juan drainage, as well as the final decades of the Developmental period (AD 900–1200), the entirety of the Coalition period (AD 1200–1350), and the initial decades of the Classic period (AD 1350–1540) in the Rio Grande drainage (Table 1.1).

The distribution of Pueblo "nations" in the Rio Grande region at the time of Spanish contact was complex (Barrett 2002; Schroeder 1979). As explorers traveled north from Mexico, they first encountered a chain of villages along the Rio Grande where Piro, a now-extinct language, was spoken. North of the Piro villages, in the vicinity of present-day Albuquerque, lay a chain of Southern Tiwa–speaking villages, and also a group of villages in the Estancia Basin east of the Rio Grande in which the now-extinct Tompiro language was spoken. North of present-day Albuquerque, settlements began to occur along tributaries of the Rio Grande, as well as along the river itself. To the west Spanish explorers encountered a group of Towa-speaking villages on the southwestern slopes of the Jemez Mountains, and a group of Keres-speaking villages along the lower Rio Jemez and along the Rio Grande north of its confluence with the Rio Jemez. To the east they encountered a group of Tewa-speaking villages along Galisteo Creek, and a pueblo of debatable linguistic affiliation at Pecos, on the southern slopes of the Sangre de Cristo Mountains. Finally they encountered the main group of Tewa-speaking villages in the Tewa Basin, and a group of Northern Tiwa-speaking villages along eastern tributaries of the Rio Grande, northeast of its confluence with the Rio Chama.

The most vexing problem in the archaeology of the Rio Grande drainage is how this complex distribution came about. Several factors suggest that migration was involved in some way. First, the center of gravity of the prehispanic Pueblo population gradually shifted from the San Juan drainage at AD 1140 to the Rio Grande drainage by AD 1400. Second, languages of two distinct families, Keresan and Tanoan, were spoken in the Rio Grande drainage in the sixteenth century, and this argues against a singular origin for these groups. Third, the distribution of languages encountered by the Spanish is not what one would expect if they had diversified in their sixteenth-century territories. For example, the closely related Northern Tiwa and Southern Tiwa languages were spoken at opposite ends of the distribution, with more distantly related languages spoken in between (Harrington 1909). Yet despite these indications that migration was involved in the formation of the Rio Grande pueblos, there is no consensus on its role, especially with regard to the Tewa pueblos. To get a sense of these varied opinions, I offer a guided tour of the many proposals that have been offered to explain how the Tewa and other Rio Grande pueblos came to be.

Previous Research on Tewa Origins

Early Models

Researchers have been offering contradictory models of Tewa origins from the very beginning of anthropological research in New Mexico. Two of the earliest statements illustrate this point very clearly. In the first decade of the twentieth century, J. P. Harrington recorded Tewa place-names and associated traditions for several locations in the Mesa Verde region of southwestern Colorado. For example, regarding the Montezuma Valley, Harrington (1916:564) wrote, "This is a large valley in southwestern Colorado. It is said that in ancient times when the Tewa were journeying south from *Sip'ophe* the *K'ósa*, a mythic person who founded the *K'ósa* society of the Tewa, first appeared to the people while they were sojourning in this valley." The data collected by Harrington and other early researchers (e.g., Jeançon 1923:75–76, 1925:39) suggest in a fairly straightforward way that the Tewa people originated in the Mesa Verde region; however, the earliest treatment of the archaeological evidence, A. V. Kidder's (1924) landmark *Introduction to the Study of Southwestern Archaeology*, suggests a somewhat different scenario.

> The best argument for a movement of people from the peripherae toward the center is provided by the marked increase in the number and size of pueblo ruins of a relatively late date in and near that center. During the early Pueblo period and even in the Great Period that had just closed, the Rio Grande and the Little Colorado were not very densely populated. The towns of those times (i.e. the Black-on-white sites) were small when numerous, and few when they became larger; now, however, just as the northern and southern districts were being abandoned, villages became much more abundant and much greater in size. As examples of this we may name the great pueblos of the Rio Grande from Socorro to the headwaters of the Chama, and the many new towns that sprang up in the Zuni country, along the Little Colorado, and about the Hopi Mesas.
>
> I think the connection between these two sets of phenomena, abandonment of the outlying districts and sudden increase in population in the central areas, cannot be mistaken. The puzzling thing about it is that the incoming people brought with them so little of their local culture. No adobe

> *casas grandes* were built in the Little Colorado, no towns of the Mesa Verde or Chaco types were erected in the Rio Grande. The old styles of pottery became extinct, or were altered so rapidly and completely that the transitional stages have escaped identification. It would seem as if the transference of people must have been by small groups, rather than by whole communities, an infiltration rather than a migration. Each successive increment became amalgamated with the resident group that it joined, adopted the local culture, probably stimulated and strengthened it, possibly influenced it to a certain extent, but seldom, if ever, succeeded in changing it radically, or in turning its course of development sharply away from the channels in which it was already running. (341–342)

These early statements evidence the contradictions that have framed debates on Tewa origins ever since. Tewa oral traditions focus on the Mesa Verde region as a prior homeland, and the correlated nature of settlement changes between the Mesa Verde region and the Northern Rio Grande also suggest movement, but if there was a migration from the Mesa Verde region to the Northern Rio Grande during the AD 1200s, the pottery and architecture of Northern Rio Grande sites do not clearly show it. Kidder took the archaeological evidence as suggesting that movement between the two regions involved a gradual infiltration by small groups who were incorporated into established Rio Grande communities upon arrival, but if this were the case, one would not expect present-day Tewa-speakers to have retained social memories of an ancient homeland in the Mesa Verde region. Also, if there are no material culture continuities to confirm that population growth in the Rio Grande was due to migration from the San Juan, perhaps the population changes that Kidder observed resulted instead from situ growth. In short, the three lines of evidence known to researchers at the time of Kidder's synthesis were already suggesting three distinct models of Tewa origins: mass migration, as indicated by oral traditions and place-names; local development without external influence, as evidenced by material culture patterns; and gradual infiltration and assimilation by small groups, as suggested by population changes combined with local continuity in material culture.

All subsequent statements on Tewa origins have gravitated toward one of these models, depending on the line of evidence that individual authors have viewed as most significant. H. P. Mera, for example, presented a model in 1935 based primarily on the distributions and relationships among pottery types in the Rio Grande drainage. Mera (1935:34) was careful to acknowledge that "pottery types often may be, but are not of necessity, indicative of the racial or linguistic status of the peoples who made and used it," but like many others who followed, he attempted to correlate pottery genealogies with ethnolinguistic groups. To understand the proposals of Mera and subsequent researchers, it is necessary to introduce the Northern Rio Grande decorated pottery sequence and Mera's view of the external influences on this sequence. Figure 1.2 summarizes

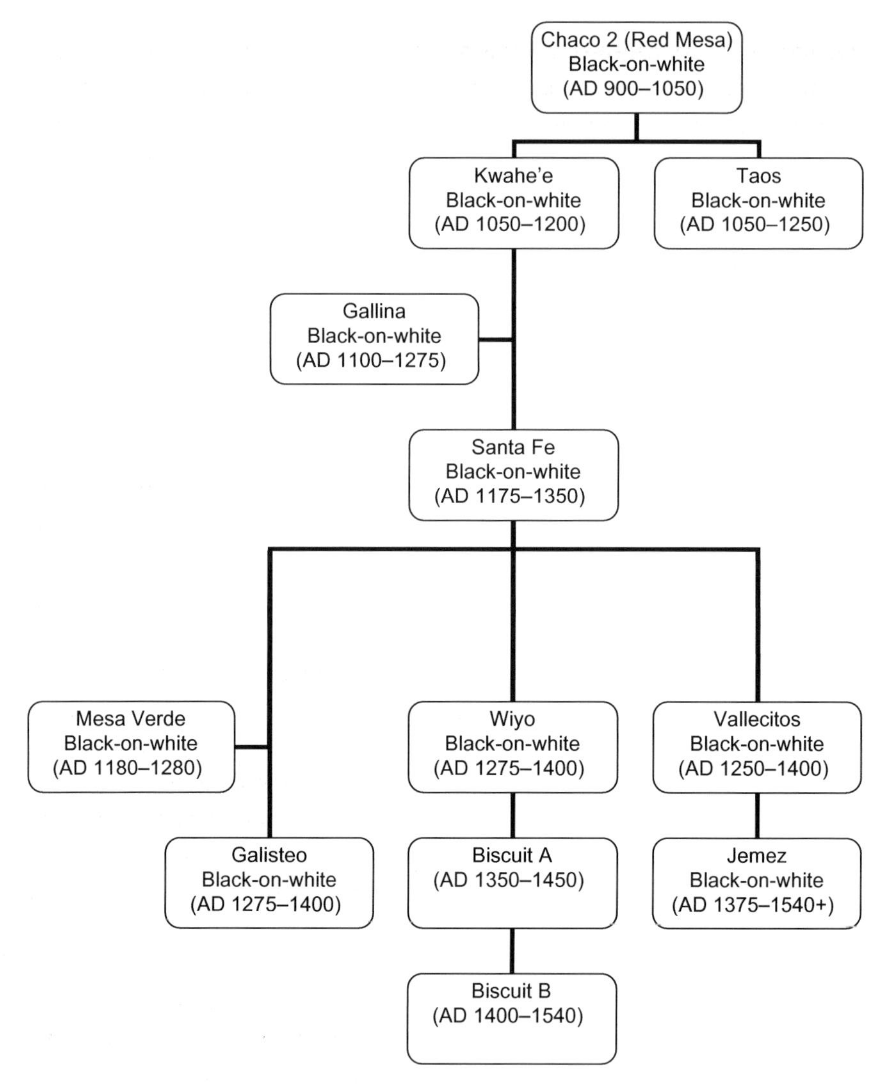

FIGURE 1.2. Mera's (1935) genealogy of Northern Rio Grande pottery types.

Mera's types and interpretations, along with current understandings of the date range for each type (see Chapter 4).

On the basis of this sequence, Mera suggested that the Tanoan-speaking Pueblos, including the Tewa, descended from early Rio Grande peoples who made Kwahe'e Black-on-white pottery, the characteristic type of the Late Developmental (AD 1050–1200) period. He reached this conclusion for the Tewa in particular because the characteristic ware of ancestral Tewa sites, known as Biscuit ware, appeared to Mera (1935:38) to have descended in an unbroken tradition from Santa Fe Black-on-white, a type that appeared well before the final depopulation of the Mesa Verde region, and which he viewed as the product of influence by Gallina Black-on-white on Kwahe'e Black-on-white. Mera also suggested that the Keres-speaking Pueblos originated in the San Juan drainage, citing a rough correspondence between the distribution of Keres-speaking

Pueblos in the sixteenth-century Rio Grande region, and the distribution of Galisteo Black-on-white, a type which did appear shortly after the Mesa Verde depopulation, and one that he viewed as the product of influence by Mesa Verde Black-on-white on Santa Fe Black-on-white. The details of Tewa Basin pottery traditions thus led Mera to lean toward an in situ development model of Tewa origins.

In 1949 Erik Reed presented a very different model by matching archaeological events with patterns of linguistic variation. Reed emphasized that the sixteenth-century Rio Grande Pueblos fell into four major language groups: (1) Tiwa, consisting of a northern and a southern group along the Rio Grande; (2) Towa, which was spoken along the upper Rio Jemez, west of the Rio Grande, and possibly also in the upper Pecos drainage; (3) Tewa, which was spoken in the Tewa and Galisteo basins; and (4) Keres, which is spoken along the lower Rio Jemez and adjacent areas of the Rio Grande Valley. Reed then postulated that the first group represents the earliest inhabitants of the Rio Grande region; that the second migrated to the Rio Puerco of the East, on the west side of the Jemez Mountains, between AD 1000 and 1200; that the third migrated from the Mesa Verde region to the Tewa and Galisteo basins around AD 1300, split the Tiwa speech community into northern and southern groups, and soon after developed Galisteo and Wiyo Black-on-white; and that the fourth migrated from the Cibola area south of Chaco Canyon in the early AD 1300s, also inserted themselves between the Tiwa subgroups, and brought glaze-painted pottery to the Northern Rio Grande region. Here, again, the differences between Mera's and Reed's views can be traced to the line of evidence each author privileged: Mera worked from his understanding of pottery sequences and influences, whereas Reed worked from Tanoan language relationships and was more willing to view generalized similarities in material culture as evidence of historical relationship.

Only a few years later Wendorf and Reed (1955) restated Mera's (1935) view in their classic article that formalized the phase sequence still used by Northern Rio Grande archaeologists. As in Mera's model, Wendorf and Reed focused on material culture and did not emphasize linguistic details, such as the Tiwa language distribution, which had formed the foundation of Reed's earlier model. Thus, with respect to the Tewa they wrote, "The unbroken continuity in the Northern Tewa area in pottery, kivas, and architectural style from the earliest known sites through the historic period would seem to favor a very long occupation of the area by the Tewa, certainly preceding the Mesa Verde intrusion. Except for the Galisteo villages, there are no features in early historic period Tewa sites, or their earlier counterparts, which could be ascribed to Mesa Verde immigrants; rather, there is a noticeable lack of specialized Mesa Verde features in Tewa sites" (Wendorf and Reed 1955:160–161). The "Mesa Verde feature" of the Galisteo Basin villages mentioned by Wendorf and Reed is Galisteo Black-on-white pottery, which Mera argued had derived in part from Mesa Verde Black-on-white. Wendorf and Reed noted, as Mera did earlier, that this type also occurs in areas that were occupied by Keresan speakers in the sixteenth century. They also observed that even though the kivas of both areas are round, several characteristic features of San Juan kivas — including benches, pilasters, southern recesses, and southern orientation — are rarely found in Northern Rio Grande sites in any period (141).[2] Wendorf and Reed thus focused on material culture continuities at the expense of language relationships in arguing that the Tanoan languages diversified within the Rio Grande, and that Keres-speaking migrants from the Mesa Verde region were responsible for the development of Galisteo Black-on-white, the putative cognate of Mesa Verde Black-on-white.

Mid-Twentieth-Century Models

In early models, migration from the Mesa Verde region was most often viewed as an event that took place shortly before AD 1300, when the last ancestral Pueblo villages in this region were vacated. However, in 1959 Charles H. McNutt developed a model (published in 1969) in which the Mesa Verde migrations began around AD 1200. This model was also innovative in that it focused on the pattern of change in the Northern Rio Grande archaeological record, as opposed to material culture continuities per se. McNutt (1969:107) began by noting that carbon-painted Santa Fe Black-on-white replaced mineral-painted Kwahe'e Black-on-white around AD 1200 in the Northern Rio Grande, and that the rate at which carbon paint replaced mineral paint was much more rapid in this area than it was in other parts of the Southwest, where carbon paint was adopted gradually by in situ populations.

Earlier researchers tended to view Santa Fe Black-on-white as a local development (Mera 1935:12; Stubbs and Stallings 1953:48; Wendorf and Reed 1955: 144), but McNutt argued that pottery traditions of the San Juan and Rio Grande regions are so similar that a number of proposals for genealogical relationships among types are equally plausible. More importantly, he noted that the adoption of carbon-painted pottery corresponded to several other changes in the Northern Rio Grande archaeological record, including population increase, the construction of larger pueblos, the replacement of trough metates by slab metates, the replacement of corner-notched projectile points by side-notched points, and the first appearance of full-grooved axes, turkey husbandry, and bird-bone artifacts (McNutt 1969:107). All of these traits appeared in the San Juan drainage at different times prior to AD 1200, but in the Northern Rio Grande they appeared as a group around AD 1200. On this basis, McNutt argued that San Juan populations began moving into the Northern Rio Grande around AD 1200, and that the process continued until the former region had emptied.

McNutt noted that the intrusive complex associated with Santa Fe Black-on-white consisted primarily of techno-functional traits, whereas socio-symbolic traits, such as architectural details of San Juan–style kivas, are not apparent at these sites.[3] Nevertheless, McNutt (1969:109) did not believe such continuities were required if one interpreted the data along the same lines as Kidder: "The absence of pilasters in Rio Grande kivas does not, in my opinion, negate the very considerable evidence for several immigrations into that area from the Chaco–San Juan. It does suggest, however, that no extremely large group entered the valley at any particular time, although their total impact upon the resident population was quite significant; that the 'immigrations' were actually results of small social units drifting into the area rather than a planned and organized population movement." McNutt thus rehabilitated Kidder's view that Rio Grande Pueblo populations derived primarily from the San Juan drainage, but the cultural impacts of their movements to the Rio Grande were muted by the social scale of the migrating units and the extended period of time over which migration took place. McNutt made no attempt to correlate his postulated movements with language groups, but under his model, it would not be difficult to imagine the ancestral Tewa population deriving primarily from the San Juan drainage, but the Tewa language deriving from early inhabitants of the Tewa Basin.

In 1967 Florence Hawley Ellis presented yet another reconstruction based primarily on oral traditions that she had compiled for the Wetherill Mesa Archaeological Project. Her goal was "to determine whether traditions still existent among the living Pueblo peoples could provide some light on which of them would claim ancestors who had lived in the Mesa Verde country" (Ellis 1967:35). As Harrington had done, she found that oral traditions suggested many Rio Grande Pueblo language groups originated in the San Juan drainage. Keres oral traditions, for example, suggested prior occupancy of a large area that included the upper reaches of the Little Colorado drainage, Chaco Canyon and the San Juan Basin, and also portions of the Mesa Verde region. Tewa oral traditions also suggested prior occupancy in the Northern San Juan, "either in the Mesa Verde country or farther upriver" (Ellis 1967:38). In addition, Jemez oral traditions suggested that their ancestors had originated in the Four Corners country and then moved to the Rio Puerco of the East, along the west side of the Jemez Mountains, before settling into their present territory. Finally, Tiwa migration traditions were not highly developed, suggesting that Tiwa speakers are descendants of the earliest inhabitants of the Rio Grande Valley.

Ellis attempted to correlate these traditions with archaeological and linguistic evidence, but tellingly, her correlations often contradicted the oral traditions. For example, Ellis (1967:37) suggested that the Tanoan languages originated in the Mogollon highlands and Sonoran Desert of southern Arizona based on the so-called Aztec-Tanoan hypothesis (Whorf and Trager 1937; also see Chapter 6), despite her acknowledgment that none of the Tanoan-speaking Pueblos maintain migration traditions of a southern origin. Also, in contradiction to Jemez oral tradition, Ellis (1967:38) suggested that the Jemez language originated in the upper San Juan drainage and then drifted south to the Gallina country, along the northwestern edge of the Jemez Mountains, before entering the Rio Puerco of the East and the Jemez Mountains (Ellis 1967:38).[4] These disjunctions suggest, once again, that the various lines of evidence related to the origins of the Rio Grande Pueblos do not tell the same story.

In the mid-twentieth century several researchers attempted to correlate linguistic evidence with archaeological and ethnohistorical data. Once again, their results were highly divergent. Davis (1959), for example, suggested that Towa diverged from the other Tanoan languages before Towa speakers entered the Rio Grande, but that the Tewa, Tiwa, and Piro languages diversified within the Rio Grande region. He also suggested that the Keres-speaking Pueblos originated in the Mesa Verde region (following Mera). Hale and Harris (1979:177) suggested a nearly identical scenario: "Linguistic knowledge of the area is not sensitive enough to permit any firm assertion with regard to this matter, but the linguistic facts appear consistent with San Juan ancestry for the Keresans and with a scheme of the following sort for the Tanoans: the Rio Grande Anasazi were ancestral to the historic Tiwa and Tewa, already differentiated from the Towa, who developed the Anasazi variety distinguished in the Largo-Gallina area." Trager (1967), however, presented a very different model, in which Keresan speakers inhabited the Rio Grande by AD 700, the Towa language derived from an early group of Tanoan speakers who entered the Rio Grande region around AD 750, and the Tiwa and Tewa languages diverged as a result of differential interaction with Keres speakers after the remaining Tanoans entered the Rio Grande from the northwest around AD 1000.

In 1972 Ford, Schroeder, and Peckham updated earlier attempts at correlating language relationships with pottery type distributions and sequences. Not surprisingly, they could not agree on many basic points. All three carried forward Ellis's (1967) view that the Jemez Pueblos descended from the Los Pinos and Rosa phases in the Upper San Juan via the Gallina District, and also agreed with Reed (1949) that the original occupants of the Rio Grande were Tiwa speakers. These authors differed, however, over the reasons for the split of Tiwa speakers into northern and southern speech communities. Ford and Schroeder believed an intrusion of Tewa speakers caused the split, whereas Peckham viewed the Tiwa split as derivative of the in situ development of the Tewa.

All three authors (Ford et al. 1972) agreed that Tewa-speaking peoples were in place in the Tewa and Galisteo basins by Late Coalition (AD 1275–1350) times, but they had substantial disagreements over how they got there. Ford and Schroeder suggested that Tewa diversified from Towa in the Upper San Juan, the archaeological trace of which is the stylistic boundary between Piedra Black-on-white (Tewa) and Rosa Black-on-white (Towa) in Upper San Juan sites dating after AD 700. Then, around AD 1000, Tewa speakers left the Upper San Juan for the western, southern, and eastern peripheries of the Jemez Mountains, where sites bearing Kwahe'e Black-on-white are found. Tewa speakers then remained in the Rio Grande region from that point to the present day. Peckham, in contrast, believed Tewa diversified from Tiwa within the Rio Grande around AD 900.[5]

These authors also disagreed over the cause of the divergence of the Tano or Southern Tewa dialect from the main body of Tewa speakers: Peckham argued, following Reed (1949), that Keres-speaking, glaze-producing migrants from the Cibola region split the Tewa speech community in the early fourteenth century, whereas Schroeder followed Mera (1935) and Wendorf and Reed (1955) in arguing that it was actually Keres-speaking migrants from the Mesa Verde region who caused this split in the late thirteenth century, and Ford argued the Southern Tewa were pushed from the Rio Puerco of the East into the Galisteo Basin by in-migrating Mesa Verde Keres in the late thirteenth century.

Recent Models

Perhaps dissuaded by the tangle of conflicting and irreconcilable claims in Ford et al. 1972, recent researchers have tended to shy away from the task of correlating Rio Grande ethnolinguistic groups with archaeological complexes. Cordell (1979:146–147), for example, emphasized the difficulties involved in her contribution to the *Handbook of North American Indians*.

> Attempts to determine the linguistic affiliation of various prehistoric groups have had a long history in the Anasazi area with less substantial results. There would seem to be at least two major problems in this regard. First, there are excellent ethnographic cases of two linguistically diverse groups sharing essentially the same material culture inventory, such as the Hopi and Hopi-Tewa (Tewa Village) of Arizona. Second, although the historic and contemporary distributions of related languages in the Pueblo area do show geographic patterning, the assumption that geographic patterning in ceramic types or architectural features represents linguistic patterning is both untested and probably untrue.

Despite these legitimate concerns, there has been a continued interest in tracing migrations to the Northern Rio Grande using archaeological evidence, especially population trends. Not surprisingly, the focus on population trends has led researchers to echo views expressed by Kidder some 55 years earlier. Cordell (1979:150–151), for example, concluded: "when abandonment became necessary the San Juan groups, probably gradually, joined the local population to the east and southeast, integrating themselves into communities in much the same way as the highland Enga do." Similar arguments have appeared in Cordell's more recent writings (e.g., Cordell 1995; Cordell et al. 2007). Once again, the unstated implication would be that the Tewa language is unlikely to have originated outside the Rio Grande drainage.

A very similar view, with nearly identical implications, was expressed by Judith Habicht-Mauche (1993:87–88) in her study of the pottery from Arroyo Hondo Pueblo. Her ideas are worth quoting at length.

> Prior to the end of the twelfth century, the population density of the northern Rio Grande appears to have remained relatively low. It has been estimated, however, that some time between AD 1150 and 1250 the area experienced as much as a tenfold increase in population.... The rapidity and scale of this population increase has been interpreted as evidence for a migration of people into the area during the thirteenth century. The archaeological record of abandonment in the San Juan Basin and Mesa Verde regions of the Colorado Plateau during this same period suggests that these areas were likely sources of this new population.... Nevertheless, not a single site has ever been identified in the northern Rio Grande that contains an assemblage of features or artifacts that can be interpreted as evidence of a wholly immigrant community. The overall continuity of northern Rio Grande culture has been cited as evidence for the local development of early Coalition culture without substantial migration. The magnitude of population changes reflected in the settlement data, however, cannot be explained readily by biological models of in situ population growth. As a result, the continuity of local material culture reflected in the archaeological record may indicate that the processes of population movement, social integration, and the emergence of the various historic ethnic groups of the area may have been much more complicated and harder to read "on the ground" than most archaeologists have imagined.
>
> As Upham and Cordell have pointed out, mass migrations of entire villages are extremely rare ethnographically. It is more likely that throughout the Coalition, families leaving the San Juan Basin and Mesa Verde areas traveled south and east to join local Rio Grande communities with whom they had existing economic or kin-based relationships. In societies like those of the Eastern Pueblos, agricultural land and other productive resources are not the property of individuals but are held in common by a community or kinship group and distributed to members on the basis of need or status. As a result, there would have been a strong impetus for newcomers to develop cultural and familial ties with the recipient community in order to gain access to these resources. This process would act to sustain the general homogeneity and continuity of local material culture by selecting against the persistence of those cultural traits that marked newcomers as "foreigners" or "outsiders." From this perspective, then, the continuity of local cultural development in the northern Rio Grande is not inherently antithetical to the proposed model of population growth and settlement expansion due, in part, to population movement into the area during the thirteenth century.

In recent years archaeologists interested in Rio Grande Pueblo origins have also turned to the modern migration literature to gain a better understanding of what migrations should look like in the archaeological record. A good example of this trend is Andrew Duff's 1998 article on late prehispanic Pueblo migration as a social process. Duff drew upon ethnographic studies to suggest that ancient migrations, even of large groups, rarely leave clear traces in material culture.

> If small family or extended family groups join existing communities, they are unlikely to express their identity in language, let alone overt material culture. In most instances, assimilation or accommodation to the established group would be expected.... For larger-scale group migration, the Hopi-Tewa case is instructive. The Tewa community moved to Hopi as a large group, yet they would be virtually indistinguishable archaeologically from the surrounding Hopi population. Only in language, history and ceremony does this large immigrant group preserve its identity; overt material culture does not differ. (Duff 1998:33–34)

Duff thus concludes that material culture is likely to change substantially with migration, regardless of the size of the migrant group, and that the best clues as to the origin of large migrant groups lie in the realm of language, technological style, and ritual practice rather than architecture and decorated pottery. He also suggests that colonization of an unoccupied area by large, homogenous groups may be the only situation in which overt material culture continuities might be expected to persist. In contrast, when large groups move into already settled areas, one may initially see "intrusive" material culture traits, but these would be expected to fade rapidly, perhaps becoming archaeologically undetectable within a generation.

The notion that population growth in the absence of an intrusive material culture could derive from incorporation of small migrant groups is not new, but Duff's second insight — that migrant groups large enough to maintain a distinct identity after migration may also adopt the overt material culture of the destination area — has obvious implications for debates on Tewa origins. Duff (1998:44–45) draws on these insights to suggest that one should not be surprised to find that Mesa Verde migrants did not produce site-unit intrusions in the Northern Rio Grande, despite indications that the final depopulation of the Mesa Verde region involved movement by community-sized groups. Duff also suggests that community-sized groups were able to migrate from the Mesa Verde region to the Northern Rio Grande because these larger groups were preceded by smaller groups that settled unoccupied portions of the region and established information networks and migration pathways that allowed larger-scale movements to occur later on. From Duff's perspective, then, it would not appear contradictory to propose that the ancestral Tewa population and language derived from the Mesa Verde region, but ancestral Tewa material culture resulted from the adoption of Rio Grande traditions by Mesa Verde migrants. This is an intriguing solution, but it leaves unanswered the question of why later migrant groups, who would have surpassed both the indigenous population and earlier migrants in numbers and social scale, adopted Rio Grande material traditions instead of continuing Mesa Verde material traditions.

Finally, it is important to note that in situ models of Tewa origins, based primarily on material culture continuities, have also continued to appear in the literature. Charlie Steen (1977:39–41, 1982:53–54), for example, argued that the Tanoan-speaking Pueblos, including the Tewa, developed within the Rio Grande region due to the existence of an unbroken archaeological tradition from the earliest settlement of this region to the present day. Specifically, he argued that: (1) Northern Rio Grande pottery styles reflect generalized patterns that are found throughout the Pueblo area; (2) there is no evidence for an intrusion of foreign construction methods at any point; and (3) the characteristics of ceremonial rooms in AD 1200s Rio Grande sites are distinct from those of earlier, small kivas in the San Juan drainage. He also suggested that the Mesa Verde region population spoke a Uto-Aztecan language that dwindled in place during the thirteenth century (Steen 1982:54). Lakatos (2007) continues this line of reasoning in a recent study focusing on continuities between Developmental period pit structures and Coalition–Classic period kivas in the Rio Grande. Wilson (2008a) restates Mera's (1934) opinion that Santa Fe Black-on-white is of local derivation and argues that the subsequent type in the Galisteo Basin, Galisteo Black-on-white, is of local derivation because it lacks the exterior designs and rim decorations so characteristic of Mesa Verde Black-on-white. He thus interprets the shared raw materials and technologies of these two types, which many have interpreted as evidence of migration, as a simple by-product of the pottery-making resources available in the two regions. Finally, Boyer and others (2010) emphasize Lakatos's and Wilson's points, and argue that in situ growth could have produced the AD 1300 Tewa Basin population from the population that was already residing there by AD 1000.

Summary

Despite a century of research, there is truly no consensus among researchers as to how the Tewa Pueblos came to be. Some believe that they developed in situ from the initial settlers of the Tewa Basin; others suggest that they are the result of gradual infiltration and assimilation of San Juan migrants into established Rio Grande communities; and still others argue that the Tewa people originated in the San Juan drainage and moved to the Rio Grande during the AD 1200s. In addition, it is clear that researchers have understood the basic evidence related to Tewa origins since the early decades of the twentieth century, yet there is no model in the literature that accounts for all of this evidence. Instead, researchers tend to privilege certain lines of evidence in developing their proposals, and to gloss over or explain away others. Thus, in situ development models emphasize the lack of evidence for intrusive Mesa Verde material culture in the Tewa

Basin, but overlook correlated population changes in the two areas; assimilation models emphasize population changes, but gloss over oral traditions and language relationships; and mass migration models emphasize oral tradition and language, but gloss over material culture continuities in the Rio Grande.

Nevertheless, resolving the puzzle of Tewa origins matters on a number of levels. For archaeology in the U.S. Southwest, the answer to the question implies the extent to which ancient Pueblo languages and cultures survive among the present-day Pueblos. Mesa Verde material culture largely disappeared from the archaeological record in the late AD 1200s. If most Mesa Verde people migrated to the Tewa Basin, then the Tewa language might have originated in the Mesa Verde region — and might preserve aspects of ancient Mesa Verde culture. If, on the other hand, Mesa Verde people died in place, moved elsewhere, or were absorbed into existing Tewa Basin communities, it would be likely that Mesa Verde language and culture have not survived to the present, and, as a result, it would not be appropriate to mine Tewa language and culture for clues regarding ancient Mesa Verde culture.

In addition, the degree to which the depopulation of the Mesa Verde region and the formation of the Tewa Pueblos are connected makes a significant difference in how one should ideally go about studying each of these processes. If the two processes were linked, then it may not be possible to understand exactly how and why one occurred without being informed about the other; however, if these two processes were not connected, then conditions during the final decades of Mesa Verde region occupation are not relevant for understanding the character of Coalition period Tewa Basin society, and Tewa Basin society is not relevant for understanding the depopulation of Mesa Verde.

The relationship between the Mesa Verde depopulation and Tewa origins is also significant in terms of how researchers imagine ancient human societies and their ability to respond to social and environmental challenges. If the Mesa Verde population scattered, declined in place, or destroyed itself in a spasm of warfare, it would suggest an utter failure of a well-established society to cope with the challenges it faced and would present a cautionary tale of just how apocalyptic such failures can be. If, on the other hand, some fraction of Mesa Verde society responded to these challenges by moving to the Tewa Basin and developing a new society there, it would present a somewhat more optimistic view of human adaptability and resiliency.

Finally, anthropology needs to provide a satisfactory account of Tewa origins if it wishes to present itself as a field that advances our understanding of human nature, history, and diversity. The Eastern Pueblo area represents one of the most completely preserved, most intensively studied, and most precisely dated archaeological regions in the world. Indeed, the sheer volume of available data is daunting even to specialists, who tend to focus on much smaller areas than are generally needed to address culture-historical questions (see Wilshusen and Ortman 1999). In addition, the Tewa language is part of a well-defined and universally accepted language family; the Rio Grande Pueblos are mentioned in historical records dating from the middle AD 1500s onward; and a large number of oral traditions and place-names have been recorded for many of these groups. Thus, if there is any region of the world where there should be enough evidence to determine the nature of the relationship between archaeological sequences of adjacent regions, the Eastern Pueblo area is it. The rich pattern of resistance provided by the evidence related to Tewa origins presents a complex puzzle, but it also provides an opportunity to develop a realistic model that approximates what actually happened. If researchers are ultimately unable to get to the bottom of this case, the prospects for producing convincing accounts of other cases, where far less evidence is available, would appear dim indeed.

Tewa Origins and Human Diversity

Why does debate persist despite the wealth of evidence? I believe the primary reason is that genes, language, and culture did not follow parallel patterns of descent in the ancient U.S. Southwest, but researchers tend to slide into thinking that they must have. It is not difficult to understand why this happens. Languages do come in families, and language is one of the primary criteria used by both analysts and subjects to define social identities in the present. Thus, there is a tendency to assume that the present-day social identity associated with a language originated and traveled along with that language in the past. A child's native language is also almost always learned from parents, and as a result there is a tendency to assume that population-level migrations also imply the movement of a speech community. Also, because oral traditions are recollections of events in the history of a social group, there is a tendency to assume that these social memories imply that the present-day group existed in its present form, and with its present identity, at the time of the events in the narratives. Finally, material cultures normally do exhibit descent with modification in local archaeological sequences, and the techniques that produce material traditions are initially learned from parents. Consequently, it is hard to imagine how a new language could be introduced to an area in the absence of a corresponding change in material culture, and the combination of population growth and local material culture continuity surely must be due to the incorporation of migrants into established communities.

These tendencies encourage researchers to assume that genes, language, culture, and identity normally travel as packages, but in this book I argue that none of the interpretations above are necessary. That is, languages are not necessarily associated with enduring social identities; ethnic groups can endure despite language shifts; oral traditions do not necessarily imply the existence of present-day groups and identities in the past; migration can transform the material culture even of large migrating groups; and cultural traditions emerge not only from social learning, but also from people's choices. Indeed, the contradictory claims that have emerged from previous research on Tewa origins leads one to suspect that the problem is not that researchers have lacked sufficient evidence, or have misconstrued this evidence, but that Tewa origins did not involve parallel descent in genes, language, and culture.

I therefore believe that the best way to reconcile the various models that researchers have offered on Tewa origins over the past century is to adopt a perspective that allows genes, language, and culture to evolve independently, and to use methods that allow one to tie past populations and speech communities directly to archaeological complexes. When approached in this way, the question of Tewa origins presents a productive field through which anthropology might extend its reach to the full range of processes involved in ethnic group formation, and might carry such studies back to periods before the advent of written documentation. My goal for this book is to provide an extended example of how this can be accomplished. The range of methods I employ enables one to move beyond analysis of descent and diversification within regions to encompass the full range of processes through which the rich tapestry of human diversity has been woven. I believe wider application of these methods will help us make major strides toward synthesizing prehistoric archaeology, historical linguistics, and population genetics in the historical study of human diversity.

Notes

1. The overall area of ancestral Pueblo settlement north of the San Juan River is often referred to the Northern San Juan region (Lipe 1995; Rohn 1989). In this study the Northern San Juan includes the Mesa Verde, Totah, and Upper San Juan regions, including the upper drainages of the Animas, Piedra, and San Juan rivers.
2. The term *kiva* refers to a subterranean or semisubterranean chamber entered through the roof and containing a fire pit and ventilation system. Kivas are specialized ceremonial structures in present-day pueblos, but most of the prehispanic kivas in the San Juan drainage, and in the Rio Grande drainage prior to the Classic period (Lipe 1989), appear to have been elements of domestic architecture.
3. Bertha Dutton (1964) subsequently looked specifically for San Juan–style kivas in her excavations at Las Madres — a site in the Galisteo Basin tree-ring dated to the late AD 1200s at which Galisteo Black-on-white was the dominant pottery type — but she found no such evidence.
4. I will consider Jemez culture history at several points in this study. For now, the important point to emphasize is that Ellis's archaeological sequence (Rosa-Piedra-Largo-Gallina-Jemez), which has been widely accepted in the literature (e.g., Cordell 1979:143; Ford et al. 1972:25; Stuart and Gauthier 1981:97), actually contradicts the Jemez oral traditions that she collected for this purpose. These traditions refer to the Four Corners region as the original home of the Jemez, and even refer to a shrine on Sleeping Ute Mountain in southwest Colorado, whereas no mention is made of the Upper San Juan or Gallina areas.
5. In this classic article (Ford et al. 1972) Ford and Schroeder based their views on Whorf and Trager's (1937) suggested subgrouping of the Tanoan languages, in which Tiwa split from Tewa-Towa before Tewa and Towa diversified, whereas Peckham followed the subgrouping suggested by Davis (1959) and Trager (1967), in which Towa split from Tiwa-Tewa before Tiwa and Tewa diversified. I examine the internal structure of Kiowa-Tanoan in Chapter 6.

Inheritance and Ethnic Groups

This book focuses on two issues that have dogged archaeology in the U.S. Southwest for nearly a century: the origins of the Rio Grande Pueblos in New Mexico, and the nature of their relationships, if any, with earlier groups of the Mesa Verde region to the northwest. To address these issues, I focus on the genetic, linguistic, and cultural backgrounds of the Tewa-speaking Pueblos, the largest contemporary Pueblo ethnic group in the Northern Rio Grande region, and the group around which the greatest controversy swirls. In this chapter I lay out the conceptual framework of this study, formalize the most plausible alternatives on Tewa origins into a series of hypotheses, and outline the method I will use to evaluate these hypotheses in the remainder of the book.

Three Systems of Human Inheritance

This study of Tewa origins is an exercise in historical anthropology, a pursuit that Kirch and Green (2001:2) characterize as "recovering and writing the deep history of 'peoples without history'" by integrating methods and data from the four traditional subfields of anthropology: ethnography, linguistics, archaeology, and physical anthropology. This approach to understanding human diversity was first formalized by Edward Sapir in his classic treatise, *Time Perspective in Aboriginal American Culture: A Study in Method* (1949 [1916]), but due to increasing specialization and the need for methodological and theoretical development in each subfield, Sapir's program was rarely pursued for much of the twentieth century.[1] Over the past few decades, however, a profusion of studies that integrate the methods, theories, and data of two or more subfields have appeared, and it is now apparent that the holistic, historical study of human diversity is a central pursuit in anthropology.[2]

A fundamental proposition of historical anthropology is that human genes, language, and culture represent distinct systems of inheritance. This notion dates from the early-twentieth-century writings of Boas, Kroeber, and Sapir (Terrell 2001) and is at the root of the contemporary division of anthropology into subfields. In recent years, however, several researchers have questioned whether language might be collapsed into culture, or both might be collapsed into biology (Barkow et al. 1992; Boyd and Richerson 1985: Chap. 5; Durham

1991: Chap. 4). Thus, an important preliminary for this study is an examination of the degree to which it remains appropriate to view genes, language, and culture as distinct systems of inheritance. Durham (1991:22) suggests that any system capable of producing descent with modification should possess five characteristics: (1) units that are transmitted; (2) sources of variation; (3) transmission mechanisms; (4) transformation forces, and (5) sources of isolation. In this chapter I illustrate that genes, language, and culture each possess these characteristics, and that they vary across systems to such an extent that it remains appropriate to view each as distinct.

Units of Transmission

The first requirement of any inheritance system is that it consist of transmissible units. For a biological system, the fundamental unit of transmission is the gene, a sequence of DNA bases that provides instructions for synthesizing proteins and regulating other genes within a cell. Because genes, as opposed to an organism's observable properties, are the units of inheritance, evolutionary biologists use the term *genotype* to refer to the specific genetic constitution of an organism, and *phenotype* to refer to its observable morphological, physiological, and behavioral properties. This distinction is critical because genes are inherited at the moment of conception, whereas phenotypes develop over the life span of an organism, partly as a consequence of the underlying genotype, and partly in response to the environment.

In the case of linguistic and cultural systems, the units of inheritance are conceptual phenomena that structure behavior and can be transmitted socially (Boyd and Richerson 1985:33; Durham 1991:8–9; Sapir 1994:37, 55; Shennan 2002:37). We still have much to learn about the structure of human concepts on the neurocognitive level, but it is clear that their scale and complexity vary widely. In the case of language, for example, phonemes, individual words, grammatical structures, manners of speaking, and entire languages can all be considered units of transmission, depending on one's frame of reference. Dawkins (1986) refers to these socially acquired conceptual models as *memes*; I will refer to them as *cultural models* to emphasize that language and culture change involves change in the socially acquired conceptual models that guide behavior, rather than behavior itself.

It is important to emphasize that surface behavior is often a poor proxy for the underlying cultural models that structure it. When children acquire their native language, for example, they do not merely store and recall the sentences spoken to them by their parents; rather, they abstract from this input general patterns which can then be used to generate infinite utterances (Pinker 1994). These patterns, which are never made explicit by parents, are what are internalized, and it is these patterns which act as a subsequent guide to speech behavior. In addition, individuals have the ability to learn and use multiple languages, each of which has a unique history and continues to develop independently, despite being stored in the same brains and externalized by the same persons. So although languages physically exist only as neural activation patterns in individual brains, they nevertheless exhibit descent with modification independent of the individuals who internalize these patterns and externalize them in speech.

Many additional domains of culture appear to work the same way. When an individual learns how to make an artifact, for example, what he or she internalizes are recipes and techniques that enable them to create new examples of the same category of object, each of which will be unique in subtle or not so subtle ways. What is transmitted in this case are not the behaviors involved in making the objects, or the objects themselves, but mental representations of the recipes and techniques required to fashion examples of a category of object (Miller 1985). Even more importantly, there is no simple one-to-one correspondence between individuals, cultural models, and surface behavior. As examples: individuals can internalize multiple social identities and behave in accordance with the one they perceive to be most advantageous in a given situation;[3] they may vary in their exposure to, and understanding of, the central concepts of their religion, despite widespread knowledge of ritual behaviors based on these canonical ideas;[4] and the same objects often have different connotations for different people, or mean many different things all at once.[5] In sum, there is no necessary correspondence between individual behavior and cultural models as there is between individual phenotypes and genes. This is a major difference between biological evolution on the one hand, and language and culture change on the other.

Sources of Variation

The second requirement of an inheritance system is sources of variation. In a biological system the primary source of variation is mutation. Changes in specific genes resulting from mutation may persist and spread in a population over time if they are not disadvantageous with respect to reproduction. Evolutionary biologists refer to these variants of individual genes as *alleles*. However, random changes in portions of the genome that are essential for proper functioning are almost always deleterious, and as a result the process of speciation is quite slow, on the order of 100,000 generations (Cavalli-Sforza et al. 1994:24).

In contrast, "variations [in language] may be induced by the processes of assimilation or differentiation, by analogy, borrowing, fusion, contamination, random variation, or any number of processes in which the language system interacts with the physiological and psychological aspects of the individual" (Labov 1972:1–2). Cultural variation arises through similar processes, including individual learning, intuition, rational calculation, and analogy (Boyd and Richerson 1985:94–98). The fact that new variations in language and culture arise under the guidance of human physiology and psychology, as opposed to randomly, is one of the factors that lead language and culture change to be much more rapid than biological evolution.

Transmission Mechanisms

The third requirement of an inheritance system is transmission mechanisms. In biology, transmission of genes occurs only one way, from parents to offspring, and only at the moment of conception. In cultural and linguistic systems, in contrast, transmission involves social interaction and occurs in a variety of ways over the course of the life span. Cavalli-Sforza and Feldman (1981) distinguish three modes of cultural transmission: vertical (parent to offspring), horizontal (among peers), and oblique (from nonparental adults). Shennan (2002: 50) adds a fourth mode, concerted transmission (from expert to novice), to this typology.

Vertical transmission is clearly an important means by which language and culture are inherited. A child's native language is almost always learned through interaction with parents during the first few years of life, and several studies demonstrate that knowledge of crafts, the local environment, subsistence practices, life skills, values, beliefs, and dispositions are also initially obtained from parents during childhood (some of these are summarized in Boyd and Richerson 1985:46–55; and in Shennan 2002:38–42). It is equally important, however, to recognize that individuals retain the ability to acquire new models, or to replace their "native" models via horizontal, oblique, or concerted transmission throughout life. In fact, horizontal and oblique transmission appears to increase in frequency during adolescence and adulthood, even for domains that are initially acquired from parents (Boyd and Richerson 1985:53–55).

During periods of "normal" social reproduction, it may be reasonable to model specific cultural domains as being acquired through specific transmission modes during certain phases in the life cycle.[6] But this may not be reasonable during periods of resource scarcity, social conflict, migration, or culture contact. For example, it is obvious from the literature on revitalization movements (Jorgensen 1972; Lincoln 2003: Chap. 6; Mooney 1896; Preucel 2006: Chap. 9; Wallace 1956) that such movements encourage rapid replacement of inherited cultural models with new models defined by leaders of the movement. Shennan (2002:50) adds the important observation that oblique transmission, which is characteristic of such movements, tends to reduce the amount of variation in a population and increase the rate of culture change relative to other forms of cultural transmission (Table 2.1). Finally, it is obvious from contemporary migration literature (Brettel and Hollifield 2008) and from archaeological studies of migration (Clark 2001; Stone 2003) that increased horizontal transmission is a fundamental consequence of migration for both migrants and locals.

Thus, the relative contribution of various modes of transmission to the store of cultural models in the brains of individuals varies not only over their life spans, but also with social context. As a result, changes in language and culture are much more sensitive to social context than is biological evolution (Cavalli-Sforza and Feldman 1981:356–357; Labov 2001; Thomason and Kaufmann 1988). A variety of processes — including migration, ethnic interaction, social

TABLE 2.1. Modes of cultural transmission

	VERTICAL	HORIZONTAL	OBLIQUE	CONCERTED
Transmitter	Parent	Peer	Teacher/leader	Expert/elder
Receiver	Child	Peer	Student/follower	Novice/ apprentice
Variation within population	High	Can be high	Low	Very low
Rate of change	Slow	Can be rapid	Most rapid	Most conservative

Source: Shennan 2002:50.

movements, social conflict, and resource scarcity—can lead to the replacement of models transmitted vertically during childhood by models transmitted via other mechanisms.[7]

Transformation Forces

The fourth requirement of an inheritance system is transformation forces. Two such forces are responsible for transformation in biological systems. The first is natural selection, or differential reproduction by phenotypes, which leads to increases in the proportion of certain alleles in a population, and decreases in others. Because selection fixes beneficial alleles and eliminates detrimental ones, most of the genetic variation in human populations is neutral variation (Cavalli-Sforza et al. 1994:15). Thus, the second force of transformation, random genetic drift, is the more important force in the study of human population history and diversity. Drift arises from fluctuations in allele frequencies from generation to generation as a result of random sampling of gametes. When selection pressures are weak, random deviations in allele proportions in each generation will outweigh differential reproduction in affecting gene frequencies in a population over time. Drift serves to reduce genetic diversity within groups, and increase genetic differences between groups, at a rate that is inversely proportional to the effective population size of a mating network. Consequently, small populations can diverge rapidly when they become isolated from each other (Cavalli-Sforza et al. 1994:13–16), but residues of common ancestry can remain for some time due to the relatively long generation length in humans.

The same process of iterative sampling error also operates on linguistic and cultural variation, but drift is not terribly important for language and culture change due to the human ability to continuously acquire new models through individual and social learning (Henrich 2004:207–208; Labov 1972:165).[8] Natural selection has also played a major role in the evolution of human cognitive abilities (Barkow et al. 1992), but is a relatively minor factor in language and culture change because humans have the ability to choose among alternative models on the basis of perceived and valued consequences, and can impose their preferred models on others in accordance with their position in society. Thus, language and culture change are governed by other processes.

A number of factors internal to language play a role in regular sound change, including limitations in the human ability to control the speech organs, limitations in human auditory perception (Campbell 1998:286), and the tendency to avoid homophony (Campbell 1998:292–293). However, the dominant force of both linguistic and cultural transformation is cultural selection, or the processes by which individuals choose among a series of cultural models related to a given domain.[9] Cultural selection incorporates several distinct processes. Boyd and Richerson (1985:134–135) and Henrich (2001:997–998) note three ways in which human psychology influences the spread, persistence, or disappearance of cultural models in a social group over time: (1) direct bias, where cultural models are adopted or rejected based on individual judgments about the models themselves; (2) prestige bias, where individuals preferentially adopt models associated with prestigious individuals in the group; and (3) conformist bias, where individuals preferentially adopt models that others have already adopted.

Social factors also exert a major influence. There are always fields of tension in society based on differential access to resources, prestige, and authority, and it is often in the interest of the privileged to impose their norms and preferences on others through hegemonic discourse, threat of sanction, or direct use of force. As a result, individuals rarely have the ability to choose freely in an absolute sense (Bourdieu 1990; Giddens 1979; Harvey 1996; Lincoln 2003; Sahlins 2000; Sewell 2005). In addition, constraints on choice tend to increase during periods of social instability or resource scarcity, when deteriorating material conditions encourage ideological competition, political factionalism, and social conflict. Thus, the degree to which individuals are free to choose varies in accordance with their position in society and the social context in which cultural selection occurs.

Durham (1991:198–205) combines these observations into a model of cultural selection as a two-dimensional process (Figure 2.1). One axis represents the continuum between choice (free decision making) versus imposition (compliance with the decisions of others), the latter of which occurs through the exercise of various forms of social power, including coercion (threat of sanction), force (elimination of dissenters), manipulation (influence or control over the values and desires of others), and authority (through which the commands of others come to be viewed as appropriate in terms of one's own values) (Durham 1991:198). The other axis represents the continuum between primary value selection (on the basis of innate psychological dispositions, motivations, and reasoning mechanisms that evolved through natural selection) and secondary value selection (on the basis of socially transmitted values, norms, and preferences that emerge from the interaction of cultural models with primary values)

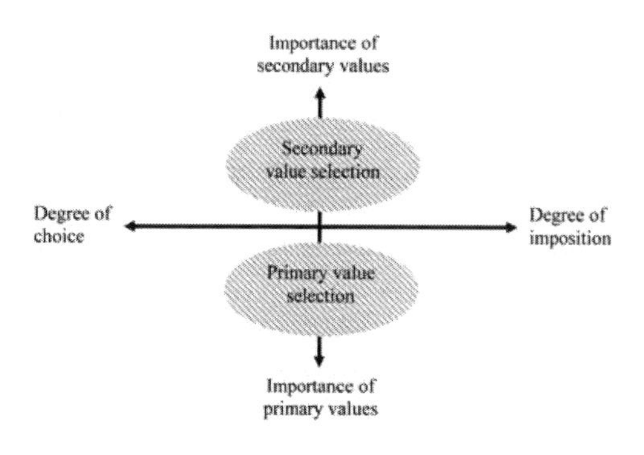

FIGURE 2.1. The structure of cultural selection (after Durham 1991: Fig. 4.6).

(Durham 1991:198–202).[10] In this model the process through which individuals decide which cultural models to adopt, maintain, or discard is primarily a function of values-based selection, with individual values dominating under conditions of free choice, and others' values dominating under conditions of imposition. In the latter case, "Imposition succeeds either because manipulation has spread the imposers' values through the reference group, or because the imposers have narrowed the range of choices to those favored by their own values, or both" (Durham 1991:433).

An important aspect of Durham's model is its implication that cultural phylogenies result not only from transmission mechanisms, but also from evaluation of the consequences of cultural models in light of primary and secondary values, under social conditions that vary from those in which free choice is dominant to those in which imposition is dominant. Thus, cultural traditions (including languages) can exhibit descent with modification across episodes of horizontal, oblique, or concerted transmission that can decouple these traditions from biological lineages.

Studies of language change clearly support this conclusion. Fine-grained studies of sound change, for example, indicate that changes in the pronunciation of phonemes initially spread horizontally among subgroups of a speech community due to their positive social value, rather than vertically from parents to offspring (Labov 1972:178–180). Yet the new dialects that result still exhibit descent with modification from earlier dialects and are subsequently transmitted from parents to children. Studies of language shift also show that this process emphasizes horizontal transmission and cultural selection. Language shift proceeds according to a characteristic pattern, where speakers first become bilingual, then the new language becomes the language of everyday communication, and finally the new language becomes the first language taught to children. The entire process may occur over a single generation (Thomason and Kaufman 1988:38–41), in which case the reasons for the shift can only be that adults determine it is in their interest to adopt the target language or they are forced to do so. As a result, the phylogeny associated with the native language is extinguished, but the phylogeny associated with the target language continues in the community that shifted to it.

The fact that cultural selection, or preservation by preference, is guided by human physiology, psychology, and social structure, as opposed to probabilistic forces, results in much faster rates of change in language and culture than in biology. Also, the fact that language change responds to factors internal to language itself, in addition to sociocultural factors, can result in a decoupling of language change from culture change, and a decoupling of both from biological evolution.

Sources of Isolation

Finally, the fifth requirement of an inheritance system is mechanisms that lead to the isolation of subgroups. In biology the primary source of isolation of gene pools is speciation. This occurs when gene flow between two portions of a mating network is reduced to the point that genetic differences accumulate independently in each portion. If gene flow remains below a critical threshold for a sufficient number of generations, the organisms in each subgroup will become so different that they are no longer able to mate and produce viable offspring. At this point a clade with two daughter species derived from a single parent species will have formed, and each daughter species will evolve independently. This process is known to biologists as *phylogenesis*.

All humans belong to a single species, but the initial stage of speciation — the independent accumulation of genetic differences due to reduced gene flow between portions of a mating network — has occurred many times in human history. Various forms of social isolation deriving from demic expansion, migration, and social conflict have also led to the accumulation of independent changes in the language and culture of local groups. Finally, a close analog of speciation actually does occur in the realm of language (Thomason and Kaufman 1988). When a speech community expands geographically or splits due to migration, distinct dialects will develop as changes in pronunciation accumulate independently in different portions of the social network. If the situation persists long enough, these dialects will lose mutual intelligibility, and a language family consisting of two or more daughter languages will have formed. Importantly, once languages become distinct from each other, they do not readily merge with subsequent contact, as genes and cultures may (Brettel and Hollifield 2008:11–14; Dixon 1997).

This is not to say that languages are immune from influence. Speakers routinely adopt individual words from other languages when they come in contact, and more significant influences in grammar and phonology can occur through a process called *interference through shift*, in which people who join a speech community learn the new language imperfectly and transmit these "errors" to native speakers (Thomason and Kaufman 1988:37–45). Nevertheless, there are only two situations in which languages that are not demonstrably descended from a single parent language arise (Thomason and Kaufman 1988:147–199). One of these is recurrent but limited social contact, which leads to the development of conventionalized jargons that are adequate for rudimentary communication but are not the native language of any community. These trade jargons are known as *pidgins*, and in some cases they can develop into full-fledged native languages that are not descended from a single parent, known as *creoles*. The other situation is extreme isolation of individuals of multiple linguistic backgrounds from any speech community, as occurred during the transatlantic slave trade. These individuals will rapidly create a creole language that allows them to communicate despite radically changed social conditions.

When previously isolated groups come into contact, genes and cultural models can, and often do, flow freely between them. Consequently, it often becomes problematic to speak of the resulting populations and/or cultures as having derived from a single parent (Moore 1994, 2001). But since pidgins rarely survive the period of contact, creoles only develop in certain situations, and most of the world's extant languages fall into language families, linguistic diversity is actually more phylogenetic in nature than either genetic or cultural diversity. In fact, residues of the phylogenetic relationships among languages persist for thousands of years, even in regions where people who speak related languages coexist for long periods. This is one of the primary reasons that language is appropriately viewed as a distinct system of inheritance from culture, despite the fact that these two systems have much more in common with each other than either has with the genetic system.

Summary

Table 2.2 summarizes the discussion above concerning genes, language, and culture as systems of inheritance. The table emphasizes that these three systems are distinct and have no necessary relationship, primarily because each bears a different relationship to population history. Neutral genetic variation provides a faithful representation of overall population history due to the mechanisms of gene flow, drift, and admixture, and the fact that individuals cannot alter their genes. Language, in contrast, preserves a stronger signal of differentiation than contact due to the prevalence of bilingualism and language shift over contact-induced change. Finally, culture bears the weakest relationship to population history due to its role in adaptation (Binford 1962), the relative ease with which cultural models are transmitted between individuals, and the mechanisms of cultural selection.

It should also be clear from this discussion that genetic evolution is a much simpler process than language or culture change, and that the latter two are quite similar in that they share neurocognitive units, variation that is generated under the guidance of human physiology and psychology, transmission through social interaction, and transformation through the interaction of human psychology with society. As a result, there is a basis for considering language as an especially well delimited domain of a single, cultural inheritance system. At the same time, however, the histories of languages are clearly distinct from the histories of other cultural domains, and linguistic change has a unique character due to the nature of language as a formal symbolic system, the habitual and unconscious nature of language use, the greater resistance of language to contact-induced change, and the limited function of language as a means of communication. Thus, even though it appears appropriate to view language as a domain of culture, and language change as part of the general process of culture change, it also remains appropriate to track language as a separate inheritance system.

TABLE 2.2. Comparison of human inheritance systems

Inheritance System	Function	Sources of Variation	Mode(s) of Transmission	Period of Transmission	Transformation Forces	Phylogenetic Signal	Results of Contact
Genes	Physiological adaptation	Mutation	Vertical	Moment of conception	Natural selection, drift	Moderate: isolation by distance, but also admixture	Gene flow
Language	Communication	Biological differences, guided variation	Vertical for acquisition, horizontal/oblique for adoption of innovations	Childhood for acquisition, then continuous throughout life span	Physiological and perceptual limitations, primary and secondary value selection	Strong: distinct languages do not merge readily	Borrowing, bilingualism, interference, language shift
Culture	Behavioral adaptation	Biological differences, guided variation	Vertical, horizontal, oblique, concerted	Continuous throughout life span	Primary and secondary value selection, influenced by imposition	Strong in stationary groups, weak in migrating groups	Hybridity, incorporation, acculturation

Ethnic Identity and Ethnic Groups

The reaffirmation of genes, language, and culture as distinct systems of inheritance raises a question of fundamental importance for this study: whether the ethnic group, in this case the Tewa, is an appropriate unit of study for historical anthropology. In his classic introduction to *Ethnic Groups and Boundaries*, Frederik Barth (1969:10–11) characterized the traditional anthropological view of the ethnic group as a population that: (1) is biologically self-perpetuating; (2) shares fundamental cultural values, realized in overt unity in practice; (3) makes up a field of communication and interaction; and (4) has a membership which identifies itself, and is identified by others, as constituting a social category distinguishable from other categories of the same order. This traditional view implies that ethnic groups form as a result of social and geographic isolation; that each group is associated with a distinctive biology, language, and culture; and that ethnic groups persist only in situations where within-group interaction dominates over between-group interaction.

It is difficult to reconcile this view with the notion that genes, language, and culture are distinct systems of inheritance. However, in the same essay Barth (1969:10–14) makes three key observations that cast doubt on the traditional view. First, ethnic groups persist despite intermarriage and gene flow between them. Thus, over the long term there is no necessary correspondence between ethnic groups and biological variation.[11] Second, stable, persistent, and even essential social relations are often maintained across ethnic group boundaries. Thus, ethnic groups persist despite regular exchange of cultural models and practices between them. In fact, their persistence often depends on the existence of other groups in a field of social interdependence. Third, there is no one-to-one correspondence between ethnic groups and cultural (and linguistic) similarities and differences. Rather, the features that matter for classifying individuals into groups are purely contextual. In other words, ethnic identities persist even as the cultural, linguistic, historical, religious, and/or physical characteristics that the members of these groups objectify as indicators of membership change over time. This means that, at any given moment, ethnic groups may be identified on the basis of biological, linguistic, or cultural differences, but that over the long term, there are no necessary material correlates of enduring ethnic identities.

These observations led Barth to formulate a view of ethnic groups as social identities to which people ascribe and are ascribed, and that assist in organizing social interaction. In other words, ethnic groups are behavioral realizations of cultural models that configure the human diversity of a region in such a way that social relations become more predictable, even if not always more peaceful or equitable. This view of ethnic groups has dominated anthropological discourse for the last 40 years. Combining Barth's insights (1969) with Bourdieu's practice theory (1977), Sian Jones (1997:72–92), developed the definitions of ethnic identity and ethnic group that I adhere to in this work. Following Jones (1997:xiii), I define *ethnic identity* as that aspect of a person's self-conceptualization that results from identification with a broader group in opposition to others on the basis of perceived cultural differentiation and/or common descent; and I define *ethnic group* as a group of people who set themselves apart and/or are set apart by others with whom they interact on the basis of perceived cultural differentiation and/or common descent. These definitions emphasize that ethnic groups are defined not on the basis of shared genes, language, and/or culture, but by cultural models that categorize people on the basis of perceptible variations construed to be important for structuring social relations in a given socio-natural environment.

This view is much more appropriate for a study of Tewa origins because it allows aspects of the biology, language, and culture of an ethnic group to evolve independent of that group as a behavioral or material entity. Defining ethnic groups as behavioral correlates of ethnic identities, as opposed to patterns in objective characteristics of groups, also clarifies that the study of ethnic origins is the study of how the concepts that bundle together a set of biological, linguistic, and cultural characteristics come into being, as opposed to the study of a population, a language, or a culture per se. The traditional view of ethnic groups conceptualizes them as individuals possessing a unique biology, language, and culture, but in fact ethnic groups do not exist as concrete individuals; rather, they emerge from cultural models that define groups. Also, if one views ethnic identity as a cultural model, then ethnic groups do not actually evolve; rather, it is ethnic identities — and the biological, linguistic, and cultural characteristics associated with them — that evolve. The importance of this conclusion is its suggestion that biological, linguistic, and cultural variation at any given moment represents the objective manifestations of ethnic identities in a region, but that over the long term, the objective characteristics that reflect these identities will evolve somewhat independently as these identities and the characteristics that define them evolve as well.

Thus, the fact that genes, language, and culture constitute distinct systems of inheritance does not pose a problem for the study of ethnic group formation so long as one frames the analysis in terms of cultural models (identities) rather than behavior (groups). When this is done, the question of whether it is most appropriate to view the inheritance of an ethnic group as derived from one or from multiple "parents" becomes an empirical problem rather than a theoretical assertion.

Inheritance, Phylogenesis, and Ethnogenesis

Ethnic groups often do arise through phylogenetic processes involving parallel descent of genes, language, and culture (Jordan 2007; Kirch and Green 2001; Mace et al. 2005; Shennan 2002, 2009). For example, when most marriages are endogamous, and the dominant mode of linguistic and cultural transmission is from parents to offspring, genes, language, and culture do tend to evolve in parallel within ethnic groups. The existence of correlated patterns of genetic, linguistic, and cultural variation across a series of groups also implies that these groups are descended from a common ancestor that diversified in response to factors that affected all three systems equally, such as migration and demic expansion. In such cases, population history will be the common factor underlying most variation in these groups' genes, language, and culture, and the three strands of human diversity will form a single evolutionary tree, with the ethnic groups in this phylogenetic unit as the leaves, and population events such as migrations being the branches (Bellwood and Renfrew 2003; Bellwood 2005; Cavalli-Sforza et al. 1994; Cavalli-Sforza et al. 1988; Kirch and Green 2001; Renfrew 1987; Thomason and Kaufmann 1988).

However, ethnic groups can also form through the process that anthropologists call *ethnogenesis*. In recent postcolonial scholarship this term has been used as a label for "peoples' simultaneously cultural and political struggles to create enduring identities in general contexts of radical change and discontinuity... imposed during the historical expansion of colonial and national states" (Hill 1996: 1). I use this term in its more general sense: as a label for the process through which "human beings occasionally create novel and original new cultures and societies by combining bits and pieces of pre-existing cultures in a fresh and enterprising manner" (Moore 1996:30). When ethnic groups originate through this process, the historical patterns of descent among genes, language, and culture will vary depending not only on the pattern of interactions involved, but also on the objective characteristics that become associated with the new ethnic identities that emerge (see Ferguson 2004). This does not necessarily mean that patterns of descent will not be apparent for the genetic, linguistic, and cultural lineages involved, but it does imply that these patterns will not be correlated. Consequently, one should not presume that a clear pattern of descent in one system necessarily reflects a parallel pattern of descent in the other systems. For example, descent with modification in a local archaeological sequence need not imply continuity in population; and conversely, the replacement of a local archaeological complex by an intrusive complex need not imply population movement if there is no supporting biological or demographic evidence.[12]

Because ethnic groups can and do arise through both phylogenetic and ethnogenetic processes, the pattern-matching procedures that are so often used to relate contemporary genetic and linguistic variation to the archaeological record (Ammerman and Cavalli-Sforza 1984; Bellwood and Renfrew 2003; Ford et al. 1972; Hill 2001; LeBlanc 2008; Ross 1998; Shennan 2002) are not appropriate for this study of Tewa origins. Such procedures assume correlated descent in genes, language, and culture, and thus presume a phylogenetic process at the outset, when in fact the nature of the process behind Tewa origins is an empirical question yet to be answered. A more appropriate approach is to forge links between past populations, speech communities, and communities of practice — one at a time. Such studies have been accomplished but have generally been limited to periods for which historic records are available (Hill 1996b; Moore 1987,

1996; Sturtevant 1971; Welsch et al. 1992). The shallow time depth of many ethnogenetic studies is due primarily to the fact that historic records often tie genes, language, and culture to specific times and places in a straightforward way; however, if one wishes to examine ethnic group formation in prehistory, one must tie genes, language, and culture to the archaeological record. This book provides an example of how this can be done.

Three Hypotheses on Tewa Origins

Previous research on Tewa origins has gravitated toward one of three models because each is a reasonable extrapolation from one of the fundamental lines of evidence related to the problem. It would therefore seem reasonable to take these three models as multiple working hypotheses to be evaluated through a series of studies that address the biological, linguistic, and cultural background of the Tewa Pueblos. In the final section of this chapter, I outline these three hypotheses; develop expectations for biological, linguistic, and cultural patterns under each hypothesis; and provide a road map to the various studies that address these expectations.

Hypotheses

The first scenario, which I call the *in situ development hypothesis*, proposes that the Tewa Pueblos developed from the initial settlers of the Tewa Basin. This hypothesis presumes that: population growth during the Coalition period was due primarily to robust intrinsic growth of the Late Developmental population; the Tewa language became distinct from other Tanoan languages in the Tewa Basin; the Tewa Basin archaeological record reflects continuous local development with no significant external inputs; and oral traditions of ancient homelands either represent memories of a distant time, prior to the emergence of a distinct Tewa identity, or narratives that should not be interpreted in historical terms.

The second scenario, which I call the *immigration hypothesis*, proposes that the Tewa Pueblos derived from the incorporation of San Juan migrants into established local communities. This hypothesis presumes that: population growth during the Coalition period reflects long-term in-migration of small groups from the San Juan; the Tewa language originated in the Tewa Basin, and subsequent migrants shifted to this language upon arrival; the Tewa Basin archaeological record reflects the hybridization of San Juan and Tewa Basin culture; and oral traditions of ancient homelands in the northwest represent the memories of San Juan migrants who joined Tewa Basin communities during the Coalition period.

Finally, the third scenario, which I call the *population movement hypothesis*, proposes that the Tewa Pueblos derived from a mass migration from the Mesa Verde region. This hypothesis presumes that: population growth during the Coalition period reflects an increasing pace and scale of in-migration from the Mesa Verde region; the Tewa language originated in the Mesa Verde region and was brought to the Tewa Basin by these migrants; the Tewa Basin archaeological record reflects the large-scale adoption of local material traditions by Mesa Verde migrants; and oral traditions referring to ancient homelands in the northwest represent social memories of the place where the Tewa population and language originated.

Expectations

The three hypotheses introduced above lead to a series of distinct but partly overlapping expectations for the various lines of evidence available for investigating Tewa origins. I summarize these expectations in Table 2.3 and briefly introduce them here, leaving more detailed treatments for specific chapters.

These hypotheses lead to different expectations not only for population growth rates in the Tewa Basin, but also for the spatial pattern of growth over time. In the in situ development model, the ancestral Tewa population is seen as resulting primarily from strong intrinsic growth of the initial Tewa Basin population. In this case the observed population history of the Tewa Basin should not imply intrinsic growth rates that exceed maximum plausible rates of natural increase, and the spatial pattern of growth should reflect an expansion of population outward from the initial area of settlement. The immigration hypothesis, in contrast, posits that the ancestral Tewa population resulted from the integration of substantial numbers of Mesa Verde migrants into the indigenous Tewa Basin population. In this case growth rates could exceed maximum plausible rates of natural increase, and the spatial pattern of growth should be one where the most robust growth occurs in areas that were already settled when the migration period began. Finally, the population movement hypothesis proposes that the ancestral Tewa population resulted from the establishment of new communities composed primarily of migrants from the Mesa Verde region. In this case growth rates could exceed maximum plausible rates of natural increase, and one would expect the spatial pattern of growth to be one in which new population centers developed during the period of migration. In addition, one would expect the pace of migration into the Tewa Basin to have increased over time as the final depopulation of the Mesa Verde region took place. I address these expectations regarding Tewa Basin population history through reviews of recent archaeological approaches to population as well as previous studies of Tewa Basin population in Chapter 3, and a new study of Tewa Basin population history in Chapter 4.

These three hypotheses also lead to different expectations for the pattern of biological variation in the late prehispanic Eastern Pueblo area. Under the in situ development model, one would expect ancestral Tewa populations of the Classic (AD 1350–1540) period to be direct descendants of Developmental (AD 900–1200) period populations of the Northern Rio Grande, with minimal evidence for admixture with peoples from outside the region. Based on the models of Mera (1935) and Wendorf and Reed (1955), one would also expect Pueblo III (AD 1150–1300) Mesa Verde populations to bear a closer affinity to ancestral Keres populations than to ancestral Tewa populations. Under the immigration

TABLE 2.3. Hypotheses and expectations

CATEGORY OF EVIDENCE	HYPOTHESIS 1: IN SITU DEVELOPMENT	HYPOTHESIS 2: IMMIGRATION	HYPOTHESIS 3: POPULATION MOVEMENT
Population history	Within limits of natural increase; expansion from area of initial settlement	Growth primarily in areas settled prior to migration period	Growth primarily in areas settled during migration period
Pace and duration of movement	Not applicable	Variable pace, long-term	Accelerating pace and scale
Biological affinity of ancestral Tewa population	With early Tewa Basin populations	With Mesa Verde region populations	With Mesa Verde region populations
Pattern of genetic admixture	No evidence of significant admixture	Proportional to numbers of locals and migrants	Proportional to numbers of locals and migrants
Date of Tewa language divergence	Prior to Spanish contact	Prior to Spanish contact	Prior to migration period
Antiquity of Tewa speech in the Tewa Basin	Same as closest relatives	Same as closest relatives	Coalition period
Homeland of the Tewa language	Tewa Basin	Tewa Basin	Mesa Verde region
Oral tradition, Spanish documents	Memories of northern homeland do not exist or have other interpretations	Vague memories of northern homeland	Widespread memories of northern homeland
Source area archaeological record	Not applicable	Gradual decline; incomplete depopulation; diffuse, long-distance contacts	Accelerating decline; permanent, long-distance moves; increasing contact with destination area
Destination area archaeological record	Gradual change in individual traits	Site unit intrusions; ethnic coresidence	Punctuated change in new sites; homeland continuities that vary with destination context

model, in contrast, one would expect Classic period ancestral Tewa populations to exhibit affinities with earlier, Mesa Verde populations, and to exhibit evidence of admixture between Developmental Rio Grande and Pueblo III Mesa Verde populations. Finally, under the population movement model, one would expect Classic period ancestral Tewa populations to be lineal descendants of Mesa Verde region populations, and would not expect this lineage to exhibit evidence of significant admixture with, or close affinity to, Developmental Rio Grande populations. I evaluate these expectations in a study of prehispanic Eastern Pueblo biological variation in Chapter 5.

These hypotheses also lead to distinct expectations for the history of the Tewa language. Under the in situ development and immigration models, the Tewa language would have originated in the Tewa Basin and would have been spoken there from the time it became distinct to the present day. Thus, the Tewa language could have become distinct at any time prior to AD 1540, when it was documented as a distinct language by the earliest Spanish explorers. Under the population movement hypothesis, in contrast, the Tewa language would have to have originated in the San Juan drainage prior to AD 1200, the beginning of the Coalition period. Because we have no inscriptions with which to trace the development of the Tewa language, evaluating these expectations will prove to be the most complex undertaking of this study. In Chapters 6 through 10 I will break these expectations down into a series of questions that are each answerable through different approaches. In Chapter 6 I examine the sequence of speech-community events that produced the Kiowa-Tanoan languages to better understand how the Tewa language became distinct; in Chapter 7 I examine reconstructed cultural vocabularies for various Kiowa-Tanoan subgroups to investigate the homelands and divergence dates of these subgroups, and to estimate where and when Tewa became a distinct language; in Chapter 8 I examine Tewa place-names in an effort to determine the minimum length of time Tewa has been spoken in the Northern Rio Grande region; and in Chapters 9 and 10 I evaluate whether Tewa was spoken in the Mesa Verde region through a study of archaeological expressions of conceptual metaphors that are also embedded in the Tewa language.

One would expect social memories of Mesa Verde region occupancy to vary substantially under these hypotheses. Under the in situ development model, one would expect any such traditions that do exist to have interpretations that do not imply former occupancy of the Mesa Verde region. Under the immigration model, one would expect these traditions to have been translated from the language of the Mesa Verde region into Tewa, and for much of this memory to have been lost due to assimilation to the historical identity of the Tewa Basin. Thus, one would expect oral traditions surrounding former occupancy of the Mesa Verde region to be vague and inconsistent in their details. Finally, under the population movement hypothesis, migration from the Mesa Verde region would be expected to have been an important element of ancestral Tewa identity, and one would expect oral traditions surrounding former occupancy of the Mesa Verde region to be consistent in their details and to have been more widespread in the past than they are at present. One might also expect to find reflections of this historical consciousness in Spanish documents concerning seventeenth- and eighteenth-century New Mexico. To address these expectations, I will examine oral traditions surrounding Tewa migrations, and their reflections in Spanish documents, along with place-names and place-lore in Chapter 8.

Finally, the competing models of Tewa origins lead to distinct expectations for the archaeological record; however, following the lead of McNutt (1969) and Duff (1996), I argue in Chapter 11 that these expectations lie not so much in the realm of material culture continuities, but in the pattern of change in the archaeological records of the Tewa Basin and Mesa Verde region. From this perspective, under the in situ development hypothesis the pattern of change in the Tewa Basin archaeological record should bear no relationship to the process of depopulation in the Mesa Verde region, but should instead be characteristic of material culture change in an in situ society. In other words, the pattern of change in the Tewa Basin archaeological record from the Late Developmental period through the Early Classic period should be one of incremental and independent change in individual items of material culture. In contrast, under the immigration and population movement hypotheses, the nature of depopulation in the Mesa Verde region should be connected to the pattern of change in the Tewa Basin. Under the immigration hypothesis one would expect to see evidence of gradual population decline in the Mesa Verde region, social contacts with a wide range of migration destinations, and a cultural mosaic deriving from the dynamics of ethnic coresidence in the Tewa Basin. Under the population movement hypothesis one would instead expect to see evidence of accelerating population decline in the Mesa Verde region, increasingly focused social contacts with the Tewa Basin, and a pattern of pervasive and punctuated culture change in the Tewa Basin itself. These expectations are evaluated for the Mesa Verde region in Chapter 12, and for the Tewa Basin in Chapter 13.

Differences in the expected patterns for each line of evidence under each hypothesis considered in this study are in some cases subtle and may not uniquely specify one of the three hypotheses when considered in isolation. These hypotheses should also be viewed as a framework to guide analyses of various lines of evidence, as opposed to rules that allow no deviation from expectations. One should not be surprised if these explorations lead to some unexpected conclusions. Nevertheless, it is clear that, on a multivariate level, each of these hypotheses suggests a unique configuration of evidence. Thus, although it may eventually turn out that none of these models adequately characterize Tewa origins, it is unlikely that more than one will remain plausible when the full range of evidence is considered.

With the conceptual framework and competing hypotheses now in place, let us begin the process of unraveling Tewa origins, beginning with population history.

Notes

1. Kirch and Green (2001:2–9) present an overview of historical anthropology and its development from Sapir to the present.

2. Examples of major studies that attempt to integrate the findings of multiple subfields of anthropology include Flannery and Marcus 1983; Ammerman and Cavalli-Sforza 1984; Rouse 1986; Renfrew 1987; Moore 1987; Mallory 1989; Durham 1991; Kirch and Sahlins 1992; Cavalli-Sforza et al. 1994; Madsen and Rhode 1994; Kirch and Green 2001; Bellwood and Renfrew 2003; Shennan 2002; Bellwood 2005; Bernardini 2005; Anthony 2007; and Gregory and Wilcox 2007.
3. Kroskrity (1993) illustrates the situational nature of identity through an analysis of "code-switching" behavior among the Arizona Tewa. The people who live in Tewa Village, on Hopi First Mesa in northeastern Arizona, are trilingual in Arizona Tewa, Hopi, and English, and tend to use the language that is most appropriate for the social identity they wish to take on in any given situation. In other words, individuals sometimes speak as an Arizona Tewa person, other times as a member of the Hopi tribe, and still other times as an American citizen. Thus, social identity can be viewed as a conceptual vantage point from which individuals address a given social situation.
4. Merrill (1988) illustrates intrasocietal variation in religious beliefs through an analysis of beliefs surrounding "souls" in Rarámuri communities of northern Mexico. He shows that Rarámuri tend to agree on ideas about souls that are conveyed in curing and death rituals, or are logically presupposed by these ideas, but disagree on ideas that are neither made explicit in these rituals nor contingent upon those that are. This finding suggests that "The reproduction of all knowledge requires at a minimum two steps: the transmission of information through social practices, and the incorporation, organization, and elaboration of this information by individuals" (Merrill 1988: 192). Merrill's study demonstrates that cultural models of the soul are not mirror images of the models expressed in ritual behavior and are not transmitted directly, in a precise parallel to language learning.
5. Thomas (1991) illustrates how the same objects mean different things to different people through his analysis of the uses of indigenous artifacts by explorers, missionaries, planters, and ethnologists in the South Pacific. For explorers, indigenous objects were testaments to "having visited remote places and observed novel phenomena" (141), thus substantiating relations of knowledge and power. For missionaries, the acquisition of idols from native converts, who gave them up as part of their conversion, symbolized the success of their efforts and the worthiness of their cause. For planters, the most important objects were those that supported the discourse of natives as lazy savages who should be swept aside by the tide of progress. Finally, for ethnologists, native objects were valuable as scientific specimens that attested to objective social facts as opposed to subjective individual histories.

   Ucko (1969) also illustrates how objects mean several things simultaneously through a comparative study of methods for sheathing the glans penis in societies where it is not obscured by other articles of clothing such as trousers, skirts, or leggings. Among most sheathing peoples, exposure of the penis is a sign of nakedness and lewdness, yet many sheathing practices are strikingly noticeable and draw greater attention to the anatomy that is obscured from view. In addition, formal variation in penis sheaths often reflects the social and political status of the people who wear them. Thus, penis sheaths are simultaneously modesty coverings, display signs of virility, and status symbols.
6. A good example of an archaeological approach built on these assumptions is the model developed by Clark (2001), which is discussed in Chapter 11.
7. This would seem to be one of the major reasons why descent with modification is often more apparent within local archaeological sequences than it is between them.

8. Neiman (1995) has developed and applied an archaeological model of cultural drift, but subsequent applications (Kohler, VanBuskirk et al. 2004; Shennan and Wilkinson 2001) have used this model primarily as a null hypothesis against which to compare the data, and have found that more than drift is necessary to account for the observed patterns.
9. For example, Labov (1972:23) argues that the primary mechanism of sound change is the assignment of a positive social value to an allophone (a phonetic variant of a phoneme, analogous to an allele), thus encouraging the new pronunciation to spread.
10. The psychological mechanisms that lead to biased cultural transmission in Boyd and Richerson's (1985) framework are considered aspects of primary value selection in Durham's framework.
11. A good example is the persistence of an Arizona Tewa identity that contrasts with Hopi identity and continues to be objectified by language differences, despite the fact that speakers of these two languages now constitute a single biological population (Dozier 1954:289).
12. In this study I define *archaeological complex* as the constellation of material culture traits that are characteristic of a particular area during a definable period of time.

Population and Movement

The primary line of evidence supporting migration models of Tewa origins, despite the apparent absence of corroborating material culture evidence, is the population history of the Rio Grande drainage. Indeed, researchers from Kidder (1924) to Duff (1998) have considered the evidence of population growth in the Rio Grande drainage, combined with evidence for coincident decline in the San Juan drainage, as the strongest argument in favor of migration between the two areas. However, recent archaeological work on population illustrates that archaeologically derived population histories represent the net result of several distinct processes, only one of which is migration into or out of an area. Estimating population from archaeological remains has always been a challenging task, and not all studies of Tewa Basin population have concluded that large-scale migration from the San Juan is required to account for the observed changes. To evaluate the role of population processes in Tewa origins, we need to understand how these processes contribute to archaeologically derived population histories, and also to review previous studies of Tewa Basin population history with an eye toward their strengths and weaknesses. I cover both topics here, and apply the insights gained to the construction and interpretation of an updated Tewa Basin population history in the following chapter.

Population Histories and Population Processes

Population histories derived from archaeological remains consist of a series of estimates of the momentary population of a given area during each of a series of chronological periods, based on quantification and apportionment of some aspect of the archaeological record, most often dwelling space. In these reconstructions, observed changes in population between adjacent periods are the net result of three processes: (1) migration into or out of the area; (2) demographic processes that result in intrinsic population growth or decline; and (3) internal migration, especially movement of individuals into or out of characteristic settlements of the ethnic group considered in the population estimates. In the following pages I take a closer look at each of these factors and how each is reflected in archaeologically derived population histories.

External Migration

Patterned movement into or out of an area is obviously one of the primary processes that can lead to increases or decreases in local populations. Prior to the development of concrete methods for estimating population, migration was inferred on a qualitative and relative basis, primarily in cases where regions were depopulated or colonized (e.g., Kidder 1924). As researchers have developed methods for estimating absolute population numbers, they have turned their attention to more subtle cases where movements into or out of continuously populated regions may have taken place. Researchers have generally followed one of two approaches to inferring migration on the basis of local population histories. In one approach, in-migration is argued to be a reasonable interpretation when the observed rate of population growth exceeds the maximum sustainable intrinsic growth rate observed in ethnographic studies of preindustrial societies (Cowgill 1975; Hassan 1981; Orcutt 1999b:229–230; Richerson et al. 2001; Varien et al. 2007). Researchers have also suggested that rapid population decline may be due to out-migration, but tying this inference to intrinsic growth rates is problematic because there is no lower limit to intrinsic population decline analogous to the upper limit on intrinsic population increase.

Another approach to inferring migration from local population histories relies on absolute population changes between potential source and destination areas. This approach is based on the seminal work of David Anthony (1990), who suggests that ancient migrations are best conceptualized as social processes involving information exchange networks, advance scouts, migration streams, and return migration. Because ancient migrations typically involved the interaction of populations in source and destination areas, and also occurred over a period of time, archaeologists who work with well-dated archaeological sequences like those in the U.S. Southwest have reasoned that it should be possible to catch migrations "in progress" by correlating population changes in likely source and destination areas (Duff 1998; Glowacki 2006; Schlanger and Wilshusen 1993; Wilshusen and Ortman 1999; Wilshusen and Van Dyke 2006). Although this correlative approach requires comparable population histories for both the source and destination areas, it is a more robust method than the intrinsic growth threshold approach because it involves tracking an absolute number of migrants from a source to a destination area. In other words, the threshold approach focuses only on the shape of an area's population history, whereas the correlative approach considers both the magnitude and the shape of the population histories in both a source and a destination area.

Intrinsic Population Processes

Although it appears relatively straightforward to infer migration from exceptional growth rates or correlated population changes, recent research on human population dynamics suggests that intrinsic population processes also play a significant role in local population histories. Stephen Shennan (2002:

102–119) provides a cogent summary of this research in his book *Genes, Memes, and Human History.* He reviews research in life-history theory — "a set of ideas from evolutionary biology concerned with the effect of natural selection in how organisms allocate their limited resources through the course of their lifetime" — to show that humans and other organisms have evolved physiological mechanisms for tailoring the energy devoted to reproduction to the availability of energy in the environment. Because these physiological mechanisms are a product of natural selection, their existence implies that maximizing reproductive fitness does not necessarily mean maximizing fertility, but rather maximizing the number of offspring who reach maturity. Thus a better indicator of reproductive success is not an individual's total number of offspring, but rather the number of grandchildren.

Shennan suggests that humans have also evolved cultural mechanisms that enhance these biological responses, and that individuals seeking to maximize their reproductive fitness — whether consciously or by habit, tradition, or instinct — will tend to put more energy into bearing and raising children when there is a surplus of resources. In this view, population effects are consequences of individual adaptive decisions about reproductive strategies. The material conditions affecting people influence individual fertility, and the resulting patterns of population growth, stability, or decline reflect the relative success of past human adaptations. From the perspective of life-history theory, then, population growth indicates the availability of new resources made possible by improvements in food sources, climate, exchange systems, social relations, or technology. Population stability, on the other hand, indicates population pressure on available resources (also see Schacht 1980:792–793).[1]

Shennan (2002:115–134) takes the argument one step further, suggesting that life-history theory provides an alternative explanation to migration for the rapid fluctuations in human population evident in many archaeological sequences. He reviews a number of studies from archaeology, computer modeling, and biological anthropology which suggest that changes in material conditions — including the colonization of new lands, the development of new technologies, climatic oscillations, and human impacts on the environment — have dramatic effects on fertility and mortality, and lead to rapid changes in population. He draws upon these studies to suggest that oscillations in population often apparent in the archaeological record are due to both density-dependent and external factors, and result in alternating periods of strong population growth followed by crashes and, in some cases, extinction of local groups.

Shennan's work suggests that over short periods intrinsic population processes can be more extreme than the maximum sustainable growth rate evidenced in ethnographic studies. Because of this, rapid population swings, and even complete depopulation of an area, might also be explained by intrinsic population processes under unusual conditions and need not imply movement. It is important, however, to emphasize that it is not possible to disentangle the role of intrinsic processes versus migration on the basis of population estimates alone.

Shennan, in fact, made no attempt to control for population movement in the archaeological studies he reviewed, and thus migration might also explain some of the changes he observed in specific archaeological sequences. The key point is that both intrinsic population processes and migration contribute, in varying degrees, to local population histories.

Internal Migration

A final factor that is often overlooked but further complicates the interpretation of archaeologically derived population histories is that these histories track the numbers of people who participated in the communities of a given society, in a given area, at a given point in time. This is not the same thing as tracking the life histories of people who were born into that society. Researchers interested in the histories of ethnic groups often focus on tracking population changes in settlements that exhibit a particular group's characteristic material culture, as opposed to the population histories of all ethnic groups in a given region. It is possible that in certain situations some of the observed changes in ethnic group populations reflect the movement of individuals between communities of different ethnic groups within a region rather than intrinsic population processes or external migration. This problem is especially thorny in multiethnic landscapes because interaction in such settings is regular and intensive, making it difficult to model internal migration rates from material culture evidence.

A clear example of this problem is reflected in accounts of Pueblo population decline in seventeenth-century New Mexico. These accounts have tended to focus on declines in fertility and increases in mortality resulting from disease and depredations by the Spanish as well as native groups (Barrett 2002; Dobyns 1993; Schroeder 1979). However, demographic modeling by Trigg and Gold (2005) shows that, in addition to these factors, a large number of Pueblo women probably married Spanish men. The departure of these women from Pueblo communities would have further reduced the communities' demographic potential. Also, according to the journals of Diego de Vargas, significant numbers of Pueblo people from Jemez Pueblo, the Galisteo Basin, and the Tewa villages of Jacona and Cuyamunge joined Navajo communities during the Pueblo Revolt (Barrett 2002:97–111). These observations suggest that migration and incorporation into non-Pueblo groups also contributed to Pueblo population decline during the seventeenth century, but the absence of population studies of Hispanic and Navajo communities of this period make it impossible to determine the scale and impact of this movement.

Solutions

The discussion above illustrates that in addition to population estimates, archaeologists need to consider other lines of evidence to assess the relative contributions of external migration, intrinsic population processes, and internal migration to a given population history. One obvious place to turn is an examination of the spatial distribution of population within a region over time, in a sort of intraregional version of the correlative approach discussed earlier. If the population of a region expanded due to intrinsic growth over time, for example, one would expect it to have expanded outward from the earliest and most densely settled areas. In contrast, if population growth was due to large-scale in-migration, one would expect the initial migrants to have settled a previously unoccupied area instead of joining existing communities. The result would be the development of a second focal area of settlement rather than enhancement of an existing focal area. This approach can be operationalized by calculating population estimates separately for subregions in order to capture spatial variation in population density over time.

A second place to turn for evidence of population history is human skeletal remains. The use of skeletal morphology to study population history and movement has a long lineage in physical anthropology (Hooton 1930; Larsen 1997; Pietrusewsky 2000). The traditional approach has been to compare morphological traits of individuals from different skeletal samples to identify population affinities. In recent years it has also become possible to identify individuals who moved to new physical environments during their lifetimes by comparing trace element concentrations in teeth, which form during childhood and reflect an individual's natal environment, versus bones, which exchange trace elements with the environment over an individual's life span. Thus, if a person lived in a different physical environment at the time of death than they lived in when their adult teeth were forming, this movement will be reflected in trace element concentrations in their teeth and bones (Ezzo et al. 1997; Ezzo and Price 2002; Knudson and Price 2007; Price et al. 1994). Such studies can be used to estimate migration rates, or even to "source" individuals to their place of birth. Both can be of use in interpreting population histories constructed from settlement pattern evidence.

Skeletal indicators of health and disease may also be useful for interpreting intrinsic population processes independent of settlement pattern evidence. In general, these indicators are expected to be correlated with intrinsic growth rates, and some researchers have assumed this to be the case, but recent work has shown that the relationship between skeletal health indicators and population processes is not so clear (Wood et al. 1992). Most skeletal indicators of disease are a result of chronic rather than acute conditions. Thus when a skeletal stress marker such as porotic hyperostosis is visible on a person's bones, it means that that person suffered from the underlying condition, in this case nutritional deficiency, for an extended period of time. Because relatively frail individuals might perish from the same condition before it manifested itself in their bones, increased incidence of a stress marker in a skeletal population could be a reflection of increased ability to withstand the underlying disease process. In other words, somewhat paradoxically, populations that exhibit more skeletal indicators of stress may have had lower mortality rates than populations in which such indicators are rare. Consequently, skeletal indicators of stress are not straightforward proxies for mortality rates, which would be most useful for interpreting population histories.

In recent years a new method for estimating intrinsic growth rates has emerged from paleodemography, the study of ancient populations on the basis of skeletal remains from archaeological sites. Early work in this field focused on matching mortality profiles from skeletal remains with age-at-death profiles recorded in a range of historically documented societies (for a review, see Chambelain 2006:81–92). This approach was challenged by Boquet-Appel and Masset (1982), who pointed out that methods in use at that time for estimating skeletons' age at death were too imprecise for paleodemographic study and tended to superimpose onto archaeological samples the age structure of the reference collections from which the age indicators were developed. In response to these problems, paleodemographers have shifted their focus from life table analysis to direct estimation of demographic parameters. The most relevant work in this area is that of Boquet-Appel (2002; also see Boquet-Appel and Naji 2006), who showed that the ratio of individuals who died between the ages of 5 and 19 to the total number of individuals who lived to be 5 years or more is highly correlated ($r^2 > .87$) with the crude birth rate and rate of intrinsic growth in preindustrial human populations. This index provides a basis for estimating the intrinsic growth rate of a population independent of settlement pattern data. These estimates of intrinsic growth can then be compared to the realized growth rates suggested by the settlement pattern evidence to assess the relative contribution of intrinsic population processes and migration to a region's overall population history.

I utilize several of these approaches to disentangle the contributions of external migration, intrinsic population processes, and internal movement to the overall population history of the Tewa Basin. First, I calculate separate population estimates for subregions of the Tewa Basin to capture previously identified trends in settlement history, and to determine whether the spatial pattern of growth is more consistent with in-migration or intrinsic population processes. Second, I estimate intrinsic growth rates using the techniques developed by Boquet-Appel and data compiled in a recent publication by Kohler and others (2008) to assess the likelihood that population increases in the Tewa Basin during certain periods were due to intrinsic growth. Finally, I present a study of biological variation across the late prehispanic Eastern Pueblo world to assess whether AD 1200s population growth in the Tewa Basin was due to in situ growth, immigration, or population movement.

Previous Studies of Tewa Basin Population

Prior to presenting my own work, it is necessary to review previous studies of Tewa Basin population, highlighting their strengths and weaknesses, as a step in developing a new Tewa Basin population history. This is important because population estimates are notorious for being at the mercy of the assumptions built into the analysis. One must therefore identify and examine these assumptions, and specify how they influence results, if one is to improve upon previous efforts. Also, population studies in the Tewa Basin have used a variety of methods leading to divergent conclusions on the role of migration in Tewa origins. When confronted by this range of methods and interpretations, one is tempted to conclude that a number of reconstructions are equally plausible. I aim to show that this is not the case. Current knowledge of Tewa Basin archaeology suggests that certain assumptions are more realistic than others, and a persuasive population history needs to work from these assumptions.

Early Studies

An important early assessment of Tewa Basin population history is H. P. Mera's *Survey of the Biscuit Ware Area in Northern New Mexico* (1934). In this study Mera identified most of the large prehispanic settlements in the Tewa Basin and established the relative periods of occupation of each based on the range of pottery types he observed on the modern ground surface. Mera's analysis of population trends is based on the number and spatial extent of occupied villages, both of which clearly declined over time; however, he noted that those towns that remained grew larger over time, and thus the regional population appears to have been stable up until mid-sixteenth century, when population decline associated with Spanish contact set in. Mera's surface studies of large settlements remain a significant data source for interpreting population history in the Rio Grande region. I have incorporated both his pottery data and room counts estimated from his sketch maps into my own analysis.

Because Mera limited his analysis to sites with Biscuit ware pottery — whose initial date of manufacture (AD 1350) is well after the ancestral Tewa population was established — his study does not address the origins of this population. The first study that I am aware of that assessed population trends for earlier phases of Tewa Basin prehistory is Susan Collins's (1975) doctoral dissertation. Collins coded data for Developmental and Coalition period sites in eight, 100 km^2 quadrats selected from a larger (4,900 km^2) area of northern New Mexico. Three of her quadrats — centered on Upper White Rock Canyon (Quadrat VII), Santa Fe (Quadrat VI), and the Cañada de Cochiti (Quadrat V) — encompass portions of the Tewa Basin. Collins (1975:247) found that the number of new settlements established in the Cañada de Cochiti quadrat during the Coalition period (in this case, AD 1200–1325) represented a tenfold increase over the number of settlements occupied in the preceding Developmental period (AD 900–1200). Collins (1975:324–337) also translated room counts and site areas into population estimates, which showed that the population of the sites in her study area increased so rapidly during the Coalition period that in situ growth was an unlikely explanation.

Collins's study deserves more attention than it has received, but several areas have been improved upon by subsequent research. First, because she did not take into account the proportion of each quadrat that had been subjected to full-coverage survey, Collins ended up projecting archaeological patterns found in areas where the most work had been done (usually those with the most sites, and thus disproportionately large populations) onto her entire study area. Second, in translating room counts and site areas into population estimates, she assumed that house occupation spans were consistent over time. Subsequent research (Kohler, Powers et al. 2004:294–296; Orcutt 1999b:225–226) has suggested that the occupation spans of both individual rooms and sites overall increased through time.

These issues were addressed to some extent in Dickson's (1979) study of settlement patterns around Arroyo Hondo Pueblo, a large Late Coalition and Early Classic period site at the southern edge of the Tewa Basin. Dickson's study included full-coverage survey of the 18-square-mile "sustaining area" surrounding Arroyo Hondo Pueblo, and sample survey of a much larger transect extending from Arroyo Hondo to the Rio Grande. Dickson (1979:22–27) devised a site weight index (Number of Structures / Number of Phases of Occupation + 1) in an attempt to control for variation in site size and occupation span. Occupation spans were determined from the date ranges of pottery types present at each site. Dickson also corrected for varying phase lengths by dividing the estimated duration of each phase by the length of the shortest phase (in this case, 25 years) and then dividing the total site weight for each phase by this value. Note that the effect of standardizing to the minimum period length is essentially the same as assuming a structure use-life equal to the duration of the shortest phase for all sites in all periods. Thus, populations for phases during which structure occupation spans were greater than 25 years are underestimated in Dickson's study, and populations for phases during which occupation spans of structures were shorter than 25 years are overestimated.

The resulting population history suggests a modest increase in population between the Middle and Late Developmental (AD 900–1200) periods, which Dickson argued could be accounted for by in situ growth, followed by robust population growth during his Early Coalition period (AD 1200–1250), a modest decline during his Middle Coalition period (AD 1250–1300), and then striking growth during his Late Coalition period (AD 1300–1325), corresponding to the foundation of Arroyo Hondo Pueblo. Dickson interprets population change during the Early and Late Coalition periods as the result of migration into the study area, but the limited geographical extent of that area means that his results do not necessarily imply movement from any great distance. It is possible the growth was simply movement from surrounding areas, as is the case in many accounts of aggregation (e.g., Adler 1994; Kintigh et al. 2004). It is therefore necessary to assess population across the entire Tewa Basin if such estimates are to have a bearing on the origins of the ancestral Tewa population.

Recent Studies

Several population studies were completed in the 1990s. Applying Dickson's methodology to a probabilistic sample survey of the Pajarito Plateau, Orcutt (1991) suggested a history of robust population growth during the Coalition period, followed by long-term decline in the Classic period. Crown and others (1996) presented curves representing changes in living space over time in several districts, all of which suggested robust growth between AD 1200 and 1400, but they refrained from translating these figures into population estimates. Dean and others (1994:68–69) presented a population reconstruction for the entire Northern Rio Grande region that showed dramatic growth beginning in AD 1100, reaching a peak of roughly 28,000 people by AD 1300. This was followed by an almost equally precipitous decline between AD 1300 and 1600, such that the population of the Northern Rio Grande at AD 1600 was less than it was at AD 1200.[2]

In an unpublished but often-cited conference paper, Maxwell (1994) developed a population history for the Chama District, which encompasses the northern portion of the Tewa Basin. Maxwell worked from maps of major sites created by Mera (1934) and Beal (1987) to estimate the total living space in each site. He then multiplied the total living space by the proportion of the total occupation span represented by each phase to estimate the living space at each site for each phase. He then standardized these figures to a 19-year structure occupation span (based on Crown's [1991] study of Pot Creek Pueblo) to estimate the total momentary living space during each phase. Based on these figures, Maxwell calculated growth rates and populations using a variety of estimates of people per square meter of roofed area. He interpreted these results as suggesting that significant in-migration was not needed to account for the population history of the Chama District.

Maxwell's (1994) study is significant because it is the first to suggest that the Classic period population in a portion of the Tewa Basin could be accounted for by in situ growth of the initial population. However, two aspects of Maxwell's method suggest that the resulting population estimates are not very realistic. First, by apportioning the total living space at each site across the periods of occupation at each site, Maxwell modeled the occupational histories of Chama villages as Dickson had done, essentially assuming that living space accumulated in the same way as pot sherds or stone flakes. Consequently, the occupancy rate of each site is no greater than the inverse of the number of periods of occupation. Excavations in Tewa Basin settlements suggest that this is not a reasonable assumption (see Chapter 4). Rather, it appears that in most cases nearly the entire architectural footprint of a site was occupied during the period of peak occupation. Thus, Maxwell's procedure reduces estimates of the peak populations of Chama villages by a factor of 2 or 3. Maxwell's procedures also average out the populations of sites over time. Given the evidence reviewed in Chapter 4 that villages actually grew over time, Maxwell's procedures overestimate population during the initial period and underestimate it during the final period.

Second, by standardizing living space estimates by a structure use-life parameter, Maxwell (1994) built in the assumption that each square meter of living area was used only for the use-life of a single room. The notion that puddled adobe structures did not last very long before needing repair or rebuilding is reasonable, but excavations in Tewa Basin sites suggest that a given square meter of mound area was used for a much longer period than the use-life of any of the rooms constructed on that spot over the history of occupation (see Chapter 4). Therefore, the concept of structure use-life appears to be inappropriate for interpreting the occupational histories of large sites in the Tewa Basin, and application of this concept in Maxwell's study has the effect of reducing the total momentary populations of large sites by a factor of 4 to 5. As a result, Maxwell produced overly conservative estimates.[3]

In what is perhaps the most analytically complex study yet accomplished within the Tewa Basin, Orcutt (1999a, 1999b) analyzed survey data from a stratified random sample of environmental zones and administrative units encompassing 16 percent of Bandelier National Monument to reconstruct the population history of the entire monument, which occupies the southwestern corner of the Tewa Basin. In the first stage of her analysis, Orcutt (1999a) performed cluster analyses of pottery assemblages from an appropriate sample of Bandelier Survey sites to define clusters that represented pottery periods. She then matched tree-ring-dated assemblages to these clusters to estimate the date range of each one. Then she used the clusters' assemblage profiles as calibration data in a multiple regression analysis (see Kohler and Blinman 1987) to establish periods of occupation for all Bandelier Survey sites.

In the second stage Orcutt (1999b) applied Dickson's methods to apportion room-block areas across periods of occupation, and to standardize estimates to the length of the shortest period. She then converted room-block areas to room counts, applied secondary weighting functions for the use-life of structures and occupancy rate, and assigned two persons to each occupied room to estimate the momentary population of the survey sample. Finally, she divided the sample population estimates by the survey proportion to estimate the total momentary population of Bandelier National Monument during each of eleven time periods. Her results suggest that Bandelier's population history was characterized by several dramatic swings that imply equally dramatic population movements and/or booms and crashes.

Although this study is, in many ways, an improvement over previous efforts, a few details require comment. To facilitate discussion, Table 3.1 presents the series of weighting functions that Orcutt applied to the Bandelier Survey data, and her average momentary population estimates. The first concern is that Orcutt's method of creating pottery periods may have resulted in chronological divisions that are too precise for practical application. For example, the shortest periods in her study are Periods 3 and 4, each of which is 15 years long, but the error terms associated with the beginning and end dates of these periods are also 15 years. Because the error terms are equal to the period lengths, statistical procedures designed to assign undated assemblages to one period or another would probably do so on the basis of very slight differences in assemblage

TABLE 3.1. Parameters in Orcutt's (1999a, 1999b) population history of Bandelier National Monument

Period	Begin Date (AD)	End Date	Period Length	Occupancy Rate	Use-Life	Period Weight[a]	Average Momentary Population
1	1150 (±25)	1190 (±20)	40	1.00	15	.1406	275
2	1190 (±20)	1220 (±15)	30	1.00	15	.2500	500
3	1220 (±15)	1235 (±15)	15	1.00	15	1.0000	1,100
4	1235 (±15)	1250 (±20)	15	.80	35	1.8667	3,240
5	1250 (±15)	1290 (±15)	40	.80	35	.2625	710
6	1290 (±15)	1325 (±10)	35	.80	35	.3429	3,610
7	1325 (±10)	1375 (±25)	50	.65	50	.1950	3,230
8	1375 (±25)	1400 (±25)	25	.65	50	.7800	2,100
9	1400 (±25)	1440 (±30)	40	.65	50	.3047	2,400
10	1440 (±30)	1525 (±30)	85	.65	50	.0675	500
11	1525 (±30)	1600 (±30)	75	.65	50	.0867	550

Sources: Orcutt 1999a:115, 1999b:225-227; Kohler, Powers et al. 2004:294.

[a] Period weight = 15 / period length \x occupancy rate \x use-life / period length. Room counts for each time period were multiplied by the period weight to produce momentary population estimates.

composition that are more likely due to sampling error than to real chronological differences.

Second, incorporating Dickson's procedures exerts strong effects on the results, as discussed earlier for Maxwell's study. In this case, Dickson's period-weighting procedure imposes a model where the occupation span of any given square meter of room block was only 15 years; this means that room counts dated to periods of 30 to 50 years (all but two of the periods are 50 years or less in duration) are discounted by a factor of 2 to 3.33, even though the average use-life of structures dating to these periods is estimated as equal to or greater than the period length. In addition, Dickson's method of apportioning rooms evenly across periods of occupation imposes a model of gradual accumulation of living space on all sites, and introduces the same bias against rooms from larger and longer-lived sites noted earlier with respect to Maxwell's study. Due to disproportionate discounting of large-site living space, and the underrepresentation of large sites in the survey sample overall, it is possible that the Classic period population decline in her reconstruction derives in part from her analysis method.

Third, standardizing for use-life on top of period weighting effectively momentizes room counts twice: first to the period-weighting use-life of 15 years, and second to the structure use-life vector in Table 3.1. Double-momentizing has significant and disproportionate impacts on resulting population estimates for certain periods. For example, it results in room counts for Period 4 being roughly doubled in her momentary population estimates, and room counts from the subsequent Period 5 being divided by 4. It is possible that these effects are responsible for the initial spike and trough in this reconstruction.[4]

A recent study that overcomes several issues related to the interpretation of large settlements is Hill and others' (2004) study of late prehispanic population across the U.S. Southwest. Hill and colleagues worked with many partners for many years to compile a database of all recorded sites containing 13 or more rooms and dating between AD 1200 and 1700. Because one goal of this effort was to develop models for the long-term decline of southwestern populations, the authors refer to it as "the Coalescent Communities Database" (also see Wilcox et al. 2007). The CCD includes room counts for each occupational component at each site, and models the population histories of these sites in 50-year increments. Hill and others applied an occupancy rate that decreases with site size to these estimates, and then applied a site life-history model (Hill et al. 2004:693) tailored to the number of periods of occupation to model the histories of large sites as one of gradual growth followed by a period of peak population and then relatively rapid decline.

The methods used by Hill and others (2004) improve upon previous studies in several ways. First, application of the variable life-history model to room counts is a significant improvement because it imposes a growth model on room counts from large sites, and models most of the architectural area as having been occupied during the period of peak occupation. This is much more realistic than dividing the number of rooms by the number of periods of occupation, as many previous studies have done. Second, given the fact that Hill and others are primarily interpreting large sites, the absence of standardization for structure use-life is an improvement because the duration of use of a given square meter of architectural area in a large site is often much longer than the use-life of any single structure. Third, even if their methods are less appropriate for interpreting small sites, it is far more important to model the occupations of large sites adequately, because far more people lived in them, and thus errors in their interpretation impact population estimates to a greater extent (see Ortman et al. 2007).

The one area where Hill and colleagues (2004) introduce disproportionate discounting of larger sites into their analysis is in applying occupancy rates that decrease with site size. These rates are "based on the assumption that smaller sites were often short-lived and had fewer abandoned rooms while they were occupied" (Hill et al. 2004:692). Although it is reasonable to assume that most rooms in small, short-lived settlements were inhabited simultaneously, and the assumption of decreasing occupancy rates with site size may be appropriate for pithouse villages, excavation data from the Rio Grande region do not suggest that a greater percentage of rooms were unoccupied throughout the occupation of larger and longer-lived pueblos. There would have always been a certain percentage of unoccupied rooms in large pueblos, but progressive discounting of the data from larger sites, peaking at 50 percent for sites with more than 1,000 rooms, appears excessive for Tewa Basin sites. Inverse correlation of occupancy rates with site size once again introduces progressive discounting of the data from the largest settlements. When applied to settlement systems characterized by gradual aggregation of people into fewer and larger settlements, it biases population estimates in favor of decreasing population through time. Southwestern populations may well have declined during the late prehispanic period, as Hill and others suggest, but it is important to recognize that the methods used contributed to this result.

A second difficulty with the CCD is that the only way it can integrate the data from sites across the Southwest in a common framework is to group the data into consistent, 50-year intervals. These intervals do not always coincide with natural breaks in local pottery chronologies. Thus, if migration took place between two regions with distinct pottery chronologies during one of their 50-year intervals, the CCD would count the people involved in this movement twice: once in the settlement they vacated early in the period, and again in the settlement they moved into later in the period. This is especially problematic for the purposes of this study because the final pottery period in the Mesa Verde region ends at AD 1280, and the most natural break between the Early and Late Coalition periods in the Northern Rio Grande is at approximately AD 1275. Consequently, the latest sites in the Mesa Verde region and Coalition period sites in the Northern Rio Grande both contribute to the AD 1250–1300 southwestern population in Hill and others' (2004) study, even though many of these sites were occupied sequentially. In light of this, it is perhaps not surprising that the peak southwestern population in Hill and others' sequence occurs during this same interval. Despite the attractiveness of equal-length periods, forcing settlement data into such periods, against the natural divisions of local pottery chronologies, introduces new difficulties that are most easily solved by grouping sites according to local pottery periods. This was not an option for the CCD, but as a result it is less than ideal for tracking migrations between regions.

The final study I consider here is a study of Developmental period population by Boyer and others (2010) that produced estimates of the populations of the Taos Valley, Tewa Basin, and Middle Rio Grande regions in 100-year increments. Their Tewa Basin study area focuses on the portion where Developmental sites are known to occur, including the Rio Grande Valley from the Santa Fe River in the south to just north of the Chama–Rio Grande confluence in the north, and from the foothills of the Sangre de Cristo Mountains in the east to the foothills of the Jemez Plateau on the west. Notably excluded from their study are areas that lack Developmental sites, including the Pajarito Plateau and the Chama drainage within the Tewa Basin, and the Galisteo Basin southeast of Santa Fe. Boyer and others (2010) divided the number of recorded Developmental sites dated to each 100-year interval by the proportion of the area surveyed to estimate the total number of Developmental sites in the Tewa Basin. Then they assumed that the average Developmental site housed 2 households of 6 persons each for 15 years to estimate momentary populations for AD 900–1000, 1000–1100, and 1100–1200. Finally, they calculated growth rates based on the population changes noted for these three intervals, and projected the regional population at AD 1300 based on these rates. They found that intrinsic growth of this population at the rate defined by their Developmental period estimates could have produced an Early Classic population of between 13,000 and 16,000 people without significant in-migration.

Many of the assumptions incorporated into this analysis are reasonable given the characteristics of Developmental sites and the nature of the available data for these sites, but there are a few problematic areas. First, Boyer and others (2010) used the data for all recorded Developmental sites and estimated the portion of their study area that has been surveyed in making their estimates. This may not be reasonable, given that many sites have been recorded individually as archaeologists encountered them over the years. By including sites outside survey areas in their sample estimates, Boyer and others may have overestimated the total population.[5]

Second, the growth rates calculated by Boyer and others (2010) for various intervals of the Developmental period, and used to extrapolate the potential AD 1300 population, are assumed to derive wholly from intrinsic growth. In other words, by assuming that their Developmental period growth rates reflect intrinsic growth rates, Boyer and others presuppose that there was no significant migration into the Tewa Basin at any time after its initial settlement. Because the Tewa Basin had very limited population prior to AD 900, there must have been in-migration during the initial period of settlement at least, and it seems unrealistic to assume that there was zero in-migration from this point onward. By assuming a migration rate of zero after initial colonization, Boyer and others have probably overestimated the intrinsic rate of growth of the Developmental period population.

Third, it is important to note that Boyer and others (2010) exclude portions of the Northern Rio Grande where ancestral Tewa sites occur that were settled only after AD 1200. Thus, even if intrinsic growth of the population in the area they modeled could have produced 16,000 people by AD 1300, migration would still seem to be required to explain the total Northern Rio Grande population by that time. For example, if the estimate of 16,000 is meant to apply only to the modeled area, then one still needs to account for the Pajarito Plateau, Chama drainage, and Galisteo Basin. Alternatively, if the estimate is meant to apply to the entire Northern Rio Grande region, it would appear far too low given the number of large settlements identified in the region. Thus, although Boyer and others' analysis suggests that a portion of the Classic period Northern Rio Grande population could have derived from the Developmental population, their analysis is insufficient to determine whether migration is needed to account for the Early Classic Tewa Basin population in particular.

Guidelines for Population Studies

In this chapter I have reviewed recent archaeological perspectives on population and previous studies of Tewa Basin population. These reviews make it clear that interpreting the mix of population processes behind local population histories is more complex than it first appears, and that it is difficult to say, on the basis of previous studies, whether or not long-distance in-migration played a significant role in Tewa origins. Accordingly, there is a need for a new study that builds on previous efforts and takes intrinsic population processes as well as external and internal migration into account in interpreting the results. As a step in this direction, the conclusions reached regarding methods for estimating population from archaeological data, and that will serve as guiding principles for the study that follows, are restated below.

1. Population histories constructed from settlement pattern evidence represent the net result of external migration, intrinsic population processes, and internal movement in the case of multiethnic landscapes. It is not possible to disentangle the contribution of each to a given population history on the basis of the population estimates themselves. Other lines of evidence, including the spatial pattern of growth and data from human skeletal remains, must be considered to assess the relative contribution of each process.
2. To control for internal movement, it is important to model population history across the entire area in which a given archaeological complex occurs. In the present case, this means that one needs to model the entire area of ancestral Northern Tewa settlement, which corresponds geographically to the Tewa Basin and culturally to the Biscuit ware area as defined by Mera (1934).
3. When extrapolating from the populations of recorded sites to the total population of a region, one needs to develop an effective stratification that takes into account ecological factors affecting the range of settlement locations, prior archaeological knowledge of the spatial extent of settlement during different time periods, and knowledge of existing survey areas and the sites found within them.
4. When working with compilations of survey data, it is best to group sites into phases that reflect natural breaks in local pottery sequences. Pottery chronologies are constructed on the basis of perceptible changes in the pottery assemblages at sites. These patterns derive from variation in rates of change in local pottery traditions, and also variation in the establishment and abandonment of sites. The latter process is neither random nor regular, but is punctuated at various points due to social, economic, and ecological processes. Because pottery periods are correlated with these settlement changes, the shape of the population history of a society is most readily captured using traditional pottery periods.
5. The larger a site is, the more likely it is to be known to researchers, and the more impact it will have on the overall population history of a region.

Because large sites are also relatively rare, extrapolating total populations on the basis of sample surveys will likely underrepresent the contribution of larger sites (see Flannery 1976:159–160). Even when it is reasonable to extrapolate the total population residing in small settlements on the basis of sample surveys, different methods should be used to account for larger settlements.

6. Both the shape and the magnitude of a population history matter. Growth rates are estimated on the basis of shape, so if this shape is inaccurate, the growth estimates will be inaccurate as well. Also, understanding the actual number of people involved in a given population history is critical for assessing potential source areas for these populations. It is therefore important to avoid methods that distort the shape of a local population history through disproportionate discounting of the data for certain categories of sites, or distort its magnitude by discounting the data for all sites. Both types of distortion have been identified in previous studies of Tewa Basin population history.
7. Methods commonly used to translate site size and occupation span into momentary populations build in the assumptions that abandoned structures accumulated horizontally rather than vertically over time, and that a given area of architectural remains was only occupied for the use-life of a single structure. This model may be reasonable for sites consisting of one or a few houses, but it is not reasonable for larger settlements, where vertical superpositioning of structures and rebuilding are typical. Thus, it is necessary to take vertical stratification into account when modeling occupational histories of large sites.
8. The concept of *use-life* is important for translating total occupied living space to momentary populations, especially for groups of small sites that are imprecisely dated; however, this concept derives from ethnoarchaeological studies of buildings, which are not the same as sites. The occupation spans of residences can be influenced by many factors, including the length of the family cycle, residence rules, the sustainability of economic practices in a given location, and the availability of unclaimed agricultural land. It is therefore necessary to consider multiple lines of evidence when estimating the occupation spans of small site residences.
9. A common method used to account for variation in the lengths of pottery periods has been to divide the period lengths by the length of the shortest period, and divide the total living space for each period by the resulting figure. This is equivalent to assuming that the use-life of residences in all periods was equal to the length of the shortest pottery period. This may or may not be reasonable depending on the situation and the goals of the analysis. More importantly, standardizing for varying period lengths is not necessary if standardization for occupation span is performed.

Notes

1. This perspective on population and resources also accounts for the findings of researchers interested in the relationship between population growth and social evolution. In the early days of processual archaeology, researchers tended to view population growth as a prime mover in such fundamental transitions as the adoption of agriculture (Binford 1968), agricultural intensification (Boserup 1965), and the emergence of urban society (Carneiro 1967; Sanders et al. 1979). However, several researchers who compared population histories and social trajectories concluded that rather than causing social change, population growth appears to have been a consequence of these changes (Adams 1966:44–45; Blanton et al. 1993:201–203; Flannery 1972). As Shennan (2002) notes, life-history theory accounts for these observations readily.
2. The source given for this reconstruction is the conference paper for which Crown and others (1996) is the published version. Unfortunately, neither source details the calculations behind this population history.
3. See Ortman 2009:97 for a discussion of additional problems with Maxwell's (1994) population estimates.
4. Orcutt (1999b:224) notes that Dickson's reconstruction for the Arroyo Hondo area also shows population decline during the Middle Coalition period, but this pattern could be an artifact of period weighting in both cases.
5. For example, in the data set compiled for this study (see Chapter 4), only 256 of 414 recorded Developmental sites (62 percent) are located within the survey area shape files maintained in the Archaeological Resource Management System (ARMS). See Ortman 2009:94–95 for additional discussion.

Population History of the Tewa Basin

In this chapter I construct a population history for the Tewa Basin and make inferences regarding the pace, scale, and character of population changes in the basin over time. I also compare this reconstruction with the most recent population history produced for the central Mesa Verde region to assess the likelihood that migration from that area contributed to the ancestral Tewa population.

Estimating Tewa Basin Population

The first half of this chapter focuses on the methods and data used to estimate population for 12 time periods spanning AD 900 to 1760. I first discuss the sources that I used to construct a database of all recorded habitation sites within the Tewa Basin. I then discuss how I estimated the total number of rooms and periods of occupation at each site. Third, I define four site size classes and develop models for the occupational histories of each class based on patterns in previously excavated sites. Finally, based on prior knowledge of regional settlement history, I define five sampling strata and use them in combination with the site data to develop a population history for the entire Tewa Basin.

Data Sources, Size Estimates, and Dating Estimates

The backbone of the database is an Archaeological Resource Management System (ARMS) data set (exported on December 3, 2007) containing information on the cultural features, date ranges, and pottery assemblages of 4,763 sites located within the rectangle shown in Figure 4.1. Several additional compilations of Tewa Basin site data have been linked to this backbone.[1] In order to produce the most useful dataset possible, I linked the data from various sources by site number in a relational database, reviewed the data from these various sources for each of the 218 sites with 50 or more rooms, and evaluated the data for smaller sites in batches using select and update queries. The resulting database contains information on 1,920 habitation components at 1,829 different sites.

The currency for the size of Pueblo occupations is the total number of rooms and/or pit structures associated with each site component. Room counts have been estimated by several researchers using sketch maps of room-block areas

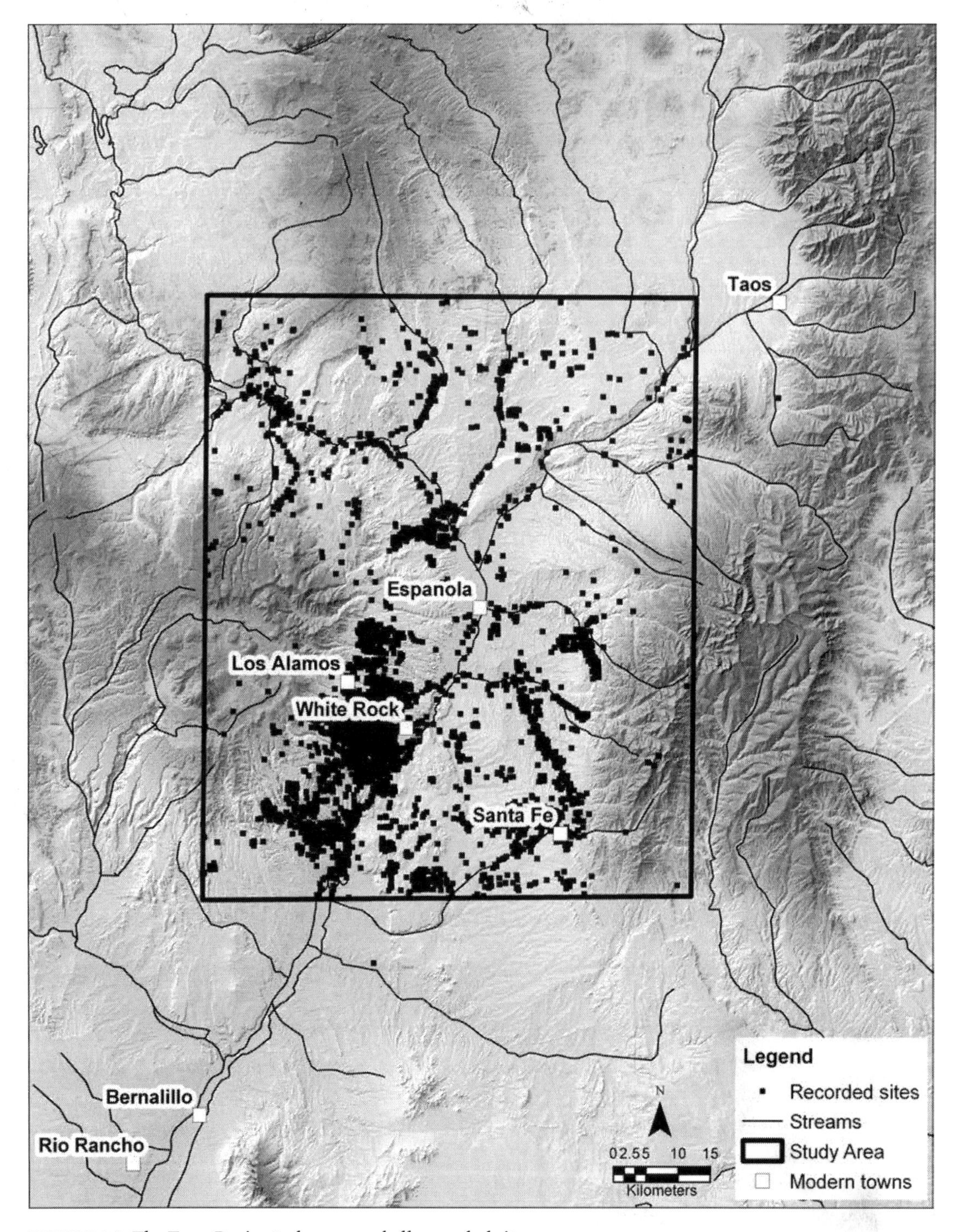

FIGURE 4.1. The Tewa Basin study area and all recorded sites.

and relationships between surface evidence and excavation results (e.g., Gabler 2008; Marshall and Walt 2007; Maxwell 1994; Scheick 2007; Wilcox et al. 2007). I simply correlated these various estimates, and carry forward the estimate that seems most reasonable for each site in light of the available data from all sources. Room counts have been estimated at least once for every site with 13 or more rooms (as part of the Coalescent Communities Database [Hill et al. 2004]); for small sites I assumed a minimum of 6 rooms per room block if no mound area is available, and use the relationship between mound area and room counts as defined by Gabler (2008) to estimate rooms in cases where mound area was available. Brown's (1987:31) revision of Naroll's (1962) constant suggests a reasonable translation of roofed space into human capacity is 1 person per 6 m^2.[2] Because the average size of rooms at Tewa Basin sites is also approximately 6 m^2 (Creamer 1993:14; Fallon and Wening 1987:145; Hill and Trierweiler 1986:23; Jeançon 1923:8; Peckham 1981:118; Stubbs and Stallings 1953:29; Wendorf 1953a:37), I assumed the capacity of a site was one person per room (also see Lang and Scheick 1991; Peckham 1996). Finally, I assumed that each Developmental pit structure was equivalent to 6 rooms and could have accommodated a household of 6 people (Lakatos 2007; Boyer et al. 2010). Note also that, under these assumptions, each rubble mound lacking size information is assumed to have housed a single household.

I estimated periods of occupation at sites using associated pottery, architectural traits, documentary evidence, and excavation results where available. I began with the date ranges recorded by surveyors and then refined these ranges as possible based on the architectural details and pottery types associated with each site. Architectural dating is based on the date of first appearance of specific features and settlement forms derived from excavation results.[3] Pottery dating is based on a phase scheme (Table 4.1) defined by the date ranges of 22 pottery types, presented in Table 4.2 and in Figure 4.2 (after Wilson 2006). Given this framework, the maximum date range for a given site is the beginning date of the earliest pottery type observed through the end date of the latest type observed. Also, if the list of types associated with a site is complete, these maximum ranges are narrowed based on the date ranges of types that are *absent* from the assemblage.[4] Finally, if the assemblage information appears complete but there are gaps in the types present within the range defined by the earliest and latest types, I assumed that there were two occupations separated by a period of disuse. For small sites, this pattern is interpreted as reflecting initial year-round habitation followed by reuse as a field house.

In addition to architecture and pottery, I used Spanish documents to estimate the resident populations and abandonment dates of sites occupied into the historic period. A recent synthesis of these documents (Barrett 2002) includes lists of sites observed as occupied by Castaño in 1591 and Oñate in 1598, and recorded on the Oñate map of 1602, as well as population estimates from the

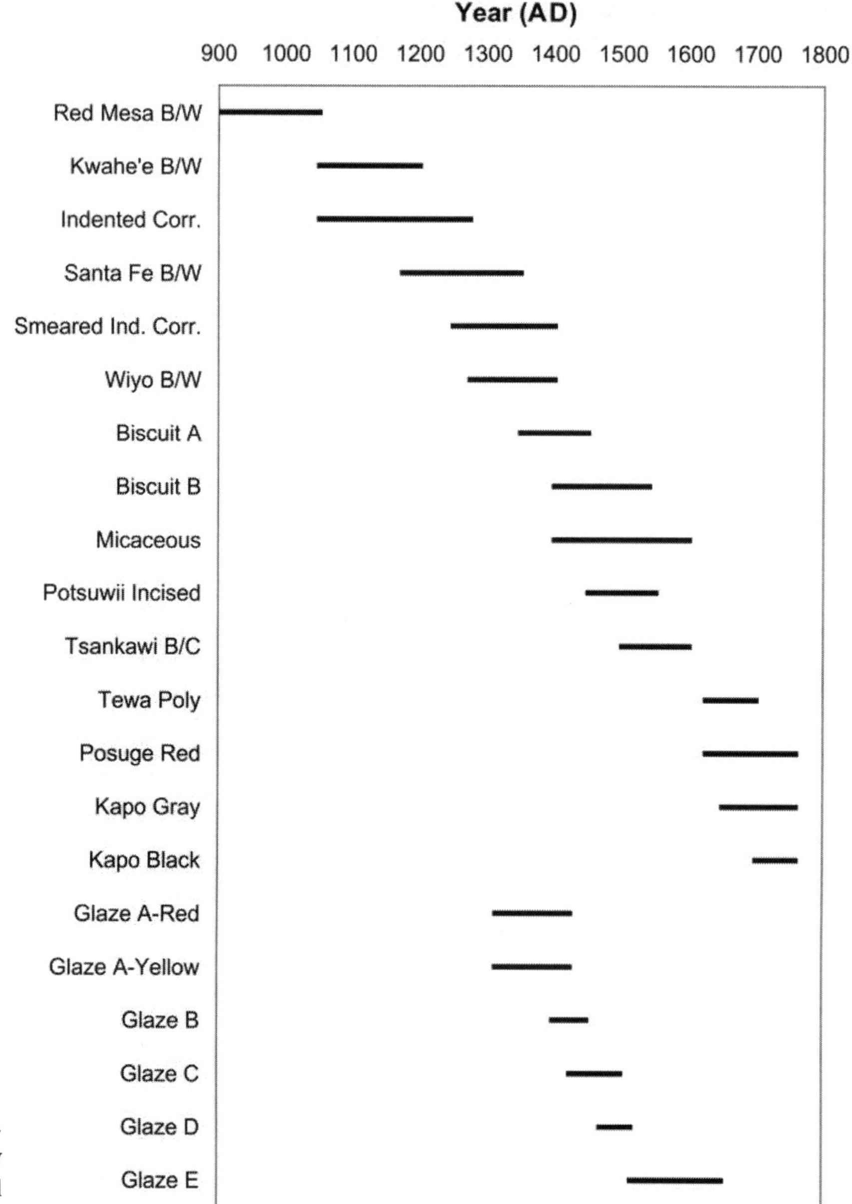

FIGURE 4.2. Chart of pottery sequence used to estimate date ranges for sites.

Benevides Memorial of 1629 and the Alvarez census of 1706. There are numerous issues with these sources (see Kulisheck 2005; Ramenofsky and Feathers 2002), but these documents provide population estimates for sites and time periods for which there are few corresponding archaeological data, and it therefore seems more appropriate to make use of these estimates than to ignore them.

TABLE 4.1. Tewa Basin phase scheme based on date ranges of 22 pottery types

PERIOD NUMBER	PERIOD NAME	DATES (AD)	PERIOD LENGTH
1	Early Developmental	900–1050	150
2	Late Developmental	1050–1200	150
3	Early Coalition	1200–1275	75
4	Late Coalition	1275–1350	75
5	Early Classic	1350–1400	50
6	Middle Classic	1400–1450	50
7	Late Classic	1450–1500	50
8	Terminal Classic	1500–1540	40
9	Contact	1540–1600	60
10	Colonial	1600–1680	80
11	Revolt	1680–1700	20
12	Reconquest	1700–1760	60

TABLE 4.2. Tewa Basin pottery types tabulated in the database

TYPE	DATE RANGE (AD)
Red Mesa Black-on-white	900–1050
Kwahe'e Black-on-white	1050–1200
Santa Fe Black-on-white	1175–1350
Wiyo Black-on-white	1275–1400
Biscuit A (Abiquiu Black-on-gray)	1350–1450
Biscuit B (Bandelier Black-on-gray)	1400–1540
Tsankawi Black-on-cream	1500–1600
Tewa Polychrome	1625–1700
Indented Corrugated	1050–1275
Smeared Indented Corrugated	1250–1400
Micaceous Slipped or Washboard	1400–1600
Potsuwii Incised	1450–1540
Posuge Red	1625–1900
Kapo Gray	1650–1900
Kapo Black	1700–1760
Glaze A-Red (Agua Fria, Sanchez)	1315–1425
Glaze A-Yellow (Cieneguilla, San Clemente, Sanchez, Arenal)	1315–1425
Glaze B (Largo)	1400–1450
Glaze C (Espinosa)	1425–1500
Glaze D (San Lazaro)	1470–1515
Glaze E (Puaray, Escondido, Pecos)	1515–1650
Glaze F (Kotyiti)	1625–1700

Occupational Histories of Sites

The next step in this analysis was to translate the estimated total rooms and date ranges of habitation sites into estimates of the resident population during each period of occupation. Following the insights gained from previous studies, I grouped habitation sites into four size classes and developed a separate model for each class based on excavation results. The four size classes are: houses, with 1 to 12 rooms; hamlets, with 13 to 49 rooms; villages, with 50 to 499 rooms; and towns, with 500 or more rooms.

Houses. Sites with 1 to 12 rooms were occupied by 1 to 2 households. I assume that the inhabitants of such sites were kin groups, that these sites were built to house such groups, and that the primary factor limiting the length of their occupation was the length of the domestic cycle, roughly equivalent to a single human generation. Data from recent excavations at Tewa Basin houses suggest that modeling the occupation spans of such sites as having been no longer than a single phase is reasonable (see below). Based on these results, I assume that houses were filled to capacity at some point during one, and only one, phase. Unfortunately, it is not possible to determine which phase this was for many houses because small sites often have limited surface pottery assemblages and can only be imprecisely dated to several consecutive phases. To prevent data from imprecisely dated houses from contributing unduly to overall population estimates, I followed Dickson's method of dividing the room counts of houses by the number of phases of occupation. It is unlikely that the momentary resident populations of individual sites were ever as low as those produced using this method, but the procedure has the effect of averaging out the aggregate capacities of houses in each phase, on the assumption that the true occupations of such sites are randomly distributed within their date ranges. This ensures that the data from houses contribute appropriately to the resulting regional population estimates.

Hamlets. The occupational histories of sites large enough to accommodate 3 to 8 households are more varied than those of houses. One possibility is that a larger group filled the living space to capacity during a single domestic cycle; another is that a smaller group occupied the site for multiple generations, constructing new living spaces as old ones wore out. Because hamlets often have larger surface pottery assemblages than houses, I assume that the available data are sufficient to distinguish between these two scenarios. If the surface evidence suggests occupation during a single phase, I modeled such sites as having been filled to capacity at some point during that phase. If, on the other hand, surface pottery suggests occupation during multiple phases, I assumed that the accumulated living space represents the end product of several domestic cycles that involved some combination of construction of new residences adjacent to old ones, and rebuilding of residences on top of old ones. As a result, I assumed that 50 percent of the total horizontal living space would have been occupied at once.

Although well reported excavations from small sites in the Tewa Basin are few, several examples do suggest that these models are a reasonable first approximation for the occupational histories of houses and hamlets. The model of full occupancy for single-phase hamlets is supported by excavations at several Coalition period sites. Excavations at Riana Ruin, near present-day Abiquiu Lake, uncovered a site with 25 rooms constructed around AD 1335 and abandoned around AD 1350 (Hibben 1937; Smiley et al. 1953), and excavations at the adjacent Palisade Ruin revealed a 48-room settlement constructed rapidly between AD 1312 and 1314, and occupied for a very short period (Peckham 1981). Neither site exhibits evidence of trash-filled rooms, remodeling, or dismantling and rebuilding, suggesting that 100 percent occupancy is a reasonable interpretation. The same pattern is apparent at LA4624, a hamlet-sized site on the Pajarito Plateau constructed in a single episode and occupied for about 22 years (Vierra et al. 2002; also see below).

The model of partial occupancy for multiphase occupations is also supported by excavations at several sites. Excavations at Tesuque By-Pass (McNutt 1969) revealed two distinct areas of living space occupied for three consecutive pottery periods. Occupation appears to have alternated between the two areas from phase to phase, such that one of the two areas, or 50 percent of the total area, was occupied during each of the three phases. A similar pattern is apparent at the Red Snake Hill site (LA6461), where excavation of two adjacent pithouses revealed that the first one was filled with trash from the second, more recently constructed pithouse (Bussey 1968:10). Also, the two small pueblos excavated by Stubbs (1954) at the Pojoaque Grant site appear to have been occupied sequentially, one during the Early Developmental and the other during the Late Developmental period (Wiseman 1995:246).

Perhaps the best example of partial occupancy of sites occupied for multiple pottery periods comes from the North Bank site near present-day Cochiti Pueblo, which has evidence of occupation during each of the first four phases defined for this study. The excavations at this site, summarized in Table 4.3, encountered ten Developmental pithouses and four Coalition room blocks with associated pit structures. Fill sequences, stratigraphic relationships, and associated pottery indicate that no more than 6 of the 10 Developmental pithouses and 4 of the 7 Coalition pit structures could have been occupied at once. It also appears that, at most, 3 of the 4 Coalition room blocks could have been occupied at once: two in the Early Coalition period only, one in the Late Coalition period only, and one throughout the Coalition period. Results from previously excavated sites thus suggest that an average occupancy rate of 50 percent is reasonable for hamlets occupied over two or more phases.

Villages and Towns. Because the social correlates of villages and towns are quite different from those of houses and hamlets, modeling their occupational histories requires a different approach. Several generalizations about Tewa

TABLE 4.3. Summary of excavations at the North Bank site, Cochiti Dam Project

Unit[a]	Feature	Excavation Comments	Sequence in Unit[b]	Phase[c] (Tree-Ring Dates)
I	Pithouse	roof salvaged		4
II	Pithouse 4		1	1
II	Pithouse 3		2	2
II	Pithouse 1	unfinished	3	2
II	Pithouse 2	unfinished	3	2
III	Pithouse	wind and water fill	1	2 (1119+vv)
III	Room block (8 rooms, 4 with hearths)	constructed as a unit	2	3
III	Kiva	roof-fall on floor, then wind and water fill, then wall-fall	2	3
IV	Pithouse	burned roof-fall, then wind and water fill	1	2
IV	Room block (9 rooms, 3 with hearths)	built over trash	2	3
IV	Kiva	trash fill over intentional rock fill	2	3
IV	Square Kiva	wind and water fill	3	3
V	Pithouse 2	trash fill	1	1
V	Pithouse 1	dismantled roof, wind and water fill	2	2
V	Storage pits (*n*=3)		2	2 (1080+vv)
VI	Pithouse	roof-fall and wall-fall	1	2
VI	Room block (20 rooms, 6 with hearths)	front row of living rooms, back row of storage rooms	2	3–4
VI	Square kiva	burned roof, trash fill	2	3
VI	Kiva	burned roof-fall, no trash fill	3	4 (cutting dates at 1103 [1], 1278 [2], and 1280 [12])
VII	Pithouse	unfinished	1	2
VII	Room block (8 rooms, 3 with hearths)		2	4
VII	Kiva	wind and water fill	2	4

Sources: Data from site reports (Bussey 1968b; Honea 1968).

[a] A concentration of artifacts and architectural remains on the modern ground surface.

[b] Inferred from feature fills, stratigraphic relationships, and chronology.

[c] Translated into the phase scheme of this study.

Basin villages and towns are useful for developing models of the occupational histories of these sites.

The first generalization is that surveyors have already identified villages and towns where different sections were occupied in a sequence. Such cases are often revealed by differences in the character of surface architectural remains and perceptible differences in surface pottery assemblages that correlate with architectural differences. A good example of this occurs at Tsama, a Coalition and Classic period settlement in the Chama River valley. The site consists of three distinct architectural areas known as the West, Middle, and East plazas. The West Plaza consists of low, single-story mounds of melted adobe arranged to form one enclosed and one open plaza; the Middle Plaza, two detached but taller mounds with some embedded cobbles; and the East Plaza, a massive quadrangle of melted, multistory adobe architecture with outlines of cobble wall foundations exposed on top of the mound. These architectural differences correlate with differences in surface pottery assemblages across the site. Together these patterns indicate that the three areas were occupied in a sequence, from west to east (see Chapter 13). Excavations have confirmed this sequence, revealing that the West Plaza was built and occupied during the Late Coalition period (Windes and McKenna 2006), and the East Plaza was occupied into the Contact period (Greenlee 1933). Finally, this sequence was also apparent to Mera (1934), who gave separate site numbers to the West Plaza (LA909) and the Middle and East plazas (LA908). These observations suggest that surveyors are likely to have identified horizontal occupational sequences at sites where they occur.

The second generalization has four parts: (1) nearly the entire architectural area with a consistent surface signature was occupied during the period of peak occupation; (2) the period of peak occupancy most often coincides with the final period of occupancy; (3) the decline and abandonment of villages and towns most often occurred rapidly, usually within a single phase; and (4) longer-term declines in site populations were most often the result of reestablishment following a period of abandonment. Note that the pattern of occupancy implied by these generalizations is in the opposite direction from that proposed for houses and hamlets. For the smaller sites, it is assumed that the percentage of rooms occupied simultaneously is lower at sites with longer occupations. For larger sites, in contrast, I assume that nearly all rooms in a site component were inhabited during the final phase of occupation.

These generalizations are supported by excavations at numerous Tewa Basin sites. Wendorf (1953:61) concluded that the entire village of Te'ewi was occupied from the Middle Classic until it was abandoned during the Contact period. Fallon and Wening (1987) also suggest that all room blocks at Howiri were inhabited during the final period of occupation, as does Snow (1963) for Sapawe, and Greenlee (1933) for the East Plaza at Tsama. This pattern of full occupancy of the site footprint during the final phase of occupation also appears to be characteristic of Late Coalition plaza pueblos, including Area 1 at Burnt Mesa Pueblo

(Kohler and Root 2004b), Palisade Ruin (Schroeder 1981), Kapo (Luebben 1953), and Nake'muu (Vierra et al. 2003). Finally, although the two components at Arroyo Hondo are superimposed, and the first was much larger than the second, Creamer (1993:152–153) estimated that nearly all the rooms associated with each component were inhabited near the end of each occupation, with a period of abandonment in between. This same pattern is apparent for several pueblos that were reestablished with smaller populations after the Pueblo Revolt (Barrett 2002). Based on these observations, I assume that nearly all rooms associated with each site component were occupied during the final phase of that component.

The third generalization is that a given area of architectural remains at a large site could have had a house on it for a much longer period than the use-life of an individual structure. A variety of stratigraphic observations support this conclusion. At Te'ewi approximately 50 percent of the excavated rooms contained evidence of multiple floors, floor levels varied across stratigraphic sections, and cultural fill consisting of melted adobe construction material mixed with refuse was found beneath nearly all the excavated rooms (Wendorf 1953: 36–42). The same patterns are apparent in the stratigraphic sections of Pindi Pueblo (Stubbs and Stallings 1953:2–8) and in the East Plaza at Tsama (Greenlee 1933). Snow (1963) also observed that most walls at Sapawe exhibited evidence of having been rebuilt on existing wall stubs using chunks of adobe from previous, disintegrated walls set in adobe mortar.

It is almost certainly the case that the use-life of individual adobe rooms at Tewa Basin sites was short. At Sapawe, for example, Snow (1963) inferred from the number of plaster layers inside certain rooms, and the rate of replastering in contemporary pueblos, that the use-life of a room was about 25 years. However, based on stratigraphic observations, it is also clear that structures were often rebuilt on the remains of earlier structures, and thus a given horizontal area of architectural remains was normally used for a much longer period of time. This means that standardizing for structure use-life, which assumes each square meter of architectural mound was only used for the use-life of a single room, is not appropriate for modeling the occupational histories of these sites.

The final generalization I make about large sites in the Tewa Basin is that their patterns of growth are reasonably approximated by logistic, or S-shaped, curves. This generalization is based on both theoretical and empirical observations. Schacht (1980) reviewed literature in cultural ecology to show that logistic curves best capture growth in systems where human populations approach local carrying capacities. This was almost certainly the case for the largest Tewa Basin settlements. Agricultural features — including check dams, cobble-bordered grid gardens, and gravel-mulched plots — were common and extensive around these sites, and appear to have improved local farmland by retaining runoff and soil, by absorbing heat and radiating it onto crops on cool evenings, and by retaining soil moisture beneath the gravel mulches (Anschuetz 1998, 2005; Bugé

1984; Marshall and Walt 2007; Maxwell and Anschuetz 1992:61–66). These constructed fields thus represent substantial intensification in food production and investment in particular plots of land. This, in turn, suggests that the inherent agricultural productivity of the Tewa Basin placed an upper limit on the number of people who could live in a village or town, and that land pressure would slow the growth of settlements as they approached this limit.

There is also a basis for suggesting that the general manner in which cultural innovations are adopted by members of a social group may also have influenced decisions on the part of ancestral Pueblo people as to where to live. Henrich (2001) illustrates that both conformist bias (the tendency to do what most other people do) and prestige bias (the tendency to copy the behavior of prestigious individuals) are central factors in human decision making. Because increasing proportions of local populations lived in larger settlements over time, and there are reasons why larger settlements may have become more prestigious than smaller ones, settlements that began growing, for whatever reason, would tend to keep on growing until the resident population approached density-dependent limits or the site was abandoned. Thus, both density-dependent resource limits and characteristics of human decision making encourage a pattern of logistic growth in settlements over time.[5]

Logistic growth of ancestral Pueblo villages is most clearly illustrated using tree-ring cutting dates from well-sampled sites. Eighmy (1979) showed that logistic curves fit the cumulative distributions of tree-ring dates in 13 of 14 cases he examined, including two Tewa Basin sites (Arroyo Hondo and Pindi), with an average $r^2 \geq .95$. He also showed that logistic curves fit these distributions better than exponential curves. Figure 4.3 illustrates a similar pattern using tree-ring cutting dates as a proxy for construction at Spruce Tree House, a cliff-dwelling in Mesa Verde National Park (data from Varien 1999b). The data clearly show a pattern of slow initial growth, followed by a period of increasingly rapid growth, and finally, a period of slowing growth. In cliff-dwellings, a likely factor limiting continued growth was the size of the alcove in which the settlement was built, but in open settings, one would expect factors such as distances to fields and agricultural potential to play a similar role.

This same pattern is apparent if one uses rooms rather than tree-ring dates as the index of growth. Graves (1983) used tree-ring dates in combination with architectural data to date the construction of each room at Canyon Creek Ruin, a cliff-dwelling in central Arizona, and found that the resulting cumulative distribution of rooms in use at this site was closely approximated by a logistic curve. Creamer (1993:140–147) also integrated tree-ring dates and architectural details to determine the construction sequence for Component I at Arroyo Hondo Pueblo, a Tewa Basin site. This particular village grew from nothing to a town of more than 1,000 rooms in just 15 years (AD 1315–1330) and appears to have been abandoned shortly after construction ended. Creamer identified and mapped out a sequence of four construction phases, and these maps can be used

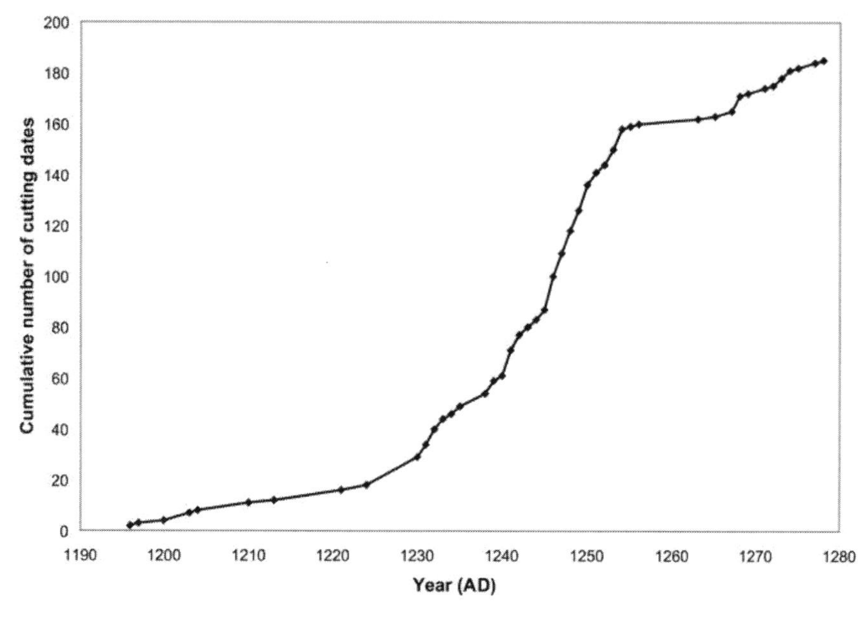

FIGURE 4.3. Tree-ring dates from Spruce Tree House, Mesa Verde National Park.

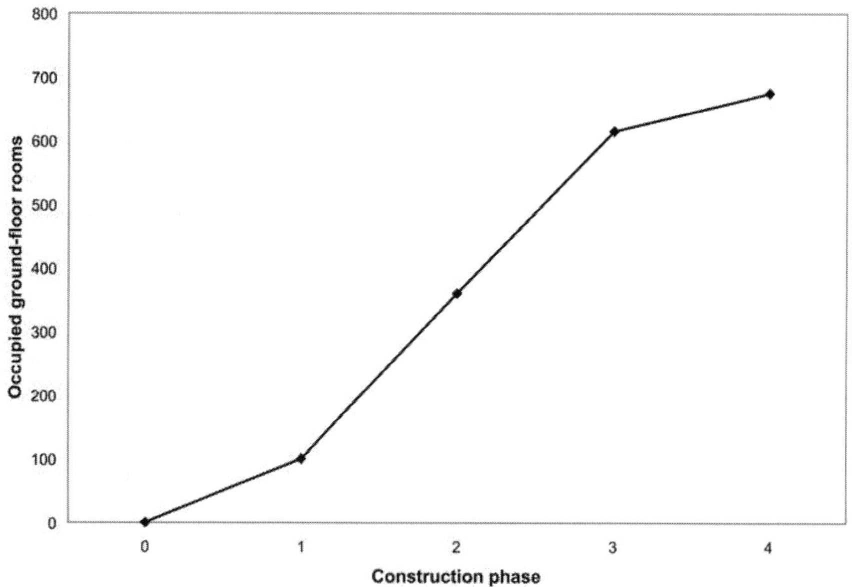

FIGURE 4.4. Rooms by construction phase, Component I, Arroyo Hondo Pueblo.

to illustrate the pace of construction over a period of 15 years. Figure 4.4 illustrates the number of occupied ground floor rooms at the conclusion of each construction phase. Here again, the data show an increasing rate of construction during the first two phases, followed by a decreasing rate during the final two phases.

Due to these theoretical and empirical observations, it appears reasonable to model the growth of Tewa Basin villages and towns as having followed a logistic pattern. In order to estimate growth curves for sites of differing occupation spans, I utilize a dataset of Tewa Basin villages and towns for which occupied-

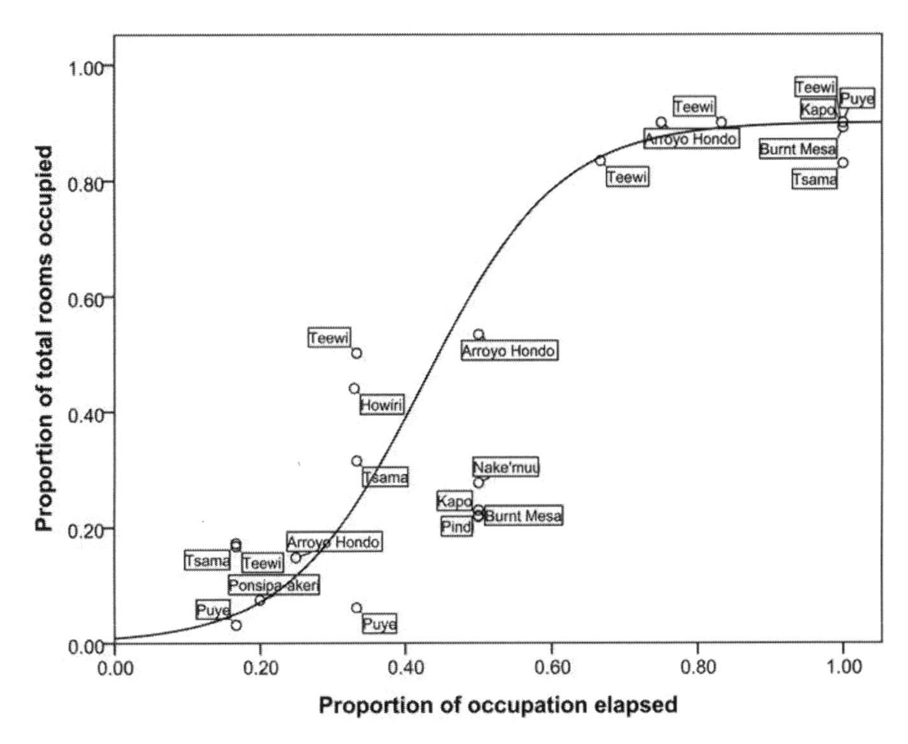

FIGURE 4.5. Logistic regression of site growth data. The fitted equation is: $y = 1 / (1 / .9 + (113.816 \times .00001865^x))$; $r^2 = .850$.

room estimates are available for more than one period in the overall development of the site (Table 4.4). I standardized these data to reflect the proportion of the total rooms and proportion of the total phases for each phase estimate, and also set the maximum proportion of occupied rooms at 90 percent following Creamer's (1993:152) suggestion for Arroyo Hondo. I then fit a logistic curve to the resulting data. Figure 4.5 presents the regression, and Table 4.5 uses the resulting equation to estimate the proportion of total rooms occupied during each phase at sites occupied for varying numbers of phases.

I used these vectors to estimate the number of occupied rooms during each phase of occupation for village and town components. To model population through time for the 208 village components, I multiplied the total room estimate by the vector corresponding to the number of phases associated with that component. This procedure imparted a model wherein villages occupied for a single phase grew to full capacity during that phase, villages occupied for two phases grew consistently throughout their occupations, and villages occupied for three or more phases grew rapidly during the first half of their occupations and more slowly during the second half.

Two factors led me to modify this approach somewhat for the 44 town components. First, the growth functions in Table 4.5 assume that the entire occupational history of a site is considered as a whole, but the occupations of most towns have already been subdivided into two or more components, most often with a village-sized Coalition period component preceding a town-sized Classic period component. As a result, the initial population of the Classic period

TABLE 4.4. Estimated numbers of occupied rooms for Tewa Basin villages and towns

LA Number	Site Name	Dates (AD)	Total Rooms	Rooms in Each Phase of Occupation						Reference
				1	2	3	4	5	6	
1	Pindi	1250–1350	175	40	175					Stubbs and Stallings 1953:9–10
12	Arroyo Hondo	1315–1330	675	100	360	615	675			Creamer 1993:140–147
47	Puye	1200–1625	1,600	50	100				1600	Peckham 1996
71	Howiri	1400–1525	1,671	734		1,671				Fallon and Wening 1987:145–146
252	Te'ewi[a]	1275–1600	600	100	300		500	600	600	Wendorf 1953:61–62
297	Ponsipa-akeri[b]	1275–1540	1,350	100				1,350		Bugé 1978
300	Kapo[c]	1250–1350	175	43	175					Luebben 1953:9–10
908/909	Tsama	1250–1600	700	120	220				580	Windes and McKenna 2006
12655	Nake'muu	1250–1325	58	16	58					Vierra et al. 2003
60372	Burnt Mesa[d]	1275–1325	73	16	65					Kohler and Root 2004a, 2004b

[a] Room counts for each phase of growth are estimated from spatial extent of occupation during different pottery periods.
[b] Initial room count from Bugé 1978; final room count from Coalescent Communities Database (Hill et al. 2004).
[c] Initial phase consists of pit structures and rooms beneath room blocks, with each pit structure equivalent to six rooms.
[d] Initial phase consists of Area 2 room block and a second room block assumed to be of equal size beneath Area 1; second phase consists of Area 1 rooms.

TABLE 4.5. Growth curves for Tewa Basin villages and towns

Number of Phases in Component	Phase of Occupation						
	1	2	3	4	5	6	7
1	0.90						
2	0.62	0.90					
3	0.24	0.84	0.90				
4	0.12	0.62	0.88	0.90			
5	0.07	0.39	0.78	0.89	0.90		
6	0.05	0.24	0.62	0.84	0.89	0.90	
7	0.04	0.16	0.46	0.75	0.86	0.89	0.90

Note: Values are the proportion of total rooms occupied during each phase of occupation for sites of varying occupation span.

component at many towns was much larger than zero, the number implied by the procedure used for villages. Thus, using the vector corresponding to the phases of occupation for town components would produce multimodal population histories for these sites purely as an artifact of the analysis. Second, excavations suggest that the growth period of some Tewa Basin towns was limited to the initial phase of occupation. This was clearly the case at Arroyo Hondo, but it is also apparent at Poshuouinge, where Jeançon (1923) did not find evidence of gradual growth, even though the settlement was inhabited for several consecutive pottery periods.

To account for these observations in modeling the population histories of towns, I used the seven-phase vector in Table 4.5 for all town components and worked backward from the seventh phase until all phases associated with that component had been accounted for.[6] For sites with multiple components I used the seven-phase growth function to work backward from the peak/final population estimate of the most recent component toward the peak/final estimate of the previous component. For sites with a single component, this procedure imparted a model wherein the period of most rapid growth was during the initial phase of occupation.[7]

Estimating Regional Population History

The next step in producing a population history for the Tewa Basin was to extrapolate the total momentary population of the study area from the population histories of recorded sites. The basic assumption I made in this step is that all sites with 50 or more rooms are known, but many smaller sites remain to be discovered in unsurveyed areas (Flannery 1976:159–160). Thus, extrapolation from surveyed to unsurveyed areas is only necessary for small site populations. In order to make reasonable extrapolations, I divided the study area into five sampling strata that take into account the distribution of arable land, prior archaeological knowledge of settlement history, and ethnohistoric information on social boundaries.

First, I excluded land above 2,400 m because very few habitation sites have been recorded above this elevation contour. Second, I subdivided the study area based on prior knowledge of the spatial distribution of settlement during the Developmental, Coalition, and Classic periods. During the Developmental (AD 900–1200) period, settlement was most extensive along the Rio Grande south of La Bajada (Lange 1968) and along its eastern tributaries to the north, including the Santa Fe, Tesuque, Nambé, Pojoaque, and Santa Cruz drainages (Lang 1995; McNutt 1969; Scheick 2007; Marshall and Walt 2007). The Santa Cruz watershed appears to represent the northern limit of this distribution, given that Marshall and Walt (2007) were unable to identify any Developmental sites in the Truchas drainage to the north despite a concerted effort to find them. During the Coalition (AD 1200–1350) period, in contrast, settlement was most extensive west of the Rio Grande, from the Cañada de Cochiti in the south to Santa Clara Canyon in the north (Collins 1975; Orcutt 1991, 1999a, 1999b; Vierra et al. 2006). Finally, neither Developmental nor Coalition sites are common north of Santa Clara Canyon and the Rio Santa Cruz, but Classic (AD 1350–1540) period settlement was extensive in this area along western tributaries of the Chama, along the El Rito and Ojo Caliente drainages, and along the Rio Grande upstream of its confluence with the Chama (Anschuetz 1998; Beal 1987; Bugé 1984; Mera 1934; Peckham 1981). Based on these patterns, I divide the Tewa Basin into four quadrants, with an east-west division defined by the Rio Grande, and a north-south division defined by an east-west line that places Santa Clara Canyon and the Rio Santa Cruz to the south, and the lands upstream of the Chama–Rio Grande confluence to the north.

I also subdivide the southwestern quadrant as defined above into two strata along the northern edge of Frijoles Canyon based on ethnohistoric information (Harrington 1916) which suggests that the boundary between ancestral Tewa and ancestral Keres territory followed this canyon. A variety of archaeological evidence — including lithic raw material distributions, rock art motifs, and pottery type distributions — support the inference that by the Early Classic period there was indeed a social boundary in this area (Kohler 2004). It therefore seems appropriate to estimate population separately for these two areas. The resulting stratification is presented in Figure 4.6, and the total area of each sampling stratum, the surveyed portion of each stratum, and the small-site population in the surveyed area of each stratum are presented in Table 4.6.

Estimating Momentary Population

Figures for the average occupation span of small sites during different time periods comprise the final set of parameters needed to translate the site data into regional population estimates. Orcutt (1999b) estimated that small, Classic

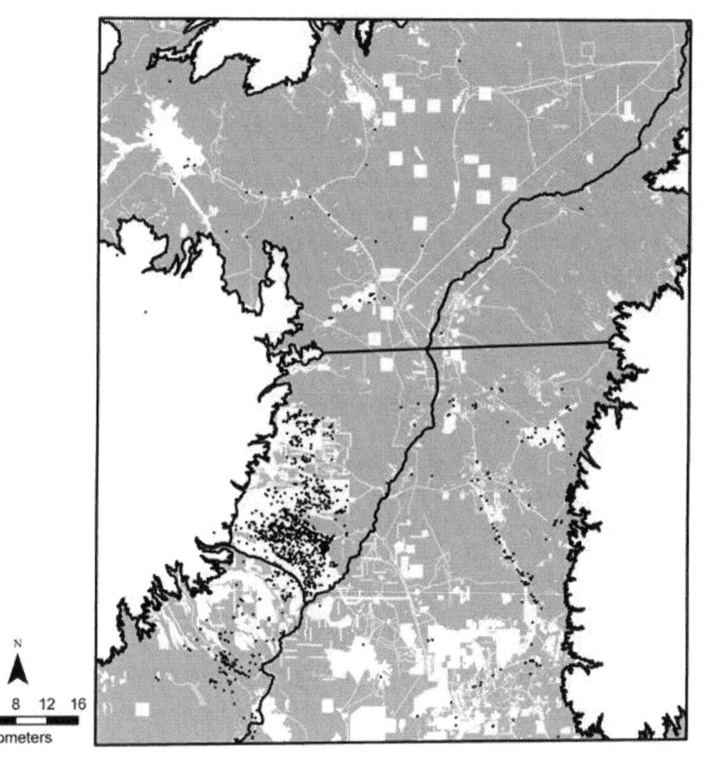

FIGURE 4.6.
Tewa Basin sampling strata, survey areas, and houses and hamlets. Land above 2,400 m elevation is excluded, sampling strata are outlined and shaded gray, survey areas are white, and hamlets and houses are shown as dots.

period habitations in Bandelier National Monument were used for an average of 50 years. Because this is equivalent to the lengths of Classic period phases in the chronological scheme of this study, there is no need to momentize small-site populations from the Early Classic period onward.

Occupation span corrections are more important for the Coalition and Developmental periods because most small habitations date to these periods, and the lengths of phases are also longer for these periods. For the Coalition period, it is possible to estimate the average occupation span of individual houses from recent excavations that emphasized absolute dating, quantification of artifact collections, and delineation of architectural features (Kohler 2004; Schmidt 2006; Vierra et al. 2002; Vierra et al. 2008). Table 4.7 presents a summary of recent excavation data relevant to estimating the occupation spans of Coalition period room block sites. I used the average occupation span of these seven sites, 30 years, as the average occupation span of Coalition period houses and hamlets.[8]

For the Developmental period, Orcutt (1999b) and Boyer and others (2010) suggest 15 years as the average use-life of a pit structure, based primarily on ethnoarchaeological studies of earthen architecture (Cameron 1990; Gilman 1987). This estimate is supported by excavations from the North Bank site, where several Coalition period room blocks are associated with a sequence of pit structures, the first of which was dismantled and filled with trash during use of the second (Bussey 1968b; also see Table 4.3). If the average occupation span of the

TABLE 4.6. Sampling strata and small-site sample data for the Tewa Basin

Stratum	Location	Total Area (km^2)	Surveyed Area (km^2)	Proportion Surveyed	Population Within Surveyed Area by Phase (Years AD)											
					1 (900–1050)	2 (1050–1200)	3 (1200–1275)	4 (1275–1350)	5 (1350–1400)	6 (1400–1450)	7 (1450–1500)	8 (1500–1540)	9 (1540–1600)	10 (1600–1680)	11 (1680–1700)	12 (1700–1760)
Velarde	Northeast	544.5	19.0	.0349	9	0	0	0	0	0	0	0	0	0	0	0
Chama	Northwest	2,057.7	171.2	.0832	46	6	45	91	16	32	22	2	0	3	3	3
Santa Fe/ Santa Cruz	Southeast	1,474.5	293.9	.1993	92	288	110	104	62	51	37	31	0	0	0	0
Cochiti	Southwest	448.0	94.5	.2110	31	96	107	210	69	38	44	76	1	28	1	1
Pajarito	West	513.3	205.7	.4007	90	290	2741	2186	471	206	105	105	52	0	14	14

TABLE 4.7. Estimates of occupation spans for Coalition period houses and hamlets

LA Number	Pottery Assemblage[a]	Total Sherd Accumulation	Rooms	Kivas	Households	Absolute Date Span (AD)	Pottery Span[b]	Best Span (years)	Notes
3852	Early Coalition	30,715	8	1	1	—	41.0	41	Assumed to be a unit pueblo residence. Total sherd estimate from probability sample.
135290	Middle Coalition	10,152	10	0	1	1180–1240	13.5	14	One square “ceremonial room” in the center of the room block. Three AMS maize dates 1180–1220; AM dates AD 1170–1240.
86534	Middle Coalition	17,949	8	1	1	1250–1275	23.9	24	Assumed to be a unit pueblo residence. Six AMS maize dates, also AM and TL dates; bulk of evidence suggests AD 1250–1275.
60372, Area 2	Middle Coalition	427,881	8	0	2	1235–1275	(285.3)	40	Total sherd estimate exaggerated due to later occupation of Area 1. Room block includes two square “ceremonial rooms.” Abandonment at AD 1275. 1207+vv to 1250B tree-ring dates; AM dates of AD 1220–1290 and 1205–1240.
4624	Middle Coalition	33,013	25	0	2	1270	22.0	22	Room block includes one square and one D-shaped “ceremonial room.” Total sherd estimate = surface sherds + (room block sherds / 10 of 25 excavated rooms); one AMS maize date.
4618	Late Coalition	9,872	13	2	2	1280–1318	(6.6)	38	One square and one round semisubterranean kiva. Sherd estimate limited to analyzed sherds from room block. Four AMS maize dates and one TL date between AD 1280 and 1318.
12587	Late Coalition	71,338	20	0	3	1270–1300	31.7	32	Total sherd estimate is total artifacts \x proportion of sherds in analyzed sample. Five AMS maize dates from AD 1270 to 1300. Household estimate based on three habitation rooms.

Sources: Data are from site reports (Harmon and McVickar 2008; Kohler, Powers et al. 2004:295; Kohler and Root 2004a:149–150, 156–161; Schmidt 2006, 2008; Vierra 2008; Vierra et al. 2002).

[a] Early Coalition: Kwahe’e B/W and Santa Fe B/W, Indented Corrugated; Middle Coalition: Santa Fe B/W dominant over Kwahe’e B/W, more Smeared-indented than Indented; Late Coalition: Santa Fe B/W dominant over Wiyo B/W, Smeared-indented.

[b] In years, based on the total accumulation of pottery and number of households present at the site. Sherd deposition rate is 750 sherds per household per year (after Nelson et al. 1994:132). Estimates in parentheses are deemed inaccurate for reason given in comments.

room blocks was 30 years (after Table 4.7), and this was equivalent to the use-life of two pit structures, then a use-life estimate of 15 years for pit structures appears reasonable; however, two factors suggest that applying this use-life correction by itself may result in overly conservative estimates of the Developmental population. First, the lengths of the Developmental phases used in this study may be generous compared to the actual dates of occupation of sites. The chronological scheme of this study has two Developmental phases, each spanning 150 years (AD 900–1200). Thus, given a 15-year structure use-life, the momentary population for each phase would be one-tenth of the total structures assigned to each phase. However, the Developmental period remains poorly tied to absolute dates, and it is not certain that these phases were actually 150 years in duration. If, in fact, these phases were each 100 years long, momentary population estimates would become one-third larger using the same data and use-life correction.[9] Because the lengths of Developmental phases are poorly defined, and one needs good estimates of both phase lengths and structure use-life to calculate momentary population estimates, applying a 15-year use-life correction to the Developmental site data may result in overly conservative momentary population estimates.

Second, the surface visibility of Developmental sites is low because their surface architecture is relatively insubstantial, and they often occur adjacent to watercourses, where they can be buried by alluvial sediment or obscured by more-recent land use. For example, initial survey of the Red Snake Hill site, on the Rio Grande floodplain near Cochiti, suggested that it dated to the Coalition period, but subsequent excavations determined that it consisted of a Developmental hamlet with intrusive Coalition material (Honea 1968:111). Also, at the North Bank site, Bussey (1968b:15) found that Developmental pithouse locations did correspond to artifact scatters but were not always indicated by depressions. It therefore seems likely that survey data underrepresent the numbers and sizes of Developmental sites. To correct for this underrepresentation, one would need to compare survey and excavation results across project areas and within individual sites, but as of this writing, appropriate data for such an analysis are not available.

Given these problems, I take a generous approach and assume that the effects of short use-life, imprecise dating of Developmental phases, and low visibility of Developmental sites and structures cancel each other out. In other words, I assume that the ratio of phase length to use-life for the Developmental period is the inverse of the proportion of the total number of Developmental structures documented on surveys.[10] As a result, the total structures assigned to each Developmental phase also provide estimates of the momentary occupied structures.

It may be useful to note the contribution of each Developmental site to regional momentary population estimates using these assumptions. In the present study, the 257 Developmental components within surveyed areas contribute an average of 3 individuals per component to the Early Developmental period, and

4 individuals per component to the Late Developmental period. Also note that the Late Developmental population estimate resulting from these assumptions—approximately 3,300 individuals—could be accommodated by placing 400 individuals in each of the Santa Fe, Pojoaque, Nambe, Tesuque, and Santa Cruz drainages, an additional 400 individuals on the Pajarito Plateau, and 400 individuals along the Rio Grande floodplain to the south and to the north of White Rock Canyon, respectively. This seems plausible given present understanding of Late Developmental settlement patterns. For example, Marshall and Walt (2007, II:6) note the presence of four Late Developmental site clusters in the Santa Cruz drainage, and Lang (1995) also identified three to four clusters of the same age in the Tesuque drainage. Marshall and Walt, as well as Lang, interpret these clusters as indications of the long-term presence of a community of several hundred people in each drainage unit. Due to the plausibility of the results obtained using these zero-sum-game assumptions, I believe this approach is reasonable for the purposes of this study. Nevertheless, it is important to keep in mind that due to these assumptions, the Developmental period population estimates are more likely generous than conservative.

Population History and Tewa Origins

Based on the data and methods outlined above, Table 4.8 presents estimates of the total momentary population of each Tewa Basin population stratum for each of 12 phases dating between AD 900 and 1760. The table presents total momentary population estimates for houses and hamlets, for villages and towns, and for the study area overall. As stated earlier, the estimates for houses and hamlets take use-life and survey coverage into account, whereas the estimates for villages and towns make use of the logistic growth model and assume that all such settlements are known. The total estimates for each stratum are presented graphically in Figure 4.7. Note that to be as generous as possible, I include the Cochiti stratum in the total Tewa Basin population estimates for the Developmental period but exclude this stratum for the Coalition period onward due to the likelihood that a boundary between Tewa and Keres territory developed along Frijoles Canyon, the northern limit of the Cochiti stratum, by the end of the Coalition period. This reconstruction suggests that the Tewa Basin population grew in a roughly linear fashion prior to AD 1200, exponentially between 1200 and 1350, was roughly stable from 1350 to 1540, and then experienced exponential decline from the Contact period through the Pueblo Revolt period.

These results suggest several points that are relevant for the competing models of Tewa origins. Most importantly, they suggest that the regional population doubled during the Early Coalition (AD 1200–1275) period and again during the Late Coalition (AD 1275–1350) period. The suggested average rate of population growth during these two phases was approximately 1 percent, or 10 per 1,000, per year, over a span of four to six generations. Intrinsic growth at this rate, over this period of time, would have been unusual relative to documented

TABLE 4.8. Momentary population estimates for the Tewa Basin

	Momentary Population by Phase (years AD)											
Stratum	1 (900–1050)	2 (1050–1200)	3 (1200–1275)	4 (1275–1350)	5 (1350–1400)	6 (1400–1450)	7 (1450–1500)	8 (1500–1540)	9 (1540–1600)	10 (1600–1680)	11 (1680–1700)	12 (1700–1760)
Houses and Hamlets												
Velarde	258	0	0	0	0	0	0	0	0	0	0	0
Chama	553	72	216	437	192	385	264	24	0	36	36	36
Santa Fe/Santa Cruz	462	1,445	221	209	311	256	186	156	0	0	0	0
Cochiti	147	455	203	398	327	180	209	360	5	133	5	5
Pajarito	225	724	2,736	2,182	1,175	514	262	262	130	0	35	35
Villages and Towns												
Velarde	0	0	74	375	404	1,057	1,540	1,684	1,809	1,830	750	565
Chama	0	0	191	2,341	6,401	9,766	10,643	11,216	6,551	225	0	0
Santa Fe/Santa Cruz	59	415	781	4,956	4,130	3,329	2,069	2,178	3,587	4,815	2,225	1,400
Cochiti	0	52	2,174	2,941	3,235	2,765	2,900	1,902	1,793	1,035	180	520
Pajarito	46	229	3,472	6,599	5,135	3,688	4,349	3,377	3,834	3,581	52	210
Total Momentary Population												
Velarde	258	0	74	375	404	1,057	1,540	1,684	1,809	1,830	750	565
Chama	553	72	407	2,778	6,593	10,151	10,907	11,240	6,551	261	36	36
Santa Fe/Santa Cruz	521	1,860	1,002	5,165	4,441	3,585	2,255	2,334	3,587	4,815	2,225	1,400
Cochiti	147	507	2,377	3,339	3,562	2,945	3,109	2,262	1,798	1,168	185	525
Pajarito	271	953	6,208	8,781	6,310	4,202	4,611	3,639	3,964	3,581	87	245
Tewa Basin Total[a]	1,749	3,340	7,691	17,099	17,749	18,994	19,313	18,897	15,911	10,487	3,098	2,246

[a] Includes the Cochiti stratum only for the Developmental period (Phases 1 and 2).

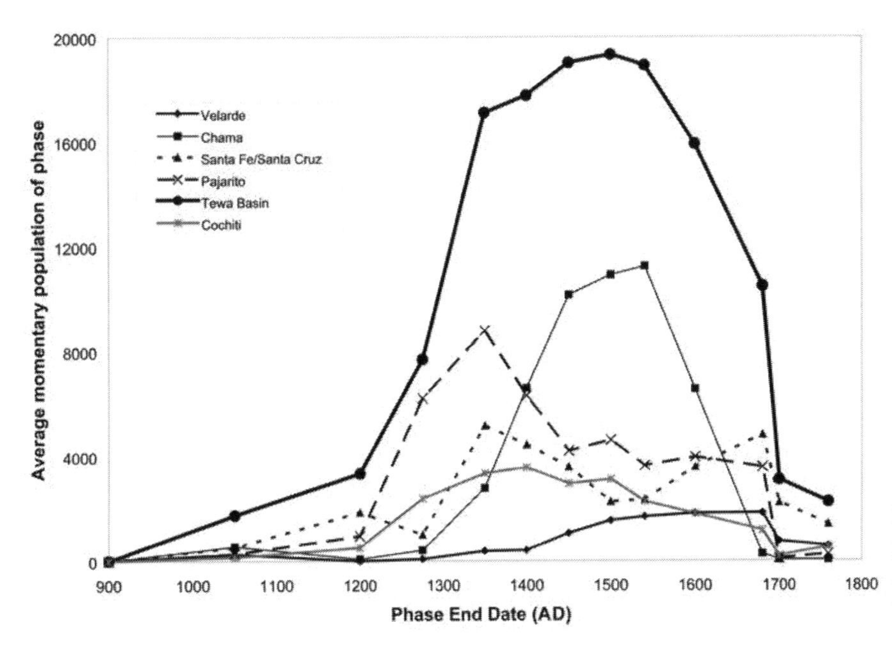

FIGURE 4.7. Population history of the Tewa Basin, by stratum.

preindustrial societies (Cowgill 1975) but may have been attainable under exceptionally advantageous conditions (Richerson and others 2001:396–397).[11] Also, this period of robust growth is bracketed by extended periods of relatively modest growth during the Developmental and Classic periods. The overall shape of Tewa Basin population history prior to Spanish contact thus appears to approximate a logistic curve that could have conceivably resulted from strong intrinsic growth of the founding population until it began to approach the regional carrying capacity.[12]

Intraregional population trends, however, appear inconsistent with this interpretation. If intrinsic growth were responsible for this history overall, one would expect population to have expanded outward from an original, densely settled core area over time. The subregional trajectories in Figure 4.7 do not show this pattern; instead they show that during the Early Coalition period a new population center developed on the Pajarito Plateau at a growth rate of greater than 1 percent per year within this stratum, and with no corresponding change in the eastern Rio Grande tributaries (the Santa Fe/Santa Cruz District) that had been the focus of Late Developmental settlement. Then, during the Late Coalition period, population expanded rapidly throughout the Tewa Basin, including on the Pajarito Plateau and along the eastern tributaries. It appears most straightforward to explain these subregional trajectories as the result of migration from outside the study area into the Pajarito and Cochiti areas during the Early Coalition period, and then throughout the Tewa Basin during the Late Coalition period.

These patterns appear more consistent with the population movement hypothesis of Tewa origins than with the immigration hypothesis for two reasons.

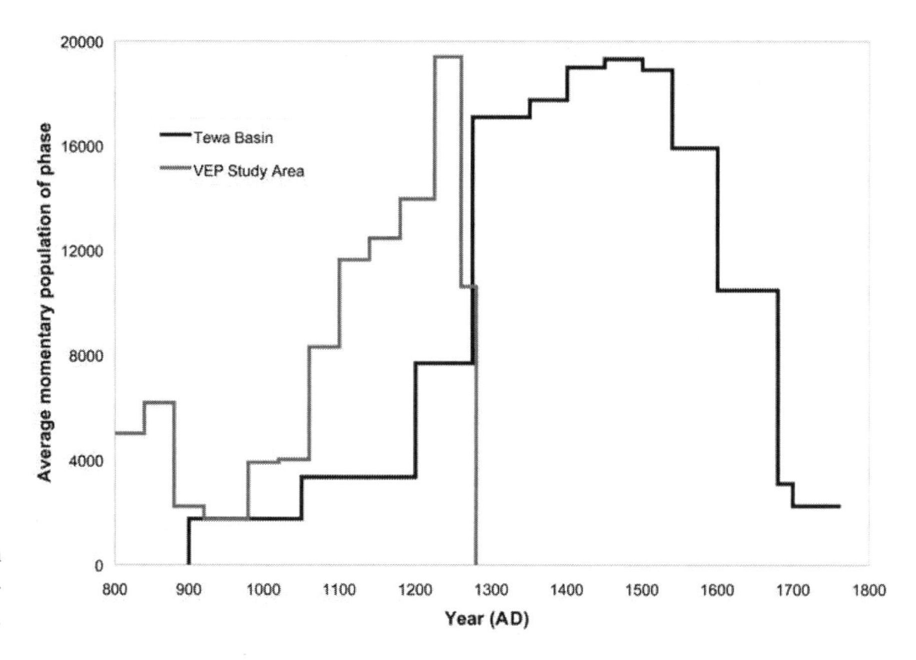

FIGURE 4.8. Correlation of Tewa Basin and VEP population histories.

First, a new population center developed on the Pajarito Plateau, a previously uninhabited area, during the Early Coalition period, even as the population of the previously settled eastern Rio Grande tributaries remained stable. Under the immigration hypothesis, one would expect more migrants to have joined communities in already settled areas than to have established new communities in previously uninhabited areas. Second, the increased scale of migration into the Tewa Basin during the Late Coalition period, combined with the establishment of many new villages and towns in the Santa Fe/Santa Cruz and Chama districts during this period (Table 4.8), suggests an influx of community-sized groups after AD 1275. One would not expect to see this pattern if Late Coalition population growth were due to the gradual infiltration of small groups into established communities, as the immigration hypothesis proposes.

This scenario leaves open the possibility that a source of the Classic period Tewa Basin population was the Mesa Verde region. To investigate the extent to which the pace, scale, and timing of migration into the Tewa Basin correspond to depopulation of the Mesa Verde region, Figure 4.8 correlates the present model of Tewa Basin population history with the most recent population history for a portion of the central Mesa Verde region. This latter reconstruction is for the Village Ecodynamics Project (VEP) study area, a 1,817 km^2 rectangle encompassing the McElmo and Yellowjacket drainages, and a portion the Dolores River valley, in southwestern Colorado (Kohler et al. 2007; for location relative to Tewa Basin see Figure 5.1). It excludes areas of likely high-density settlement on Mesa Verde proper and in southeastern Utah, but does encompass the most densely settled portion of the region. The VEP population history is derived from a comparable database of all recorded sites. The methods used to assess the occupational histories of these sites (Ortman et al. 2007) are more intricate than those used in this study, because the Mesa Verde region archaeological record is more precisely dated and has more complete surface indications that can sustain a more complex analysis. However, the principles used to translate these site-level occupational histories into a regional population history (Varien et al. 2007) are similar to those used in this study.

In order to emphasize the fact that population histories consist of average momentary population estimates over a period of time rather than point estimates for specific years, Figure 4.8 presents the data in the form of bar charts, where the width of each bar corresponds to the length of each phase. Note also that changes in average momentary population between periods did not occur instantaneously at period boundaries, but instead occurred continuously, so, for example, the Tewa Basin population must have been somewhat lower than the average momentary estimate at the beginning of the Early Coalition period and somewhat higher by the end of that period.

Some of the parallels between the two reconstructions are probably coincidental. The comparable size of the VEP population prior to AD 1260 and the Tewa Basin population after AD 1275 is probably not meaningful because the VEP study area encompasses only a portion of the Mesa Verde region, and a reconstruction for the entire region would have a somewhat larger peak population; however, other details may inform on the potential role of migration from the Mesa Verde region in producing the ancestral Tewa population. For example, Early Coalition (AD 1200–1275) population growth on the Pajarito Plateau coincides with the period during which the central Mesa Verde population density reached the highest level of the entire ancestral Pueblo sequence and then began to decline (AD 1225–1260). In other words, both population pressure and population decline characterized the AD 1200s in the Mesa Verde region, and both could be related to the formation of a migration stream from the Mesa Verde region to the Tewa Basin during this same period. Also, the fact that more than 14,000 people inhabited the central Mesa Verde region at AD 1200 is significant because it indicates that this region had enough people at the right time to have possibly been a major source for the 14,000 person increase in the Tewa Basin population during the Coalition period. Finally, the precipitous decline in the central Mesa Verde region during the second half of the AD 1200s corresponds quite closely to the dramatic rise in Tewa Basin population at this same time. In short, enough people were leaving the Mesa Verde region at the right time for it to have been a major contributor to the increase of roughly 10,000 people in the Late Coalition Tewa Basin.

Although these parallels appear to support models of Tewa origins that involve migration from the Mesa Verde region, this is by no means the only possible explanation. Another possibility is that environmental changes taking place across the Southwest during the thirteenth century were deleterious to Mesa Verde region populations but encouraged robust intrinsic growth in the

Tewa Basin. An examination of potential environmental factors related to these population histories is beyond the scope of this study but is well treated in several publications, most recently by Wright (2010). Here I merely investigate the suggestion that the Mesa Verde region population experienced in situ decline at the same time the Tewa Basin population experienced robust intrinsic growth.

To investigate intrinsic growth independent of the settlement data, I drew upon Kohler and others' (2008: Table 1) compilation of age-at-death data from human skeletal assemblages across the Southwest. As noted in Chapter 3, the ratio of individuals aged 5 to 19 years to all individuals aged 5 and older, also known as 15P5, is strongly correlated with intrinsic growth rates across a wide range of preindustrial societies (Boquet-Appel 2002; Boquet-Appel and Naji 2006; Kohler et al. 2008). Sampling problems associated with the recovery and analysis of human remains from archaeological sites mean that there are likely to be significant errors in 15P5 estimates for individual sites. To control for these errors to some extent, I aggregated samples from sites across the Northern Rio Grande, which includes the Pecos drainage and Galisteo Basin in addition to the Tewa Basin, and across the Northern San Juan, which includes the Totah in addition to the Mesa Verde region. I also lump samples from each regional grouping into major cultural periods to maximize sample sizes while still capturing broad demographic trends. The resulting data are presented in Table 4.9 and Figure 4.9.

These data suggest that intrinsic growth was more robust in the Northern San Juan during the Pueblo III period than it ever was in the Northern Rio Grande. This is the opposite of what one would expect under the in situ development model of Tewa origins. If the Coalition period population increase were due primarily to intrinsic growth, one would expect the Coalition period 15P5 ratio to be at least comparable to that of the Pueblo III Northern San Juan, where population was also growing for most of the Pueblo III period. The fact that strong population growth does not correlate with high 15P5 ratios in the Tewa Basin, as it appears to do in the Mesa Verde region, suggests that intrinsic growth was not a major factor in producing the Late Coalition Tewa Basin population. If anything, these data suggest that robust intrinsic growth in the Mesa Verde region was one of the catalysts behind the formation of a migration stream out of this region in the thirteenth century.

The Blossoming of Tewa Basin Population

In this chapter I have developed a model of Tewa Basin population history, compared it to the most recent population history for a portion of the central Mesa Verde region, and compared both to independent indicators of intrinsic growth rates. The results suggest that the Tewa Basin population doubled during the Early Coalition period, and again during the Late Coalition period, at an annual rate of growth of roughly 1 percent per year. In contrast, growth was relatively

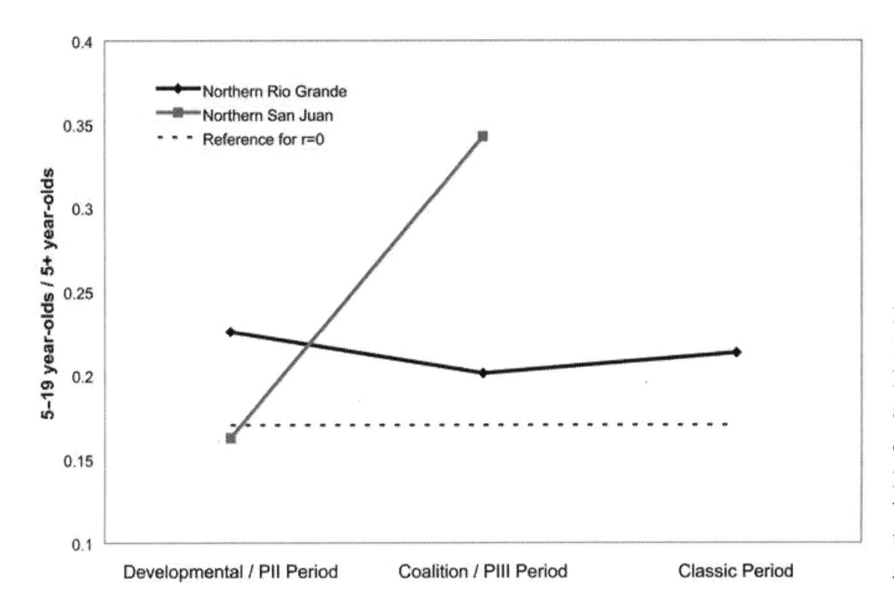

FIGURE 4.9. 15P5 ratios for Northern Rio Grande and Northern San Juan regional samples; $r = 0$ at a 15P5 value of .170, based on the analysis in Boquet Appel 2002:639–640.

TABLE 4.9. 15P5 ratios in regional samples

Period	Samples[a]	Total n[b]	Total 15P5
Rio Grande Developmental	Pena Blanca I–II, NRG1150	38.46	.226
Rio Grande Coalition	Pecos B/W, Forked Lightning, NRG1250	155.92	.201
Rio Grande Classic	Arroyo Hondo, San Cristobal, Pecos Glaze I–III	573.28	.213
Northern San Juan Pueblo II	La Plata, NSJ950, NSJ1050	93.18	.163
Northern San Juan Pueblo III	NSJ1150, NSJ1250	148.07	.343

[a] Sample names correspond to those listed in Kohler et al. 2008: Table 1.
[b] Total individuals are not whole numbers because Kohler and others (2008) reapportioned counts for samples that grouped individuals into age classes that crosscut ages 5 and/or 19 (following procedures in Boquet-Appel 2002: online supplemental materials).

modest during the preceding Developmental period and in the subsequent Classic period.

Intrinsic growth is not impossible as an explanation for the overall magnitude of Coalition period population changes, but the spatial pattern of growth is more consistent with models that involve migration from outside the Tewa Basin. This is because, instead of an Early Coalition florescence of the Developmental population in the eastern Rio Grande tributaries, Early Coalition growth involved the formation of a new population center on the Pajarito Plateau that subsequently spread across the basin during the Late Coalition period. This pattern also lends greater support to the population movement hypothesis than to the immigration hypothesis because it indicates that early migrants colonized an uninhabited area instead of moving into an established population center, and that later migrants colonized additional, previously uninhabited areas in village-sized groups.

The results of this study also indicate that the initial colonization of the Pajarito Plateau took place during the same decades that the central Mesa Verde region population peaked and began its initial decline. Continued growth throughout the Tewa Basin during the Late Coalition period also corresponds to the departure of at least 10,000 people from the central Mesa Verde region. Thus, it appears that the Mesa Verde region could have donated substantial populations to the Tewa Basin in the late thirteenth century.

Finally, age-at-death distributions from the Northern Rio Grande and Northern San Juan regions suggest that Coalition period population growth was not due to exceptional intrinsic growth. On the contrary, these data suggest that robust intrinsic growth in the Mesa Verde region may have been one of the factors that led to the formation of a migration stream out of that region during the thirteenth century.

Overall, these results are inconsistent with the in situ development hypothesis of Tewa origins and lend support to models that involve migration from beyond the Tewa Basin. Subregional patterns of growth are also more consistent with expectations of the population movement hypothesis than with the immigration hypothesis. The population history of the central Mesa Verde region meshes well with that of the Tewa Basin and suggests the former region as a possible source area for at least some of these migrants, but in the absence of comparable demographic studies across the northern U.S. Southwest, one cannot rule out additional source areas, or multiple source areas, for the eventual Tewa Basin population. The next step in the analysis, then, is to evaluate whether the Mesa Verde region was a primary source for the ancestral Tewa population. I tackle this problem using an additional line of biological evidence — namely, osteometric traits of human skeletal remains.

Notes

1. These include data from Biscuit ware sites compiled by Mera (1934); data on large sites (50+ rooms) compiled by Crown, Kohler, and Orcutt (1996) and available at (http://csanet.org/archive/adap/usa/prepueb/prepw.html); data on large sites compiled by Fowles (2004) and Snead and others (2004), and made available by Andrew Duff; data on Tewa Basin villages compiled by Anschuetz (2005) and made available by him; data for all Tewa Basin sites with 13 or more rooms from the Coalescent Communities Database, made available by Brett Hill; data for Developmental sites in the Santa Fe area compiled by Scheick (2007); data for all recorded sites and several previously unrecorded sites in the Santa Cruz and Truchas drainages compiled by Marshall and Walt (2007); data on the size and periods of occupation of sites on Los Alamos National Laboratory property analyzed by Brandon Gabler (2008) and made available by him; data on Tewa Basin villages abandoned in historic times from Span-

ish documents synthesized by Barrett (2002); and excavation and survey reports for specific sites (see Ortman 2009: App. A).

2. The often-cited figure of 10 m^2 per person from Naroll's (1962) classic paper is the result of a calculation error that Brown (1987) corrected in his reanalysis of Naroll's constant.
3. For architectural dating, I assume that the earliest Tewa Basin sites date from AD 900 onward (McNutt 1969); that no cavate rooms were constructed prior to AD 1200 (Toll 1995:62); that sites on the Pajarito Plateau with rubble mounds do not predate AD 1150 (Vierra et al. 2006:70); that plaza-oriented sites do not predate AD 1275 (Steen 1977:13–14); and that one- to three-room structures dating to the Classic period were used as field houses rather than year-round residences (Snead 2008a: 49–80).
4. For example, a site lacking Santa Fe B/W but with Wiyo B/W is inferred to have been established after AD 1350 (the end date of Santa Fe B/W), and a site with Biscuit B but lacking Potsuwii Incised is inferred to have been abandoned by AD 1450 (the beginning date of Potsuwii Incised).
5. Henrich couched this analysis in terms of Boyd and Richerson (1985), but in light of the discussion in Chapter 2, I believe it is preferable to view prestige bias and conformist bias as deriving from primary values that guide human decision making as opposed to influences on cultural transmission itself.
6. For example, the site of Yungue (LA59) has two components: the later encompasses four phases (Middle Classic through Contact) and is associated with a town of 520 rooms; the earlier encompasses two phases (Late Coalition through Early Classic) and is associated with a village of 160 rooms. To estimate the population history of the later, town-sized component, I multiplied 520 by the vector of proportions for Phases 4 through 7 (.75, .85, .86, .90) in the seven-phase equation (Table 4.5) to estimate the occupied rooms during the Middle Classic (390), Late Classic (447), Terminal Classic (463), and Contact (468) periods. Then, to estimate the population history of the earlier, village-sized component, I multiplied 160 by the vector of proportions for phases 1 and 2 (.62, .90) in the two-phase equation (Table 4.5) to estimate the occupied rooms during the Late Coalition (99) and Early Classic (144) periods.
7. The resulting population histories of villages and towns are available in Ortman 2009: App. A.
8. This figure is slightly shorter than the 35-year estimate that Orcutt (1999b) used for Middle and Late Coalition period components in Bandelier National Monument.
9. Early Developmental sites dating to AD 900 or even earlier have been excavated in the Cochiti District (Akins et al. 2003), but in other areas of the U.S. Southwest the same pottery assemblage associated with Phase 1 of the present study (consisting of Red Mesa style decorated wares and neckbanded culinary wares) was being produced even after AD 975 (Ortman et al. 2007).
10. For example, with 150-year phase-lengths and a 15-year use-life, this model implies that one-third of all Developmental sites are identified on surveys, and that one-third of the structures within these sites were identified from surface evidence.
11. For example, Patrick Kirch (2010:138) recently estimated intrinsic growth rates of between 1.2 and 1.8 percent for the Hawaiian population between AD 1100 and 1500, a span of 400 years.
12. The overall S shape of this reconstruction is not a result of the logistic growth model applied to villages and towns, because most Early Coalition growth is due to the establishment of smaller sites on the Pajarito Plateau, and the robust growth observed

during the Late Coalition period is due in large part to the establishment of many larger sites that continued to grow during the Classic period. The primary effect of the logistic growth model is to produce stable population estimates for the Classic period. This is because, over the course of the Classic period, population aggregated into fewer, larger sites, and it appears logistic growth in the remaining towns was sufficient to accommodate the populations leaving abandoned settlements.

In the present model, initial population decline during the Contact period (AD 1540–1600) is the result of abandonment of several towns in the Chama District. See Ortman 2009:136–137, n. 29, for additional discussion of this issue.

Biological Variation and Tewa Ancestry

Indeed, if such a hypothesis of migration can be corroborated by the association of distinctive skeletal remains, the probability of migration will be established insofar as it is possible for an archaeologist to do so.

—Charles McNutt, 1969

In the previous chapter I constructed and interpreted a population history for the Tewa Basin in which the overall pace and spatial pattern of growth are more consistent with a past history of migration than with a history of in situ development. I also compared Tewa Basin and central Mesa Verde population histories to suggest that if migration was involved in the formation of the ancestral Tewa population, the Mesa Verde region is a plausible source area for at least some of the migrants. In this chapter I further examine the origins of the ancestral Tewa population through analysis of biological variation across the Rio Grande, San Juan, and Little Colorado drainages. Migration, by definition, involves the movement of people from one place to another, regardless of other processes that may have been involved. And whereas people can change material practices or adopt a new language during their lifetimes, they cannot alter their genes. Thus, to the extent that humans exhibit heritable, group-level variation resulting from historical differences in mating networks, biological variation should provide a reliable means of discerning whether or not migration has occurred, and if it did, what its biological consequences were.

I first review previous studies of ancestral Pueblo biological variation, several of which address Tewa ancestry specifically, to better appreciate the data requirements for a study of this kind and to identify the most useful data sources. Based on this review, I conclude that craniometric traits provide the most practical data source for investigating Tewa ancestry, given the current state of data and methodology. Next I review the theoretical and empirical bases for the use of craniometric and other quantitative phenotypic traits in studies of population history, and introduce the methods most commonly used in biodistance analyses of such traits. Finally, I present a study of previously collected cranial measurements from late prehispanic Pueblo skeletal remains to address the sources of the ancestral Tewa population.

Previous Studies of Pueblo Biological Variation

Given the potential of biological variation for illuminating the population history of Pueblo peoples, it is not surprising that a large number of such studies have been done. As examples, El-Najjar (1986) used craniometric data to suggest that the inhabitants of Canyon de Chelly migrated to the Hopi mesas in the late thirteenth century; Akins (1986) and Schillaci (2003) examined craniometric variation in Chaco Canyon, and both found evidence for a highly variable population that had diverse origins and affinities; and LeBlanc and others (2007) extracted ancient mitochondrial DNA from quids and aprons found at Basketmaker cave sites and compared the resulting mtDNA haplogroup frequencies with those of living populations to suggest that the western Basketmakers were a migrant group from Mexico who introduced maize agriculture to the Colorado Plateau.

I focus here on recent studies of biological variation that address Tewa ancestry to some extent. A brief review of these studies is helpful for understanding the data requirements for an effective examination of Tewa ancestry. Corrucini (1983) examined craniofacial, dental, and postcranial metric and nonmetric traits of samples from Pueblo Bonito (in Chaco Canyon), Hawikuh (an ancestral Zuni town), and Puye (an ancestral Tewa town near present-day Santa Clara Pueblo). He found that these three populations were too different from each other to have been drawn from a single population, but also that these three populations were more similar to each other than they were to non-Pueblo populations from other parts of North America. One implication of this study is that Pueblo people appear to have derived from several distinct ancestral populations that were still distinct in the late prehispanic period. More importantly, Corrucini's study suggests that the degree to which Pueblo populations appear homogeneous or heterogeneous depends upon the frame of reference.

Barnes (1994) compared developmental defects of the axial skeleton, which appear to be under strong genetic control, in skeletal populations from Mesa Verde National Park and from Puye. She found a number of relatively rare defects in both populations, and on this basis suggested that the Mesa Verde region population was likely ancestral to the Tewa Basin population. Kuckelman (2008: 120) identified several of the same anomalies among the skeletal remains from Sand Canyon Pueblo, one of the final Pueblo villages constructed in the Mesa Verde region. These findings are suggestive because the heritability of the traits examined is known to be high based on medical records; however, their applicability is limited because comparable data do not exist for skeletal populations across the Southwest. Thus, while both of these studies suggest a Tewa–Mesa Verde linkage, they cannot rule out other possible sources for the Puye population, and cannot be taken in isolation as definitive confirmation of a Mesa Verde to Tewa Basin migration.

Mackey (1977) used craniometric data to investigate Jemez culture history. His study was designed to test Ellis's (1967) contention that Jemez Pueblo descended from earlier populations of the Rosa-Piedra and Largo-Gallina districts, in the Upper San Juan and eastern San Juan Basin, respectively (see discussion in Chapter 1). He found that samples from the Largo-Gallina District are not likely ancestral to the protohistoric Jemez population; that samples from the Rosa-Piedra District are relatively similar to ancestral Jemez, Tewa, and Tompiro populations; and that the Pecos population is more closely related to ancestral Tewa and Tompiro populations than it is to the ancestral Jemez population. These results are largely replicated by the present study for those samples that are common to both. Mackey's study included samples from several ancestral Tewa sites, as well as earlier populations from the Rosa-Piedra and Largo-Gallina districts, but it did not include samples from the Rio Grande Developmental period or the Mesa Verde region and thus does not address the full range of possibilities for Tewa ancestry.

Turner (1993) examined dental nonmetric traits of more than 4,600 individuals, both living and dead, across the U.S. Southwest and northern Mexico, including Mogollon, Hohokam, Salado, Sinagua, ancestral Pueblo, living Native American, and northern and central Mexican samples. His study includes a regional grouping from southwestern Colorado, comprised equally of Basketmaker and Pueblo period samples, and also an Eastern Pueblo group that contains samples from Puye (Tewa), San Cristobal (Southern Tewa), Giusiwa (Jemez), and Pecos. Turner's most relevant finding was that, out of 25 regional groupings, the population most similar to the Eastern Pueblo group was the southwestern Colorado group, thus suggesting an ancestor-descendant relationship between these two samples. Turner's results are significant because they are based on analysis of large samples from many sites. However, Turner's database does not include samples from Mesa Verde proper or from Developmental Rio Grande sites, and covers such a broad area that one could imagine the southwest Colorado and Eastern Pueblo samples being similar simply as a function their geographic proximity.[1]

Additional studies have examined biological affinities among ancestral Tewa villages and found evidence that biological variation maps closely onto culture history even at this relatively fine scale. Mackey (1980) used cranial nonmetric traits to show that the inhabitants of several ancestral Tewa villages were more similar to each other than they were to inhabitants of an ancestral Jemez village. Schillaci and Stojanowski (2005) used craniometric traits to examine population structure among ancestral Tewa populations from Otowi, Tsankawi, Puye, Sapawe, and San Cristobal, and found a good correlation between geographical and biological distances; specifically, the three samples from sites on the Pajarito Plateau were most similar to each other, whereas the samples from Sapawe (to the northeast) and San Cristobal (to the southeast) were distinct from the Pajarito group and from each other. These results support the contention of Stojanowski and Schillaci (2006) that given sufficient sampling, phenotypic traits can reliably identify aspects of population structure even at small spatial and temporal scales.

Finally, Schillaci and others (2001) used craniometric traits to examine biological relationships across the northern U.S. Southwest. Two findings are of interest. First, they found the thirteenth-century population of Aztec Ruin (in the Totah District of the Northern San Juan, southeast of the Mesa Verde region) to be biologically similar to that of several Rio Grande sites at which Tanoan languages (Tiwa, Tewa, and Towa) were spoken, suggesting that the population of the former site spoke a Tanoan language. Second, they were unable to demonstrate the affinity of a small sample from Mesa Verde ($n = 7$) with ancestral Tanoan populations of the Rio Grande. Schillaci and others (2001) nevertheless leave open the possibility of a migration from the San Juan drainage into the Rio Grande, based on Morris's (1928) view that the late population of Aztec represents a reoccupation by people from the Mesa Verde region.[2]

Summary

The studies reviewed above suggest several guidelines for an effective examination of Tewa ancestry. First, multiple lines of evidence suggest that Pueblo people derive from a number of distinct ancestral groups (Corruccini 1972; Hill 2001, 2008b; LeBlanc 2008; LeBlanc et al. 2007; Matson 2002; Turner 1993: 45). Even if between-group gene flow has been continuous over the course of Pueblo history, one would expect these differences to have been preserved into the late prehispanic period so long as within-group mating was more common than between-group mating. This means that ancestors of the Classic period Tewa Basin population should be identifiable if one can sample the full range of potential source populations, the Tewa Basin population itself, and other contemporary populations in the Rio Grande region and in potential source areas.

Second, because all biological relationships within a single species are relative, an effective analysis of Tewa ancestry should be tailored to the geographical and temporal scale appropriate to the problem. Even if the Pueblos derive from multiple ancestral populations, Corrucini's (1972) study suggests that between-group differences have been reduced over time due to gene flow. As a result, one would expect any pair of late prehistoric populations to be somewhat similar. Thus in order to claim that an ancestor-descendant relationship exists between specific populations, one should ideally show that the two populations are more similar to each other than they are to other possible pairings. However, it is also important not to include geographically distant populations because the inclusion of outliers will reinforce the homogeneity of the more relevant populations and may obscure patterns of affinity that betray regional population history.

Third, previous studies suggest that a variety of data — including dental morphology, cranial metric and nonmetric traits, and ancient DNA — can produce results that are broadly compatible despite the fact that the underlying genetic bases of these traits differ.[3] This suggests that sampling and analytical issues are more important than the type of variation being examined in analyses of human population history. Because population history is the dominant factor underlying biological variation in general, a variety of genotypic or phenotypic data should reveal this history with adequate regional sampling and appropriate analytical methods. Certain types of data may provide a clearer signal than others, but capturing the range of variation appears to be more important.

These observations suggest that an effective analysis of Tewa ancestry needs to employ a comprehensive regional database with large sample sizes from as many relevant subregional populations of the right time periods as possible. For a variety of reasons, craniometric data offer the most practical means of achieving these objectives. Craniometric data collected from skeletal remains are preferable to other types of osteological data — including dental measurements, dental nonmetric traits, and cranial nonmetric traits — because these other types of data have not been collected as consistently for as many samples. Direct studies of genetic variation among living American Indian populations are also not an option because no Pueblo people remained in the Mesa Verde region within a few years of AD 1280 (Varien 2010; also see Chapter 12), so there is no direct relationship between people who live in the Mesa Verde region today and its thirteenth-century inhabitants.

Finally, it will be many years before sufficient ancient DNA evidence to address Tewa origins has accumulated. Techniques for extracting ancient DNA are progressing rapidly, and studies using these data are beginning to produce exciting results (Kaestle and Smith 2001; LeBlanc et al. 2007; Parr et al. 1996). At present, however, ancient DNA evidence is largely limited to mtDNA, which only provides information about maternal lineages. Also, due to partial preservation, the most productive way of analyzing mtDNA strands at present is to screen them for the specific nucleotide sequences characteristic of the five major Native American mtDNA haplogroups. As a result, ancient DNA analyses often resolve into cluster analyses of haplogroup frequencies across sample populations. Such analyses are informative, but they can also be misleading due to microevolutionary forces acting on small populations (Cabana et al. 2008; Relethford and Lees 1982). Work is proceeding on the identification of additional ancient DNA markers that would allow more reliable phylogenetic analyses, but due to the expense of ancient DNA analysis, limitations in the currently available samples, the destructive nature of current analysis methods, and the data requirements for an analysis of Tewa ancestry, it will probably take many years for a sufficiently large ancient DNA database to accumulate.[4]

Because cranial measurements have been collected from human remains using standardized protocols since the early twentieth century, and many relevant collections of human skeletal remains are no longer available for study, I utilize craniometric data for the analysis of Tewa ancestry in this chapter. In the following section I introduce the theoretical basis for using metric phenotypic traits, including craniometric data, to study population history, and describe current methods used to analyze these data.

Metric Traits and Biodistance Analysis

The conceptual basis of contemporary biodistance studies was established by John Relethford and Francis Lees (1982) in their classic article, "The Use of Quantitative Traits in the Study of Human Population Structure." This essay makes the case that population genetic theory provides a basis for viewing traditional anthropometric and osteometric traits as indicators of underlying genetic variation. Relethford and Lees built on Cavalli-Sforza and Bodmer's (1971: 508–626) classic work on human population genetics, which grouped quantitative traits into three categories: (1) single-gene traits, for which phenotypic variation associated with each genotype is due to environmental influences; (2) threshold traits, where phenotypes are discontinuous but are governed by continuous underlying genetic variation; and (3) polygenic traits, which exhibit continuous phenotypes that are determined by the equal and additive effects of several genes in combination with environmental influences. Most commonly occurring skeletal traits are either threshold or polygenic traits. Examples of the former are cranial ossicles and shovel-shaped incisors, and examples of the latter are long-bone lengths and craniofacial measurements.

Although the underlying genetic bases of many metric phenotypic traits remain largely unspecified, a model in which such traits derive from the equal and additive effects of many genes is a reasonable approximation. Also, even if the underlying genetic bases of metric traits vary from trait to trait, deviations from the equal and additive model will tend to be averaged out if one examines several such traits in a multivariate analysis to estimate the overall genetic relationships between groups (Relethford and Lees 1982:114–116). In fact, for several reasons, multivariate analyses of polygenic traits may be among the most useful ways to investigate human population history. Random genetic drift can have a dramatic effect on frequencies of single-gene traits, but it appears to have less of an effect on polygenic traits because random fluctuations in the many contributing genes tend to cancel one another out. Also, polygenic traits appear to respond more slowly to gene flow than do single-gene traits. Finally, expressions of polygenic traits track genetic variation for every individual, whereas in threshold traits, phenotypic expressions will underrepresent the underlying genetic variation. Thus, it may require larger sample sizes to estimate between-group genetic variation using nonmetric data, which usually reflect threshold traits, than with metric data.

Of course, the primary shortcoming of any phenotypic traits for population genetic analysis is that only a portion of the total phenotypic variation in a population is due to genetic variation, and only a portion of the genetic variation is due to population history. In fact, phenotypic variation derives from nongenetic influences on the developing organism and natural selection, as well as population history. Several studies have shown that craniometric traits are subject to environmental influences. In an influential early study, Franz Boas (1912) compared the phenotypes of migrants who were born and raised in Europe versus individuals who were born to European migrants in the United States. He found that the phenotypes of Europeans raised in the United States differed systematically from those of Europeans raised in Europe, and concluded that developmental plasticity, or the effects of the environment on gene expression, was responsible (for a supportive reanalysis of these data, see Gravlee and others [2003]). Boas therefore concluded that craniometric traits were poorly suited to the investigation of population history. Additional studies (e.g., Beals 1974; Guglielmino-Matessi et al. 1979; Manica et al. 2007; Roseman and Weaver 2004) have also investigated the role of natural selection in worldwide craniometric variation by correlating craniometric variation with environmental and geographic variation. These studies indicate that natural selection has influenced human craniometric variation to some extent.

Nevertheless, additional studies of global craniometric variation demonstrate that population history is also a significant factor in phenotypic variation. Relethford (2002) demonstrated that global patterns of human variation apparent in studies of classical genetic markers are mirrored in patterns of craniometric variation; that is, most of the total variation in human phenotypes occurs within populations, with less occurring between regions, and very little within regions.[5] He also showed that global variation in skin color does not follow these patterns, but is more consistent with a model of strong selection (driven by exposure to UV radiation), as opposed to the largely neutral variation in craniometrics and genetic markers. In another study, Relethford (2004b) demonstrated that global patterns of human craniometric variation show the same patterns of isolation by distance as DNA markers and blood types. Finally, Manica and others (2007) showed that, after controlling for the effects of climate-based selection, levels of craniometric variation are inversely correlated with distance from Africa, consistent with the African origin hypothesis for modern humans. These studies provide ample evidence that craniometric variation reflects genetic variation resulting from population history and microevolution. In the words of Manica and others (2007:348), "after allowing for the impact of heritability and selection, the signal of ancient demography in human skull variability should properly be seen as remarkably strong."

A common misconception among researchers skeptical of biodistance analysis is that traits affected by natural selection or environmental conditions during development cannot be trusted for studies of population history. In fact, the real issue, as Relethford (2004a) points out, is not whether craniometric traits are subject to selection or developmental plasticity, but the relative contributions of selection, plasticity, and population history to the pattern of variation in the traits under study. For example, if a certain trait is under selection, but the selection pressure is weak, the history of population movements and resultant changes in mating networks will exert a stronger influence on the resulting patterns than selection. Also, even if a trait is influenced by the environment, it is possible to control for this influence. For example, when the populations under study lived in a single environmental zone, it is reasonable to assume that environmental effects were distributed randomly, in which case selection would be expected to play a negligible role, and developmental plasticity would simply blur, rather than skew, variation related to population history (Larsen 1997: 304). And when environmental variation is structured, it is possible to control for this variation using a variety of statistical procedures, as Manica and others (2007) did in their study of craniometric evidence for an African origin of modern humans.

Finally, reanalyses of Boas's data illustrate that the same data can be analyzed to investigate all three sources of phenotypic variation. Sparks and Jantz (2002) showed that developmental effects are relatively small compared to the effects of inheritance for these data; Relethford (2004a) also showed that developmental effects do not obscure genetic relationships among the sampled populations; and Konigsberg and Ousley (1995) demonstrated that phenotypic variation is proportional to genetic variation, as estimated by kinship coefficients in the Boas data. In fact, I am not aware of any studies of craniometric variation in which selection and plasticity (other than the obvious case of intentional cranial deformation) obscure the effects of population history. Thus, so long as one works with adequate samples of individuals who lived in similar environments and had similar diets, it is reasonable to view craniometric variation as proportional to the underlying genetic variation among groups.

Quantitative Genetic Methods for Metric Traits

The use of metric traits to study population affinities has a long lineage in physical anthropology (see Larson 1997 and Pietrusewsky 2000 for reviews), but analytical methods for such studies have advanced considerably since Relethford and Lees's (1982) essay through the development of quantitative genetics models that use anthropometric and osteometric data as input. The most important such model is that of Relethford and others (Relethford 2003; Relethford and Blangero 1990; Relethford et al. 1997; Relethford and Harpending 1994), which enables one to derive the genetic relationship (R) matrix for a group of populations directly from metric trait data. The R matrix is a standardized variance-covariance matrix, which also turns out to be a matrix of average kinship coefficients, or deviations from panmixis, among a group of populations (Konigsberg 2006:279). R matrices therefore have a number of useful properties (see Relethford and Harpending 1994:252–255).

One advantage of R matrix analysis is that it allows one to estimate three distinct population genetic parameters that are useful for investigating regional population structure. First, the average diagonal element of the R matrix, weighted according to the census size of each population, represents the average genetic distance of populations from the regional centroid, or the average within-population kinship coefficient, and is also an estimate of Wright's F_{ST}, a measure of regional genetic differentiation. Second, genetic distances between populations are easily calculated from the elements of the R matrix, and these distances can be projected onto two dimensions using principal coordinates analysis to summarize regional patterns of genetic relationships. Third, one can compare the observed phenotypic variance of a population to an expected variance under a model of equal mate exchange with extraregional sources — based on the genetic distance of that population to the regional centroid, the pooled mean within-group phenotypic variance across subpopulations, and Wright's F_{ST} — to identify greater- or less-than average gene flow into that population (Relethford and Blangero 1990). This last type of analysis has come to be known as Relethford-Blangero analysis.

R matrix analysis has many benefits, but also more extensive data requirements than model-free methods. Specifically, one needs to estimate relative population sizes for the sampled groups and the mean narrow-sense heritability (h^2) of the traits in the analysis to translate phenotypic variation into estimates of underlying genetic variation. Relative population sizes are important because genetic drift tends to influence phenotypes more rapidly in small populations. As a result, the relative sizes of the populations being compared must be factored into the analysis if one is to distinguish the effects of drift from the effects of gene flow or common ancestry. Narrow-sense heritability is defined as the ratio of additive genetic variance to phenotypic variance for a given trait and population. Essentially, this is the proportion of phenotypic variation in a population that can be accounted for by the underlying genetic variation for that trait in that population. Estimates of craniometric heritabilities (Carson 2006; Cheverud 1988; Devor 1987; Konigsberg and Ousley 1995; Relethford 1994; Relethford and Lees 1982) range from near zero to more than .7, with a mean of approximately .55. Although craniometric heritabilities vary widely across traits and populations, precise estimates are not essential for R matrix analysis because patterns of relative phenotypic variance are stable over a range of heritability values (Relethford and Blangero 1990:16–18).

In addition, it is important to not overinterpret the significance of heritability values. Heritability is, in fact, a momentary property of a population that varies significantly across traits and environments (Vitzthum 2003), and traits with high heritability are not necessarily under stronger genetic control or necessarily more useful. For example, traits such as eye number would have very low heritability values if one were to calculate them because the genes governing eye number are under strong selection. As a result, nearly all phenotypic variation in eye number is due to injury during development, and the ratio of genetic variance to phenotypic variance for eye number would therefore be very low. In contrast, a trait like cranial breadth can have a high heritability value if expression of the genes governing cranial breadth is constrained by cradleboarding practices (environmental effects). As a result, variation in cranial breadth will underrepresent the underlying genetic variation, leading to a high heritability estimate that has more to do with culture than with genes. These extreme cases illustrate that the heritability of craniometric traits does not necessarily determine their usefulness for biodistance analysis. Rather, what matters is that the traits are transmissible to some extent, and that environmental factors are either randomly distributed or controllable. The extensive literature on craniometric variation suggests that these conditions can be satisfied in most cases.

Quantitative genetic methods based on the R matrix are widely used in biodistance studies (Relethford 2003; Relethford and Blangero 1990; Relethford and Harpending 1994; Sparks and Jantz 2002), and their use has been facilitated by a computer program written by Relethford (RMET 5.0) and available online (http://konig.la.utk.edu/relethsoft.html) that performs the analysis. I also use R matrix methods in this examination of Tewa ancestry.

Biodistance Analysis of Tewa Ancestry

To evaluate biological expectations of the competing hypotheses on Tewa origins, I used a data set of standard cranial measurements collected in previous studies of human skeletal remains from sites across the northern U.S. Southwest dating between AD 1000 and 1600, including the Rio Grande drainage, the San Juan drainage, and the upper reaches of the Little Colorado River drainage. The data derive from archives, published literature, and personal files graciously shared by fellow researchers (see acknowledgments). In accordance with U.S. law and the wishes of affiliated tribes, many remains from which these data were collected are no longer available for study. The data set includes 16 measurements of the face, frontal region, palate, and mandible because these were both widely available and are not affected significantly by cradleboarding (Droessler 1981:110–116; Kohn et al. 1995).[6] I include all individuals for which at least 4 of the 12 measurements actually included in the analysis are available (see below).

I grouped these samples into two chronological periods, with a break point corresponding to the date of final abandonment of the San Juan drainage and the beginning date of the Late Coalition period, and also by archaeological district following the definitions in Adler (1996) for the pre-AD 1275 period, and Adams and Duff (2004) for the post-AD 1275 period. The result is a data set of 858 individuals grouped into 22 district-level populations dating to one of the two time periods (Table 5.1). The number of individuals in each population varies between 6 and 89, with a median of 32. Figure 5.1 illustrates the general location of each population, along with the Tewa Basin and Village Ecodynamics Project (VEP) study areas that were the focus of attention in the previous chapter.[7]

A basic assumption I make in defining populations from archaeologically defined districts is that individuals in each district can be used to model phenotypic variation in a corresponding panmictic biological population. Strictly speaking, skeletal samples are samples of lineages rather than populations because: (1) many of the individuals in such samples were not simultaneously alive

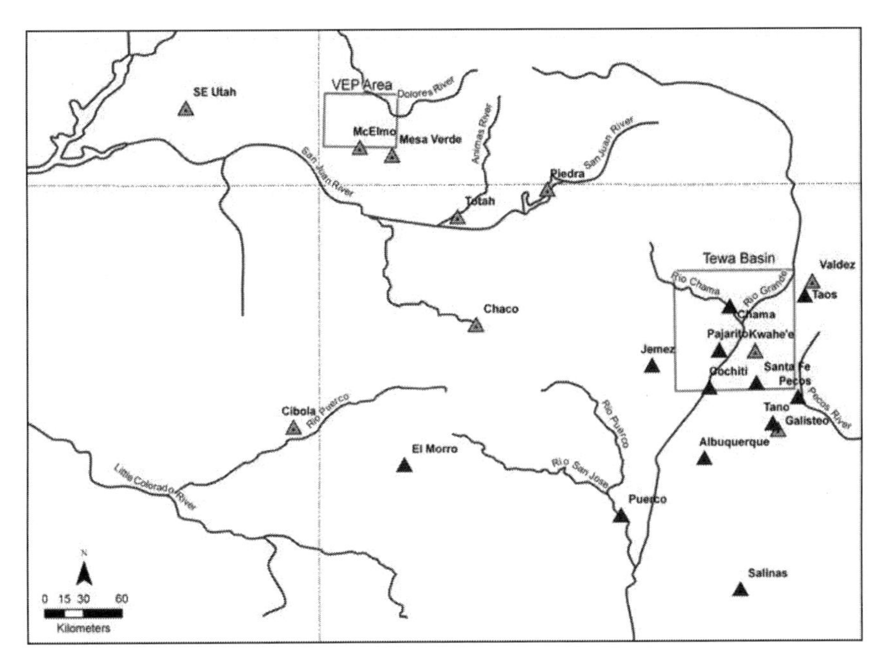

FIGURE 5.1. Distribution of samples in the craniometric data set. Triangles mark the geographic centroid of sites contributing samples to each population. Pre-AD 1275 populations are marked with a light gray triangle, and post-AD 1275 populations with a dark gray triangle. Open gray rectangles demarcate the Village Ecodynamics Project and Tewa Basin study areas.

and thus could not have interbred (Cadien et al. 1974); and (2) the distribution of mating probabilities for each individual within a district was not equivalent with respect to individuals from adjacent districts. Given these realities, it is important to not lose sight of the goal of the analysis, which is to infer population parameters from samples. Given that craniometric traits are at least moderately heritable, and that drift over time is normally distributed (Lande 1977), it is reasonable to suggest that the pattern of genetic variance within a district can be estimated for the temporal midpoint of a lineage using a random sample of individuals from several generations on either side of this midpoint. Thus, the distinction between lineages and populations does not pose a significant problem for this analysis.

Data Preparation

Before conducting an R matrix analysis of craniometric data, one must first control for interobserver variation, missing data, and sexual dimorphism; estimate relative population sizes for the sampled groups; and estimate the mean narrow-sense heritability of the traits in the analysis.

Interobserver Variation. A factor one must consider when working with data collected by many analysts over many decades is interobserver variation, which comes in two forms. The first is systematic variation due to observers using different skeletal landmarks when taking measurements.[8] Such variation is easy to identify when the landmarks used for each measurement are reported, but it is also possible to identify unreported cases by comparing distributions of measurements collected by specific analysts for specific samples to global

TABLE 5.1. Populations and data sources

Population	Dates (AD)	Affiliation	*n* (M/F)	Analysts[a]	Sites (*n*)	Sources[b]
Southeastern Utah	1080–1260	Mesa Verde region	33 (21/12)	AB, AH, BL, ER	42SA7005 (1), 42SA738 (3), Butler Wash (1), Graham Canyon (1), Grand Gulch (15), Alkali Ridge (12)	2, 8, 22, 23, 30
McElmo/ Monument	1020–1275	Mesa Verde region	58 (24/34)	AH, BL, CB, DM, KEB, LS, MD, MS, PL, SU	Mitchell Springs (3), Southern Ute Piedmont (25), Ackmen/Lowry (13), Castle Rock (3), Dominguez (1), Montezuma Canyon (5), Sand Canyon (3), Wallace (5)	1, 2, 5, 9, 10, 11, 12, 13, 15, 16, 30
Mesa Verde (landform)	1020–1275	Mesa Verde region	56 (33/23)	BL, DM, ER, KAB, MS	5MV1676 (5), 5MV1241 (1), 5MV1253 (1), 5MV80 (1), 5MV866 (1), Big Juniper House (3), "Cliff Dweller" (11), Coyote Village (2), Lister Site 1 (1), Lister Site 2 (1), Long House (8), Mancos Canyon (1), Mug House (7), Site 34 (7), Two Raven House (6)	1, 6, 17, 30
Totah	1020–1275	Totah	57 (18/39)	ER, JHS, MG, MS	Aztec (24), La Plata Highway (9), Lone Kiva (2), Mine Canyon (7), Salmon (7), Tommy site (8)	1, 20, 31
Piedra District	850–1050	Upper San Juan	13 (7/6)	ER, KAB	Navajo Reservoir (13)	35, 36
Chaco Canyon	920–1120	S. San Juan	65 (26/39)	BL, ER, MS, NA	Small sites (33), Kin Kletso (1), P. Bonito (30), P. del Arroyo (1)	1, 18, 24, 25
Cibola	1000–1275	S. San Juan	33 (12/21)	AH, MS, TDS	Kintiel (10), Manuelito (5), Vill. of the GK (8), White-water (10)	1, 2, 28
Taos Valley (Valdez)	1100–1200	N. Rio Grande	8 (1/7)	ER, MS	Johnson Pit House (2), LA3643 (1), TA 47 (3), Taos (2)	1, 21
Tewa Basin (Kwahe'e)	1000–1200	N. Rio Grande	10 (5/5)	ER, MS, NA	Kearney and Sunset (1), Kwahe'e site (2), LA742 (1), LA103919E (1), LA103919W (2), LA391 (3)	1, 18, 32
Galisteo Basin	1100–1250	N. Rio Grande	6 (3/3)	MS	LA 3333 (6)	1

Taos	1300–1550	Tiwa	17 (4/13)	MS	Picuris (7), Pot Creek (10)	1
Chama	1350–1600	Tewa	30 (16/14)	AH, ER, MS	Poshuouinge (2), Sapawe (17), Te'ewi (9), Yunque (2)	1, 2, 26
Jemez	1325–1550	Towa	42 (15/27)	AH, MS	Amoxiumqua (7), Giusiwa (7), Kwasteyukwa (28)	1, 2
North Pajarito	1325–1550	Tewa	81 (36/45)	AH, MN, MS	Burnt Mesa (1), Otowi (11), Puye (58), Tsankawi (3), Tsirege (8)	1, 2, 33
Santa Fe	1250–1400	Tanoan	27 (12/15)	AP, ER, EO, MS	Agua Fria (1), Arroyo Hondo (13), Pindi (13)	1, 7
Pecos (B/W-Gl. A)	1275–1400	Tanoan	89 (48/41)	EH	Bandelier Bend (1), Loma Lothrop (1), Pecos (87)	3
Galisteo (Tano)	1275–1550	S. Tewa	55 (30/25)	ER, MS	LA183 (9), LA25 (5), San Cristobal (41)	1, 27
Cochiti	1275–1600	Keres	29 (14/15)	MOS	LA6455 (10), LA70 (17), LA9154 (2)	4
Albuquerque	1300–1550	Tanoan	28 (22/6)	DW, SR	Pa-ako (prehispanic period only, 23), Tijeras (5)	24, 34
Rio Puerco (East)	1300–1500	Tiwa?	27 (14/13)	MS	Pottery Mound (27)	1
El Morro	1275–1375	Keres/Zuni?	29 (12/17)	CT, LS, MS	Atsinna (1), Heshatauthla (22), P. de los Muertos (6)	1, 14
Salinas	1400–1680	Tompiro	65 (33/32)	ER	Gran Quivira (57), Pueblo Pardo (8)	29

[a] AB = Alice Brues; AH = Ales Hrdliçka; AP = Anne Palkovich; BL = Brian Lesley; CT = Christy Turner; CB = Cindy Bradley; DM = Debra Martin; DW = David Weaver; EH = Ernest Hooton; ER = Erik Reed; EO = Eric Ozolins; JHS = Jeff Shipman; KAB = Kevin Bennett; KEB = Kay Barnett; LS = Linda Smith; MD = Michael Dice; MG = Michelle Greene; MN = Marco Niskkanen; MOS = Maria Smith; MS = Michael Schillaci; NA = Nancy Akins; PL = Patricia Lambert; SR = Spencer Rogers; SU = Sally Underwood; TDS = T. D. Stewart.

[b] 1 = Schillaci, p.c.; 2 = Hrdliçka 1931; 3 = Beck, p.c.; 4 = M. Smith, p.c.; 5 = Martin, p.c. a; 6 = Martin, p.c. b; 7 = Palkovich 1980; 8 = Brues 1946; 9 = Karhu 2000; 10 = Bradley, p.c.; 11 = Underwood, p.c.; 12 = Lambert, p.c.; 13 = L. Smith, p.c. a; 14 = L. Smith, p.c. b; 15 = Barnett 2000; 16 = Dice 1993; 17 = Bennett 1975; 18 = Akins, p.c.; 19 = Reed 1956; 20 = Reed 1957; 21 = Reed 1963b; 22 = Turner 1961; 23 = Reed 1963a; 24 = Reed 1962; 25 = Reed 1964b; 26 = Reed 1953; 27 = Rogers 1954; 28 = Stewart 1940; 29 = Reed 1981; 30 = Pestle, p.c.; 31 = Greene, p.c.; 32 = Reed 1964a; 33 = Niskanen 1990; 34 = Weaver 1976; 35 = Bennett 1966; 36 = Reed 1966.

distributions for that measurement, and to summary statistics for the same samples reported by previous analysts. Whenever possible, I used two different methods to correct or rescale such sets of divergent measurements;[9] however, when there was no basis for rescaling or adjusting a set of divergent measurements, I treated them as missing data.

The second form of interobserver variation is equivalent to intraobserver error; that is, random errors in taking individual measurements. If a single observer were to measure a given specimen many times, the resulting data would contain a distribution of values with a mean and standard deviation. This means that there are standard errors associated with every measurement in a data set, regardless of the number of observers who collected the data. Given that error is always present, the key question is whether such errors affect multivariate centroids and variances enough to influence the results. Comparisons of measurements collected by different analysts for the same specimens suggest that this is unlikely. For example, measurements collected from the same specimens by analysts responsible for about 60 percent of the data set used here are highly correlated ($r^2 > .99$), with standard errors ranging from 1.08 mm for paired measurements by Schillaci and Reed, to 1.28 mm for paired measurements by Schillaci and Hrdlička. The average standard deviation of the 16 measurements tabulated for this study is 3.26 mm; thus, random errors on this order are unlikely to affect subpopulation summary data enough to obscure multivariate patterns (see Ortman 2009:172).

Missing Data. The multivariate methods used in biodistance analysis require data sets that contain no missing values. This is a significant problem for all osteological data sets derived from archaeological samples due to partial preservation of specimens, and it is even more significant for multiple-observer data sets because, in addition to missing data due to preservation, not all measurements are available for all samples. There are two solutions to such problems. One is to exclude cases and variables to produce a data set in which no data are missing. This is not a good solution because the potential for sampling error to influence results rises as the number of cases and variables decline. A more productive solution is to estimate the missing data. This enables one to use all the cases and a larger number of variables, and to fill in the missing data with estimates that reinforce patterns in the available data.

The simplest way of estimating missing data is to replace missing values by the mean of existing values for each variable. This is not ideal because it tends to homogenize the data set and make groups with more missing data appear more similar than they are likely to actually be. A better alternative is to use the intercorrelated nature of the variables to estimate the missing values individually (Pietrusewsky 2000:385–386). For this study I used an iterative, multivariate, maximum-likelihood method known as *EM estimation*, as implemented in Systat version 11, to estimate missing values (see Allison 2001). The EM algorithm first calculates a covariance matrix from the actual data, and uses this matrix to es-

TABLE 5.2. Cranial measurements, raw data

MEASUREMENT	ABBREVIATION	LANDMARKS	*n*	MIN.	MAX.	MEAN	STD	LILLIEFORS P[b]
Mandibular symphysis height	MandHt	gn-id	633	22	44	33.47	3.17	< .01
Zygomatic breadth	ZYB	zy-zy	557	100	153	132.96	6.93	< .01
Nasion-prosthion height[a]	NPH	n-pr	346	52	85	67.43	4.59	< .05
Nasion-alveolon height	Na-Alv	n-ids	670	52	96	70.17	4.79	< .01
Mean orbital height	MOBH	⊥ dk-ek	823	26	40	34.45	1.81	< .01
Mean orbital breadth	MOBB	dk-ek	819	27	44	38.27	2.19	< .01
Interorbital breadth	DKB	dk-dk	459	13	31	22.24	2.31	< .20
Biorbital breadth[a]	EKB	ek-ek	348	86	106	96.26	3.82	> .20
Nasal height	NLH	n-ns	816	33	62	49.16	3.11	< .01
Nasal breadth	NLB	al-al	817	17	31	24.94	1.85	< .01
Maxillo-alveolar length	MAL	pr-alv	599	37	66	51.40	3.90	< .01
Maxillo-alveolar breadth	MAB	ekm-ekm	569	51	75	63.08	3.64	< .01
Internal palate length[a]	IntPall	ol-sta	308	31	53	43.72	3.01	< .10
Internal palate breadth[a]	IntPalb	enm-enm	310	30	44	36.74	2.59	> .20
Minimum frontal breadth	WFB	ft-ft	582	81	112	93.30	4.78	< .01
Upper facial breadth	UFB	fmt-fmt	418	92	117	104.13	4.35	> .20

Note: 113 cases have no missing values in this data set.

[a] Measurement used in EM estimation but not in R matrix analysis.

[b] Significance test for normality of the distribution.

timate missing values. It then calculates a new covariance matrix from the data set that includes the estimated data, and compares it to the previous covariance matrix. This process continues iteratively until the two covariance matrices converge at a specified level of error.

Table 5.2 presents summary statistics for the raw data, and Table 5.3 presents the same information after EM estimation. Table 5.4 also summarizes the pattern of missing data in the raw craniometric data set. Two aspects of these data deserve comment. First, note that 4 of the 16 tabulated measurements (nasion-prosthion height, biorbital breadth, internal palate length, and internal

TABLE 5.3. Craniometric data after EM estimation

Measurement	Abbreviation	Landmarks	*n*	Min.	Max.	Mean	STD	Lilliefors P[b]
Mandibular symphysis height	MandHt	gn-id	858	22	44	33.44	2.88	< .01
Zygomatic breadth	ZYB	zy-zy	858	100	153	132.77	6.26	< .01
Nasion-prosthion height[a]	NPH	n-pr	858	52	91	67.66	4.49	< .01
Nasion-alveolon height	Na-Alv	n-ids	858	52	96	70.10	4.69	< .01
Mean orbital height	MOBH	dk-ek	858	26	40	34.46	1.78	< .01
Mean orbital breadth	MOBB	dk-ek	858	27	44	38.27	2.16	< .01
Interorbital breadth	DKB	dk-dk	858	13	31	22.32	1.87	< .01
Biorbital breadth[a]	EKB	ek-ek	858	81	107	96.09	3.62	> .20
Nasal height	NLH	n-ns	858	33	62	49.16	3.06	< .01
Nasal breadth	NLB	al-al	858	17	31	24.94	1.82	< .01
Maxillo-alveolar length	MAL	pr-alv	858	37	66	51.37	3.49	< .01
Maxillo-alveolar breadth	MAB	ekm-ekm	858	51	75	63.02	3.20	< .01
Internal palate length[a]	IntPall	ol-sta	858	31	55	44.55	2.78	< .10
Internal palate breadth[a]	IntPalb	enm-enm	858	30	44	36.78	2.03	< .05
Minimum frontal breadth	WFB	ft-ft	858	80	112	92.97	4.43	< .01
Upper facial breadth	UFB	fmt-fmt	858	89	117	103.89	4.15	> .20

Note: 858 cases have no missing values in this data set.

[a] Measurement used in EM estimation but not in R matrix analysis.

[b] Significance test for normality of the distribution.

palate breadth) are used in EM estimation but not in the biodistance analyses. These measurements are included in missing value estimation because each is strongly correlated with a more commonly taken measurement (nasion-alveolon height, upper facial breadth, maxillo-alveolar length, and maxillo-alveolar breadth, respectively), and the distributions of these two sets are somewhat complementary; that is, individuals missing data for the second set of measurements often had data for the first set (see Table 5.4). I therefore use the first set to aid in estimating missing data for the second set, but exclude the first set from the actual analysis due to the high percentages of missing values for these measurements overall.

Second, it is clear that EM estimation is both appropriate and essential for these data. Only 113 of the 858 cases have no missing data for the 16 variables

TABLE 5.4. Percent of individuals with each measurement in each population

POPULATION	N	MANDHT	ZYB	NPH	NA-ALV	MOBH	MOBB	DKB	EKB	NLH	NLB	MAL	MAB	INTPALL	INTPALB	WFB	UFB
SE Utah	33	63.6	81.8	33.3	57.6	97.0	100.0	42.4	42.4	100.0	97.0	39.4	69.7	0.0	0.0	57.6	12.1
McElmo	58	58.6	46.6	34.5	36.2	94.8	89.7	48.3	65.5	81.0	89.7	63.8	58.6	5.2	5.2	72.4	72.4
Mesa Verde	56	64.3	60.7	41.1	58.9	85.7	85.7	67.9	69.6	83.9	85.7	57.1	53.6	3.6	3.6	80.4	58.9
Totah	57	80.7	56.1	86.0	57.9	93.0	93.0	91.2	80.7	91.2	89.5	84.2	77.2	52.6	52.6	91.2	82.5
Piedra	13	84.6	92.3	53.8	46.2	100.0	100.0	0.0	53.8	92.3	84.6	53.8	53.8	0.0	0.0	92.3	0.0
Chaco	65	69.2	61.5	20.0	96.9	96.9	98.5	47.7	23.1	96.9	98.5	72.3	64.6	41.5	41.5	32.3	46.2
Cibola	33	42.4	69.7	0.0	87.9	100.0	100.0	24.2	0.0	100.0	100.0	57.6	54.5	24.2	21.2	30.3	21.2
Valdez	8	100.0	75.0	75.0	87.5	100.0	100.0	75.0	50.0	100.0	100.0	87.5	87.5	62.5	62.5	100.0	62.5
Kwahe'e	10	90.0	80.0	50.0	30.0	90.0	90.0	70.0	60.0	70.0	90.0	70.0	70.0	10.0	10.0	90.0	70.0
Galisteo	6	100.0	100.0	83.3	100.0	100.0	100.0	100.0	66.7	100.0	100.0	83.3	66.7	83.3	83.3	100.0	100.0
Taos	17	82.4	52.9	94.1	94.1	100.0	100.0	100.0	100.0	100.0	94.1	88.2	94.1	88.2	94.1	100.0	100.0
Chama	30	66.7	36.7	0.0	93.3	96.7	96.7	83.3	0.0	96.7	100.0	30.0	26.7	76.7	76.7	30.0	76.7
Jemez	42	83.3	81.0	23.8	95.2	92.9	92.9	23.8	23.8	97.6	95.2	81.0	69.0	23.8	23.8	23.8	23.8
Pajarito	81	77.8	75.3	71.6	97.5	100.0	100.0	88.9	70.4	97.5	97.5	91.4	91.4	86.4	88.9	70.4	87.7
Santa Fe	27	66.7	33.3	25.9	96.3	100.0	77.8	88.9	25.9	100.0	96.3	48.1	44.4	77.8	77.8	44.4	70.4
Pecos	89	79.8	70.8	0.0	91.0	97.8	97.8	0.0	0.0	98.9	98.9	79.8	73.0	0.0	0.0	76.4	0.0
Tano	55	74.5	85.5	74.5	100.0	98.2	98.2	89.1	74.5	100.0	98.2	92.7	76.4	74.5	74.5	96.4	74.5
Cochiti	29	65.5	31.0	89.7	0.0	82.8	86.2	89.7	58.6	86.2	93.1	72.4	65.5	0.0	0.0	41.4	34.5
Albuquerque	28	78.6	82.1	82.1	17.9	100.0	100.0	0.0	0.0	96.4	96.4	82.1	78.6	0.0	0.0	100.0	0.0
Puerco	27	81.5	48.1	96.3	100.0	85.2	92.6	88.9	74.1	96.3	92.6	85.2	85.2	92.6	92.6	88.9	88.9
El Morro	29	72.4	10.3	0.0	96.6	100.0	100.0	75.9	20.7	100.0	96.6	20.7	20.7	75.9	75.9	20.7	75.9
Salinas	65	87.7	92.3	0.0	100.0	100.0	100.0	0.0	0.0	100.0	96.9	56.9	56.9	0.0	0.0	95.4	0.0
Total	858	633	557	346	670	823	819	459	348	816	817	599	569	308	310	582	418

Note: Measurements for NPH, EKB, IntPall, and IntPalb were included in EM estimation but not in R matrix analysis.

tabulated, and only 418 cases have no missing data for the 12 measurements used in the biodistance analysis. At the same time, most measurements are available for most samples, and the pattern of missing data is essentially random. Also note that EM estimation has little effect on the summary statistics for the tabulated variables, but increases the sample size for all variables to the total number of cases. EM estimation thus appears to be the best solution for maximizing the utility of the available data.

Sexual Dimorphism. There are three options for controlling sexual dimorphism. One is to analyze the data for each sex separately. This introduces the same problem that arises when one excludes cases or variables with missing data: it reduces the sample size of each population by about 50 percent, and thus increases the potential for sampling error to affect the results. The other two options involve standardizing the data. In Q-mode standardization, each measurement for an individual is divided by the geometric mean of measurements for that individual (Schillaci et al. 2001:138). This may be a good option when one is unsure of the sex of specimens; however, the distribution of means for measurements in the data set (Table 5.3) is not normal, and thus it is not clear that the mean of measurements for an individual is a reasonable characterization of that individual's "size." In R-mode standardization, measurements for individuals of each sex are converted to Z-scores before pooling the data for analysis. This second method is more intuitive because the mean of a measurement across males or females in a population does reflect the central tendency of those measurements. The underlying questions with regard to Q-mode vs. sex-specific R-mode standardization are whether sexual dimorphism is more of a size or a shape phenomenon for the measurements used (it is obviously both to some extent), and which method accounts for sexual dimorphism in such a way that the resulting data better reflect overall patterns of genetic variation. I use sex-specific R-mode standardization in this study because it is easier to visualize how this approach affects the data, and this method has been used most often in previous studies (e.g., Relethford and Harpending 1994; Schillaci and Stojanowski 2005; Steadman 1998, 2001).

Effective Population Sizes. R-matrix methods require estimates of the effective population size, or the number of potentially interbreeding individuals, in each district-level population. These estimates are used to weight the data in various calculations to control for the effects of drift, which correlate with population size. Weighting is relative, so these estimates only need to reflect proportionate differences in population size rather than actual numbers of people. To calculate such estimates, I used the data in two recently published, pan-southwestern syntheses of large settlements for districts where a significant portion of the total population lived in such settlements (Adler 1996; Adams and Duff 2004), and consulted previous settlement pattern studies of small sites for areas where the majority of the population resided in small settlements (Dickson 1979; Eddy 1972; Matson et al. 1988; Windes 1987). I use these sources and very simple assumptions to calculate momentary population estimates for each district-level population in the data set. These estimates, and descriptions of the methods used to produce them, are presented in Table 5.5. Note that the spatial extents of several district-level populations correspond somewhat with the Tewa Basin population strata defined in Chapter 4. The simpler methods applied here produce estimates that differ from those produced in Chapter 4, but these estimates are sufficiently close to be adequate for weighting purposes.

Heritability. The final step in preparing the data for analysis is to estimate the mean, narrow-sense heritability of the traits in the analysis. As mentioned earlier, heritability estimates for craniometric traits vary widely across populations and from trait to trait, but relative patterns of phenotypic variance appear relatively stable over a range of values (Relethford and Blangero 1990:16–18). Because precision is not critically important, I estimate $h^2 \approx .55$, which corresponds to the mean heritability value across all traits and populations in previous studies of craniometric heritability (Carson 2006; Devor 1987; Konigsberg and Ousley 1995; Relethford 1994; Relethford et al. 1997).

R-Matrix Analyses

In this section I present four analyses of the prepared craniometric data set, all of which derive from the unbiased R matrix for these data.[10] I also evaluate the extent to which sample size and EM estimation have influenced these results.

Genetic Distances. Table 5.6 presents the matrix of minimum genetic distances between each pairing of the 22 district-level populations in the prepared craniometric data set. These distances are analogous to Mahalanobis distances and should be thought of as estimates of the minimum standardized genetic distances between each pair of populations. The distances below and to the left of the dividing lines represent distances between populations dating to different time periods, and distances above and to the right of the lines represent distances between populations dating to the same period.

These data show that, on a pair-wise basis, affinities among the sampled populations are complex. The overlapping patterns of affinities among populations from different portions of the Pueblo region confirms that by the late prehispanic period, Pueblo populations were relatively similar throughout the Southwest due to a long prior history of population movement and gene flow. One pattern that does emerge from inspection of the data is that most post-AD 1275 populations of the Northern Rio Grande region — including those from the Santa Fe, Pajarito, Chama, Cochiti, Tano, Pecos, and Salinas districts — appear more closely

TABLE 5.5. Census estimates for populations

POPULATION	DATES (AD)	CENSUS	METHOD
Southeastern Utah	1080–1260	4,500	Cedar Mesa District (Matson et al. 1988: Fig. 8) + Cottonwood District and Montezuma District west of Montezuma Creek (total PIII kivas [Adler and Johnson 1996] × 5 persons per kiva, 50 percent of population in large sites) + Red Rock Plateau (500 = minimal population estimate)
McElmo/Monument	1020–1275	14,200	Total PIII kivas from McElmo/Yellow Jacket, Ute Mountain, and Montezuma Creek (E. of Montezuma Creek) districts ([Adler and Johnson 1996] x 5 persons per kiva × 2 (50 percent of population in sites > 50 rooms)
Mesa Verde (landform)	1020–1275	3,600	Total PIII rooms from district (Adler and Johnson 1996), 1 person per room, 50 percent of population in sites > 50 rooms
Totah	1020–1275	7,400	Total PIII rooms in district (Adler and Johnson 1996), 1 person per room, 50 percent of population in sites > 50 rooms
Piedra District	850–1050	1,400	Eddy (1972: Table 9) estimate for the Piedra Phase population, based on Brown's revision of Naroll's formula (total m^2 floor area in structures / 6)
Chaco Canyon	920–1120	1,500	Windes's (1987) estimate of momentary Bonito phase population
Cibola	1000–1275	9,500	Total rooms abandoned AD 1275–1300 in Zuni, Defiance, Rio Puerco West, and Manuelito districts (Adler and Johnson 1996), 1 person per room, 50 percent occupancy, 50 percent of population in sites > 50 rooms
Taos Valley (Valdez)	1000–1200	500	Minimal population estimate (Wobst 1977a)
Tewa Basin (Kwahe'e)	1000–1200	2,000	Communities of approximately 400 people each in the Santa Cruz, Tesuque, Pojoaque, Santa Fe, and Arroyo Hondo drainages
Galisteo	1100–1250	500	Minimal population estimate (Wobst 1977)
Taos	1300–1550	1,700	Total PIV rooms in cluster (Adams and Duff 2004), 1 person per room, 50 percent occupancy
Chama	1350–1600	8,800	Total PIV rooms in cluster (Adams and Duff 2004), 1 person per room, 50 percent occupancy
Jemez	1325–1550	8,000	Total PIV rooms in cluster (Adams and Duff 2004), 1 person per room, 50 percent occupancy.
Pajarito Plateau (N. of Frijoles Cyn.)	1325–1550	2,000	Total PIV rooms in Pajarito cluster north of Frijoles Canyon (Adams and Duff 2004), plus 400 rooms each for San Ildefonso and Santa Clara pueblos, 1 person per room, 50 percent occupancy
Santa Fe	1250–1400	1,700	Total PIV rooms in cluster (Adams and Duff 2004), 1 person per room, 50 percent occupancy

TABLE 5.5. (cont'd.) Census estimates for populations

Population	Dates (AD)	Census	Method
Pecos (B/W-Glaze A only)	1275–1400	600	Total rooms in cluster abandoned by AD 1400 (Adams and Duff 2004), 1 person per room
Galisteo (Tano)	1275–1550	4,800	Total Classic period rooms in cluster (Adams and Duff 2004), 1 person per room, 50 percent occupancy
Cochiti	1275–1600	2,000	Total rooms in cluster (Adams and Duff 2004), 1 person per room, 50 percent occupancy
Albuquerque	1300–1550	4,700	Total rooms in cluster (Adams and Duff 2004), 1 person per room, 50 percent occupancy
Lower Rio Puerco (East)	1300–1500	500	Minimal population estimate (Wobst 1977)
El Morro	1275–1375	6,700	Total PIV rooms in eastern Zuni region cluster (Adams and Duff 2004; Huntley and Kintigh 2004), 1 person per room, 50 percent occupancy
Salinas	1400–1680	3,300	Total PIV rooms in Salinas District (Adams and Duff 2004), 1 person per room, 50 percent occupancy

related to earlier populations of the Four Corners region than they are to earlier populations of the Northern Rio Grande, including the Valdez, Kwahe'e, and Galisteo populations.

To summarize overall patterns of similarity and dissimilarity among the sampled populations, Figure 5.2 plots each population according to a principal coordinates analysis of the genetic distance matrix, with the two axes scaled in accordance with their eigenvalues.[11] Many details of Figure 5.3 are interesting, but I focus here on three clusters of samples that appear to represent biological lineages. First, there is a clearly defined cluster of populations in the central area of the chart which includes post-AD 1275 samples from the Pecos, Chama, Pajarito, Tano, and Salinas districts, as well as pre-1275 samples from the Mesa Verde, McElmo, and Southeast Utah districts. In addition, populations from other portions of the Four Corners region (including Chaco, Cibola, El Morro, and Totah) and from the Rio Grande region (including Albuquerque, Cochiti, Jemez, Puerco, Santa Fe, and Taos) are all excluded from this cluster. The internal cohesion and external isolation of samples in this cluster suggest that these samples represent a biological lineage that originated in the Mesa Verde region and includes ancestral Tewa populations among its descendants.

Figure 5.2 also suggests that the Chaco, Cibola, El Morro, and Cochiti samples form a second, more loosely defined lineage. The El Morro District lies between present-day Zuni and Acoma pueblos, and was home to a large population between AD 1275 and the early decades of the AD 1300s (Schachner 2007). Inhabitants of post-1275 Cochiti district sites were probable ancestors of present-day Cochiti people (Preucel 2005). Because both Acoma and Cochiti are

TABLE 5.6. Minimum genetic distance matrix

Population	SE Utah	McElmo	Mesa Verde	Totah	Piedra	Chaco	Cibola	Valdez	Kwahe'e	Galisteo	Taos	Chama	Jemez	Pajarito	Santa Fe	Pecos	Tano	Cochiti	Albuquerque	Puerco	El Morro
McElmo	.024																				
Mesa Verde	.037	.012																			
Totah	.152	.067	.137																		
Piedra	.124	.117	.153	.251																	
Chaco	.066	.083	.041	.211	.305																
Cibola	.036	.047	.032	.168	.207	.021															
Valdez	.145	.167	.180	.290	.354	.148	.174														
Kwahe'e	.204	.224	.211	.327	.256	.255	.315	.581													
Galisteo	.570	.551	.638	.468	.693	.854	.733	.763	.965												
Taos	.108	.042	.094	.052	.169	.174	.146	.106	.326	.410											
Chama	.044	.063	.090	.165	.088	.119	.032	.211	.361	.670	.120										
Jemez	.019	.043	.018	.176	.099	.072	.032	.251	.187	.718	.144	.046									
Pajarito	.027	.026	.031	.092	.129	.058	.026	.225	.216	.591	.077	.021	.021								
Santa Fe	.061	.029	.099	.042	.161	.158	.095	.172	.310	.350	.000	.064	.124	.044							
Pecos	.055	.118	.147	.224	.071	.221	.133	.197	.323	.544	.115	.072	.075	.101	.099						
Tano	.055	.029	.032	.111	.114	.109	.059	.185	.235	.561	.025	.066	.042	.032	.040	.085					
Cochiti	.185	.242	.219	.505	.229	.229	.173	.426	.499	.927	.357	.125	.178	.172	.289	.253	.230				
Albuquerque	.122	.049	.105	.088	.181	.234	.173	.383	.343	.554	.109	.125	.104	.085	.093	.204	.106	.308			
Puerco	.230	.153	.241	.097	.335	.316	.226	.236	.602	.317	.033	.167	.285	.172	.030	.223	.156	.504	.185		
El Morro	.081	.066	.044	.207	.295	.025	.015	.112	.414	.828	.134	.096	.073	.070	.138	.192	.085	.185	.164	.253	
Salinas	.047	.097	.083	.216	.124	.095	.080	.142	.283	.636	.147	.092	.062	.071	.136	.067	.119	.210	.237	.294	.115

Notes: Data are standardized minimum genetic distances derived from the unbiased R matrix of the craniometric data set. Cells above and to the right of the dividing lines represent within-period distances, and cells below and to the left of the dividing lines represent between-period distances.

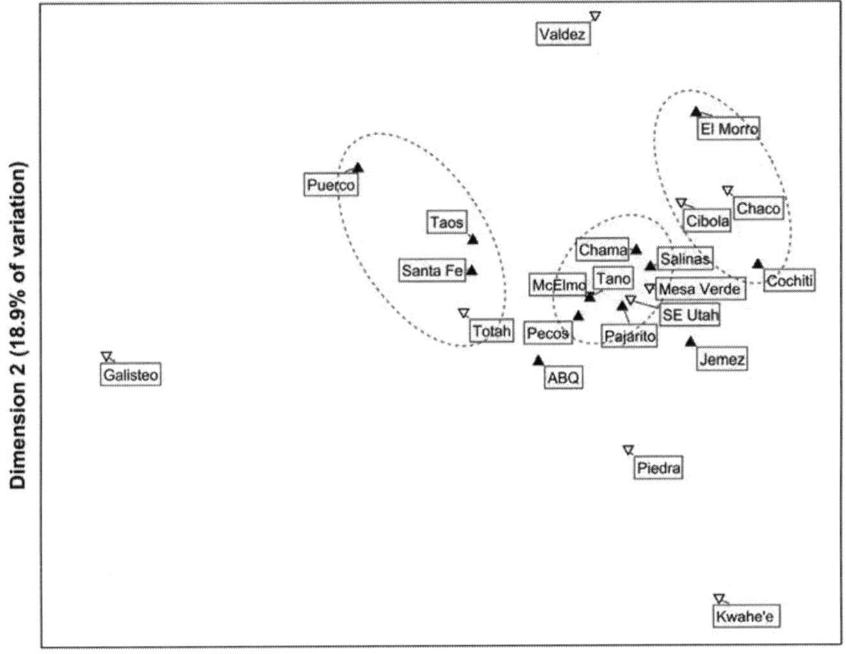

FIGURE 5.2. Principal coordinates analysis of the craniometric data set. The first two eigenvectors have been scaled by the square roots of their eigenvalues. Up-facing, solid triangles indicate post-AD 1275 populations, and down-facing, open triangles indicate pre-AD 1275 populations. Suggested lineages are circled.

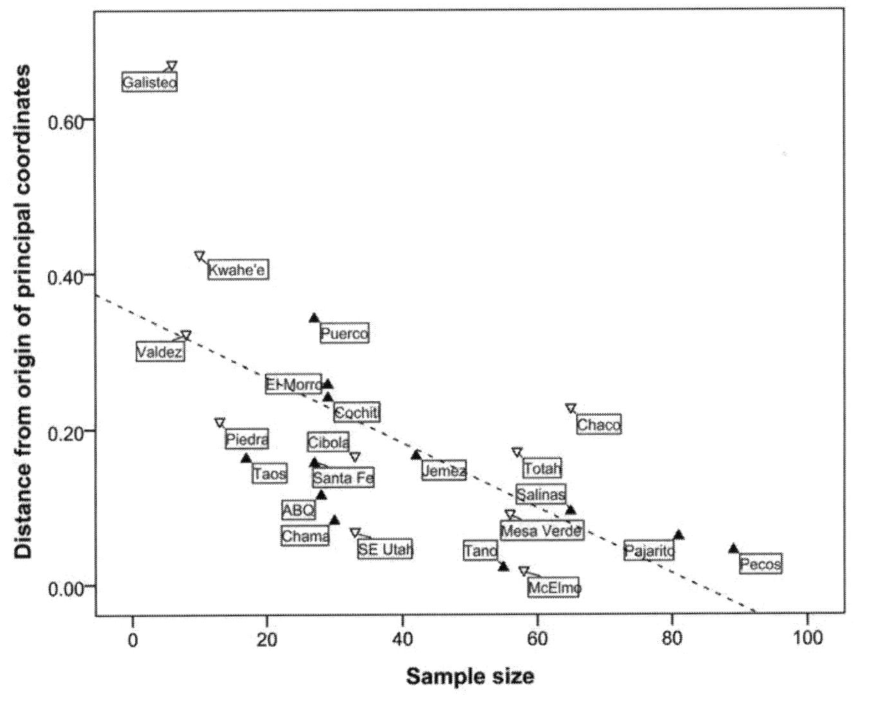

FIGURE 5.3. Relationship between principal coordinates analysis and sample size. Up-facing, solid triangles indicate post-AD 1275 populations, and down-facing, open triangles indicate pre-AD 1275 populations. $r^2 = .4230$ for these data.

Keresan-speaking pueblos, the biological affinity between Cochiti and earlier Cibola and Chaco samples suggests that inhabitants of ancestral Keres pueblos in the Rio Grande were primarily descendants of San Juan Basin and Cibola region populations. In addition, the fact that the post-1275 Cochiti and Pajarito populations have affinities with different pre-1275 populations is consistent with the notion that an ethnic boundary existed in the Frijoles Canyon area during the Classic period. Finally, the fact that the populations in this second cluster are not included in the Mesa Verde lineage suggests that ancestral Keres populations did not originate primarily in the Mesa Verde region, in contrast to the views of many previous researchers (Boyer et al. 2010; Ford et al. 1972; Mera 1934; Wendorf and Reed 1955; also see Chapter 2).

A third suggested lineage includes samples from the Puerco, Taos, Santa Fe, and Totah districts. The affinity between the Puerco and Taos samples, despite the fact that these samples come from opposite ends of the Rio Grande region, is consistent with Reed's (1949) model that the initial inhabitants of the Rio Grande were split by migrating groups from the west into northern and southern groups during the Coalition period. The Santa Fe sample is closely related to samples from the Mesa Verde lineage, but it is even more similar to the Taos and Puerco samples and is plotted closer to them on this basis. This is consistent with the fact that the Santa Fe sample corresponds to the portion of the Tewa Basin that was most densely occupied during the Developmental period, and thus represents an area where admixture between locals and migrants would be most expected. However, under this model one might expect the Kwahe'e phase population of the Tewa Basin to be more similar to the Taos, Puerco, and Santa Fe samples than the data suggest. This discrepancy will be explored further below.[12]

A final point regarding the potential lineages indicated in Figure 5.2 is that pre-1275 samples from the Rio Grande region — including LA3333 in the Galisteo Basin, Kwahe'e phase sites in the Tewa Basin, and Valdez phase sites in the Taos Valley — all appear quite dissimilar from all other populations, including post-AD 1275 Rio Grande region populations. This pattern suggests that post-1275 Rio Grande populations consisted primarily of descendants of migrants, which is consistent with the idea that early populations of the Rio Grande were small and part of several distinct and localized mating networks.

Gene Flow Analysis. Table 5.7 presents an analysis of gene flow following the model developed by Relethford and Blangero (1990). This model compares the observed phenotypic variance in each population to an expected variance defined as:

$$E[\bar{v}_i] = \frac{\bar{v}_w(1 - r_{ii})}{1 - F_{ST}} \tag{5.1}$$

where $E[\bar{v}_i]$ = the expected variance for population i, $\bar{v}_w$ = the pooled mean within-group variance, r_{ii} = the distance of population i from the regional centroid (equivalent to the diagonals of the R matrix), and F_{ST} = the mean distance

TABLE 5.7. Relethford-Blangero analysis of the craniometric data set

Period	Population	n	Distance from Regional Centroid	Phenotypic Variance (V_p)	Expected Variance (V_e)	Residual Variance (V_r)	S.E. (V_r)	P ($V_r \approx 0$)
1	Cibola	33	.0218	0.657	0.931	-0.274	.0179	.0000
1	Piedra	13	.1163	0.610	0.841	-0.231	.0471	.0005
1	SE Utah	33	.0159	0.738	0.937	-0.199	.0209	.0000
1	Totah	57	.0932	0.898	0.863	0.035	.0214	.1308
1	Mesa Verde	56	.0171	1.000	0.936	0.065	.0264	.0316
1	McElmo	58	.0048	1.034	0.947	0.087	.0226	.0027
1	Valdez	8	.1681	1.011	0.792	0.219	.0617	.0045
1	Galisteo	6	.5856	0.848	0.394	0.453	.0872	.0003
1	Kwahe'e	10	.2378	1.424	0.726	0.698	.1348	.0003
1	Chaco	65	.0624	1.699	0.892	0.807	.0803	.0000
2	Jemez	42	.0196	0.655	0.933	-0.278	.0299	.0000
2	Taos	17	.0592	0.686	0.896	-0.210	.0210	.0000
2	El Morro	29	.0501	0.728	0.904	-0.176	.0146	.0000
2	Pecos	89	.0863	0.699	0.870	-0.171	.0242	.0000
2	Salinas	65	.0681	0.832	0.887	-0.055	.0244	.0459
2	Pajarito	81	.0062	0.917	0.946	-0.029	.0291	.3396
2	Tano	55	.0225	0.934	0.930	0.003	.0138	.8322
2	Chama	30	.0302	0.951	0.923	0.027	.0185	.1714
2	Puerco	27	.1625	0.910	0.797	0.113	.0370	.0110
2	Santa Fe	27	.0386	1.217	0.915	0.302	.0353	.0000
2	Cochiti	29	.1914	1.082	0.770	0.312	.0496	.0001
2	Albuquerque	28	.0760	1.265	0.880	0.386	.0575	.0000

Notes: Period 1 < AD 1275, Period 2 > AD 1275. Sample populations for each time period are in ascending order of residual variance. Standard errors are estimated by jackknifing across variables. Significance is estimated from the Student's T distribution (2-tailed, $N_{var}-1$ degrees of freedom) of the residual variance over its standard error (after Relethford and Harpending 1994:256). Regional populations are presented in ascending order of residual variance within each time period.

to the regional centroid across populations, weighted according to the census size of each subdivision. The most important parameter to focus on in interpreting these results is the residual variance. When this value is less than zero, it indicates that the population in question experienced less-than-average gene flow; when it is greater than zero, it indicates that the population experienced greater-than-average gene flow. The samples are listed in order of increasing residual variance within each time period.

These results suggest several points. First, post-1275 samples from the Pajarito, Tano, and Chama districts had not recently experienced greater than average gene flow, despite their affinity with earlier Mesa Verde region populations. This suggests that the ancestral Tewa populations of these areas were descended primarily from Mesa Verde migrants, as opposed to significant admixture of migrants and earlier Rio Grande populations. Second, samples from the post-1275 Santa Fe and Cochiti districts, both of which were home to significant Late Developmental populations, do appear to have experienced greater than average gene flow. This result — combined with the affinity of Santa Fe with the Taos, Puerco, and Mesa Verde region samples (Table 5.6), and the affinity of Cochiti with the San Juan Basin and Cibola samples — suggests that the Classic period populations of these districts did result from admixture of locals and migrants during the Coalition period. Third, the Kwahe'e, Valdez, and Galisteo populations all appear to have been experiencing significant gene flow due to in-migration prior to the Coalition period. This pattern is consistent with their placement around the edges of the principal coordinates plot, and suggests that the pre-1275 Rio Grande region was quite fluid in biogeographic terms.

Finally, it is important to note that high residual variance is not limited to populations with small sample sizes. The highest residual variance observed in the entire data set is associated with Chaco Canyon, which also has one of the largest sample sizes. This result is consistent with previous analyses of remains from Chaco Canyon, all of which have found evidence for a highly variable population that encompassed individuals from a much larger catchment area than the average southwestern population (Akins 1986; Schillaci 2003; Schillaci and Stojanowski 2002; Stojanowski and Schillaci 2006).[13] These results are consistent with studies that suggest Chaco Canyon was the central place of a regional system organized at a larger geopolitical scale than any other prehispanic Pueblo society (Lekson 2006). These details are not relevant to the question of Tewa ancestry, but they do reinforce the conclusion that biodistance analyses can, and do, reveal the biological correlates of culture-historical processes suggested by archaeological evidence.

Possible Confounding Effects on Genetic Distances and Gene Flow Estimates. An important question with respect to this analysis is the extent to which sample size and missing data estimation have influenced genetic distances and gene flow estimates. In a previous work (Ortman 2009:189–191) I compared the percentage of estimated data in each sample with the distance of that sample from the principal coordinates centroid calculated from the minimum genetic distance matrix, and I found no relationship between these variables. This suggests that EM estimation has not created patterns that did not already exist in these data. I also assessed the influence of sampling error and estimated data on the Relethford-Blangero analysis and found that there is no relationship between either of these estimators and phenotypic variance. Thus, it is clear that sampling error and data estimation are not driving the patterns in Table 5.7.

There is, however, a modest relationship between sample size and distance. Figure 5.3 illustrates this relationship by comparing sample size with distance from the principal coordinates centroid for each sample. The chart shows that these variables are moderately correlated, and that the three most-divergent samples, from the pre-1275 Rio Grande, also have the smallest sample sizes. This suggests that it is important to assess the potential error in estimating population parameters for pre-1275 Rio Grande samples before concluding that these populations are actually as divergent as the genetic distance matrix suggests. This assessment is incorporated into the analysis of drift probabilities below.

Drift and Admixture Analyses. A third way of assessing the contribution of the Developmental period population to the Classic period population of the Tewa Basin is to ask how often random genetic drift acting on each of the pre-1275 populations would be expected to produce each of the post-1275 populations. In other words, what is the likelihood that a given pre-1275 population, characterized by its phenotypic mean and variance, could have drifted to match a given post-1275 population, characterized by its phenotypic mean and variance, in the absence of natural selection and under conditions of complete endogamy? These conditions approximate those that would have occurred if the Classic period Tewa Basin population resulted primarily from intrinsic growth of the Developmental population. Lande (1977:323) showed that after *t* generations in the absence of selection, the probability distribution of the resultant average phenotype in a population will be normal, with a mean equal to the initial phenotypic mean and variance given by:

$$\sigma^2_{\varphi}(t) = \frac{h^2 \sigma^2 t}{N} \tag{5.2}$$

where h^2 is the heritability of the phenotype (.55 in this case), σ^2 is the phenotypic variance, t is the number of generations passed, and N is the effective population size. Given this relationship, we can estimate the probability of the observed distances between each between-period population pairing under the null hypothesis that they formed a lineage evolving in the absence of selection or migration.[14] In these tests, $h^2 = .55$, $\sigma^2 =$ the mean phenotypic variance of the compared populations (from Table 5.7), $t = 10$ generations between the midpoints of the two time periods, and $N =$ the mean census size of the two populations divided by 3. The results of these tests are given in Table 5.8.

These tests show that in most cases, even with no directional selection or exogamy, one would expect pre-1275 Mesa Verde region populations to drift to match the ancestral Tewa populations of the Tewa and Galisteo basins more often than once in 7 trials, and in some cases as often as once in 3 trials. These tests also suggest that the Cibola population could have easily drifted to match the El Morro population in the absence of selection or exogamy, and that the Valdez population would drift to match the Taos population in approximately 1 of 7 trials. This latter result suggests that a significant component of the ancestral Taos population was in place by the Late Developmental period. In contrast,

TABLE 5.8. Drift probabilities between pre-AD 1275 and post-AD 1275 populations

POPULATION	SE UTAH	MCELMO	MESA VERDE	TOTAH	PIEDRA	CHACO	CIBOLA	VALDEZ	KWAHE'E	GALISTEO
Taos	.0249	.1333	.0726	.1409	.0115	.0400	.0001	.1476	.0001	.0000
Chama	.1437	.0316	.0243	.0000	.0250	.0204	.1747	.0000	.0000	.0000
Jemez	.3073	.0878	.3432	.0000	.0097	.1052	.1575	.0000	.0002	.0000
Pajarito	.3210	.2560	.3199	.0349	.0468	.2791	.2738	.0130	.0070	.0000
Santa Fe	.1730	.2544	.0923	.2234	.0341	.0745	.0213	.0679	.0007	.0008
Pecos	.1830	.0014	.0222	.0000	.2234	.0362	.0008	.0841	.0009	.0000
Tano	.1298	.2163	.2833	.0063	.0232	.0709	.0610	.0039	.0003	.0000
Cochiti	.0011	.0000	.0009	.0000	.0023	.0128	.0001	.0000	.0000	.0000
Albuquerque	.0115	.1111	.0406	.0351	.0023	.0016	.0000	.0000	.0000	.0000
Puerco	.0002	.0001	.0011	.0387	.0006	.0080	.0000	.0694	.0000	.0188
El Morro	.0250	.0238	.1739	.0000	.0000	.3444	.3275	.0237	.0000	.0000
Salinas	.1794	.0047	.0793	.0000	.0252	.1276	.0201	.0375	.0001	.0000

Notes: Column heads represent pre-AD 1275 populations, and row heads represent post-AD 1275 populations. Values are the probabilility that the pre-AD 1275 population could have evolved into the post-AD 1275 population in the absence of selection and migration.

the Kwahe'e and Galisteo populations would drift to match one of the post-1275 Rio Grande populations in less than 1 of 100 trials. Because strong directional selection seems unlikely for populations occupying the same physical environment and eating similar foods, it appears unlikely that the Classic period Tewa Basin and Galisteo Basin populations could have derived solely, or even primarily, from populations with characteristics of the Kwahe'e and Galisteo samples, respectively.

But before accepting these conclusions, it is important to recall that the Kwahe'e and Galisteo populations are characterized on the basis of very small samples (10 and 6, respectively), and there are indications of sample size effects on patterns of between-group variation in this data set. It is therefore necessary to investigate the level of sampling error one might expect with samples of this size, and whether this level of imprecision should affect one's interpretation of the analysis results. To accomplish this, I estimated the probability that a subsample of the Pajarito population of equal size to the Kwahe'e population, and a subsample of the Tano population of equal size to the Galisteo population, would yield distances that approach those observed between the total Pajarito and Kwahe'e samples, and the total Tano and Galisteo samples. To accomplish this, I took 10 random samples of the appropriate size from the Pajarito and Tano samples, and then calculated the R matrix and minimum genetic distances between the random subsample and the total sample for each trial. These data allow me to construct 90 percent confidence intervals for the Kwahe'e and Galisteo samples on the assumption that these pre-1275 populations were actually closely related to the post-1275 populations, but that small samples have obscured this relationship. I then subtracted the 90 percent confidence interval from the Kwahe'e-Pajarito and Galisteo-Tano distances, recalculated drift probabilities using this distance, and compared these to the mean distances and drift probabilities between all Mesa Verde region samples and the Pajarito and Tano samples. The results, presented graphically in Figure 5.4, show that even with this allowance for sampling error, Mesa Verde region populations appear far more likely as progenitors of the Pajarito and Tano populations than do the Kwahe'e and Galisteo populations, respectively.

The fourth and final model I applied to the craniometric data is an analysis of admixture rates. As mentioned earlier, the genetic distance matrix and Relethford-Blangero analysis suggest that the post-1275 population of the Santa Fe District resulted from the blending of Mesa Verde region migrants with the district's previous inhabitants. What was the relative contribution of locals and migrants to this hybrid population? One simple model for estimating admixture rates from polygenic traits, on the assumptions that drift and selection played negligible roles, is given by:

$$m = \frac{(R_H - R_1)}{(R_2 - R_1)} \tag{5.3}$$

where m = the proportion of admixture from population 2, R_H = the value of the trait in the hybrid population, and R_1 and R_2 are the values of the trait in the parent populations. This model has been used with reasonable success in studies of skin color in admixed populations (Relethford 2002:320–321; Relethford and Lees 1982:125–126), and is also the basis of Cavalli-Sforza and others' (1994:54–57) model for estimating past episodes of admixture from contemporary gene frequency data. In this context the appropriate calculation is simply the genetic distance between the hybrid and one of the source populations over the genetic distance between the two source populations.

I used this model to assess the relative contributions of Mesa Verde region migrants and the indigenous Kwahe'e population to post-1275 populations of the Santa Fe and Pajarito districts in the Tewa Basin on the assumption that the post-1275 populations of these areas derived solely from these two sources.[15] The admixture estimates, presented in Figure 5.5, suggest that the Kwahe'e population contributed approximately 30 percent of the genes in the Santa Fe population and 15 percent of the genes in the Pajarito population. The remainder of the Classic period genes in these populations derived from Mesa Verde region migrants. These admixture rates correspond closely to the ratio of Late Developmental to Early Classic populations in the corresponding population stratum from Chapter 4, as shown in the chart. These data are thus consistent with a model in which Coalition period population growth in the Tewa Basin was due

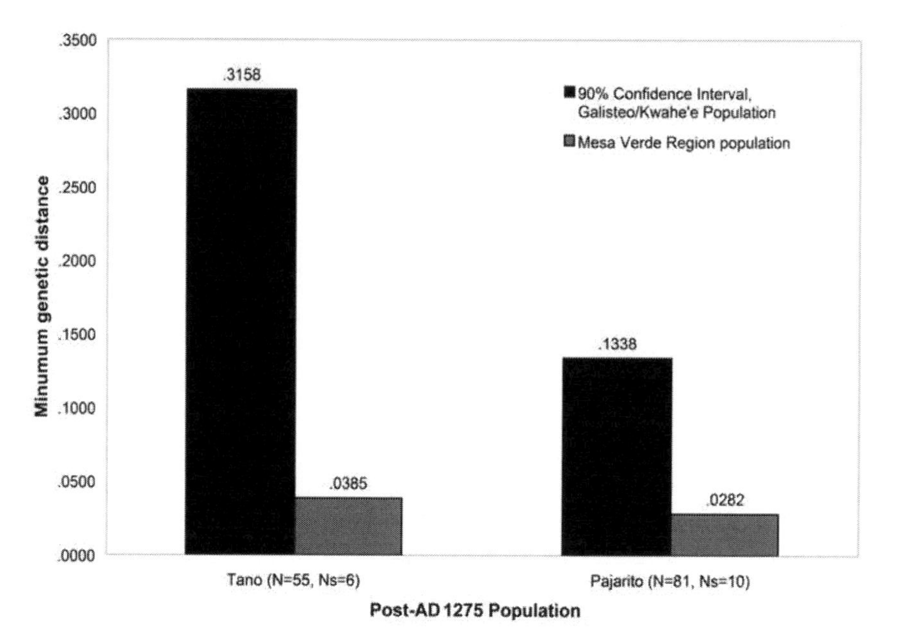

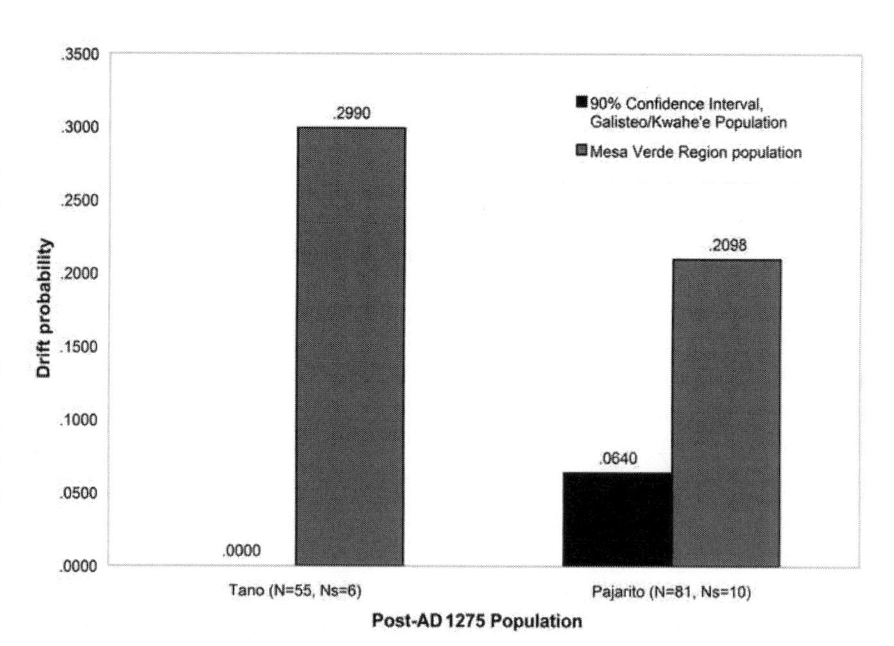

FIGURE 5.4. Results of sampling error analysis. The confidence interval for the distance between the indigenous population and the post-AD 1275 population was constructed by taking 10 subsamples from the post-AD 1275 population (Tano, Pajarito) of sample size equal to the pre-AD 1275 sample size (Galisteo, Kwahe'e) and calculating the distance of the subsample from the total sample for each trial. Drift probabilities were calculated as in Table 5.5.

almost entirely to migration from the Mesa Verde region, and that both migrants and locals contributed genes in proportion to their numbers to the resulting Classic period population.

Shared Ancestry as an Alternative Explanation. A final issue I consider here is the possibility that biological affinities among post-1275 ancestral Tewa populations and pre-1275 Mesa Verde region populations are due to shared ances-

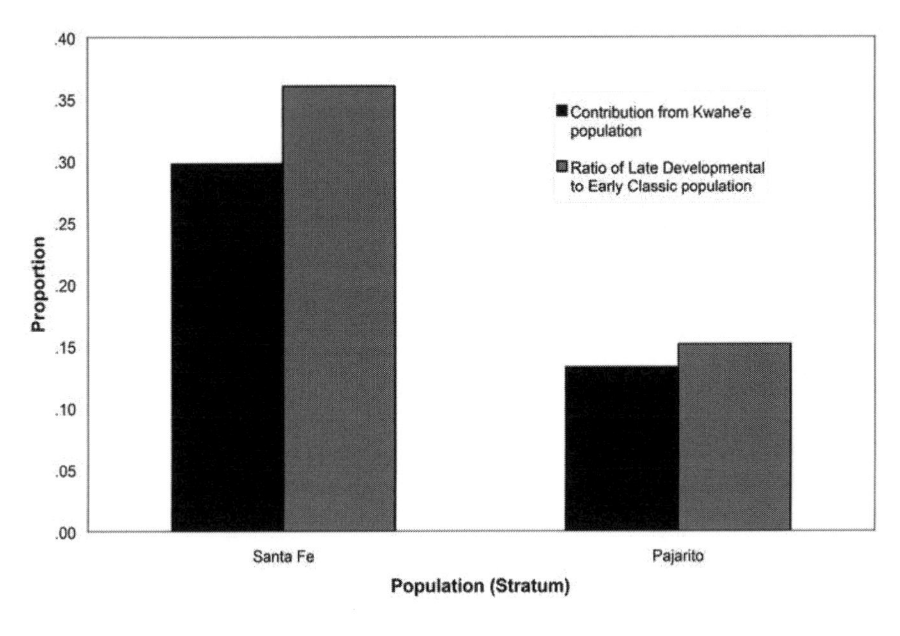

FIGURE 5.5. Admixture analysis results. The black bars indicate the proportion of admixture (*m*) from the Kwahe'e population in each of the post-AD 1275 populations (1 – m = the proportion of admixture from Mesa Verde Region migrants), and the gray bars indicate the ratio of the Phase 2 (AD 1050–1200) population to the Phase 5 (AD 1350–1400) population for the corresponding Tewa Basin population stratum from Chapter 4.

try rather than an ancestor-descendant relationship. It is reasonable to ask this question due to the evidence presented in Chapter 7 that suggests Proto-Kiowa-Tanoan, the ancestral language from which Tewa descended, was spoken in Eastern Basketmaker II communities (also see Hill 2008a; LeBlanc 2008; Matson 2002). Given this, it is possible that Northern Rio Grande and Mesa Verde region populations are biologically similar because they are cousins — that is, both are descended from a common ancestor population. In this scenario the Mesa Verde region population would have spoken a Tanoan language that has not survived to the present day, and the ancestral Tewa population would have descended from early migrants to the Rio Grande region from the northwest, as suggested by Ford and others (1972).[16]

Although this scenario does provide a reasonable alternative explanation for the similarities between Mesa Verde region and ancestral Tewa populations in isolation, it does not appear consistent with the overall pattern of biological relationships summarized in Figure 5.3. If the ancestral Tewa population had descended primarily from the earliest settlers of the Rio Grande, and it retained evidence of shared ancestry with Mesa Verde region populations, one would expect other Rio Grande populations that descended from this common parent population to have also remained similar to Mesa Verde region populations. Yet even if the small Kwahe'e, Galisteo, and Valdez samples are excluded, this expectation is not met for other samples that would have descended from the same common ancestor under this model. Note, in particular, that the Taos and Santa Fe samples — both of which represent areas settled by people of a closely related cultural tradition during the Developmental period — are similar to each other but do not cluster with samples from areas settled during the Coalition period, including the Pajarito, Chama, Tano, and Pecos districts. If, in fact, the Early

Classic populations of these areas descended from early Northern Rio Grande populations, and samples from areas that were initially settled during the Coalition period retain evidence of shared ancestry with Mesa Verde region populations, one would expect samples from areas that were initially settled during the Developmental period to do so as well. The fact that this is not the case is difficult to explain under the shared ancestry scenario, but it is readily explained under an ancestor-descendant scenario. In the latter case, samples from the Pajarito, Chama, Tano, and Pecos districts exhibit close biological affinity with Mesa Verde region samples because these areas were settled primarily by Coalition period migrants from the Mesa Verde region, whereas samples from the Santa Fe and Taos districts do not exhibit such affinity because these areas were initially settled prior to the Coalition period by people from elsewhere.

One area where a shared ancestry interpretation may be just as plausible as an ancestor-descendant interpretation is the close similarity of the Totah sample with the Santa Fe and Taos samples. The eastern Totah contains large numbers of sites that were abandoned shortly after AD 900 and exhibit a very similar material culture to Developmental Rio Grande sites (see Chapter 13). Thus later Totah populations and Developmental Rio Grande populations may have descended from a common ancestor population of the Totah–Upper San Juan. But shared ancestry appears less plausible than an ancestor-descendant relationship in the case of Mesa Verde region and ancestral Tewa populations, because, in this case, samples in the lineage implied by the shared ancestry hypothesis do not exhibit the same degree of relationship.

Moving, Blending, and Descending

The analyses presented in this chapter suggest that the Classic period population of the Rio Grande region derived from at least three distinct biological lineages: one rooted primarily in the Rio Grande region, a second rooted in the Mesa Verde region, and a third rooted in the San Juan Basin and Cibola regions. The geographical distribution of samples included in each lineage is presented in Figure 5.6.

Of the many avenues one could explore in these results, one tempting direction is to correlate biological variation with linguistic variation. For example, there appears to be a reasonable basis for correlating the Rio Grande lineage with Tiwa speakers, the San Juan Basin lineage with Keres speakers, and the Mesa Verde region lineage with Tewa speakers.[17] It is important, however, to keep in mind that such correlations assume that mating networks have mirrored the social networks of speech communities across several episodes of migration. Many studies of human biological diversity take this next step, as Cavalli-Sforza and others (1994) have done on a global scale, and in many cases linguistic distances do correlate with biological distances because a child's first language is normally obtained from parents, as his or her genes always are.

Languages, though, are much more resistant than phenotypes to hybridization when people from different backgrounds come into contact. Each parent

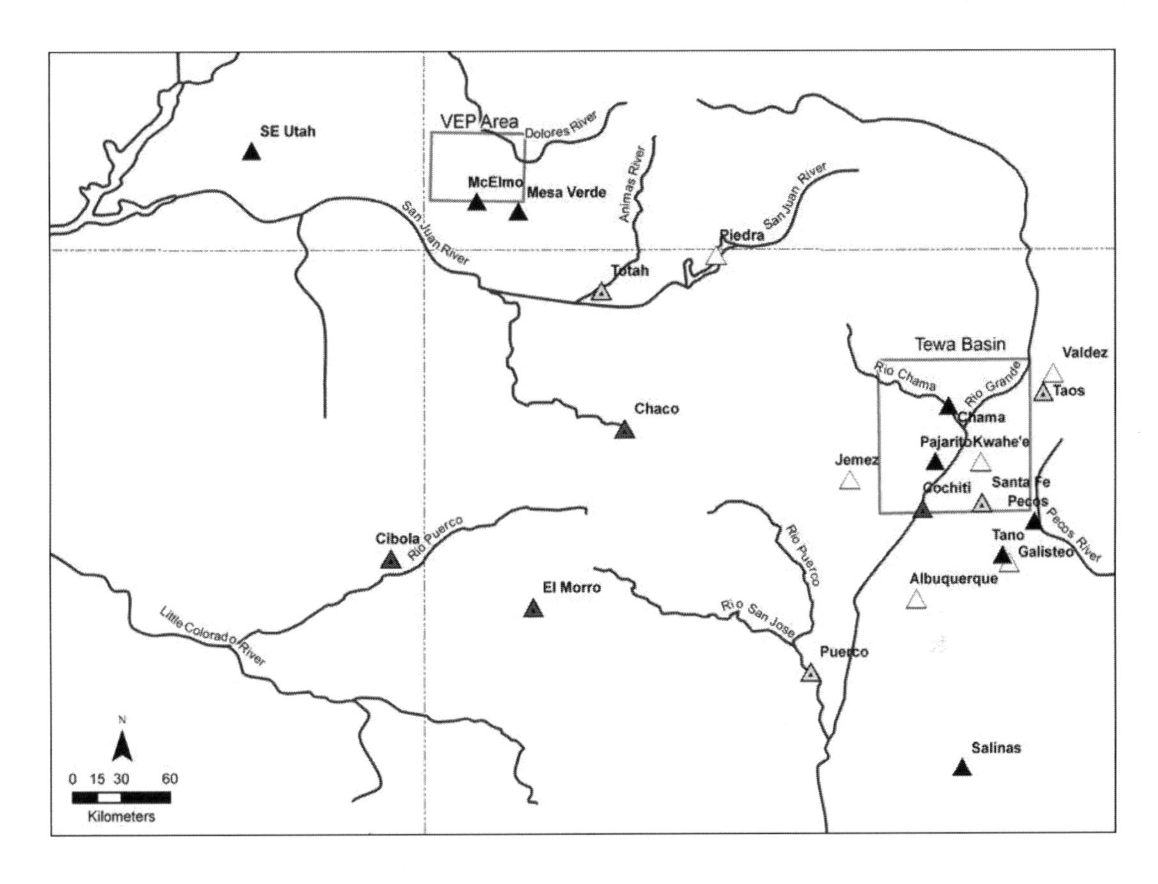

FIGURE 5.6. Distribution of lineages identified in biodistance analysis. Triangles mark geographic centroids of sites contributing samples to each population. Populations in the Mesa Verde region lineage are indicated in black, the Cibola lineage in dark gray, the Rio Grande lineage in light gray, and unaffiliated populations with a white triangle. Gray rectangles demarcate the Village Ecodynamics Project and Tewa Basin study areas.

contributes half the genes of each offspring, but when the first languages of parents differ, offspring will most often become bilingual or learn the dominant language of their community as their first language rather than create a new language that blends the languages of their parents equally. Once established, languages do not readily blend or recombine, whereas the genes of previously isolated groups can and often do. It is also important to keep in mind that the linguistic consequences of population movement are often not predictable from the demographic parameters of this movement, as biological consequences necessarily are. In his book *The Horse, the Wheel, and Language*, David Anthony (2007:108–113) reviews several cases in which the group that established a new social system had an inordinate cultural and linguistic influence on later generations of migrants. A good example is the adoption of English language, house forms, and settlement types by nineteenth-century German migrants to Ohio, even though they far outnumbered the earlier English settlers (see Wilhelm 1992). Anthony (2007:113) explains, “As a font of tradition and success in a new land, the charter group exercised a kind of historical and cultural hegemony over later generations. Their genes, however, could easily be swamped by later migrants, which is why it is often futile to pursue a genetic fingerprint associated with a particular language.” In the present context, then, the biological evidence cannot rule out the possibility that the Late Developmental population of the Tewa Basin already spoke Tewa and served as the charter group to which later Mesa Verde region migrants assimilated linguistically and culturally.

These observations suggest that it may not be appropriate to put too much faith or effort into language-biology correlations in the absence of additional analyses which demonstrate that languages traveled with genes in any given case. This will be the emphasis of several chapters that follow. Here I interpret the biodistance analysis results more narrowly, focusing on their implications for the origins of ancestral Tewa and Tano populations of the Tewa and Galisteo basins, respectively.

First, the post-1275 Pajarito and Chama populations of the Tewa Basin, and the Tano population of the Galisteo Basin, all exhibit a much closer genetic relationship to the latest populations of the Mesa Verde region than they do to other, pre-1275 populations, including those of the Rio Grande. This suggests that these populations derive primarily from earlier Mesa Verde region populations.

Second, the Relethford-Blangero model of gene flow suggests that the Pajarito, Chama, and Tano populations had not recently experienced greater than average gene flow, as one would expect if these populations were the product of significant admixture between indigenous Rio Grande populations and migrants from the Mesa Verde region and/or elsewhere. This lack of evidence for significant gene flow correlates with settlement pattern evidence suggesting that these specific districts had small resident populations prior to the Coalition period. This analysis also suggests that the post-AD 1275 Cochiti and Santa Fe populations had recently experienced greater than average gene flow, consistent with a model of admixture between locals and migrants. This result correlates with settlement pattern evidence indicating that these districts were home to significant Late Developmental populations.

Third, the analysis of genetic drift suggests pre-1275 populations of the Tewa and Galisteo basins could not have drifted to match the post-1275 populations of these same areas in the absence of significant exogamy and/or directional selection on craniofacial shape. Because changes in selective forces over the period of this study are unlikely, and sampling error cannot explain the degree of divergence between these sequential populations, the in situ development model of Tewa origins is not supported by the biological evidence.

Fourth, admixture analysis suggests the Late Developmental population contributed between 15 and 30 percent of the genes in the Classic period gene pools of the Pajarito and Santa Fe districts, respectively. These admixture rates correspond to the relative sizes of Late Developmental and Early Classic populations of these districts. Thus, combined biological and settlement pattern evidence suggests that Late Developmental Tewa Basin populations and thirteenth-century Mesa Verde migrants contributed genes in proportion to their numbers to the resultant Classic period Tewa Basin populations. This correspondence also implies an absence of barriers to gene flow among migrant and local populations during the Coalition period.

Finally, an alternative explanation for the close biological affinities between Mesa Verde region and ancestral Tewa populations — shared ancestry — appears less plausible than the interpretation of a lineal relationship because other Rio Grande samples that one would expect to be in the clade defined by common ancestry under this hypothesis do not cluster with samples in the Mesa Verde lineage.

The fact that four different population genetic models applied to the craniometric data provide a consistent picture of Tewa ancestry, and that the results are consistent with the population history developed in Chapter 4, make a strong case that most of the Classic period Tewa Basin population derives from earlier populations of the Mesa Verde region and not from earlier populations of the Rio Grande. Nevertheless, it is important to emphasize that earlier inhabitants of the Tewa Basin, especially in the Santa Fe District, also appear to have contributed their genes to the Classic period Tewa Basin population. It thus appears most accurate to state that the ancestors of present-day Tewa people include people who lived on both Developmental Rio Grande and Pueblo III Mesa Verde region sites. Also, the absence of significant admixture in ancestral Tewa populations suggests that many Mesa Verde migrants adopted local Rio Grande material traditions upon entry to the Tewa Basin. In other words, a close look at the population biology of Tewa origins reinforces the suspicion that genes, language, and culture did not travel as a package in this case. Thus, what is needed is a set of methods that make it possible to examine each mode of inheritance separately. This approach will be followed in the remainder of this book, starting with an analysis of Kiowa-Tanoan languages.

NOTES

1. It is also interesting to note that LeBlanc and others' (2007) ancient DNA study of Basketmaker populations replicates the relevant portion of Turner's (1993) results. Specifically, Turner found that samples from southeastern Utah and northeastern Arizona, which contained both Basketmaker and Pueblo period remains, appear more similar to samples from central and northern Mexico than they do to the Eastern and Central Pueblo samples. One should probably group Turner's data differently and perhaps use different statistical methods to investigate these patterns in more detail, but it is nevertheless important to note that analyses of phenotypic variation can yield results that are compatible with analyses of ancient mtDNA variation.
2. The data compiled by Schillaci and analyzed in several recent publications form the nucleus of the data set analyzed for this study, but with a greatly expanded sample from the Mesa Verde region and other relevant sites. I am grateful to Schillaci for making these data available.
3. Droessler (1981) reached a similar conclusion after comparing the results of her craniometric study of Late Woodland and Mississippian remains with the results obtained by Buikstra (1977) on the basis of nonmetric traits from the same specimens. Sokal and Sneath (1963:85) also recognized that patterns of biological relationship are stable across a wide range of traits, and suggested this pattern derives from the fact that the effects of most genes are nonspecific — which is to say, broadly distributed throughout the phenotype.

4. This also begs the question of whether sources of ancient DNA other than skeletal remains are subject to the consultation process mandated by the Native American Graves Protection and Repatriation Act.
5. Hanihara and Ishida (2005) obtained the same result working with worldwide odontometric variation, thus providing another example of consistent biodistance analysis results across multiple forms of biological variation.
6. Most ancestral Pueblo infants were fastened to cradleboards for the first few months of life. The weight of the head on the cradleboard, perhaps augmented by wrappings that held the head in place, flattened the occipital or lambdoid region of the cranial vault, and encouraged compensatory widening of the lateral portions. As a result, measurements of the cranial vault are not reliable indicators of genetic affinity in ancestral Pueblo populations. However, a comparison of modified and nonmodified Hopi skulls from the village of Walpi by Kohn and others (1995) demonstrates that the unintentional deformation caused by cradleboarding does not impact the cranial base or face. Droessler (1981:116) made similar comparisons for skulls from the eastern United States and found that the cranial vault is most susceptible and the facial skeleton least susceptible to the effects of artificial cranial deformation.
7. The raw craniometric data set is available in Ortman (2009: Appendix B). Unfortunately, I was not able to obtain craniometric data for two districts that may have played a role in Tewa origins. Mera (1935) suggested the Upper Rio Puerco of the East as a possible source of "Mesa Verde" influences in Tewa Basin pottery designs, and both Mera (1935) and Lang (1982) have suggested the Largo-Gallina District as a possible source for several technological traits of Santa Fe Black-on-white pottery. I do not think this is a critical omission for two reasons. First, even if these districts were sources of certain traits of Classic period Tewa Basin culture, the suggested thirteenth-century populations of these districts (Crown et al. 1996:193–194; Roney 1995, 1996) were not sufficiently large to account for the magnitude of population increase suggested by the analysis in Chapter 4. Second, Mackey (1977) included samples from the Largo-Gallina District in his analysis of Towa ancestry and found that this population was most closely related to the Piedra District population included in this study, and was not closely related to any Classic period Pueblo populations.
8. I encountered this problem primarily for orbital breadth and interorbital breadth measurements because the landmarks used for these measurements in Howells's (1973) system are different from those used in Buikstra and Ubelaker's (1994) system. I standardized the data to the Howells system because most measurements were collected following Howells's definitions.
9. In some cases I could identify a subset of specimens for which a measurement was taken using both the standard and the divergent landmark. In such cases I used linear regression to generate an equation that estimates the standard measurement based on the nonstandard measurement, and applied this equation to the nonstandard measurements. In other cases I did not have multiple measurements for individual specimens, but did have summary statistics reported in previous studies of the same samples. In this situation I rescaled the divergent measurements based on the descriptive summaries provided by previous researchers. If I only needed to adjust the mean, I subtracted the mean difference of the two sets of measurements from each divergent measurement. If I needed to adjust both the mean and standard deviation, I multiplied each divergent measurement by the proportionate difference between the means of the two sets of measurements.

10. As noted by Relethford and others (1997:462), the diagonals of the R matrix are subject to sampling bias, especially for small sample sizes. To correct for this bias, RMET 5.0 subtracts $1/2n_i$, where n_i is the sample size of the ith population, from the ith diagonal of the R matrix for all values of i. In some situations this will result in a negative value for r_{ii}. In this case, the bias correction procedure sets $r_{ii} = 0$. The diagonals of the R matrix are involved in calculating minimum genetic distances and the expected variance in Relethford-Blangero analysis. Thus, all analyses presented here are affected by bias correction.
11. In generating this plot, I did not weight the site coordinates by the square root of population size, as Relethford (2003) recommends to control drift effects among contemporaneous samples, because it is likely that ancestor-descendant relationships exist among several of these populations, and the number of generations between the midpoints of the two time periods considered is relatively small. Weighting by population size would hinder the identification of ancestor-descendant relationships in this case because samples would need to have similar population sizes as well as phenotypic parameters to plot near each other. Thus Figure 5.2 does not attempt to control for drift in assessing patterns of relatedness among populations of the two time periods. I address potential drift effects using a different method in a subsequent analysis.
12. Inclusion of the Totah sample in this group also appears somewhat puzzling at first. The pottery style of the Totah District is very similar to that of the Mesa Verde region. This has led previous researchers to include the Totah in a Northern San Juan culture area that also includes the Mesa Verde region. However, recent studies suggest that painted pottery vessels made in the Mesa Verde region ended up in the Totah more often than Totah vessels ended up in the Mesa Verde region (Glowacki 2006:115), and that a number of architectural features of thirteenth-century Mesa Verde region villages—including plazas, towers, D-shaped structures, and enclosing walls—are rare to nonexistent in the Totah (Glowacki 2006:62–70). If the Totah constituted a distinct biocultural region, the suggested affinity of the Totah sample with the Santa Fe, Taos, and Puerco samples may indicate that the Totah population was ancestral to, or shares common ancestry with, the Santa Fe and Taos populations. Shared ancestry may be a more plausible interpretation than lineal relationship in this case, as explained later in this chapter.
13. It is also interesting to note that the Totah sample does not exhibit the same level of phenotypic variance observed for the Chaco sample. This may be because the great house population of the Totah is not well sampled by this data set (most of the samples derive from the late occupations at Aztec, Salmon, and other typical residential sites), but if there had been a period of interaction between locals and intrusive, Chaco-related populations during the early AD 1100s, one would expect this interaction to be reflected in higher residual variance, and smaller distances than those observed between the Totah and Chaco samples. These results thus suggest that if individuals with Chacoan ancestry did occupy the Totah great houses at one time, they either did not marry into local lineages or were so few in number that their genetic effects were minimal.
14. Scuilli and Mahaney (1991) used this model to investigate the role of selection in tooth size reduction among prehistoric Ohio Amerindians.
15. I did not estimate admixture rates for the post-AD 1275 Chama population because the Classic period population of this district appears to have resulted in part from internal migration from the Pajarito and Santa Fe/Santa Cruz districts (see Figure 4.7).

Thus, it is not realistic to estimate Mesa Verde–Kwahe'e admixture rates for this population.

16. I am grateful to Michael Schillaci for this suggestion.
17. One result that deserves more attention is the inclusion of Salinas and Pecos samples in the Mesa Verde region lineage. The Salinas Pueblos spoke Tompiro, a now-extinct Tanoan language whose relationships to other Tanoan languages is unknown (Hayes et al. 1981:6). This fact, combined with the location of the Salinas District southeast of Albuquerque, might lead one to hypothesize that the Salinas population was most closely related to Southern Tiwa or Piro populations. Yet the Salinas sample bears a close affiliation with the Mesa Verde region, Cibola, and Chaco samples (Table 5.6). Why this should be so deserves more research. One possibility is that ancestors of the Salinas Pueblos derived from earlier inhabitants of the Magdalena District, approximately 100 km to the west. There are a number of settlements in this area dating from the AD 1290s that bear pottery reminiscent of Mesa Verde Black-on-white (Lekson et al. 2004:57–58; Lekson et al. 2002).

    If the Pecos population also consists largely of descendants of Mesa Verde Region migrants, this may only add to the mystery surrounding the language affiliation of Pecos Pueblo and its relationship with Jemez. If the inhabitants of Pecos spoke Towa but derived from the same ancestral population as the Tewa-speaking Pueblos, it would follow that the ancestral Jemez population also derived from Mesa Verde region migrants. The Jemez population is, in fact, more closely related to Mesa Verde region populations than to earlier populations of the Piedra or Gallina districts (see Mackey 1977), and recent studies of Jemez area archaeology find little evidence to support Ellis's (1967) contention that the Jemez population derived from the earlier Gallina tradition (Elliott 1998; Kulisheck and Elliott 2005). However, the evidence of biological affinity among ancestral Jemez and Tewa populations is also somewhat surprising, given evidence that the Towa language is more distant from Tewa than is Tiwa (see Chapter 6). One possible explanation for the lack of correspondence between linguistic and biological distances in this case could be that the Towa, Tewa, and Keres speech communities were all located in the Four Corners region at one time, and there was continuing gene flow among them for a period of time after the group whose descendants would comprise the Tiwa speech community left the Four Corners for the Rio Grande.

    Alternatively, Jemez and Pecos may derive from different ancestral populations—a scenario which would raise the possibility that the inhabitants of Pecos spoke a Tanoan dialect more closely related to Tewa than to Towa. A variety of evidence supports this view, as explained in Chapter 6.

The Tewa Language in Kiowa-Tanoan Context

The studies of population history and biological variation in previous chapters make a strong case that most Classic period inhabitants of the Tewa Basin were descendants of Coalition period migrants from the Mesa Verde region. This possibility raises the question of whether these migrants brought the precursor of the Tewa language with them, whether they adopted this language upon arrival, or whether the Tewa language formed as a product of migration and culture contact. Although the pattern of population growth and evidence of biological affinity suggests the first scenario may be most likely, the fact that population movement took place over several generations and involved interaction between locals and migrants suggests that all three scenarios are possible. Thus, it is necessary to examine the history of the Tewa language independent of demographic and genetic evidence to evaluate these various scenarios.

To make this task more tractable, I have broken down the question posed above into three subquestions that are easier to answer one at a time: How long has Tewa been a distinct language? How long ago can this language be documented as having being spoken in the Tewa Basin? And what aspects of the Tewa language might one expect to see expressed in the material culture of ancestral Tewa speakers, and where and when do we see them? This chapter and the following one focus on the first question. The other two are considered in Chapters 8 through 10.

The Tewa language is part of the largest and most diverse language family of the Pueblo culture area. This family is known as Kiowa-Tanoan because it includes Kiowa, a language spoken on the Southern Plains, as well as several Pueblo languages often grouped together as Tanoan. To say that these languages constitute a language family is to say that these languages are all descended from a common ancestral language. This implies that the Tewa language has not been distinct since remote antiquity; rather, it became distinct at some point in the development of the Kiowa-Tanoan languages. Dating when Tewa became a distinct language is important for the study of Tewa origins because it has a bearing on where the Tewa language originated. If the Tewa language became distinct only after AD 1280, for example, it could not have originated in the Mesa Verde region because its last Pueblo inhabitants had left within a few years of this date. In contrast, if the Tewa language became distinct prior to AD 1280, it could have originated in the Mesa Verde region and been brought to the Tewa Basin by migrants from that region. Thus, the first step in evaluating whether Mesa Verde migrants brought the Tewa language to the Rio Grande is to estimate the length of time that Tewa has been a distinct language.

To determine how long Tewa has been distinct, one first needs to establish the sequence of events that produced the various languages of the Kiowa-Tanoan family to which Tewa belongs. Then one needs to estimate when these events took place. Here I provide some background on the Kiowa-Tanoan languages, introduce current methods for establishing historical relationships among languages, and apply these methods to these languages to investigate their sequence of development.

The Kiowa-Tanoan Languages

Languages of the Kiowa-Tanoan family for which there is at least minimal documentation include Northern Tiwa, Southern Tiwa, Tewa, Towa, Piro, and Kiowa. Kiowa is spoken by a community of the Southern Plains today, and was spoken along the front range of the Rocky Mountains in southwestern Montana at the beginning of the eighteenth century (Harrington 1939; Meadows 2008:116–117; Mooney 1898). The other languages were all spoken in various pueblos of the Rio Grande region at the time of Spanish contact (Harrington 1909). At present, the pueblos of Taos and Picuris speak closely related languages often grouped as Northern Tiwa (Trager 1942, 1969), the pueblos of Isleta and Sandia speak nearly identical dialects of Southern Tiwa, and Jemez Pueblo speaks Towa. Tewa is spoken in six pueblos in the Tewa Basin — Ohkay Owingeh, Santa Clara, San Ildefonso, Tesuque, Pojoaque, and Nambe — and also at Tewa Village on Hopi First Mesa. Figure 6.1 illustrates the distribution of present-day Pueblo lands and languages.

Several Tanoan dialects known to have been spoken at the time of Spanish contact are now extinct. Piro was spoken in several pueblos along the Rio Grande south of Albuquerque in the sixteenth century (Barrett 2002). All these villages were abandoned by AD 1680, when the remnant Piro population accompanied the Spaniards retreating to El Paso during the Pueblo Revolt. Bartlett collected a brief vocabulary of Piro in 1850, but by 1909 Harrington was unable to locate a living Piro speaker. A Tanoan language was also spoken at Pecos, a pueblo that was abandoned in 1838. Most of the remaining inhabitants joined Jemez Pueblo at that time, but it is not clear whether the language of Pecos was Towa: "the scant Pecos material remembered by descendants of Pecos at Jemez is not sufficiently clear to demonstrate a Towa identity, but Pecos is clearly a Tanoan language" (Campbell 1997:139; also see Hale and Harris 1979:171).[1]

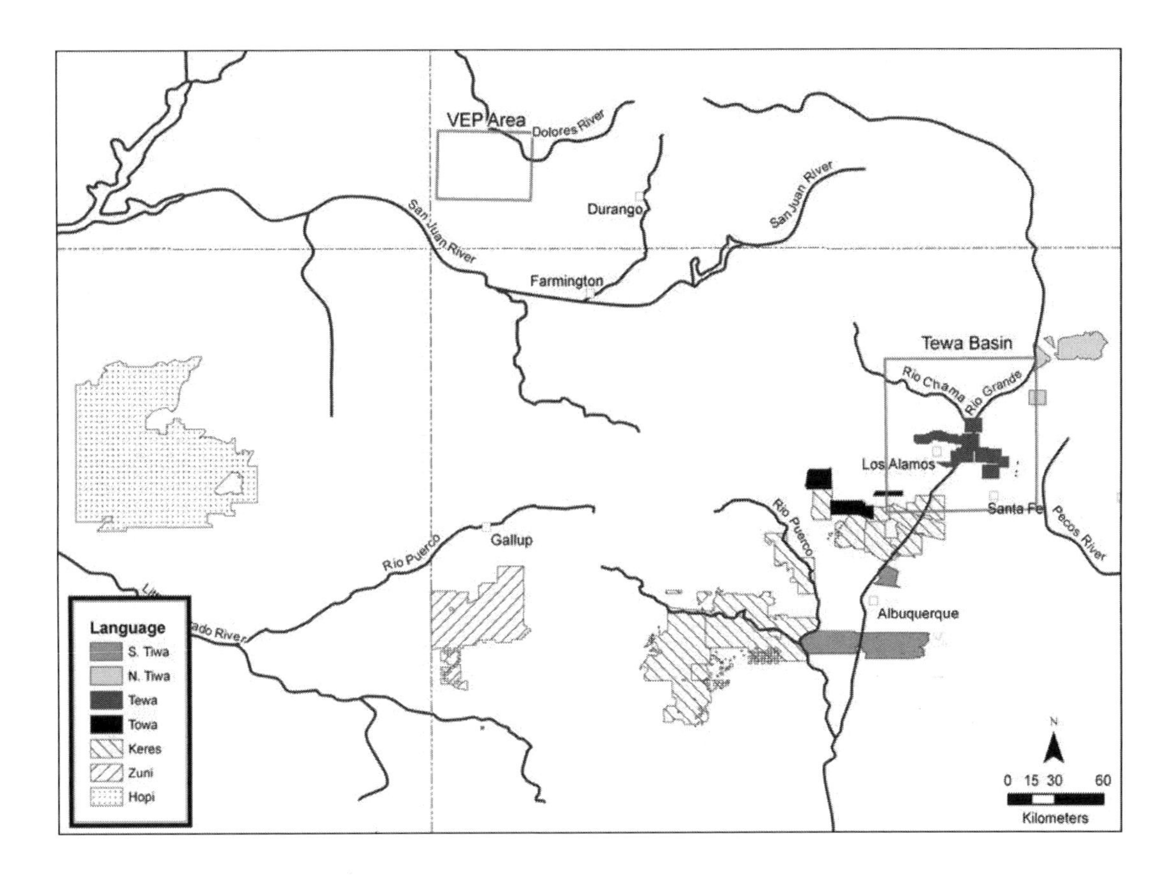

FIGURE 6.1. Distribution of present-day Pueblo lands and languages. Tanoan languages are indicated by solid colors, and other Pueblo languages by hatch patterns. Boundaries of the Tewa Basin and Village Ecodynamics Project study areas are depicted as open rectangles.

Finally, a dialect of Tewa was spoken at several pueblos in the Galisteo Basin southeast of Santa Fe at the time of Spanish contact. This dialect is known as Southern Tewa, or "Tano," after the Northern Tewa appellation T^{h}anut'owa 'down country people' for their southern brethren. The Tano Pueblos dwindled during the historic period, until the last inhabitants of Pueblo Galisteo moved to Santo Domingo in 1794 (Harrington 1916:483–485). Although the Tano Pueblos no longer exist, the fate of the Southern Tewa dialect is less clear. It is important to determine whether this dialect is preserved in any present-day Tewa-speaking communities, because an understanding of historical relationships among extant Tewa dialects is a prerequisite for reconstructing Proto-Tewa and the history of the Tewa speech community. This history may, in turn, provide important clues regarding where and when Tewa became a distinct language. I summarize the available evidence related to the history of Tewa dialects below.

Tewa Dialect Variation

The existing literature suggests that it is most reasonable to distinguish three Tewa dialects. Speirs (1966:30–36) identified a number of dialect differences that crosscut different subsets of Tewa-speaking villages in northern New Mexico, but viewed the most important variation, /ẓ̌/ (often written as 'j') in Santa Clara versus /y/ in other villages, as distinguishing a Santa Clara dialect from that of the other Rio Grande Tewa villages. Several writers have also suggested that Santa Clara fricatives /f, θ, x/ correspond to aspirated stops /p^h, t^h, k^h/ in the other villages (Hale 1967:116–117; Hoijer and Dozier 1949). Thus, there appears to be some basis for subdividing Rio Grande Tewa into a Santa Clara dialect and the dialect spoken in the other villages, often referred to as the "San Juan" dialect.[2]

The third dialect, Arizona Tewa, is spoken at Tewa Village on Hopi First Mesa in Arizona. Tewa Village formed as a result of migration from the Rio Grande in 1696, a few years after the reconquest of New Mexico. Most previous writers have considered these migrants to have derived from Southern Tewa villages of the Galisteo Basin (Dozier 1954; Kroskrity 1993; Parsons 1994). According to this view, the Arizona Tewa dialect is also descended from Southern Tewa speech of the Galisteo Basin. However, a case can be made that many of the Tewas who migrated to the Hopi mesas in 1696 derived from Northern Tewa villages (Marshall and Walt 2007:40–47; Yava 1978). Several accounts suggest that Hopi-Tewa migrants came from Ts'ą̨wad̲i, a Tewa Basin village on the lower Rio Santa Cruz, across the Rio Grande from Santa Clara Pueblo. It is also clear that inhabitants of several Southern Tewa villages moved north and joined their northern cousins during the Pueblo Revolt, and that many people from San Cristobal in particular ended up at Ts'ą̨wad̲i by the early 1690s (Marshall and Walt 2007). However, Ts'ą̨wad̲i may have already been established when the Southern Tewas settled there, and Hopi-Tewas remember their homeland village by its Northern Tewa name, rather than the Southern Tewa names "Yam P'ham-ba" or San Cristobal, both of which were transferred to Ts'ą̨wad̲i when the Southern Tewas moved there (Harrington 1916:486). In addition, living Ohkay Owingeh tribal members claim that many of the occupants of Phíˀôege, a seventeenth-century village along the Rio Grande a few miles north of Ohkay Owingeh, moved to the Hopi mesas along with people from Ts'ą̨wad̲i, and that the remainder moved to Ohkay Owingeh (Richard Ford, personal communication, April 27, 2009).

In fact, a variety of evidence suggests that the Southern Tewa dialect has been preserved in the Santa Clara dialect rather than the Arizona Tewa dialect. This includes archaeological evidence that a group of glaze-producing potters moved from the Galisteo Basin to Puujé (LA47) in the early AD 1500s and subsequently to Santa Clara Pueblo (Peckham and Olinger 1990:210–211); that Santa Clara tribal members maintain social memories of this movement (Naranjo 2006:49) and view their dialect as having derived from these Southern Tewa migrants (Swentzell 1993:48); and that Ts'ą̨wad̲i, the village to which Southern Tewas from San Cristobal moved in the 1690s, lay across the Rio Grande from Santa Clara Pueblo. In addition, Arizona Tewa is spoken using the /y/ and the aspirated stops /p^h, t^h, k^h/ of the San Juan dialect, and not the /ẓ̌/ or the fricatives /f, θ, x/ of the Santa Clara dialect (Hale 1967:116–117; Kroskrity 1993:58). This is consistent with the derivation of Arizona Tewa from San Juan Tewa, and Santa Clara Tewa from Southern Tewa.[3]

Thus, available evidence suggests that the Santa Clara dialect preserves dialect distinctions that developed among Southern Tewa speakers in the Galisteo Basin, and that the Arizona dialect is descended from the Northern Tewa, or San Juan, dialect. This is not to say that the people who migrated to the Hopi mesas in AD 1696 all spoke the Northern Tewa dialect. Indeed, variations in oral traditions surrounding the origins of Tewa Village suggest that both Northern and Southern Tewas were involved. What this model does suggest, however, is that the San Juan dialect became the standard in the early Arizona Tewa speech community.

This model has significant implications for this study. For example, if Arizona Tewa is descended from San Juan Tewa, it would imply that phonological differences between these two dialects could not predate 1696, when the two speech communities became isolated. The shallow time depth of Arizona Tewa is supported by Kroskrity's (1993:55–60) comparison of Arizona Tewa and San Juan Tewa vocabulary, which found that 94 percent of the compared forms share common ancestry. In addition, if Santa Clara Tewa is descended from Southern Tewa, then comparisons of the Santa Clara and San Juan dialects may provide the best means of reconstructing Proto-Tewa, the common ancestor of all extant Tewa dialects.

The comparisons that have been made to date suggest that Proto-Tewa was spoken in a single speech community in the not-too-distant past. For example, Harrington (1916:483–485) compared a short vocabulary he collected from a Pueblo Galisteo descendant in 1908 with "Ordinary Rio Grande Tewa" and found that these two dialects were nearly indistinguishable in AD 1794, when the last inhabitants of Pueblo Galisteo moved to Santo Domingo Pueblo.[4] Speirs (1966:30–36) also identified a number of dialect variations in Rio Grande Tewa, but found none that suggest extended periods of isolation. Thus, the Santa Clara and San Juan dialects must have diverged before the Southern Tewa migration to Puujé in the sixteenth century, and after the formation of the Galisteo Basin villages in the late thirteenth century AD. This model will prove important for the analysis of shared phonological innovations later in this chapter.

Previous Kiowa-Tanoan Research

The name *Kiowa-Tanoan* is a product of the history of scholarship on these languages. John Wesley Powell recognized the relationship between Northern Tiwa, Southern Tiwa, Tewa, and Towa in the late nineteenth century (Powell 1891) and labeled this group "Tañoan," after the Mexicanized name for the Southern Tewa (Harrington 1910a:12). Harrington (1909) compared Bartlett's Piro vocabulary with data he collected from Isleta, Taos, Jemez, and San Ildefonso to show that Piro was also a Tanoan language closely related to the languages of Taos and Isleta. Harrington (1910a) was also the first to propose the tripartite classification of the Tanoan languages into Tiwa, Towa, and Tewa, and the first to suggest a relationship between Tanoan and Kiowa (Harrington 1910b,

1928). Miller (1959) and Trager and Trager (1959) set up sound correspondences between Tiwa, Tewa, and Kiowa in support of Harrington's proposed relationship, and Hale (1962) presented correspondences between Kiowa and Jemez. Hale (1967) finally proved the existence of the Kiowa-Tanoan family by reconstructing the sound system of the protolanguage from which all these languages descended. As a result, there is universal agreement today on the validity and membership of the Kiowa-Tanoan family.

Despite the relatively small size of the Kiowa-Tanoan family, it has received considerable attention by linguists due to its role in the so-called "Aztec-Tanoan hypothesis." John Wesley Powell (1891) was the first to suggest a relationship between Tanoan and "Shoshonean" (the Uto- [or northern] branch of today's Uto-Aztecan language family). Harrington (1910b) also suggested that Kiowa-Tanoan was related to "Nahuatlan" (the -Aztecan [or southern] branch of Uto-Aztecan), and Sapir considered Aztec-Tanoan to be one of the six major groups of American Indian languages in his classification (1949 [1926]:173). In 1937, Whorf and Trager proposed a reconstruction of Aztec-Tanoan based on comparisons of Tanoan and Uto-Aztecan forms. The conclusion of this study, that there was a Proto-Aztec-Tanoan language spoken in a single speech community in the distant past, was widely accepted for decades. Thirty years later, Ken Hale (1967: 112) referred to Whorf and Trager's study as "undoubtedly among the very best examples available of the use of the comparative method in support of broader linguistic relationships suggested by earlier workers."

Recent work has gradually undermined the Aztec-Tanoan hypothesis, but in the process many aspects of Proto-Kiowa-Tanoan (PKT), the protolanguage at the root of the Kiowa-Tanoan family tree, have been reconstructed. Hale (1967: 112) couched his reconstruction of Kiowa-Tanoan phonology as a step in testing the Aztec-Tanoan hypothesis. As part of this work Hale also produced a Kiowa-Tanoan cognate list of 210 items (Hale n.d.) that is extremely useful for cultural reconstruction. In a later publication Hale concluded, with regard to Aztec-Tanoan, "while the case looks considerably more convincing than the comparison of randomly selected language families not believed to be related, a cautious view must leave the question open" (Hale and Harris 1979:171). Davis (1989) used Hale's work to reconstruct additional Kiowa-Tanoan forms in his more recent assessment of Aztec-Tanoan. Davis rejected many of Whorf and Trager's proposed cognate sets for various reasons, but still found about half of them to be plausible. On this basis he suggested that there is a relationship between Kiowa-Tanoan and Uto-Aztecan, but that it is impossible to tell how close or distant the relationship is from the available data. Most recently, Campbell (1997:269–273) examined the proposed cognate sets that survived Davis's scrutiny, and found that all but five could be dismissed as chance resemblances, loan words, onomatopoeic words, words that do not correspond semantically, nursery words, or pan-Americanisms. He thus concluded that the evidence for Aztec-Tanoan is weak.

Recently researchers have begun to consider language contact as an alternative to shared descent as an explanation for similarities between Uto-Aztecan and Kiowa-Tanoan. Shaul (1985) suggested that some of the sound correspondences proposed by Whorf and Trager may be the result of contact between Kiowa-Tanoan and the northern branch of Uto-Aztecan. Hill (2006:640–642, 2008) expands on this argument, suggesting that a number of specific words in Proto-Kiowa-Tanoan (PKT) related to maize cultivation are loans from Proto-Northern Uto-Aztecan (PNUA), and that several words for plants and animals in PNUA are loans from PKT. She suggests that this pattern is a residue of early contact between migrant, PNUA-speaking farmers from Mexico who brought maize cultivation to the Southwest, and indigenous hunter-gatherers of the Colorado Plateau who adopted farming and spoke PKT (also see Matson 2002; LeBlanc 2008). I will revisit Hill's hypothesis when I examine the age of Kiowa-Tanoan subgroups in Chapter 7.

In 1979 Irvine Davis suggested, "The working out of Kiowa-Tanoan interrelationships in more detail may shed light on Tewa prehistory and the origin of the Kiowas, among other questions" (1979:426). Unfortunately, despite universal agreement that Kiowa-Tanoan is a legitimate family, debate continues on the internal relationships of its languages. The traditional view is based on vocabulary comparisons. Harrington (1909:593) compared the 180 words in Bartlett's Piro vocabulary with corresponding forms in other Tiwa dialects, and found 59 forms that closely resembled forms in both Isleta and Taos, 29 that resembled Taos forms only, and 25 that resembled Isleta forms only. On this basis Harrington inferred that Piro, Northern Tiwa, and Southern Tiwa were three equally divergent dialects of Tiwa.[5] Using similar logic but on an impressionistic basis, Harrington (1910a, 1910b) proposed that Kiowa separated from the Tanoan group long ago, and that Tanoan subsequently split into three branches (Tiwa, Tewa, and Towa) before Tiwa split into Northern Tiwa, Southern Tiwa, and Piro. Whorf and Trager (1937) agreed with Harrington on the Tanoan dialects, and Trager (1967:339–342) agreed with Harrington's conclusions for the entire family based on phonological and grammatical comparisons.

Davis (1959) made this traditional model more concrete by comparing the percentage of basic vocabulary that is cognate among each pair of Kiowa-Tanoan languages. His results, reproduced in Table 6.1, suggest that Kiowa is the most divergent dialect, followed by Towa, then Tewa, and finally the Tiwa dialects. Based on the principle that languages that separated recently will share more vocabulary than languages that separated long ago, these data suggest that the ancestral Kiowa-Tanoan speech community first split into Kiowan and Tanoan; then Towa split from Tiwa-Tewa before Tiwa and Tewa split from each other. Finally, Tiwa diversified into Northern Tiwa, Southern Tiwa, and Piro. Davis (1959) also produced glottochronological estimates for the divergence dates of these subgroups, but most researchers, including Davis himself, now view these

TABLE 6.1. Cognate densities among Kiowa-Tanoan languages (percent)

	S. Tiwa	Piro	Tewa	Towa	Kiowa
Northern Tiwa	82.8	74.2	56.8	45.8	27.1
Southern Tiwa		71.0	56.8	47.9	22.9
Piro			56.5	45.2	?
Tewa				47.4	26.0
Towa					28.9

Source: Davis 1959:75–77.

estimates as misleading (Campbell 1997:139; Davis 1979:414; Ford et al. 1972: 36–37; Hale and Harris 1979:171; Trager 1967:339–340).

A variety of alternative views have since been proposed. One alternative alluded to by Trager (1967:338) is that the first split formed a Kiowa-Towa group and a Tiwa-Tewa group, rather than Kiowa and Tanoan groups. A second, more subtle view was developed by Davis on the basis of shared innovations in the sound systems of the languages. Based on the fact that innovations are shared among Tiwa, Tewa, and Towa, and also among Towa and Kiowa, Davis (1979: 402–403) concluded:

> Further Kiowa-Tanoan work may clarify the picture, although the possibility remains that the relationships among the languages are of the nature that one would expect from slow differentiation in a context of incomplete isolation rather than clean breaks.
>
> In summary, it appears that classifications (1) placing all four branches of Kiowa-Tanoan on par, or (2) pairing Tiwa and Tewa and/or Kiowa and Towa (with perhaps stronger evidence for the former pairing) would be compatible with presently available data. On the other hand, pairing either Tewa or Tiwa with either Kiowa or Towa would seem unrealistic.

Several researchers have leaned toward the first option suggested by Davis. Hale and Harris (1979:171) suggested that "a case could perhaps be made for the view that Kiowa is coordinate with the Tanoan branches and its apparent divergence is a result of geographic and cultural separation rather than a reflection of purely linguistic differentiation." Also with regard to Kiowa, Watkins (1984: 2) opined that "it is difficult to point to any constellation of features that might indicate a particularly long period of separation from Tanoan before the Tanoan languages split from each other." Kroskrity (1993:56) takes this argument even further, suggesting "a radical adaptive shift towards a Plains orientation on the part of the Kiowa might have produced linguistic consequences which give an unwarranted impression of great divergence from the other Kiowa-Tanoan languages," and asserting "the consensus among specialists has switched to a view of the family consisting of four coordinate branches" (Kroskrity 1993:243).

The primary difficulty with most models of Kiowa-Tanoan internal structure is that only Davis's treatment explicitly addresses shared innovations in the sound systems of the languages, which is the strongest basis for subgrouping (Campbell 1998:170; Ross 1997:220–222, 1998:153). Because it is not possible to estimate how long Tewa has been a distinct language in the absence of a well-justified subgrouping, it is necessary to further examine shared innovations in Kiowa-Tanoan to assess these proposals.

The Comparative Method and Subgrouping

In an effort to make the following analysis accessible for nonspecialists, I first introduce how one goes about establishing that a language family exists, and how one reconstructs aspects of the protolanguage as a step in identifying shared innovations.

The existence of a language family implies two historical facts. First, it implies that at some point in the past there was a social network of individuals who used the ancestral language for everyday communication. Following Ross (1997:214), I will refer to such social networks as *speech communities*. Second, the existence of a language family implies that at some point in the past the density of communication links in different parts of the ancestral communication network were reduced to such an extent that changes in the manner of speaking in one portion of the network did not spread throughout. Over time this process led to two or more dialects that were no longer mutually intelligible. Thus, to say that there is such a thing as a Kiowa-Tanoan language family is to imply, first, that somewhere and at some point in the past, there was a speech community in which Proto-Kiowa-Tanoan was the language of everyday discourse; and second, that at some point the single social network within which Proto-Kiowa-Tanoan was spoken split into several distinct networks.

Linguists use something called *the comparative method* to prove the existence of language families. Two basic properties of language change make the comparative method possible. First, phonological change in language is systematic. Languages are complex symbolic systems whose primary function is communication. Languages constantly change in response to the conditions experienced by their speakers, but because language use is so habitual and the system is so integrated, haphazard changes in pronunciation hinder rather than improve communication. As a result, the phonological aspects of language are more resistant to change than biological and cultural forms of human inheritance; related languages preserve a residue of their common origin for millennia; and the differences that gradually accumulate between them tend to be systematic in nature (Campbell 1998:16–56).

Second, languages split much more readily than they merge. When a single speech community splits into two as a result of migration or population expansion, the language of each community will change independently over time, eventually resulting in two, nonmutually intelligible dialects. But when two previously isolated speech communities come into contact, their languages do not normally blend as their genes and cultures may. Every aspect of language is influenced through contact with other languages, but in most cases it is more appropriate to speak of one language influencing another than it is to speak of two languages merging (Thomason and Kaufman 1988; Dixon 1997:11–14; Ross 1997:251–253; Bellwood 2005:196–199). In most cases of language contact, bilingualism followed by the shift of all speakers to one of the languages involved is the long-term outcome, rather than the merging of previously distinct dialects. Because languages are more resistant to blending than are genes and culture, the relationships among languages are actually more phylogenetic in nature than are biological or cultural relationships.

The comparative method builds on these twin axioms of language change to provide a means to establish that a group of languages derive from a common ancestor and to reconstruct elements of this language. The first step is to discover the phonemes, or meaningful units of sound, for each language to be compared. This is accomplished by studying the distribution of sounds in a language. When similar sounds have complementary distributions — meaning that they occur only in different phonetic environments — then the sounds in question do not represent phonemes but, instead, allophones, or different ways of pronouncing the same phoneme. However, when similar sounds occur in the same phonetic environments, and the words in these minimal pairs have different meanings, it indicates that the differences in sound are meaningful, and represent distinct phonemes. For example, in Tewa *po* means 'squash,' whereas *p'o* (pronounced with a popping *p*) means 'water'; and *pín* means 'heart' whereas *p'in* means 'mountain' (see Hoijer and Dozier 1949). On the basis of many comparisons like these, one can establish that in Tewa */p/* and */p'/* are perceived as different, meaningful sound units, and are therefore separate phonemes.

Once the phonemes are known and phonemically written vocabularies have been collected for the languages to be compared, the next step is to search for words that resemble each other in sound and meaning across these languages. If the languages being compared derive from a common ancestor, one will begin to notice systematic sound correspondences, or "sound laws," among words of similar meaning across these languages. Sound correspondences need not involve the same sound in every language; what matters is that everywhere a given phoneme appears in one language, a corresponding phoneme occurs in the second. Table 6.2 provides an example, comparing words for 'big,' 'tobacco,' and 'prickly pear' in Kiowa-Tanoan languages. The table shows that everywhere an /s/ appears in Tewa and Kiowa, a /t^y/ appears in Jemez, and a /ł/ appears in Northern Tiwa and Southern Tiwa. This pattern implies that there was a word for 'big,' 'tobacco,' and 'prickly pear' in the Proto-Kiowa-Tanoan language, and that the words in the present-day daughter languages are phonetically transformed reflexes of those original words. Such sets of words, which are similar in sound and meaning, are called *cognates*. By comparing hundreds of such sets, it is possible to define all the sound correspondences among a group of related languages.[6]

TABLE 6.2. Example of sound correspondence in Kiowa-Tanoan dialects

	TAOS (N. TIWA)	ISLETA (S. TIWA)	SAN JUAN (TEWA)	JEMEZ (TOWA)	KIOWA
'Big'	*łó* 'big'	*ła* 'big'	*só* 'big'	*tʸæ* 'wide'	*sɔ:-* 'big'
'Tobacco'	*łá* 'tobacco'	*łe* 'tobacco'	*sa:* 'tobacco'	*tʸu-ne* 'tobacco'	*sɔ́:-tóp* 'pipe'
'Prickly pear'	*łę́-* 'cactus, thorn'	*łį-feura* 'prickly pear'	*sǽ̜:* 'prickly pear'	*tʸǽ̜:* 'prickly pear, cactus'	*sę́:* 'cactus, stickers, peyote'
Correspondence	*ł-*	*ł-*	*s-*	*tʸ-*	*s-*

Sound correspondences are a residue of past changes in the way speakers in one of a group of related speech communities pronounced the words of their language. Sound changes originate from individuals who articulate a certain phoneme differently than others within their speech community. In most cases phonetic variants do not spread beyond the individuals who utter them. But in certain situations, such as the appearance of prestigious foreigners or changes in the frequency with which certain articulatory patterns occur, a variant will become favored and begin to spread to other speakers. As more speakers use the alternate pronunciation, pressure mounts on others to follow suit. Through a combination of increasing rates of adoption and generational turnover, the new pronunciation can become fixed in the speech community, and the language will have changed. The residue of this change will be systematic sound correspondences among words in the innovating dialect and in the unchanged dialect.

Once all the sound correspondences among a group of related languages have been established, the final step in the comparative method is to reconstruct the sound system of the protolanguage. Historical linguists use a number of principles to accomplish this (see Campbell 1998:114–131). The most basic principle is that of economy: all other things being equal, the proposal which requires the fewest number of sound changes is most likely to be correct. The second principle is "majority rules": all other things being equal, the sound which occurs most often in a correspondence set is the most likely to be the original sound of the protolanguage. In Table 6.1, for example, /s/ occurs in Tewa and Kiowa, whereas /ł/ occurs only in Tiwa, and /tʸ/ occurs only in Jemez. Thus, the most likely original sound in Proto-Kiowa-Tanoan was *s (the asterisk is a convention used to represent a reconstructed form).

A third principle is directionality: certain directions of change are more likely than others. For example, voiceless stops — sounds where the flow of air is cut off by the tongue or lips, and the vocal chords do not vibrate — commonly change to voiced stops between vowels, because vowels are inherently voiced.

TABLE 6.3. Analysis of Tiwa vowels

RECONSTRUCTION	TAOS	PICURIS	SANDIA	ISLETA
*i	i	e, i(w)	i	i
*e	e	e	i	i
*a	a	e, ´ia, a(j)	e, ia(j)	e
*o	o	a	a	a
*ɨ	ɨ	ɨ	ɨ	ɨ
*u	u	o, u(j)	u	u
*į	į	ę	ę	ę
*ę	ę	ę	į	į
*ą	ą	ą	ą	ą
*ǫ	ǫ	ą	ą	ą
*ɨ̨	ɨ̨	ɨ̨	ɨ̨	ɨ̨
*ų	ų	ǫ	ų	ų
*ie	i, ie	i	ie	i, ie
*ia	ia	i	ia	ia
*ɨo	ɨo	ɨ	ɨa	ɨa
*uo	uo	u	ua	ua
*įę	įę	į	ę	ę
*ɨ̨ą	ą	ą	ɨ̨ą	ɨ̨ą

Source: Trager 1942.
Note: I represent the central, close, unrounded Tiwa vowel that Trager represents as /ə/ using /ɨ/, following the recommendation of Laurel Watkins (personal communication, 2009).

Thus, /p, t, k/ often change to /b, d, g/, respectively, between vowels, but the reverse almost never happens because it takes more, rather than less, effort for a speaker to devoice a voiced stop between vowels. Another example is that the change *s* > *h* is relatively common in the world's languages, but *h* > *s* is not, because the former eases articulation of the following vowel, whereas the latter makes this articulation more difficult (Campbell 1998:115).

Two additional principles take into consideration characteristics of the reconstructed sound system overall. The first principle is that of naturalness: the reconstructed sound system should present symmetric patterns and should not imply a language inconsistent with known linguistic universals. This principle is illustrated by Table 6.3, which presents Trager's (1942) reconstruction of Proto-Tiwa vowels. In this table the columns represent dialects, and the rows represent phonemes. The data in each row are sound correspondences worked out by Trager. The left-hand column presents Trager's reconstruction of the Proto-Tiwa vowel system based on the sound correspondences in the other columns. This reconstruction is symmetrical with respect to oral and nasalized vowels (pronounced with air resonating in the nasal septum), even though it violates the "majority rules" principle in some cases.

The second, total system principle is that of no overlap: the reconstruction should not include two instances of the same sound. In Table 6.3, for example, Trager reconstructed *ǫ (a nasalized /o/) for the tenth correspondence set, even though /ą/ is the most commonly occurring sound in this set, because *ą is required for the ninth set, and /ǫ/ occurs in all phonetic environments in Taos. The alternative reconstruction would have to combine the ninth and tenth rows, and propose a Proto-Tiwa *ą which changed to /ǫ/ in certain phonetic environments in Taos, but remained /ą/ in others. Because Trager could not find any systematic basis for this change, he was forced to reconstruct two distinct phonemes for Proto-Tiwa, and infer that /ą/ merged with /ǫ/ in the other dialects. The only other alternative would have been to propose unsystematic change from /ą/ to /ǫ/ in Taos, and this would violate the axiom of regular sound change.

Once a plausible reconstruction is developed, one can compare changes that have occurred in each of the languages from the protolanguage to reconstruct the branching sequence in the history of the language family. Because language change is conservative, the most parsimonious explanation for a shared innovation is that it occurred once, before the dialects that share these innovations diverged from a common ancestor. The logic is essentially the same as that used in constructing biological phylogenies on the basis of shared derived characters. For example, in Table 6.2, the fact that /s/ corresponds to /ł/ in both Northern and Southern Tiwa suggests that the change s > ł occurred in a single language (Proto-Tiwa) descended from Proto-Kiowa-Tanoan before it split into Northern and Southern Tiwa. The strongest evidence of subgrouping occurs when a group of languages in a family share a bundle of innovations, at least some of which are highly unlikely to occur independently. Note, however, that continuity from the protolanguage is not relevant for subgrouping because this simply means that the original sound has not changed in certain of the daughter languages. In Table 6.2, for example, the fact that Proto-Kiowa-Tanoan /s/ is unchanged in Tewa and Kiowa does not suggest a closer relationship between these two dialects than between Tewa and Jemez. Analysis of shared innovations is generally accepted as the strongest basis for defining subgroups of a language family (Campbell 1998: 170; Ross 1997:220–222, 1998:153).

Shared Innovations and Kiowa-Tanoan Subgroups

With this background in place, I here examine the phonological system of Kiowa-Tanoan vis-à-vis its reflexes in various daughter languages to determine the history of diversification of these languages. In his work on Kiowa-Tanoan phonology, Hale (1967) reconstructed Proto-Kiowa-Tanoan consonants, established sound correspondences for the vowels, and identified a system of morphophonemic alternations (predictable changes in pronunciation in certain

TABLE 6.4. Kiowa-Tanoan consonant correspondences and shared innovations

PKT	TAOS	PICURIS	SANDIA	ISLETA	PROTO-TIWA	SAN JUAN	SANTA CLARA	JEMEZ	KIOWA
*p	p	p	p	p	*p	p	p	p	p
*p’	p’	p’	p’	p’	*p’	p’	p’	p’	p’
*p^h	p^h	p^h	p^h	p^h	*p^h	p^h	f	ɸ	p^h
*b	m	m	b	b	*mV̨, bV	mV̨, bV	mV̨, bV	mV̨, bV	b
*t	t	t	t	t	*t	t	t	t	t
*t’	t’	t’	t’	t’	*t’	t’	t’	t’	t’
*t^h	t^h	t^h	t^h	t^h	*t^h	t^h	θ	š	t^h
*d	nV̨, lV	nV̨, lV	nV̨ dV	nV̨ dV	*nV̨, dV	nV̨, dV	nV̨, dV	nV̨, dV	d
*c	c	c	š	š	*c	c	c	s	t
*c’	c’	c’	c’	c’	*c’	c’	c’	t’	t’[a]
*c^h	s	s	s	s	*s	s	s	š	t^h[b]
*z̨	y[c]	c	c	c	*ž̨[c]	y[c]	ž̨[c]	z	d
*k	k	k	k	k	*k	k	k	k	k[d]
*k’	k’	k’	k’	k’	*k’	k’	k’	k’	k’[d]
*k^h	x	x	k^h	k^h	*k^h	k^h	x[e]	h	k^h[d]
*g	g	—	g	g	*g	g	g	k	g
*k^w	k^w	k^w	k^w	k^w	*k^w	k^w	k^w	g	k
*$k^{w’}$	$k^{w’}$	$k^{w’}$	$k^{w’}$	k’u	*$k^{w’}$	$k^{w’}$	$k^{w’}$	g	k’
*k^w	x^w	x^w	h^w	h^w	*x^w	k^{wh}	x^w[e]	h	k^h
*g^w	w	w	w	w	*w	w	w	k^w	g
*m	m	m	m	m	*m	m	m	m	m
*n	n	n	n	n	*n	n	n	n	n
*s	ɬ	ɬ	ɬ	ɬ	*ɬ	s	s	t^y	s
*ʔ	ʔ	ʔ	ʔ	ʔ	*ʔ	ʔ	ʔ	ʔ	ʔ
*h	h	h	h	h	*h	h	h	ɦ	h
*w	w	w	w	w	*w	w	w	w	y

Sources: Kiowa-Tanoan (KT) reconstruction from Hale 1967; Proto-Tiwa reconstruction from Trager 1942.
Note: PKT = Proto-Kiowa-Tanoan. Shared innovations are indicated by shading.

[a] The change *c’ > t’ is part of a systematic change from affricates */c, c’, c^h/ to apical stops /t, t’, t^h/ in Kiowa. In Jemez two of the three affricates descended as sibilants, but the third changed in accordance with Kiowa, and is therefore considered a shared innovation (see Davis 1979:402).

[b] It is also possible that in Towa *c^h > t^h as in Kiowa before t^h > š, but there is no direct evidence. KT *c could not have merged with /t/ in Towa, as it did in Kiowa, because KT *c descended as /s/ in Towa, whereas *t descended unchanged. Regardless, the shared innovation *c’ > t’ is sufficient to demonstrate an early lectal linkage involving KT dialects.

[c] Hale noted that KT z̨ descended as /y/ in Taos and /y, ž̨/ in San Juan and Santa Clara, respectively. However, Trager (1942) reconstructed *ž̨ as the Proto-Tiwa (PTi) reflex of this phoneme. I follow Trager for the following reasons. First, the PTi reflex could not have been *c because in this case one could not account for the presence of

phonetic environments) that must have characterized the protolanguage. As a by-product, he identified the changes in consonants from the protolanguage in each of the extant dialects. Hale did not consider the implications of this reconstruction for subgrouping, but the shared innovations that it implies are useful for this purpose.

Kiowa-Tanoan Consonants

Table 6.4 presents Hale's Proto-Kiowa-Tanoan consonant reconstruction and the sound correspondences on which it is based. Hale developed this reconstruction using data from Taos, Santa Clara, San Juan, Jemez, and Kiowa. He did not include data from Southern Tiwa in a systematic way, but Taos is an appropriate representative for the Tiwa languages because Trager (1942) showed that Taos phonology is little-changed from Proto-Tiwa, and Trager (1942) and Harrington (1909) had previously demonstrated Tiwa to be a valid subgroup. I have also incorporated Trager's Tiwa correspondences and Proto-Tiwa reconstruction in this table to expand the number of dialects considered. Finally, shared innovations from Proto-Kiowa-Tanoan are indicated by shading.

An initial look at the pattern of shared innovations in Table 6.4 appears to support the traditional view of subgrouping in these languages; namely, that Kiowa diverged from the Tanoan languages first, followed by Towa and then by Tewa before the Tiwa languages diverged from each other. For example, in Tiwa, Tewa, and Towa — but not in Kiowa — Proto-Kiowa-Tanoan voiced stops (*b, *d) became corresponding nasals (m, n) before nasalized vowels. Conditional changes such as these are unlikely to occur multiple times independently,

---

/y/ and /c/ as distinct phonemes in Taos, or /c/ and /š/ in Southern Tiwa. Second, the change PTi *ž̨ > c is more natural than PTi *y > c because the former primarily involves a loss of voicing, whereas the latter also involves a change from a palatal glide to a dental affricate. Third, *z̨ and *c were ablaut partners in KT, and Hale (1967:115) reconstructed KT ablaut as involving a loss of voicing in stops. This would have provided stronger motivation for the former change than for the latter. Finally, both ž̨ and y are represented in Tewa dialects, so either phoneme is a plausible reconstruction for Proto-Tiwa-Tewa. The implication of PTi *ž̨ for present purposes is that it suggests the change *ž̨ > y occurred in both Taos and San Juan after the Tiwa dialects diverged. This shared innovation thus appears to reflect subsequent contact between the San Juan dialect of Tewa and the Taos dialect of Tiwa.

[d] Laurel Watkins (personal communication, 2008) suggests that KT velars */k, k', k^h/ have also descended as affricates /c, c', c^h/ in certain environments in Kiowa. Because these changes are restricted to Kiowa, they have no impact on the pattern of shared innovations.

[e] These innovations in Santa Clara are considered to be independent of Tiwa because in Santa Clara all aspirated stops */p^h, t^h, c^h, k^h, k^{wh}/ descended as fricatives /f, θ, s, x, x^w/, and four of these five changes occurred after the Santa Clara dialect became distinct from the San Juan dialect (Hale 1967:116–117), whereas in Tiwa aspirated stops either remained unchanged or changed individually at different stages of development.

and thus make a strong case that the changes occurred after that portion of the Proto-Kiowa-Tanoan speech community that spoke a dialect ancestral to Kiowa became isolated from the portion we can refer to as the Proto-Tanoan speech community. Three additional changes, which are shared by Proto-Tiwa and Tewa but not by Towa or Kiowa (*c^{h} > s, *z̢ > ž̢ and *g^{w} > w), suggest that the next major event in the history of these languages took place when a portion of the Proto-Tanoan speech community that spoke a dialect ancestral to Towa became isolated from the Proto-Tiwa-Tewa speech community. Finally, a number of changes reconstructible to Proto-Tiwa are absent in Tewa, Towa, and Kiowa, and additional changes occurred among the dialects of Northern Tiwa and Southern Tiwa, respectively. These changes suggest that a portion of the Proto-Tiwa-Tewa speech community which spoke a dialect ancestral to Tewa became isolated from the Proto-Tiwa speech community before the Proto-Tiwa speech community itself split into Northern Tiwa and Southern Tiwa speech communities.

However, a closer look at this table suggests a messier history than the traditional view proposes. Note, for example, that Towa and Kiowa share an innovation (*c' > t') which by itself would suggest an initial bifurcation into Tiwa-Tewa and Towa-Kiowa, as Davis (1979) suggested. Also, note that the three shared innovations which define Tiwa-Tewa as a subgroup involve Proto-Kiowa-Tanoan consonants (*c^{h}, *z̢ and *g^{w}) that also changed in Jemez. Thus, from these data, one could not rule out the possibility that the innovations shared only by Tiwa and Tewa were also originally shared with Towa but have been obscured by subsequent changes. This would in turn undermine the validity of Tiwa-Tewa as a subgroup, and would strengthen the view that Tiwa, Tewa, and Towa are coordinate branches. Finally, there is an innovation that involves San Juan Tewa and Taos. By itself, and under a strict phylogenetic interpretation, this innovation would suggest a closer genealogical relationship between Taos and San Juan Tewa than between Northern Tiwa and Southern Tiwa.

Kiowa-Tanoan Vowels

Given these inconsistent results, it may prove useful to incorporate Kiowa-Tanoan vowels into the analysis. Unfortunately, existing reconstructions of Proto-Kiowa-Tanoan vowels are not suitable for this purpose. Hale (1967) identified correspondence sets for vowels and went so far as to number these sets, but refrained from assigning them phonetic values. Hale's vowel data therefore cannot be used as is to analyze shared innovations because he did not reconstruct protovowels, which are necessary for identifying shared innovations. Davis (1989) has proposed a reconstruction of Proto-Kiowa-Tanoan vowels, but this reconstruction also has several shortcomings. First, Davis assumed that Proto-Kiowa-Tanoan had three nasalized vowels, when five are suggested by Hale's correspondence sets, and six are reconstructed for Proto-Tiwa by Trager (1942). The reduced number of nasalized vowels in Davis's reconstruction derives from his use of an unpublished analysis of Taos vowels that combined /ǫ/

and /ą/ as a single phoneme (1989:367). This led Davis to merge several of Hale's vowels, even though Hale's correspondence sets combined with Trager's Proto-Tiwa reconstruction suggest that they should be kept separate (see below). Second, Davis proposed a number of Proto-Kiowa-Tanoan diphthongs that were not noted by Hale and, by Davis's own admission, "should be regarded as highly tentative" (1989:367). It is therefore not appropriate to use these proposals in an analysis of shared innovations within Kiowa-Tanoan.

In order to incorporate information on Kiowa-Tanoan vowels in this analysis, I propose a revised reconstruction that incorporates Trager's Proto-Tiwa reconstruction (see Table 6.3) into Hale's vowel correspondence sets, and uses the principles of reconstruction described earlier in this chapter. Table 6.5 presents the data I used to develop this proposal. Each row represents a Hale vowel, and the correspondences themselves (which Hale gives for Taos, Tewa, Jemez, and Kiowa) are listed in the far right-hand columns of the table. I also list the values that Davis (1989) proposed for each Hale vowel and Trager's Proto-Tiwa reconstruction along with the Proto-Kiowa-Tanoan reconstruction proposed here. This revised reconstruction follows Davis for most of Hale's non-nasalized vowels and diphthongs, but refrains from merging Hale's V_1 and V_2 and reconstructs *æ for Hale's V_1 because Jemez /æ/ is closer than Jemez /a/ to the other reflexes of V_1 and V_2. Also, it proposes a different series for the nasalized vowels and diphthongs. Proto-Kiowa-Tanoan *ą, *ǫ and *ų are reconstructed for Hale's V̨_4, V̨_6 and V̨_2, respectively, on the basis of "majority rules"; *ǽ is reconstructed for Hale's V̨_{5a} because it is the closest front vowel of the various reflexes of V̨_{5a} and V̨_{5b} to Proto-Tiwa *į̨ę; and *ę and *į are reconstructed for Hale's V̨_3 and V̨_{1a}, respectively because these are the only plausible values among the daughter language reflexes that are not already reconstructed for other vowels, and because these values produce a more symmetrical system of nasalized and non-nasalized vowels. Finally, *įą is proposed for Hale's V̨_{1b} based on Trager's reconstruction, which shows Taos /ą/ as a reflex of Proto-Tiwa *įą.

Table 6.6 presents this reconstruction of the Hale vowels and their reflexes in Proto-Tiwa, the Tiwa dialects, San Juan Tewa, Jemez, and Kiowa. As in Table 6.4, I highlight shared innovations implied by this reconstruction in various daughter languages using shading. These data reinforce patterns seen the analysis of consonants. Although there are no innovations from the protolanguage shared by all the Tanoan dialects, there are three innovations shared by Proto-Tiwa and Tewa (*e > *i, *æ > *o, and *ǫ > *ų) for which the Proto-Kiowa-Tanoan value is unchanged in Kiowa and/or Jemez. This reinforces the view that Tiwa-Tewa is a valid subgroup of Kiowa-Tanoan which excludes Jemez and Kiowa. Also, several innovations shared among the Southern Tiwa dialects reinforce the division of Tiwa into a northern and southern group. Note, however, that the pattern of overlapping innovations observed in the consonants is also present for the vowels. One innovation is shared by Jemez and Kiowa, another is shared by Tewa and Jemez, two are shared by Tewa and one or both Northern Tiwa dialects, and two are shared by the Southern Tiwa dialects and Picuris.

TABLE 6.5. Proposed reconstruction of Kiowa-Tanoan vowels

HALE VOWEL[a]	PKT (DAVIS)	PKT[b] (PROPOSED)	PTI[c] (TRAGER)	TAOS	TEWA	JEMEZ	KIOWA
V_9	*i	*i	*i	i	i	i	e
V_4	*e	*e	*i	i	i	e (ɨ after labio-velars)	a
V_7	*a	*a	*a	a	a	æ	a
V_1	*o	*æ	*o	o	o	æ (e after velars)	ɔ
V_2	*o	*o	*o	o	o	a	ɔ
V_3	*ɨ	*ɨ	*ɨ	ɨ	a	o	a
V_6	*u	*u	*u	u	e~u[d]	ɨ	o
V_8	*ia	*ia	*ia	ia	i	e	e
V_5	*ɔa	*ɔo	*ɔo	ɔo	e~u[d]	o	o
V_{10}	*ua	*uo	*uo	uo	u	a	o
V̨$_4$	*ǫ	*ą	*ą	ą	ą	ǫ	ɔ̨
V̨$_3$	*ę	*ę	*ę	ę	æ̨	æ̨	ą
V̨$_{1a}$	*ǫ	*ɨ̨	*ǫ	ǫ	ą	į	ɔ̨
V̨$_6$	*ų	*ǫ	*ų	ų	ų	ǫ	ǫ
V̨$_2$	*ų	*ų	*ų	ų	ų	ɨ̨	ǫ
V̨$_{5a}$	*ęǫ	*æ̨	*įę	įę	æ̨	ǫ	ǫ(?)[e]
V̨$_{5b}$[f]	*ęǫ	*įę	*įę	įę	ą	ǫ	ɔ̨
V̨$_{1b}$	*ǫ	*ɔ̨ą	*ɔ̨ą	ą	ą	į	ɔ̨

Note: PKT = Proto-Kiowa-Tanoan; PTi = Proto-Tiwa.

[a] Hale identified and gave correspondence sets for each vowel but did not reconstruct phonetic values.

[b] My proposal differs from Davis's (1989) in that I have not combined any of the Hale vowels and do not include diphthongs that are absent from Hale's vowel correspondence sets.

[c] Four vowels reconstructed by Trager for Proto-Tiwa (*e, *ie, *į and *ɨ̨, see Table 6.3) do not appear in this table because they are absent from Hale's correspondence sets. Proto-Tiwa *e is attested only in noun endings in Northern Tiwa, and *ie is also poorly attested. In addition, Trager (1942:9) believed *ɨ̨ was very rare, and viewed the reversal of vowel quality involving *į and *ę in Southern Tiwa to be puzzling. There are clearly a number of unresolved issues surrounding Kiowa-Tanoan vowels, but Trager knew the Tiwa languages well, and I therefore work from his assessment in this study.

[d] I have listed Tewa /e~u/ based on widespread sound symbolism in this language in which front vowels refer to small entities, and back vowels to large entities. As a result it is not always clear which of these constitutes the original correspondence.

[e] Hale believed the Kiowa reflex of V̨$_{5a}$ to be questionable as it was based on a single correspondence set.

[f] Davis did not list V̨$_{5b}$ in his Table 2, but appears to have meant to include it under his *ęǫ. If so, the Kiowa correspondence identified by Hale for this vowel is incorrect in his Table 2.

TABLE 6.6. Kiowa-Tanoan vowel correspondences and shared innovations

Hale Vowel	PKT	Taos	Picuris	Sandia	Isleta	PTi	Tewa	Jemez	Kiowa
V_9	*i	i	e, i(w)	i	i	*i	i	i	e
V_4	*e	i	e, i(w)	i	i	*i	i	e (ɨ after labio-velars)	a
V_7	*a	a	e, ´ia, a(j)	e, ia(j)	e	*a	a	æ	a
V_1	*æ	o	a	a	a	*o	o	æ (e after velars) [a]	ʃ
V_2	*o	o	a	a	a	*o	o	a [a]	ʃ
V_3	*ɨ	ɨ	ɨ	ɨ	ɨ	*ɨ	a	o	a [b]
V_6	*u	u	o, u(j)	u	u	*u	e~u	ɨ	o
V_8	*ia	ia	i	ia	ia	*ia	i	e	e
V_5	*ɨo	ɨo	ɨ	ɨa	ɨa	*ɨo	e~u	o	o
V_{10}	*uo	uo	u	ua	ua	*uo	u	a	o
V̨$_{3}$	*ę	ę	ę	į	į	*ę	æ̨	æ̨	ą
V̨$_{4}$	*ą	ą	ą	ą	ą	*ą	ą	ǫ	ʔ̨
V̨$_{1a}$	*ɨ̨	ǫ	ą	ą	ą	*ǫ	ą [c]	į	ʔ̨
V̨$_{6}$	*ǫ	ų	ǫ	ų	ų	*ų	ų	ǫ	ǫ
V̨$_{2}$	*ų	ų	ǫ	ų	ų	*ų	ų	ɨ̨	ǫ
V̨$_{5a}$	*æ̨	įę	ɨ̨	ę	ę	*įę	æ̨	ǫ	ǫ [d]
V̨$_{5b}$	*įę	įę	ɨ̨	ę	ę	*įę	ą	ǫ	ʔ̨
V̨$_{1b}$	*ɨ̨ą	ą	ą	ɨ̨ą	ɨ̨ą	*ɨ̨ą	ą	į	ʔ̨

Note: In this chart the Tiwa dialects are listed left to right according to their geographical arrangement north to south.

[a] The Jemez reflex is the only difference in the correspondences for Hale's V_1 and V_2, and as a result, the reconstructions for these vowels are uncertain; however, it appears that either V_1 or V_2 should be reconstructed as /*o/, and as a result, the pattern of shared innovations is the same regardless of the reconstruction. Specifically, Tiwa and Tewa share an innovation, as do the three southernmost Tiwa dialects.

[b] Kiowa reflexes of Hale's V_3 in his Kiowa-Tanoan cognate sets are variable, and there is no other evidence of subsequent contact between Kiowa and Tewa, so I do not consider the correspondence with Tewa /a/ to be a shared innovation.

[c] Because the change was * ʔ̨ > ą in Tewa but *ǫ > ą in the Tiwa dialects, the changes in Hale's V̨$_{1a}$ in Tiwa and Tewa are unrelated.

[d] The Kiowa reflex of Hale's V̨$_{5a}$ only occurs in one cognate set in Hale's list, but Jemez and Kiowa also share *c' > t', and on this basis I suggest the correspondence with Jemez /ǫ/ is a shared innovation linking Jemez and Kiowa.

Interpretation of Shared Innovations

Patterns of overlapping innovations like these have caused considerable argument and anxiety in the past, but Ross (1997:222–225, 238–241, 1998:151–156) has shown that such patterns are quite common and can be explained as resulting from one of two processes. The first is called *lectal differentiation*. Clean and rapid fissioning of a single speech community into two isolated communities, as is implied by phylogenetic models of language relationship, is in fact relatively rare. The more common scenario involves the gradual differentiation of a communication network as the population of speakers grows and expands. As the density and complexity of communication links between adjacent settlement systems declines, innovations that begin in one portion of the network become less likely to spread throughout, but a few still do spread to adjacent dialects. The long-term residue of this process is a combination of shared innovations that reflect the dialects of the spreading social network and overlapping innovations that reflect linkages between adjacent dialects.

The second process is called *linkage rejoining*. This occurs when communication links between two networks (or portions of a network) are established (or reestablished) such that innovations begin to pass between adjacent dialects. Among related languages the long-term residue of this process is a pattern of changes that indicate a period of isolation between dialects before innovations began to flow between them once again. In this case, overlapping innovations are the result of renewed contact between previously isolated speakers of distinct dialects.

It is likely that sequences of lectal differentiation and linkage rejoining are responsible for the patterns of shared innovations illustrated in Tables 6.4 and 6.6. The key to understanding these data is to notice that the majority of shared innovations map onto the traditional subgroups, whereas remaining innovations link dialects that diverged in the sequence suggested by the subgroups. For example, while there are innovations shared by Kiowa and Towa, and by Towa and Tewa, there are no innovations shared by Proto-Tiwa and Towa, or by Tewa and Kiowa. This pattern of overlapping innovations suggests that the history of the Kiowa-Tanoan speech community involved aspects of all previous proposals on the internal structure of this language family. It was treelike in the sense that there are bundles of innovations that define the traditional subgroups, but it was also chainlike in the sense that innovations appear to have diffused among dialects that were spoken in adjacent speech communities, even as they gradually diverged.

Analysis of the patterns of shared innovations in Tables 6.4 and 6.6, following the methods outlined by Ross (1997, 1998), leads to an overall interpretation of the sequence of speech community events in the history of the Kiowa-Tanoan language family. This interpretation is presented in Figure 6.2. Lectal linkages are identified using Ross's convention of a double horizontal line; the innovations which define subgroups are shown in a box between the previous linkage

FIGURE 6.2. Kiowa-Tanoan speech community history.

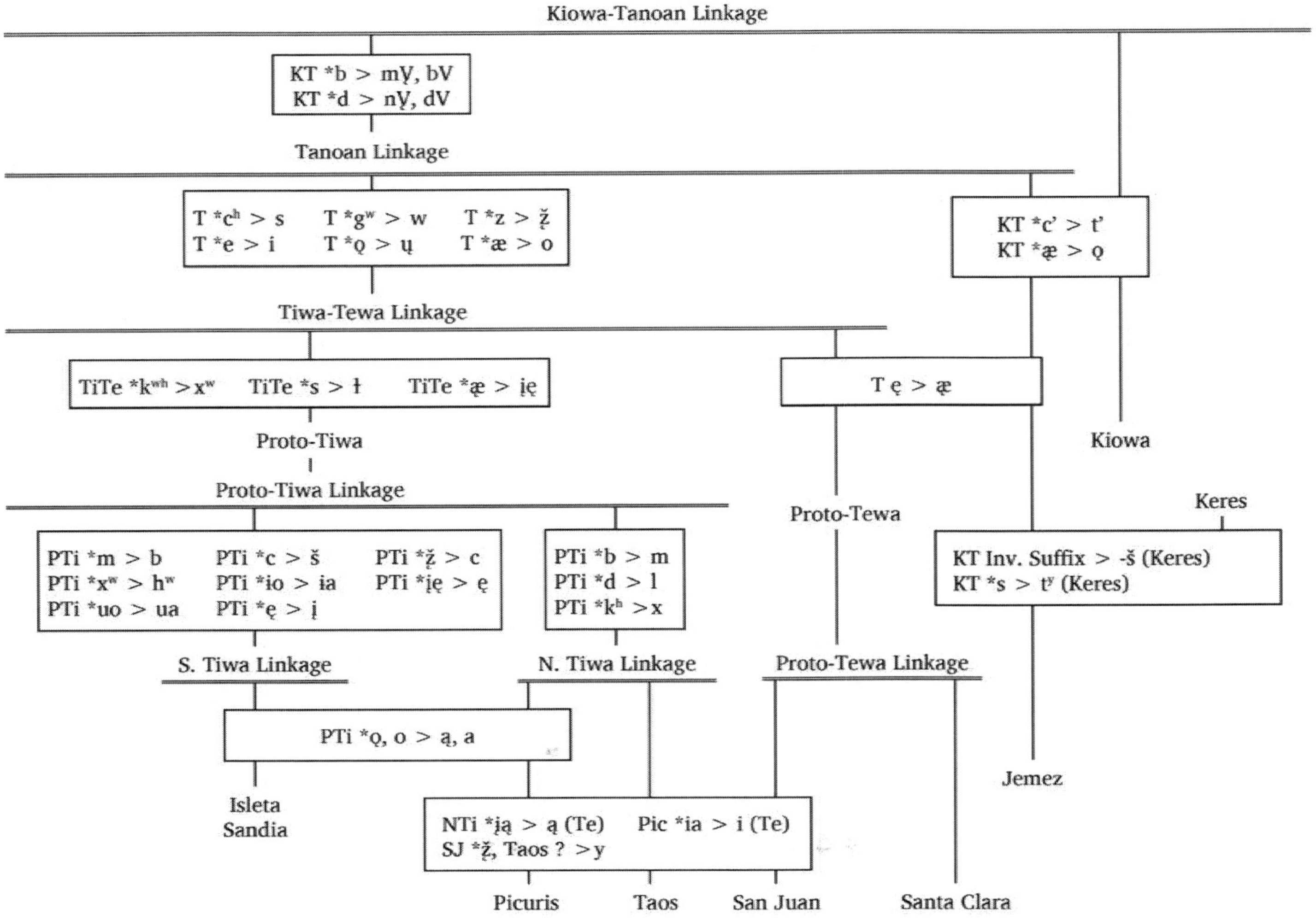

Kiowa-Tanoan Linkage

KT *b > mỴ, bV
KT *d > nỴ, dV

Tanoan Linkage

T *cʰ > s T *gʷ > w T *z > ž̧
T *e > i T *ǫ > ų T *æ > o

KT *c' > t'
KT *æ̨ > ǫ

Tiwa-Tewa Linkage

TiTe *kʷʰ > xʷ TiTe *s > ɫ TiTe *æ̨ > įę

T ę > æ̨

Kiowa

Proto-Tiwa

Proto-Tiwa Linkage

Proto-Tewa

Keres

PTi *m > b PTi *c > š PTi *ž̧ > c
PTi *xʷ > hʷ PTi *io > ia PTi *įę > ę
PTi *uo > ua PTi *ę > į

PTi *b > m
PTi *d > l
PTi *kʰ > x

KT Inv. Suffix > -š (Keres)
KT *s > tʸ (Keres)

S. Tiwa Linkage

N. Tiwa Linkage

Proto-Tewa Linkage

PTi *ǫ, o > ą, a

Isleta
Sandia

Jemez

NTi *įą > ą (Te) Pic *ia > i (Te)
SJ *ž̧, Taos ? > y

Picuris

Taos

San Juan

Santa Clara

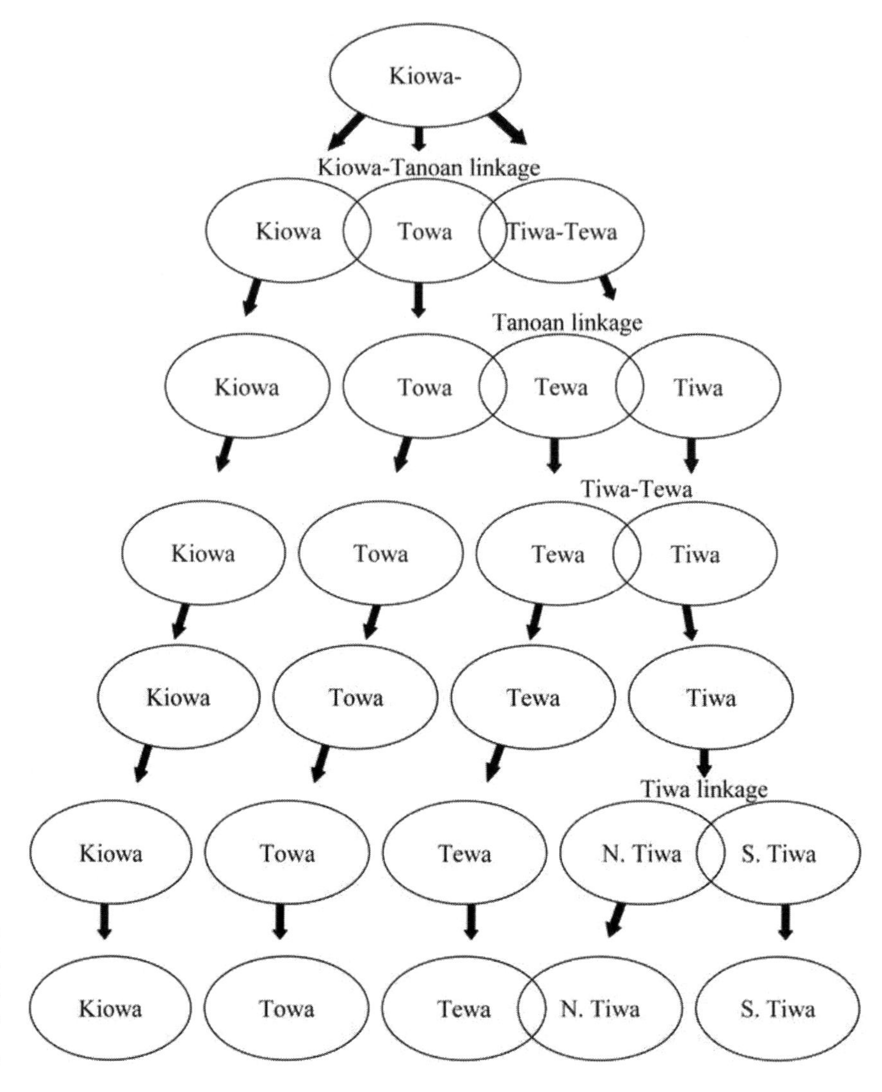

FIGURE 6.3. Schematic model of Kiowa-Tanoan speech community history.

and the innovation-defined subgroup; and innovations that reflect lectal differentiation or linkage rejoining are shown in boxes below the subgroups that diverged or rejoined during a given stage, with the box intersecting the vertical lines representing the affected dialects. Figure 6.3 presents a simplified version of this history, using ellipses to represent speech communities, and overlap in these ellipses to indicate contact between them.

These figures show that the first events in the history of the Kiowa-Tanoan speech community involved the gradual growth and differentiation of the Proto-Kiowa-Tanoan speech community into four dialects: one ancestral to Kiowa, a second ancestral to Towa, a third ancestral to the Tewa dialects, and a fourth ancestral to the Tiwa languages. These four dialects appear to have taken shape early in the history of the language family and were arranged in this order on the landscape such that innovations diffused between adjacent dialects, but not throughout the Kiowa-Tanoan network. The data also imply that these dialects formed in a sequence, with Kiowa becoming distinct first, followed by Towa, and then Tewa. They also suggest that isolation of the ancestral Kiowa dialect was not complete until after the ancestral Towa dialect had formed, and that isolation of the ancestral Towa dialect was not complete until after the ancestral Tewa dialect had formed. All of this is consistent with a model of gradual demographic and geographic expansion of Kiowa-Tanoan speech communities over many centuries, as Davis (1979:402–403) suggested.

The next major event, which is relevant for models of Tewa origins, involved a fissioning of the Tiwa-Tewa speech community into Proto-Tiwa and Proto-Tewa speech communities. Notice that this event differed from the earlier divergences in that there are no subsequent innovations shared by Proto-Tewa and either Northern Tiwa or Southern Tiwa, as was characteristic of the divergence of Kiowa from Tanoan, and Towa from Tiwa-Tewa. The absence of overlapping innovations in this case suggests the Proto-Tiwa speech community became isolated from the Proto-Tewa speech community relatively quickly, as would occur if speakers of one dialect migrated away from speakers of the other. These data are thus contrary to expectations of the in situ development and immigration models for Tewa origins because, under these models, the Tiwa-Tewa split would have taken place in the Rio Grande region. As a result, the Proto-Tewa speech community would have remained in contact with the Proto-Tiwa speech community, and one would therefore expect phonetic innovations to have diffused between these dialects as they gradually separated. However, these data are consistent with the population movement model because they suggest the Tiwa-Tewa split involved a relatively rapid fissioning of a lectal linkage into two, isolated speech communities, as would occur if Proto-Tiwa speakers migrated from the eastern San Juan drainage to the Rio Grande, leaving Proto-Tewa speakers behind. The Proto-Tiwa speech community subsequently differentiated into a lectal linkage containing the ancestral dialects of Taos, Picuris, and Southern Tiwa (and probably Piro), in that arrangement from north to south. This is indicated by the presence of three innovations linking Southern Tiwa and Picuris, which are closer geographically than are Taos and Southern Tiwa. The pattern of overlapping innovations among Tiwa dialects suggests that at one time they formed a continuous dialect chain. This inference is paralleled by the biological data discussed in Chapter 5, which suggest that the original occupants of the Rio Grande region were split into northern and southern groups by in-migrating populations from the west.

The next major event of relevance for Tewa origins involved a rejoining of portions of the earlier Tiwa-Tewa linkage. There appears to have been a period after the separation of Northern Tiwa from Southern Tiwa where innovations flowed between speakers of the eventual San Juan Tewa dialect and speakers of Northern Tiwa dialects. Three such innovations are apparent, but the clearest example is the change from Proto-Tewa *ž̯ to San Juan Tewa /y/, and a parallel change in Taos from either /ž/ or /c/ to /y/. This change occurred prior to AD 1696, under the assumption that Arizona Tewa, which shares the change *ž̨ > y, is descended from the San Juan dialect, as discussed earlier in this chapter. It is also important to note that this change did not occur in the Santa Clara Tewa dialect (which preserves Proto-Tewa and Proto-Tiwa-Tewa *ž). This suggests that the San Juan and Santa Clara dialects were already separated when the former dialect came into regular contact with Northern Tiwa speakers.

All of this is consistent with the model of Tewa dialects presented earlier, in which the Santa Clara dialect preserves the Southern Tewa speech of the Galisteo Basin, and the San Juan dialect reflects the history and contacts of Northern Tewa speakers in the Tewa Basin, because there is much less evidence of Developmental period occupation in the Galisteo Basin than there is in the Tewa Basin (Spielmann 1996). The overall picture is also consistent with the scenario suggested by biological evidence in Chapter 5; namely, that the Proto-Tiwa linkage represents early inhabitants of the Rio Grande region, that this linkage was broken in part by Tewa-speaking migrants who settled the Tewa and Galisteo basins, and that the group that settled in the Tewa Basin interacted intensively with Northern Tiwa speakers who had previously settled there.

The final speech community event I highlight here involved contact and bilingualism among ancestral Towa and Keres speakers. Keresan is a separate language family that exhibits less differentiation than Kiowa-Tanoan and has no known external relationships, but is spoken in seven extant pueblo communities, from Cochiti in the northeast to Acoma in the southwest. Ethnologists have long noted that the social organization of Jemez Pueblo, where Towa is spoken today, is far more similar to that of the Keres-speaking Pueblos than it is to the other Tanoan-speaking Pueblos (Ellis 1964b; Parsons 1925). This evidence of cultural influence is mirrored in at least two changes in Towa that appear to derive from Keres.

First, a phonological change in Towa appears to be the result of Keres influence. Towa contains a palatal stop /tʸ/ that is otherwise absent in Kiowa-Tanoan languages and is relatively rare in the world's languages overall, but is reconstructible to Proto-Keresan (Miller and Davis 1963). It is thus reasonable to hypothesize that contact with Keresan-speakers was responsible for this unique sound change in Towa.

Second, innovation in a Towa grammatical feature suggests that there was an episode in Towa speech community history where a significant number of Towa speakers were native Keres speakers. Based on shared grammatical features, it is clear that Proto-Kiowa-Tanoan had an inverse suffix which gave nouns the inverse number of their unmarked state (Speirs 1974:46; Sutton 2010; Trager 1946:204–206; Watkins 1984:78–79; Yumitani 1998:97–98). If the noun was prototypically singular, the suffix would make it plural, and if the noun was prototypically plural, the suffix would make it singular.[7] The Towa inverse suffix -š functions in a nearly identical fashion to the Kiowa inverse suffix -gɔ́, but is not cognate with the Kiowa or other Kiowa-Tanoan forms. There are, however, phonetically and functionally similar forms in Keresan. For example, the Acoma dialect of Keres does not mark inverse number in nouns; instead, all nouns are prototypically singular and the suffix -iši is added to nouns to indicate plural number (Miller 1965:148). Similar suffixes, -šɪ and -šᴇ, are members of a series of allomorphs used to indicate plural subject in the Santa Ana dialect of Keres as well (Davis 1964:86). The fact that the Towa inverse suffix is unique within Kiowa-Tanoan, but is similar phonetically to these Keres plural suffixes, suggests that at some point Towa speakers adopted the Keres plural suffix as their inverse suffix.

This sort of innovation is characteristic of a form of contact-induced change that Thomason and Kaufman (1988:38–39) call interference through shift, which occurs when a group of speakers shifting to a target language fail to learn the target language perfectly, and the errors in speaking the target language by members of the shifting group subsequently spread to the target language speech community as a whole when they are imitated by its original speakers. In this case, the direction of change implies that at some point in the past, a group of Keres speakers who were shifting to Tanoan failed to learn the noun class and inverse number marking system of Tanoan perfectly, and instead continued to use the method of indicating plural number from their native Keres language. This error led to the adoption of the Keres plural suffix as the Towa inverse suffix. One might expect such changes to occur only if the shifting Keres speakers were viewed as prestigious relative to the native Tanoan speakers.

These influences from Keres on the Towa language make a good case that at some point in the past, the ancestral Towa speech community incorporated a group of Keres speakers, and the dialect and culture of this latter group were viewed as prestigious on the part of the native Towa speakers. The fact that many aspects of Keresan social organization were also adopted by ancestral Jemez people in the past is consistent with this notion, and suggests that these social changes occurred during the same period. This period of influence could have taken place at any point from the time Towa became a distinct dialect through the early historic period, but there are clues which suggest it may have taken place as Towa diverged from Tiwa-Tewa. The change from Tanoan *s > t^y in Towa was probably due to Keres influence, and as a result Towa and Tewa cognates exhibit an s~t^y correspondence (Table 6.2). However, other changes resulted in Towa retaining /s/ in its phonemic inventory. Thus, resemblant forms in Towa and Tewa that both begin with /s/ may represent loans into one or both languages after the change *s > t^y in Towa, which is to say, after the period of Keres linguistic influence. For example, the resemblant set Towa *zǽ̨ya* 'manta' and Tewa *segá* 'white manta' probably reflects a loan from Spanish (*saco* 'a woolen jacket without sleeves' [Cobos 2003]) into both languages during the historic period. Another, potentially more significant example is Towa *sa̲de* 'quiver' and Tewa *súd̲eh* 'quiver'. The latter incorporates the Tewa form for 'arrow' (*sú*), but the former does not incorporate the Towa cognate (*tʸá:*), which is also part of the set that allows the reconstruction of Proto-Tanoan **suo* 'arrow' (Appendix A, no. 35). The implication of this is that Towa *sa̱de* 'quiver' is in fact a loan from Tewa that postdates the period of Keres influence on Towa. Because bows and arrows first appeared in the Pueblo archaeological record during the Basketmaker III period (AD 450–725), quivers for storing arrows probably date from around this period as well. Thus, the adoption of the Tewa loanword, and the period of Keres influence, could have both taken place relatively early in the history of this language.

Phonology and Genealogy

In this chapter I have introduced the Kiowa-Tanoan languages and conducted a study of their shared phonetic innovations to better understand the sequence of speech community events that produced them. The results are dependent on the accuracy of Hale's Proto-Kiowa-Tanoan consonant reconstruction, Trager's Proto-Tiwa reconstruction, my proposed phonetic values for the Hale vowels, and my construal of Tewa dialect variation.

If all four are valid, this analysis suggests that the best model of Kiowa-Tanoan speech community history lies somewhere between the traditional view — in which subgroups fissioned in a stepwise, treelike manner — and more recent views — in which the major branches of Kiowa-Tanoan diverged nearly simultaneously. The overall pattern in shared phonetic innovations is one in which most shared innovations define the traditional subgroups of Kiowa-Tanoan, but there are also innovations that link each subgroup to the closest outgroup language. This suggests that at a relatively early stage in the development of these languages, there were four dialects whose associated speech communities were arranged geographically in a chainlike manner, with the dialect ancestral to Kiowa being adjacent to the ancestral Towa dialect, ancestral Towa adjacent to Proto-Tewa, and Proto-Tewa adjacent to Proto-Tiwa.

For much of its history, it is most accurate to characterize Kiowa-Tanoan language development as a gradual process of lectal differentiation as the population of Kiowa-Tanoan speakers expanded demographically and geographically. Thus, the dialect ancestral to Kiowa gradually became isolated from the ancestral Towa dialect, and the Towa dialect from Proto-Tewa, in that sequence. However, the separation of Proto-Tewa from Proto-Tiwa was more rapid and more complete than earlier divergences, and appears to reflect the isolation of Proto-Tiwa speakers from Proto-Tewa speakers, perhaps caused by migration of one of the two groups.

After Proto-Tiwa diversified into Northern and Southern Tiwa, the portion of the Proto-Tewa speech community ancestral to the Northern (San Juan) dialect came back into contact with the Northern Tiwa speech community. The Santa Clara dialect does not share any innovations with Northern Tiwa dialects, but did undergo additional changes that did not occur in Northern (San Juan)

Tewa. In addition, current evidence suggests that the Arizona Tewa dialect descended from the San Juan dialect. These findings are consistent with nonlinguistic indications that Santa Clara Tewa preserves the Southern Tewa dialect of the Galisteo Basin, and that Arizona Tewa originated in AD 1696 when a group of Northern Tewa speakers migrated to the Hopi mesas.

Finally, at some point after Towa became isolated from the other Kiowa-Tanoan languages, Towa speakers absorbed a group of prestigious Keres speakers into their community, leading to linguistic and cultural changes that made Jemez culture and the Towa language more similar to Keresan language and culture than it had been previously. This period of influence may have occurred soon after Towa became distinct from Tiwa-Tewa.

Sequences of speech community events like the one developed here are detailed enough to provide some basis for linking with the archaeological record, as Ross has argued in various publications (1997, 1998). For example, this reconstruction contradicts expectations of the in situ development and immigration models of Tewa origins because, under both models, Proto-Tewa would have differentiated from Proto-Tiwa in the Rio Grande region. If this had occurred, the differentiating dialects would have remained in regular contact, and one would therefore expect Northern Tiwa and Proto-Tewa to share phonetic innovations, yet no such innovations are evident.

In contrast, this reconstruction is consistent with the population movement hypothesis because it suggests Proto-Tewa was a single speech community that diversified only after a period of isolation from Proto-Tiwa, when San Juan Tewa speakers came in contact with Northern Tiwa speakers. This pattern is consistent with Reed's (1949) model, in which Tewa speakers inserted themselves within the Tiwa dialect chain, splitting the latter into northern and southern groups. Notice also that if, in fact, Mesa Verde migrants spoke Proto-Tewa, the sequence reconstructed here would be consistent with the view suggested by biological evidence; namely, that migrants who entered the Tewa Basin and developed the Northern (San Juan) Tewa dialect came into regular contact with existing, Tiwa-speaking inhabitants of this area, whereas migrants who entered the Galisteo Basin and developed the Southern (Santa Clara) Tewa dialect entered a relatively empty landscape. Although these parallels are suggestive, one would have an even stronger basis for correlating linguistic and archaeological sequences if the speech community events identified through this analysis were dated reasonably well. This is the topic to which I turn next.

Notes

1. In fact, a range of nonlinguistic evidence suggests that the language of Pecos was more closely related to Southern Tewa than to Towa: (1) the biological evidence presented in Chapter 5 suggests that the Pecos population was more closely related to ancestral Tewa populations than to the ancestral Jemez population; (2) a shrine assemblage characteristic of other Tewa Basin villages exists at Rowe Pueblo, a Late Coalition period village in the Pecos Valley (Anschuetz 1999); (3) the governor of

Pecos Pueblo in 1731 was a Southern Tewa (Kessell 1987:541, n. 32); (4) no actual documentation of the language spoken at Pecos has been obtained; and (5) the last inhabitants of Pecos moved to Jemez only after a failed attempt to resettle at Sandia, and after a few remained at Santo Domingo, the same village to which the last remnants of Pueblo Galisteo, a Southern Tewa village, had moved in 1794 (Harrington 1916:477).

2. For a discussion of the evidence supporting a distinction between Santa Clara Tewa and San Juan Tewa, see Ortman 2009:215–216 n. 47).
3. For a discussion of alternative views of Tewa dialect variation, see Ortman 2009:217 n. 48).
4. Harrington did not distinguish San Juan /y/ from Santa Clara /ž̧/ in his writings. Although he appears to have transcribed Tewa in the Santa Clara dialect, the fact that he did not distinguish dialects makes it impossible to determine whether this short vocabulary from Pueblo Galisteo reflects San Juan or Santa Clara pronunciation.
5. Leap (1971) has argued that Piro became distinct from Tiwa as a result of influence from a non-Tanoan language.
6. In addition to discovering sound correspondences, it is also important to look for correspondences in grammar and morphology among putatively related languages to confirm that they do in fact derive from a common protolanguage. In Kiowa-Tanoan, for example, a striking detail that confirms its validity as a language family is a pattern of alternations between related sounds in certain circumstances that Hale (1967) was able to reconstruct for the protolanguage.
7. Sutton (2010) provides the most comprehensive description and analysis available of the noun class and number marking systems in all extant Kiowa-Tanoan languages. These systems involve four noun classes, a three-way number distinction (singular, dual, and plural [3+]), and noun suffixes and pronominal prefixes on verbs. That these systems are so complex, share so many features, and are so rare in languages overall strongly reinforce Kiowa-Tanoan as a proven language family, and indicate that Proto-Kiowa-Tanoan must have had such a system.

Homelands and Dating of Kiowa-Tanoan Subgroups

Shared phonetic innovations indicate that, in addition to the Proto-Kiowa-Tanoan speech community itself, a number of intermediate speech communities existed at various points in the history of diversification of Kiowa-Tanoan languages. In this chapter I use reconstructed vocabulary to date and roughly locate these proto-speech communities. I focus on words for concrete objects, especially words for material culture, cultigens, and plants and animals to delimit the Kiowa-Tanoan homeland and date Kiowa-Tanoan subgroups. This analysis is necessary because it answers the question of whether the Tewa language could have originated outside the Rio Grande region. If the Tewa language had not become distinct prior to the depopulation of the Mesa Verde region, it would be unlikely to have originated anywhere but the Rio Grande region. If, on the other hand, it was already distinct prior to the beginning of the Coalition period, it could have originated elsewhere.

This chapter is an exercise in linguistic paleontology, which is essentially the use of historical linguistic findings to make inferences about where and when a protolanguage was spoken and what the culture of its speakers was like (Campbell 1998:339; Sapir 1949 [1916]:432–460). Such methods have been widely used in the investigation of large and diverse language families such as Indo-European (Campbell 1998:34–345; Mallory 1989; Renfrew 1987; Anthony 2007), Athapaskan (Sapir 1936), Uto-Aztecan (Fowler 1972, 1983, 1996; Hill 2001), and Polynesian (Kirch and Green 2001). They can be equally well applied to smaller families, but only one study that applies these methods to Kiowa-Tanoan has been published to date (Hill 2008). Thus, Davis's (1979:427) statement that for Pueblo languages, a "systematic follow-up of Sapir's (1916) suggestions...would still be relevant with respect to fully exploiting linguistic clues to prehistory," still rings true.

To redress this problem, I first discuss the logic behind and implications of the reconstructed forms I developed for this study. I then consider two approaches to defining the homeland of the Proto-Kiowa-Tanoan speech community as a step in evaluating where Tewa became a distinct language. Both methods point to a homeland within the northern reaches of the Pueblo culture area. Finally, I consider terms related to cultigens and material culture that are reconstructible to various stages in the breakup of Kiowa-Tanoan, and correlate these terms with the appearance of these items in the archaeological record, to estimate when various subgroups of Kiowa-Tanoan formed.

Reconstructing Kiowa-Tanoan Vocabulary

The analysis in this chapter relies on reconstructions of terms related to plants, animals, and material culture for various subgroups of Kiowa-Tanoan. A number of such terms have been reconstructed in previous works (Whorf and Trager 1937; Hale 1967, n.d.; Davis 1989; Hill 2008), but previous investigators have not considered the implications of subgrouping for these reconstructions. The forms reconstructed by Whorf and Trager (1937), for example, did not consider evidence from Kiowa, and thus are only securely reconstructed to Proto-Tanoan.[1] Hale's (n.d.) Kiowa-Tanoan cognate list also assumes that the presence of cognates in dialects from two of the four major branches (Kiowa, Towa, Tewa, and Tiwa) is sufficient to reconstruct a Kiowa-Tanoan form, even though this is not necessarily true, because the major branches of Kiowa-Tanoan did not diversify simultaneously. Finally, previous reconstruction work has not been geared toward ecological and cultural vocabulary per se, and as a result, previous work has not exhausted the possibilities in the available material for these languages. It is therefore necessary to reconstruct additional ecological and cultural vocabulary working from available lexical data and using the reconstruction of Kiowa-Tanoan phonology presented in Chapter 6.

Using these sources, I have reconstructed 101 forms and associated meanings for various subgroups of Kiowa-Tanoan. The cognate sets, reconstructions, sources of lexical data, and cross-references to previous reconstruction efforts are presented in Appendix A.[2] The logic used to reconstruct these forms follows from the treelike aspects of Kiowa-Tanoan speech community history. Because Kiowa appears to have been the first dialect to become isolated from the rest, Proto-Kiowa-Tanoan reconstructions must be based on cognates in Kiowa and at least one Tanoan language. By the same logic, Proto-Tanoan reconstructions are based on the presence of cognates in Towa and at least one other Tanoan language, and the absence of a Kiowa cognate; Proto-Tiwa-Tewa reconstructions are based on the presence of cognates in Tewa and either Northern Tiwa or Southern Tiwa, and the absence of cognates in Kiowa and Towa; and Proto-Tiwa reconstructions are based on the presence of cognates in Northern Tiwa and Southern Tiwa, and the absence of cognates in other languages.[3]

Several aspects of these reconstructions require comment. First, one must keep in mind limitations in the available data and in my ability to identify cognates. A dictionary comparable in scope to the one recently produced for Hopi (Hill 1998) is not available for any Kiowa-Tanoan language. Thus, it is not possible to know whether the absence of a cognate for a given form in a given language is due to true absence, vocabulary replacement, or missing data. Also, although I have made a serious effort to comb all major available sources of lexical material for Kiowa, Jemez Towa, San Juan Tewa, Taos (Northern) Tiwa, and Isleta (Southern) Tiwa — and have probably identified many of the obvious relevant cognates in this material — additional cognates are likely present but difficult to spot due to morphophonemic processes that distort the systematic sound correspondences among these languages. The reconstructions in Appendix A should therefore not be taken as a comparative lexicon for these languages. It is simply a list of cognates and associated noncognate forms I have identified in the available sources of lexical material that are relevant for my purposes. Readers may imagine additional terms that would be useful for dating and locating Kiowa-Tanoan subgroups that are absent from Appendix A. Their absence may indicate that no cognates are present in the available lexical material, that appropriate forms for comparison are not present, or that I have not examined words for these items. Despite these shortcomings, I believe the data in Appendix A are sufficient to identify chronological and locational patterns related to the differentiation of Kiowa-Tanoan subgroups.

Second, it is important to keep in mind that terms reconstructible to lower-order subgroups of Kiowa-Tanoan may in fact date to higher-order subgroups, with the supporting evidence having been lost through vocabulary replacement. This problem is most significant for Proto-Tanoan reconstructions because: (1) Kiowa is the only outgroup language in which to search for cognates; (2) although there has been recent contact between Kiowa and Taos people,[4] Kiowa speakers were isolated from Tanoan speakers for many centuries; (3) Kiowa speakers have lived along the front range of the Rocky Mountains for at least three centuries (Harrington 1939; Meadows 2008); and (4) present-day Kiowa culture is more akin to that of other Plains tribes than to the Pueblo Southwest. The problem of vocabulary replacement is less severe for Proto-Tiwa-Tewa and Proto-Tiwa reconstructions because in these cases there are two or three outgroup languages in which to search for cognates, separation times are shorter, and at least one of the outgroup languages is still spoken in one or more Pueblo communities of the Southwest. Thus, the probability of cognates being replaced independently in two or three languages which have been separated from the subgroup for progressively shorter periods of time is fairly low. Following this same logic, it is reasonable to conclude that Tiwa-Tewa reconstructions could conceivably date to Tanoan, but not likely to Kiowa-Tanoan, and that Tiwa reconstructions could conceivably date to Tiwa-Tewa, but not likely to Tanoan or Kiowa-Tanoan. As I will show, this chain of reasoning makes it possible to construct statistical tests to evaluate the dating significance of reconstructed vocabulary.

Third, despite limitations in the available data, the nature of linguistic reconstruction, and limitations in understanding of more subtle details of Kiowa-Tanoan phonology such as tone and stress, it is nevertheless true that reconstructed vocabulary represents the closest thing to written texts that archaeologists will ever have for reconstructing ancestral Pueblo culture and history.[5] Archaeological method and theory have undergone a rapid maturation process over the past 50 years, and today archaeology is a distinct branch of social science that allows researchers to reliably infer certain aspects of past human behavior from material remains. Archaeologists continue to struggle, however, with reliable methods for inferring the cultural models that structured this behavior. Linguistic reconstruction helps with this problem, providing direct evidence of the culture and worldview of people who lived in the archaeological sites at which a protolanguage was spoken. The reconstructions in Appendix A approximate words that were actually spoken at ancestral Pueblo sites. In fact, some of them appear to have been uttered in some of the earliest farming communities in the U.S. Southwest. Even though these reconstructions are phonetic idealizations, lacking details that must have been present in the actual language, it is truly remarkable that one can pronounce, however stiffly, words that were spoken by Pueblo people who in some cases lived more than 2,000 years ago. Linguistic reconstructions represent strong and direct evidence of the language and culture of past societies. My hope is that this chapter will encourage historical anthropologists to pay more attention to them.

Kiowa-Tanoan Homelands

The "homeland" of a language family refers to the geographical area over which the protolanguage of that family was spoken. The protolanguage of every language family must have been spoken in a single speech community located in a contiguous geographical area. Thus, the existence of a Kiowa-Tanoan language family implies that there was a definable geographic area within which people who communicated using Proto-Kiowa-Tanoan actually lived. One technique commonly used to estimate the area over which a protolanguage was spoken is referred to by Campbell (1998:352) as "linguistic migration theory." This technique combines two principles to estimate the geographical area in which a protolanguage was spoken. The first is called the "center of gravity" principle (Sapir 1949 [1916]:452–458), which states that the homeland of a language family tends to be in the area where the most members of higher-order subgroups of a language family occur, and that the distribution of lower-order subgroups reflects the direction of later migration or spread of speech communities in the family. The second, known as the "least moves" principle, states that the homeland is also most likely to be in the area that would require the fewest number of migrations to produce the resulting distribution of languages. The underlying assumption of both principles is that when a language family diversifies, the various daughter languages are more likely to stay close to the region where they diversified as opposed to moving very far or very frequently (Campbell 1998:352).

Linguistic migration theory has been used to postulate the homeland of the Athapaskan (Sapir 1949 [1916]:456–457) and Austronesian (Bellwood 2005:

227–229) language families, but may be misleading in the case of Uto-Aztecan (Fowler 1972; Hill 2001; Lamb 1958; Miller 1986) and Indo-European (Anthony 2007; Mallory 1989; Renfrew 1987), depending on one's point of view. When this technique is applied to Kiowa-Tanoan, it appears to produce inconsistent results. On the one hand, representatives of all major branches of Kiowa-Tanoan, with the exception of Kiowa, are spoken in the Rio Grande region today (see Figure 6.1). This has led several scholars (Foster 1996; Hale and Harris 1979:174; Trager 1967:347–348) to conclude that the Kiowa-Tanoan homeland was within the Rio Grande region. This, in turn, supports the hypothesis that Tewa diverged from Tiwa within this region, and thus the in situ and immigration models of Tewa origins. On the other hand, the fact that Kiowa is spoken far from the Rio Grande region; that Kiowa, Towa, and Tiwa-Tewa differentiated gradually, whereas Tiwa and Tewa did not; and that all Tiwa dialects are spoken within the Rio Grande region could also be taken as evidence for a spread of the language family from the San Juan drainage toward the Rio Grande. This would support a Kiowa-Tanoan homeland outside the Rio Grande.

The "least moves" principle does little to clarify the picture. It certainly would not have required very many moves for the Kiowa-Tanoan languages to reach their historic distribution if their homeland were within the Rio Grande; however, the distribution of the Tiwa and Tewa speech communities is difficult to reconcile with the model that Tewa, Northern Tiwa and Southern Tiwa developed in situ (Davis 1979:417). If this had occurred, one would expect the Northern Tiwa and Southern Tiwa speech communities to have ended up adjacent to each other, with Tewa to one side. Instead, Northern Tiwa and Southern Tiwa are spoken at opposite ends of the Rio Grande, with Tewa, Towa, and Keres in between. This distribution could have resulted in one of two ways (see Davis 1979:415–416). First, a group of Tiwa speakers could have migrated northward from the Southern Tiwa area, through or around other speech communities, at some point after the Tiwa-Tewa split (Davis 1959:81; Wendorf 1954). Second, in-migrating groups from the west, including Tewa speakers, could have split the Tiwa dialect chain into northern and southern groups (Reed 1949). The early Kiowa-Tanoan linkage — with dialects ancestral to Kiowa, Towa, Tewa, and Tiwa arranged in that order on the landscape — could be accommodated to either scenario.[6]

Given these conflicting results, it may prove worthwhile to cite Campbell's (1998:359–360) caution regarding linguistic migration theory:

> It is not difficult to imagine rather straightforward situations in which linguistic migration theory would fail to produce reliable results. For example, suppose a language family with a number of subgroups had once been found in one geographical area, but something forced all their speakers to abandon that area, say, a volcanic eruption, a drought, an epidemic or the onslaught of powerful aggressors. In such a case, it is possible that many of the migrating

> speakers of the different subgroups could end up bunched relatively closely together in a new area, particularly if driven until they encountered some serious obstacle such as insurmountable mountains, an ocean, inhospitable lands without sufficient subsistence resources, or other peoples who prevented entry into their territory.... In such scenarios, it is in principle possible that we might find that the greatest linguistic diversity would in fact not be in the original homeland, but in the new area where the groups came to be concentrated.

Campbell's comment may well be applicable to the Kiowa-Tanoan language family. In fact, it reflects one interpretation of linguistic migration theory for Kiowa-Tanoan so well that he may have had it in mind when he wrote this passage.

A second method commonly used to establish a homeland is to consider the natural habitats of the plants and animals for which terms are reconstructible in the protolanguage (e.g., Anthony 2007: Chap. 5; Campbell 1998: Chap. 15; Fowler 1983; Kirch and Green 2001: Chap. 4; Mallory 1989: Chap. 6). It is reasonable to infer that an ancestral speech community was located in an area where the historic ranges of these species overlap. Table 7.1 presents Proto-Kiowa-Tanoan and Proto-Tanoan reconstructions for plants and animals taken from Appendix A. These data contain several clues regarding the early locations of Kiowa-Tanoan speakers. First, the list of plants reconstructible to Proto-Tanoan or Proto-Kiowa-Tanoan includes many of the major species found in middle- and upper-elevation contexts in the western United States, from cottonwood, pinyon, juniper, yucca, and prickly pear to Gambel oak, ponderosa pine, aspen, and spruce. The environment suggested by this list is mirrored by several terms for middle- and high-elevation fauna, including skunk, deer, bighorn sheep, wolf, and elk. This suggests that early Kiowa-Tanoan speakers lived in upland environments, most likely adjacent to the Rocky Mountains.

Second, Figure 7.1 presents the distributions of three plant species, all of which have reconstructible terms in Proto-Kiowa-Tanoan. Taken together, these data suggest that the Kiowa-Tanoan homeland was in the northern U.S. Southwest. Gambel oak (*Quercus gambelii*) occurs in upland environments throughout the U.S. Southwest, including western Colorado and Utah. Blue and Englemann's spruce (*Picea pungens* and *englemannii*), on the other hand, occur only in alpine environments and are rare south of the Jemez and Sangre de Cristo mountains in the Rio Grande drainage (Little 1971–1978). Finally, the wild potato species *Solanum jamesii* occurs throughout the U.S. Southwest but has a northern boundary corresponding to the northern San Juan drainage (Bamberg, et al. 2003). The distributions of these three species overlap most extensively in the northern San Juan and Rio Grande drainages, whereas wild potato does not occur in areas to the north, and spruce is rare in areas to the south. Thus, the present-day distributions of these specific species suggest that the Kiowa-Tanoan homeland was somewhere in the northern U.S. Southwest.

TABLE 7.1. Proto-Kiowa-Tanoan and Proto-Tanoan terms for plants and animals

I. PROTO-KIOWA-TANOAN[a]	II. PROTO-TANOAN[b]
a. Wild plants	**a. Wild plants**
21. *´*eya* 'willow'	53. *p^h*uol-* 'yucca'
22. **sę* 'prickly pear'	54. **t'o* 'pinyon nut'
23. **siw-* 'wild onion'	55. *g^w*ę* 'ponderosa'
24. *k^w*ę* 'oak'	56. **nǫ-* 'aspen'
25. **tu* 'cottonwood'	57. **hų* 'juniper'
26. **k'uo* 'spruce'	
90. **sęgo* 'wild potato'	
b. Wild animals	**b. Wild animals**
27. *k^w*œl* 'coyote, wolf'	58. **ti* 'elk'
28. **kiu* 'prairie dog'	59. **k'uo* 'bighorn sheep'
29. *k'^w*uo* 'jackrabbit'	60. **sǫ* 'skunk'
30. **t'o* 'antelope'	62. **ce* 'eagle'
31. **pę* 'deer'	63. **pi* 'fish'
32. **kol-* 'bison'	
33. **kodo* 'crow' (?)[c]	
34. *k^h*œwį* 'grasshopper' (?)[c]	

Note: Sound correspondences for reconstructions are as given in Tables 6.4 and 6.6. Reconstructed forms are numbered in accordance with Appendix A, which provides the data on which these reconstructions are based, and cross-references the work of other researchers.

[a] Terms reconstructed for Proto-Kiowa-Tanoan possess cognates in Kiowa and at least one other language.

[b] Terms reconstructed for Proto-Tanoan possess cognates in Towa and either Tiwa or Tewa. The binomial probability that Kiowa cognates never did exist for all five Proto-Tanoan wild plants, given that Kiowa shares about 26 percent of its basic vocabulary with other Kiowa-Tanoan languages (see Table 6.1), is .22. Thus, one cannot rule out the possibility that cognates for these five items have been replaced in Kiowa.

[c] These reconstructions are questionable, for the reasons stated in Appendix A.

Before accepting this conclusion, however, it is important to address two details of Table 7.1 that may suggest an alternative location. First, several terms for high desert and alpine trees — including pinyon, juniper, ponderosa pine, and aspen — reconstruct only to Proto-Tanoan, which means that they lack Kiowa cognates. Second, several animal names that do reconstruct to Kiowa-Tanoan — including terms for jackrabbit, antelope, and bison — refer to species that prefer open grassland environments. One could take the environmental differences suggested by these Proto-Kiowa-Tanoan versus Proto-Tanoan terms as a reflection of real differences in the locations of these two speech communities. In this scenario, Proto-Kiowa-Tanoan would have been spoken in a relatively open grassland environments east or north of the Colorado Plateau, and the subsequent development of the Kiowa-Tanoan linkage would have involved the spread of speakers toward the mountains of southwest Colorado or north-central New Mexico.

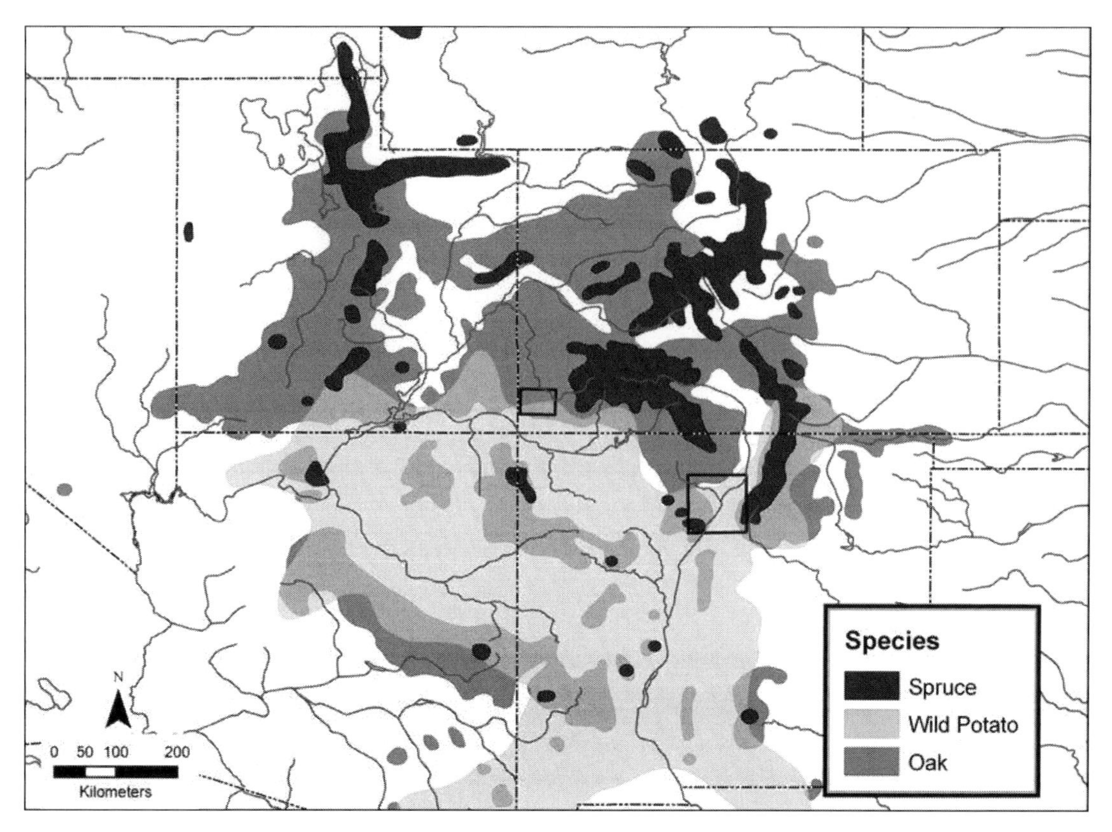

FIGURE 7.1. Distribution of plant species with Kiowa-Tanoan terms. The Tewa Basin and Village Ecodynamics Project study areas are shown as open black rectangles. (The wild potato [*Solanum jamesii*] distribution is based on Bamberg et al. 2003, courtesy of Scott Ure. The blue spruce and Gambel oak distributions are from Little 1971–1978, available at http://esp.cr.usgs.gov/data/atlas/little/.)

I believe this scenario is less plausible than the first for the following reasons. In the case of the plant names, vocabulary replacement is a reasonable interpretation for the Tanoan terms that lack Kiowa cognates because there is no consistent environmental difference suggested by the list of Tanoan versus Kiowa-Tanoan species, and it is not possible to rule out vocabulary replacement based on the number of terms involved and the percentage of vocabulary that Kiowa still shares with Tanoan (see Table 7.1, note b). Also, in the case of animal terms, although they prefer open grassland environments, bison, jackrabbit, and antelope did range over the northern U.S. Southwest in the past and have been found in archaeological sites in this area.

Thus, the most reasonable interpretation of the data in Table 7.1 is that the entire list reflects the environment experienced by Proto-Kiowa-Tanoan speakers. This implies that Proto-Kiowa-Tanoan was spoken in a region where people had regular access to montane forests, pinyon-juniper woodlands, and open grasslands. Consequently, the most plausible locations for the Kiowa-Tanoan homeland lie along the margins of the high mountains of the northern U.S. Southwest, including the Sangre de Cristos, the Jemez, and the southern and western slopes of the San Juans in New Mexico and Colorado.

This scenario does not rule out the Northern San Juan or the Northern Rio Grande as potential homelands for the Tanoan languages, including Tiwa and Tewa, but it does argue against the Southern Plains, the Central Rockies, and the Rio Grande drainage south of Albuquerque. Also, given that the San Juan drainage was occupied by Pueblo peoples earlier in time than the Northern Rio Grande, it may be possible to rule out the latter region as a homeland based on the age of subgroups suggested by reconstructed vocabulary.

Dating Kiowa-Tanoan Subgroups

In the remainder of this chapter, as a step in determining whether Tewa could have originated in the Mesa Verde region, I estimate when various Kiowa-Tanoan subgroups formed. As stated earlier, the Tewa language would have to have become distinct prior to AD 1200, when migration into the Tewa Basin began, for this language to have originated anywhere other than the Northern Rio Grande region.

One method for estimating the age of subgroups is glottochronology, a technique that estimates the length of time that two related languages have been separated, based on the percentage of vocabulary that is cognate between them. This method assumes that the rate of replacement of "basic" vocabulary is roughly constant across languages and over time, and that the residue of common ancestry between two related languages will decay in a fashion analogous to radioactive decay.

Several researchers have used this method to estimate time depths for Kiowa-Tanoan subgroups. Davis (1959:74–77) produced the earliest glottochronological study of these languages based on the 100-word list of basic vocabulary items developed by Morris Swadesh (1955) (see Table 6.1). His estimates, which are presented in Table 7.2, suggest that Kiowa and Tanoan diverged more than 4,000 years ago; Towa from Tiwa-Tewa about 2,500 years ago; Tiwa from Tewa about 1,800 years ago; and Northern Tiwa from Southern Tiwa about 600 years ago. Hale and Harris (1979:171) used updated information to calculate a more modest estimate of 3,000 years for the separation of Kiowa from Tanoan, and 2,000 to 2,500 years for the diversification of Tanoan.

These estimates suggest that Kiowa became isolated from Tanoan prior to the adoption of full-time agricultural subsistence in the northern U.S. Southwest (Matson 2002, 2006); however, this scenario is contradicted by studies of reconstructed vocabulary, most of which suggest that Proto-Kiowa-Tanoan was spoken by an agricultural group (Brown 2006; Campbell 2002; Hill 2006, 2008). Fortunately, most linguists today view glottochronological estimates as coarse at best, and misleading at worst, so errors on the order of 1,000 years or more are not unexpected. Researchers continue to propose refinements of the method (see, for example, chapters in Renfrew et al. 2000), and even the most

TABLE 7.2. Glottochronological time depths (years) for Kiowa-Tanoan languages

	S. TIWA	PIRO	TEWA	TOWA	KIOWA
Northern Tiwa	595	985	1,790	2,470	4,130
Southern Tiwa		1,085	1,790	2,330	4,660
Piro			1,809	2,516	?
Tewa				2,470	4,230
Towa					3,930
Average	595	1,015	1,796	2,446	4,238

Note: Estimates were calculated by Davis (1959) using the cognate densities in Table 6.1 and the formula $t = \log C / 2 \log r$, where t represents the time depth in millennia, C represents the cognate density between two dialects, and r represents the retention rate of basic vocabulary. Davis (1959:75) set $r = 85.4\%$ per 1,000 years.

strident critics continue to cite glottochronological estimates along with the requisite disclaimers.[7] Linguists have also continued to work with cognate percentage data to define subgroups using the more basic principle that more similar languages are more closely related (see papers in Forster and Renfrew 2006). Nevertheless, it has become clear that shared innovations are more reliable for defining subgroups, and that other tools of linguistic paleontology are more reliable for estimating the time depths of these subgroups (Anthony 2007: Chap. 5; Campbell 1998:339–368; Fowler 1983; Hill 2001; Kirch and Green 2001: Chap. 4; Mallory 1989:143–185). Thus, I will utilize such methods here to estimate the time depths of Kiowa-Tanoan subgroups.

The technique that has proven most reliable for dating subgroups is known as the *Wörter und Sachen*, or "words and things," approach (Sapir 1949 [1916]). The principle behind this method is that when one can reconstruct a word for a cultural item in a protolanguage, one can also assume that the associated item was known to the speakers of that language. If it is also possible to date the initial appearance of the item using archaeological evidence, one can argue that the protolanguage diversified after the introduction of that item. Terms for cultigens and material culture are most useful for this type of analysis, and together provide one of the strongest and most direct links between archaeology and language.

The speech community history developed in Chapter 6 suggests that there are four potentially datable subgroups in the Kiowa-Tanoan language family: Kiowa-Tanoan itself, Tanoan, Tiwa-Tewa, and Tiwa. These four subgroups reflect the long-term differentiation of the ancestral speech community and occurred in the sequence given. If the speech community events behind this sequence occurred in the Southwest, and reconstructible vocabulary is useful for dating these events, it should be possible to identify words for cultigens and material culture items that map onto culture trait inventories of archaeological sequences in potential Kiowa-Tanoan homelands, including the San Juan and Rio Grande drainages. Because these sequences are some of the best-dated in the world, this procedure should provide a strong basis for correlating Kiowa-Tanoan speech community history with absolute dates.

In Appendix B I list terms related to cultigens and material culture (taken from Appendix A) that are reconstructible to various subgroups of Kiowa-Tanoan, and discuss evidence for the earliest appearance of each item in the archaeological record of the northern U.S. Southwest. Because many of these reconstructions refer to perishable items, the discussion in Appendix B leans heavily on reports of excavations in dry caves and alcoves across the Colorado Plateau. The major sources I consulted in preparing the appendix include reports on Hogup Cave, Danger Cave, Cowboy Cave, and a number of sites in the Fremont drainage for Archaic and Fremont material culture (Aikens 1970; Jennings 1957, 1980; Morss 2009 [1931]); the Falls Creek rockshelters and Tabeguache caves in southwestern Colorado for Eastern Basketmaker II (Hurst 1940, 1941, 1942, 1944, 1945, 1947; Morris and Burgh 1954); Sand Dune Cave (Lindsay et al. 1968) and White Dog Phase sites near Marsh Pass, Arizona (Guernsey 1931; Guernsey and Kidder 1921; Kidder and Guernsey 1919) for Western Basketmaker II; the Prayer Rock District sites in northeastern Arizona for Basketmaker III (Morris 1980); Antelope House and Mesa Verde for Pueblo II and Pueblo III perishables (Kent 1957; Morris 1986; Osborne 2004), and Arroyo Hondo for Rio Grande Classic period perishables (Lang 1984). Perishable material culture is very poorly known for the Rio Grande region due to the absence of sites and settings that are conducive to preservation. Fortunately, the goal of this analysis is simply to establish time horizons for major Kiowa-Tanoan speech community events, and for this purpose it is reasonable to assume that new cultigens and items of material culture appeared roughly simultaneously in both the San Juan and Rio Grande drainages.

Appendix A includes noncognate terms for the item referred to by the cognate set when available for the outgroup languages. These noncognate forms are listed using gray text so as to emphasize the cognate forms; however, it is important to keep in mind that in many cases the linguistic data are insufficient to rule out the possibility that a term reconstructible to a given subgroup actually dates from an older, higher-order subgroup. Thus, even though terms reconstructible to a given subgroup could not be younger than the subgroup, they could be older. Also, even if the absence of a cognate in an outgroup language is not due to vocabulary replacement, the presence of a noncognate term only confirms that speakers of the outgroup language obtained knowledge of the item some time after its speakers became isolated from the subgroup. Based on the archaeological record, I believe it is reasonable to assume that knowledge of newly introduced items spread to whatever Kiowa-Tanoan speech communities existed at that time relatively quickly, but the linguistic data are largely silent on this issue.

It is therefore necessary to consider patterns in the archaeological correlates of these cultural inventories to assess their significance for dating.

Finally, although English glosses are given for each reconstruction, the reconstructions refer to aspects of ancestral Pueblo culture, not to the meanings and connotations of the English words. In several cases it is the imagery of the actions and objects the cognates refer to that offer the best guide to the proto-meaning, and thus to the archaeological record. The English glosses are most properly viewed as translations of this imagery into Western categories.

Proto-Kiowa-Tanoan Reconstructions

Appendix B discusses 20 terms that are reconstructible to Proto-Kiowa-Tanoan. The English glosses of these terms are: 'house,' 'to dwell,' 'ladder,' 'sleeping mat,' 'stone point,' 'hammer,' 'hide,' 'bag,' 'sinew,' 'shoe,' 'snare,' 'to sound,' 'flute,' 'tobacco,' 'to smoke,' 'ripe corn,' '(pop)corn,' 'squash, gourd,' 'to boil,' and 'to lay down.' All of the associated objects or activities were known in the Kiowa-Tanoan speech community before the dialect ancestral to Kiowa became isolated from the Tanoan dialect chain. With the possible exceptions of 'ladder' and 'to lay down,' these items and activities are all associated with Basketmaker II sites in the northern U.S. Southwest. In addition, the cultural inventory in this list appears to reflect Eastern Basketmaker culture, for two reasons. First, the existence of terms for cultigens ('corn,' 'squash') and high-elevation trees ('oak,' 'spruce') but absence of terms related to intensive agriculture ('to plant,' 'field') in Proto-Kiowa-Tanoan is more consistent with an indigenous foraging group that gradually adopted agriculture (Eastern Basketmaker) than with a migrant, fully agricultural group from the south (Western Basketmaker). Second, sleeping mats have been found only in Eastern Basketmaker II sites, and a word for this item is reconstructible to Proto-Kiowa-Tanoan. Third, many additional items in the Kiowa-Tanoan cultural inventory are found in Archaic sites of the Colorado Plateau, and the textiles from Eastern Basketmaker II and Colorado Plateau Archaic sites were made using nearly identical techniques (Geib 1996: 68–69; Matson 2006). All of this evidence is consistent with recent proposals that Proto-Kiowa-Tanoan descended from an earlier indigenous, Late Archaic, hunter-gatherer language of the Colorado Plateau, and began to diversify as its speakers adopted agriculture (Hill 2008; LeBlanc 2008; Matson 2002). The earliest maize from the Eastern Basketmaker area dates to 1500 BC, but the Durango Basketmaker II sites are more recent, dating between 300 BC and AD 450 (Charles et al. 2006). If, in fact, Proto-Kiowa-Tanoan was the language of the Eastern Basketmakers, it would suggest that this language was spoken in the northern U.S. Southwest as recently as AD 450.

Finally, the strong evidence in cultural vocabulary that Proto-Kiowa-Tanoan was spoken by people with a material culture consistent with an Eastern Basketmaker II affiliation is relevant for delimiting the geographical extent of the Kiowa-Tanoan speech community. Maize macrofossils dating as early as 1200 BC have been found at Jemez Cave in the Rio Grande region (Vierra and Ford 2006), but Basketmaker II sites are far more numerous in the drainages of the San Juan and Colorado rivers to the northwest (compare Charles and Cole 2006 with McNutt 1969). This suggests that the focal area of Kiowa-Tanoan settlement was also north and west of the Rio Grande region.[8]

Proto-Tanoan Reconstructions

Appendix B also discusses 20 terms that are reconstructible to Proto-Tanoan. The glosses of these terms are: 'arrow,' 'pithouse,' '(coiled) basket,' 'pottery (bowl),' 'bow,' 'axe,' 'thread,' 'to sew,' 'road,' 'dance,' 'metate,' 'to grind,' 'to plant,' '(flour) corn,' 'kernel,' 'bean,' 'field,' 'sunflower,' 'turkey,' and 'cornstalk.' All of the associated objects or activities were known in the Tanoan speech community before speakers of the dialect ancestral to Towa became isolated from it. The fact that terms for 'field' and 'to plant' are reconstructible only to Proto-Tanoan, whereas terms for 'maize' and 'squash' reconstruct to Proto-Kiowa-Tanoan, suggests that Kiowa-Tanoan speakers adopted an agricultural lifeway somewhat gradually. This reinforces an association of Kiowa-Tanoan languages with the Eastern Basketmaker area, where the archaeological record suggests that agriculture was adopted by an in situ population (Sesler and Hovezak 2002), as opposed to the Western Basketmaker area, where the earliest agricultural peoples appear to have been migrant farmers from the south (LeBlanc 2008; LeBlanc et al. 2007; Matson 2002, 2006). With the exceptions of 'coiled basket,' 'thread,' 'to sew,' 'cornstalk,' and 'sunflower,' these items all occur for the first time in sites dating after AD 450, and are absent from earlier sites. It therefore appears that Proto-Tanoan was spoken during the Basketmaker III period. In addition, the absence of sites of this age in the Tewa Basin (McNutt 1969; this study, Chap. 4) indicates that the Tanoan dialect chain did not extend into the Northern Rio Grande at this time.

Proto-Tiwa-Tewa Reconstructions

Appendix B includes nine terms that are reconstructible to Proto-Tiwa-Tewa. The glosses of these terms are: 'string,' 'rooftop,' 'cooking pot,' 'olla,' 'dipper,' 'cradleboard,' 'knife,' 'pick,' and 'squash.' These nine items were all known to the Tiwa-Tewa speech community before Proto-Tewa became isolated from it. With the exceptions of 'string' and 'knife,' the remaining seven items all appear for the first time in sites dating to the Pueblo I period. This pattern suggests that Proto-Tiwa-Tewa was spoken in the northern U.S. Southwest as early as AD 725, and as recently as AD 920.

Proto-Tiwa Reconstructions

Finally, Appendix B discusses 15 terms that reconstruct to Proto-Tiwa. The glosses of these terms are: 'moccasin,' 'thread,' 'hoe,' 'quiver,' 'dish,' 'gourd rattle,' 'viga,' 'adobe,' 'racetrack,' 'shirt,' 'turquoise,' 'cotton,' 'blanket,' 'tortilla,' and 'macaw.' The terms for these 15 items were part of the Tiwa language before it split into Northern Tiwa and Southern Tiwa. Proto-Tiwa terms for 'moccasin,' 'thread,' 'hoe,' 'quiver,' and 'dish' appear to reflect neologisms, and the initial construction of racetracks is poorly dated. Of the remaining 9 items, none appear widely in sites dating prior to AD 980, and all but 'shirt' (ca. AD 1200) and 'tortilla' (ca. AD 1250) appeared by AD 1100. Also, the presence of cognates in Northern and Southern Tiwa for several items whose first widespread appearance is associated with the Chacoan regional system ('viga,' 'turquoise,' 'macaw') suggests that the Tiwa dialect chain had not yet split into northern and southern branches during the heyday of this system.

These Proto-Tiwa reconstructions hold additional clues to the locations of the Proto-Tiwa and Keres speech communities after AD 980. The Proto-Tiwa word for 'turquoise' was adopted before the Tiwa speech community split into northern and southern speech communities, and appears to be a loan from Keres. The earliest widespread occurrence of turquoise ornaments is attributed to the development of the Chacoan regional system (Harbottle and Weigand 1992; Windes 1992), and a major source of this turquoise is in the Cerrillos hills south of Santa Fe. There is also direct evidence that participants in the Chacoan regional system mined this source (Wiseman and Darling 1986). Finally, note that the Tewa word for 'turquoise' is not a loan from Keres, but a neologism that incorporates the Tewa word for 'stone' (Appendix A, no. 84). Taken together, this evidence suggests the following scenario: (1) Keres was the dominant language of Chaco Canyon; (2) the Tiwa speech community was located in the Northern Rio Grande by AD 980 and adopted their word for turquoise from Keres-speaking Chacoans who were mining it from the Cerrillos source; and (3) the Tewa speech community was not involved in this interaction and adapted a native term when turquoise ornaments began to be distributed to Tewa speakers from Chaco. This scenario is consistent with the biological evidence discussed in Chapter 5.

Summary of Subgroup Dating Analysis

Based on archaeological dating of cultural inventories of Kiowa-Tanoan subgroups, it is possible to date the periods of time during which these various subgroup languages were spoken, and to estimate when the most closely related out-group language to each subgroup became isolated from it. Two principles allow one to do this:

1. The dialects comprising a subgroup must have been linked at the time the newest item in the cultural inventory of that subgroup appeared in the archaeological record; and
2. So long as vocabulary replacement is not distorting the overall picture, an out-group dialect must have become isolated from its closest subgroup before the oldest item in the cultural inventory of this subgroup appeared in the archaeological record.

Although the chronological implications of Principle 1 are firm, the same cannot be said for Principle 2 due to the possibility of vocabulary replacement. If the closest out-group language of a subgroup once had cognates for some of the items reconstructible to that subgroup, but these words have been replaced in the out-group language, this would push the separation date of the subgroup and out-group forward in time.

Fortunately, it is possible to test the likelihood of vocabulary replacement as an alternative explanation for the patterns in reconstructed cultural vocabulary identified in this chapter. The null hypothesis in these tests is that a given out-group language separated from its closest subgroup more recently than is suggested by the cultural inventory of the subgroup because cognates for all the items suggestive of a split date that are reconstructible to that subgroup have been replaced by noncognate terms in the out-group language. The question being asked is what the probability of all these cognates being replaced would be, given that the associated items first appeared at roughly the same time, and a certain percentage of vocabulary is still shared among the subgroup and its closest out-group. Table 7.3 presents a summary of the subgroup dating analysis and statistical tests of the null hypothesis described above. These tests show that vocabulary replacement is unlikely as an explanation for the patterns in reconstructed vocabulary identified in this chapter. Thus, it appears that the out-group language in each row of Table 7.3 did indeed become isolated from its closest subgroup at some point during the span of time that items in the cultural inventory of that subgroup first appeared.

The data are now in place to assess whether or not the Tewa language was distinct prior to the onset of the Rio Grande Coalition period. The data in Table 7.3 show that: (1) cultural items for which cognate terms are attested in Tiwa and Tewa, but not in Towa, had all appeared in the archaeological record by AD 920; (2) cultural items for which cognate terms are attested in Northern Tiwa and Southern Tiwa, but not in Tewa, began to appear in the archaeological record around AD 980; and (3) the probability that the seven words for cultural items that are reconstructible only to Proto-Tiwa once had a Tewa cognate, given the fact that about 56 percent of Tiwa and Tewa words are cognate, is $<.005$. Thus, these data indicate that Tewa could have been distinct as early as AD 920, and was probably distinct by AD 980. This means a distinct Tewa language was spoken somewhere several centuries prior to the Rio Grande Coalition period, and several centuries prior to depopulation of the Mesa Verde region.

Comparison with Glottochronological Estimates

The analysis of Kiowa-Tanoan speech community history presented in this work is a major undertaking involving reconstruction of Kiowa-Tanoan consonants and vowels, analysis of shared phonetic innovations, reconstruction of cultural vocabulary, and archaeological dating of the objects and activities corresponding to the reconstructed terms. Given the amount of work involved, it is important to ask whether it leads to an improved dating of Kiowa-Tanoan speech community history relative to results obtained using the much simpler and more

TABLE 7.3. Summary of subgroup dating analysis

Subgroup	Closest Out-Group Language	Cultural Inventory (Number of Items)	Time Period of Complex	Items for Which a Noncognate Term Is Recorded for the Out-Group	Estimate of Sub-Group–Out-Group Shared Vocabulary[a]	Probability of Out-Group Vocabulary Replacement[b]
1. Kiowa-Tanoan	none	'house,' 'to dwell,' 'sleeping mat,' 'stone point,' 'hammer,' 'hide,' 'bag,' 'sinew,' 'shoe,' 'snare,' 'flute,' 'tobacco,' 'to smoke,' 'ripe corn,' '(pop)corn,' 'squash, gourd,' 'to boil,' 'to lay down' (18)	?–AD 450	n/a	n/a	n/a
2. Tanoan	Kiowa	'arrow,' 'pithouse,' 'pottery (bowl),' 'bow,' 'axe,' 'road,' 'dance,' 'metate,' 'to grind,' 'to plant,' '(flour) corn,' 'kernel,' 'bean,' 'field,' 'turkey' (15)	450–725	12	.2622	.0260
3. Tiwa-Tewa	Towa	'rooftop,' 'cooking pot,' 'olla,' 'dipper,' 'cradleboard,' 'pick,' 'squash' (7)	725–920	6	.4703	.0221
4. Tiwa	Tewa	'gourd rattle,' 'viga,' 'adobe,' 'shirt,' 'turquoise,' 'cotton,' 'blanket,' 'tortilla,' 'macaw' (9)	980–1100	7[c]	.5680	.0028

Note: This table presents a statistical test I devised to assess the likelihood that vocabulary replacement is responsible for the apparent chronological trends in these data. The null hypothesis is that the subgroup and closest out-group diverged more recently than is suggested by the dating of the reconstructed cultural complex. The question being asked is what the probability is that cognates for all the forms in the cultural inventory for the subgroup were replaced by the noncognate terms in that out-group, given that the subgroup and out-group still share a certain percentage of vocabulary.

[a] Mean proportion of cognates between the out-group and the subgroup languages, from Davis's (1959) analysis of the Swadesh 100-word list (Table 6.1).

[b] The test statistic is the binomial probability that all noncognate terms in the out-group language for the subgroup cultural inventory are due to vocabulary replacement.

[c] I exclude "shirt" and "tortilla" from consideration in this test because these two items first appeared after AD 1200, whereas the remaining seven items appeared by AD 1100.

TABLE 7.4. Comparison of linguistic dating estimates (years before present)

Speech Community Event	Vocabulary Estimate (This Study)	Davis's (1959) Estimate[a]	Hale and Harris's (1979) Estimate[b]
Kiowa from Tanoan	1,550	4,250	3,000
Towa from Tiwa-Tewa	1,275	2,450	2,500
Tewa from Tiwa	1,020	1,800	2,500
N. Tiwa from S. Tiwa	800	600	

Note: All data are in years before present, which is AD 2000 for the vocabulary-based estimates, and approximately AD 1950 for the other estimates.

[a] Rounded to the nearest half-century.

[b] Hale and Harris did not estimate the date of the Proto-Tiwa split and assumed that the major branches of Tanoan diversified simultaneously.

readily applied method of glottochronology. To facilitate comparison, Table 7.4 presents the dates of major splits in Kiowa-Tanoan speech communities developed on the basis of archaeological correlations with reconstructed vocabulary in this study, and compares them to the glottochronological estimates of the dates of these same events produced by Davis (1959) and Hale and Harris (1979).

It is important to note that Davis's glottochronological estimates are based on the cognate densities presented in Table 6.1, and that this matrix implies the same sequence of branching events produced through analysis of shared phonetic innovations. Although lexicostatistical methods cannot reconstruct details of lectal differentiation, linkage breaking, and linkage rejoining, they do appear adequate for discovering the basic structure of the Kiowa-Tanoan language tree. However, it is also clear that the glottochronological estimates of when these various branching events occurred are markedly different from those produced through the vocabulary-based dating method. According to the glottochronological estimates, Kiowa was already a distinct language when maize agriculture entered the northern U.S. Southwest, and Towa, Tewa, and Tiwa were already distinct by the end of Basketmaker II.

This suggested chronology is very difficult to reconcile with the patterns in cultural vocabulary identified in this chapter. To view the glottochronological estimates as more accurate, one would have to argue, first, that Proto-Kiowa-Tanoan reconstructions related to tobacco, maize, and squash—and Proto-Tanoan reconstructions related to bow and arrow technology, pottery, beans, and turkeys—are all erroneous; and second, that vocabulary replacement has produced patterns that mimic an archaeologically coherent chronology of language splits merely by chance. This seems much less likely than the alternative conclusion, which is that the rate of basic vocabulary replacement in Kiowa-Tanoan speech communities has varied through time and across languages, and as a result, glottochronological estimates for the dates of various language splits are too imprecise for correlation with archaeology.

Words, Things, and Tewa Origins

The analyses presented in this chapter help tie the sequence of speech community events reconstructed through phonological analysis to specific times and places. The geographical distributions of several key species suggest that the Kiowa-Tanoan homeland was not located exclusively to the south of the Jemez and Sangre de Cristo mountains in the Rio Grande region, but neither linguistic migration theory nor reconstructed plant and animal terms can rule out the northern Rio Grande or the northern San Juan as potential homelands.

Fortunately, the "words and things" approach allows one to get more specific. It suggests that Proto-Kiowa-Tanoan was spoken in Eastern Basketmaker II sites, in which case it would have been spoken along the foothills of the southern Rocky Mountains, from the Upper San Juan region of northwest New Mexico to the area surrounding Montrose, Colorado. Because Basketmaker II sites do not occur widely in the Rio Grande drainage but are common throughout the San Juan and Colorado drainages, it appears most likely that the Proto-Kiowa-Tanoan speech community did not extend into the Rio Grande region.

The "words and things" approach also suggests that Tewa and Tiwa became distinct from each other as early as AD 920, and almost certainly by AD 980. There is also evidence for interaction between Keres and Tiwa speakers in the Rio Grande region prior to the Coalition period, but no corresponding evidence for Tewa speakers in the Rio Grande at that time. Finally, words for "shirt" and "tortilla," which reconstruct to Proto-Tiwa but are not in evidence in the archaeological record prior to AD 1200, suggest that the Tiwa dialect chain was not broken into Northern Tiwa and Southern Tiwa prior to the period of time during which migration from the Mesa Verde region began.

These results demonstrate that Tewa was a distinct language that was spoken somewhere in the northern U.S. Southwest from at least AD 980, well prior to the beginning of the Rio Grande Coalition period. Because these results also suggest Proto-Kiowa-Tanoan was spoken in Eastern Basketmaker II sites, but Proto-Tiwa was spoken in the Rio Grande, they imply a general southeastward movement of Tanoan speakers over time. The question raised by these results is how long ago the Tewa language can be documented as having been spoken in the Rio Grande. The analysis of place-names and place-lore that follows will suggest that it has not been spoken there for as long as it has been a distinct language, and that Tiwa has been spoken in the Rio Grande region for a longer period of time than has Tewa, as suggested here.

Notes

1. This has proven to be an insidious problem. Hill (2008), for example, cites several forms for which a cognate is not known for Kiowa in her study of postulated contact between Proto-Kiowa-Tanoan speakers and Proto-Uto-Aztecan speakers in the early agricultural period of the northern U.S. Southwest. It is quite possible that several of the Kiowa-Tanoan forms cited as part of this exchange actually date to more recent periods.

2. This appendix corrects minor errors and expands slightly upon Appendix C in Ortman 2009. Although this version adds a few additional PKT and PT reconstructions, I have chosen to add these to the end of the list instead of inserting them within the list in order to maintain the numbering system of the previous version. Here again, I thank Laurel Watkins for her assistance with this work.
3. Kiowa-Tanoan phonology does not include *l initially, but does include a medial * -l- as suggested by Hale (1967:116) and Davis (1989:366), based on the cognate sets in the following table:

RECONSTRUCTION	TAOS	ISLETA	TEWA	JEMEZ	KIOWA
**-l-*	*-l-*	*-r-*	*-Ø*	*-l/d-*	*-l-*
KT **hɨol* 'canyon'	*hɨ́olúna*	*p'ahɨa*	*heˀe~huˀu* 'small/large arroyo'	*wé:ɦo:la*	*hil*
PT **búlu* 'pottery bowl, round'	*múlu* 'pottery'	*búru* 'pottery, bowl'	*bé:ˀe~bú:ˀú* 'small/large roundish place'	*bɨ́do* 'round'	
KT **k'ǽl-* 'eat'	*k'ólą*	*k'ar*	*k'o'*		*k'ɔle*
PT **delu* 'turkey'	*lilú* 'chicken'	*diru* 'chicken'	*di* 'chicken, turkey'	*dél'ī* 'chicken, fowl'	

4. There is a "kiowa" kiva at Taos (Elizabeth Brandt, personal communication, 2009), and in the mid-twentieth century some cases of Kiowa-Taos marriages were noted (Trager and Trager 1959:1079).
5. The Kiowa-Tanoan languages are tonal, which means that particular languages contain minimal pairs that mean different things, but differ in sound only in the "tonal" pitch of the vowel. For example, in Tewa, *p'o:* (with a low tone) means 'water,' whereas *p'ó:* (with a high tone) means 'moon,' and *p'ô:* (with a rising then falling tone) means 'road.' The development of tonal contrasts in Kiowa-Tanoan languages is still not fully understood, and is not taken into account in the reconstructions given in Appendix A.
6. Under the first scenario, however, Tewa would have to have been spoken in the Northern Rio Grande region for a longer period of time than Northern Tiwa, whereas under the second scenario, Northern Tiwa would have priority over Tewa. The different expectations of these two scenarios can be tested through analyses of paired placenames in Tewa and Northern Tiwa, and will be addressed further in Chapter 8.
7. As an example, in his well-received textbook, Lyle Campbell, one of the foremost practitioners of historical linguistics, states (1998:186): "In summary, glottochronology is not accurate; all its basic assumptions have been severely criticized. It should not be accepted; it should be rejected." Yet Campbell cites glottochronological estimates throughout his book on American Indian languages published the previous year. For example, Campbell (1997:139) states: "glottochronological time depths have been calculated to be approximately 3,000 years for the separation of Kiowa from Tanoan and 2,000 or 2,500 years for the breakup of Tanoan (Hale and Harris 1979:171). While this reflects the original view that Kiowa is more divergent, it should be kept in mind that glottochronology is at best a rough gauge, rejected by most linguists."
8. See Appendix D for a hypothesis concerning movements of the Kiowa speech community between AD 450 and the present.

Place-Names, Place-Lore, and Oral Tradition

Chronological patterns in reconstructed vocabulary suggest that the ancestral Tewa speech community became isolated from the Proto-Tiwa speech community between AD 920 and 980, well before the onset of the Rio Grande Coalition period. This raises the question of *where* Tewa was spoken when it became distinct, the answer to which has an obvious bearing on Tewa origins. If Tewa has been spoken in the Tewa Basin since it became distinct from Tiwa, it would suggest that any Coalition period migrants to the Tewa Basin shifted their language to Tewa upon arrival. If, on the other hand, Tewa speech can only be documented in the Tewa Basin from the Coalition period, it would leave open the possibility that this language was brought to the Tewa Basin by migrants from elsewhere. In the latter case, a likely homeland for the Tewa language would have to be the Mesa Verde region, based on demographic and biological evidence. Patterns in shared phonetic innovations reviewed in Chapter 6 lend support to the second scenario. This chapter will further evaluate these two possibilities through studies of Tewa and Tiwa place-names, and Tewa oral traditions that reference ancient homelands.

In the first section I examine paired terms for specific topographical features in the San Juan Tewa and Taos Tiwa dialects. This analysis will assess whether speakers of these two dialects have inherited a common stock of toponyms for the Rio Grande landscape from their most recent common-ancestor language, Proto-Tiwa-Tewa. If some of these paired toponyms are cognate, it would suggest that Tewa has been spoken in the Rio Grande region from the time it became distinct from Tiwa, and Tewa therefore could not have been brought to the Rio Grande from elsewhere. If, on the other hand, there is no evidence for shared descent, and some of these paired terms are the result of subsequent contact, it may be possible to determine which of these two languages has been spoken for a longer period in the Rio Grande by examining the direction of borrowing. For example, if Tiwa was spoken in the Rio Grande during the Developmental period, and Tewa entered during the Coalition period, one would expect to find certain Tewa place-names that are loans from Tiwa, but not the reverse.

In the second section I examine Tewa names for archaeological sites to assess how far back in time it is possible to document the Tewa language in the Tewa Basin. The basic assumption of this analysis is that Tewa has been spoken there for at least the length of time implied by the longest-abandoned sites associated with traditional Tewa names. If the oldest sites with Tewa names date from the Developmental period, one can rule out the possibility that Tewa was brought to the Rio Grande during the Coalition period. But if the oldest sites with Tewa names date to the Coalition period, this would leave open the possibility that Tewa was spoken outside the Rio Grande region from the time it became distinct from Tiwa until the time of occupation of these sites.

In the final section I consider recorded statements in the Tewa ethnographic literature and Spanish documents concerning an ancient Tewa homeland in the north. If the ancestral Tewa population does derive from the Mesa Verde region, and the Tewa language was spoken outside the Rio Grande for some portion of its history, one might expect Tewa people to have retained social memories of this prior homeland. To illustrate that such memories were widespread in the early historic period and remain to some extent to the present day, I compile and analyze these statements for clues to the location of the ancestral Tewa homeland.

Analyzing Place-Names

The major source I have consulted for information on Tewa and Taos Tiwa place-names is John Peabody Harrington's (1916) *Ethnogeography of the Tewa Indians*. Harrington collected the data reported in this work in the first decade of the twentieth century, and due to its completeness and accuracy it remains one of the foundational references for northern Rio Grande archaeology and Pueblo Indian studies, savored by generations of scholars and Tewa people alike. Alfonso Ortiz, a Tewa anthropologist, praised it as "one of the most comprehensive treatises ever assembled for the geographical terminology of any non-Western society" (Ortiz 1979a:295). What is less well known is that this work also contains a large number of toponyms for other Pueblo languages, including Taos Tiwa. Taos place-names are also available from archival sources, including the personal papers of J. P. Harrington (available on microfilm [Mills and Brickfield 1981]), and the personal papers of George L. Trager, currently housed at the University of California, Irvine. I consulted these and several additional sources to compile a list of San Juan Tewa and Taos Tiwa names for specific topographical features and archaeological sites.

The techniques I used to analyze these toponyms are essentially the ones laid out by Edward Sapir (1949 [1916]) for cultural vocabulary generally.[1] The most basic technique is to examine the degree to which a name can be broken up into meaningful parts, also known as morphemes. It is generally the case that a name with a transparent morphological analysis in a given language was coined by speakers of that language. In contrast, names that cannot be analyzed into meaningful parts were either coined long ago or represent loans (see Campbell and Kaufman 1976; Shaul and Hill 1998). In the latter case it is usually appropriate to infer that the donor language preceded the recipient language in that region.[2] In addition, the occurrence of cognate toponyms referring to the same geographic features indicates that speakers of the most recent common-ancestor language had knowledge of these features, and that this ancestral language was likely spoken in the vicinity. Finally, in the case of names for archaeological sites, it is reasonable to infer that a site was not occupied prior to being named, unless the name implies that it was already a ruin at the time of naming.[3] As a result, one can use archaeological dating evidence for named sites to estimate the minimum length of time a language has been spoken in a region. These techniques will all come into play in the following analyses of San Juan Tewa and Taos Tiwa place-names.

Analysis of Paired Toponyms

Working from the sources mentioned above, I have identified 20 topographical features for which place-names recorded in sufficient phonetic detail are available for both the San Juan Tewa and Taos Tiwa dialects. If Tewa and Tiwa diversified within the Rio Grande region, one might expect a certain percentage of these paired toponyms to date from the period prior to the Tewa-Tiwa split, and thus to be cognate. If, instead, this diversification occurred outside the Rio Grande region, one would expect to find evidence of loans from the language with historical priority into the more recently arrived language instead of cognates. Table 8.1 lists these 20 paired toponyms with English translations, and interprets the nature of the relationship between each pair.

It is unfortunately difficult to distinguish true cognates from calques (loan translations) for several of these pairs because most of the toponyms are transparent compounds that could have easily been translated. When loan translation occurs between closely related languages, as Tewa and Tiwa are, the resultant toponyms will combine morphemes that are often themselves cognate. In addition, toponyms can be simplified during the translation process or through the loss of morphemes over time, making it even more difficult to distinguish true cognates from calques. With this caveat in mind, I discuss each of these pairs below:

1. Ute Mountain (San Juan *P^{h}a:p'in*; Taos *Puot'ep'íanenemą*). This pair of names refers to a prominent laccolith near Cortez, Colorado, in the Mesa Verde region. It is difficult to say what the relationship between the Taos and San Juan forms is. The first part of the Taos form, *Puot'ę-*, refers to a plaited yucca basket used for sifting cornmeal. This word is in turn most likely a compound of *p^{h}uol-* 'yucca' and *t$^{?}$įęne* 'dish,' but is not cognate with the San Juan word for "yucca basket," *p^{h}a:yo* (*p^{h}a:* 'yucca' + *yo* 'big'). In addition, the first morpheme in the San Juan form refers to the yucca plant and not to a basket, and also occurs in the San Juan name for the adjacent Montezuma Valley (*P^{h}a:p'innae'ahkongeh* 'Plain

TABLE 8.1. Paired Tewa and Tiwa place-names

Landform (Harrington Reference)	San Juan Tewa Place-Name	Translation	Taos Tiwa Place-Name	Translation	Relationship
1. Ute Mountain (Unmapped:565)	Pʰa:p'in	Yucca Mountain	Puot'ep'íanenemą[a]	Basket Mountain	Calque from Tewa
2. Tres Piedras ([8:12]:173)	K'úwák'u:	Mountain Sheep–Rocks	K'uwaxúną	Mountain Sheep–Rocks	Loan, calque, or cognate
3. Tusas Mountains ([8:4]:172)	Kíp'in	Prairie Dog Mountain	Kitʰɨp'ianena	Prairie dog–dwelling Mountain	Calque from Taos or cognate
4. Ojo Caliente ([6:7]:159)	P'osíp'o:	Moss Greenness–Water	P'oˀuop'ó'ona	Water-hot Creek	Unrelated
5. Sierra Blanca Lake (Unmapped: 567)	Sip'opʰe	[Unexplained]	Cip'opʰúntha[b]	Eye-water-black-at	Tiwa loan
6. Taos Peak ([8:40]:177)	Mąxwolop'in	[Unexplained]-mountain	Mąxʷoluna	covering?, -high?	Taos loan
7. Taos Mountain ([8:24]:175)	Tʰawíp'in	Taos [Dwell-gap] Mountains	Poxʷiap'íanenemą[a]	Lake Mountain	Taos priority
8. Taos Creek ([8:43]:178)	Tʰawíp'o:	Taos [Dwell-gap] Creek	ˀIałopʰayp'ó'ona	Red Willow Water	Taos priority
9. Santa Fe ([29:6]:460)	ˀOgap'o:geh	Shell-water-at	Hulp'ó'ona	Shell River	Calque
10. Orejas Mountain ([8:37]:177)	Deˀoyep'in	Coyote Ears Mountain	Tuxʷat'ołɨotʰuntʰo[a]	Fox Ear Place	Calque
11. Sierra Blanca (Unmapped:564)	P'inc'ǽˀii	Mountain-white	P'ianp'otʰɨbo[a]	Mountain-white-place	Calque
12. Tierra Amarilla ([1:10]:111)	Nąnc'eyiwe	Earth-yellow-at	Nąmc'úlito[a]	Earth-yellow-place	Independent, calque, or cognate
13. Jicarilla Peak ([22:9]:339)	T'ųmp'in	Basket Mountain	P'uot'įęp'ientʰa[b]	Basket-mountain-at	Calque
14. Sandia Peak ([29:83]:513)	O:ku:p'in	Turtle Mountain	Kep'íanenemą[b]	[?]-mountain	Unrelated
15. Abiquiu Mountain ([3:2]:130)	Ábešup'inˀây	Abiquiu [Chokecherry-end] Mountain-little	P'íanp'omúluna[b]	Mountain Water Jar	Unrelated
16. Abiquiu ([3:36]:135)	Pʰéšúbú:ˀu	Stick-end-town	Kultʰɨtta[b]	[?]	Unrelated
17. Red River ([8:19]:174)	P'îp'ogeˀinp'o:	Red Water Creek	Tɨsiup'ó'ona	[?]-creek	Unrelated
18. Horse Lake ([1:1]:108)	Kabayup'okwin	Horse-lake	Ka'up'oxʷia'ana	Horse-lake	Calque
19. Boulder Lake ([1:2]:109)	K'u:p'okwin	Stone-lake	Xúp'oxʷia'ana	Stone-lake	Independent, calque, or cognate
20. Stinking Lake ([1:3]:109–110)	P'okwisų'ii	Lake-smell-at	P'oxʷiaława'ana	Lake-smell-which	Independent or calque

Note: All data are from Harrington 1916 unless otherwise noted, and have been retranscribed into Martinez's (1982) and Trager's (1946) orthographies.

[a] George L. Trager Papers, University of California, Irvine, Box 40. [b] J. P. Harrington Papers, microfilm edition, Reel 49, Frame 0195–0197.

of the Yucca Mountain' [Harrington 1916:564]). Thus it appears that the Taos and San Juan names for Ute Mountain are not cognate.

It is possible that the Taos form is a calque from Tewa, but the San Juan form is less likely as a calque from Tiwa based on the evidence of Tiwa-Keres interaction presented in Chapter 7, which suggests that Tiwa has been spoken in the Rio Grande from the time it became isolated from Tewa. Given this scenario, it would seem unlikely that there was ever a time when Taos Tiwa speakers knew about Ute Mountain but San Juan Tewa speakers did not. It therefore seems most likely that the Taos form is the result of a loan translation from Tewa or some other language into Northern Tiwa.

Complicating this picture is the possibility that the Jemez name for Ute Mountain is cognate with the Tewa form. Ellis (1967:42) reports the Jemez name as "Banana Mountain," a translation derived from the association of yucca fruit with bananas in Towa (*fʷâ:lā* 'yucca,' *fâ:* 'banana'). Thus, the Towa name for Ute Mountain is probably *Fʷâ:lā-p'é:* 'yucca-mountain' (also see Parsons 1925:43), a transparent compound for which each morpheme is cognate with the corresponding morpheme in Tewa *Pʰa:-p'in*. These forms are either cognates or calques. If they are cognates, it would imply that Proto-Tanoan was spoken in the vicinity of Ute Mountain, in which case one would have to propose that Proto-Tiwa speakers lost knowledge of this landform, only to be reintroduced to it via subsequent contact with Tewa speakers. If, on the other hand, the Tewa and Towa forms represent a separate episode of calquing, it would imply a period of interaction among Tewa and Towa speakers in the vicinity of Ute Mountain, after Towa, Tewa, and Tiwa had become distinct languages. Either scenario suggests that Tewa differentiated from Tiwa outside the Rio Grande region.

It is also important to note that the Ute name for Ute Mountain, *Wiisi-kaa=pɨ* 'Yucca-fruit Mountain,' is semantically related to the Tanoan names for this landform (Goss 1972:233), whereas the Navajo name for this mountain, *Dził naajiní* 'Black Mountain Sloping Down,' is not (Linford 2000:165). Although Ute-speaking people have lived in the northern San Juan drainage since the time of Spanish contact (see Wroth 2000), it is unclear when Ute-speaking peoples first entered this area, or whether Ute ancestors might have arrived prior to the departure of ancestral Pueblo peoples.[4] At minimum, the fact that the Ute name is unambiguously associated with Ute Mountain, and that the Ute, Tewa, and Towa names are all loan translations of each other, confirms that all of these names refer to this landform. The possibility that the Ute name derives from interaction with Tanoan-speaking peoples at some point in the past also deserves further research.

2. Tres Piedras (San Juan *K'úwák'u:*; Taos *K'uwaxúną*). This pair of names refers to a set of three large rocks located just to the west of the modern town of Tres Piedras, northwest of Taos Pueblo. Both the San Juan and Taos names are identical transparent compounds. They are probably not independent because they do not describe physical characteristics of the place they name. This pair could represent cognates, a loan from one language to the other, or a calque from one language to the other. The available data do not allow one to distinguish among these alternatives.

3. Tusas Mountains (San Juan *Kíp'in*; Taos *Kit*^{h}*ip'ianena*). This pair of names refers to the mountain range in which Ojo Caliente Creek originates, north of the towns of Ojo Caliente and El Rito, and northwest of Taos Pueblo. Both names begin with cognate forms for 'prairie dog' (*ki*), and both end with cognate forms for 'mountain' (Tewa *p'in* ~ Taos *p'ianena*), but the Taos form also includes the intermediate morpheme *t*^{h}*i* 'to dwell,' which is absent in the San Juan form. These two forms are possibly cognate, with the Tewa form undergoing subsequent simplification, but the more probable interpretation is that the San Juan form represents a partial loan translation from Taos.

4. Ojo Caliente (San Juan *P'osíp'o:*; Taos *P'oƚuop'ó'ona*). This pair of names refers to the hot springs in the Ojo Caliente drainage north of Ohkay Owingeh and west of Taos Pueblo.[5] The Taos form is a transparent compound (*P'o* 'water' + *ƚuo* 'hot' + *p'ó'ona* 'creek'). The first part of the Tewa form, *P'o-* 'water,' is cognate with the initial Taos morpheme; however, the second morpheme, *-sí-*, is not cognate; in fact, the Tewa cognate of the second Taos morpheme is *suwa* 'hot.' Harrington (1916:162) provides the following etymology of *P'osí*: "old absolute form of *P'osíwi'i*, *P'osíwįn* 'moss-greenness' 'moss-green,' this adjective being applied to water, stain, paint, and things stained or painted which have this color, while of ordinary green and blue colors *cą:wą̈ ´*^{ʔ}*i*^{ʔ} is used." The Taos and San Juan forms therefore cannot be cognates. They must have been coined independently, because these two names pick out different characteristics of the Ojo Caliente hot springs, the Taos name emphasizing the temperature of the water, and the San Juan name its effect on the rocks it flows over.

5. Sierra Blanca Lake (San Juan *Sip'op*^{h}*e*; Taos *Cip'op*^{h}*úntha*). These names refer to a brackish lake in the sand dunes north of Alamosa, Colorado. The Taos form is a transparent compound (*Ci* 'eye' + *p'o* 'water' + *p*^{h}*ún* 'black' + *tha* 'at') that appears to be cognate with Isleta *šíp'ap*^{h}*ún*^{ʔ}*ai* 'Eye-water-black-at.' This place therefore appears to have been known to speakers of Proto-Tiwa; however, the San Juan name, *Sip'op*^{h}*e*, is unanalyzable in Tewa, and is not cognate with the Tiwa forms because the initial consonant correspondence is incorrect. The Tewa form is thus most likely a loan from Tiwa. This finding is significant because Sierra Blanca Lake figures prominently in Tewa origin narratives and is often referred to as ^{ʔ}*Ok*^{h}*ą ngep'ok*^{w}*inge* 'Sandy Lake Place' in these narratives (Harrington 1916:568–569; Parsons 1994 [1926]; Ortiz 1969). The likelihood that the Tewa name for this place is a loan from Tiwa suggests that Tewa speakers learned of it from Tiwa speakers. This, in turn, suggests the Tewa-Tiwa split did not occur within the Rio Grande region.

6. Taos Peak (San Juan *Mą̧xwolop'in*; Taos *Mą̧x^{w}oluna*). This Taos name for Taos Peak appears to derive from the Taos word for a covering or lid. The San Juan name for this landform appends the San Juan word for 'mountain' to the end of the Taos name, which is unanalyzable in Tewa. Thus the San Juan name for Taos Peak is a loan from Taos.

7. Taos Mountain (San Juan *T^{h}awíp'in*; Taos *Pox^{w}iap'íanenemą̧*). These names are not truly pairs, because the Taos form presents a second name for Taos Peak, whereas the Tewa form presents the name for the Taos mountain range overall. The San Juan form incorporates the Tewa name for Taos Pueblo, *T^{h}awi'ówînge* (Dwell-gap-village), and therefore postdates the establishment of this pueblo. The Taos form reflects the fact that Taos Mountain contains Blue Lake, a Taos emergence place. Taken together, these data suggest that the Taos names for Taos Mountain have historical priority over the Tewa names.

8. Taos Creek (San Juan *T^{h}awíp'o:*; Taos *$^?$Iałop^{h}ayp'ó'ona*). This pair of toponyms refers to the creek that runs through Taos Pueblo. The Taos name is descriptive of the plants that grow along its banks and has been adopted as one of the Taos names for their pueblo, *$^?$Iałop^{h}ayt^{h}a* 'Willow-red-at' (Harrington 1916:180). In contrast, the San Juan form incorporates the Tewa name for Taos Pueblo. Because the San Juan name postdates the establishment of Taos Pueblo, whereas the Taos name describes a feature of the natural landscape, the Taos name probably has historical priority over the Tewa name.

9. Santa Fe (San Juan *$^?$Ogap'o:geh*; Taos *Hulp'ó'ona*). Both the Taos and San Juan names for this town derive from the Santa Fe River, which flows through it. The two forms are not cognate but are clear loan translations of each other. There is no evidence to suggest whether the Taos form, the San Juan form, or neither is the original source.

10. Orejas Mountain (San Juan *De$^?$oyep'in*; Taos *Tux^{w}at'ɨołot^{h}unt^{h}o*). This pair of names refers to two peaks near Taos Junction which are said to resemble ears in some way (Harrington 1916:177). The Taos and San Juan forms are not cognate but are clear loan translations of each other. There is no evidence to suggest whether the Tiwa or Tewa form is the original source.

11. Sierra Blanca (San Juan *P'inc'ǫ̨e$^?$ii*; Taos *P'ianp'ot^{h}ɨbo*). This pair of names refers to Mount Blanca, which rises above the Great Sand Dunes in the San Luis Valley, Colorado. The Taos and San Juan forms are not cognate but are loan translations of each other. There is no evidence to suggest whether the Taos or San Juan form is the original source.

12. Tierra Amarilla (San Juan *Nąnc'eyiwe*; Taos *Nąmc'úlito*). This pair of names refers to the Tierra Amarilla region to the north of Ohkay Owingeh and Taos Pueblo. Both refer to the yellow pigment that can be obtained a short distance northwest of the modern town and is used for yellowing the walls of rooms near the floor (Harrington 1916:112–113). The Taos and San Juan names are transparent compounds for which each of the morphemes is cognate. In addition, both are descriptive of the location they name. As a result, these forms could represent cognates, calques with an unknown direction of borrowing, or independent coinages. However, these two forms appear too different phonetically to represent loaning.

13. Jicarilla Peak (San Juan *T'ųmp'in; Taos P'uot'įęp'ient^ha*). These toponyms refer to the northernmost peak of the Sangre de Cristo Mountains northeast of Santa Fe. Harrington (1916:339) states that the San Juan name derives from the rounded shape of the peak, which looks like an inverted basket. It is also known as the principal peak of Picuris Pueblo. The Taos and San Juan forms are not cognate but are clear loan translations of each other. The Spanish name for this landform is also a calque of the Tewa and Tiwa names. There is no evidence to suggest whether the Tiwa or Tewa form is the original source.

14. Sandia Peak (San Juan *O:ku:p'in*; Taos *Kep'ianenemą*). This pair of names refers to the peak that rises to the northeast of Albuquerque, New Mexico. The first part of the Taos name is of unknown etymology but does not refer to the turtle of the San Juan name. Thus, the two forms are unrelated and were coined independently. It is also notable that the Isleta name for Sandia Peak recorded by C. T. Harrington (1920:50), *Nąp^hį́p'ien,* is not cognate with the Taos form, as one might expect if Proto-Tiwa was spoken in the vicinity of Sandia Peak.

15. Abiquiu Mountain (San Juan *Ábešup'in^ʔây*; Taos *P'ianp'omúluna*). These names refer to a small mountain that rises southwest of Abiquiu, New Mexico. Based on the etymologies of the Taos and San Juan forms, they were coined independently.

16. Abiquiu (San Juan *P^héšúbú:^ʔu*; Taos *Kult^hɨtta*). This pair refers to the modern town of Abiquiu, New Mexico. Although the etymology of the Taos form is unknown, it is clearly not related to the San Juan etymology. Thus, the two forms were coined independently.

17. Red River (San Juan *P'îp'oge^ʔinp'o:*; Taos *Tɨsiup'ó'ona*). This pair of names refers to an eastern tributary of the Rio Grande which flows out of the northern end of the Taos Mountains. Although the etymology of the Taos form is unknown, it is clearly not related to the San Juan etymology. Thus, the two forms were coined independently.

18. Horse Lake (San Juan *Kabayup'okwin*, Taos *K'owp'ox^{w}ia'ana*). This pair of names refers to a lake on the present-day Jicarilla Apache reservation west of Tierra Amarilla. The first part of the San Juan name derives from a Spanish loan (*kabayu* 'horse' (< Spanish *caballo* 'horse'). Trager (1944:149) questioned whether the initial Taos morpheme was also a Spanish loan, but in either case, horses were clearly unknown to speakers of both languages prior to the historic period. Thus, these toponyms could not be cognate. They are also not likely independent because they do not describe the physical characteristics of the place they name, and they could not represent a loan from one language to the other because the initial morpheme is too different phonetically. They are thus most likely calques.

19. Boulder Lake (San Juan *K'u:p'okwin*, Taos *Xúp'ox^{w}ia'ana*). This pair refers to a lake a short distance south of Horse Lake, on the Jicarilla Apache reservation, that is surrounded by a rim of rocks. The Jicarilla Apaches hold a dance on the shore of this lake on the night of September 15 every year (Harrington 1916:109). Each of the morphemes in this pair is cognate, but both toponyms are descriptive of the landform and thus could also represent calques or independent coinages. They do not likely represent a loan from one language into the other because they are so similar in sound and meaning that it would have been straightforward for speakers of one language to translate the name into the pronunciation of the other.

20. Stinking Lake (San Juan *P'okwisų'ii*, Taos *P'ox^{w}iaława'ana*). This pair refers to a lake a short distance south of Boulder Lake that is fed by a spring that emits a strong odor. The two forms are not cognate because the final Taos morpheme is *wa* 'which' whereas the final San Juan morpheme is the locative postfix *'ii*. Both toponyms are descriptive of the landform and thus could represent calques or independent coinages. They are too different phonetically to represent loans in either direction.

Summary

Although as many as 4 of the 20 pairs discussed above may be cognate, none are clearly so. Thus, there is no definite evidence in these data that San Juan Tewa and Taos Tiwa speakers have inherited a common stock of place-names for elements of the Rio Grande landscape from the period of time before their languages became distinct. This leaves open the possibility that Tewa diversified from Tiwa outside the Rio Grande region. Among the 6 pairs that are clearly loan translations, the direction of borrowing can only be specified for two: the Tewa name for the Tusas Mountains is probably a loan translation from Taos Tiwa; and the Taos Tiwa name for Ute Mountain appears to have been a faulty translation of the Tewa name ('Yucca Mountain'), perhaps due to interference from the Taos name for Jicarilla Peak ('Yucca-dish-mountain'). The fact that the Tewa name for Ute Mountain is also a cognate or calque of the Towa name for this landform is evidence that Proto-Tanoan, or Tewa and Towa, speakers interacted in the vicinity of Ute Mountain, in the Mesa Verde region, at some point in the past.[6]

There are two pairs of place-names (for Taos Peak and Sierra Blanca Lake) for which it is clear that the Taos or perhaps Proto-Tiwa form represents the older toponym that was loaned into Tewa, because the Taos form has a transparent morphological analysis, whereas the San Juan form does not. There are also two additional pairs (for Taos Mountain and Taos Creek) for which it is clear the Taos form is older than the San Juan form, because the San Juan form incorporates the Tewa term for the Taos people. These four pairs provide evidence that Tiwa has been spoken in the Rio Grande region for a longer period than Tewa. Five of the seven remaining pairs are not related and appear to have been coined independently. Overall, then, these data suggest that Proto-Tanoan, or Tewa and Towa, were once spoken in the Mesa Verde region, and that Tiwa has been spoken in the Rio Grande region for a longer period of time than has Tewa. This, in turn, argues against the hypothesis that the Tiwa-Tewa split occurred within the Rio Grande region.

Tewa Names for Archaeological Sites

In this section I examine the abandonment dates of archaeological sites for which Tewa names were remembered in the early twentieth century to determine the minimum length of time that Tewa has been spoken in the Tewa Basin. If sites that were abandoned prior to the Coalition period had traditional Tewa names, it would suggest that Tewa was spoken in the Rio Grande prior to the period of in-migration suggested by demographic and biological data, and would weaken the argument that migrants brought the Tewa language to the Tewa Basin during this period. Starting once again from Harrington (1916), augmented by Ellis (1964a) and a variety of other sources, I have correlated Tewa names for ancestral village sites with New Mexico state site numbers, and with the occupation spans for these sites determined using the procedures discussed in Chapter 4. Appendix C presents the resulting data set, which includes Tewa names, English translations, and occupation spans for 60 archaeological sites in the Tewa Basin, along with the notes and references that justify these correlations.

The most important pattern to emphasize at the outset is that nearly all Tewa ruin names have transparent morphological analyses, and I have been unable to identify a Taos cognate for any Tewa site name. This is strong evidence that all Tewa names for ancient Tewa Basin settlements were coined by Tewa speakers. It is also clear that Tewa names were established for these sites when they were occupied. Tewa names for sites that are ruins today typically end in *'ówînkeyi*

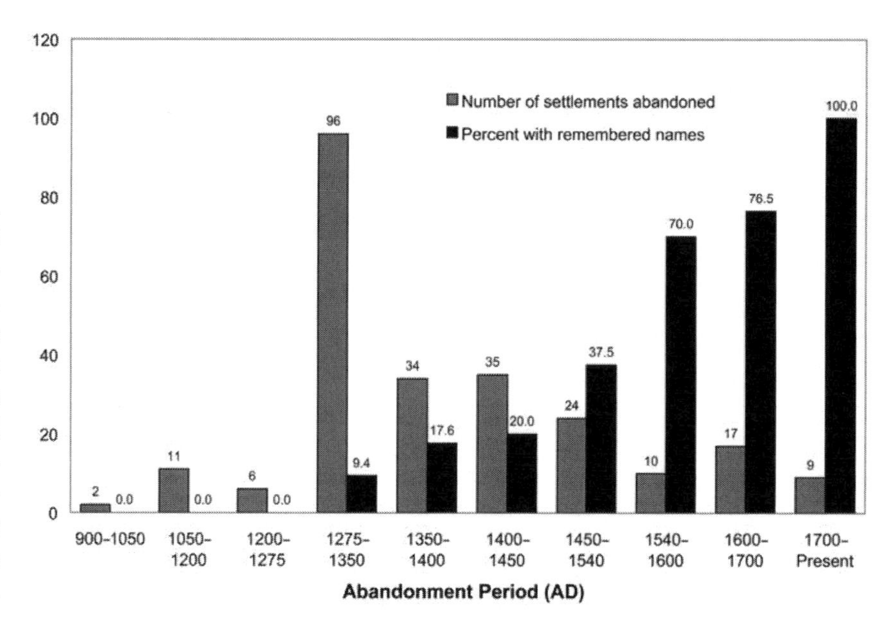

FIGURE 8.1. Settlements and Tewa names by abandonment period. *Settlements* are sites or site clusters that housed 50 or more total persons, and the final "abandonment" period includes pueblos that remain occupied to the present day.

(*'ówîn* 'village' + *keyi* 'ruin') to distinguish them from *'ówînge,* or occupied villages (e.g., *Oke'ówînge,* 'San Juan Pueblo'; *Thawi'ówînge,* 'Taos Pueblo'). There is also evidence, however, that *'ówînkeyi* were originally *'ówînge.* For example, the site known today as Yûnge'ówînkeyi was occupied in the sixteenth-century and recorded as "Yûnge'ówînge" in Spanish sources (Harrington 1916:227). Also, the ancestral Keres site of Tyuonyi (occupied ca. AD 1350–1550) is known in Tewa as *Puqwige'ówînkeyi*, 'Pueblo ruin where the pottery bases were wiped thin' (Harrington 1916:411; Kohler et al. 2004:239). Tewa oral tradition indicates that this name derives from the practices of its ancient inhabitants, which suggests that the name originated when the site was occupied and was probably Puqwige'ówînge at that time. Finally, many ancestral Tewa sites named as *'ówînkeyi* by Harrington's informants were referred to as *'ówînge* by Antonio Trujillo, a Tewa elder who worked with Ellis (1964a) on Nambe land claims in the middle decades of the twentieth century.[7] These examples suggest that *'ówînkeyi* are sites that were named by Tewa speakers when they were occupied, which means that the Tewa language must have been spoken in the Rio Grande region prior to the abandonment of the oldest archaeological sites for which names in the Tewa language are remembered.

With this framework in mind, the graph in Figure 8.1 summarizes the total number of villages and towns in the Tewa Basin settlement database (Ortman 2009: App. A) that were abandoned during each of a series of chronological periods, and the proportion of such settlements for which a Tewa name was remembered in the early twentieth century. Several aspects of these data deserve comment. First, it is clear that the probability of a Tewa site name being remembered is inversely proportional to the length of time the site has been abandoned. Tewa names are known for all villages and towns presently occupied, and

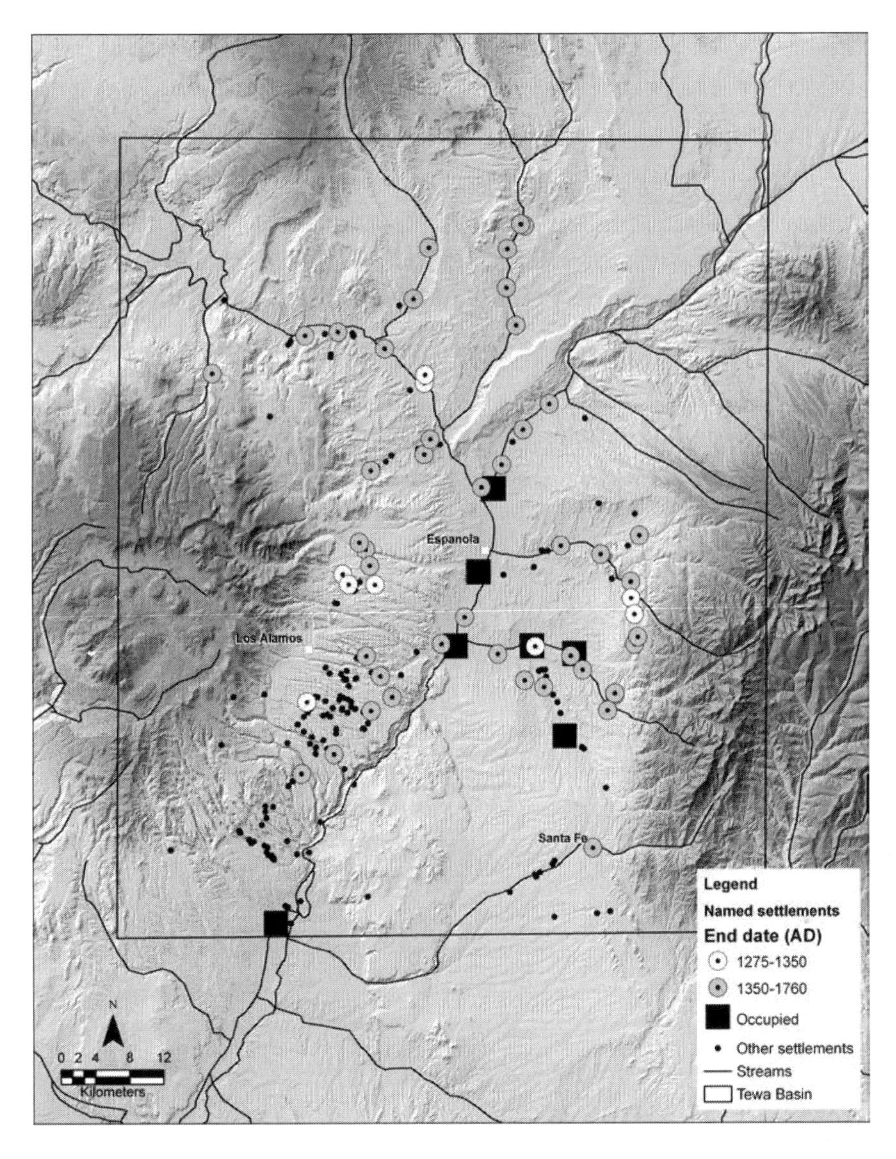

FIGURE 8.2. Distribution of named settlements, by abandonment date.

all that have been abandoned since AD 1700, but sites abandoned earlier in time are less likely to be remembered. It is not appropriate to analyze this decay process statistically because several idiosyncratic factors in addition to the passage of time are responsible for the list of named sites in Appendix C. But it is clear that decay in social memory of abandoned settlements is one of the major factors structuring these data.[8]

The second important pattern is that the earliest sites for which Tewa names are remembered were abandoned during the Late Coalition period (AD 1275–1350). Figure 8.2 illustrates the distribution of these sites within the Tewa Basin, along with that of all other abandoned settlements with Tewa names, currently occupied pueblos, and other settlements for which there was no Tewa name in the early twentieth century. This map illustrates that these oldest named sites occur throughout the area encompassed by more recently abandoned sites with Tewa names, including the Pajarito Plateau, the Chama Valley, and the eastern Rio Grande tributaries. These data make a strong case that Tewa was being spoken throughout the Tewa Basin by the early AD 1300s.

The third point is that although large settlements abandoned prior to the Late Coalition period are not numerous, the Tewa Basin settlement database contains 11 Late Developmental aggregates that could have housed 50 people or more, and none of these are associated with Tewa names in the extant literature. Due to decay in memory of site names over time, it is certainly possible that these settlements once had Tewa names that have since been forgotten. Thus, we could not say on the basis of these data that Tewa was not spoken in the Tewa Basin during the Late Developmental period. There are, however, ancillary data that increase the likelihood of this scenario.

Table 8.2 presents a list of site numbers, native names, morpheme-by-morpheme translations, and occupation spans for the oldest archaeological sites for which names are remembered in the Tewa (San Juan and Santa Clara dialects) or Taos Tiwa languages. The first nine sites in this list correspond to the sites highlighted in Figures 8.1 and 8.2. The names for all these sites are transparent compounds that follow typical Tewa naming conventions, and all of them were established, as well as abandoned, during the Coalition period. Large Tewa Basin settlements abandoned during the Late Developmental period, such as the Pojoaque Grant site (LA835), do not have Tewa names, and there are no sites with Tewa names that were occupied continuously from the Late Developmental period into the Coalition period.[9] In addition, Table 8.2 includes two ancestral Northern Tiwa sites, one of which (LA12741) was abandoned during the Late Developmental period, approximately AD 1190. This is the longest-abandoned, village-sized settlement in the Northern Rio Grande region for which a name in the Tewa or Taos language has been recorded. The fact that no Late Developmental sites have Tewa names, but at least one such site has a Tiwa name, generally supports the conclusions of the paired-toponym analysis — namely, that Tiwa has been spoken in the northern Rio Grande for a longer period of time than Tewa.

Finally, and perhaps most importantly, the only site abandoned prior to the Late Coalition period for which a Tewa name is remembered is actually a site in the Mesa Verde region. Its name is inferred from an oral tradition surrounding it recorded by Jean Jeançon (1925:39) in the early twentieth century.

> In the early days of his contact with the Tewas of Santa Clara, the writer was told stories of the coming of these people from a great village in southwestern Colorado in the dim past. The accounts were so graphic and exact that he copied a map made by his informant of the village, which must have been in ruins at that time, and located in a part of the country in which the man had never been, and only knew from traditions, and a few years later visited a

TABLE 8.2. Early villages and towns with Tewa or Tiwa names

Site Number[a]	Name[b]	Translation	Occupation Dates (AD)[c]
LA180	Pʰinikʰą̈wiˀówînkeyi	Dwarf cornmeal gap pueblo ruin	1250–1325
LA245	K'aatayˀówînkeyi	Cottonwood grove pueblo ruin	1275–1350
LA264	P'ibiḏiˀówînkeyi	Little red mound pueblo ruin	1275–1350
LA271	Tekʰeˀówînkeyi	Cottonwood bud pueblo ruin	1200–1350
LA300	Kaap'oeˀówînkeyi	Leaf water pueblo ruin	1250–1350
LA918	Shųp'óḏéˀówînkeyi	Cicada head pueblo ruin	1275–1350
LA12655	Nakeˀmuu	Land-point village	1250–1325
LA21422	Tsipiwiˀówînkeyi	Flaking-stone issuing gap pueblo ruin	1250–1350
LA21427	Navahuˀówînkeyi	Cultivable field arroyo pueblo ruin	1250–1325
LA12741[d]	P'ôkutʰo (Taos)	Water-dry-at (El Pueblito site)	1050–1190
LA260[e]	T'oytʰɨna (Taos)	People-house (Pot Creek Pueblo)	1260–1320
5MT5006[f]	Phaap'in-	Yucca mountain (village) (Yucca House)	1240–1280

[a] The basis for associating native language names with site numbers is provided in Appendix D, unless otherwise noted.
[b] Tewa names are written using the practical orthography established by the Ohkay Owingeh (San Juan Pueblo) Bilingual Program (Martinez 1982; San Juan Pueblo 2000). Taos names are written using the orthography of Trager (1946).
[c] Occupation spans were determined following the procedures discussed in Chapter 4.
[d] George L. Trager Papers, University of California, Irvine, Box 40; Fowles 2004:230.
[e] George L. Trager Papers, University of California, Box 40; Crown 1991.
[f] Jeançon 1925:39; Glowacki 2001.

> ruin which in situation and surrounding corresponded with the description given him, and was able to identify the place as the one from which the Tewa claimed that they came. While the ruin is a great mound at present, there is enough of outline left to positively identify it with the map and as a result of information given by the writer and from other sources, the name of the ruin was changed from the one by which it had been known to that by which it is known to the Tewa. The site here referred to was formerly known as the Aztec Springs ruins, but is now known as the Yucca House, which is the name that the Tewa call it.

The archaeological site of Yucca House (5MT5006), around which this tradition centers, is a large ancestral Pueblo village on the east flank of Sleeping Ute Mountain in southwest Colorado (see Figure 12.1 for location). The site was first described by W. H. Jackson (1876:377–378), mapped by W. H. Holmes (1878: Plate XL), and later mapped and described by Fewkes (1919:26–27). The site contains a McElmo style great house that may have been constructed during the Chacoan era (AD 1060–1140) (Marshall et al. 1979:313; Powers et al.

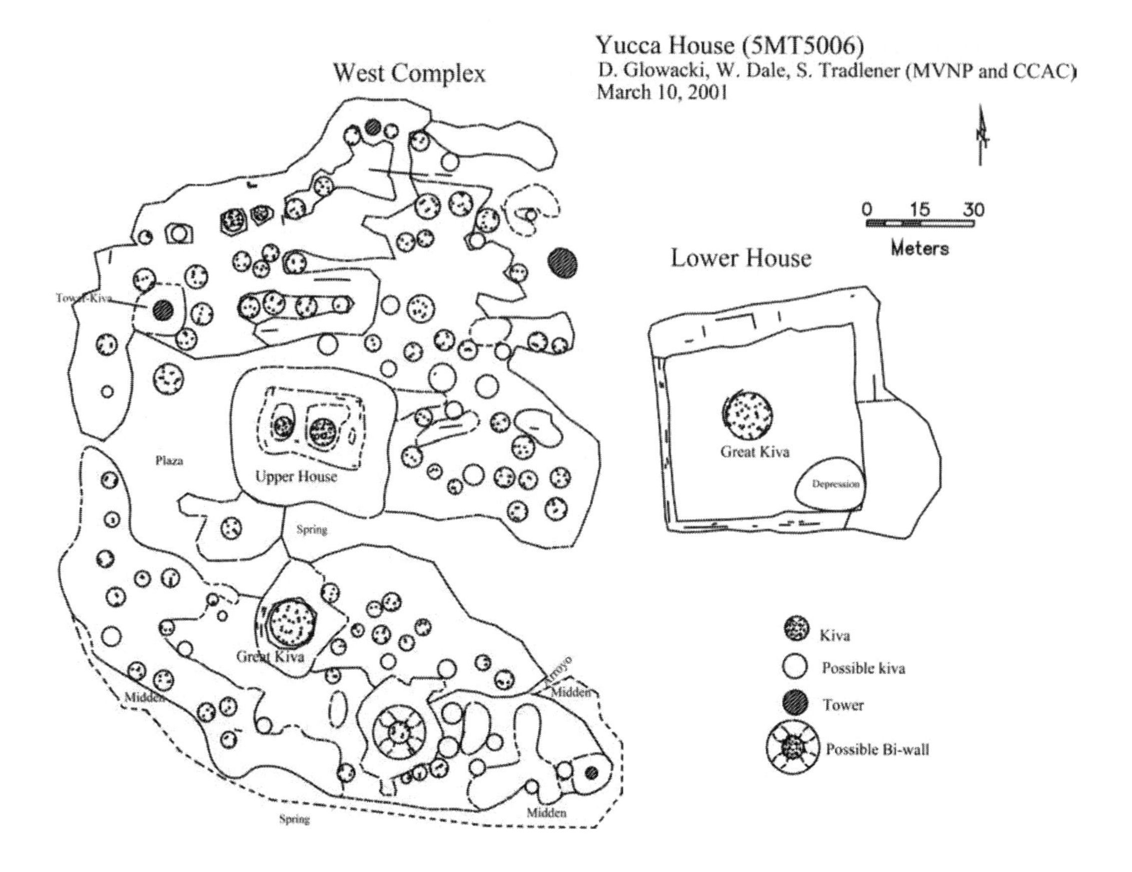

FIGURE 8.3. Plan map of Yucca House (© 2001 Crow Canyon Archaeological Center).

1983:174–177), but a recent review of pottery, tree-ring dates, and architectural details (Glowacki 2001) indicates that the surrounding village dates from the Late Pueblo III period (AD 1240–1280) and represents a "canyon-rim pueblo" analogous to Sand Canyon Pueblo (Lipe and Ortman 2000; Ortman and Bradley 2002). Yucca House was thus one of the last villages occupied by ancestral Pueblo people in the Mesa Verde region, and its inhabitants were likely involved in the final depopulation.

Although it is not known what Jeançon's informant's map looked like, Yucca House (Figure 8.3) contains several architectural features that distinguish it from other large sites in the area, and as a result it would have been identifiable even from a rough sketch map.[10] These include the Upper House — a rectangular, multistoried room block with two enclosed, circular kivas — and the Lower House — a large, rectangular enclosure with a circular kiva in the plaza that may represent an early expression of the plaza-oriented village plan that became the standard form throughout the Pueblo world by the early AD 1300s. In light of the Tewa tradition surrounding this site, it may not be a stretch to view the Lower House as a prototype of this new settlement form.[11]

It is also significant that Harrington independently recorded place-names for topographical features in the vicinity of Yucca House in his ethnogeography. As mentioned earlier, he recorded the name *Phaa p'in* ('Yucca Mountain') for "a mountain somewhere near the Montezuma Valley in southwestern Colorado.

The mountain gives Montezuma Valley its Tewa name" (Harrington 1916:565). It appears that neither Harrington nor his informant knew precisely where this mountain was, but the term clearly refers to Ute Mountain because this landform is labeled *Sierra del Datil*, 'Mountain of Yucca Bananas,' in the 1778 Pacheco map of the Domínguez-Escalante Expedition (Warner 1995:144–145). The Spanish name likely derives from the Ute name for this landform, given that Ute people inhabited this area at the time of Spanish contact, the Dominguez-Escalante Expedition was led by Ute guides, and Utes who live in the area today refer to the mountain as *Wiisi-kaa=pɨ* 'Yucca-fruit mountain' in their native language. The Ute name may in turn derive from the Tewa and/or Towa name for this same landform. Finally, Harrington recorded a Tewa name for the Montezuma Valley (*Phaa p'innae'ahkongeh* 'Plain of the Yucca Mountain'), along with statements to the effect that ancestors of the Tewa lived in this area in the past: "This is a large valley in southwestern Colorado. It is said that in ancient times when the Tewa were journeying south from *Sip'ophe* the *K'ósa*, a mythic person who founded the *K'ósa* society of the Tewa, first appeared to the people while they were sojourning in this valley" (Harrington 1916:564). Thus, the tradition surrounding Yucca House recorded by Jeançon, and the related place-names and traditions recorded by Harrington, provide substantive evidence that Tewa ancestors once inhabited the Mesa Verde region because these traditions concern an ancestral village and link to an archaeological site and its environs that were occupied during the late 1200s, plausibly by people who emigrated to the Tewa Basin.

This analysis of ancestral site names suggests that the Tewa language has definitely been spoken in the Tewa Basin from the Late Coalition period onward. There is no evidence to suggest whether or not Tewa was spoken in the Rio Grande during the Late Developmental period, but there is positive evidence that Tiwa was spoken in this region at that time. Finally, there is positive evidence that Tewa ancestors lived in the Mesa Verde region in the thirteenth century. This implies that the Tewa language was either spoken there at that time, or place-names and place-lore surrounding the Mesa Verde region were translated into the Tewa language as these Tewa ancestors moved to the Rio Grande.

Deciphering Oral Tradition

The third line of evidence I examine in this chapter is Tewa oral tradition. Ethnographers have published numerous statements by Tewa people regarding their history and migrations, and several of these accounts mention the Mesa Verde region as a prior homeland. I have already presented accounts of the traditional lore surrounding specific locations within the Mesa Verde region. Other accounts reference the Mesa Verde region in a more general way. For example, Aniceto Swaso, a Tewa from Santa Clara Pueblo, offered the following statement to Jeançon (1923:75–76) in the early twentieth century.

> We were a long time coming down to this country; sometimes we stop long time in one place, but all the time it was still too cold for us to stay, so we

> come on. After while some people get to what you call Mesa Verde, in Colorado.... Then they began to get restless again and some go west on the San Juan River, some of them come by way of the Jicarilla Apache country, some come the other way by way of Cañon Largo, Gallinas, and the Chama.

Tewa people also refer to the north as the general direction of their ancestral homeland in traditional songs. A good example was composed for the Turtle Dance at Santa Clara Pueblo in the early twentieth century (Spinden 1933:97).

> Long ago in the north
> Lies the road of emergence!
> Yonder our ancestors live,
> Yonder we take our being.
>
> Yet now we come southwards
> For cloud flowers blossom here
> Here the lightning flashes,
> Rain water here is falling!

Finally, the Tewa origin narrative specifically states that in the beginning, Tewa ancestors lived in the distant north (e.g., Ortiz 1969:13). These statements reinforce Alfonso Ortiz's (1969:148–149) observation that "Many Tewa elders show a very detailed knowledge of the region north and northwest of San Juan into what is now southwestern Colorado. This is true even if they have never been there themselves.... such detailed knowledge does lend credence to the Tewa's migration traditions and claims that they once occupied an area considerably to the north and northwest of where they are now." These statements and texts demonstrate that Tewa people generally view the north as the direction from which they originated in the distant past. What I wish to focus on here, however, are accounts that actually mention the legendary Tewa homeland by name.

Tewayó: The Ancient Tewa Homeland

Harrington (1916:572) reported that "the old cacique of Nambé seemed to know a vague place in the north named *Tewayóge* 'great Tewa place' (*Tewa* name of the tribe; *yó* augmentative; *ge* 'down at,' 'over at')." Florence Hawley Ellis (1974:2) confirmed this in a report on the past use of territory for agriculture by Nambé Pueblo.

> The Tewas on the east side of the Rio Grande referred to their territory as Teguayo, 'Place of the Tewas,' even as they also referred to their earlier home in the northwest on the San Juan, apparently either in Mesa Verde or a little farther east in the Upper San Juan around Aztec and the basin of the Navajo

Reservoir. As 'Teguayo' was also used to designate a mythical ancestral place of origin, the term puzzled the Spaniards, but causes little difficulty if one realizes that the Pueblos (like ourselves) often duplicate some old names in new areas.

Statements such as these are intriguing, but because they refer to a place that, if real, would not have been occupied for more than 600 years, the historical value of these statements would be strengthened considerably if it could be shown that references to Tewayó that link it with the Mesa Verde region also occur in Spanish documents written closer to the period in which it would have been inhabited. It turns out that such references do exist, and date as far back as the middle seventeenth century. It is difficult to perceive the significance of these references on a surface reading, however, because the Spanish became confused regarding the location and significance of Tewayó, and this has led many scholars to overlook or misinterpret these accounts. Hodge (1912:712), for example, concluded that Tewayó was nothing more than "the name of the country of the Tewa (Tegua) and perhaps of the Tigua, in New Mexico, around which, as in the case of Quivira, considerable mystery arose among the Spanish writers of the seventeenth century, who, losing sight of the exact application of the term, transplanted the 'province' to the then unknown north" (also see Sanchez 2006; Tyler 1952). According to Ellis, Hodge was partly right: Tewa people do call their current homeland "Tewayó." Nonetheless, Harrington's and Ellis's statements suggest that it is worthwhile to examine Spanish references to Tewayó in greater detail.

To make sense of these references, I first take a short detour into the literature surrounding the Lake of Copala, another mythic place in the unknown north with which the Spanish became infatuated during the Age of Exploration.[12] According to Chavez (1967:121–122), the legend of Copala derived from Toltec, Nahua, and Chichimec legends recorded by sixteenth-century Spanish writers. These legends refer to Aztlán, Huehuetlalpallan, and Tlalpallan as places in the north from which these peoples came down into Mexico. One group lingered at a place called "Seven Caves" on their way down. Tlalpallan came to be identified with Seven Caves, and then merged with "the Seven Cities" of a Portuguese romance to become "the Seven Cities of Cibola" that Marcos de Niza and Coronado searched for in 1539–1540. By the middle of the sixteenth century Spanish adventurers and fortune seekers had begun to refer to Copala as the northern homeland of the Mexica, and as the birthplace of Montezuma, the Hispanicized name of the last Mexica emperor and a major Nahua deity.

As Spanish explorers pushed northward into New Mexico, they inquired about these Nahua narratives with the local people they encountered. One such encounter occurred in 1604 during the journey of Oñate from Santa Fe toward "the Sea of the South." This encounter was later described by Fray Gerónimo de Zarate Salmerón, summarized by Tyler (1952:317–318) as follows.

> As the expedition proceeded on its way some Indians were encountered who had news of the Lake of Copala. These Indians described the lake, the surrounding lands, and all its banks, saying the area was thickly populated. One Indian said "Copala" plainly. Captain Geronimo Marquez told Father Zarate that upon hearing the Indians from Copala talk to a Mexican Indian, the servant of the soldier, one of them asked, "Where is that man from? Is he by chance from Copala? For the people there speak as he speaks." The Indians encountered told them that those Indians who spoke the Mexican language wore gold bracelets on their wrists and upper arms, and earrings in their ears. They said it was fourteen days' journey from that point to Copala, in a northwesterly direction.

What appears to have happened is that Oñate's party met some Northern Uto-Aztecan-speaking people (probably Ute, Southern Paiute, or Chemehuevi) who could communicate to some extent with their Nahua servants and guides, and who, when asked about lakes to the north, responded as best they could. Through communications like these, the Spanish came to believe that fabulously rich Copala, the birthplace of Montezuma, was several hundred leagues northwest of Santa Fe, in the area of present-day Utah Lake and the Great Salt Lake.

The real confusion began when the Spanish began to learn of Pueblo Indian traditions concerning lakes and kingdoms in the northwest. One of the places they learned about was Tewayó. The earliest references to this place are associated with Don Diego de Peñalosa Briceno, governor of New Mexico from 1661 to 1664. During his reign he learned of Tewayó through his dealings with Pueblo Indians and tried in vain for many years to mount an expedition to the place they described. The earliest depiction of Tewayó occurs on "The Peñalosa Map," dating from the AD 1680s, which locates it northwest of Santa Fe, beyond the mountains along the west side of the Rio Chama (Figure 8.4) (also see Bloom 1934).

Veiled references to Tewayó also occur in Spanish documents related to the Pueblo Revolt. In fact, it appears that social memories of an ancient homeland in the north were part of the discourse behind the rebellion itself.[13] According to the Spanish account of the testimony of two Tesuque runners who were interrogated by Otermín on August 9, 1680, "They said that the most that has come to their knowledge is that it is a matter of common report among all the Indians that *there had come to them from very far away toward the north a letter from an Indian lieutenant of Po he yemu* to the effect that all of them in general should rebel, and that any pueblo that would not agree to it they would destroy, killing all the people" (Hackett and Shelby 1942, I:4–5, emphasis added).

Additional details emerge from the Spanish account of the testimony obtained from Tewa and Tiwa warriors captured by Otermín's forces during the siege of Santa Fe.

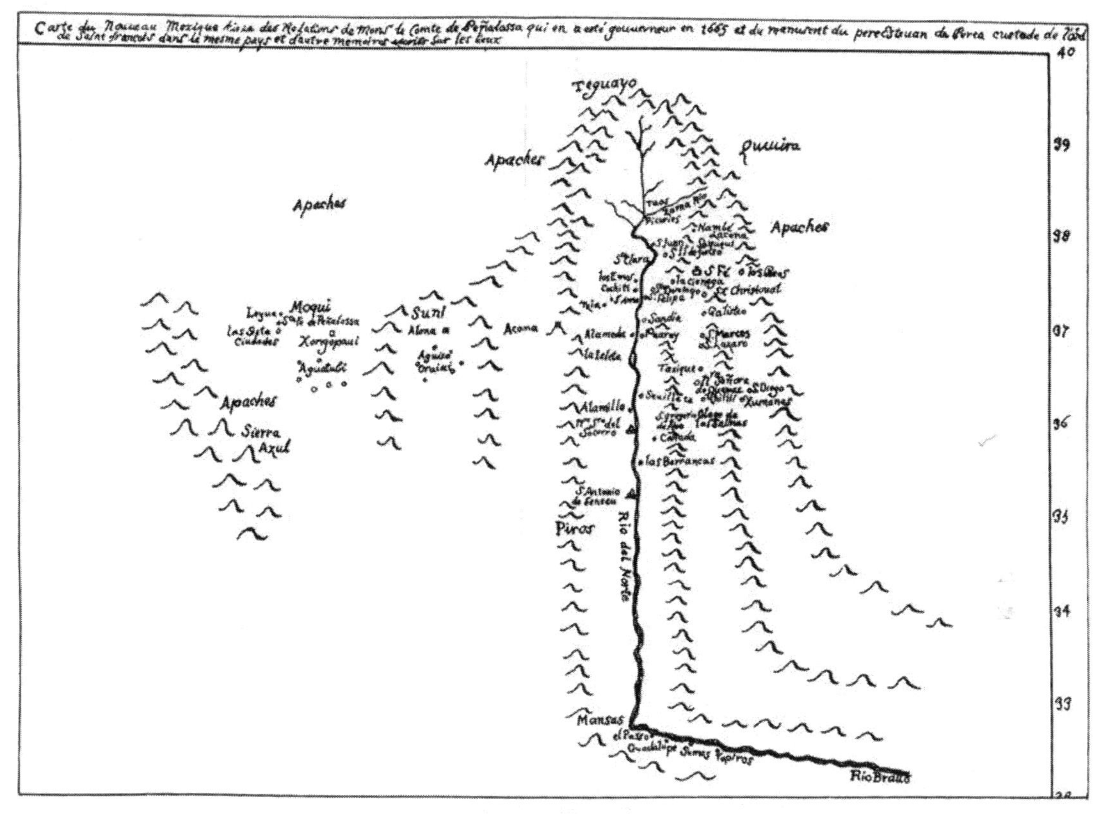

The latter were executed, having first revealed the treason, saying it had been planned a long time before by the Teguas Indians of the pueblo of Tesuque, and that now, in order to carry it out, *they had the mandate of an Indian who lives a very long way from this kingdom, toward the north, from which region Montezuma came, and who is the lieutenant of Po he yemu*; and that this person ordered all the Indians to take part in this treason and rebellion, saying that they would kill immediately anyone who refused to agree to it. (Hackett and Shelby 1942, I:15–16, emphasis added)

FIGURE 8.4. "Tracing of a French Map." Note the location of "Teguayo" northwest of New Mexico. (From Jose Manuel Espinosa, "The Legend of Sierra Azul with Special Emphasis upon the Part It Played in the Reconquest of New Mexico," *New Mexico Historical Review*, 9 (April 1934): 113. Reproduced by permission.)

Finally, during his attempted reconquest, Otermín's forces captured an elderly man from San Felipe named Pedro Naranjo who was fluent in Keres, Tewa, and Spanish. The account of his testimony concerning the causes of the revolt, given in Spanish on December 19, 1681, reads as follows.

Finally, in the past years, at the summons of an Indian named Popé who is said to have communication with the devil, it happened that in an estufa of the pueblo of Los Taos there appeared to the said Popé three figures of Indians who never came out of the estufa. *They gave the said Popé to understand that*

> *they were going underground to the lake of Copala*. He saw these figures emit fire from all the extremities of their bodies, and that one of them was called Caudi, another Tilini, and the other Tleume.... as soon as the Spaniards had left the kingdom an order came from the said Indian, Popé, in which he commanded all the Indians to break the lands and enlarge their cultivated fields, *saying that now they were as they had been in ancient times*, free from the labor they had performed for the religious and the Spaniards, who could not now be alive. He said that this is the legitimate cause and the reason they had for rebelling, *because they had always desired to live as they had when they came out of the lake of Copala*. (Hackett and Shelby 1942, II:246–247, emphasis added)

Naranjo's testimony, in particular, has been much commented upon by scholars of the Pueblo Revolt, but for present purposes the following points are most relevant.[14] First, in seventeenth-century New Mexico it was commonly understood that Montezuma came from Copala, and that Copala lay far to the northwest of Santa Fe. Second, the accounts also place Po he yemu, the Tewa culture hero, in the direction of Copala. Third, the conflation of Montezuma and P'oseyemu that had clearly taken place by the early twentieth century (see Bandelier 1892b; Read 1926), as reflected in Harrington's (1947) use of "Montezuma" as an English translation of *P'oseyemu*, appears to have been underway in the seventeenth century based on the captive testimonies. Finally, Naranjo's testimony presents Copala as the lake from which the Pueblos emerged in ancient times. Given Naranjo's knowledge of Spanish, we may surmise that he used the word *Copala*, which appears in the original Spanish text (De Marco 2000:418–419) and may have been more familiar to the Spanish, to refer to Tewayó.

This analysis, which suggests Tewayó and Copala had become conflated by the late seventeenth century, is supported by other documents dating from the Pueblo Revolt period. The most important of these is the report of Fray Alonso de Posada to the Spanish Council of the Indies on the northern provinces of "Quivira" and "Teguayo." The report was completed in 1686, partly in response to Peñalosa's scheming among Spain's enemies after his exile from New Spain, and perhaps also in response to suspicions regarding messengers from the unknown north as instigators of the Pueblo Revolt. It is clear from Posada's report that he believed Tewayó and Copala were a single place located in the area of Utah Lake, as suggested by Zarate Salmerón. Posada's directions to Tewayó began as follows:

> To provide some understanding of this land, let us recall again the location of the villa of *Santa Fe*, the capital of New Mexico which is as stated at thirty-seven degrees. Taking from this villa a straight line to the northwest between north and south and crossing the *sierras* called *Casafuerte* or *Navajo*, one reaches a large river which runs directly west for a distance of sixty leagues

> which are possessed by the *Apacha* nation. Crossing this river, one enters the nation called the *Yuta*, a warlike people. (Thomas 1982:42)

The river forming the southern boundary of Ute (Yuta) territory and the northern boundary of the territory of the Apaches de Navajo was the San Juan River, as indicated by Tewa names for this feature. In the early twentieth century the San Juan was known to Tewas as *Yutaˀîmp'oe,* 'Ute Indian river,' and also *Wän Sáveh'împ'oe*, 'Navajo Indian river' (Harrington 1916:560). The passage thus indicates that the initial steps in the journey from Santa Fe toward Tewayó involved crossing the Jemez Mountains, the Dinetah, and then the San Juan River.

The initial stages of the journey would have taken one into the northern San Juan drainage, heading toward the Mesa Verde region, but Posada believed Tewayó/Copala was located much farther to the northwest.

> Beyond this nation some seventy leagues in the same northwest direction one enters afterwards between some hills at a distance of fifty leagues more or less, *the land which the Indians of the North call Teguayo, and the Mexican Indians by an old tradition call Copala*. In the Mexican language this means a congregation of many different peoples and nations. The same old tradition states that from that region came not only the Mexican Indians, who were the last, but also all the rest of the nations which in different times were settling in these lands and kingdoms of New Spain.... For a brief resumé let us consider the direction of the nations which are on the north according to the needle by taking Santa Fe as the center of its four directions.... Looking from the said villa to the northwest we will have at seventy leagues the *Yuta* nation. Beyond at a distance of some one hundred and eighty leagues from the villa are the kingdom and provinces of *Teguayo*. (Thomas 1982:42–45, emphasis added)

A Spanish league in the eighteenth century was defined as the distance a man on horseback could travel on level ground at a normal gait in one hour, approximately 2.63 statute miles, or 4.23 km (Warner 1995:5, n. 17). Assuming that Posada used the same unit, the Yuta territory would have been approximately 185 miles northwest of Santa Fe, in the vicinity of the present-day Southern Ute reservation, and Tewayó/Copala would have been approximately 475 miles in the same direction, in the vicinity of Lake Timpanogo, or Utah Lake, near present-day Provo, Utah (Tyler 1952:323).

The conflation of Tewayó and Copala that is explicit in Posada's report, and implied by the Otermín captive accounts, probably resulted from several factors. First, tales of Tewayó must have derived primarily from Tewa speakers because *Tewayó* is a native Tewa word, and Tewa origin narratives describe their place of origin as a lake in the north (Ortiz 1969; Parsons 1994 [1926]). This is important because the Tewa word for 'lake' can mean many things in addition to a still body of water.

> P'oquin is a high-context word [that] simply means 'lake' [in English]. But in Tewa that's not the case. P'oquin is a metaphor that means many things. [For example,] the p'oquin is a kiva too, so it's a sacred place. Where there is a kha-je, there is a p'oquin, or sacred place. Therefore, those places that are p'oquin [include] not only the kiva but where you collect Douglas fir for ceremonial dances; where you bring the Douglas fir to is a prayer shrine, a p'oquin. If we came from P'oquingeh, it does not mean that we came from a body of water, literally, although that's the way anthropologists and archaeologists have interpreted it. That's the only way they can interpret it if they don't know Tewa [and] they don't understand the many contexts and meanings of p'oquin. (Naranjo 2006:53–54)

In this context it is reasonable to presume that when asked where they came from, Tewa people would have responded that they came from a *p'o:kwin* in the northwest also known as Tewayó, and the Spanish interpreted this as a reference to an actual lake. Second, the Yuta territory and Mesa Verde region lay on the same azimuth from Santa Fe as Utah Lake, and the initial stages of the journey to both places would have been identical, up the Rio Chama toward the northwest. Thus, it would have been easy to confuse Tewayó with Spanish understandings of Copala based on information provided by Tewas regarding the former place. Third, although early accounts, such as those reflected on the Peñalosa Map, appear to have placed Tewayó adjacent to and northwest of New Mexico, the Spanish had very little knowledge of the "unknown north" in the seventeenth century, and thus could have inferred that Tewayó lay a much greater distance northwest of Santa Fe so as to bring it into accord with their developing understanding of Copala as Utah Lake. Fourth, one of Posada's primary sources was a Jemez Indian named D. Juanillo, who claimed to have been a captive in the provinces of Tewayó and reported "that they have in them a very large number of people of different languages some of which were spoken in New Mexico, and also a large lake with its entire circumference populated" (Thomas 1982:44). This passage may well refer to Utah Lake. Finally, Pueblo people may have intentionally contributed to the conflation of Tewayó and Copala to connect their resistance of Spanish domination to Mexica legends and prophecies in the hope of arousing fear and anxiety among the Spanish.

The conflation of Tewayó with Copala, and the association of both with Utah Lake, persisted in New Mexico for nearly a century after the completion of Posada's report. For example, "Laguna de Teguyo" appears northwest of New Mexico, at 40 degrees north latitude, on a map of New Spain prepared by Alzate-Ramírez in 1768 (O'Crouley 1972). This lake is depicted at the same latitude and direction from Santa Fe as the actual Utah Lake, and is annotated with a short

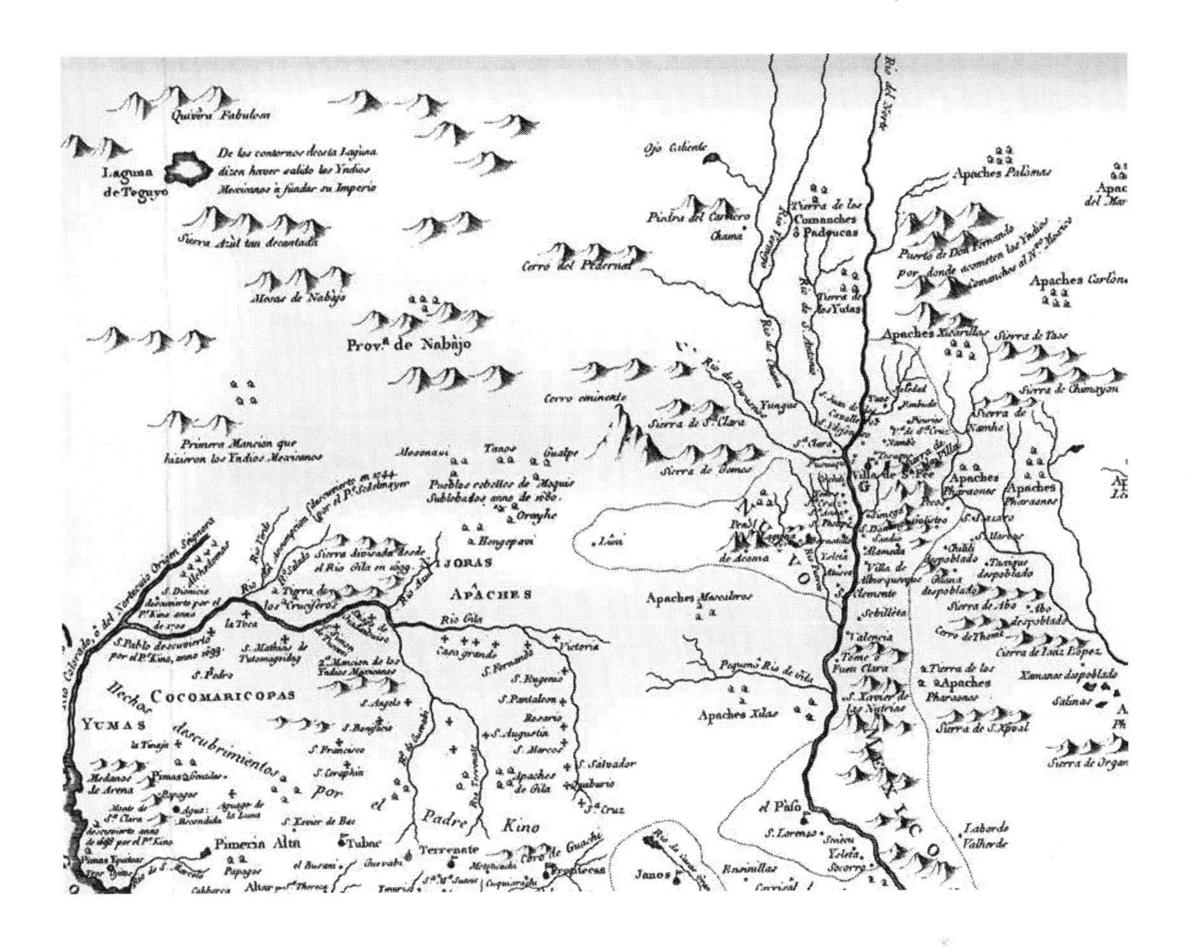

passage that identifies it as the origin place of the Mexica (Figure 8.5). This map suggests that, from the time of the Pueblo Revolt through the mid-eighteenth century, Spanish geographers viewed *Tewayó* as a synonym for *Copala*.

This confusion was finally cleared up by Fray Silvestre Vélez de Escalante in a letter he wrote to Fray Morfi in 1778, a few years after the Domínguez-Escalante Expedition. Escalante reported camping on the banks of the Dolores River in southwestern Colorado, visiting some ruins in the vicinity, and journeying all the way to Lake Timpanogo, or Utah Lake, where he observed the Indian settlements on its shores (Warner 1995). In closing the letter, he wrote,

> Before finishing this letter I desire to indicate what is my opinion, at least, upon the Tehuayo and upon the Gran Quivira, whose imaginary greatness has given much to think over from the beginning of the last century to the present. The Tehuayo, according to the diary of Oñate and other ancient narratives, should be considered at the most two hundred leagues to the northwest from Santa Fe; and it is nothing but the land by way of which the Tihuas, Tehuas, and the other Indians transmigrated to this kingdom; which is clearly shown by the ruins of the pueblos which I have seen in it, whose

FIGURE 8.5. Detail of "Nuevo mapa geográfico de la America septentrional," by Alzate-Ramírez, 1768 (from O'Crouley 1972). Note the location of "Laguna de Teguyo" northwest of Nuevo México, Cerro Pedernal, and the Provincia de Nabajo, and the caption identifying it as the mythic homeland of the Mexica.

> form was the same that they afterwards gave to theirs in New Mexico; and the fragments of clay and pottery which I also saw in the said country are much like that which the said Tehuas make today. To which is added the prevailing tradition with them, which proves the same; and that I have gone on foot more than three hundred leagues in the said direction up to 41 degrees and 19 minutes latitude and have found no information whatever among the Indians who today are occupying that country of others who live in pueblos. (Twitchell 1914:278–279)

Note that the "diary of Oñate" refers to the account of Zarate Salmerón, and the distance of "at most two hundred leagues" refers to a distance of approximately 525 miles. Also, note that this passage implies that Escalante continued to treat *Tewayó* and *Copala* as interchangeable names for the same place (recall that Zarate Salmerón's diary does not actually mention Tewayó, but only Copala). Escalante argues here, however, that the land of Tewayó is actually closer to Santa Fe than Posada suggested, and represents the former homeland of the Tewa and Tiwa people. The basis for this argument was Escalante's finding of ruined pueblo style dwellings and black-on-white pottery in southwestern Colorado, his knowledge of Tewa oral traditions regarding a former homeland in the northwest, and the fact that he had traveled to Utah Lake and beyond and found no evidence of present or past occupancy of these areas by people who lived in pueblo style dwellings.

Escalante thus determined through archaeological and ethnographic observation that the most likely location of Tewayó, the ancient homeland of the Tewa people, was in the Mesa Verde region — and not in the vicinity of Utah Lake. He thus brought Spanish understanding of Tewayó in line with Tewa oral traditions that are remembered to this day. His conclusion also appears to have been accepted by other Spanish geographers, such as Juan López, who prepared a map of New Mexico in 1795 on which the area northwest of Santa Fe and between the Río de Nabajo (the San Juan River) and the Río Tizón (the Colorado River) — in other words, the Mesa Verde region — is labeled as "Teguayo, Pais de los Teguas" (Figure 8.6).

Oral Tradition, Geography, and Cosmography

Before concluding this chapter, I wish to comment on one aspect of Tewa oral tradition that could be construed as evidence that the Tewa people originated in the Rio Grande region as opposed to the Mesa Verde region. The Tewa origin narrative has been recorded independently by several researchers, including Alfonso Ortiz (1969:13–14), Elsie Clews Parsons (1994 [1926]:9–15), and Jean Jeançon (n.d.). In all cases this narrative refers to the primordial place of emergence as *Sip'op^{h}e*, which lies beneath a brackish lake called *ˀOkhą̨ngep'o:kwinge* 'Sandy Place Lake.' Harrington (1916:567) associated these names with Sierra Blanca Lake in the San Luis Valley of Colorado. The question these data raise is

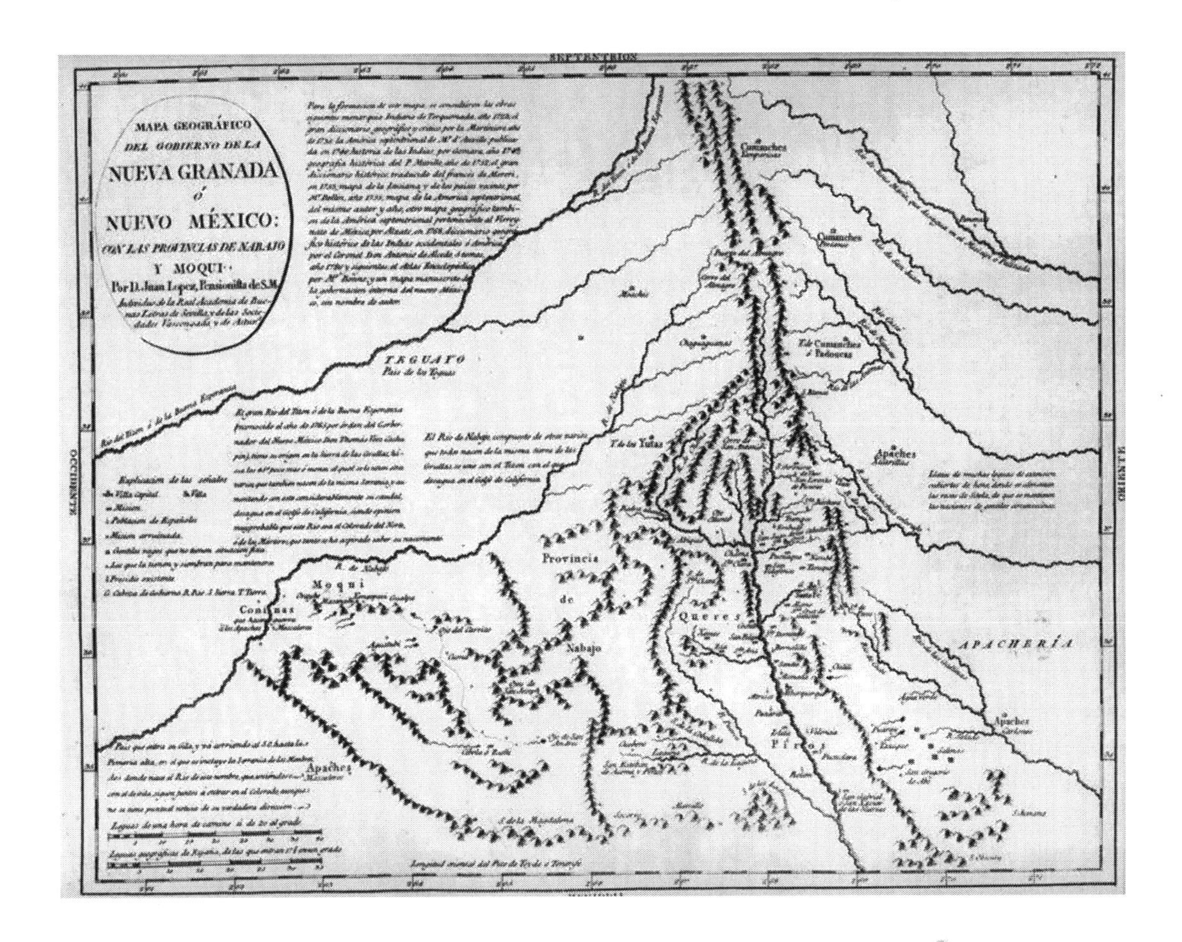

FIGURE 8.6. Detail of "Mapa geográfico del gobiernio de la Nueva Granada o Nuevo México," by D. Juan López, 1795 (photocopy). Note the location of Teguayo northwest of New Mexico, between the "Rio Tizon" (Colorado) and "Rio de Nabajo" (San Juan). (Map Collection 78.9 1795, Fray Angélico Chávez History Library, Santa Fe, New Mexico, USA. Reproduced by permission.)

why Tewas consistently talk about their place of emergence as a lake near the headwaters of the Rio Grande if, in fact, they lived to the northwest, in the Mesa Verde region, before migrating to the northern Rio Grande region.

There are a few reasons why I think Tewa origin narratives do not undermine the hypothesis suggested by other lines of evidence. First, following the earlier discussion of *p'o:kwin* and *Tewayó*, the notion that Tewa people emerged from a lake does not necessarily mean that they emerged from a specific lake. Thus, ˀOkhąngep'o:kwinge, in the San Luis Valley, may simply represent the prototypical "lake" based on its characteristics and geographical relationship to the historic Tewa territory rather than being the actual place where the Tewa people originated. Tewa worldview provides ample basis for thinking of "Sandy Place Lake" this way. As Alfonso Ortiz explains,

> All peoples try to bring their definitions of group space somehow into line with their cosmologies, but the Pueblos are unusually precise about it. This precision has many, almost inexhaustible, implications because the Pueblos attempt to reproduce this mode of classifying space on a progressively smaller scale. Since all space is sacred and sacred space is inexhaustible,

> these models of the cosmos can be reproduced endlessly around them.... All the Pueblos also have a well-elaborated conception and symbolization of the middle or center of the cosmos, represented by a sipapu, an earth-navel, or the entire village. Usually there are many centers because sacred space can be recreated again and again without ever exhausting its reality.... The elaboration of the notion of the center has the further implication that the dominant spatial orientation, as well as that of motion, is centripetal or inward.... Thus a Pueblo priest, when setting out a dry painting, will first carefully set out the boundaries and then work his way inward toward the center. (Ortiz 1972:142–143)

This centripetal orientation reinforces Naranjo's explanation that Tewa people conceive of the world as having layers of lakes that are located at the far edges of the world, on the tops of their cardinal mountains, at springs closer to home, and within the kivas in their villages. Notice also that due to this centripetal orientation, events that happened longest ago happened farthest away. Finally, the characteristic Tewa ritual circuit — which is followed in recounting emergence narratives, kiva ceremonies, and plaza dances — begins in the north (Kurath and Garcia 1970; Laski 1959; Ortiz 1969). What all this means is that the prototypical emergence place must be a lake located in the far north, beyond the edge of the current Tewa world. 'Sandy Place Lake' fits these criteria perfectly.

Second, as Ellis hinted in her discussion of Tewayó, Pueblo people tend to map preexisting cosmographical ideas onto whatever environment they find themselves in. In other words, as one moves through the world, the system of lakes that place that person in the center moves as well.[15] A documented example of this process is the fact that the primary cardinal mountain and associated lake of each Tewa pueblo varies in accordance with its geographical location (see Ortiz 1969; Ortman 2008a). This leaves open the possibility that Tewa cosmographical ideas developed elsewhere and were translated to the northern Rio Grande landscape as ancestral Tewas settled into it. This process appears to be reflected in the transfer of directional shrine systems and translation of cardinal mountains from the Mesa Verde region to the Tewa Basin (see Chapter 13; also Ortman 2008a). It is also suggested by the analysis of paired Tewa-Tiwa place names discussed earlier in this chapter. Specifically, the Tewa name for the actual emergence place, *Sip'op^{h}e*, appears to be a loan from Proto-Tiwa **tsip'aphún-* 'eye-water-black.' This toponym loan suggests that Tewa speakers learned of 'Sandy Place Lake' from Tiwa speakers who were already resident in the Rio Grande region when they began to migrate into the Tewa Basin.

Remembering Tewa Origins

The analyses of place-names, place-lore, and oral traditions in this chapter lead to several conclusions regarding Tewa origins. First, analysis of San Juan Tewa and Taos Tiwa names for specific topographic features provides no evidence that Tewa and Tiwa speakers have inherited a common stock of place-names for topographic features in the Rio Grande region from Tiwa-Tewa, their most recent common-ancestor language, as one might expect if these languages had diversified within that region. However, the existence of several Taos place-names that have been translated or loaned into San Juan Tewa does provide evidence that Tiwa has been spoken in the Rio Grande region for a longer period of time than Tewa. In addition, the identification of Tewa and Towa names for Ute Mountain that are either cognates or calques provides evidence that Proto-Tanoan speakers inhabited, or Tewa and Towa speakers interacted in, the general vicinity of Ute Mountain, in southwest Colorado, at some point in the past.

Second, the identification of Taos Tiwa names for an ancestral site abandoned around AD 1190 provides concrete evidence that Northern Tiwa has been spoken in the Northern Rio Grande region from at least the Late Developmental (AD 1050–1200) period onward. In contrast, the spatial distribution and abandonment dates of sites with Tewa names indicate that the Tewa language can only be documented as having been spoken in the Tewa Basin from the Late Coalition (AD 1275–1350) period onward. Furthermore, identification of the Tewa name for an ancestral site in the Mesa Verde region that was occupied ca. AD 1240–1280, along with names for surrounding topographic features and oral traditions of past occupation in this area, provides concrete evidence that the Tewa language was spoken in the Mesa Verde region during the final decades of ancestral Pueblo occupation in that region.

Third, statements by Tewa people regarding a former homeland in the north and/or northwest are common in the ethnographic literature. Knowledge of this former homeland and its location in the Mesa Verde region was widespread among Tewa people in seventeenth- and eighteenth-century New Mexico, and analyses of Spanish documents indicate that Tewa people called this homeland "Tewayó" and placed it within the present-day Ute territory in southwest Colorado. At least a few Tewas could recall the name and location of this homeland well into the twentieth century.

Finally, the emergence place in Tewa origin narratives, which Tewa people call 'Sandy Place Lake' and locate near the Great Sand Dunes in the San Luis Valley, Colorado, was learned of through contact with Tiwa speakers, and probably represents the translation of more ancient cosmographical concepts to the landscape of the Rio Grande region.

These findings provide strong support for the inference that Tewa was the dominant language of the Tewa Basin from the early decades of the AD 1300s into the Spanish Colonial period. These findings are also consistent with a scenario in which: (1) the Tewa language became distinct from Proto-Tiwa outside the Rio Grande region; (2) the Tewa language was brought to the Rio Grande by people who left the Mesa Verde region in the AD 1200s; and (3) these Tewa-speaking migrants encountered people who spoke Tiwa when they arrived in the Rio Grande. This scenario also matches up well with the biological and demographic evidence for population movement presented in previous chapters.

Despite the fact that place-names, place-lore, and oral traditions are consistent with this scenario, this evidence is not conclusive because a number of alternative explanations remain for these data. For example, the place-names and oral traditions surrounding Yucca House and Tewayó could have been translated into Tewa after Mesa Verde people migrated to the Rio Grande and encountered local Tewa speakers. Also, perhaps the reason Late Developmental sites lack a Tewa name is that such names are unlikely to be remembered for so long. Finally, the existence of social memories of Mesa Verde occupancy among seventeenth-century Tewas does not necessarily mean that the Tewa people came from the Mesa Verde region. Oral traditions take shape after the events they describe, and often trace the roots of the group that maintains them further back in time than the actual genesis of the present-day identity of that group. In other words, oral traditions surrounding Tewayó indicate that social memories of Mesa Verde occupancy were an element of seventeenth-century Tewa identity, and support the notion that ancestors of many present-day Tewa people migrated to the Tewa Basin in the past. However, these stories do not necessarily indicate that "*the* Tewa" migrated from the Mesa Verde region to the Northern Rio Grande as a self-identified ethnic group that maintained its identity as it moved. Instead, the stories may indicate that Tewa identity developed as part of, or in response to, this movement. In other words, memories of the migration from the Mesa Verde region to the Tewa Basin may have been an element of the discourse surrounding the construction of a new Tewa identity in the Rio Grande.[16]

In this way oral traditions can be accommodated to immigration models in which migrants adopted the local language of the destination area but retained social memories of their former homeland, or to population movement models in which migrants brought their language as well as social memories with them. Thus, even if oral traditions do provide evidence of ancient migrations, and do provide a unique window into representations of the past that support social identities, they do not necessarily provide evidence for past movements of languages and identities. So to determine conclusively whether Tewa was once spoken in the Mesa Verde region, one should ideally seek to identify aspects of the Tewa language that would not have become a part of this language if it had never been spoken in the Mesa Verde region. In the following chapter, I argue that this can be accomplished by identifying "dead" metaphors embedded in language and correlating these with "material" metaphors in the archaeological record.

Notes

1. Also see Campbell 1998:362–371; Miller 1986; and Silver and Miller 1997:57–60.
2. Thus, names for English settlements with transparent meanings, such as *Oxford* (the place where oxen crossed the Thames River), were coined more recently than names for settlements ending in *-cester* or *–chester*, which were originally Roman military camps (cf. Latin *castra* 'camp' > OE *ceastra*) (Campbell 1998:368–371). These data

reflect the fact that Latin was spoken in England before Old English speakers migrated there from the continent, soon after the fall of the Roman Empire.

3. For example, Navajo names for ancestral Pueblo archaeological sites often incorporate the term *kits'iilí* 'shattered house' (Linford 2000:43–63), indicating that these sites were ruins at the time of naming.
4. In 1874 Ernest Ingersoll recorded a Hopi tradition of conflict between Hopi and Ute ancestors during the occupation of Castle Rock Pueblo, a thirteenth-century ancestral Pueblo site in McElmo Canyon, just to the north of Ute Mountain (see Kuckelman 2000). Micaceous brown ware sherds typically associated with Numic (Northern Uto-Aztecan) peoples have also been found in association with ancestral Pueblo pottery at several unexcavated artifact scatters on the rim of the Dolores River valley (Errickson and Wilson 1988). However, one cannot rule out scavenging of ancestral Pueblo artifacts by later Ute people as an explanation for these sites, and Ute people themselves do not appear to have maintained social memories of interaction with inhabitants of ancestral Pueblo sites in the Mesa Verde region (Kayser 1965).
5. It may be relevant to the question of Tiwa priority over Tewa in the Northern Rio Grande region to note that Jeançon (1930:7–8) recorded a Taos oral tradition that refers to Ojo Caliente as the initial home of "the Summer People" before they migrated to the Taos Valley and joined with "the Winter People" who had already been living there.
6. This finding is consistent with the study of biological variation presented in Chapter 5, which suggests that ancestral Tewa and Towa speakers both originated in the Mesa Verde region.
7. Perhaps Trujillo referred to them in this way to strengthen Nambe arguments concerning their ancestral territory. This is not inconsistent with Tewa worldview, in which the past continues to exist simultaneously with the present, and thus there is a sense in which all ancestral places are still occupied, regardless of their current condition as ruins.
8. In this analysis I use the term *settlement* as shorthand for sites or site clusters that contained enough roofed space to house 50 or more persons, following the conventions discussed in Chapter 4 (1 person per room, 6 persons per pit structure).
9. Evidence of Late Developmental occupation has been found at two sites listed in Appendix C (LA36 and LA68), but in both cases there is a more recent occupation that is discontinuous with the earlier component.
10. I have combed through the personal papers of Jean Jeançon, which are currently housed at the Denver Public Library and the Colorado History Museum, for the original sketch map referred to in the published account, but have not been able to find it.
11. In Chapter 13 I suggest that plaza pueblos also exhibit formal continuities with earlier, Chaco-era great houses.
12. It is beyond the scope of this study to present a thorough treatment of the Spanish literature surrounding Copala and Tewayó. The best summaries I have encountered are by Tyler (1952), Chavez (1967), and Sanchez (2006), and I rely heavily on these sources here.
13. In Chapter 14 I draw upon these accounts to argue that the Pueblo Revolt was promoted by its leaders as a reenactment of the Mesa Verde migration.
14. For example, Chavez (1967) and Beninato (1990) present alternative theories concerning possible connections between the lieutenant of Po he yemu and Pedro Naranjo. Also see Preucel 2002. De Marco (2000) presents the original Spanish texts

for all of the Pueblo Indian testimonies recorded by Otermín, as well as commentaries on these testimonies.

15. That P'oseyemu dwelled in both Tewayó and P'osí'ówînkeyi (see Chap. 14, n. 12) may also be a reflection of this translation process.
16. This possibility emphasizes how unfortunate it is for historical anthropology that the language and ethnonym of so many groups in the "ethnographic present" are identical. It leads to such confusing but in fact unremarkable statements as "the Tewa language originated in the Mesa Verde region but the Tewa people never existed in Mesa Verde." It does not appear strange to state that the language of the United States originated in England, but Americans never existed there, yet anthropologists routinely and unjustifiably assume the histories of languages and ethnic groups are isomorphic, when in fact they are not. This conflation would be much less tempting if anthropologists did not use the same word to describe both a people and their language.

Metaphors, Language, and Archaeology

In this investigation of Kiowa-Tanoan speech community history I have thus far examined: (1) shared phonetic innovations that imply the Proto-Tewa and Proto-Tiwa speech communities were isolated for a period of time before their northern dialects came back into contact; (2) reconstructed vocabulary that indicates the Kiowa-Tanoan homeland was in the San Juan drainage and the Tewa language became distinct some time between AD 920 and 980; (3) place-names that indicate Tiwa has been spoken in the Northern Rio Grande region for a longer period than Tewa, and that Tewa can only be documented as having been spoken in that region from AD 1275; and (4) oral traditions that indicate historic Tewa people have maintained social memories of a former homeland in the Mesa Verde region from the time of the earliest written documentation to the present. When combined with demographic and biological evidence, these findings generally support the population movement hypothesis of Tewa origins, and especially the expectation that the Tewa language was brought to the Tewa Basin by thirteenth-century migrants from the Mesa Verde region.

Despite the fact that multiple lines of evidence appear contrary to expectations of the in situ development hypothesis, the analyses conducted to this point cannot rule out the immigration hypothesis — that the Tewa language diversified from Tiwa within the Rio Grande region and was subsequently adopted by Mesa Verde migrants — because the evidence presented to this point does not involve necessary links between the Tewa language and Mesa Verde archaeology: Proto-Tewa and Proto-Tiwa could have been geographically isolated in different portions of the Rio Grande region; the same plant species occur in both the Mesa Verde region and the Tewa Basin; the basic material culture and economy reflected in Proto-Tiwa-Tewa and Proto-Tiwa lexicons occur in sites of the same age in both regions; and Tewa place-names and oral traditions related to past Mesa Verde region occupancy could have been translated as Mesa Verde migrants relocated to the Tewa Basin. So to truly determine where the Tewa language originated, a method that forges direct and necessary links between archaeology and language is required. Archaeological evidence suggests that the society and culture that took shape in the Tewa Basin during the Coalition period was quite different from the society and culture of the Mesa Verde region.

So if the Tewa language was spoken in the Mesa Verde region before it came to be spoken in the Rio Grande, perhaps it retains traces of Mesa Verde culture that were left behind when Tewa speakers migrated to the Tewa Basin.

To establish such links, it is necessary to work with an aspect of human culture that is observable in the archaeological record, can become enshrined in language, and is more culturally specific than the basic elements of environment and material culture examined previously. I believe the aspect of human culture that best meets these requirements is an aspect of cultural cognition known as *conceptual metaphor*. Research on semantic change in linguistics has shown that the conceptual metaphors of ancient speech communities are often fossilized in the languages of their descendants (Campbell 1998:254–273; Sweetser 1990: 23–48; Traugott 1989; Pinker 2007:235–278), and archaeological research shows that these metaphors are also identifiable from patterns in material culture (Hays-Gilpin 2008; Ortman 2000b, 2006, 2008b; Ortman and Bradley 2002; Potter 2002, 2004; Potter and Ortman 2004; Sekaquaptewa and Washburn 2004; Tilley 1999; Whitley 2008; Whittlesey 2009). It should therefore be possible to link protolanguages with archaeological complexes by linking conceptual metaphors embedded in language with material metaphors expressed in the archaeological record.

The techniques I have used to investigate Tewa origins to this point have been, other than a few methodological wrinkles, standard approaches in archaeology, bioarchaeology, linguistics, and history. I now turn onto a different path and seek to expand the range of tools that historical anthropologists might use to integrate archaeology and language by introducing the contemporary theory of metaphor in cognitive science, and reviewing how one can identify these metaphors in language and the archaeological record. In the following chapter I use these methods to adduce strong evidence that the Tewa language did in fact originate in the Mesa Verde region.

What Are Conceptual Metaphors?

In contemporary cognitive science, *conceptual metaphor* is a label for the highly developed human ability to model relatively complex or abstract phenomena using the structure of simpler or more concrete phenomena. It also refers to the cognitive models resulting from this process that humans use in thinking, reasoning, and speaking. Conceptual metaphors arise in our brains from correspondences in the image-schematic structure of two domains of experience. Attending to these correspondences encourages a conceptual projection of additional entities, properties, and relations from the more concrete source domain onto the more abstract target domain. This makes it possible for people to better comprehend the target domain using the structure provided by the source domain.

For example, most readers of this study know what I am doing when I "lay the foundations of my argument" because English speakers have internalized the metaphor ARGUMENTS ARE BUILDINGS, and of course no building can stand without a solid 'foundation.'[1] If one thinks for a moment about the process of 'constructing' an argument, one will see that architectural imagery is thoroughly involved. When 'building' an argument, one needs to identify its 'parts' and the order in which they should be 'put together.' One also needs to ensure that the conclusions 'rest squarely' on a 'secure foundation,' and that the argument 'holds together,' can 'withstand' criticism, and will not 'crumble under its own weight.' It is possible to talk about intellectual arguments without using metaphorical language, but when one tries to do this, it usually takes more specialized vocabulary and more complex grammatical constructions to convey concepts that are more directly and readily expressed using the concrete terminology of buildings and other tangible objects. And even if one succeeds in avoiding metaphorical language, it is very difficult to think about intellectual arguments without using general metaphors such as MENTAL PROCESSES ARE PHYSICAL PROCESSES, of which ARGUMENTS ARE BUILDINGS is an example. The key point, then, is that conceptual metaphors are not just poetic tropes used to communicate nonmetaphorical concepts. Rather, these metaphors, which arise through manipulation of mental imagery, are a significant component of the concepts themselves.

The dominant theory of conceptual metaphor in contemporary cognitive science was first proposed by the linguist George Lakoff and the philosopher Mark Johnson in their book *Metaphors We Live By* (1980). In this work and subsequent writings Lakoff and Johnson demonstrate the pervasiveness of conceptual metaphor in everyday language and thought, and apply this insight to such diverse realms as linguistics, literature, philosophy, psychology, mathematics, and politics (Johnson 1987; Lakoff 1987, 1993; Lakoff and Johnson 1980, 1999; Lakoff and Kövecses 1987; Lakoff and Núñez 2000; Lakoff and Turner 1989). Others have considered the implications of their theory for anthropology (Shore 1996), religious studies (Slingerland 2004), archaeology (Ortman 2000b), and historical linguistics (Sweetser 1990). These studies make a very strong case that conceptual metaphor is a basic mechanism of human thought, and a basic building block of language and culture. As Steven Pinker (2007:237) explains, research on language and thought turns up conceptual metaphors "under every stone."

The most remarkable achievement of the Lakoff and Johnson theory is that it has promoted metaphor from the status of literary trope to a central component of the human capacity for abstract thought, of interest to a wide range of researchers throughout the social and biological sciences. As a result, a phenomenon that was previously of interest primarily to philosophers, cultural anthropologists, and literary theorists is now the subject of research in psychology (Gibbs 1994), neuroscience (Damasio 1994, 1999), and linguistics (Regier 1996) as well. An illustrative example of such studies is a series of ingenious experiments that examined the role of spatial metaphors in structuring thought about time (Boroditsky 2000). English speakers generally conceive of time using one of two spatial schemas: in the object-moving schema, you are standing still as objects pass by, as in "the weekend is almost here," whereas in the ego-moving schema, you are moving and the objects are standing still, as in "I barely made it through the week." These two schemas lead to different answers for ambiguous questions such as "Wednesday's meeting has been moved forward two days. To what day has the meeting been moved?" If one interprets this question using the object-moving schema, the day of the meeting has moved two days closer to you, or to Monday; whereas if one uses the ego-moving schema, the meeting has moved two days further from you, or to Friday. When subjects answer this question with no previous guidance as to which schema to use, they answer "Friday" and "Monday" with equal frequency. But when subjects are primed with pictures of objects moving in space, they answer "Monday" more often, and when they are primed with pictures of an individual moving through space, they answer "Friday" more often. Thus, reasoning about time is influenced by spatial imagery. Additional experiments show that subjects can also be influenced by temporal schemas when thinking about time, but are not influenced by temporal schemas when thinking about space.

These results are consistent with several aspects of the Lakoff and Johnson theory. First, they show that conceptual metaphors involve understanding abstract domains using the imagery of more concrete domains, but not the reverse. Second, they illustrate that humans use conceptual metaphors to reason and communicate about abstract phenomena. Third, because statements reflecting temporal schemas (expressed in metaphorical language) have the same influence as spatial imagery in structuring subjects' interpretation of ambiguous temporal statements, it is apparent that with repeated use, the image-schematic structure of spatial imagery comes to be linked to the domain of time and is used automatically and unconsciously. In other words, metaphors that are initially processed consciously can become so deeply ingrained that people lose sight of the fact that they are thinking and communicating metaphorically.

In their writings, Lakoff and Johnson show that English speakers use hundreds of conventional metaphors like TIME IS SPACE unconsciously and automatically in everyday thinking and communicating. These widely shared metaphors are part of the cognitive unconscious of our culture and are fundamental to our worldview and language. Metaphors that are rooted in basic bodily experience, such as ANGER IS HEAT ("he was steaming mad") are probably present in all languages and cultures (see Kövecses 2002:163–182), but other metaphors occur only in certain languages and cultures due to differences in socio-natural environments, social memory, and inherited thought traditions. Nevertheless, cross-cultural variation in conceptual metaphors is limited by the fact that all humans live on the earth and share the same basic physiology and nervous system (Johnson and Lakoff 2002). Thus, conceptual metaphors are neither universal and objective, nor radically relative and subjective.

It is difficult to overstate the fundamental advance in our understanding of human language, culture, and cognition represented by the Lakoff and Johnson theory. In Steven Pinker's words,

> metaphor really is a key to explaining thought and language. The human mind comes equipped with an ability to penetrate the cladding of sensory experience and discern the abstract construction underneath — not always on demand, and not infallibly, but often enough and insightfully enough to shape the human condition. Our powers of analogy allow us to apply ancient neural structures to newfound subject matter, to discover hidden laws and systems in nature, and not least, to amplify the expressive power of language itself.... Lakoff is right to insist that conceptual metaphors are not just literary garnishes but aids to reason — they are "metaphors we live by." And metaphors can power sophisticated inferences, not just obvious ones. (Pinker 2007:276, 253)

In this chapter I propose that conceptual metaphor theory also offers tremendous opportunities for historical anthropology. In addition to providing a currency for describing and comparing the worldviews of human societies, conceptual metaphors provide a new means of integrating archaeology and language. The key points that make conceptual metaphors relevant for this task are, first, that metaphors are consistently enshrined in language as semantic fossils; and second, that metaphors are routinely expressed in concrete nonlinguistic behavior, including the design, manufacture, and use of objects. In the following pages I examine each of these processes in turn.

How Metaphors Become Enshrined in Language

In every society new metaphors are constantly being invented by creative individuals who notice parallels among diverse realms of experience. The same individuals express these newly perceived connections in their words and actions, and if others find them appealing, the new concept will become part of a community's collective consciousness. When first exposed to a new metaphor in poetry, song, or discourse, people notice its novelty and immediately begin to work through its implications for the realm of experience it proposes to frame. As these implications are worked out, and the new metaphor is invoked in everyday thought and discourse, speakers repeatedly recruit the language of the source domain to communicate about the target domain. Over time this recruitment becomes habitual, new compound words are coined that bring together source and target domain vocabulary, and new senses related to the target domain of the metaphor become attached to source domain vocabulary. With continued use, the fact that people are using a conceptual metaphor to think about the target domain, and to communicate about it using figurative language, fades from awareness. At this point the newer, metaphoric sense of source domain words may replace the original sense, and what were once transparent, metaphoric compounds may become indivisible words with nonmetaphoric referents. It is at this point—when a metaphor has become so ingrained in the collective unconscious of a community that it influences the default meanings of words in their language—that it exerts the strongest influence on their thoughts and actions.

An excellent study of how conceptual metaphors influence semantic change is Eve Sweetser's (1990:23–48) analysis of Indo-European perception verbs in which she showed that historical changes in the meanings of these verbs followed a regular pattern, generally from concrete to abstract (also see Campbell 1998:270–273; Traugott 1989). Verbs for the physical act of seeing repeatedly came to refer to knowledge and intellection (e.g., Greek *eĩdon* 'see' > English *idea*); verbs for the physical act of hearing came to refer to listening or obeying (Greek *klúo* 'hear' > English *listen* and Danish *lystre* 'obey'); verbs for the act of smelling or tasting came to refer to personal likes or dislikes (the Latin root meaning 'touch' > English *taste*, from the French *tâter* 'to touch or try'); and verbs for touch came to refer to emotions or feelings (Classical Greek *aísthe:ma* 'object of perception' > Modern Greek 'feeling, emotion'). From these patterns Sweetser hypothesized that for several millennia people in Indo-European speech communities have used the metaphor THE MIND IS THE BODY to conceptualize cognitive and emotional aspects of experience in terms of physical sensation. Sweetser thus showed that semantic change in one area of the lexicon was not haphazard or idiosyncratic, but instead followed regular patterns, the basis of which was a specific conceptual metaphor.

Sweetser did not examine whether the mind-as-body metaphor is part of the specific cultural inheritance of Indo-European speakers or is in fact universal. It is quite possibly universal, as it draws upon basic physiological experiences that all humans share. Regardless, the key point is that Sweetser's methods can be used to reconstruct metaphors that were specific to individual protolanguages, including metaphors that are no longer active among present-day speakers of daughter dialects.

To see how, it is important to first recognize that humans are not enslaved by their metaphors. People usually maintain several distinct ways of conceptualizing a given domain and draw upon the one that best serves their needs in a given situation. Also, people can become aware of the metaphors they live by and can change them. As a group learns of the implications and limitations of their metaphors, the conditions of their lives change, or they gain additional knowledge of the world, new and perhaps more useful concepts may be invented that eventually replace the old ways of conceptualizing specific domains. The key point, however, is that discarding a metaphor does not lead to a purging of the changes that it has already wrought in a language. People generally do not retain awareness of the semantic histories of the words they use. As a result, traces of these 'dead' metaphors will remain in their language—enshrined in the form of multiple senses of words, compound words, and words whose meaning has changed — for as long as the words that betray them remain. In this way, every language contains residues of the metaphors of its past speakers. This remarkable aspect of language allows one to reconstruct components of past speakers' worldviews, irrespective of the degree to which these concepts remain active among present-day speakers. In other words, the fact that language preserves traces of the metaphors of past speakers provides an avenue for tracing culture change within a language family.

Previous work in historical semantics suggests three methods that can be used to reconstruct the metaphors of past speech communities. The first is analysis of compound words. When two morphemes that refer to distinct semantic domains have been brought together to make a single word, it is often possible to discern a conceptual metaphor that motivated this conjunction. It is also safe to assume that the underlying metaphor implied by the compound was either widely shared when the word was coined, or became widely shared as the compound was adopted into the language; otherwise the word would not have made sense to speakers of the time. An example is the etymology of English *phosphorus*, which today refers to a flammable, nonmetallic element commonly used in fertilizer, explosives, toothpaste, and detergents. The roots of this word are Greek *phos* 'torch' and *phoros* 'bearer,' which were combined in ancient times to coin the name for Venus as the morning star, which "lights the way for the sun" before the dawn. By the seventeenth century, *phosphorous* had become an adjective used to describe a substance or organism that shines of itself, and this was the meaning transferred to the substance discovered by an alchemist that glowed when exposed to oxygen (Harper 2001). The morphological analysis of *phosphorus* thus implies the metaphor CELESTIAL OBJECTS ARE ANIMATE BEINGS, which is an accurate reflection of ancient Greek belief, but clearly did not characterize the minds of early scientists.

The second method is analysis of polysemy, especially the relationships among multiple senses of words. Metaphor is often involved in extending or adding new senses to a word, and in such cases it is often possible to discern the metaphor that links these related senses. In this case, it is reasonable to infer that the metaphor was conventional in the speech community at the time the extended senses of the word became conventional. For example, the modern English word *economy* is a compound that derives from the Ancient Greek *oikos* 'household' and *nomos* 'managing.' In its adjectival form this word retains the ancient sense of managing personal resources ("hybrids are economical cars"), but the word is most often used today to label a system of labor and exchange, as in "the American economy." This shift in meaning, from management of household resources to a system of labor and exchange, implies that THE NATION IS A HOUSEHOLD is one way that English speakers conceptualized nation-states when the newer sense of *economy* developed.[2]

The third method is analysis of semantic change in specific words within a language family. This method is an extension of the polysemy approach, but in this case one pays attention to the meanings of cognates. Metaphor is again commonly involved in the replacement of an older sense of a word by a newer sense, so when the older and newer senses can be identified through comparison of cognates, one can posit the metaphor that motivated the change among speakers of the innovating language. For example, the French terms *pasteur* and *congrégation* today refer to a minister and an assembly of the faithful in a church, but the Latin roots of these words meant 'shepherd' and 'herded together,' respectively. The pattern and direction of change in these words indicates that Latin speakers in the early Roman Catholic Church conceptualized the relationship between priests and followers using metaphors related to shepherding drawn from passages in the Bible, and French retained only the metaphorical meanings of these words.

As there has been very little linguistic paleontology focused specifically on conceptual reconstruction using the methods outlined here, the strengths and limitations of such work still need to be worked out through review and debate of specific studies. Several caveats are initially apparent, and others will probably come to light as work in this area proceeds. First, conceptual reconstruction is subject to the same methodological issues discussed previously for lexical reconstruction, including vocabulary replacement, data limitations, and analyst abilities. Second, no studies have been done to determine how faithfully or regularly the metaphors of a speech community actually become embedded in their language, so it is possible that some conventional metaphors of past speech communities have faded without leaving residues in their descendant languages. Third, no studies have been done to examine how readily metaphors spread across language boundaries, whether metaphors involving certain domains are more or less likely to spread, or whether it is possible to distinguish the natal language in which a metaphor was invented from the languages into which it was adopted. Finally, if the goal is to relate protolanguages to the archaeological record, metaphors that incorporate material culture items into the source or target domain are most likely to be useful.[3]

How to Find Metaphors in the Archaeological Record

There is no question that conceptual metaphors reveal themselves in all forms of human expression, including language, ritual, poetry, oral tradition, and material culture. This has been demonstrated by numerous anthropological studies across a wide range of societies.[4] For the purposes of this study, however, the critical question is whether one can decipher such metaphors from archaeological evidence alone. This is what one needs to do if one wishes to link protolanguages to archaeological complexes using conceptual metaphors. In previous work I have shown that one can decipher conceptual metaphors archaeologically by comparing the structure of material expressions of a proposed metaphor in the archaeological record with the structure of figurative speech in everyday conversation.

Research on figurative speech in cognitive linguistics (Fauconnier 1997; Fauconnier and Turner 1994; Lakoff 1993; Lakoff and Johnson 1980) suggests six

TABLE 9.1. Generalizations on the structure of metaphoric expression

1. **Directionality:** onceptual metaphor is a cognitive, point-for-point mapping of image-schematic structure from a concrete source domain to an abstract target domain.

   Example: TIME IS MONEY, but money is not time. You can "save," "spend," or "waste" time just as easily as money, but saved time does not accumulate interest.

2. **Superordinate principle:** Metaphors exist at the superordinate level of classification, but are expressed at the basic level of concrete imagery.

   Example: Expressions of LIFE IS A JOURNEY involve specific modes of transportation, as in "his marriage is off-track," "they hit some roadbumps," "she's drifting," "he's really flying high."

3. **Invariance principle:** Image-schematic properties of the source domain that contradict properties of the target domain are not mapped.

   Example: Even if LIFE IS A JOURNEY, you cannot go back and take the other "fork in the road" if you change your mind later on because time is irreversible, whereas space exists continuously.

4. **Constitutive principle:** Metaphors do more than express the results of thinking; they constitute conventionalized ways of thinking and reasoning.

   Example: Because POLITICS IS WAR, you can "give ground," "attack," "defend," or "mobilize your allies," even though you are not engaged in physical combat.

5. **Blended sources:** Multiple source domains can be combined for mapping onto a single target when they share image-schematic structure. The resulting constructions are conceptually coherent but physically impossible.

   Example: "Brainstorming" is a desirable activity, even though there is no such thing as a storming brain.

6. **Experiential principle:** Metaphors derive from the concrete, bodily experiences of individuals in specific contexts.

   Example: The metaphor ANGER IS HEATED FLUID IN A CONTAINER derives from the physiological experience of anger. Your body temperature actually does rise when you get "steaming mad" and "blow your top."

Note: Adapted from Ortman 2000:616–619.

generalizations on the structure of metaphoric expressions that ultimately derive from the ways humans manipulate mental imagery (see Ortman 2000b: 616–621; Ortman 2008b). Table 9.1 presents these patterns and examples of each one in everyday American English. These generalizations are critical because they provide something like "grammatical" rules for metaphoric expressions in material culture. In other words, expressions of a proposed metaphor in an archaeological complex should reflect these generalizations if the metaphor really was widely shared among the people who created that complex. If one analyzes an archaeological complex in terms of a hypothesized metaphor and finds patterns consistent with its expected expressions, then it can be said that one has supported that hypothesis. In addition, if one identifies patterns that clearly contradict this structure, this hypothesis can be rejected. The process of deciphering material metaphors is more involved than the identification of metaphors in language, and the approach may only be possible in certain archaeological situations, but I believe it is possible to make strong inferences regarding material metaphors following this methodology.

An Example of Material Metaphor Analysis

To illustrate how one goes about inferring ancient material metaphors, I will work through an example of a metaphor that was expressed in architecture and community organization in the Mesa Verde region during the Pueblo III period (AD 1140–1280).[5] Prior to AD 1140, most aggregated settlements in this region were established on upland ridges and consisted of rows of houses oriented east to west and facing south (Lipe and Ortman 2000; Ortman and Bradley 2002: 73; Ortman et al. 2000). Over the course of the Pueblo III period, however, new villages were increasingly constructed in canyon-rim environments that have concave, earthen basins of rock and soil. These canyon-rim villages were also commonly built around springs. Figure 9.1 illustrates these changes in settlement location using environmental setting attributes compiled for all community centers (settlements containing evidence of 9 or more pit structures, 50 total structures, or public architecture) in the Village Ecodynamics Project (VEP) Area (Kohler et al. 2007; Ortman et al. 2007; Varien et al. 2007; also see Figure 5.1).[6] This chart shows that over the course of the Pueblo III period, the locations chosen for new community centers emphasized canyon heads, springs, rimrock, and talus slopes; in other words, bowl-shaped settings that "contained" groundwater sources.

A series of innovations in community center architecture occurred coincident with these changes in site setting (Figure 9.2). Over the course of the Pueblo III period, great kivas were superceded by plazas as the most common setting for public rituals; villages were increasingly demarcated by enclosing walls that surrounded the entire village or its central, civic-ceremonial precinct (Kenzle 1997; Lipe and Ortman 2000); and the houses constructed within the enclosing walls generally followed the canyon-head topography and thus faced inward and terraced downward, toward the low center of the immediate built environment (Lipe and Ortman 2000: Figs. 4–5). These changes also appear to express serving bowl imagery: the plaza and spring correspond to the center of the bowl, the enclosing wall to the rim, and the inward-facing houses to the painted designs that run around bowl interiors (Figure 9.3) (see Ortman and Bradley 2002: 71–77; Potter and Ortman 2004:185–186).

These correspondences lead to the hypotheses that during the Pueblo III period, Mesa Verde people came to conceptualize the communities in which they lived as containers—especially as pottery serving bowls (Ortman 2006; Ortman and Bradley 2002; Potter and Ortman 2004). If THE COMMUNITY IS A

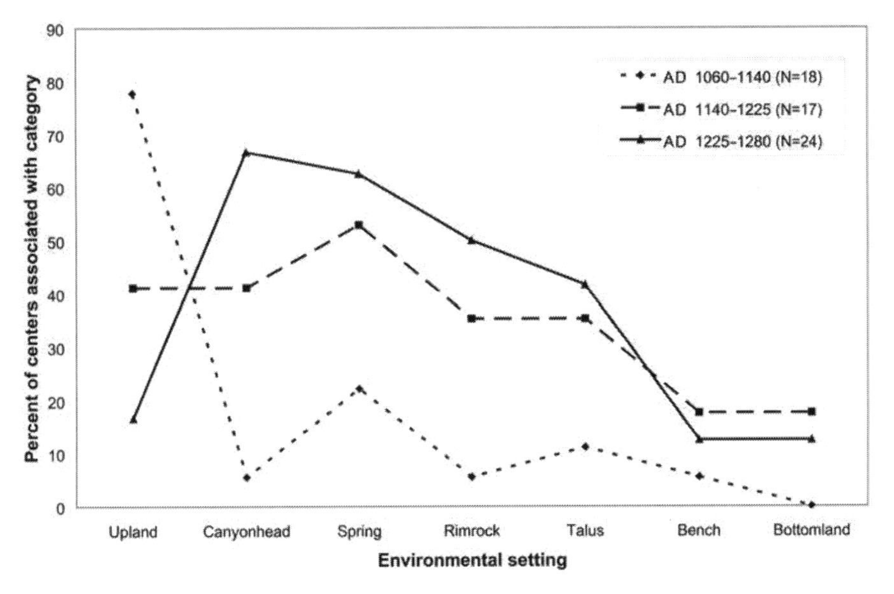

FIGURE 9.1. Environmental settings of new community centers in the Village Ecodynamics Project study area. Each line presents the profile of centers established during the stated period.

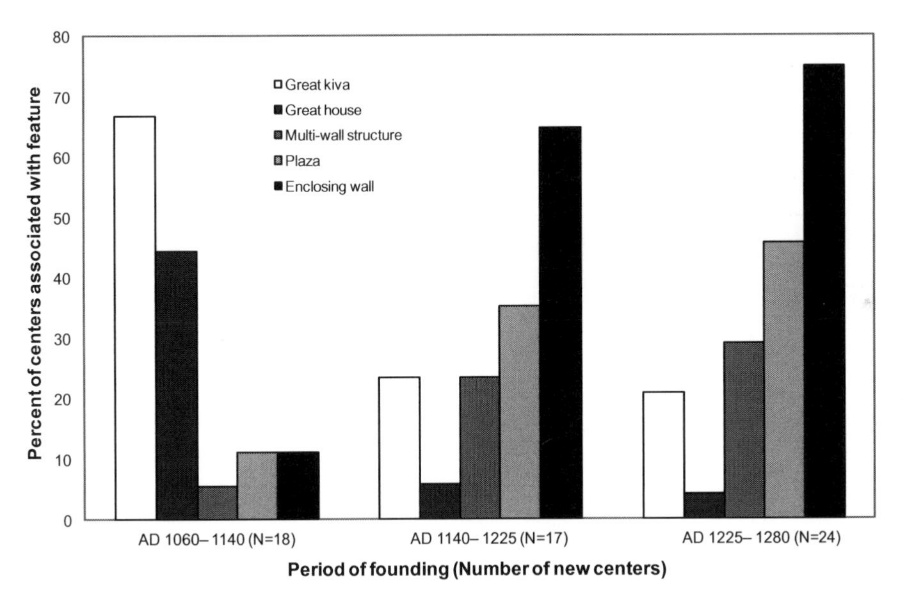

FIGURE 9.2. Architectural features of community centers in the Village Ecodynamics Project study area.

CONTAINER was in fact a metaphor that structured these changes in village architecture and community organization, one would expect material expressions of this concept to be patterned in accordance with the six generalizations on figurative expression summarized in Table 9.1. In the following paragraphs I illustrate that the archaeological record of canyon-rim villages does in fact exhibit patterns consistent with all six of these generalizations.

The Directionality Principle. The first generalization concerning metaphoric expression is that it involves the projection of imagery from a relatively concrete source domain to a more abstract target domain. The Pueblo III archaeological

FIGURE 9.3. Serving bowl imagery in canyon-rim villages: *from top*, Sand Canyon Pueblo, Yellow Jacket Pueblo, serving bowl from Sand Canyon Pueblo. (Reconstructions by Dennis Holloway, © Crow Canyon Archaeological Center.)

record is consistent with this principle because the settings and architecture of villages increasingly expressed serving bowl imagery, but architectural imagery was not painted on bowls. There is no physical reason why villages could not have been represented on bowls, but I have never encountered a Mesa Verde Black-on-white pottery bowl upon which elements of village architecture were depicted on the interior surface.[7] This suggests that the mapping of imagery between bowls and villages was directional—which is to say, the target domain of communities appears to have been structured by the source domain of containers, but not the reverse.

The Superordinate Principle. The second generalization is that conceptual metaphors are stored in the brain at a relatively abstract level of categorization, but are expressed at the basic level of concrete imagery. The archaeology of canyon-rim village communities reflects this principle because most expressions of THE COMMUNITY IS A CONTAINER were realized as expressions of a more basic and easily imaged concept, THE VILLAGE IS A SERVING BOWL. In addition, serving bowl imagery is expressed in the form and use of plazas as well as villages overall. Plazas with varying degrees of formality occur in most canyon-rim villages, usually in relatively flat areas that were intentionally kept free of other structures (Lipe and Ortman 2000). Plazas at several sites were defined by enclosing walls in combination with structures (Ortman and Bradley 2002; Ortman et al. 2000; also see Figure 13.11), but in other cases, such as Castle Rock Pueblo, plazas were defined by boulder alignments (Kuckelman 2000). The characteristic that unifies these plazas is that they are more round than rectilinear in shape. The most striking example occurs at Yellow Jacket Pueblo, where a bowl-shaped plaza occurs in a shallow basin surrounded by terraced, inward-facing house blocks connected by enclosing walls (Figure 9.3, center) (see Kuckelman 2003; Varien and Ortman 2005; Varien et al. 2008).

The notion that plazas were modeled after serving bowls is supported by evidence that communal feasting was common in canyon-rim villages and likely occurred in the plazas. The houses in these villages contained more very large cooking pots suitable for "fiesta" cooking than was the case in earlier villages (Figure 9.4, top) (Ortman 2000a: paragraphs 41–77), and many communities maintained room-dominated architectural blocks adjacent to the plazas that have been interpreted as communal food storage structures (Lipe and Ortman 2000; also see Figure 13.11). The pottery bowls used for serving food in these villages were often decorated on the outside, suggesting that they were regularly viewed from the side at communal feasting events (see Mills 2007), and exterior decoration is more frequent on pottery vessels found at sites with plazas than it is on vessels at smaller sites (Figure 9.5) (Ortman and Bradley 2002). In addition, these bowls come in two sizes: a large size that could hold enough food to feed a family, and a small size that was suitable for individual servings (Figure 9.4, bottom) (Ortman 2000a: paragraphs 41–77). Finally, serving bowl sherds are

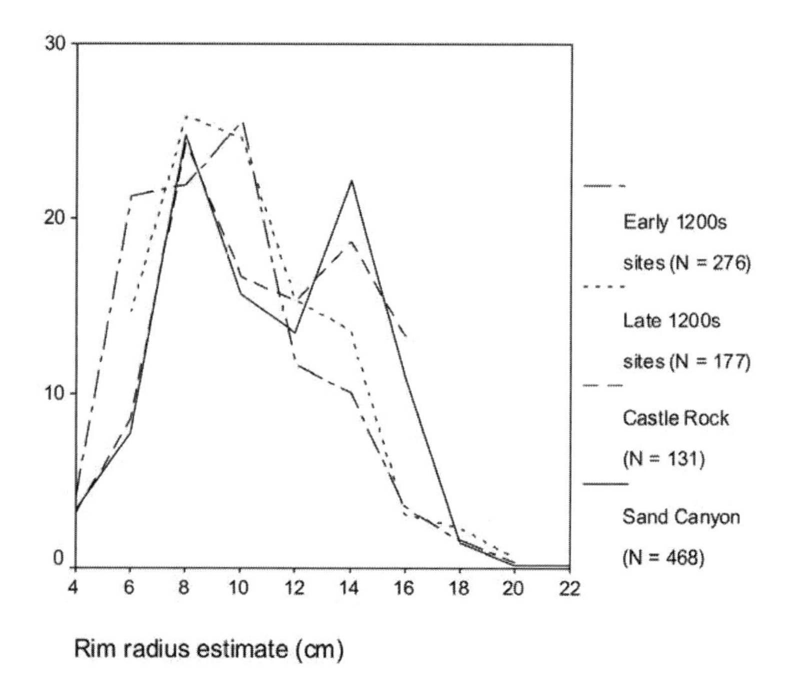

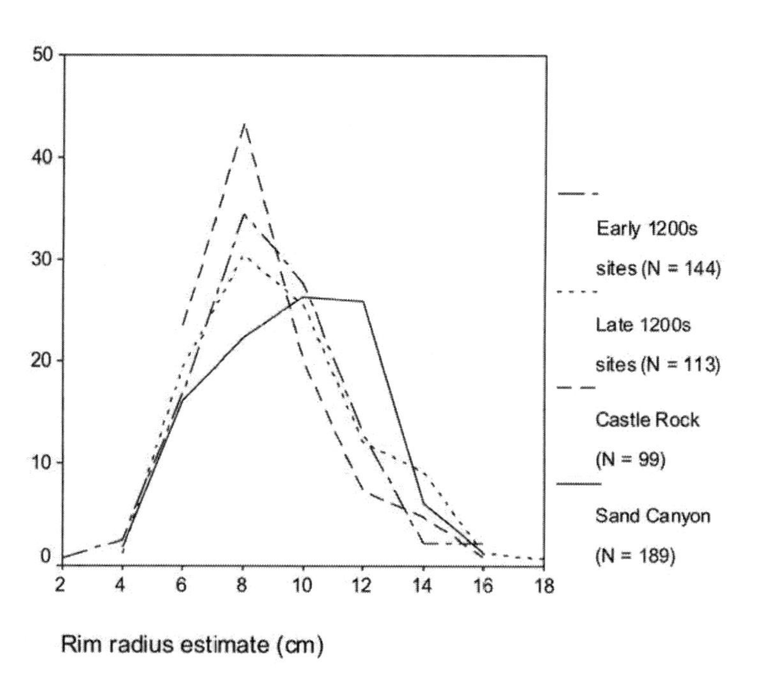

FIGURE 9.4. Pottery vessel size distributions in the Sand Canyon locality. Sand Canyon Pueblo is a large canyon-rim village, and Castle Rock Pueblo is a small canyon-rim village. Both sites had plazas. Data are degrees of arc encompassed by large ($\geq 20^{\circ}$ of arc) rim sherds of each radius class: *top*, serving bowl distributions; *bottom*, cooking pot distributions. (After Ortman 2000a: Figs. 4 and 7. Courtesy of Crow Canyon Archaeological Center.)

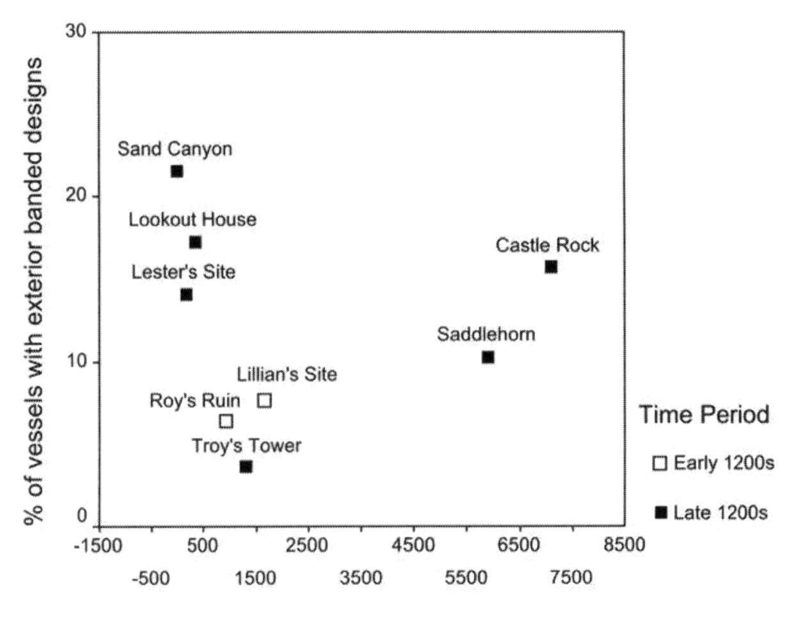

FIGURE 9.5. Exterior decoration on serving bowls in the Sand Canyon locality. Sand Canyon Pueblo was a large canyon-rim village, and Castle Rock Pueblo a small canyon-rim village. Both sites had plazas. (After Ortman and Bradley 2002: Fig. 3.9. Courtesy of Crow Canyon Archaeological Center.)

overrepresented in the trash associated with the plaza at Yellow Jacket Pueblo (Ortman 2003: paragraph 165). All of this suggests that communal meals were often served and consumed in the plazas in these villages.

Additional public structures called *great kivas* also occur within canyon-rim villages (Lipe and Ortman 2000; Ortman and Bradley 2002), but several patterns suggest that these structures were not modeled as serving bowls. First, great kivas have a deep history in the Mesa Verde region (Lightfoot 1988; Martin 1936) and were locations for periodic group assembly many centuries before the changes in pottery assemblages suggestive of regular public food sharing. Second, although the great kivas at some canyon-rim villages, such as Sand Canyon Pueblo and Goodman Point Pueblo, are round, examples at Long House (Cattanach 1980) and New Fire House (Fewkes 1923) are rectangular, and all contain four masonry pillars forming a square oriented to the cardinal directions (Ortman and Bradley 2002). Third, mural imagery suggests that great kivas could be imagined as microcosms of the landscape, but not as bowls. When the walls of small household kivas were decorated, they were painted with murals that depict the walls as a pottery bowl or as the distant horizon. Mural paintings on the walls of great kivas, in contrast, are only of the horizon type and not the pottery bowl type (Ortman 2008b:242–243). Likewise, although a few small household kivas in canyon-rim villages are rectangular, and landscape imagery has been identified on a few of these, pottery design murals occur only on the walls of round kivas. This suggests that great kivas were not imagined as pottery bowls in the same way that villages, plazas, and small round kivas appear to have been.[8] This conclusion is important because it shows that the framework utilized here can be used to reject a metaphor hypothesis, and to distinguish metaphors that characterized ancient minds from those invented by present-day analysts.

The Invariance Principle. The third generalization regarding the structure of metaphoric expression is that aspects of the source domain that are contradicted by the inherent structure of the target domain are not mapped. This principle is evident in the archaeology of canyon-rim villages, where houses constructed by community members beyond the bowl-shaped area defined by the village enclosing walls did not conform to the inward-facing layout, but instead continued the south-facing tradition of earlier settlements (Figure 9.3) (Kuckelman 2003; Kuckelman and Ortman 2003; Ortman and Bradley 2002; Ortman et al. 2000; Varien 1999b; Varien and Ortman 2005; Varien et al. 2008). These houses could have been built facing inward, but they were not. This pattern is consistent with the fact that canyon-rim environments correspond only to the inside and rim of a bowl, not to the outside. Thus, there would have been no correspondence motivating the arrangement of houses outside the enclosing wall, or "rim," of these villages.[9]

The Constitutive Principle. The fourth generalization is that a conceptual metaphor is not merely a means of expressing thought, but is actually the thought itself. The archaeological record of canyon-rim villages reflects this principle: many communities designed new villages, or modified existing ones, to express serving bowl imagery at the same time that communal feasting developed. In other words, the architecture of canyon-rim villages expresses what community members were actually doing in these settlements: sharing food from common bowls. At Sand Canyon Pueblo, for example, the round, enclosing wall was built in a single construction event early in the village's history (Bradley 1992, 1993). At Woods Canyon Pueblo, habitation shifted from the canyon bottom up its slopes and to an enclosed plaza constructed on the rim (Churchill and Ortman 2002), and at the Hedley Main Ruin (see Figure 13.11), a number of existing house blocks arranged around a central slickrock area were linked together with enclosing walls (Ortman et al. 2000). These details suggest that the imagery and actual behavior of eating from a common vessel structured the development of canyon-rim villages, regardless of how conscious people were of this influence.

The Blending Principle. The fifth generalization is that two source domains can be blended to produce concepts that are physically impossible but conceptually coherent (Fauconnier 1997; Fauconnier and Turner 1994). The archaeological record of canyon-rim villages reflects blending because the serving bowl community combines the imagery of households, people, and corn. Ancestral Pueblo households had granaries in which dried corn was stored throughout the year. In everyday domestic life this corn was transformed into food through grinding and the addition of water and heat in a cooking pot. Once the cornmeal was cooked, it would be placed in a pottery serving bowl for consumption by the household. These aspects of daily domestic life are mirrored at the community scale in the communal storage structures and plaza-oriented feasts of canyon-rim villages, as mentioned earlier. But villages were also places where children were raised to become the mothers and fathers of future generations. Add to this the likelihood that Mesa Verde people likened themselves to corn, and canyon-rim villages become images of a serving bowl in a double sense: they were places where actual corn was stored, transformed into food, and shared among community members, and they were also places where young children were nurtured into adults who could create future generations. In a society where the life cycles of people and corn were mirror images of each other, a serving bowl would be a potent symbol of the successful completion of both cycles.

The Experiential Principle. This final generalization states that metaphors are grounded in the direct, bodily experiences of individuals in a given socio-natural context. The range of experiential correspondences between the construction, form, and use of serving bowls and canyon-rim villages is consistent with this principle. Table 9.2 arranges these correspondences in two groups. The first consists of correspondences (and one case of noncorrespondence) that are inherent between pottery bowls and canyon-rim environments or villages in general. These are image-schematic parallels that would have motivated or reinforced a metaphor linking bowls and villages. The second consists of correspondences that were brought about through the transfer of conceptual structure from the source domain of pottery serving bowls to the target domain of the community, as reflected in the actual behaviors of the people who created and lived in canyon-rim villages.

Most of these correspondences have been discussed already, but the final two have not. First, the evidence for centralized planning of canyon-rim villages appears to correspond to evidence in the form of polishing stones, pottery sherd scrapers, and unfired sherds that at least one person in each household made pottery serving bowls (Ortman 2000a: paragraphs 68–75; Pierce et al. 2002; Pierce et al. 1999). If the ethnographic record (summarized in Jorgensen 1980: 428) is any guide, these persons were often maternal heads of households, so just as bowls were made by household heads, villages would have been planned by community leaders. Second, the food served in pottery bowls during everyday domestic meals was likely prepared by the mothers and grandmothers of the household (Crown 2000). This act corresponds to the activities of community leaders, who scheduled and orchestrated feasts in association with the ritual calendar (Ortman and Bradley 2002). Taken as a whole, the list of correspondences in Table 9.2 illustrates both the experiential basis of THE COMMUNITY IS A CONTAINER, and the degree to which this metaphor assisted in "fleshing out" how canyon-rim villages were to look and how their associated communities were to function.

TABLE 9.2. Correspondences between pottery serving bowls and canyon-rim villages

	Serving Bowls	Canyon-Rim Villages
A.	**Image-schematic correspondences**	
1.	Clay	Earth
2.	Ground rock temper	Building stone
3.	Clay and water make paste	Earth and water make mortar
4.	Fuelwood	Timbers for roofs, heating, and cooking
5.	Round, open, concave interior	Canyon-head slopes
6.	Center	Spring
7.	Holds water	Contains water issuing from spring
8.	Contains corn	Contains people (PEOPLE ARE CORN)
9.	Exterior surface	(Does not correspond to canyon-rim environment)
B.	**Additional structure mapped onto villages**	
1.	Rim	Enclosing wall
2.	Inward-facing band of terraced geometric designs painted just below the rim	Inward-facing houses abut the enclosing walls and also terrace downslope toward the low, geographic center of the canyon-rim environment
3.	Center left undecorated	Spring area left undeveloped
4.	Contains household food	Contains community food
5.	Household eats out of a bowl	The community feasts in the plaza
6.	Household members sit around a bowl to eat	Community members sit around the perimeter of the plaza to feast
7.	Pottery made by mothers	Village layouts planned by leaders
8.	Meals prepared by mothers	Feasts scheduled by leaders

Summary

The preceding paragraphs demonstrate that the archaeological record of canyon-rim villages exhibits a range of patterns that are consistent with generalizations concerning the structure of metaphoric expression under the hypothesis that THE COMMUNITY IS A CONTAINER was a metaphor that actively structured village architecture and community organization in Pueblo III Mesa Verde society. It seems unlikely that the range of patterns identified here would exist if the proposed metaphor was not widely shared among the creators of this archaeological complex.

Metaphors, Society, and Worldview

What sort of inferences can be made about the roles of specific metaphors in ancient societies? This is a trickier question than it may seem at first because metaphors relate to the people who express them in a variety of ways: some are used consciously and strategically, whereas others are used unconsciously and habitually; some are part of everyday thinking and communicating, whereas others are restricted to the activities of specialists; and finally, some actively structure thought and action in the present, whereas others are mere semantic fossils. The ethnographic literature is not very helpful for distinguishing these varied relationships between metaphoric expressions, society, and worldview,[10] but it is possible to construct some general guidelines from the cognitive linguistics literature.

The first generalization I draw from research on conceptual metaphor is that people are almost always aware of novel metaphors, whether they appear in the form of poetry, scientific proposals, or political discourse, but over time and with repeated use the source domain imagery comes to be permanently linked with the target domain. After this point the metaphor is used habitually and unreflectively. The shift is one from discourse to language, from phrases intended to invoke analogical reasoning to the unreflective habits of everyday conversation. Thus, the person who coined the term *computer virus* did so to draw explicit parallels between malicious computer programs and pathogenic microorganisms, but today this metaphor is so ingrained that people use it without a second thought. When someone says, "I've got a virus," many interpret it to mean their computer has been "infected" by a malicious program. Translated to the archaeological record, this suggests that new conceptual metaphors are first expressed consciously and strategically in discourse, and that expressions in material culture follow later, after the concept has been added to the conceptual repertoire of the society. Over time one might also expect material expressions to become habitual, such that people were no longer aware of why they designed, constructed, and used certain objects in certain ways.

The second generalization is that metaphors that constitute specialized knowledge, or are restricted to certain subgroups in society, tend to be used consciously, whereas metaphors that are frequently used in mundane contexts tend to be used unreflectively. Thus, the "Big Bang" theory is intended to convey to Western scientists the correspondences between the origin of the universe and the properties of an explosion, whereas all humans use ANGER IS HEAT so habitually that it does not require conscious awareness to interpret such phases as "he exploded with rage." Translated to the archaeological record, this generalization suggests that when the dominant form, appearance, or use of an object reflects a metaphor, it is likely that the associated concept was deeply ingrained and used unconsciously. In contrast, when a material metaphor is only apparent in certain contextually specific instances, it is more likely that the metaphor was used discursively and consciously.

Finally, a third generalization concerning the relationship between metaphors and society is that it is possible to distinguish active metaphors from dead ones based on the degree to which they generate novel expressions over time. The maintenance of a conceptual metaphor in a speech community will enable its members to create novel expressions that are instantly recognizable and interpretable by others, whereas dead metaphors will have ceased to create novel expressions and will be expressed only as semantic fossils. Thus, novel expressions of TIME IS MONEY, such as "this research paid no dividends," are readily interpretable, but most readers would be hard-pressed to interpret statements like "he's too salty for my taste" in terms of personal wealth unless they happened to know that modern English *salary* derives from the Latin *salarium*, 'a soldier's allotment of salt' (Campbell 1998:256). Translated to the archaeological record, this generalization suggests that one can be confident a metaphor was active if it was expressed in a variety of ways, and especially if these expressions expanded over time. In contrast, a metaphor is likely to have been inactive if its expressions appear static or stereotyped.

Using these generalizations, it is possible to make inferences regarding the role of a material metaphor in past societies. In the present context this may help one assess the likelihood that a specific archaeologically deciphered metaphor became enshrined in the language of the people who expressed it. For example, it is clear that THE COMMUNITY IS A CONTAINER was active in the social consciousness of Mesa Verde people because this concept was expressed in many different ways, and represents one of a family of metaphors linking actual containers and community life that developed over several centuries (see Chapter 10). In addition, it is likely this concept was widely shared because most thirteenth-century villages express serving bowl imagery. We should therefore expect this metaphor to have been expressed routinely in discourse in Mesa Verde society, and for this concept to have influenced the language of the people who created canyon-rim villages.

To say, however, that a metaphor circulated widely in an ancient society is not to say that everyone in that society agreed with its entailments. Rather, the metaphors that become embedded in language often represent the privileged discourses of past speech communities as opposed to a representative sample of the discourses of individual speakers. In fact, the only metaphors that are likely to be materialized in patterned ways that archaeologists can recover are those connected to these hegemonic discourses. In other words, the central tendencies in social action reflected in the archaeological record reflect the hegemonic discourses that circulated in the society that created this record, but there will always be variation that does not reflect these discourses because human behavior is responsive to local, contextual factors as well. Thus, to claim that THE COMMUNITY IS A CONTAINER was a metaphor that structured village architecture and community organization in the Pueblo III Mesa Verde region is not to claim that this concept and its entailments were universally shared, accepted, or acted on by all members of this society. Rather, it is to suggest that most people in Mesa Verde society had been exposed to expressions and entailments of this metaphor, that the privileged fraction of Mesa Verde society accepted it as valid, and that all knew how to behave in accordance with it.

Knowing Ancient Minds

In this chapter I have introduced the contemporary theory of metaphor in cognitive science, and have reviewed methods for identifying metaphors of past speech communities through polysemy, etymology, and semantic change. I have also outlined a new method through which one can decipher some of the conceptual metaphors that circulated in ancient societies using archaeological evidence. This method works from generalizations on the structure of metaphoric expression in figurative speech to provide expectations for the structure of metaphoric expression in material culture. I illustrated this method by applying it to the archaeological record of canyon-rim villages in the Mesa Verde region, and found good evidence that THE COMMUNITY IS A CONTAINER was a metaphor that structured village architecture and community organization during the Pueblo III period. Finally, I returned to previous research on metaphor in cognitive linguistics to suggest three generalizations about the relationship between material metaphors and society. These may assist one in predicting which concepts expressed in an archaeological complex are most likely to have also influenced the language of the people who created this complex.

Armed now with methods for discovering dead metaphors in language, deciphering ancient metaphors from archaeological evidence, and interpreting the role of material metaphors in society, I turn to an examination of the extent to which specific material metaphors of thirteenth-century Mesa Verde society are mirrored in Northern Rio Grande material culture and embedded in the Tewa language. I will argue that conceptual metaphor analysis provides the strongest evidence available that the Tewa language was spoken in the Mesa Verde region before it came to be spoken in the Tewa Basin.

Notes

1. The use of small caps to indicate conceptual metaphors is a convention established by Lakoff and Johnson (1980).
2. One difficulty with this approach to identifying metaphor in language, especially for poorly documented languages, is that it can be difficult to distinguish homonyms — distinct words that sound the same as an accident of history — from polysemic terms that imply the influence of a specific metaphor. A good example of this problem is discussed by Alfonso Ortiz with respect to the religious hierarchy of present-day Tewa communities (1969:79–80). The individuals in the religious hierarchy of these villages are called *paat'owa*. Many previous investigators translated this term as "fish-people" based on the fact that the initial morpheme *paa* can mean 'fish' (Bandelier 1892a; Laski 1959; Parsons 1974 [1929]); however, the verb 'to make' is also pronounced *paa*, and this raises the question of whether these forms reflect a single, polysemous term or are homonyms. It turns out that they are homonyms, because Towa cognates of *paa* 'fish' and *paa* 'to make' are different (*pô* 'fish'; *pǽ:* 'make, fix, repair'), and imply that the Tewa forms derive from different Proto-Tanoan forms (**pɔ* 'fish'; **pa* 'make'), and only ended up sounding the same due to the history of sound changes in Tewa. This would be difficult to determine if one had not studied Kiowa-Tanoan as

well as Tewa, and as a result one might mistakenly view *paa* as a single, polysemous term that metaphorically connects ceremonial leaders and fish. Of course, this does not rule out the possibility that Tewa people coined the term *paat'owa* because of the ambiguous meaning of *paa*, which encourages an association of "made people" with life in the lake. The point is that homophony complicates the analysis and makes it more difficult to identify conceptual metaphors on the basis of linguistic data in isolation.

3. The metaphor PEOPLE ARE CORN, for example, is common throughout agricultural societies of North America and is documented in the ethnographic literatures of the Hopi (Black 1984), Tewa (Ortiz 1969), Huichol (Shelton 1996), Nahua (Sandstrom 1991), Mixtec (Monaghan 1995), and Maya (Carlsen 1997). Based on this widespread distribution, it appears likely that this metaphor spread along with maize agriculture itself and is of little use for correlating archaeology and language.
4. Examples include Bird-David 1990; Bourdieu 1973, 1990:271–283; Carlsen 1997; Edmonson 1993; Knab 2004; MacKenzie 1991; Preston Blier 1987; Sandstrom 1991; Schaefer 1996; Shore 1996: Chap. 11; Sillar 1996; Tilley 1999: Chap. 4; Turner 1991; Vogt 1976; Walens 1981.
5. It is important to lay out the evidence for this particular metaphor here because this argument has not been formally developed in earlier work, and this reconstruction plays an important role in the analysis presented in Chapter 10.
6. The Village Ecodynamics Project interprets each community center site as the focal settlement of a community because such sites often contain public architecture such as a great kiva or plaza, and they are typically the largest site within a cluster of sites. These centers generally have longer histories than smaller sites in the region (Varien 1999:202–207; Varien and Ortman 2005), and excavations at these centers show that they were locations of social, economic, and political activities that did not occur at smaller sites (Adler and Varien 1994; Bradley 1988, 1993, 1996; Driver 1996; Lipe 2002; Muir 1999; Muir and Driver 2002; Ortman and Bradley 2002; Potter 1997; Potter and Ortman 2004).
7. One element of Pueblo III architecture that may have been projected onto pottery is the T-shaped doorway. This form appears as a cutout on the handles of mugs and the openings of waterfowl effigies dating to this period (see, for example, the vessel photographs in Morris 1939). The T-shaped door itself may derive from the painted terrace motif that first appeared on pottery during the AD 1000s (Ortman 2000b), and doorways are important symbols in and of themselves. Thus, the T-shaped cutout may have come to be associated with mugs and effigies due to their use in ritual. In this case, the actual projection appears have been from a concrete source domain — doorways — onto an abstract target domain — ritual passage between realms of existence. Furthermore, whereas T-shaped doors do appear on the exterior doorways of inward-facing houses in canyon-rim villages, T-shaped openings were not cut out around the perimeters of pottery bowls. In other words, if anything, the projection in this case was from painted terrace designs on pottery to exterior doorways on houses, not the reverse.
8. In Ortman and Bradley 2002:76–77 we argued that the great kivas of canyon-rim villages also expressed serving bowl imagery. With the benefit of subsequent study, especially of mural painting (Ortman 2008a), it now appears that this inference was incorrect.
9. For a discussion of changes in village architecture prior to the development of canyon-rim villages, see Lipe and Ortman 2000 and Ortman et al. 2000.

10. Anthropologists have generally treated behavioral realizations of metaphor in an undifferentiated way, essentially assuming that expressions in oral tradition, native testimony, poetry, song, etymology, material culture, and ritual practice all bear a consistent relationship to a present-day group of people. The contemporary theory of metaphor shows that this view is incorrect. Thus, anthropological studies of world-view could be greatly improved by keeping track of these varied modes of expression and considering their varied historical implications.

Mesa Verde Metaphors in the Tewa Language

In this chapter I apply my framework for deciphering conceptual metaphors in language and the archaeological record to the question of whether the Tewa language originated in the Mesa Verde region or in the Tewa Basin. These are the only two reasonable possibilities that remain after considering the demographic, biological, and linguistic evidence presented thus far. If the Tewa language originated in the Mesa Verde region, one would expect to find traces of Mesa Verde culture enshrined as semantic fossils in the Tewa language. If, instead, this language originated in the Tewa Basin, one would not expect to find such evidence.

To distinguish between these two possibilities, I examine archaeological and linguistic reflexes of a series of material metaphors involving pots and baskets in Mesa Verde archaeology, Tewa Basin archaeology, and in the Tewa language itself. I have presented reconstructions of these metaphors for Mesa Verde culture in previous publications (Ortman 2000b, 2006, 2008b; Ortman and Bradley 2002; also see Chapter 9).[1] Here I summarize this research and examine the extent to which these concepts were expressed in Tewa Basin material culture and embedded in Tewa and other Kiowa-Tanoan languages. The presentation is organized by concept, according to the sequence in which expressions of each metaphor first began appearing in Mesa Verde material culture.

Pottery Vessels Are Textiles

Reconstruction to Mesa Verde Culture

From the early AD 1000s through the final depopulation of the region, Mesa Verde pottery was decorated in a thoroughly geometric style with designs in black paint on a white-slipped surface. Many researchers have noted parallels between the painted designs on this pottery and the woven objects recovered from contemporaneous cliff dwellings in Mesa Verde National Park and southeast Utah (Brew 1946; Holmes 1886; Nordenskiöld 1979 [1893]). I have studied these correlations and found abundant evidence that they result from a conceptualization of pottery vessels as woven objects, especially coiled and plaited baskets. Specifically, Mesa Verde pottery designs exhibit the structure that one would expect under the hypothesis that pots were imagined as woven objects (after Ortman 2000b:625–637).

1. Directionality: Weaving must have been the source domain and pottery the target domain in this relationship because motifs, surface textures, design structures, and minor by-products of specific weaving methods are all represented on pottery. These correspondences could not have resulted from weavers inventing new methods of weaving in order to represent painted pottery designs as woven textures. In addition, more than two dozen analogous features of pottery design appear on pottery only after they appeared in weaving. This systematic, time-lagged response of pottery design to weaving innovations demonstrates that the direction of transfer was from weaving to pottery.
2. Superordinate principle: Imagery from four different weaving methods—coiled basketry, plaited basketry, non-loom weaving, and loom-based weaving—all appear in pottery designs. In other words, the conceptual relationship was between pottery and textiles as generic craft media, not between specific vessel forms and/or weaving methods.
3. Invariance principle: Rim decorations and framing patterns on pottery derive solely from basketry and not from warp-weft weaves. This is expectable because warp-weft weaving does not produce actual containers with rims, as basket-weaving does.
4. Constitutive principle: Over a period of two and a half centuries, all design structures and motifs that became common can be traced to specific weaving innovations, whereas pottery designs that utilized nontextile imagery were consistently rare.
5. Blended sources: The imagery of loom-based, warp-weft weaves was transferred to pottery via basket weaving imagery. As a result, framing patterns, which represent the coils of coiled baskets, are nearly absent on pottery vessels with "draped" warp-weft designs because these designs were mapped onto pots via plaited baskets (Figures 10.1 and 10.2).
6. Experiential principle: Regional variation in pottery designs correlates with potters' exposure to different weaving industries. Specifically, elements of design that derive from loom-woven cotton cloth are more common on vessels produced in areas where cotton was cultivated and woven, whereas elements of design that derive from coiled basketry were more common in areas where cotton was not grown.

Based on this evidence, the inference that Mesa Verde people conceptualized pottery vessels as mirror images of woven objects appears quite secure. In addition, the pervasiveness of weaving imagery in Mesa Verde pottery and the number of generations over which this metaphor structured pottery design suggest that this concept was conventional, widely shared, and used unreflectively. One

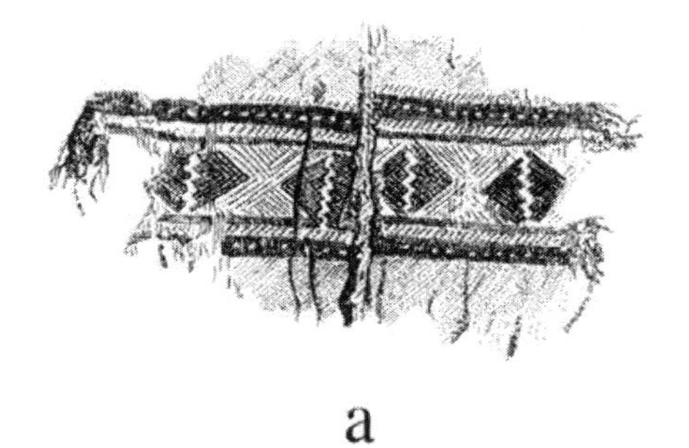

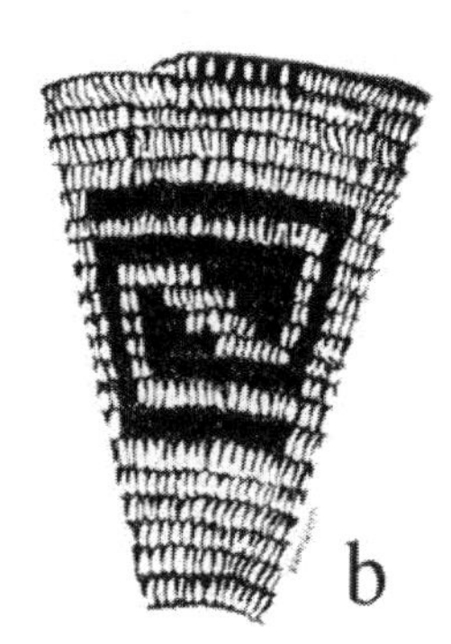

FIGURE 10.1. Derivation of banded pottery design (*c*) from mapping of loom-woven cotton cloth (*a*) onto coiled basketry (*b*). (After Ortman 2000b: Fig. 12.)

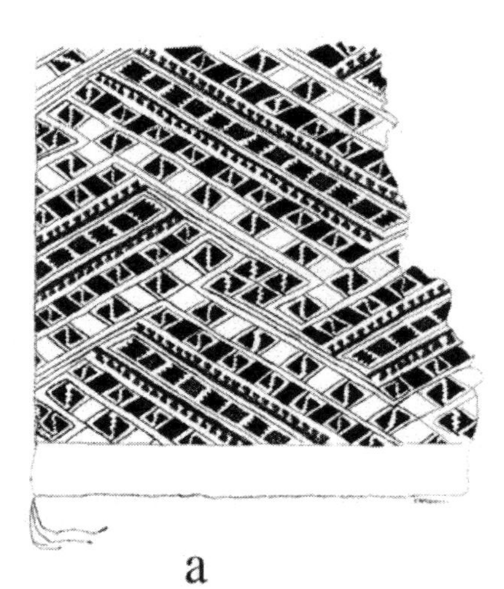

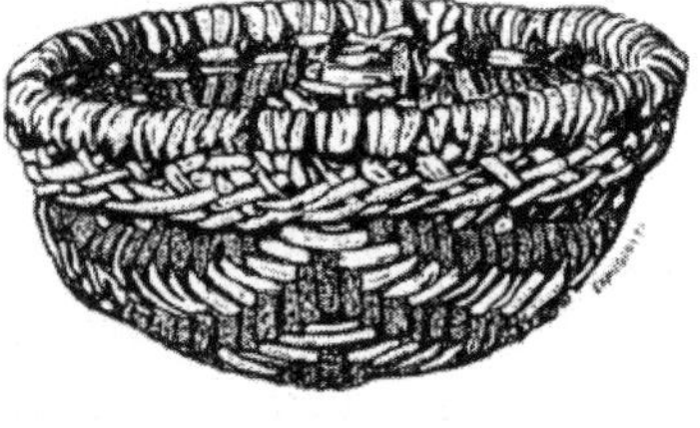

FIGURE 10.2. Derivation of "draped" pottery design (*c*) from mapping of loom-woven cotton cloth (*a*) onto twill-plaited basketry (*b*). (After Ortman 2000b: Fig. 13.)

might therefore expect this metaphor to have influenced the language of Mesa Verde people.

Cooking pots also appear to have been designed and constructed through analogy with basketry. These vessels were made by coiling and had "corrugated" surface textures created by indenting the coil onto the edge of the growing pot on the exterior using a finger or a thin tool. The coil junctions on the inner surface, in contrast, were obliterated by scraping. Decorative patterns were also incorporated into the exterior surface textures through patterned indentation during vessel construction, in precise analogy with the process of sewing or weaving designs into baskets (Morris and Burgh 1941).[2] Experiments with replica corrugated vessels by Christopher Pierce (2005a, 2005b) show that corrugated cooking pots were not easier to make but were somewhat more durable than plain-surfaced or neck-banded cooking vessels of earlier periods. In addition, full-body corrugation increased cooking control by radiating excess heat more effectively, thus reducing the likelihood that starchy foods such as corn mush would boil over during cooking (Pierce 2005a:137–138). Independent evidence for this benefit of corrugation can be seen in the changes in cooking pot shape, especially the development of more restricted openings, which followed the adoption of corrugation (see Morris 1939: Plates 218–221, 261, 270–279). This change increased heat retention and thus would have been counterproductive if potters were seeking to limit boilovers; but if boilovers were no longer a problem due to the radiator effect of corrugation, this change would have been an improvement because it would better protect the vessel contents from spillage and contamination. Thus, it appears that the application of basket-weaving imagery to cooking pottery produced vessels that functioned better when cooking mushes and gruels.

Expressions in Tewa Basin Archaeology

Tewa Basin pottery of the Late Developmental and Coalition periods was decorated with geometric, black-on-white designs, but weaving processes do not appear to have structured Tewa Basin pottery designs as they did for Mesa Verde designs. A recent stylistic analysis of Coalition period pottery from the Pajarito Plateau (Wilson 2008b: Table 58.23) shows that many of the geometric motifs on Mesa Verde Black-on-white vessels were also painted on contemporaneous Santa Fe and Wiyo Black-on-white vessels in the Tewa Basin; however, qualitative comparisons of designs on Coalition period vessels from the Santa Fe area (Habicht-Mauche 1993:47–57; Stubbs and Stallings 1953: 62–91) with coeval Mesa Verde designs (e.g., Morris 1939: Plates 299–320) suggests that motifs were combined more freely in the Tewa Basin. In addition, rim ticking and complex framing patterns derived from coiled basket imagery, and "all-over" or "draped" design layouts derived from a blending of loom-based weaving and plaited basketry (Figure 10.2) are both rare on Coalition period vessels (Wilson 2008b: Tables 58.18, 58.19). Finally, geometric elements were used even more freely in

Classic period designs (Harlow 1973:23, 148–153), with the result that there is rarely a consistent relationship between figure and ground as occurs in weaving-inspired designs. It therefore appears that even if elements of Tewa Basin designs were originally inspired by weaving, the use of these elements does not exhibit the structure one would expect if POTTERY VESSELS ARE TEXTILES continued to structure pottery decoration from the Coalition period onward.[3]

The Tewa Basin utility ware tradition suggests a similar scenario. "Indented-corrugated" vessels analogous to Mesa Verde "corrugated" do appear in Late Developmental sites, but such vessels never fully replaced plain-surfaced cooking pots, and indented-corrugated surfaces exhibit far less care and embellishment than Mesa Verde corrugated vessels.[4] In addition, indented-corrugated surface treatments were rapidly replaced by "smeared indented-corrugated" treatments during the middle decades of the AD 1200s. The latter surface treatment essentially represents indented-corrugated surfaces that were wiped or smeared immediately after construction. This had the effect of obliterating the coiled basket texture while maintaining the increased exterior surface area produced through the indented-corrugated construction method. It is as though potters intended to obliterate weaving imagery from these vessels while maintaining their functionality.[5]

During the subsequent Classic period, cooking pots drifted ever farther from their basket-inspired precursors. Increased exterior surface area was initially maintained through ribbing, but by the end of the Classic period, cooking pot exteriors looked more similar to early ancestral Pueblo gray ware than to the indented-corrugated and smeared-indented-corrugated vessels of the Late Developmental and Coalition periods. It is important to ask why this drift took place, given that corrugation is argued to have improved the functionality of cooking pots. One possibility is that changes in cuisine during the Coalition period, which involved increased consumption of tortillas cooked on griddle stones (Stubbs and Stallings 1953:124), may have resulted in corn mush being cooked less often. Beans and stews are less starchy than mushes and gruels, and less likely to boil over. As a result, the exterior surface textures of cooking pots could have drifted with no corresponding loss of functional utility.

In summary, it appears that the Tewa Basin pottery tradition can be characterized as one in which techniques and elements that originated through analogy with weaving elsewhere in the Southwest came to be freed of the constraints of this idiom. It would therefore appear that from the Coalition period onward, POTTERY VESSELS ARE TEXTILES was vestigial, at best, among Tewa Basin potters.

Reflections in the Tewa Language

One of the Tewa words for pottery, *natˀú*, is a compound of *nan* 'earth, clay' and *tˀún* 'basket' (plural *tˀú*), and thus translates as 'clay-baskets.' This term clearly reflects the metaphor POTTERY VESSELS ARE BASKETS that is so thoroughly expressed in Mesa Verde pottery. Cognates or transparent compounds of this term are not found in Northern Tiwa (*muluʔune* 'pottery,' from Proto-Tanoan **búlu* 'pottery, bowl' (Appendix A, no. 36), Southern Tiwa (*natʔę* 'clay-dish'), or Towa (*nǫ́:šī* 'clay-dish'), so there is no evidence to suggest that *natʔú* was coined prior to the differentiation of Tewa from Tiwa (prior to AD 980).[6] These data thus imply that there was a period after Proto-Tewa had become distinct from Proto-Tiwa during which a metaphor linking pottery to basketry was so pervasive among Proto-Tewa speakers that a compound word expressing this metaphor became an everyday word for pottery. It is difficult to imagine this semantic innovation taking place in the Tewa Basin because weaving imagery never appears to have played a generative role in structuring pottery design in this area. It is relatively easy, however, to imagine this innovation taking place in the Mesa Verde region, where weaving imagery was clearly generative.

BUILDINGS ARE CONTAINERS

Reconstruction to Mesa Verde Culture

Drawing upon the ancient and widespread metaphor PEOPLE ARE CORN, Mesa Verde people appear to have conceptualized buildings as containers for people in the same way that actual pots and baskets contained food. This is revealed by architectural details dating from the AD 1000s onward. Patterns in the form and decoration of buildings exhibit the structure one would expect under the hypothesis that buildings were imagined as containers (after Ortman 2008b: 231–241).

1. Directionality: Pottery designs were painted on the walls of buildings (Figure 10.3a–t), but architectural imagery was not painted on pots. In addition, the specific designs mapped onto structure walls all have antecedents in pottery designs, which were in turn inspired by innovations in weaving. Conceptual "chaining" is the most parsimonious explanation for the appearance of weaving-inspired imagery on structure walls, because structure walls share more image-schematic structure with pottery vessels than they do with weavings themselves.
2. Superordinate principle: Imagery of several different kinds of containers appears in architecture. Kiva walls were painted as pottery bowls; cribbed kiva roofs reflect the form and construction of coiled baskets; and granaries were painted as seed storage jars (Figures 10.3 and 10.4).
3. Invariance principle: Due to correspondences between the walls of buildings and the bases and sides of coiled baskets, design motifs from banded pottery designs were transferred to structure walls; however, the floors and walls of buildings do not have counterparts in plaited baskets, and as a result "draped," or all-over, pottery designs (Figure 10.2) were not painted on structure walls.
4. Constitutive principle: Cribbed roofs, which mimic the form and construction of coiled baskets, were expensive, not structurally necessary, and not load-bearing; nevertheless, they were characteristic of the small kivas associated with residential architecture.

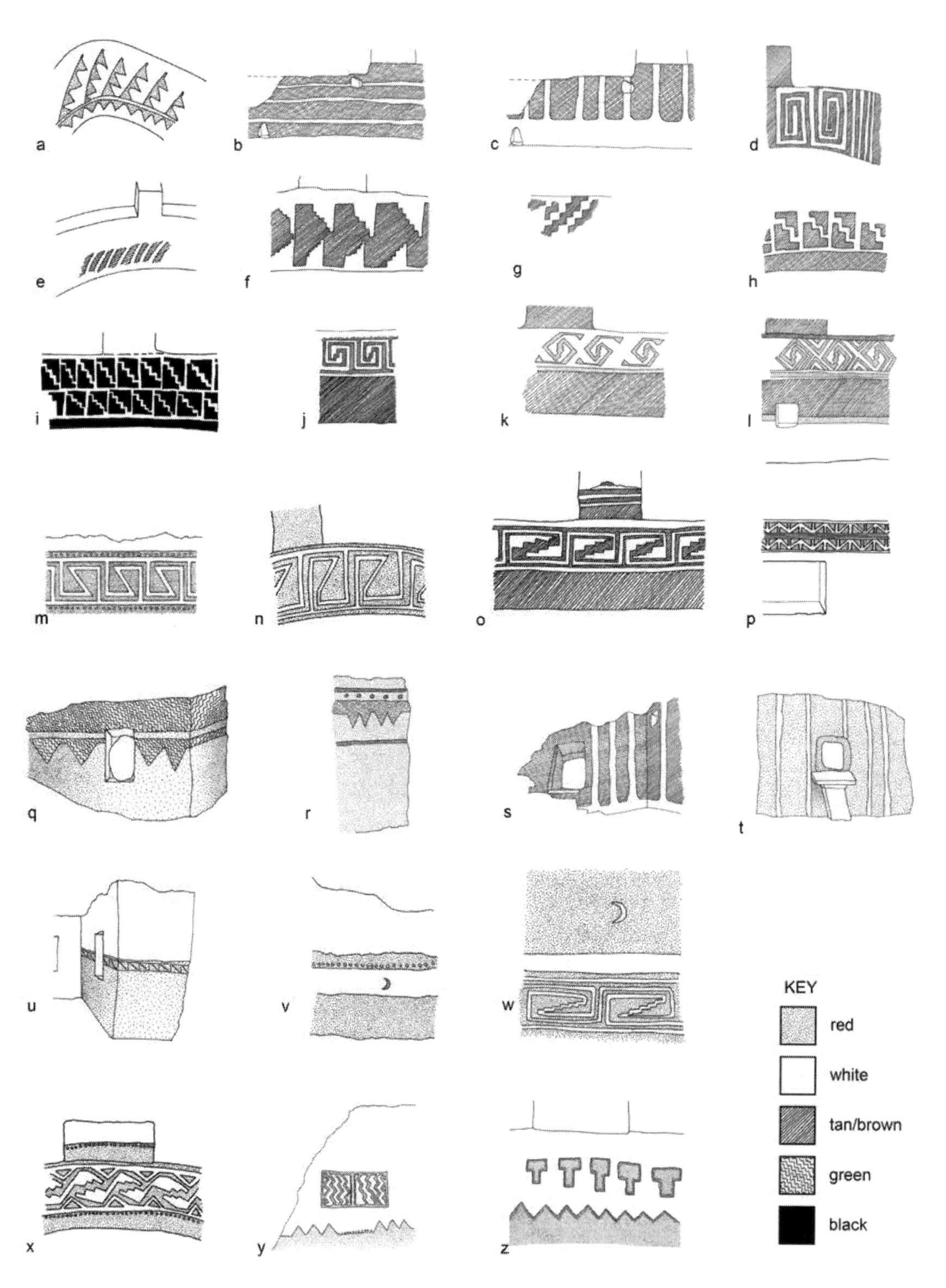

FIGURE 10.3. Container imagery in Mesa Verde mural painting: *a–p*, pottery-band murals on kiva interiors; *q–t*, pottery-band murals on granary exteriors; *u–z*, blends of landscape and container imagery. (After Ortman 2008b: Figs. 12.2–12.3.)

FIGURE 10.4. Mesa Verde region kiva with cribbed (coiled basket) roof above and pottery-band mural below. (Photo by author.)

5. Blended sources: Pottery designs painted on structure walls were themselves blends of loom-based weaving and coiled basketry. In addition, the kiva combined imagery from pottery bowls and coiled baskets in a single structure.
6. Experiential principle: Numerous formal and experiential properties of buildings are analogous to those of pottery vessels, and these correspondences would have been as apparent in the past as they are today.

Based on these patterns, it appears that Mesa Verde people drew a conceptual parallel between architectural spaces in which people lived and actual pots and baskets used in storing, preparing, and serving food. The metaphor KIVA ROOFS ARE COILED BASKETS was expressed in the standard architecture of Mesa Verde kivas, indicating that this concept was probably conventional, widely shared, and used unreflectively. One might expect this concept to have also influenced the language of Mesa Verde people, but the more limited distribution of other expressions suggests that these concepts may not have influenced their language to the same extent. For example, KIVA WALLS ARE POTTERY BOWLS was only expressed in a small proportion of kivas, and several of these appear to have been significant ceremonial structures within their respective communities (Martin 1936; Ortman 2008b). This suggests that knowledge of this metaphor was limited, or that it was only appropriate to express this knowledge in kivas used for specific purposes. Because this concept may not have been expressed in everyday life, it is less likely to have had linguistic consequences for Mesa Verde people. In addition, GRANARIES ARE SEED JARS was expressed so infrequently that it is unlikely to represent a widely shared concept, and thus was probably of no linguistic consequence.

Expressions in Tewa Basin Archaeology

There is little to no evidence for the conceptualization of buildings as containers in the Tewa Basin archaeological record. The only clear example of a Northern Rio Grande kiva decorated with a pottery-band mural is a kiva at San Lazaro, a Classic period Southern Tewa (Tano) town in the Galisteo Basin (Fenn 2004: 208). It is possible that additional pottery-band murals that have not been preserved once existed in Tewa Basin sites; for example, traces of a "zig-zag design in red pigment" were identified around the base of a kiva wall at Te'ewi (Wendorf 1953:46), and traces of painted geometric lines in white, black, red, green, and yellow were also encountered on fallen wall material in five rooms and a kiva at Pindi (Stubbs and Stallings 1953:29). Nonetheless, zigzag designs and geometric lines need not imply the presence of a pottery-band mural. Zigzag lines in the relatively well-preserved Classic period kiva murals at Picuris Pueblo appear to represent lightning instead of woven patterns, and the asymmetrical, multicolored, stepped-pyramid motifs in these murals clearly depict clouds and cloud beings, even if their terraced form originated in weaving imagery of earlier periods (Crotty 1999:157–163). It is also important to note that murals in the more typical representational style of the Classic period also occur in Tewa Basin sites (Tichy 1947) and are well preserved in several sites south of the Tewa Basin, including Kuaua (Dutton 1963), Pottery Mound (Crotty 2007), Gran Quivira (Peckham 1981), and Pueblo del Encierro (Snow 1979). No examples of pottery-band murals have been documented in Developmental or Coalition period pit structures, kivas, or granaries in the Tewa Basin.

The roofs of kivas and pit structures do not express coiled basket imagery either. Late Developmental pit structure roofs were generally flat and were supported by four posts arranged in a square within the main chamber (Lakatos 2007). Coalition and Classic period kiva roofs were also supported by posts in various arrangements (Creamer 1993; Lange 1968; Stubbs and Stallings 1953; Wendorf 1953; Windes and McKenna 2006). Evidence of cribbed roofs, in the form of pilasters or preserved crib logs, is completely lacking in Tewa Basin kivas. Thus, if Tewa had diversified from Tiwa within the Rio Grande, Tewa speakers would have had no experience with cribbed roofs that mimic the construction and appearance of coiled baskets.

In sum, there is no evidence to suggest that Pueblo inhabitants of the Northern Rio Grande conceptualized buildings as containers prior to the Classic period, and the only clear analog to Mesa Verde pottery-band murals is the Classic period San Lazaro kiva mural. The Picuris kiva murals do not depict pottery-band designs; rather, they depict motifs whose form originated in pottery designs and weavings of earlier periods. The absence of additional evidence

TABLE 10.1. People and corn in Kiowa-Tanoan context

Reconstruction	N. Tiwa	S. Tiwa	Tewa	Jemez	Kiowa
1a) KT _*k^{h}æy_ 'skin, hide' (Appendix A, no. 7)	_xójna_ 'skin, hide'	_k^{h}ay_ 'skin'	_k^{h}owa_ 'skin, bark, cornhusk'	_wǽhæ_ 'skin, hide'	_k^{h}ǫ́y_ 'skin, cloth, mat'
1b) PT _*k^{h}æ_ 'cornhusk'				_hæ̂:_ 'cornhusk'	
2) TT _*k^{hw}ę́d-_ 'pick, hoe' (Appendix A, no. 70)	_x^{w}ę́l-_ 'pick, digger'		_nan-whę́ḏi_ 'hoe'	_hę́_ 'bury, inter'	

Note: Sources are listed in Appendix A.

for pottery-band designs on kiva walls suggests that the metaphor KIVA WALLS ARE POTTERY BOWLS was either vestigial or never widely shared in the Northern Rio Grande.

Reflections in the Tewa Language

That PEOPLE ARE CORN is older than the Tewa language itself is supported by the fact that this metaphor appears to have been involved in shifts in meaning of at least two Kiowa-Tanoan terms. For example, meanings associated with Proto-Kiowa-Tanoan _*k^{h}æy_ 'skin, hide' were extended to include 'cornhusk' in Proto-Tanoan times, and a Tiwa-Tewa word for 'hoe' (_*k^{hw}ę́d-_) appears to derive from a Proto-Tanoan verb that refers to the interment of the dead (Table 10.1). Additional reflexes of PEOPLE ARE CORN are scattered throughout Kiowa-Tanoan dialects. For example, the Tewa Corn Mother, a perfect ear of corn wrapped with feathers and beads, is called _k^{h}ų̀lų̀ŋ^{ʔ}aa_ 'corn-clothed' (Parsons 1974 [1929]:249; Robbins et al. 1916:88). These examples suggest that metaphorical relationships between people and corn have been part of Pueblo culture from at least the Basketmaker III period, when Proto-Tanoan was spoken.

An expression of BUILDINGS ARE CONTAINERS is also embedded in the Tewa language. The San Juan Tewa dictionary prepared by the Ohkay Owingeh Bilingual Program (Martinez 1982:34) contains a word glossed as 'pitched roof.' This word, _t^{ʔ}úp^{h}á^{ʔ}di^{ʔ}_, is a metaphoric compound (_t^{ʔ}ún_ 'coiled basket' + _p^{h}e_ 'stick, timber' + _di_ 'of') that translates 'basket of timbers,' thus clearly expressing the metaphor ROOFS ARE COILED BASKETS. Although words related to roofs are recorded for other Kiowa-Tanoan languages (Appendix A, nos. 66, 79), cognates or transparent compounds of _t^{ʔ}úp^{h}á^{ʔ}di^{ʔ}_ are not apparent in the available data for these languages. It thus appears that at some point after Proto-Tewa became distinct from Proto-Tiwa, the metaphor ROOFS ARE COILED BASKETS came to be so widely shared in the Proto-Tewa speech community that a new term was coined that enshrined this relationship. Because roofs that mimic the design and form of coiled baskets were characteristic of household kiva architecture in the Mesa Verde region but were never created in the Tewa Basin, the most parsimonious explanation for these data is that *tˀúpʰáˀdiˀ* represents a residue of Mesa Verde culture that remained enshrined in the Tewa language after its speakers moved from the Mesa Verde region to the Tewa Basin.

It may also be significant to note that the specific expression of BUILDINGS ARE CONTAINERS that is embedded in the Tewa language (KIVA ROOFS ARE COILED BASKETS) corresponds to the most common expression of this metaphor in Mesa Verde architecture (cribbed kiva roofs). In contrast, I have not identified any Tewa language reflexes of KIVA WALLS ARE POTTERY BOWLS or GRANARIES ARE SEED JARS, even though these concepts are also expressed in Mesa Verde archaeology. This is not a surprising result because the knowledge and/or authority to express KIVA WALLS ARE POTTERY BOWLS appears to have been restricted in Mesa Verde society, and expressions of GRANARIES ARE SEED JARS were quite rare. Thus, neither of these metaphors was expressed often enough in everyday life to have had linguistic consequences.

The World Consists of Containers

Reconstruction to Mesa Verde Culture

In addition to imagining buildings as containers, Mesa Verde people conceptualized the world itself as consisting of containers. One of the ways this was expressed was through mural paintings that combined container and landscape imagery (Figure 10.3u–z). Patterns in these compositions exhibit the structure one would expect under the hypothesis that the world was imagined as a pottery vessel earth and a textile sky. This evidence is summarized below (after Ortman 2008a:241–246).

1. Directionality: Landscape imagery — including abstractions of the horizon with projecting landforms, the sun and/or moon, and animals — was commonly painted on the inside walls of buildings, and was also combined with container imagery in architectural murals; however, landscape scenes were not painted on actual containers. This is consistent with the notion that conceptual projection was from actual containers to buildings and then the larger world, but not vice versa.
2. Superordinate principle: Loom-woven fabrics were depicted in the upper, "sky" field of horizon scene murals, and pottery-band murals were depicted in the lower "earth" half. Additional compositions present the pottery bowl walls of the kiva as the earth, and the coiled basket roof as the sky (Figure 10.4). Thus three different types of "containers" were used to represent elements of the world in these compositions.
3. Invariance principle: Compositions that blend container and landscape imagery occur almost exclusively on the interior walls of buildings, presumably because there is no correspondence between the exterior surfaces of containers/buildings and the "outside" of the world.

4. Constitutive principle: Loom-weaving imagery is combined with horizon imagery in several structures that appear to have been used to observe the movements of celestial objects. This suggests that Mesa Verde people used the imagery of loom-based weaving to model the rhythmic, back-and-forth movements of celestial objects with respect to the horizon over time.
5. Blended sources: As mentioned above, several murals combine landscape and container imagery in single compositions that are only coherent as expressions of conceptual metaphors.
6. Experiential principle: Numerous formal and experiential properties of the earth, sky, and celestial motion correspond to pottery, basketry, and loom weaving, respectively. These correspondences must have been as apparent in the past as they are today. In addition, the relationship between weaving and the sky was grounded in the experiences of Mesa Verde people weaving cotton cloth. This activity took place on upright looms set up inside buildings, with the frame attached to a ceiling beam above and loops set into the floor below (Kent 1983: Fig. 58). The loom thus spanned the distance between the floor and ceiling of the room, and the tension of the warp threads literally pulled the ceiling/sky and floor/earth toward each other. The process of weaving on an upright loom was thus the process of stitching the world together (see Newsome 2005).

Based on these patterns, it is clear that Mesa Verde people used actual pots, baskets, blankets, and rooms as models for the larger world around them. Additional patterns suggest that pottery vessels were used to represent the emergence place itself. Many kivas and pit structures in ancestral Pueblo sites have a small, round hole in the floor that represents the emergence place among present-day Pueblo groups. Archaeologists have labeled these features "sipapus" after their Hopi name. In AD 1200s Mesa Verde kivas, sipapus were often created using an olla neck or mug that was recessed into the floor, with the rim at floor level and the bottom broken out (Cattanach 1980:51; Morris 1991:674; Ortman and Bradley 2002:60–62; Rohn 1971:74). Because both mugs and ollas contained liquids, the use of these forms for sipapus suggests that Mesa Verde people imagined the emergence place as a watery underworld, or a pottery vessel containing water.

The distribution of expressions of THE WORLD CONSISTS OF CONTAINERS in Mesa Verde sites is similar to that of KIVA WALLS ARE POTTERY VESSELS; that is, expressions are limited to a small proportion of structures rather than being elements of standard architectural forms. In addition, many structures in which expressions of THE WORLD CONSISTS OF CONTAINERS occur appear to have been used by ritual-knowledge specialists. This suggests that knowledge of this metaphor, or perhaps the authority to express it, was restricted in Mesa Verde society. Thus, one might not expect this metaphor to have exerted much influence on the everyday language of Mesa Verde people.

Expressions in Tewa Basin Archaeology

It is possible that THE WORLD IS A BUILDING was present in ancestral Tewa culture of the Classic period. Although wall plaster is rarely preserved in the adobe habitation rooms of most Classic period Tewa Basin villages and towns, Snow (1963:4) encountered a room at Sapawe decorated with a dado pattern, in which the lower third of the wall was painted red to brown and the upper two-thirds painted tan to white. This type of mural probably originated in the San Juan drainage (Ortman 2008b) and subsequently spread to ancestral Tewa culture, either through diffusion or the movement of Mesa Verde people to the Tewa Basin. In Mesa Verde culture such patterns were clearly abstractions of the horizon: several examples include projecting landforms and/or depictions of celestial objects in the upper field (Figure 10.3u–z); however, such embellishments have not been found in Tewa Basin examples, suggesting that ancestral Tewa people were never aware of the original symbolism of dado murals, or that knowledge of this symbolism had faded by the Classic period.

There is stronger evidence for THE UNDERWORLD IS A KIVA. Classic period kivas throughout the Rio Grande were clearly viewed as microcosms of the spirit world based on murals depicting underworld scenes populated by plants, animals, and people (Crotty 1999, 2007).[7] In addition, the presence of ritual features in Late Developmental pit structures — including sipapus, ash pits, and a consistent southeastern orientation (Lakatos 2007) — clearly indicate their symbolic importance and probably reflect a conceptualization of pit structures as microcosms.

Expressions of THE UNDERWORLD IS A KIVA are not terribly useful for tracing the Tewa speech community because similar symbolic features occur in pit structures throughout the ancestral Pueblo area from at least the Basketmaker III period onward.[8] However, given that Tewa Basin pit structures and kivas were imagined as microcosms, the upright looms which "connected" the floor and ceiling in such structures (Bussey 1968; Creamer 1993; Stubbs and Stallings 1953; Wendorf 1953; Windes and McKenna 2006) may well reflect the association between the sky, cotton/clouds, and weaving apparent in Mesa Verde mural painting. This inference is reinforced by the ethnolinguistic evidence discussed below, and suggests that THE SKY IS A WOVEN OBJECT has been part of Tewa culture for some time.

The clearest example of THE WORLD CONSISTS OF CONTAINERS in Tewa Basin archaeology consists of ceremonial bowls with terraced rims (Harlow 1965). These terraces represent the mountains or clouds that rim the world, and thus these vessels clearly express THE EARTH IS A POTTERY BOWL. According to Harlow (1965:18), terraced-rim bowls first occur in Jemez Black-on-white and Rio Grande Glaze ware during the Colonial period, but this form does not occur in Tewa pottery until the mid-nineteenth century. Based on Tewa ethnolinguistic evidence (discussed below), it would seem most likely that terraced-rim bowls represent an innovative means of expressing a concept that had been part of Tewa culture all along, as opposed to a readoption of this concept.

Reflections in the Tewa Language

THE WORLD CONSISTS OF CONTAINERS is thoroughly embedded in Tewa ritual language, and remains active in Tewa culture to the present day. One area where this is clearly revealed is in the multiple senses of *p'o:kwin*. The core sense of this word is 'lake' because this is its primary meaning in Tewa; the word incorporates the Tewa term for "water" (*p'o:*); and the term is cognate with Tiwa terms for "lake" (Taos *p'axwiane*, Isleta *p'ahwi:re*). Yet the Tewa term can also be applied to the emergence place, a kiva, or a ceremonial bowl. These extended senses form what Lakoff (1987) calls a semantic chain. In Tewa belief, the first people emerged from beneath the surface of a lake, and so the first link in this chain is THE SPIRIT WORLD IS A LAKE. The second link is provided by the kiva, which is taken as a model for the lake of emergence. The compound *p'o:kwi-k*^{h}*oyi* 'lake roof-hatch' (*k*^{h}*oyi* 'roof-hatch of a kiva') provides linguistic evidence of THE LAKE IS A KIVA. This concept is also embedded in an Arizona Tewa story recorded in 1920 (Parsons 1994 [1926]:199). In this tale, Cactus Flower Girl is led by Spider Grandmother to a lake in which there were "two poles coming out of the water. As they watched, the poles grew higher and higher, soon there was a big ladder coming out of the water. They heard a sound, someone was talking under the ladder. They saw the head of someone coming out of the water. This was a kiva, and coming out of it was a good-looking woman." The girl then walks out into the middle of the lake on a cornmeal road and descends into the lake-kiva, in which she meets a number of ancestral spirits.

Finally, the lake is modeled using an actual container. The primary object of ceremonial leaders whose activities take place inside the kiva is a ceremonial bowl (*p'o:kwingéh* 'lake-place' *or p'o:kwisą̈* ^{ʔ}*ą̈wéh* 'lake-bowl') that is filled with water and used to represent *p'o:kwin* during ceremonies (Laski 1958:165; Ortiz 1969:90). The multiple senses of *p'o:kwingéh*, the etymology of *p'o:kwisą̈* ^{ʔ}*ą̈wéh*, and the fact that objects with these names continue to be used in ceremonies today clearly indicate that THE LAKE IS A POTTERY BOWL has been and continues to be an important concept in Tewa culture. This specific metaphor may in fact be older than the Tewa language itself, because Isleta forms related to *p'o:kwingéh* are known: Isleta *p*^{ʔ}*akwimp'a* 'medicine bowl' clearly expresses the same metaphor, and Isleta *p*^{ʔ}*ahwié-ài* 'lake-place, ceremonial bowl' may in fact be cognate with the Tewa form. These multiple senses and uses of *p'o:kwin* in Tewa ritual language clearly reflect the metaphorical connections between pottery bowls, kivas, and the underworld expressed in Mesa Verde material culture.

THE SKY IS A WOVEN OBJECT also remains active in Tewa language and culture. A poem recorded prior to 1912 (Spinden 1993:116), and a song performed during the Basket Dance in 1964 (Kurath and Garcia 1970:189), both used the phrase *póvitsą́ąwą̈* ^{ʔ}*i*^{ʔ}*t*^{ʔ}*ún* 'dew basket' (*póvi* 'flower, cloud' + *tsą́ąwą̈* ^{ʔ}*i*^{ʔ} 'blue-green' + *t*^{ʔ}*ún* 'coiled basket') to refer to the sky. It may also be relevant that Tewas model the sky using vegetative metaphors in contemporary poetry (e.g., *ok*^{h}*úwá-póvi* 'cumulus cloud,' from *ok*^{h}*úwá* 'cloud' [^{ʔ}*ok*^{h}*u* 'down, fluff'+

wá 'wind'] + *póvi* 'flower'), and that historically most weaving was done using vegetal materials. Another striking image of weaving associated with the sky is developed in the following poem, also recorded in the early twentieth century.

> Oh our Mother the Earth, oh our Father the Sky,
> Your children are we, and with tired backs
> We bring you the gifts that you love.
> Then weave for us a garment of brightness;
> May the warp be the white light of morning,
> May the weft be the red light of evening,
> May the fringes be the falling rain,
> May the border be the standing rainbow.
> Thus weave for us a garment of brightness
> That we may walk fittingly where birds sing,
> That we may walk fittingly where grass is green,
> Oh our Mother the Earth, oh our Father the Sky!
> (Spinden 1933:94)

This poem beautifully develops the metaphor A THUNDERSTORM IS WEAVING IN THE KIVA, and likens the effects of rain on the world to the effect of men weaving cotton garments on upright looms in the kiva, stitching the earth and sky together. This concept may have been active in Tewa culture for as long as there have been upright looms inside pit structures/kivas, but the earliest clear expressions of this metaphor occur in thirteenth-century Mesa Verde mural paintings.

Finally, THE EARTH IS A POTTERY VESSEL is reflected in the etymology of Tewa *bé:ˀe~bú:ˀú*, which was glossed as 'small~large, low roundish place' by Harrington (1916:71). This form is also translated 'corner' in several place-names for concave geographic features in the update of Harrington's ethnogeography produced by San Juan Pueblo (2000).[9] The alternation *bé:ˀe~bú:ˀú* reflects a pattern of sound symbolism unique to Tewa among Kiowa-Tanoan languages that was first identified by Harrington (1910a:16). In a large number of Tewa terms, the front vowels /e/ and /a/ indicate smaller scale, whereas the back vowels /o/ and /u/ indicate larger scale.[10] These data indicate that at some point after it became distinct from Tiwa, the Tewa language developed a system of sound symbolism in which the manner of articulation of vowels reflects the size of entities. As a result, one might expect *bé:ˀe~bú:ˀú*, 'small~large, low roundish place' to have derived from a single ancestral word, and in fact this ancestral form turns out to be Proto-Tanoan **búlu* 'pottery (bowl)' (Appendix A, no. 36). The original meaning of the Proto-Tanoan form survives in Tewa *be:* 'pottery bowl,' but the extension of meaning from pottery bowls to geographic features did not take place in Towa or Tiwa. Thus, the Tewa word used to describe concave, roundish geographical features derives from an older word for "pottery," and this semantic extension took place at some point after Tewa became a distinct language.

Overall, then, there is abundant evidence that THE WORLD CONSISTS OF CONTAINERS has been active in Tewa culture for some time. Several basic-level expressions of this metaphor are characteristic of both Tewa Basin and Mesa Verde material culture. For example, metaphors implied by the multiple senses of *p'o:kwin* and the etymology of *bé:ˀe~bú:ˀú* are clearly reflected in the cloud-mountain symbols associated with terraced-rim bowls and kivas in historic Tewa material culture, and with the kivas with pottery-band murals and pottery-lined sipapus in Mesa Verde material culture. Also, words and expressions that link woven objects with the sky are reflected in the upright looms of pit structures and kivas in both regions, and are represented explicitly in thirteenth-century Mesa Verde mural paintings. So even though expressions of THE (UNDER)WORLD IS A POTTERY VESSEL, THE (UNDER)WORLD IS A KIVA, and THE SKY IS A WOVEN OBJECT in recent Tewa language and culture are consistent with the model that Tewa was originally spoken in the Mesa Verde region, a range of models involving diffusion or independent invention that would not require the Tewa language to have been spoken anywhere outside the Tewa Basin are also consistent with these data.

The Community is a Container

Reconstruction to Mesa Verde Culture

The archaeological record of canyon-rim villages, discussed in Chapter 9, is consistent with the structure one would expect under the hypothesis that this metaphor, and especially the more basic concept, THE VILLAGE IS A SERVING BOWL, was an active element of thirteenth-century Mesa Verde culture:

1. Directionality: Serving bowl imagery is expressed in the setting of canyon-rim villages, the architecture of these villages, and in community organization; however, village architecture is not represented on bowls.
2. Superordinate principle: Bowl imagery was mapped onto two innovative architectural forms, canyon-rim villages and enclosed plazas, but not onto older elements of community organization such as great kivas. Communal feasting modeled on household meals was also a prevalent activity in canyon-rim villages.
3. Invariance principle: Houses built outside the enclosing walls of canyon-rim villages are oriented in the traditional way, with south-facing houses, instead of continuing the inward-facing orientation. This reflects the fact that only the interior of a bowl corresponds to the canyon-rim environment.
4. Constitutive principle: New villages were planned and existing villages modified to correspond with a pottery bowl image at the same time that communal feasting was developing. Also, the central spring area was left undeveloped, as the centers of pottery bowls with banded designs were typically left free of designs.
5. Blended sources: The canyon-rim village combined the image of a family eating from a common bowl, and of corn transformed into food inside a bowl, in a single community concept.

6. Experiential principle: Numerous experiential properties of canyon-rim villages and community organization correspond to the manufacture, form, and use of pottery serving bowls. These correspondences must have been as apparent in the past as they are today.

Based on these patterns, it is clear that during the final century of occupation, Mesa Verde people began to apply the container imagery that had been associated with individual buildings since the early AD 1100s to the community as a whole. Because canyon-rim villages and plaza-oriented feasting were characteristic of the mid-AD 1200s, and village architecture and plaza ceremonies were public by nature, one would expect THE COMMUNITY IS A CONTAINER to have been widely shared and openly expressed in public discourse. One might therefore also expect this concept to have impacted the language of Mesa Verde people.

Expressions in Tewa Basin Archaeology

There is very limited evidence for THE COMMUNITY IS A CONTAINER in Northern Rio Grande archaeology. The only Tewa Basin village I am aware of in which houses were constructed facing inward in a concave geographical environment is the cavate village (LA50976) along the south rim of Tsankawi Mesa (Toll 1995: 55). This and other cavate settlements of the Pajarito Plateau date from the Coalition period, and there may well be additional cavate sites that are reminiscent of Mesa Verde canyon-rim pueblos. Nonetheless, with the possible exception of cavate villages, Tewa Basin villages and towns from the Late Coalition period onward were constructed on mesa tops or on terraces above watercourses, and consisted of rectilinear room blocks arranged to create formal or informal plazas (Figure 10.5). These settlements were constructed in more or less flat settings and contain plazas that are distinctly rectilinear in plan. None of these villages were bowl-shaped, none contain roundish plazas, and none were built in concave geographical environments. Thus, it is clear that ancestral Tewa people of the Tewa Basin had little to no experience with bowl-shaped villages or plazas. As a result, THE COMMUNITY IS A CONTAINER would not be expected to have influenced the Tewa language if Tewa-speakers had always resided in the Tewa Basin.

Reflections in the Tewa Language

Despite its absence from Tewa Basin archaeology, THE COMMUNITY IS A CONTAINER is clearly fossilized in the Tewa language. I have previously discussed the Tewa forms *bé:ˀe~bú:ˀú*, 'small~large low roundish place' and *be:* 'pottery bowl,' both of which are reflexes of Proto-Tanoan **búlu* 'pottery (bowl)' (Appendix A, no. 36). *Bú:ˀú* is also used to refer to villages, especially towns inhabited by other ethnic groups (e.g., *Ą́ˀnúbúˀú* 'Alcalde Town,' *Mokíbúˀú* 'Hopi Town,' *P'osíbúˀú* 'Green Town' (Ojo Caliente), *Tewháp'îbúˀú* 'Red House Town,' *Tsímáyôbúˀú* 'Chi-

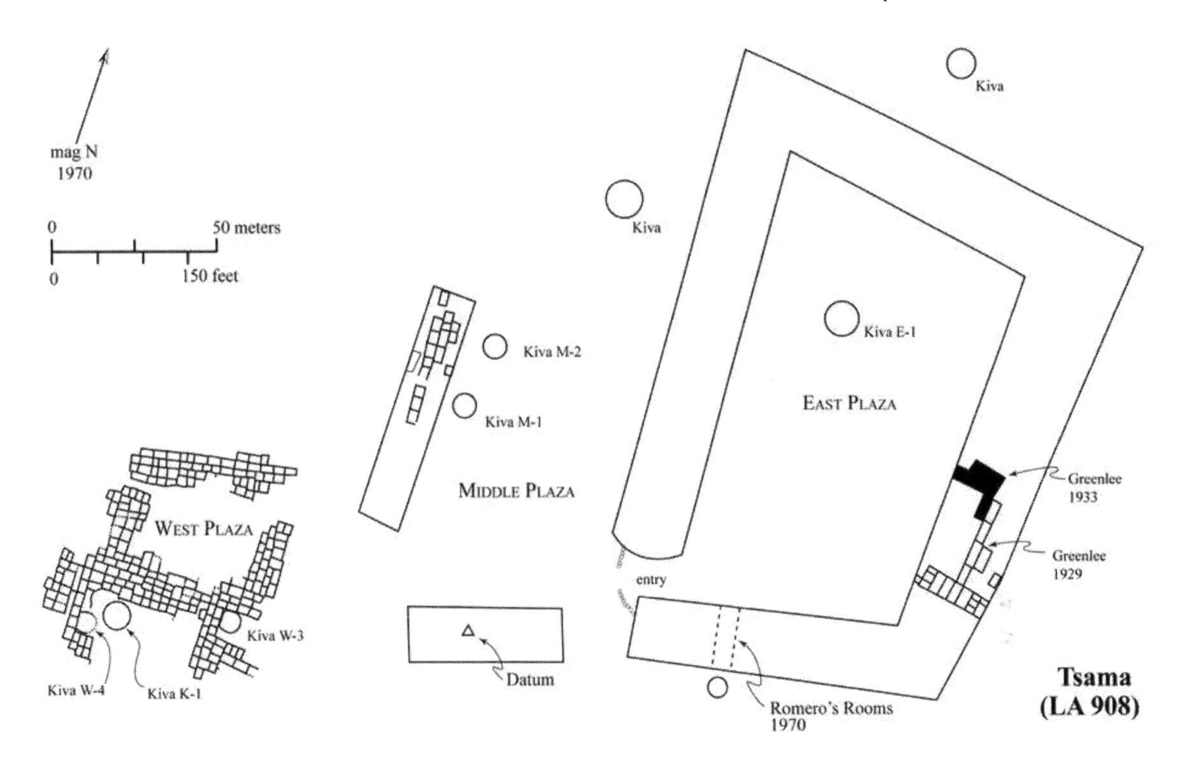

FIGURE 10.5. Plan map of Tsama Pueblo, a Tewa Basin town. The West Plaza dates from the Late Coalition period, the Middle Plaza from the Early Classic period, and the East Plaza from the Middle Classic period. (Windes and McKenna 2006: Fig. 1. Courtesy of Tom Windes.)

mayo Town'); and also plazas (e.g., *P'oqwogeˀimbúˀú* 'San Ildefonso (water cuts down through) plaza' (Harrington 1916:305–306); also *búpíngéh* 'plaza' [*bú:'ú* + *pín* 'heart, middle' + *géh* 'place']). Although the Tewa and Taos words for "plaza" contain cognates for "heart" and may imply Proto-Tiwa-Tewa **pian-* 'plaza, heart-middle place,' the metaphoric reflexes of Proto-Tanoan **búlu* in Tewa are not evident in Tiwa or Towa (Table 10.2). These data indicate that THE COMMUNITY IS A CONTAINER influenced the Tewa language after it became isolated from Tiwa. Because expressions of this metaphor are widespread in thirteenth-century Mesa Verde archaeology, but are largely absent from the Tewa Basin, it is difficult to imagine how *bú:ˀú* could have come to possess the range of meanings it has in the Tewa language today if this language had never been spoken in the Mesa Verde region.

It is also significant to note that the more commonly used word for "village" in Tewa today enshrines different metaphors. Inhabited Tewa villages are referred to as *'ówînge*, a form which contains the verb *wį́nú* 'to stand' (from Proto-Tanoan **gʷin* 'stand'), and thus translates as 'there-standing-at.' The verb *wį́nú* is also applied to growing corn plants or to female dancers in the plaza (see below). Thus, the etymology of *'ówînge* appears to reflect a conceptualization of the village as a garden. *Ówînge* has no cognates in other Kiowa-Tanoan languages (Table 10.2) and was therefore coined after Tewa became distinct from Tiwa. It was also probably coined prior to AD 1350 because the oldest ancestral Tewa sites labeled *'ówînkeyi* 'village ruin' were abandoned during the Late Coalition period (see Chapter 8).

TABLE 10.2. Villages and plazas in Kiowa-Tanoan context

TEWA	TAOS	ISLETA	JEMEZ	KIOWA	RECON- STRUCTION
be: 'pottery bowl, vessel, fruit'	*muluˀune* 'pottery'	*búru* 'pottery bowl'	*bɨ́ dó* 'round, fat, chubby' *tʸa:bɨ* 'sacred bowl'	*cę̨nd´ɔ´atdɔ* 'clay dish'	PT **búlu* 'pottery (bowl), round'
bú:ˀú 'village, plaza' *bé:ˀe~bú:ˀú,* 'small~large, low roundish place'	*tɨo-* 'village'	*natɨy, tɨy* 'community, home, pueblo'	*tû:kʷa* 'village' *tɨ́:yò* 'home, place where we live'	*to-byų̨ˀę* 'house-circle'	
pín 'heart, middle'	*píana* 'heart, middle'	*pia* 'heart' *pianład* 'center middle'	*pé:* 'heart' *pó:kʷa* 'in the middle'	*tʰę̨n* 'heart'	PT **pian-* 'heart'
búpíngéh 'plaza' (*bú:ˀú* + *pín* + *géh* 'place')	*píanto* 'plaza, center-middle' (lit. "heart-within")	*nap'ahɨa* 'place, town, plaza' *p'ahɨad* 'plaza' (cf. *p'ahɨa* 'well')	*pó:tˀu* 'plaza, middle, center' *ɦó:pɨtā* 'plaza' *ɦó:lá* 'inside a circle, in the plaza' (cf. *ɦó:-* 'inside')	*guɔn-dą̨m* 'dance-ground'	TT **pian-* 'plaza' (?)
'ówînge 'village' ('there-standing-at) *wį́nú* 'to stand' *ˀawį́n* 'to grow in a standing position'	*kʷínmą̨* 'to stand'	*wini* 'stand up'	*kʷípˀæ̀* 'stand up'	*pʰɔ̨* 'to stand up'	PT **gʷin* 'stand'

Notes: Sources are as listed in Appendix A. Noncognate forms for each row are presented in gray text.

The imagery of plazas, growing corn, and female dancers brought together by *'ówînkeyi* continues to be expressed in ceremonies that take place in Tewa villages today. During these performances, the elder women of the pueblo stand around the edges of the plaza wrapped in blankets while elder men sing songs and direct the movements of the male and female dancers within. The lyrics of these songs present the plaza and surrounding pueblo as a garden. For example, during the Butterfly Dance at Ohkay Owingeh the singers chant (Kurath and Garcia 1970:152):

> In San Juan Pueblo right in the middle of the plaza outside the kiva here, white corn goddess stands.
> With her living plants she stands prepared at dawn.

And during a later portion of this same dance, they sing (Kurath and Garcia 1970:153):

At (soul) village, over there where the rivers join at confluence lake.
They come right here, carrying flowers; the *ók^{h}ùwà* have flowers there.
They come to see our fields.

The second lyric states that "right here," the pueblo where the dance is taking place, is "our fields," and describes the ancestral site across the Rio Grande as a lake from which the *ók^{h}ùwà* 'cloud-beings' (cf. *ok^{h}úwá* 'cloud') bring *ok^{h}úwá-póvi,* 'cloud-flowers' or rain clouds, to water the fields.[11] Both lyrics thus present the village as a garden, the female dancers within the plaza as corn plants, and the male dancers who move through the plaza as clouds.

THE VILLAGE IS A GARDEN is also vividly expressed in the following poem (Spinden 1993:95):

Ready we stand in San Juan town,
Oh, our Corn Maidens and our Corn Youths!
Oh, our Corn Mothers and our Corn Fathers!
Now we bring you misty water
And throw it different ways,
To the north, the west, the south, the east
To heaven above and the drinking earth below!
Then likewise throw your misty water
Toward San Juan!
Oh, many that you are, pour water
Over our Corn Maidens' ears!

Here again, the village is presented as a garden, and the people as growing corn plants who beseech the *ók^{h}ùwà* to enter the plaza and bring them life, just as rain causes corn to grow. These reflections of THE VILLAGE IS A GARDEN in contemporary poetry demonstrate that the metaphor enshrined in *'ówînge* and first applied to settlements abandoned at the end of the Coalition period continues to be active in Tewa culture to the present day. It may therefore be the case that *bú:'ú* and *'ówînge* form a sequence, with *'ówînge* reflecting the way Tewa speakers have conceptualized the community since the Late Coalition period, and *bú:'ú* fossilizing an older manner of doing so.

Implications

In this chapter I have presented reconstructions of four general container metaphors and numerous submetaphors of thirteenth-century Mesa Verde culture, examined the extent to which each of these was expressed in the archaeological record of the Tewa Basin, and documented the extent to which each is embedded in the Tewa language and/or reflected in contemporary discourse. A summary of this analysis is presented in Table 10.3. This analysis identified three native Tewa words that enshrine specific container metaphors that were never characteristic of Tewa Basin material culture, but were characteristic of thirteenth-century Mesa Verde region material culture:

1. *natˀú* 'pottery' (*nan* 'earth, clay' + *tˀú* 'coiled baskets') (POTTERY VESSELS ARE COILED BASKETS).
2. *tˀúpʰáˀdiˀ* 'pitched roof' (*tˀún* 'coiled basket' + *pʰe* 'stick, timber' + *di* 'of') (KIVA ROOFS ARE COILED BASKETS).
3. *bú:ˀú* 'large, low roundish place, plaza, village' (from Proto-Tanoan **búlu* 'pottery bowl') (THE VILLAGE IS A SERVING BOWL).

This analysis also identified several native Tewa words that reflect metaphors expressed in both Mesa Verde region and Tewa Basin archaeology, and which remain active in twentieth-century Tewa culture:

1. *p'o:kwingéh* 'ceremonial bowl,' lit. "lake-place" (THE UNDERWORLD IS A POTTERY VESSEL).
2. *p'o:kwisą̈ˀą̈wéh* 'ceremonial bowl,' lit. "lake-bowl" (THE UNDERWORLD IS A POTTERY VESSEL).
3. *p'o:kwi-kʰoyi* 'lake roof-hatch' (*p'o:kwin* 'lake' + *kʰoyi* 'roof-hatch of a kiva') (THE UNDERWORLD IS A KIVA).
4. *póvitsą́ąwą̈ˀ́iˀtˀún* 'dew basket' (*póvi* 'flower, cloud' + *tsą́ąwą̈ˀ́iˀ* 'blue-green' + *tˀún* 'coiled basket') (THE SKY IS A WOVEN OBJECT).
5. *béˀe~bú:ˀú*, 'small- -large, low roundish place' (from Proto-Tanoan **búlu* 'pottery bowl') (THE EARTH IS A POTTERY BOWL).

For the latter group of words, all one can say for certain is that the concepts embedded in these Tewa words were part of both Mesa Verde and ancestral Tewa culture. It is possible that the words expressing these concepts derive from the language and culture of the Mesa Verde region, but other scenarios which do not require the Tewa language to have originated in the Mesa Verde region are also possible. For example, it is likely that THE UNDERWORLD IS A KIVA is older than the Tewa language itself based on the occurrence of sipapus in pithouses of the Northern Rio Grande (Lakatos 2007) and the San Juan drainage (Wilshusen 1989) from the seventh century AD onward. THE UNDERWORLD IS A POTTERY VESSEL may also date from Proto-Tiwa-Tewa times (AD 725–920) due to the existence of a possible cognate of Tewa *p'o:kwingéh* in Isleta (*pˀahwié-ài* 'ceremonial bowl,' lit. "lake-place"). These data could be accommodated to a model in which the underlying metaphors were part of the cultural inheritance of an indigenous Tewa language of the Tewa Basin, and a Tanoan language of the Mesa Verde region that has not survived into historic times. A second scenario that could account for the remaining items is that an indigenous Tewa language adopted the underlying metaphors as a result of contact with Mesa Verde migrants.

TABLE 10.3. Summary of conceptual metaphor analysis

	MESA VERDE ARCHAEOLOGY	TEWA BASIN ARCHAEOLOGY	TEWA LANGUAGE
1. pottery vessels are textiles			
a) POTTERY BOWLS ARE COILED BASKETS	Widespread	Vestigial	Fossilized
b) POTTERY BOWLS ARE PLAITED BASKETS	Widespread	Absent	Absent
c) COOKING POTS ARE COILED BASKETS	Widespread	Vestigial	Fossilized
2. buildings are containers			
a) GRANARIES ARE SEED JARS	Rare	Absent	Absent
b) KIVA WALLS ARE POTTERY BOWLS	Restricted	Vestigial	Fossilized
c) KIVA ROOFS ARE COILED BASKETS	Widespread	Absent	Fossilized
3. the world consists of containers			
a) THE SKY IS WOVEN	Restricted	Restricted	Active
b) THE EARTH IS A POTTERY BOWL	Restricted	Restricted	Active
c) THE LAKE IS A KIVA	Restricted	Restricted	Active
d) THE LAKE IS A WATER-FILLED VESSEL	Restricted	Restricted	Active
4. the community is a container			
a) THE VILLAGE IS A POTTERY BOWL	Widespread	Vestigial	Fossilized
b) THE PLAZA IS A POTTERY BOWL	Widespread	Absent	Fossilized

The situation is different for the first group of words. In this case, native Tewa words enshrine metaphors that were never characteristic of Tewa Basin culture, but which were characteristic of earlier Mesa Verde region culture. These words have no cognates in other Kiowa-Tanoan languages, and thus there is no evidence to suggest they represent a residue of Proto-Tiwa-Tewa or Proto-Tanoan culture. They also could not be loans from another language because they are comprised of native Tewa morphemes in all cases. Thus, the existence of these words in the Tewa language poses a substantial challenge to the hypothesis that Tewa diversified from Tiwa within the Rio Grande region. For this to have occurred, one would have to propose a scenario whereby Proto-Tewa speakers of the Northern Rio Grande were somehow influenced by migrants who spoke a different language to coin new compound words or to extend the meanings of existing words in ways that enshrined foreign metaphors, even as material expressions of these concepts — in the form of weaving patterns on pottery, basket-like kiva roofs, and bowl-like villages — disappeared from the archaeological record. If these material expressions had become characteristic of Tewa Basin culture, this scenario might be plausible, but it is exceedingly difficult to imagine a migrant group exerting this level of linguistic influence in the absence of a comparable cultural influence.[12] In contrast, it is relatively straightforward to imagine a migrant group discarding elements of their homeland culture as they moved to a new environment, even as they continued to speak a language that enshrined residues of these discarded elements.[13] Thus, a far more parsimonious explanation for these data is that they imply that Proto-Tewa was originally spoken in the Mesa Verde region and was brought to the Tewa Basin by Coalition period migrants from this region.

It is also important to emphasize how precisely residues of Mesa Verde metaphors in the Tewa language map onto expectations derived from the distribution of their material expressions in Mesa Verde archaeology. The earliest and most common expressions of POTTERY VESSELS ARE TEXTILES in Mesa Verde culture involved a mapping of coiled basket imagery onto pottery vessels, and the residue of this concept in the Tewa language (*natˀú*) follows suit by incorporating a word that refers specifically to coiled baskets (*tˀú*). Likewise, the residue of BUILDINGS ARE CONTAINERS that is most clearly enshrined in Tewa (*tˀúpʰáˀdiˀ* ‘pitched roof,’ lit. “basket of timbers”) corresponds to the most widespread material expression of this metaphor in Mesa Verde architecture (cribbed kiva roofs). Finally, the residue of THE VILLAGE IS A POTTERY BOWL enshrined in Tewa (*bú:ˀú* ‘large, low roundish place, plaza, village’) links both of its expressions in Mesa Verde archaeology (roundish plazas and canyon-rim villages) in a single polysemous term. The probability that such detailed correspondences might exist between Mesa Verde archaeology and the Tewa language if this language had not been spoken by creators of the Mesa Verde archaeological complex would seem vanishingly small.

The analysis presented in this chapter thus provides strong evidence that Tewa diversified from Tiwa outside the Rio Grande region and was spoken in the Mesa Verde region during the final centuries of ancestral Pueblo occupation in the San Juan drainage. This conclusion is also consistent with the most parsimonious interpretation of population history, biological variation, shared phonetic innovations, reconstructed vocabulary, place-names, and oral traditions discussed in previous chapters — all of which support the population movement model of Tewa origins. The fact that the most straightforward interpretation of multiple, logically independent lines of evidence is the same in all cases makes a strong argument that most Tewa genes and the Tewa language were brought to the Tewa Basin by Coalition period migrants from the Mesa Verde region.

Even if the language and most of the genes of the Tewa Pueblos derive from the Mesa Verde region, this should not be taken as suggesting that ancestral Tewa society and culture bear an equally straightforward relationship to previous Mesa Verde society and culture. The discussion in this chapter has alluded to what many previous researchers have concluded; namely, that Tewa Basin society and culture were quite distinct from earlier Mesa Verde region society and culture. Yet the analyses presented to this point also make a strong case that the Tewa language and most Tewa genes derive from the Mesa Verde region. The remaining task, then, is to examine the Mesa Verde and Tewa Basin archaeological records to determine the nature of the relationship between these two complexes.

NOTES

1. Although the results of these studies are summarized qualitatively here, it is important to emphasize that they include quantitative analyses of symbolic expressions that demonstrate statistically significant patterns consistent with the expectations of specific metaphor hypotheses.
2. In a previous version of this work (Ortman 2009:392–393) I suggested that the characteristic shape of Mesa Verde corrugated vessels may derive from twilled wicker baskets; however, only one such basket, from Mancos Canyon, has been tentatively associated with ancestral Pueblo people, and first-hand examination of this basket (Laurie Webster, personal communication, 2011) suggests a more recent Ute affiliation.
3. In Chapter 13, however, I show that POTTERY VESSELS ARE BASKETS did continue to structure pottery decoration in areas of the Tewa Basin first settled during the Late Coalition period.
4. Rio Grande archaeologists use a slightly different terminology when discussing utility pottery: the surface textures labeled as "corrugated" in Mesa Verde are known as "indented-corrugated" in the Rio Grande region, and the textures labeled as "banded" in Mesa Verde are known as "corrugated" in the Rio Grande.
5. The fact that these changes in the utility ware industry correspond in time to the period of most rapid influx of Mesa Verde populations to the Tewa Basin suggests that these changes may well represent a conscious reaction against Mesa Verde material traditions on the part of migrants. This possibility and its implications for our understanding of Tewa origins are discussed in greater detail in Chapter 13.
6. Isleta *natˀë* 'pottery' (lit. "clay-dish") is not cognate with Tewa *natˀú* 'pottery' (lit. "clay-baskets") because the final vowels do not correspond, and Isleta *tˀë* and Tewa *tˀú* appear to derive from different words (see Appendix A, nos. 35, 35a).
7. Terraced motifs that originated in pottery/weaving were commonly used to represent mountains and/or clouds in these murals, and also appear in the roof lines and stairways of historic kivas (e.g., Parsons 1974 [1929]: Plate 11a), but these motifs appear to have lost their connection with pottery/weaving by the Classic period, and thus did not present the kiva or the world as a pottery bowl.
8. The kiva was used to model the underworld in an Acoma origin narrative recorded in 1928 (see Ortman 2008b). This, combined with Tewa ethnolinguistic evidence, reinforces the likelihood that THE UNDERWORLD IS A KIVA was widespread in ancient Pueblo societies.
9. As examples: *Awaphábúˀú* 'cattail corner,' *Áyiˀbúˀú* 'sunflower corner,' *Pap'îbếˀé* 'red fish corner,' *Shugóbếˀé* 'mosquito corner,' *Tsaywíbúˀú* 'eagle gap corner,' *Tsígubúˀú* 'Chico corner,' *Tsikhówábếˀé* 'little firefly corner.'
10. As examples, compare: *'i piye* 'to this place,' *hae piye* 'to yonder place,' and *'o piye* 'to that remote place; *heˀe* 'small groove, arroyito' with *huˀu* 'large groove, arroyo'; and *pʰigi* 'small and flat' with *pʰagi* 'large and flat.'
11. Tonal contours that reflect the movements of clouds and souls are the only contrast between *okʰúwá* 'cloud' and *ókʰùwà* 'cloud-being.' Clouds form high over the mountains and remain in the sky, a pattern reflected in the high tone of *okʰúwá*. In contrast, cloud-beings are ancestral spirits that leave the bodies of the deceased, travel up to the mountains, and then return to the village in the form of male impersonators. This pattern of movement is reflected in the rising-then-falling tone of *ókʰùwà*. This correspondence also appears to be reflected in the tonal contours of *p'o:* 'water,' which only flows downhill (low tone), and *p'ô* 'road, trail,' along which initiated men travel to and from the mountains (retroflex tone) (see Ortman 2008a).

12. In addition, the level of influence of Mesa Verde migrants on an indigenous Tewa speech community required under this scenario would be expected to lead to significant contact-induced change in Tewa phonology, comparable to the influence that Keres exerted on Towa, as Mesa Verde migrants shifted to Tewa. Yet the analysis of phonetic innovations in Chapter 6 (Figure 6.2) shows that in fact Tewa is little changed from Proto-Tiwa-Tewa, whereas the Tiwa languages have undergone numerous phonological changes. In other words, the relative stability of Tewa phonology is the opposite of what one would expect under the hypothesis that residues of Mesa Verde metaphors in the Tewa language are contact-induced.
13. When Latin speakers spread from Italy into France during the first millennium AD, for example, the resulting French culture was a distinct hybrid of Roman and Gaulish/Celtic culture, but the French language is descended directly from Latin, contains few words inherited from Gaulish, and enshrines aspects of Roman culture that have been lost over time (Woolf 1998).

Immigration, Population Movement, and Material Culture

I have so far examined settlement evidence which suggests that the Classic period ancestral Tewa population was in large measure a result of migration during the Coalition period; bioarchaeological evidence which suggests that the primary source area of these migrants was the Mesa Verde region; and archaeolinguistic evidence which suggests that Mesa Verde migrants brought the Tewa language with them. Individually and collectively, these results support the population movement hypothesis of Tewa origins and contradict expectations of the in situ development and immigration hypotheses.

Given the range of evidence consistent with the population movement hypothesis, one might assume that it should be straightforward to identify this movement archaeologically by tracing material culture continuities between Mesa Verde region sites and Tewa Basin sites dating to the thirteenth century. As mentioned in Chapter 1, however, such continuities are neither abundant nor obvious. Archaeologists have been searching for concrete signs of a lineal relationship between these two archaeological complexes for more than a century, but in light of the negative results of previous archaeological studies, it is not unreasonable to question whether the two traditions are related at all (e.g., Boyer et al. 2010; Dutton 1964; Steen 1977:39–41, 1982:53–54; Wendorf 1953:95–96). Tewa Basin material culture quite simply does not exhibit the sort of continuities one would ideally like to see if, in fact, the Tewa population and language originated in the Mesa Verde region (Boyer et al. 2010; Habicht-Mauche 1993:87–89; Lipe 2010).

The absence of clear-cut evidence for an intrusive material culture complex is the primary reason there remains no consensus among archaeologists concerning Tewa origins. In light of the studies presented in previous chapters, this is a fascinating situation that raises several questions. Does the absence of evidence for an intrusive material culture complex necessarily undermine the population movement hypothesis? Should one expect strong material culture continuities under this hypothesis? Do migrations leave traces other than material culture continuities in the archaeological record? Are there more subtle aspects of material culture that do exhibit continuity from the Mesa Verde region? This chapter develops a framework for addressing such questions as a step in evaluating whether or not the archaeological evidence follows the biological and linguistic evidence in supporting the population movement hypothesis of Tewa origins. I focus on recent studies of migration in archaeology to develop methods for identifying population-level movements like the one suggested for this case. Then, in subsequent chapters, I turn to the archaeological records of the Mesa Verde region and Tewa Basin to evaluate whether or not the evidence supports the population movement scenario.

Identifying Migration from Archaeological Evidence

Immigration, Ethnicity, and Continuity

One of the earliest attempts to define concrete methods for detecting migration was published by Emil Haury in 1958. In this classic paper, Haury suggested that migration is the most likely, although not the only, explanation if the following minimum conditions are met: (1) a constellation of new traits appears suddenly, and without local prototypes, in a given area; and (2) the products of the hypothesized migrant group reflect elements of their homeland culture as well as borrowed elements from the culture of the destination area (Haury 1994 [1958]:415). Haury further argued that the inference of migration is even stronger if: (3) it is possible to identify an area in which the constellation of new traits was the normal pattern; and (4) expressions of the "at home" and displaced traits occur simultaneously, or in a sequence, in the homeland and destination areas.

Haury applied this methodology to the archaeological record of Point of Pines Pueblo, in the mountains of east-central Arizona, finding evidence to support all four of these conditions. This supportive evidence included a number of traits that could be traced to the Kayenta-Hopi area of northeastern Arizona, such as a D-shaped kiva, unusual floor features in domestic architecture, distinctive maize morphology, a cache of wooden ritual objects, imported Kayenta-Hopi pottery vessels, and a number of vessels decorated in the northern style but made from local materials. Haury also found that construction of the intrusive architectural block corresponded in time to the abandonment of many Kayenta-Hopi area sites. This evidence made a strong case for migration, and indeed the conclusion of Haury's study has been widely accepted ever since (e.g., Lowell 2007; Mills 1998; Stone 2003; Zedeño 1994).

Another especially clear archaeological example of migration is the so-called Oaxaca Barrio at Teotihuacan (Spence 1992). The existence of a Zapotecan enclave at Teotihuacan was first suggested by a concentration of Oaxacan-looking sherds near the western edge of the city, in an area known today as Tlailotlacan. Excavation of a portion of this area revealed a patio-platform apartment compound that would have been at home in either Teotihuacan or Monte Alban, but also included Oaxaca style tombs and mortuary remains, and a lintel on which

Zapotec glyphs were carved. Morphological traits of skeletal remains suggest that the individuals buried in these tombs were members of a high-status lineage within the enclave (Spence 1994:365). The pottery assemblage is for the most part typical of other apartment compounds at Teotihuacan and includes only a few vessels made of Oaxacan clays, but about 3 percent of the assemblage represents Oaxaca style pottery made using local materials. In addition, there is evidence that Zapotec potters continued to produce Oaxacan types that were popular when they first migrated to Teotihuacan centuries after production of these types ceased in Oaxaca. Spence (1992:78–79) interprets this "frozen" pottery tradition as evidence that the minority Zapotecans attempted to maintain their ethnic identity in a situation of limited subsequent contact with the homeland.

Intrusions such as those presented by Point of Pines and Tlailotlacan are difficult to explain as anything other than results of migration, but the clear-cut nature of these and other cases (e.g., Di Peso 1958) have encouraged some unwarranted generalizations. One such detour has been the concept of the site-unit intrusion as a characteristic marker of migration. Although it is obvious that site-unit intrusions and ethnic enclaves result from migration, the absence of such intrusions does not necessarily indicate the absence of movement. A good example, cited by Adams and others (et al.1978:500–501), is the inconsistent material signature of ethnic enclaves in the ancient Near East. Emberling (1997:316) contrasts intrusive settlements of expanding Uruk period states — which exhibit Mesopotamian styles of public architecture, seals, and mass-produced pottery — from later enclaves of Assyrian merchants that are only apparent from written records. Both involved migration, but only one produced site-unit intrusions.

A second unfortunate generalization is the notion that migration is only plausible when the intrusive complex bears a clear genealogical relationship with the material culture of a definable homeland. Although it certainly strengthens the argument, a close reading of Haury's (1994 [1958]) article shows that he viewed the identification of a new complex as sufficient. Matson and Magne (2007:6–7) reinforced this point in their study of northern Athapaskan migrations, arguing that migration is indicated when a new material culture complex appears in an area, even as continuity from the previous period prevails in an adjacent area. Spence's (1992) analysis of Tlailotlacan also suggests that overt continuities in material culture may only result when migrants choose to maintain their ethnic identity in the destination area and express it using homeland material practices that contrast with those of the local tradition (also see Stone 2003). In other words, phylogenetic relationships in material traditions may represent social consequences of migration in certain situations, rather than necessary correlates.

Even if it is not a necessary correlate, identifying the source area of an intrusive material culture complex does constitute a strong basis for identifying migration, and this has led recent researchers to spend considerable effort defining those attributes of material culture that most reliably distinguish social groups with distinct histories. These studies have shown, first, that humans actively manipulate material traditions in contextually specific ways to create, express, and maintain social identities (Bowser 2000; Carr and Neitzel 1995; Conkey and Hastorf 1990; Hodder 1982; Weissner 1983; Wobst 1977); and second, that technical choices made during the production of artifacts are transmitted through social networks just as decorative or "stylistic" traits are (Hegmon 1998; Lechtman 1977; MacEachern 1998; Sackett 1990; Stark 1998).

Because technical choices, in particular, represent "ways of doing" that have low visibility, are unlikely to send social messages, and are difficult to replicate on casual exposure with finished objects, technological style has been argued to provide a more reliable indicator of social networks and boundaries than more highly visible traits such as form and decoration (Carr 1995; Stark 1998; Stark et al. 1995). Clark (2001, 2004) has taken this argument one step further, suggesting that a variety of low-visibility attributes do not send social messages and therefore are primarily transmitted vertically during development, whereas high-visibility attributes often do send messages about social groups and thus tend to be transmitted horizontally throughout life. As a result, one would expect postmigration expressions of high-visibility attributes to reflect identity politics which need not map onto the original migrant and local groups. In contrast, low-visibility attributes are more likely to continue being produced without conscious reflection by migrants, and thus represent a more reliable means of tracking them.[1]

Summarizing ethnographic and ethnoarchaeological studies worldwide, Clark (2001:14–22) demonstrates that a variety of low-visibility attributes — including artifact manufacturing techniques, domestic spatial organization, and food preferences — do, in fact, reliably distinguish social groups in contexts of ethnic coresidence. In contrast, high-visibility attributes — including textile and pottery designs, personal adornment, burial practices, and projectile point morphology — cross-cut social groups fairly often in these studies. Clark (2001: 41–71) also applies this methodology to the archaeological record of the Tonto Basin, in east-central Arizona, and finds a strong signal of Western Pueblo immigration into a region that was initially settled by Hohokam populations from the Phoenix Basin. The indicators of migration in this case include: (1) the appearance of sites organized around room blocks as opposed to local courtyard compounds; (2) the appearance of coursed masonry, firebox entries, and high-elevation tree species in room block sites, all of which contrast with local sites; and (3) the association of corrugated pottery made using the coil-and-scrape technique with room block sites, as opposed to the local, paddle-and-anvil technique of cooking pot manufacture.

Clark's work constitutes a significant advance in archaeological approaches to migration and is convincingly applied in his case study. As a result, there appears to be a strong basis for viewing continuities in low-visibility attributes as a reliable means of distinguishing migrants from locals, and for determining the source area from which the migrants have come. Nevertheless, it is important to keep in mind that, as in earlier studies, Clark's research does not demonstrate the converse: that the absence of continuities in low-visibility attributes indicates the absence of migration. In fact, there are several reasons why migrants might not always express continuities even in low-visibility attributes.

One reason is that the visibility of material culture attributes is influenced by the social context of use as well as their physical characteristics. Artifact makers may not be aware of the enculturative traditions they participate in at home, but after migration, these traditions and the subtle details which result from them may suddenly become much more apparent as the migrants encounter people who do things differently. In fact, in a postmigration context, distinct social identities may already exist in the minds of migrants and locals before anyone starts behaving, and in such cases people will be motivated to find the behavioral differences that identify people as belonging to one group or another. As a result, attributes with low physical visibility can become highly perceptible and consciously manipulated in the postmigration social context. This raises the possibility that, in some cases, low-visibility attributes will continue to be expressed not so much because the migrants remain unaware of them, but because these attributes are sufficiently subtle to communicate group membership among the migrants without advertising it to the locals. If awareness and choice, based on perceived interests, can become entangled with low-visibility attributes, then it would seem that even low-visibility attributes might fade away when migrants choose not to maintain their homeland identity upon arrival in the destination area.

A second and more general concern that has been raised several times already is that material traditions map onto speech communities and biological populations in a variety of ways (e.g., Carr 1995; MacEachern 1998; Terrell et al. 1997). Anthony (2007:104–106) argues that it is reasonable to infer a language boundary at robust frontiers defined by bundles of opposing customs which persist over time because such distributions imply a barrier to interaction that would not permit the maintenance of a single speech community. It may also be reasonable to propose that visible ethnic enclaves or site-unit intrusions were usually created by people who at least initially spoke a different language from that of the locals. However, language boundaries can also persist in the absence of material culture boundaries, as in the case of the Hopi-Tewa of Arizona (Dozier 1954), and mating networks often cross-cut both. So even if some migrations betray their presence in material culture, and low-visibility attributes do so most reliably, it is not difficult to imagine situations in which migrants might adopt the host material culture wholesale while maintaining their distinctiveness in nonmaterial ways (i.e., language or oral tradition; see Duff 1998). Also, migrations of distinct ethnic groups that share material traditions may not leave clear traces because, in such cases, differences in migrant practices will be slight to nonexistent. Successful studies of migration have only been possible in cases where the pottery and architectural traditions of the source and destination areas happen to contrast. Movements within the area encompassed by single material traditions, or between areas with closely related material traditions, may be more difficult to identify from material culture evidence because in such cases the material culture of the migrants may exhibit continuities with both the homeland and the destination area.

A final concern is that migrations do not always result in a proliferation of ethnic groups in the destination area. The ethnographic record synthesized by Clark, and previous studies of site-unit intrusions and ethnic enclaves, involve situations where two or more ethnic groups have come to live in close proximity. These situations result when neither the migrants nor the locals immediately absorb or displace the other. But migrants can also colonize a frontier, driving out or absorbing the locals, in which case the result of migration will be a replacement of the ethnic group that occupies the destination area. Previous researchers have tended to overlook such cases on the assumption that when they occur, they should result in the obvious spread of an archaeological complex from the homeland to the destination area. This is what archaeologists have not been able to find in the Tewa Basin archaeological record, and the reason why many researchers have argued that if a migration did occur, it must have involved small groups that blended in with the local population (e.g., Cordell 1979: 144; Habicht-Mauche 1993:87–89). But do migrant populations necessarily continue material traditions of the homeland when they move long distances and colonize a lightly inhabited frontier? I argue that they often do not.

Population Movement, Colonization, and Change

One of the few studies to address the degree to which the material cultures of ethnic groups change as they move is Irving Rouse's *Migrations in Prehistory* (1986), a comparative study of ancient population movements. Rouse examined four case studies of large-scale population movement (the spread of Austronesian speakers across the Pacific, the spread of Thulean people in the Arctic, the spread of the Yayoi people in Japan, and the origins of the Caribbean Taino people in South America) that were either still under way or recently concluded at the onset of written records in each area. Written texts confirm that population movement had taken place in each case, and as a result Rouse was able to compare the archaeological data with linguistic and genetic reconstructions to assess the extent to which archaeological evidence corresponded to the biological and linguistic evidence.

Through these studies, Rouse (1986:175–180) identified two fundamentally different types of migration. The first, which Rouse labels "immigration," refers to the intrusion of a relatively small social group into an already populated area. Movements that result in site-unit intrusions and ethnic coresidence fall into this category. The second type, which Rouse labels "population movement," refers to the colonization of a previously uninhabited area or migration by a group that is large enough to absorb or drive out the existing population. Rouse argues, and several additional studies support, that the social consequences of these two types of movement and their resulting archaeological traces are markedly different.[2]

As alluded to earlier, the social consequences and archaeological traces of immigration will depend on a number of factors, including the relative size of the migrant and local groups, the relative social power and prestige of each group, and the interests of the migrants and their descendants. When the migrant group is large enough to maintain itself through endogamy, and most of its people decide it is in their interest to maintain their premigration identity and express it in material terms, they will express high-visibility attributes of their homeland material culture consciously, and low-visibility attributes out of habit. A migrant group may also remain distinct in nonmaterial ways by becoming bilingual in their native language and the host language, or by maintaining knowledge of their distinct history, even as they assimilate culturally and biologically to the host community. But if the migrant group is not large enough to maintain itself, lacks social power and/or prestige, or its members determine it is not in their interest to remain distinct, the initial migrants may betray their presence only through habitual, low-visibility attributes, and their descendants will assimilate to the majority group, making a greater or lesser contribution to the host culture depending on a variety of contextual factors.

The archaeological traces of population movement, on the other hand, follow a different logic. When a population colonizes a frontier and absorbs or displaces the indigenous population, the dynamics of ethnic group interaction do not develop. As a result, the migrants can develop and/or maintain a distinctive identity regardless of the extent to which they continue their homeland material practices because their language will continue to be spoken, all will share a recent migration experience, and all will retain knowledge of the homeland from which they have come. The moving population will thus be free to modify its cultural models and associated practices to suit the socio-natural environment of the destination area, to adopt local practices, and to comment positively or negatively on their homeland (see Pauketat 2008) without jeopardizing their identity as a distinct people. Somewhat counter-intuitively, the more dominant the migrant group is, the more readily it may change as it moves.

What factors encourage culture change in the case of population movement? I think there are at least five. One obvious factor, which applies equally well to immigration, is that technological traditions are tailored to the resources used in producing artifacts. For example, many choices involved in making pottery are connected to the performance characteristics of clays, and many choices involved in constructing buildings are connected to the qualities and availability of building materials. When people move to a new environment, familiar resources may not be available, or it may not be possible to make artifacts as efficiently or in the same way using local resources. In such situations, technological traditions of the destination area may be adopted by the migrants out of convenience or necessity, or a new tradition that utilizes local resources more effectively may become established rapidly. As a result, continuities one might otherwise expect will not occur.

A second major factor follows from the structure of migration as a social process (Anthony 1990). When factors that encourage migration from the homeland develop, communities often send out scouting parties to establish residency in potential destination areas, prepare fields, and begin producing food (Anthony 1990:905; Lefferts 1977; Stone 1996:86–87). If the destination is a lightly occupied frontier, these scouts will not join existing communities, but will establish pioneer settlements with their compatriots. Scouts are initially drawn toward areas that present similar productive resources to the homeland (e.g., Wilhelm 1992:64), but these pioneers, far away from the traditions and institutions of home, may have neither the time nor the inclination to reproduce homeland ritual architecture, houses, and household items. Instead, they may obtain household items from local manufacturers, marry local people, and adopt destination-area traditions that work well in that environment. Scouts also tend to cooperate economically with affines to a greater extent than in the homeland due to the shortage of labor on the frontier (Herr 2002; Stone 1996), and they also tend to simplify their cultural practices to suit the simpler and more fluid social context of the frontier (Anthony 2007:112–113; Noble 1992:4–5). Finally, due to the institutional vacuum of the frontier, pioneers have the opportunity to manifest ideas that circulated in the homeland society but which ran counter to entrenched interests at home (Kopytoff 1987:13). These factors can combine to produce communities that are quite different in appearance and organization from those of the homeland. Finally, the new adaptation worked out by these pioneers can become the model for subsequent migrants to follow as a migration stream develops from positive reports of return migrants in the homeland. In Anthony's (2007:112–113) terms, the pioneers become the charter group for a new society.

A third factor which encourages culture change in cases of population movement is that success on the frontier creates options for those who remain in the homeland. As positive reports of migrants' successes make their way back home, the growing body of information provides opportunities for people in the homeland to examine the conditions under which they live and make a judgment as to whether moving to the frontier would provide a better future than would staying at home. As more people decide to move, it becomes easier and less threatening for others to do the same (Boyd and Richerson 1985; Henrich 2001; Rogerson 1984), and it takes more extreme measures to keep others from following suit. The decreased risks associated with moving, combined with a hardening of traditional ways at home, can result in factional conflict and social movements that promote migration as a means of reorganization. The result of this process will be a stream of migrants who have already chosen to adopt frontier ways when they leave home.

These observations suggest "push" factors normally precede the development of "pull" factors during population movements. Pushes—such as land pressure, land degradation, or climatic fluctuations—provide the impetus for scouting and colonization, but pulls toward particular destinations develop only after the initial settlers develop a viable alternative to the homeland society. This is extremely important for the archaeology of population movement because it suggests that population should show a time-lagged response to push factors in the homeland, and pushes will tend to shift over the course of the movement from material factors to sociopolitical and ideological factors.

A fourth factor derives from the nature of culture itself. The culture of every ethnic group is in reality a palimpsest of ideas, beliefs, techniques, and values derived from multiple sources that have converged to create the constellation of traits characteristic of a group at a given moment (Sapir 1949 [1916]). Although some cultural models do form packages (Shennan 2002:78–83), many others have unique histories and are not transmitted as part of a functional system. So even if the members of an ethnic group imagine themselves as a unitary whole, the same cannot be said for their culture. Identities are unitary and momentary categories of self-ascription, whereas cultures are historical products, and always complex hybrids (Comaroff and Comaroff 1997:59; Pauketat 2008).

When members of a social group become an ethnic minority after immigration, the continued performance of homeland cultural practices often becomes linked to the survival of their identity as migrants from a particular place. Practices that were performed for a variety of reasons in the homeland are suddenly transformed into ethnic markers, and those practices that the migrants choose to continue become exhibits testifying to their enduring identity and history (Kroskrity 1993; Spence 1992). Thus, the choice facing ethnic minorities often boils down to assimilation versus resistance through a hardening of tradition. If the migrants choose the latter, they will continue to perform homeland material practices in an increasingly stereotyped and anachronistic way, and thus leave archaeological traces that are easy to spot.

When a population colonizes a new environment, in contrast, the survival of their identity does not become linked to the maintenance of homeland traditions. Thus, there are no barriers to cultural innovation, and the culture and practices of the group may continue to evolve with no threat to the survival of their identity. In addition, colonists have the opportunity to comment on the homeland they have left behind by continuing homeland practices, inverting them, or avoiding them all together. This fact, combined with the changed socionatural conditions people experience after migration, can lead to rapid culture change, and even a conspicuous absence of continuity. Indeed, the fundamental difference between immigration and population movement appears to be that in the former case, migrants are often motivated to preserve aspects of their homeland culture, whereas in the latter, they are freed to change them.

The fifth and final factor that can encourage rapid culture change — and can make population movements difficult to identify on the basis of material culture continuities — is that such movements involve leap-frogging more often than a wave of advance (e.g., Ammerman and Cavalli-Sforza 1984). Agricultural economies are often characterized as focal (Anthony 1990:901) in the sense that they focus on the intensive utilization of a single resource: agricultural land. In many regions of the world, including the U.S. Southwest, suitable land for intensive agriculture is not distributed evenly, but occurs in patches separated by expanses of less desirable land. When conditions that encourage migration develop in the homeland, potential migrants learn about possible destinations through information relayed back to the homeland by scouts and previous migrants. This cyclical movement between homeland and destination leads to well-developed routes of travel between the two areas (Anthony 1990:903) and to communication networks that encourage migrants to follow kin and coresidents to targeted locations where social support is already in place (Anthony 2007:112). These factors encourage long-distance migration between desirable patches, where migrants skip over less-desirable or unavailable areas in between. Thus, even if migrants continue to express homeland material traditions, there will not be a continuous distribution of such expressions from the destination area back to the homeland, as would occur in a wave of advance. Also, due to the distance and isolation of pioneer settlements, and the limited and irregular contact between homeland and frontier, the migrants are freed to modify elements of their homeland culture, adopt elements of the local culture, or invent new elements as the local environment dictates.

Reconfiguring Migration

It should be clear that the distinction between immigration and population movement is fundamental to an understanding of Tewa origins. Much recent research on migration in archaeology has focused on forms of migration that result in ethnic coresidence, either within specific sites or among adjacent sites in a region. This is also the situation addressed by the modern migration literature that archaeologists have drawn from so productively in recent years. Yet if the paleodemographic, bioarchaeological, archaeolinguistic, and oral tradition evidence is to be believed, Tewa origins were not the result of immigration. Rather, it involved the colonization of a frontier area by a much larger social group than had existed there previously. As a result, according to the framework developed here, one would not necessarily expect to see the site-unit intrusions or straightforward continuities in material culture that many have assumed should be apparent (e.g., Davis 1965; Dutton 1964). Indeed, the only material culture continuities one might expect are those suggested by Clark (2001): domestic spatial organization, artifact manufacturing techniques, and food preferences.

This perspective on the social consequences of population movement calls into question the basis of immigration models of Tewa origins. Immigration models tend to interpret the absence of obvious material culture continuities in Northern Rio Grande sites as evidence that Mesa Verde migrants came in small groups over a long period of time and were gradually absorbed into communities originally established by the indigenous population or by migrants from other homelands (e.g., Beal 1987; Cordell 1995; Habicht-Mauche 1993; Kidder 1924; Kohler 2004; Lipe 2010). The net result of this process would have been replacement of the local gene pool but the loss of Mesa Verde material traditions. Under these circumstances one would also expect the Tewa language to have originated in the Rio Grande drainage, and for this language to have been influenced by Mesa Verde migrants who shifted to Tewa upon arrival in the Rio Grande. However, the analyses presented in previous chapters suggest that the Tewa language originated in the Mesa Verde region and is little changed phonologically from Proto-Tiwa-Tewa. Also, under the immigration hypothesis, one would expect the dynamics of ethnic coresidence to have developed, and thus one would expect at least some ethnic enclaves or site-unit intrusions. As many have noted, Mesa Verde site-unit intrusions do not occur anywhere in the Northern Rio Grande, with the possible exception of a few small, early sites on the Pajarito Plateau (see Chapter 13).[3]

Under the assumption that population movements should result in the spread of a single material culture complex, the interpretation of material culture patterns under the immigration hypothesis leads to models that are contradicted by the evidence from language and oral tradition. From the perspective on population movement developed here, however, it would not appear exceptional for a population to refashion its culture as it shifts its location, even as it maintained its language and identity.

The Archaeology of Population Movement

Due to the factors discussed above, one should not expect to be able to trace population movements on the basis of overt material culture continuities, even if they can exist. In Rouse's (1986:179) words,

> The foregoing analysis explains why the successful participants in my case studies, whether archaeologists, linguists, or physical anthropologists, have all used some form of developmental classification to reconstruct patterns of change, and have traced population movements in terms of these patterns of change, instead of working with similarities in cultural, linguistic, or morphological traits. Patterns of change are indicative of the divergence that takes place during population movements, while similarities, if they have not resulted from independent invention or casual contact, are an indication of the convergence caused by immigration.

Thus, the archaeology of population movement should focus on: (1) continuities in traits with low contextual visibility; (2) an awareness of the structure of population movement as a social process; and (3) an understanding of the causes of various patterns of change in the archaeological record of the destination area. The first two elements have been covered over the course of this discussion. As for the third element, the key is to develop expectations for the pattern of change produced by population movement vis-à-vis other sociocultural processes. Rouse (1986:11–12) offers several guidelines.

First, when the changes in a local archaeological complex are due to weak interaction — such as trade, intermarriage, and other types of sociable activity — the pattern will be one where isolated traits appear individually and at different times, with no change in the social identity or biology of the people. This process is what many archaeologists label "diffusion," the linguistic analog of which would be the adoption of loan words, and the biological analog, gene flow.

Second, when the changes are due to strong interaction — such as warfare, political conquest, economic pressure, or other forms of forcible activity — the local group may gradually lose its identity as a separate people. The pattern of cultural change in this case will be one where a new complex gradually replaces the previous one, but the new complex is integrated into the structure of the old complex, often in the same settlements, and there is no corresponding change in the biological makeup of the population. The linguistic analogs of this process, which Rouse labels "transculturation," include language shift and interference through shift (Thomason and Kaufman 1988); however, the biological consequences are indistinguishable from gene flow.

Finally, when changes are due to population movement, the pattern of cultural change will be one where a new complex appears as a package in new sites. If the migrants are sufficiently numerous in comparison to the indigenous population, the migrants will absorb or displace the indigenous population, and the language and biological makeup of the population will shift to that of the incoming population.

These general guidelines, combined with observations made throughout this chapter, lead to specific expectations for the archaeology of population movement. In the source area:

1. one should be able to identify material push factors that correspond in time to initial colonization of the eventual destination area;
2. one should observe a decline in homeland population that takes place over decades rather than all at once;
3. one should be able to identify intensified interaction with the destination area during the period of population decline;
4. one should observe permanent, long-distance movement associated with the abandonment of sites, and an accelerating pace and scale of abandonment over time; and
5. one should find evidence for social conflict and cultural "retrenchment" during the period of population decline.

And in the destination area:

1. initial colonization should occur during a period of time corresponding to material push factors in the proposed homeland;
2. the economy of the initial settlers should exhibit continuity with that of the homeland;
3. the material culture of the colonists should appear as a package in new sites. It also should be simplified from that of the homeland and should exhibit continuities in food preferences, technological styles, and domestic spatial organization;
4. one should observe an accelerating pace and scale of in-migration over the course of the movement; and
5. material expressions of the homeland culture should vary in accordance with social conditions experienced by migrants in different portions of the destination area.

With this framework in place, I now turn to the archaeological records of the Mesa Verde region and Tewa Basin to assess whether the evidence from these two regions is consistent with population movement between the two areas.

Notes

1. This perspective on low-visibility attributes — namely, that they are likely to continue being performed by migrants because they are habitual and have low message potential — bears a strong similarity to the argument developed in Chapter 10 concerning fossilized metaphors in language. In the latter case, dead metaphors continue to be expressed in language after they are no longer active because speakers use words out of habit, irrespective of their semantic histories.
2. The distinction between immigration and population movement is also fundamental in human population genetics. When immigration occurs, the genes of the migrants and the hosts will blend together to produce a hybrid population in which each parent population has contributed genes in proportion to their numbers. In population movements, on the other hand, the degree to which the genes of the colonizing population will change depends on random genetic drift, the size of the founding population, and selection pressures in the new environment (Cavalli-Sforza et al. 1994:15).
3. Researchers have suggested that Mesa Verde site-unit intrusions occur in other portions of the Southwest (e.g., Lekson et al. 2002), but these arguments are often based solely on the presence of locally made, Mesa Verde-style pottery. Even if such sites are site-unit intrusions, they are too small and too few in number to account for more than a small proportion of the thirteenth-century Mesa Verde region population (Varien 2010).

The End of Mesa Verde Society

In AD 1200 the Mesa Verde region was the most densely populated portion of the ancestral Pueblo world. A century later the region lay vacant, literally in ruins, and the Northern Rio Grande had replaced it as the demographic center of gravity. Demographic, genetic, and linguistic evidence all suggest that population movement was involved in this dramatic reorganization of the Pueblo world. In the following two chapters, I utilize the framework for archaeological study of population movement to assess the degree to which the archaeological evidence is consistent with this view.

Here I consider population decline in the Mesa Verde region, focusing on the Village Ecodynamics Project (VEP) study area. This was the most densely settled portion of the Mesa Verde region, and it is also the best-known due to long-term research by the Crow Canyon Archaeological Center, the Dolores Archaeological Program, and the Village Ecodynamics Project. The analyses in this chapter emphasize two bodies of evidence. The first consists of various data sets developed by the VEP, and the second is the Crow Canyon Archaeological Center excavation database representing more than two decades of excavation results from sites in the VEP study area. Locations of the various sites discussed are given in Figure 12.1. If, in fact, the Tewa language and most of the Tewa population originated in the Mesa Verde region, one would expect the archaeological record of this region to exhibit characteristics of the source area of a population movement. I evaluate this hypothesis here by examining the Mesa Verde region archaeological record in light of these characteristics.

Initial Push Factors

The first expectation for the homeland of a population movement is that initial scouting of eventual destinations should correlate in time with the development of strong material push factors in the homeland. The analyses presented in previous chapters suggest that the ancestral Tewa population began to enter the Tewa Basin shortly before AD 1200 (Orcutt 1999a; Smiley et al. 1953). Were there good reasons for people to begin leaving the Mesa Verde region at this time? This question can be addressed using the paleoproductivity reconstruction created for the VEP (Kohler et al. 2007). This reconstruction models the po-

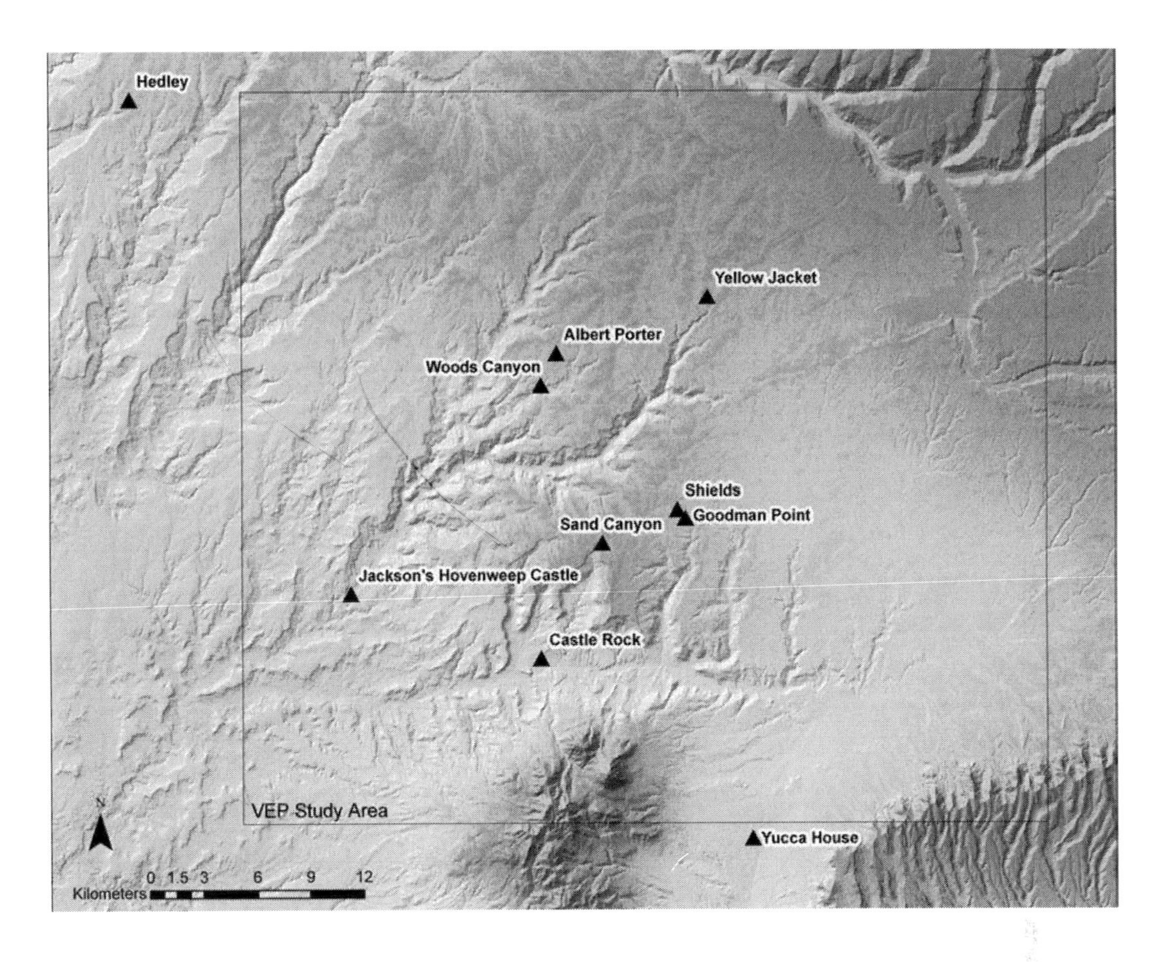

FIGURE 12.1. Locations of sites mentioned in the text.

tential production of each 4 ha plot of land within the 1,817 km^2 VEP study area based on tree-ring indices indicative of annual precipitation and temperature, soils data, historic crop yields and weather station data, and recent experimental grow-outs of Pueblo maize varieties (Varien and others 2007:276–280). Figure 12.2 presents the mean potential paleoproductivity of all 4 ha plots in the study area for each year between AD 1100 and 1300, in comparison with the long-term mean and standard deviation for this value. These data show that the VEP experienced an extended period of below-average conditions for agriculture during the first half of the AD 1200s. This downturn began in AD 1198 and extended through AD 1245, during which time 37 years were below average, and 16 years were more than one standard deviation below average. Notice also that, according to the suite of factors incorporated into this reconstruction, the period between AD 1198 and 1245 was even worse than the mid-AD 1100s drought (see Ryan 2010) and the so-called "great drought" of the late AD 1200s. The former corresponded with the collapse of the Chacoan regional system, and the latter with the final depopulation of the Mesa Verde region.

Additional indicators suggest that land pressure was high during the late AD 1100s and early 1200s. Figure 12.3 presents two such measures. The first

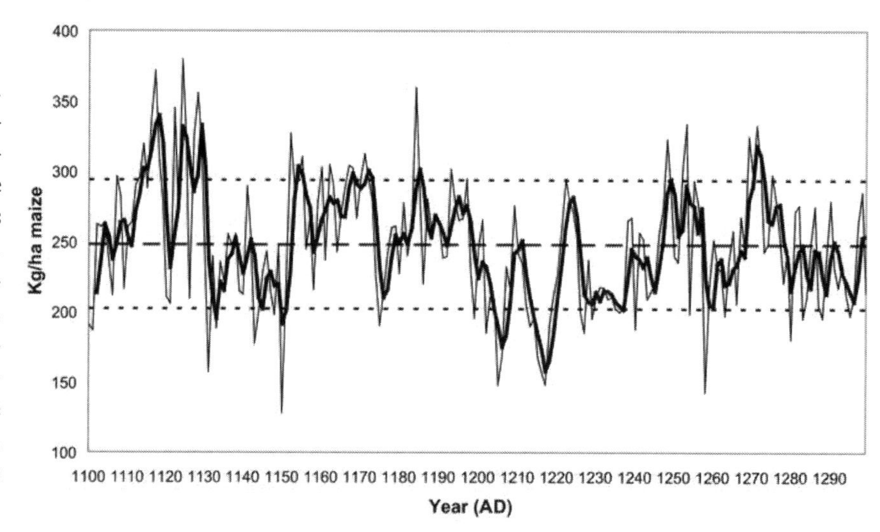

FIGURE 12.2. Potential paleoproductivity reconstruction for the Village Ecodynamics Project study area. The thin line indicates annual values, the bold line a three-year moving average, the dashed line the long-term mean, and dotted lines the standard deviation.

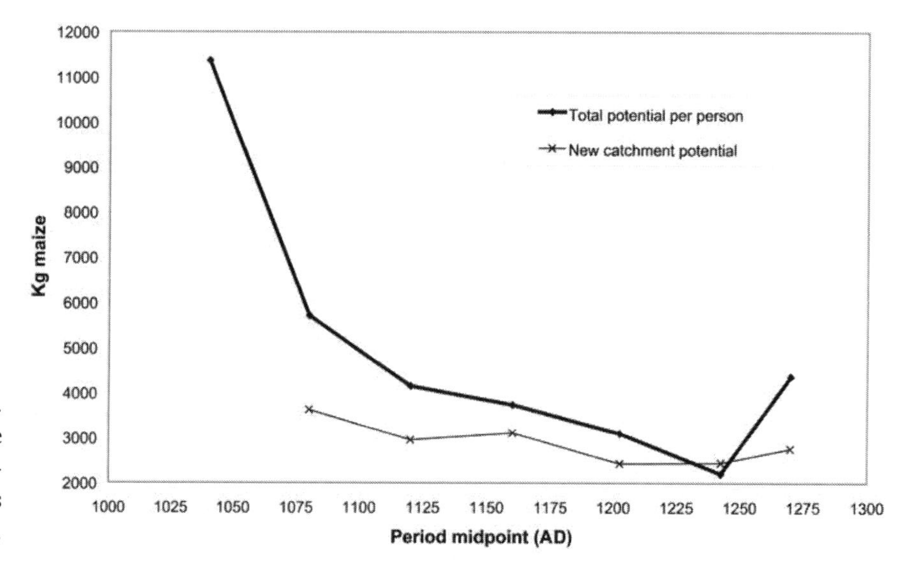

FIGURE 12.3. Land pressure indicators in the Village Ecodynamics Project study area.

represents the mean study area productivity across all years in a modeling period divided by the population density for that modeling period in the VEP population reconstruction (see Chapter 4; also Varien et al. 2007: Table 4). This measure primarily tracks population density, but also takes low-frequency environmental variation (Dean 1988) into account. The second measure is the mean productivity of land in the 2 km catchment surrounding community centers founded in each period (from Varien et al. 2007: Fig. 5E).[1] Both measures show that land pressure reached the highest levels of the entire ancestral Pueblo sequence during the first half of the AD 1200s as a result of population increase during an extended period of below-average conditions. Note also that land pressure eased during the final decades of occupation as population declined.

Population growth in the first half of the AD 1200s was probably the result of robust intrinsic growth (see Figure 4.9) combined with in-migration from more marginal areas (Glowacki 2006, 2010). The central Mesa Verde region was one of the most productive farming regions in the northern U.S. Southwest, and as a result it would have been relatively attractive to farmers residing in more marginal areas during this period. However, most of the best locations for farming had already been claimed by the early AD 1200s, and as a result new communities were forced to develop on less than optimal land (Varien et al. 2007: Fig. 5E). The Castle Rock community, for example, formed in the early AD 1200s in the sloping canyon country of McElmo Creek, on land that was only about half as productive as adjacent upland areas that had been settled since the AD 1000s (Ortman 2008a:128–131; Ortman and Varien 2007; Varien 1999b; Varien et al. 2000). These conditions would have encouraged some individuals who were forced to farm more marginal lands to seek out better, unclaimed lands farther afield, where the upland, rain-fed farming they were accustomed to would be viable.

Long-Term Population Decline

The second expectation for the homeland of a population movement is that population decline should take place over a period of decades rather than all at once. Duff and Wilshusen (2000) were the first to suggest that this occurred in the case of the Mesa Verde depopulation, and the VEP population history bears out their prediction. As shown in Figure 4.8, and as suggested by Figure 12.3, the net result of intrinsic population processes, in-migration, and out-migration tipped in favor of population decline at least two decades prior to the final depopulation of the region. This does not necessarily mean that out-migration had not been going on for an even longer period, only that the pace of out-migration came to outweigh the combined effects of in-migration and intrinsic growth at that time. Glowacki (2006, 2010), for example, suggests that people from western portions of the Mesa Verde region clustered into the VEP area during the first half of the AD 1200s, and this in-migration could have outpaced the rate of out-migration from the VEP area in producing net population growth prior to the AD 1250s. Because population histories reconstructed from settlement pattern evidence reflect the average momentary population of each modeling period, and population was clearly in decline by the onset of the final modeling period, net population decline probably set in prior to AD 1260, and it is clear that the region was completely depopulated within a few years of AD 1280 because there is no evidence of tree cutting for construction or remodeling of pueblo-style dwellings after AD 1280. Given the accumulated database of several thousand tree-ring dates from the region, and the existence of at least one cutting date for every five-year interval between AD 1080 and 1280, the probability of continued habitation at AD 1285 is vanishingly small (Varien 2010).

Return Migration

The third expectation for the homeland of a population movement is intensified interaction with the destination area during the period of population decline. Social interaction between the source and destination areas should increase primarily due to the development of a migration stream following defined routes, along which scouts can return to the source area to visit relatives, relay information about the destination area, and encourage others to follow. Return migrants may in some cases bring objects made of materials available in the destination area as tokens of that area. One would expect some of these objects to find their way into the archaeological record of the source area. Thus, archaeological traces of return migration in the source area should consist of evidence for an increased flow of objects made of materials available in the destination area, but not in the source area. In addition, because the sex ratio of scouts and return migrants tends to be male-biased (Anthony 1990; Lefferts 1977; Stone 1993), one might expect the objects brought back to the source area to be objects typically made and used by males.

The objects that best meet these requirements in this context are artifacts made of obsidian. There are no sources of obsidian in the Mesa Verde region, but several major sources occur in the Jemez Mountains on the western edge of the Tewa Basin, and artifacts from these sources can be identified with high reliability using X-ray fluorescence (Shackley 1988, 1995, 2005a). In addition, although obsidian was never common in central Mesa Verde region sites, several decades of excavation in AD 1060–1280 sites by Crow Canyon Archaeological Center has produced a very large chipped stone artifact database suitable for analyses of obsidian procurement through time.

Several hundred obsidian artifacts from the central Mesa Verde region have been sourced, and most of these derive from Jemez Mountain materials (Arakawa 2006; Arakawa et al. in press). In addition, the emphasis on Jemez Mountain sources increased over time, such that more than 90 percent of all obsidian found in Mesa Verde sites dating from the middle AD 1000s onward came from these sources (Table 12.1, upper register).[2] Inhabitants of the Mesa Verde region clearly had a long history of at least indirect contact with the Jemez Mountains area, and thus it is reasonable to view it as one that would have been explored by scouts in the early decades of the AD 1200s.

A closer look at the specific sources of Jemez obsidian artifacts suggests increasing flows from areas of the Tewa Basin where population was growing as the Mesa Verde region population declined. There are three distinct obsidian sources in the Jemez Mountains. The first, El Rechuelos, is located northeast of the Valles Caldera and erodes into the Rio Chama and ultimately the Rio Grande. The second source, Valles rhyolite, occurs only within the Jemez Caldera and thus must have been procured from there. Finally, the third source, Cerro Toledo rhyolite, erodes from the eastern and southeastern flanks of the Jemez Mountains through the canyons of the Pajarito Plateau and into the Rio Grande. This

TABLE 12.1. Obsidian sourcing data from the central Mesa Verde region

	AD 600–920 SITES		AD 1060–1280 SITES	
SOURCES	*n*	%	*n*	%
Government Mountain	6	5.6	0	0.0
Mount Taylor	12	11.2	10	6.0
Cow Canyon	0	0.0	1	0.6
Jemez Mountains (all sources)	89	83.2	156	93.4
Total	107	100	167	100
Jemez Sources[a]				
El Rechuelos (Chama)	54	60.7	44	28.2
Valles Rhyolite (Caldera)	33	37.1	61	39.1
Cerro Toledo (Pajarito)	2	2.2	51	32.7
Total	89	100	156	100

Note: Data from Arakawa et al., in press.

[a] Kilmogorov-Smirnov $P < .05$ for these data.

last material is common at sites on the Pajarito Plateau and is available in secondary deposits along the Rio Grande all the way to Chihuahua, Mexico (Church 2000; Shackley 2005b, 2008). All three obsidians make excellent chipped stone tools, so changes in the relative abundance of Jemez obsidians over time most likely reflect changes in the structure of long-distance exchange networks as opposed to raw material preference.

Based on this framework, the lower register of Table 12.1 shows that during the early centuries of occupation, most of the obsidian that ended up in Mesa Verde region sites came from the closest Jemez source, El Rechuelos, with less coming from the Valles Caldera and very little from Cerro Toledo. During later centuries, however, a much higher percentage of obsidian came from Cerro Toledo sources on the Pajarito Plateau. Cerro Toledo obsidian is available primarily in the area of the Tewa Basin that was colonized during the Early Coalition period, as detailed in Chapter 4. These data thus suggest an increasing emphasis on areas of the Tewa Basin where population grew during the AD 1200s.

Because nearly all obsidian in AD 1060–1280 Mesa Verde region sites came from the Jemez Mountains, changes in the relative frequency of obsidian artifacts should approximate changes in the frequency of contact with the Jemez Mountains region. Figure 12.4 presents these data for all contexts in the Crow Canyon research database dating to three sequential time periods. These data show that the flow of obsidian to the central Mesa Verde region was strongest during the heyday of the Chacoan regional system, AD 1060–1140. Long-distance exchange of a variety of items was relatively frequent during this period (Lipe 1995:158). The flow of obsidian into the region declined during

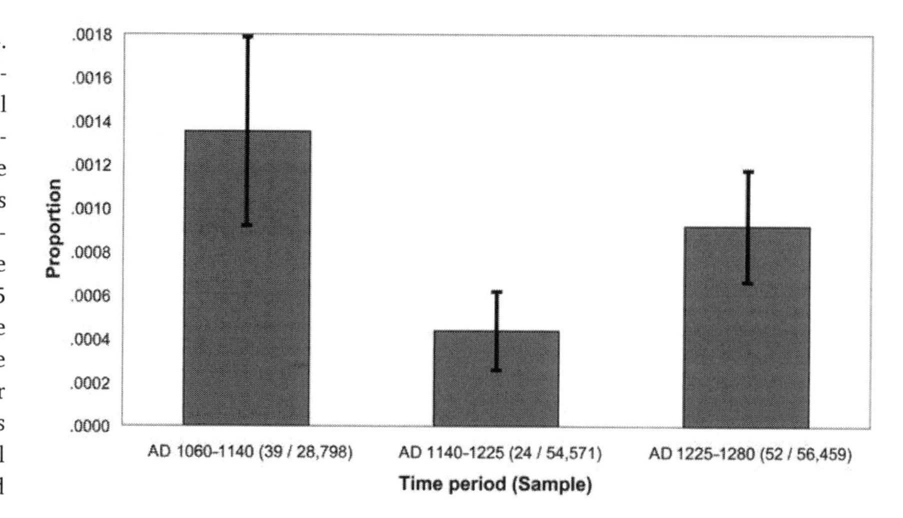

FIGURE 12.4. Frequency of obsidian artifacts in total chipped stone assemblages, by time period. Error bars represent two standard errors of the proportion (> 95 percent confidence intervals). Sample data are the number of obsidian artifacts divided by the total number of chipped stone artifacts assigned to a raw material category in the Crow Canyon Research Database (January 2009).

the post-Chacoan period but increased again during the AD 1200s. The proportion of obsidian artifacts in AD 1225–1280 contexts does not overlap the 1140–1225 proportion to two standard errors; thus, it appears that the flow of obsidian from the Jemez Mountains did, in fact, increase during the period of population decline.

Given that obsidian was always quite rare in Mesa Verde region sites, it is important to ask whether the absolute quantity of obsidian recovered from these sites reflects the level of interaction one might expect between the source and destination area of an ongoing population movement. Several lines of evidence suggest that even small quantities of obsidian likely reflect significant interaction between the Mesa Verde region and Tewa Basin. First, nearly all obsidian tools found in Crow Canyon excavations are small projectile points, bifaces, modified flakes representing projectile point blanks, or tools made from reworked projectile points. No cores suggesting primary reduction of raw material have been found (Table 12.2). This pattern contrasts with that of Dakota silicified sandstone, a local, high-quality material that was procured as raw material and worked into a variety of tool types. In addition, most of the obsidian debitage recovered from Crow Canyon excavations consists of small pieces with no evidence of cortex, whereas larger pieces and pieces with cortex are fairly common in Dakota silicified sandstone debitage (Figure 12.5). This evidence suggests that nearly all obsidian that ended up in Mesa Verde region sites entered these sites as complete arrows, arrow points, or arrow point blanks as opposed to chunks of raw material. This, in turn, suggests that nearly every piece of obsidian found in Mesa Verde region sites represents the exchange of a finished product, whereas one would expect thousands of pieces of chipped stone to derive from a raw material procurement event. So even though obsidian artifacts are small and rare, each piece is quite significant in terms of the human behavior it represents.

These observations suggest that an alternative means of assessing the significance of obsidian exchange may be to compare the proportion of projectile

TABLE 12.2. Cores and tools of obsidian and Dakota silicified sandstone

	Obsidian		Dakota Silicified Sandstone	
Artifact Category	*n*	%	*n*	%
Core			254	11.3
Modified core	1	2.5	6	0.3
Pecking stone			522	23.2
Chipped stone tool	2	5.0	44	2.0
Modified flake	6	15.0	487	21.6
Biface	3	7.5	406	18.0
Drill	2	5.0	75	3.3
Projectile point	26	65.0	456	20.3
Total	40	100	2,250	100

Note: Data represent the total number of chipped stone artifacts from AD 1060–1280 Mesa Verde region sites assigned to the given raw material category in the Crow Canyon Research Database (January 2009).

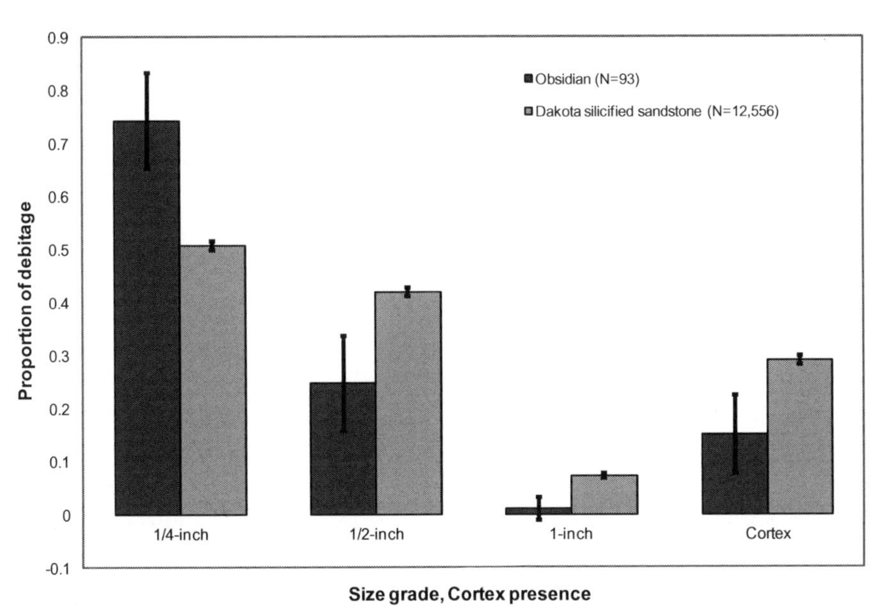

FIGURE 12.5. Attributes of obsidian and Dakota silicified sandstone debitage. Error bars show two standard errors (> 95 percent confidence intervals). Data represent all analyzed debitage in the Crow Canyon Research Database, January 2009.

points made of obsidian to the proportion of bowl sherds from nonlocal vessels in sites occupied during the migration period. Figure 12.6 presents these data for three villages with peak occupations during the AD 1225–1260 period, and three villages with peak occupations during the 1260–1280 period. During the former period, the Mesa Verde region population reached its peak and began to decline; the latter period was characterized by population decline associated with out-migration. These data show that the proportion of projectile points

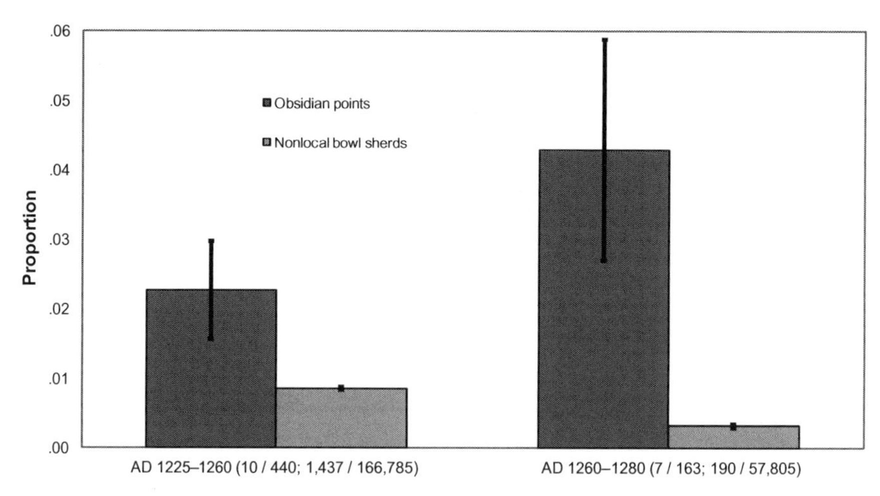

FIGURE 12.6. Obsidian points and nonlocal sherds in total site assemblages. Error bars represent one standard error (> 68 percent confidence intervals). Sites and sources: AD 1225–1260: Shields Pueblo, Till, in prep.; Yellow Jacket Pueblo, Ortman 2003: Table 28; Albert Porter Pueblo, CCAC Research Database, January 2009; AD 1260–1280: Sand Canyon Pueblo, Till and Ortman 2007: Table 61; Castle Rock Pueblo, Ortman 2000a: Table 25; Woods Canyon Pueblo, Ortman 2002: Table 37. Bowl sherd data for these sites are taken from the Crow Canyon Research Database, January 2009. Local bowl sherds are of Mesa Verde White ware; nonlocal bowl sherds are of San Juan Red ware, Tsegi Orange ware, White Mountain Red ware, Cibola White ware, Tusayan White ware, and Chuska White ware.

made of obsidian in assemblages dating from the period of population decline was almost twice as high as it was in earlier times. Due to low proportions and small sample sizes, the standard errors of these proportions overlap somewhat, so it is possible that the increase suggested by these data was not as large as it appears here. However, obsidian points do comprise larger proportions of projectile point assemblages than do nonlocal sherds for bowl assemblages during both periods. Indeed, it appears long-distance pottery exchange declined during the final decades of occupation, whereas acquisition of obsidian projectile points from the Tewa Basin increased during this same period.

In summary, the obsidian found in Mesa Verde region sites came almost exclusively from the Jemez Mountains, and increasingly from areas of the Tewa Basin where population was growing during the AD 1200s. The flow of this material increased during the period of population decline, and it entered the region primarily in the form of finished products, including complete arrows, arrow points, and arrow point blanks. These artifacts were made and used by men for hunting and protection, and thus were likely to have been carried by scouts visiting from the destination area. In addition, small obsidian points or blanks would have been appropriate objects for return migrants to bring as gifts due to their small size, light weight, and association with the landscape of the destination area. All of this is consistent with a model in which return migration from the Tewa Basin was a primary mechanism behind the increased flow of Jemez obsidian to the Mesa Verde region during the period of population decline.

Long-Distance Movement at an Accelerating Pace and Scale

The fourth expectation for the homeland of a population movement is permanent, long-distance movement associated with the abandonment of sites, and an accelerating pace and scale of abandonment over the period of out-migration. I investigate this expectation here by examining the manner in which unit pueblo residences were abandoned over time. A range of evidence suggests that a small pit structure or kiva, approximately 4 m in diameter, was the central domestic and symbolic space in ancestral Pueblo residences of the Mesa Verde region (Cater and Chenault 1988; Lekson 1988; Lightfoot 1994; Lipe 1989; Ortman 1998, 2008b). The floors and walls of these structures preserve well, and the main chamber creates a sink for falling roof material and sediment after abandonment. Consequently, it is often possible to document the sequence of events that took place around the time of abandonment by exposing a stratigraphic profile and a section of the floor. Between 1983 and 2004, archaeologists at the Crow Canyon Archaeological Center documented the fill stratigraphy and floor deposits of more than 120 kivas that can be dated relatively precisely. Table 12.3 summarizes the distribution of these structures in time and space, and Table 12.4 summarizes the stratigraphic observations recorded in these structures. These data provide an outstanding means of investigating abandonment behavior.

The middle range theory for inferring abandonment behaviors from fill stratigraphy and floor deposits is well developed and indicates that abandonment behaviors are structured by several factors, including the speed with which a site is vacated, whether its inhabitants anticipate returning, the distance of the new residence from the old one, and whether it is deemed necessary to perform abandonment rituals (Binford 1981; Lightfoot 1993; Montgomery 1993; Schiffer 1987; Schlanger and Wilshusen 1993; Stevenson 1982; Varien 1999b; Wilshusen 1986, 1988). These studies lead to a number of behavioral correlates of kiva abandonment and post-abandonment deposits.

First, the presence of trash filling an abandoned structure indicates that habitation activities continued to produce domestic refuse in the immediate vicinity of the structure after it was abandoned. In contrast, natural wind and water-deposited fill indicates the absence of subsequent habitation in the vicinity.

Second, the absence of usable artifacts on the floor of a structure is an indication that its inhabitants moved a short distance and were able to make several trips back to their old residence to gather up their belongings and carry them to their new dwelling. In contrast, the presence of usable artifacts on the floor is an indication that the inhabitants moved a great distance and thus were not able to take all of their belongings with them.

TABLE 12.3. Excavated kivas from the central Mesa Verde region

Site Number	Site Name	Abandonment Period (AD) 1060–1140	1180–1225	1225–1260	1260–1280	Total
5MT10246	Lester's Site			1	1	2
5MT10459	Lookout House			3		3
5MT10508	Stanton's Site			1		1
5MT11338	G & G Hamlet	1		1		2
5MT11842	Woods Canyon Pueblo		4	1	4	9
5MT123	Albert Porter Pueblo	2	19	5		26
5MT181	Mad Dog Tower				1	1
5MT1825	Castle Rock Pueblo				16	16
5MT262	Saddlehorn Hamlet			1		1
5MT3807	Shields Pueblo	2	14	13		29
5MT3918	Shorlene's Site		1			1
5MT3930	Roy's Ruin		1			1
5MT3936	Lillian's Site		1			1
5MT3951	Troy's Tower				1	1
5MT3967	Catherine's Site			2		2
5MT5152	Kenzie Dawn Hamlet	2	1			3
5MT765	Sand Canyon Pueblo			8	15	23
Total		7	41	36	38	122

Note: Data are the number of kivas dating to each time period from each site, based on information in the Crow Canyon Research Database (January 2009).

TABLE 12.4. Kiva abandonment modes through time

Abandonment Period (AD)	*n*	Trash Fill	Usable Artifacts on Floor	Burned Roofing	Burned and Artifacts	Burned or Artifacts
1060–1140	7	57.1	0.0	14.3	0.0	14.3
1180–1225	41	14.6	26.8	17.1	14.6	29.3
1225–1260	36	8.3	41.7	52.8	30.6	63.9
1260–1280	38	2.6	57.9	76.3	47.4	86.8

Note: Column heads are attributes of kiva stratigraphy; data are the percentage of structures in which a given attribute occurs.

TABLE 12.5. Association between floor artifacts and burning

		Usable Artifacts on Floor		
		Absent	Present	Total
Burned Roofing	Present	21	35	56
	Absent	53	13	66
	Total	74	48	122

Note: Chi-square $P < .00001$ for these data.

Third, the absence of timbers in roof-fall indicates that the inhabitants of a structure moved a short distance and salvaged usable timbers along with household items (Varien 1999:116–117). This practice is suggested by the occurrence of multiple clusters of cutting dates, separated by gaps of several decades, in roofs that eventually did burn (Bradley 1993:26–28; Ortman and Bradley 2002: 48–53), and also by the fact that unburned roofs that collapsed naturally are rare (Varien 1999:117).

Finally, the presence of burned roofing is evidence of an abandonment ritual associated with a long-distance move. Experiments indicate that kiva roofs were unlikely to catch fire accidentally or as a result of wildfire (Wilshusen 1986), and in many sites only the kivas burned. It therefore appears that in most cases burning represents intentional destruction of the largest and most important architectural space of a house. Violence is a possible explanation for this destruction in cases where the burning is associated with unburied human remains, but in most such cases, burning appears to be associated with disposal of the dead after an episode of violence rather than the cause of death itself (Kuckelman et al. 2002; Kuckelman and Martin 2007: para. 197). Thus, it would appear that ritual destruction is the most frequent cause of burned roofing in kiva fills.[3] Such rituals would have been most appropriate prior to long-distance moves with no intention of returning, such that it was impractical or impossible to transport construction timbers to the new residence. This is supported by the positive association of burned roofing and floor artifacts in kivas, as indicated by Table 12.5.

Based on this framework, Figure 12.7 illustrates the percent of kivas abandoned during each of four time periods within which trash fill is present, burned roofing occurs, usable artifacts occur on the floor, and either burned roofing or floor artifacts are present. These data show that the frequency with which occupation continued in close proximity of abandoned kivas declined over time and is inversely proportional to the frequency of ritual closure suggestive of long-distance movement. It is also intriguing to note the correlation between the proportion of ritually closed kivas in the final two time periods and the proportion of population decline suggested by the VEP population reconstruction. About 64 percent of kivas abandoned during the AD 1225–1260 period exhibit

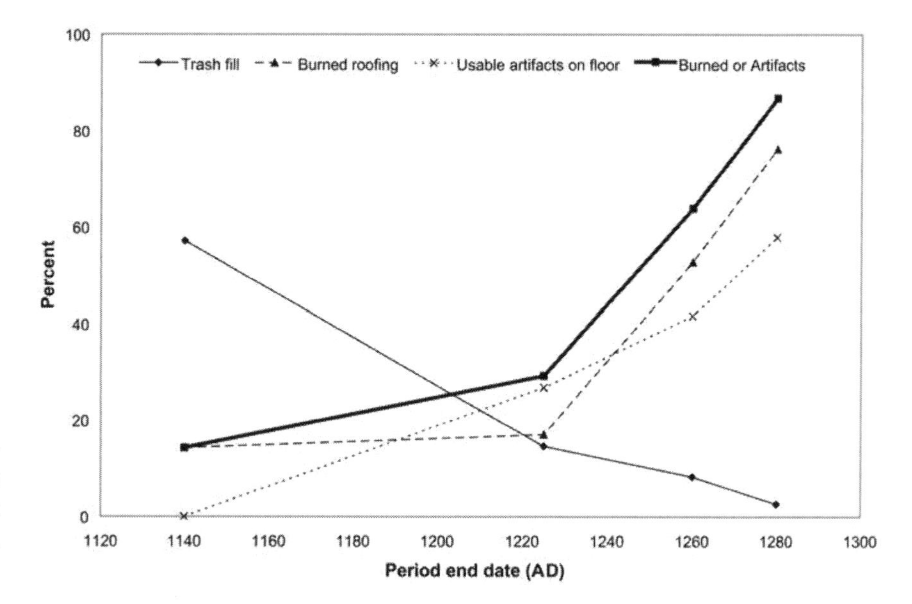

FIGURE 12.7. Summary of kiva abandonment modes through time.

evidence of ritual closure, and about 86 percent were so closed during the 1260–1280 period. These ratios correspond in a rough way to the 55 percent drop in momentary population between the 1225–1260 and 1260–1280 periods in the VEP reconstruction, and the 100 percent drop in population between 1260 and 1280. Thus, there is ample evidence to suggest that ritual closure, associated with long-distance moves, was taking place throughout the 1200s, and that out-migration was therefore the primary cause of population decline during this period.

Structure abandonment data also suggest an accelerating pace and scale of abandonment over time, as material push factors came to be augmented by social and ideological pull factors. Due to the durability of cribbed kiva roofs, the construction (or most recent roofing) date of many kivas can be estimated to the nearest decade from the latest-dated timbers used in constructing the roof. Thus, the abandonment modes of kivas with roofs constructed during each decade can serve as a proxy for the pace and scale of out-migration. Figure 12.8 summarizes roof treatments at abandonment of tree-ring dated kivas by decade, as defined by the decadal year after the latest tree-ring date from the structure.[4] Unburned kivas are underrepresented in these data because datable timbers are more likely to be preserved in burned structures, so the sample reflected in this chart is by no means a representative sample of all kivas. Nevertheless, these data highlight two general points. First, kivas that burned at abandonment were roofed during every decade of the AD 1200s. Second, most of the well-dated, burned kivas in this data set were roofed during the AD 1250s, 1260s, and 1270s. This suggests that kivas roofed during the final decades of occupation were more likely to be burned at abandonment than kivas roofed in earlier decades. In other words, the probability that the inhabitants of a unit pueblo made a long-distance move when their kiva was abandoned appears to have increased over time.

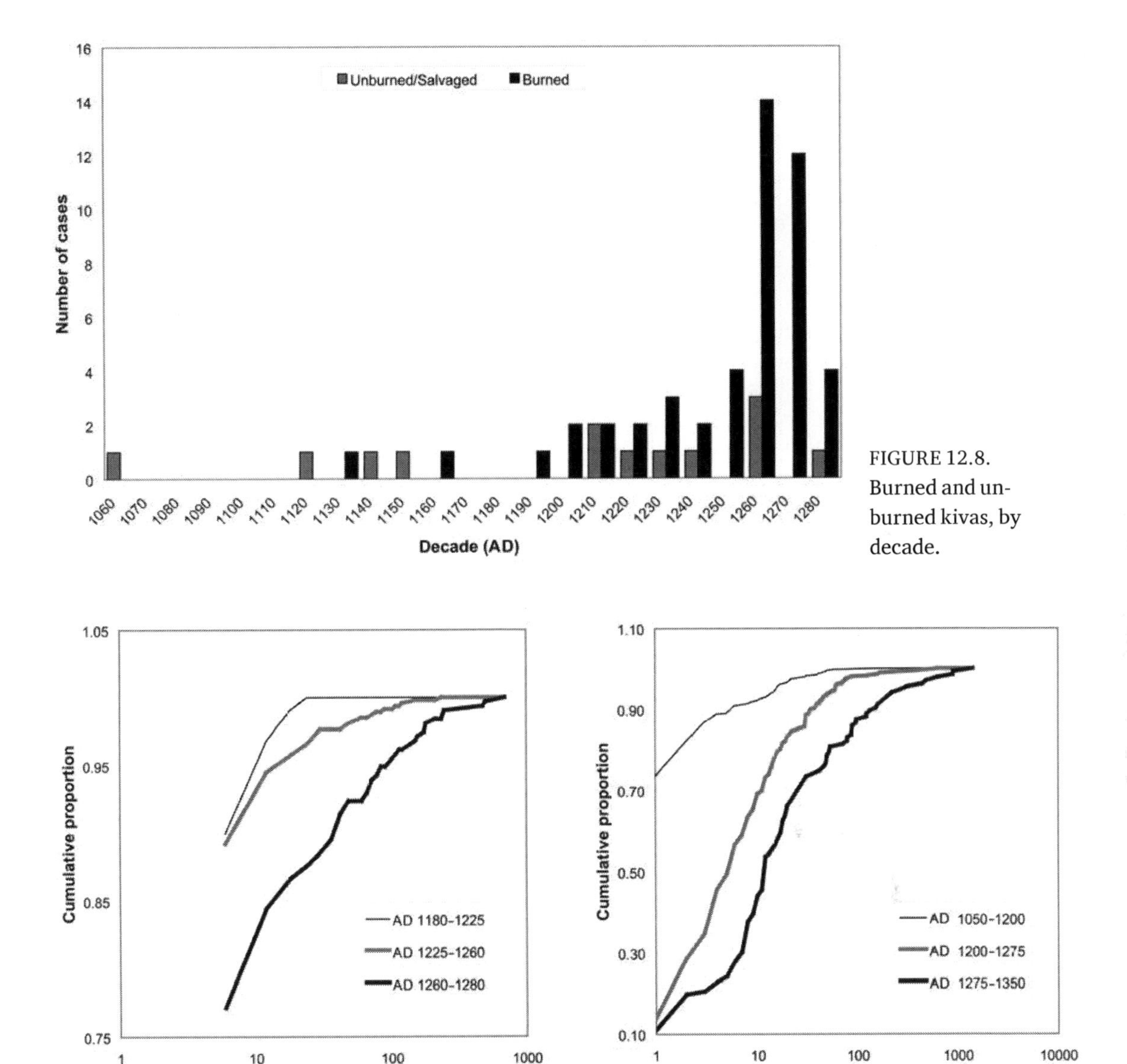

FIGURE 12.8. Burned and unburned kivas, by decade.

FIGURE 12.9. Final populations of sites in the Village Ecodynamics Project study area (*left*) and initial populations of sites in the Tewa Basin (*right*). The minimum population of VEP sites is six persons because this data set tracks pit structures which are assumed to represent six persons each. The minimum population of Tewa Basin sites, in contrast, is based on rooms which are assumed to represent one person each.

Another way of looking at the pace and scale of out-migration over time is to examine the size distributions of sites abandoned during each modeling period in the VEP settlement pattern reconstruction (Ortman et al. 2007). These data are presented in the form of cumulative distributions in Figure 12.9 (also see Figure 12.10a–d). These data clearly illustrate that the sites abandoned in the AD 1180–1225 period were almost exclusively individual houses; that a wider range of sites, including hamlets and some villages, were abandoned in the

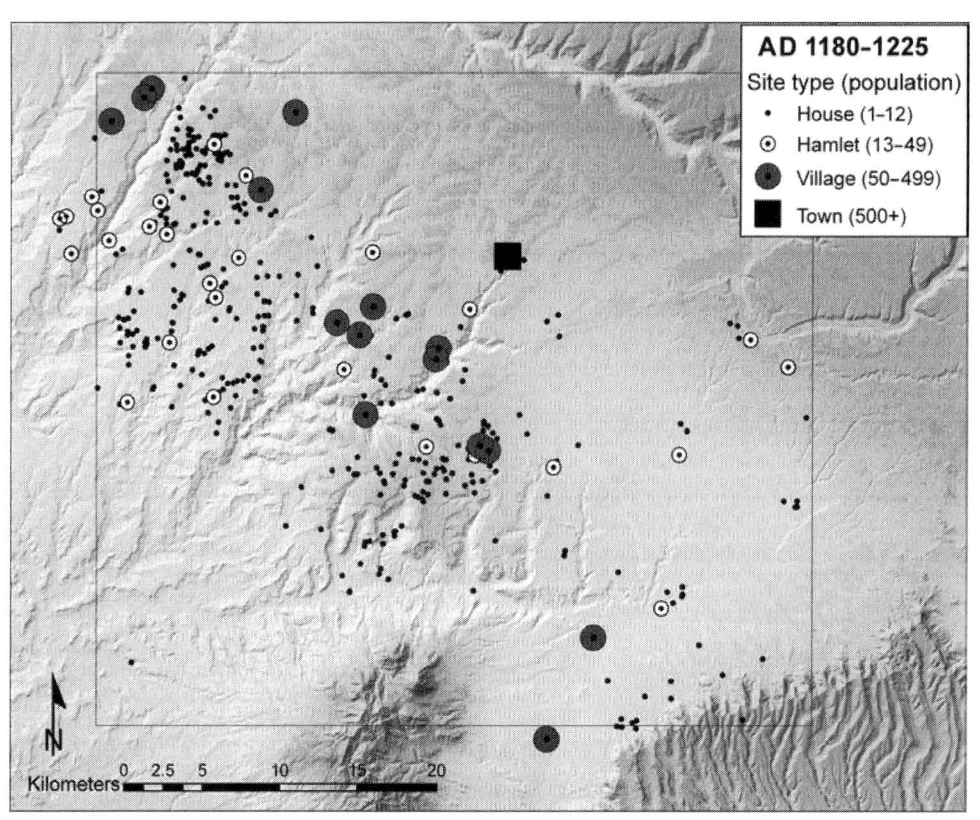

FIGURE 12.10A. Settlement pattern changes in the Village Ecodynamics Project study area, AD 1180–1225.

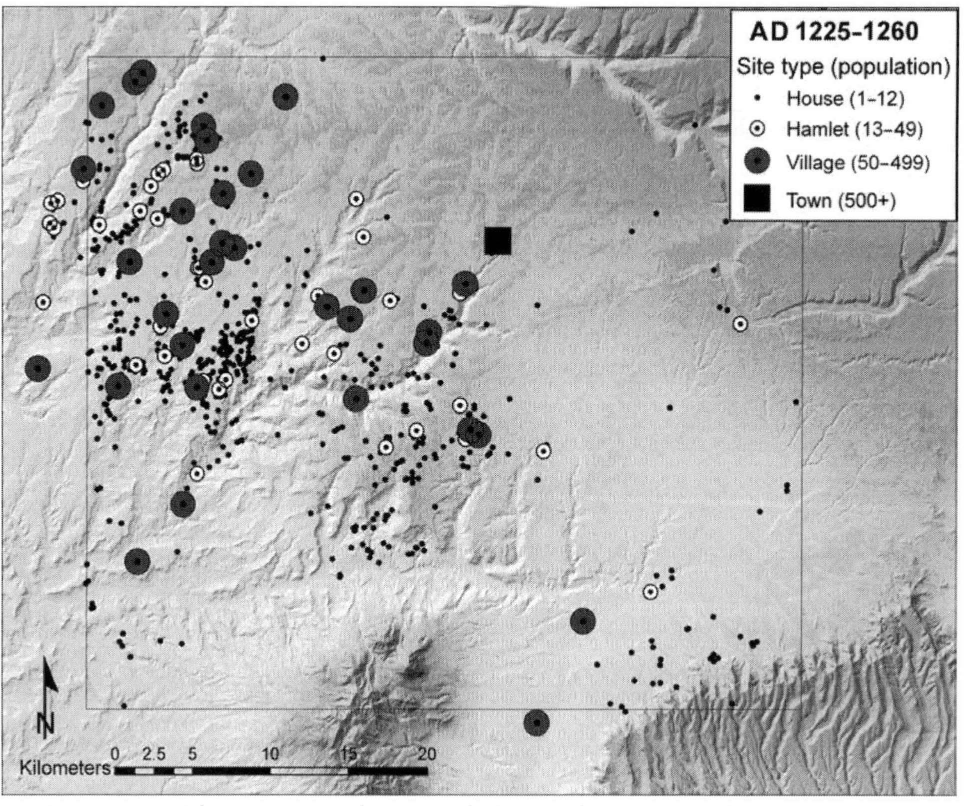

FIGURE 12.10B. Settlement pattern changes in the VEP study area, AD 1225–1260.

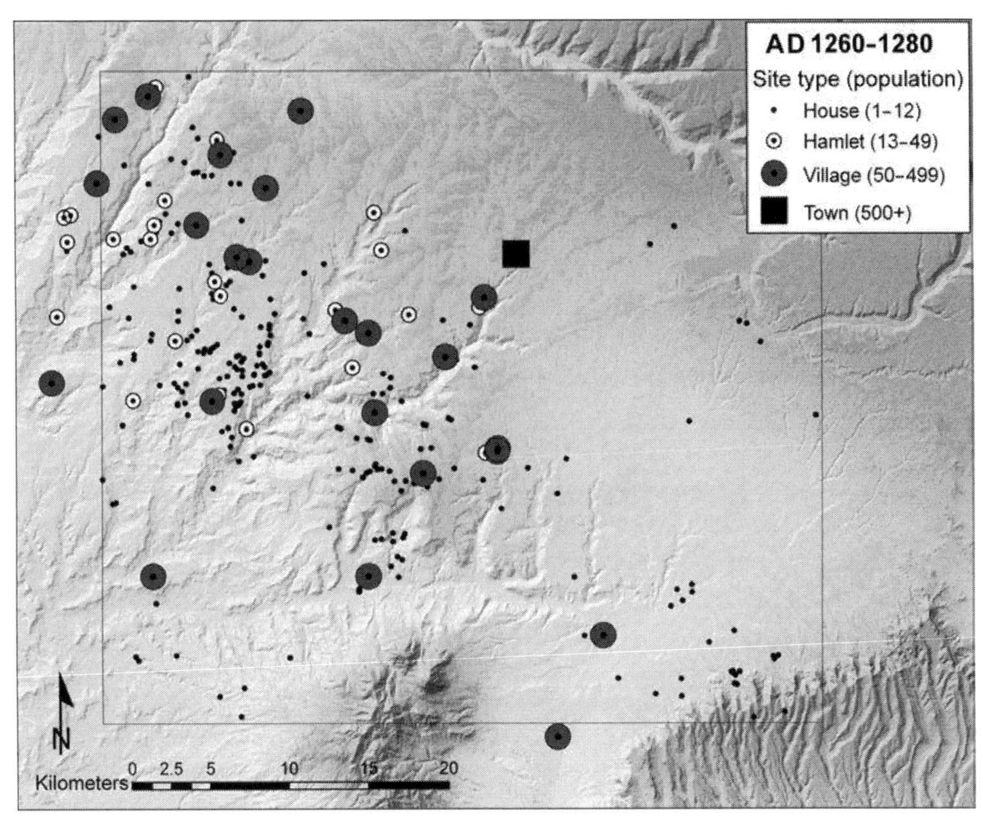

FIGURE 12.10C. Settlement pattern changes in the VEP study area, AD 1260–1280.

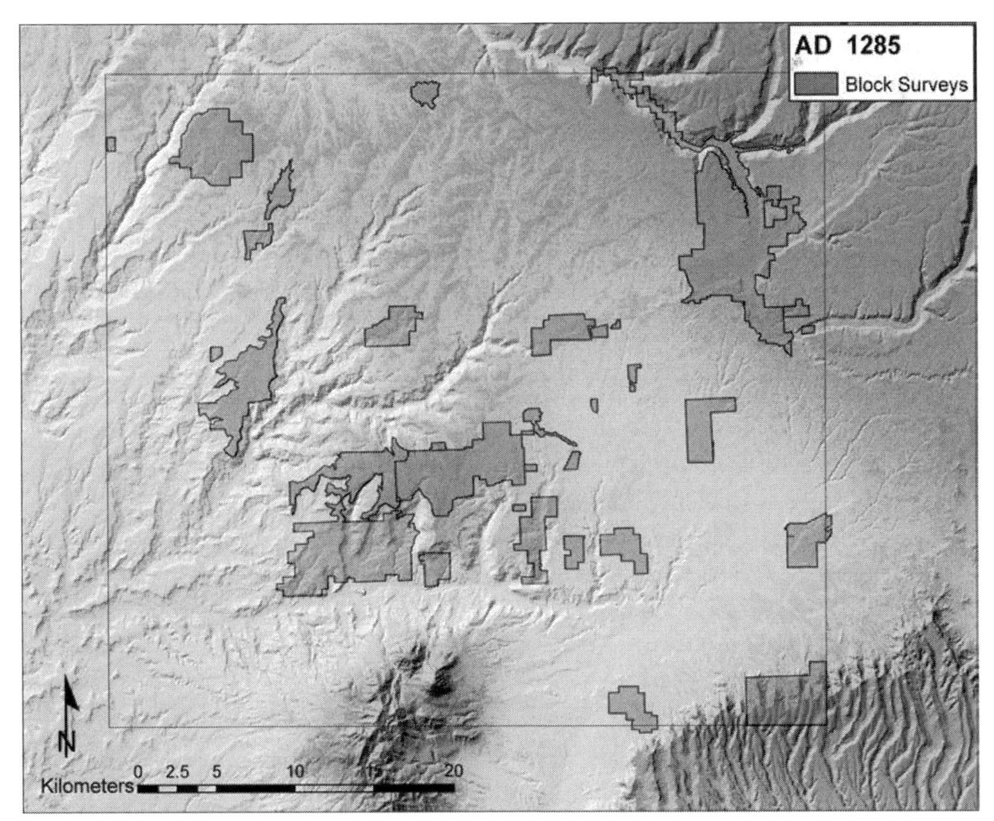

FIGURE 12.10D. Settlement pattern changes in the VEP study area, AD 1285.

subsequent AD 1225–1260 period; and that all sites, including villages of all sizes, were abandoned during the final AD 1260–1280 period.

This sequence is mirrored in the initial sizes of sites founded in the Tewa Basin between AD 1050 and 1350 (Figure 12.9). New settlements founded in the Tewa Basin prior to 1200 were almost entirely hamlet-sized and smaller. In the 1200–1275 period many new settlements grew to be village-sized, and this trend intensified in the AD 1275–1350 period, when some new settlements grew to be town-sized. Thus, the increasing proportion of burned kivas, the increasing size of settlements being abandoned in the VEP study area, and the increasing size of new settlements being established in the Tewa Basin are all consistent with the expectation that out-migration initially involved individuals and families but gradually became a movement by extended kin groups, village factions, entire communities, or even groups of communities.

Conflict and Retrenchment

The final expectation for the homeland of a population movement is escalating social conflict and cultural retrenchment during the period of population decline, as material push factors were augmented by social and ideological pull factors. An upswing in social conflict clearly occurred as population declined during the final decades of Pueblo occupation. Kohler and others (2009) tabulated incidences of skeletal trauma in central Mesa Verde region sites and found that violent death was most frequent following the collapse of the Chacoan regional system in the mid-AD 1100s. Violent death rates then subsided during the early 1200s, despite difficult conditions for farming, and then increased sharply during the final decades of occupation. The available evidence suggests that the social scale of violence was different during these two episodes. In the earlier period most incidences of violence involved extreme perimortem processing of the inhabitants of small residences, prototypical examples of which include the Cowboy Wash site on the Southern Ute Piedmont and 5MTUMR2346 in Mancos Canyon (Billman et al. 2000; Kuckelman et al. 2000; White 1992). These occurrences have a characteristic signature: piles of commingled, heavily fractured, and burned remains of family-sized groups on the floors of individual houses.

In the later period, in contrast, violence appears to have involved entire villages, as exemplified by massacres at Castle Rock and Sand Canyon pueblos (Kuckelman 2010; Kuckelman et al. 2002; Kuckelman and Martin 2007; Lightfoot and Kuckelman 2001). Violence during the final decades of Pueblo occupation, then, appears to have involved intervillage warfare and factional conflict. Increases in aggregation, defensive architecture, defensible site settings, and healed fractures during this period reinforce the fact that social conflict was endemic, and that most of the population was concerned for their safety (Kuckelman 2002). There is also no clear evidence to suggest that the aggressors were anyone other than Pueblo people (Kuckelman 2008; Kuckelman et al. 2002; Till and Ortman 2007; Ortman 2000a). Thus, the conflict was probably internecine in nature.

The onset of population decline in the middle AD 1200s is also associated with dramatic changes in settlement patterns and village plans. As population declined, the remaining population coalesced into villages surrounding springs in canyon-rim environments. Many details of these canyon-rim villages have been discussed in Chapter 9. Excavations and survey in several communities within the VEP study area suggest that these canyon-rim villages formed in a variety of ways.

In the Woods Canyon community, the upland village of Albert Porter Pueblo was abandoned and a portion of its inhabitants made long-distance moves with no intention of returning (Ryan 2008; Varien et al. 2008). The remaining population of this and other sites in the vicinity coalesced into Woods Canyon Pueblo, a settlement established in the late AD 1100s in the bottom of Woods Canyon that expanded upslope by the 1270s, at which time an enclosed plaza and public architecture were constructed on the canyon rim and talus slope (Churchill 2002; Ortman et al. 2000).

A similar process occurred in the Goodman Point community. In this case, the upland village of Shields Pueblo was abandoned, and once again a portion of its inhabitants made long-distance moves with no intention of returning (Duff et al. 2010). As Shields was being deserted, a new village, Goodman Point Pueblo, was constructed around a major spring at the head of the adjacent canyon (Kuckelman et al. 2009; Ortman and Varien 2007). This village probably took in that portion of the Shields population that did not emigrate, as well as households from the surrounding area, because there are not enough pit structures at Shields from which roof timbers were salvaged to account for the Goodman Point Pueblo population.

In the Hedley community, located just to the west of the VEP study area, the upland village known as the Middle Ruin appears to have burned catastrophically in the middle decades of the AD 1200s. Unlike the pattern seen in many sites, both surface rooms and kivas burned at the Hedley Middle Ruin, and excavations encountered charred and vitrified corn kernels and cobs on the roofs of burned structures, inside them, and even stacked against their north walls (Leh 1942; Ortman and Wilshusen 1996; Prudden 1918). Thus, a catastrophic fire, some time after the fall harvest and possibly caused by intervillage conflict, was responsible for the abandonment of the Middle Ruin. Soon after, the survivors salvaged usable building stone from the Middle Ruin and incorporated it into a canyon-rim village known as the Main Ruin, constructed around a room-dominated, McElmo style great house adjacent to a spring (Ortman et al. 2000: 135–142; also see Figure 13.11).

In the Sand Canyon community, many small upland settlements surrounding the head of Sand Canyon were abandoned by people who moved a short distance and curated usable materials (Varien 1999a). These people and others from farther afield moved into Sand Canyon Pueblo, a canyon-rim village that grew rapidly in the AD 1260s, and at which many roof timbers were recycled from earlier residences (Bradley 1993; Kuckelman 2007; Ortman and Bradley 2002; Ortman and Varien 2007).

In the Castle Rock community, in lower Sand Canyon, a portion of the existing community aggregated into Castle Rock Pueblo, a defensive village built around the base of a butte near the confluence of Sand Canyon and McElmo Creek. However, in this case about half the community population remained in small, defensively sited settlements in the cliffs of lower Sand and Rock canyons, apparently due to the lower productivity of local farmland relative to the adjacent uplands (Ortman 2008a).

Finally, in the Yellow Jacket community, the only town-sized settlement in the Mesa Verde region continued to be occupied but with a reduced population. Recently constructed room blocks around the periphery of the site were abandoned, but areas that had been established early in the town's history continued to be occupied, and a new, kiva-dominated architectural block with public architecture was constructed along the canyon rim adjacent to the local springs (Kuckelman 2003; Ortman 2003; Ortman et al. 2000; Varien and Ortman 2005; Varien et al. 2008).

The common denominator of these changes was an emphasis on canyon-rim environments surrounding springs as dwelling areas, an emphasis on bowl-shaped village layouts (see Chapter 9), and an elaboration of architectural forms. Especially noteworthy are multiwalled structures in highly visible locations within canyon-rim villages. These were either circular or D-shaped, and contained one or two small kivas surrounded by a tier of surrounding, interconnected rooms. Excavations in these structures indicate that they contained residences, presumably of community political and/or religious leaders, as well as ceremonial spaces with restricted access (Kuckelman 2003; Lipe 2002; Lipe and Ortman 2000; Ortman 2002; Ortman and Wilshusen 1996; Ortman and Bradley 2002; Till and Ortman 2007). Many details of these structures — including the suites of tall, interconnected rooms surrounding the kivas, and the vaults and subfloor ventilation systems in the kivas themselves — are reminiscent of great house architecture dating from the heyday of Chaco Canyon (Figure 12.11). Although Mesa Verde great houses were constructed primarily between AD 1080 and 1140, many continued to be used into the 1200s (Bradley 1988; Ryan 2008) and probably provided models for multiwalled structures.

Partly on this basis, Bradley (1996) suggests that a revival, or perhaps a reinvention, of Chacoan ideology swept through the Mesa Verde region during the final decades of Pueblo occupation.[5] I have found additional evidence for such a revival in the form of a directional shrine system, which appears to have drawn upon Chacoan notions of "the middle place," surrounding Castle Rock Pueblo (Ortman 2008a). Finally, the serving bowl imagery of canyon-rim village architecture and community organization (discussed in Chapters 9 and 10) appears

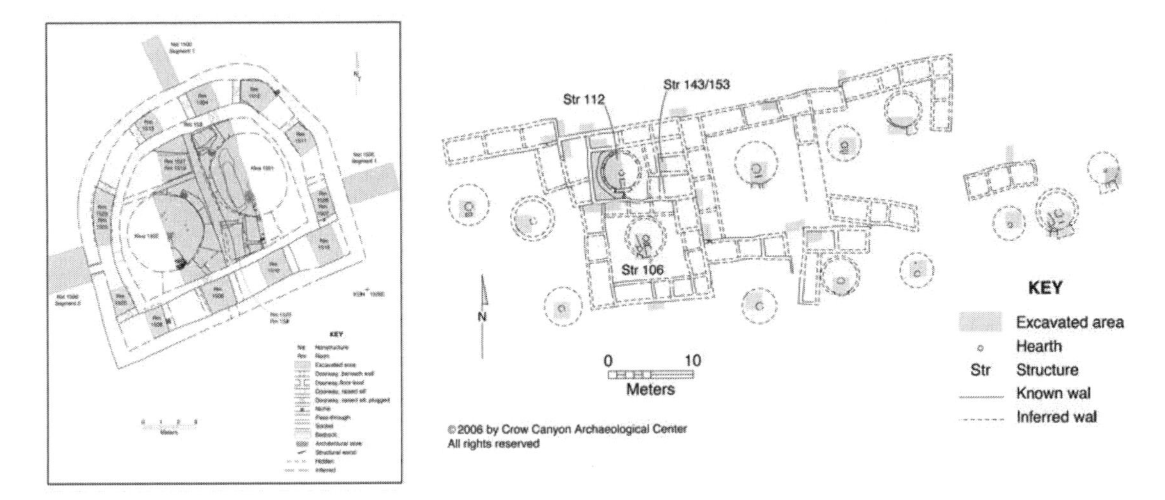

FIGURE 12.11. Relationship between multiwalled structures and Chaco era great houses: *left*, Block 1500, Sand Canyon Pueblo; *right*, Block 100, Albert Porter Pueblo. Note the lateral floor vault and subfloor ventilation system in Kiva 1501 (constructed ca. AD 1260) and in Structure 106 (constructed ca. AD 1100), and the bank of enclosing rooms surrounding both structures. (Courtesy of Crow Canyon Archaeological Center.)

to represent an extension of existing ideas related to the small, kin-based kiva to the community writ large (see Ortman 2008b), and thus appears to represent an additional effort to reinforce the status quo in the homeland society. These observations suggest that political leaders in the Mesa Verde region promoted a revivalistic discourse that reasserted central ideas of the past, expanded on existing ideas, and perhaps dampened dissent through violence in an attempt to hold Mesa Verde society together during the period of population decline. These sorts of revitalization movements are characteristic of societies under stress (Bradley 1996; Liebmann et al. 2005; Preucel 2000, 2002; 2006: Chap. 9; Wallace 1956).

Collapse and Movement

The evidence reviewed in this chapter indicates that the depopulation of the Mesa Verde region was a process that took nearly a century to complete. It began with the development of land pressure that probably motivated certain people to begin seeking out new lands shortly before AD 1200. Based on the obsidian data, one of the places these scouts explored and returned from appears to have been the Pajarito Plateau. Over time the pace of emigration quickened, and the social scale of out-migrating groups also increased. As a result, population began to decline by the middle 1200s. During the period of decline the remaining population coalesced into canyon-rim villages under an overt political leadership that promoted revitalization as a counter to migration, but to no avail. Mesa Verde society finally collapsed amid a spasm of factional conflict and rapid, large-scale out-migration associated with the onset of drought in the late 1270s. In short, the archaeological record of the central Mesa Verde region is consistent with the hypothesis that a long-term population movement, which began as a trickle and ended as a flood, was the underlying process that led to depopulation of the region.

Although I have focused on long-distance contacts between the Mesa Verde region and the Tewa Basin during the AD 1200s, there is also evidence of long-distance contacts with other areas. For example, both Tsegi Orange ware and White Mountain Red ware indicating contacts with the Hopi and Zuni areas occur in AD 1200s Mesa Verde region sites (e.g., Ortman 2003: para. 113–119). Based on the range of long-distance contacts maintained by Mesa Verde people — and the fact that population increased rapidly in the Western Pueblo area as well as in the Rio Grande region during the late AD 1200s — it would seem likely that Mesa Verde people migrated to a variety of destinations throughout the Pueblo world (e.g., Lekson et al. 2002).

It is also important to emphasize that the alternative explanation for depopulation, in situ decline, is not supported by the evidence reviewed above. Patterns in kiva abandonment, in particular, show that long-distance movement was the predominant process behind regional population decline. This conclusion is also supported by physical anthropological evidence. Age-at-death distributions in human skeletal remains suggest robust intrinsic growth rates during the Pueblo III period (Table 4.9). In addition, the incidence of enamel hypoplasia declined and adult stature increased during this period (Malville 1997). A wide range of skeletal indicators of health indicate that the individuals who died at Sand Canyon Pueblo, whether through violence or other causes, were relatively healthy at the time of death (Kuckelman and Martin 2007: para. 92). These patterns suggest that chronic starvation and disease were not primary factors in regional population decline.[6] Finally, it is important to emphasize that the models developed by the Village Ecodynamics Project — which incorporate demographic processes, environmental impacts, and climate change, but do not allow migration out of the study area — never produce a demographic collapse during the period of the final depopulation (Kohler et al. 2007). In other words, even if there had been no place for Mesa Verde people to move in the late AD 1200s, it appears that the local environment could have continued to support a sizeable population during this period.[7]

To be sure, a portion of the population that remained in sites such as Sand Canyon and Castle Rock pueblos in the AD 1270s did perish as a result of violence (Kuckelman et al. 2002), and there is also evidence to suggest that the Mesa Verde region economy collapsed in the late 1270s (Kuckelman 2008, 2010). However, the archaeological record of the last days of ancestral Pueblo occupation may inform primarily on the fate of the remnant population rather than the causes of population movement as a decades-long social process. For example, by the time the last inhabitants of Sand Canyon Pueblo were killed, many houses had already been abandoned, community institutions had ceased to function, and public buildings had become campsites (Ortman and Bradley 2002:69–70).

This suggests that the evidence for subsistence stress associated with the onset of the great drought may have more to do with the collapse of social institutions and kinship networks that had buffered the effects of previous droughts than with the direct effects of drought per se. By the same token, the spike in disturbance species in the plant record during this period (Duff et al. 2010; Adams and Bowyer 2002) may reflect an increase in abandoned fields as population declined as opposed to land degradation. Thus, even though the final collapse of Mesa Verde society has left a striking archaeological record, I believe it is most appropriate to view it as a record of the final act in a long-term historical and social process rather than a record of its causes.

Other than a consideration of initial push factors, I have not dwelled upon the "causes" of the Mesa Verde depopulation for several reasons. First, due to the multigenerational period over which depopulation of the region played out, it would seem unrealistic to imagine that a single prime mover exists that could explain the details of the entire process. The depopulation of the Mesa Verde region was clearly a long-term historical and social process in which different factors played greater or lesser roles at different points, and the influence of any given factor at any given point was likely contingent upon previous stages in the overall chain of events.

Also, it is important to keep in mind that historical sciences, in general, have great difficulty addressing the causes of any particular outcome because the systems they seek to understand are extremely complex; it is impossible to know whether the conditions associated with a given outcome in a specific case would necessarily lead to the same outcome in other cases; and it is not possible to run experiments on history, varying prior conditions and observing how they influence outcomes (Gould 1989). The Village Ecodynamics Project addressed these methodological problems by developing a computer simulation of Mesa Verde society and the environment it inhabited, and running the simulation multiple times for various parameter settings (see Kohler et al. 2007). Yet even this model can only investigate the influence of factors that are incorporated into the model, and thus far there is no combination of parameters that produces the known outcome of depopulation, so it would appear that research on why Mesa Verde society collapsed still has a long way to go.

Finally, if the Tewa Basin was a primary destination of people leaving the Mesa Verde region, it would be premature to speculate on the social dynamic associated with depopulation of the source area without first examining the archaeological record of the destination area, and considering how the new society that took shape differed from the old. Accordingly, I consider the social processes involved in the depopulation of the Mesa Verde region only in the concluding chapter of this work, after I examine the Tewa Basin archaeological record.

The Mesa Verde region was the most densely occupied portion of the Pueblo world at AD 1200 (Hill et al. 2010), with a total regional population of at least 30,000 people (Varien et al. 2007; Varien 2010). By 1285, this same region was completely empty. There is no evidence to suggest that more than a small portion of this decline in population was due to intrinsic demographic processes. Rather, the primary factor appears to have been a population movement that played out over a period of decades. The VEP population history suggests that around AD 1270, in the midst of population decline, at least 10,000 people remained in the Mesa Verde region. The abrupt halt in tree cutting after AD 1280 indicates that all 10,000 had left by AD 1285. Based on current understandings of migration as a social process, it is highly unlikely that these people scattered randomly across the landscape. Their movements were almost certainly directed toward a few specific destinations where Mesa Verde people could join with previous migrants in relative social and economic security. The Tewa Basin population grew by about 10,000 people during the same period in which the final depopulation of the Mesa Verde region occurred. A range of studies presented in earlier chapters suggest that these population trends are connected. Is the Tewa Basin archaeological record consistent with this view?

Notes

1. The Village Ecodynamics Project defines "community centers" as sites with 9 or more pit structures, 50 or more total structures, or sites with public architecture. See Chapter 9 for further discussion of such sites.
2. Sourcing of 147 items in Table 12.1 was funded by National Science Foundation Doctoral Dissertation Improvement Grant # 0753828. All items were sourced by the Archaeological XRF Laboratory at the University of California, Berkeley.
3. In previous studies, researchers distinguished roofs that were "burned intact" from "salvaged and burned" roofs. The archaeological signature of the latter category is chunks of charcoal mixed with roof sediments (Varien 1999b:114–117). The absence of large charred timbers, as occur in burned intact roofs, has been interpreted as an indication that such timbers were salvaged for use elsewhere before the unusable timbers were burned. However, usable artifacts are also often found on the floors of structures with salvaged and burned roofs, and it is difficult to reconcile the recycling of construction timbers with the discard of usable household items in the same structures. As a result, I interpret "salvaged and burned" and "burned intact" roofs as archaeological signatures of different methods of roof destruction, in which case the behavioral implications of the two signatures are nearly identical for the purposes of this analysis.
4. I also verified that tree-ring dates provide a reasonable estimate of the construction decade by cross-checking the tree-ring data with the architectural style and pottery associated with each structure, and excluded structures for which these lines of evidence were contradictory.
5. Regardless of whether the great house at Yucca House was constructed during the Chaco (AD 1060–1140) or post-Chaco (1140–1280) period, the construction of a bowl-shaped village around it during the final decades of occupation also reflects this revitalization of Chacoan ideology.
6. These patterns contrast with those observed on remains from the Hohokam Classic period, where poor health leading to low fertility and high mortality appears to have contributed to population decline in some parts of the Phoenix Basin (Abbott 2003; Hill et al. 2004).

7. The VEP climate models take annual precipitation and temperature fluctuations into account, but do not consider long-term temperature cycles that are not reflected in tree-ring series. Thus, it remains possible that a long-term cooling trend could have shortened the growing season to the point that maize agriculture was no longer feasible. I am skeptical of this hypothesis for two reasons. First, growing season lengths in various locations depend on aspect and cold air drainage patterns in addition to elevation and temperature, so it is difficult to imagine a decline in temperature dramatic enough to have made maize agriculture impossible throughout the San Juan drainage that would not have also made it impossible in adjacent high-elevation areas. Since population actually grew in high-elevation areas such as the El Morro Valley, the Mogollon highlands, and the Pajarito Plateau during this same period (see Varien 2010), it appears that any declines in regional temperatures were not of sufficient magnitude to have made maize agriculture impossible across the entire San Juan drainage.

   Second, the climate reconstructions on which "little ice age" models are based propose continent-wide temperature trends that should have made maize agriculture even more difficult in more northerly parts of North America. If so, one would expect a southward movement of the northern limit of maize cultivation during the AD 1200s, when in fact maize agriculture was spreading northward along the middle Missouri River in North Dakota at this same time (Bamforth 2008). It is difficult to reconcile such patterns with the hypothesis that declining temperatures made maize agriculture impossible throughout the San Juan drainage at the time of regional depopulation.

The Archaeology of Tewa Origins

In this chapter I examine the Tewa Basin archaeological record using the framework developed in Chapter 11 to assess whether it is consistent with the model of population movement suggested by demographic, bioarchaeological, and archaeolinguistic evidence. My analysis focuses on the settlement pattern database described in Chapter 4, published research results, and new data from Tsama Pueblo, an ancestral Tewa site in the Chama District. The locations of various sites discussed in this chapter are given in Figure 13.1.

If the conclusions suggested by other lines of evidence are to be believed, most Coalition period Tewa Basin population growth was due to in-migration by Tewa speakers from the Mesa Verde region. The initial colonists would have been scouts seeking unclaimed land where familiar farming techniques were feasible. Over time, additional colonists would have overwhelmed the existing population, either displacing them or absorbing their genes and forcing them to shift their language to Tewa. The population movement framework suggests that such movements do not necessarily leave clear-cut continuities in material culture, as is typical of migrations that result in ethnic coresidence. However, the archaeological record of the destination area of a population movement should exhibit characteristics that betray this process. Here I evaluate the extent to which these characteristics are present in the Tewa Basin archaeological record.

Initial Colonization

The first expectation for the destination area of a population movement is that initial colonization should correspond to a period of time in which material push factors existed in the putative homeland. The population history developed in Chapter 4 (Figure 4.7) shows that in the AD 1100s, most of the Tewa Basin population was located along eastern tributaries of the Rio Grande and along the Rio Grande floodplain in the Cochiti area. Shortly before 1200, however, a new population center began to develop on the Pajarito Plateau, in an area that had not been inhabited previously. Figure 13.2 maps this population reconstruction for four time periods spanning the Late Developmental to Early Classic periods. Many of the sites assigned to the initial, AD 1050–1200 period are small, one- to three-room sites on the Pajarito Plateau to which surveyors assigned broad date

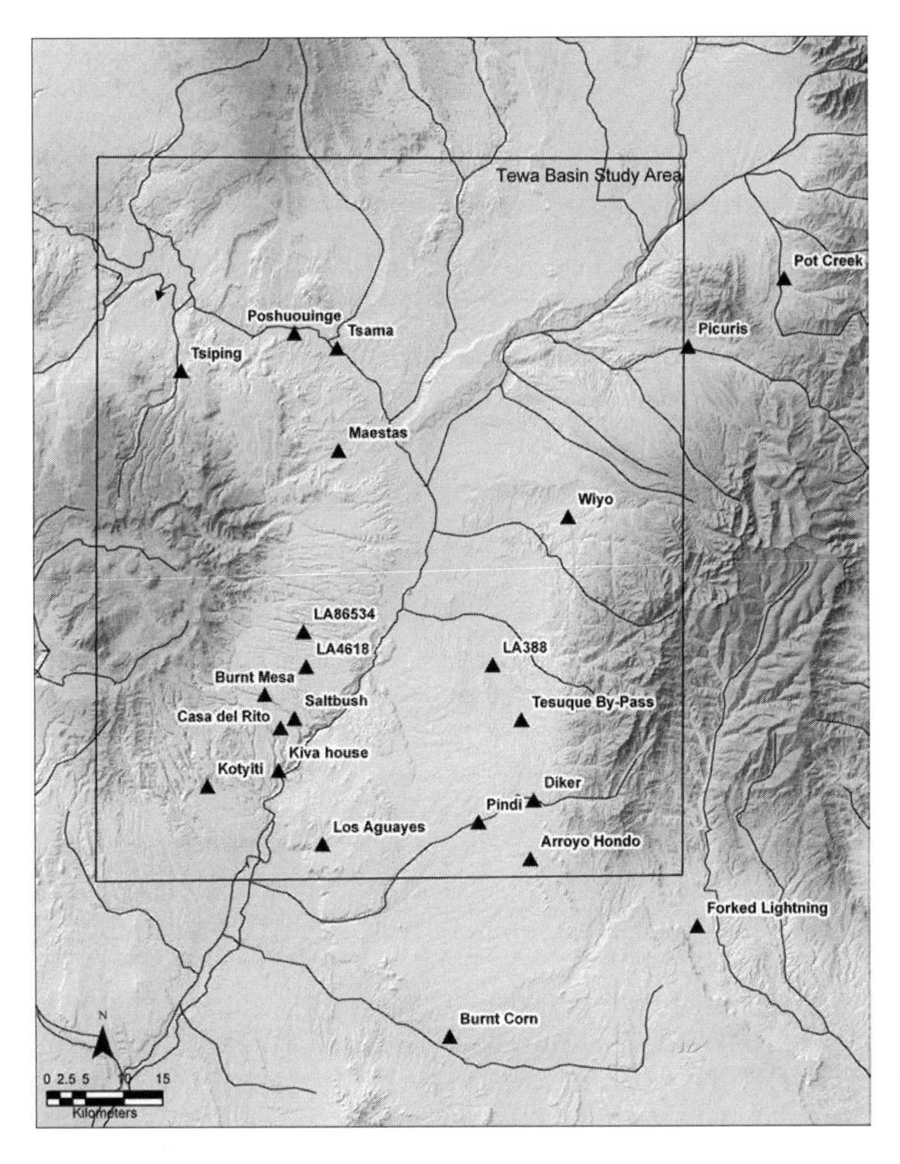

FIGURE 13.1. Locations of sites mentioned in the text.

ranges due to limited data and an awareness that the earliest occupation of the Pajarito dates from the late AD 1100s (Kohler and Root 2004a; Orcutt 1999a).[1] Thus, most of the sites shown as occupied on the Pajarito Plateau between 1050 and 1200 were probably established near the end of this period. Expansion of settlement on the Pajarito Plateau then accounts for nearly all Tewa Basin population growth during the subsequent, AD 1200–1275 period. The VEP potential paleoproductivity and settlement pattern reconstructions reviewed earlier show that land pressure in the Mesa Verde region reached the highest levels of the entire ancestral Pueblo sequence during the final decades of the AD 1100s and early decades of the 1200s. Thus, colonization of the Pajarito Plateau corresponds in time with the development of strong material push factors in the Mesa Verde region.

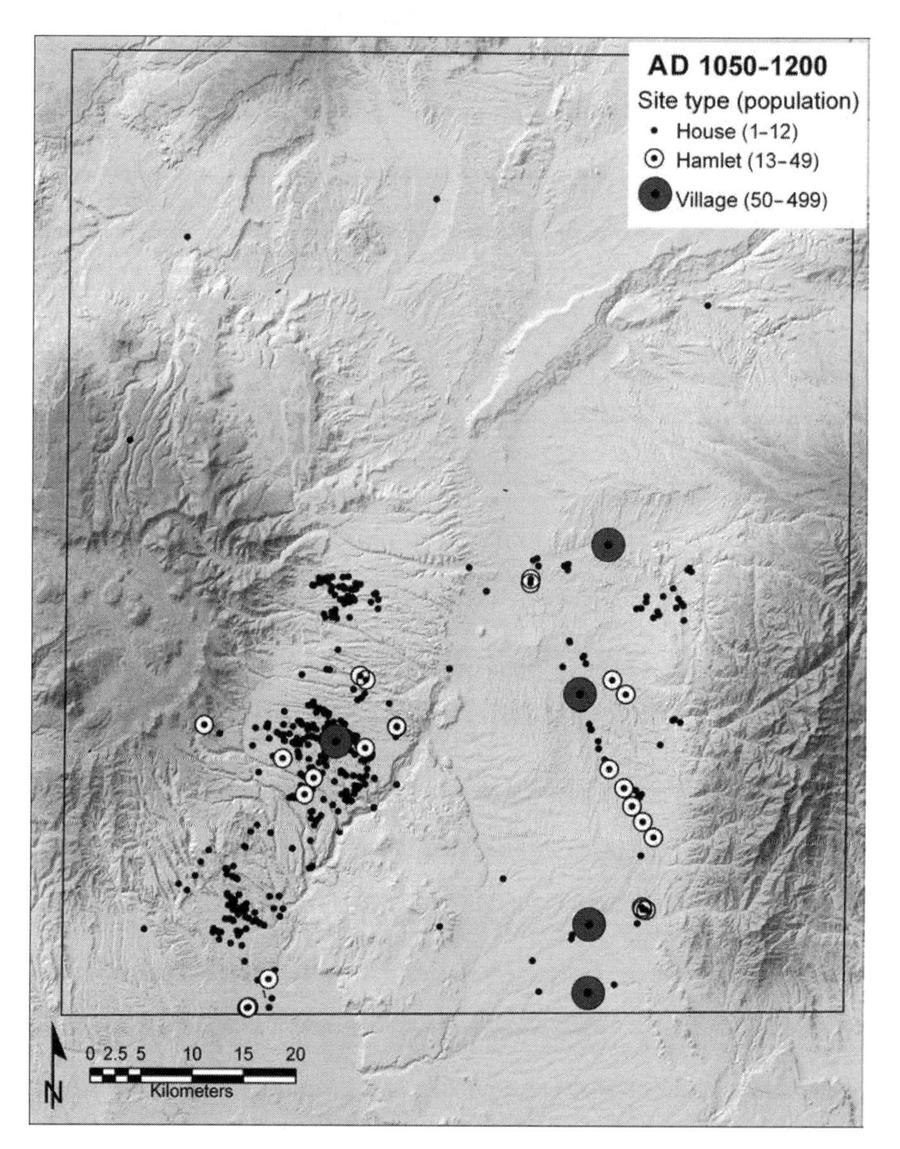

FIGURE 13.2A. Settlement pattern changes in the Tewa Basin, AD 1050–1200.

The Pioneer Subsistence Economy

The second expectation for the destination area of a population movement is that the initial colonists should attempt to re-create the agricultural economy of the homeland. In this case, one would expect continuities in subsistence practices between the Mesa Verde region and the Early Coalition Pajarito Plateau. The agricultural strategies of Early Coalition colonists are revealed most directly by the locations of their sites. When pioneers enter an open landscape, they are most likely to settle on patches of land they find desirable for farming based on prior experience. The characteristics of the land surrounding these settlements thus reflect the farming strategies these pioneers pursued.

Early Coalition sites on the Pajarito were primarily houses and hamlets scattered across upland mesa tops, on lands suitable for direct precipitation

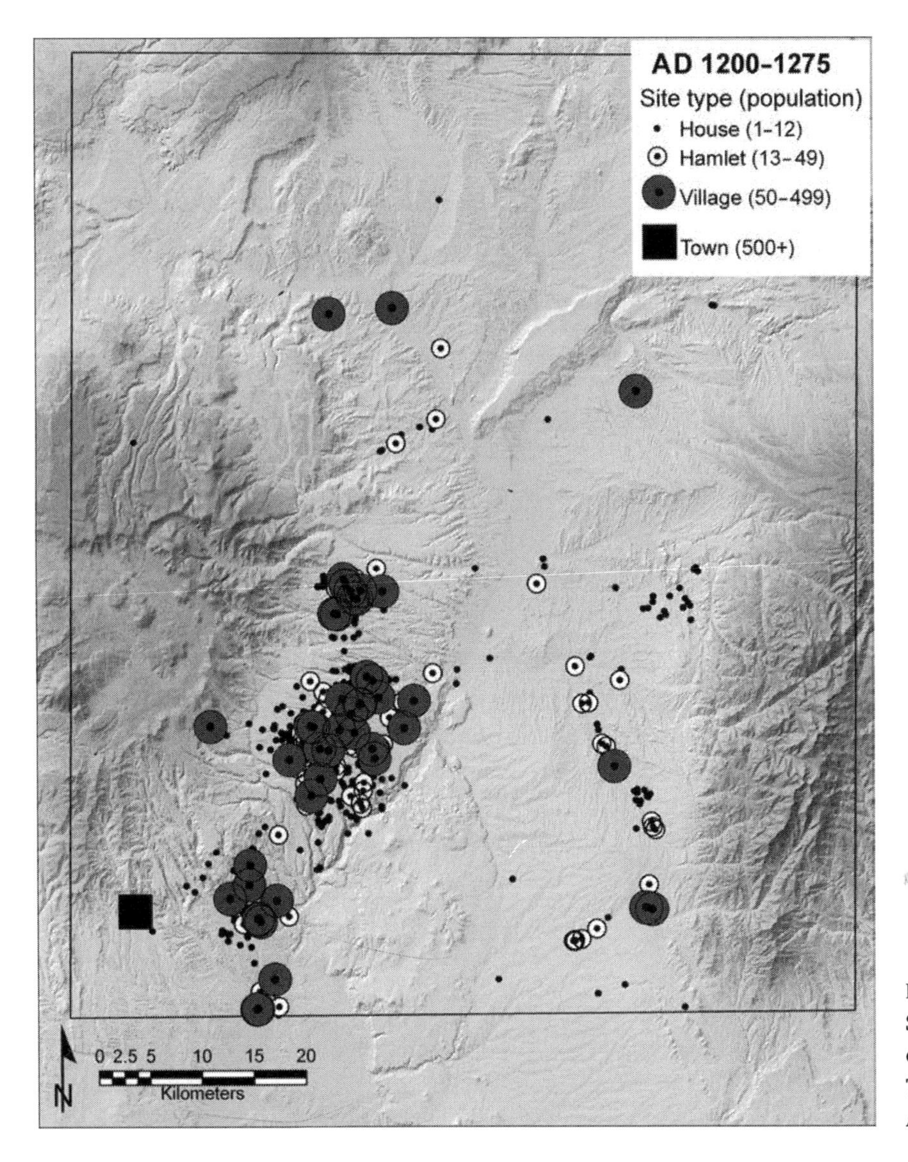

FIGURE 13.2B. Settlement pattern changes in the Tewa Basin, AD 1200–1275.

agriculture (Orcutt 1999b:251–277; Vierra et al. 2006:192). This agricultural strategy contrasts with those implied by Late Developmental sites elsewhere in the Tewa Basin, which occur primarily in settings better-suited to *ak-chin*, run-off, and floodwater strategies (Marshall and Walt 2007, II:6–12; Bussey 1968a, 1968b). However, Early Coalition farming methods were quite similar to those of the central Mesa Verde region. Prior to AD 1225 most people in this region lived in dispersed houses and hamlets in upland areas where direct precipitation or "dry" farming was the dominant agricultural strategy (see Figure 12.7; also see Adler 1992; Fetterman and Honeycutt 1987; Kendrick and Judge 2000; Ortman and Varien 2007; Varien et al. 2007). As discussed in Chapter 12, increasing land pressure appears to have pushed some farmers into the less productive canyons by AD 1200, around the same time colonization of the Pajarito Plateau began (see

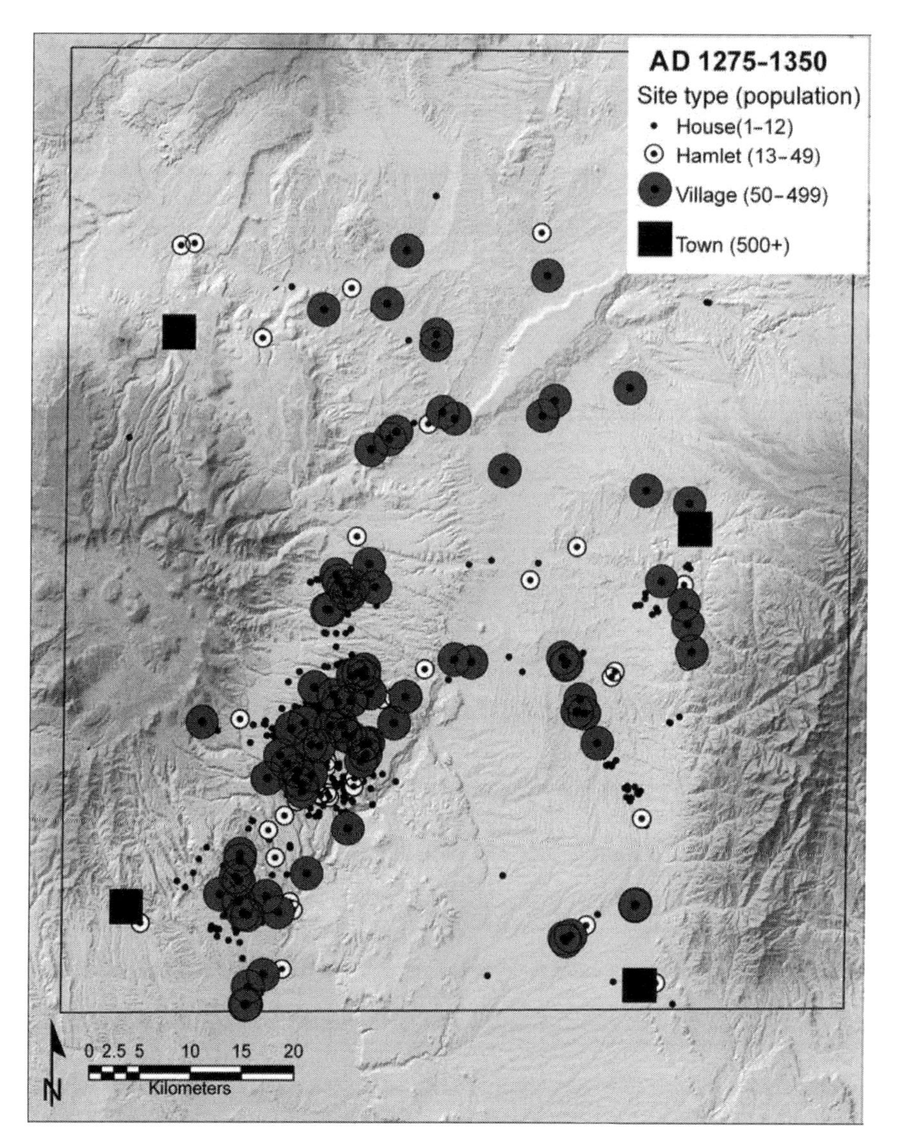

FIGURE 13.2C. Settlement pattern changes in the Tewa Basin, AD 1275–1350.

Figure 12.8; also see Ortman 2008a; Ortman and Varien 2007; Varien 1999a). In other words, migrants entering the Tewa Basin in the early AD 1200s colonized a niche where the same farming strategies that had been used for generations in the central Mesa Verde region could be pursued, even as this same niche overflowed in the Mesa Verde region itself.[2]

A second component of the Pajarito subsistence economy that was not part of the Late Developmental economy, but was part of the Mesa Verde region economy, was keeping turkeys as a source of meat. Turkey bones occur in low frequencies in Early Coalition trash deposits on the Pajarito, but turkey remains have not been recovered from Developmental sites elsewhere in the Tewa Basin, including the Peña Blanca Project sites (Akins et al. 2003), Tesuque By-Pass (Jelinek 1969), and the Diker Site in Santa Fe (Cordero 2005:202; also see Lang and Harris 1984:97). In the central Mesa Verde region, in contrast, turkey bones occur

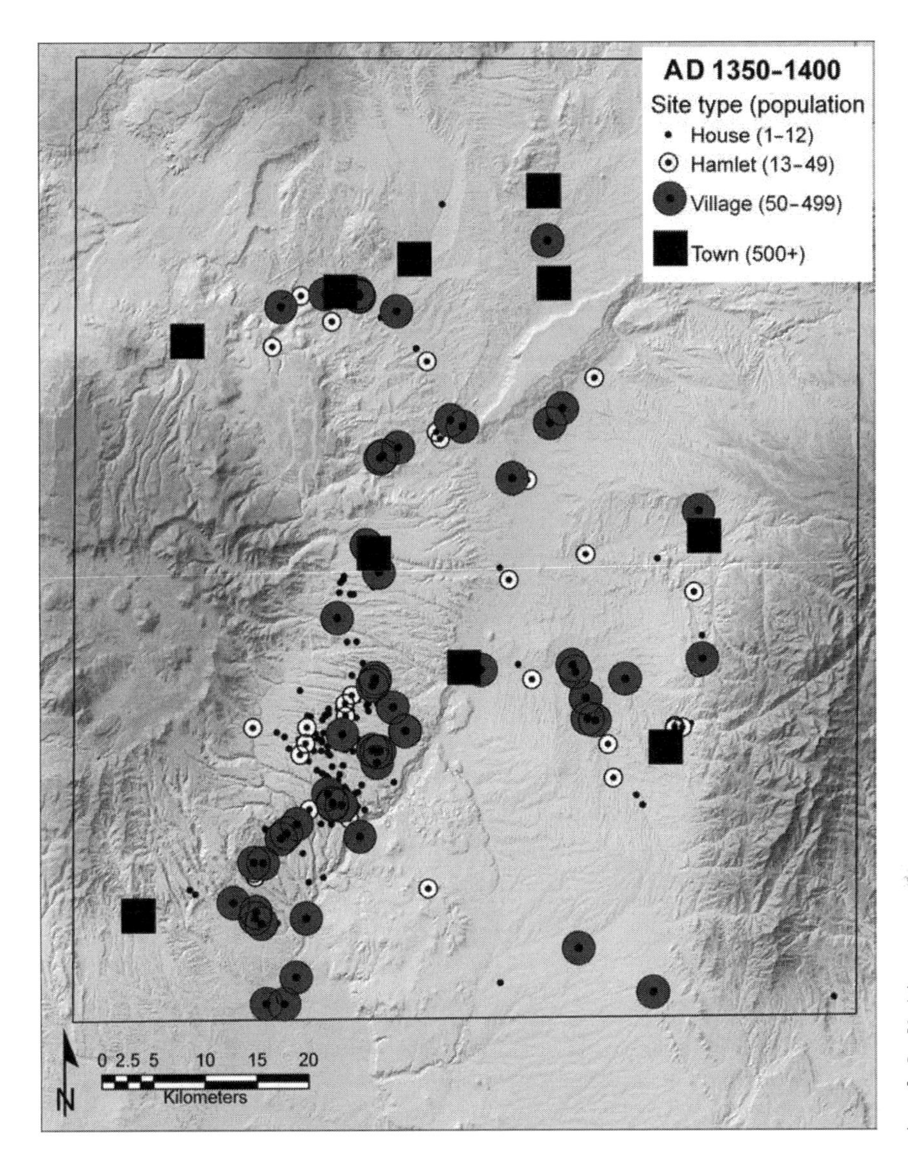

FIGURE 13.2D. Settlement pattern changes in the Tewa Basin, AD 1350–1400.

in sites dating as early as AD 600. From AD 600 until 1060, turkeys were kept primarily as a source of feathers, especially down for blankets, and were often buried whole rather than eaten (McKusick 1980:227–228). But after AD 1060 the occurrence of burned and broken bones in domestic trash signals that turkeys began to be raised for their meat as well. Recent ancient DNA studies suggest that most if not all turkey remains in Pueblo sites derive from domesticated or tame birds (Speller et al. 2010). This suggests that the keeping and eating of turkeys should be viewed as an element of cuisine as well as the agricultural economy. It also implies that the earliest turkeys in Tewa Basin sites arrived via human agency.

Figure 13.3 summarizes the relative abundance of turkey bones in faunal assemblages from sites in the Mesa Verde region and on the Pajarito Plateau. These data show that turkey husbandry intensified in the late AD 1100s in the Mesa

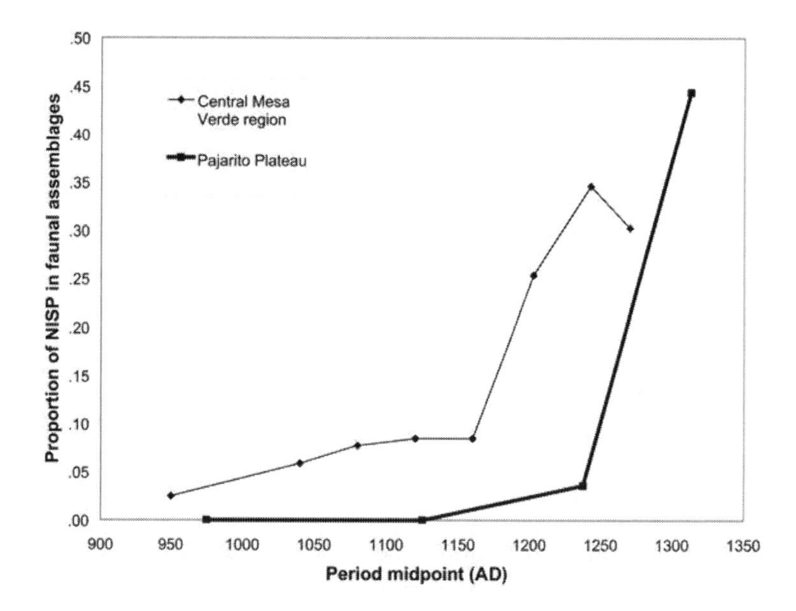

FIGURE 13.3. Relative abundance of turkey bones in faunal assemblages (Badenhorst 2008; Driver 2002; Neusius 1986; Rawlings 2007; Schmidt 2007: Table 1; Trierweiler 1990a: Table 7.7, 1990b: App. B, 1992: Table 8.7). Mesa Verde region faunal assemblages were assigned to Village Ecodynamics Project modeling periods, and Pajarito Plateau assemblages were assigned to the phase scheme of this study.

Verde region, and that Early Coalition colonists on the Pajarito Plateau appear to have brought some turkeys with them. They also show that by the Late Coalition period, turkey consumption on the Pajarito Plateau contributed to the diet at a comparable level to the mid-AD 1200s Mesa Verde region. This rapid expansion in turkey consumption suggests that turkeys came along with migrants to the Pajarito. The Mesa Verde region would be a plausible homeland for these migrants because turkey consumption was well established in that region prior to AD 1200.

In summary, the available evidence suggests that an economic system that included direct precipitation farming and turkey husbandry was introduced to a previously unoccupied portion of the Tewa Basin during the same period that land pressure began to push people off the preferred farming niche in the central Mesa Verde region. The area colonized at this time presented characteristics similar to the niche that was overflowing in the Mesa Verde region, and the subsistence economy established by the initial settlers was more similar to that of the Mesa Verde region than it was to the Late Developmental Tewa Basin subsistence economy.[3] In addition, areas such as the Chama River valley, which were available but less suited to direct precipitation farming, were not settled by the earliest migrants. All of this is consistent with the hypothesis that Early Coalition Tewa Basin migrants originated in the Mesa Verde region.

Early Coalition Society and Culture

The third expectation for the destination area of a population movement is that the material culture of the early colonists should appear as a package in new sites. It should also be simplified from that of the homeland and should exhibit continuities in food preferences, technological styles, and domestic spatial organization. In the following pages I evaluate the extent to which Early Coalition society and culture are consistent with these expectations.

Domestic Architecture

The strongest architectural evidence in favor of long-distance colonization comes from the earliest residential sites of the Pajarito Plateau. Three excavated sites from Bandelier National Monument constructed prior to AD 1200 (Kiva House, Saltbush Pueblo, and Casa del Rito) contain small kivas that exhibit architectural traits of kivas in the San Juan drainage, such as a southern orientation, benches, lateral floor vaults, and a keyhole shape in plan view (Carlson and Kohler 1990:11–18; Kohler and Root 2004a:134–138; Snow 1974). These features were characteristic of AD 1100s kivas in the Mesa Verde region and greater San Juan drainage, but do not occur in Developmental pit structures. However, none of these structures possess the pilasters and cribbed roofs of Mesa Verde region kivas, and two of the three possess ash pits that are more common in Late Developmental pit structures (Boyer et al. 2010). So even in these sites, there is no evidence for a wholesale movement of architectural traditions.

Based on the fact that these early, south-facing, semisubterranean kivas occur south of Frijoles Canyon, and that a different type of structure known as the "ceremonial room" eventually became most common north of Frijoles Canyon (see below), several researchers have argued that these early kivas reflect an initial migration of ancestral Keres people to the southern Pajarito Plateau (Boyer et al. 2010; Kohler and Root 2004a:170–171). This may be the case, but several lines of evidence suggest that the inhabitants of these earliest sites could also have been Tewa-speaking colonists from the Mesa Verde region. First, architectural traits of these early kivas are consistent with an origin anywhere in the San Juan drainage. Second, the ethnic boundary documented in historic times in the area of Frijoles Canyon is only clear in the archaeological record from the Early Classic period onward (Kohler, Herr et al. 2004:216–218). The notion that this boundary existed in the late AD 1100s is based solely on the presence of kivas with generalized San Juan traits in sites south of Frijoles Canyon. Third, there are no sites north of Frijoles Canyon that are well dated to the late AD 1100s or associated with mixtures of Santa Fe Black-on-white and Kwahe'e Black-on-white (Carlson and Kohler 1990:10–20; Orcutt 1999a:104–107; Vierra et al. 2006:190). In other words, the northern Pajarito was essentially unoccupied at this time, and as a result there was no boundary between distinct groups; there were only a small number of sites containing kivas with mixtures of San Juan and Rio Grande architectural traits to the south of Frijoles Canyon. So the existing data are also consistent with a model in which initial colonization of the southern Pajarito Plateau was by Tewa speakers, with the earliest sites exhibiting the clearest evidence of their homeland.

Regardless of the interpretation of these early sites, it is clear that architectural traits of San Juan kivas are absent from the subsequent archaeological record of the Pajarito Plateau. Indeed, kivas dating after AD 1200 present far more evidence of derivation from local forms (Wendorf 1953:95; Steen 1977:40). Examples from LA86534 (Schmidt 2008) and LA4618 (Schmidt 2006) near Los Alamos are circular or square semisubterranean structures excavated into tuff bedrock, with masonry walls above the pit edge. The floors of these structures contain an adobe-collared circular-hearth, ash pit and deflector complex, and a vent tunnel opening to the east. These structures also lack pilasters, southern recesses, and benches. The roofs were flat and supported by vigas that rested on top of the masonry walls. The eastern orientation and floor feature complex of these structures clearly continue architectural traditions of Late Developmental pit structures found throughout the Rio Grande region (Lakatos 2007) and bear no relationship to architectural traditions of Mesa Verde region kivas. So it is clear that the form of Coalition period kivas derives from that of Late Developmental pit structures.

There is less evidence for functional continuity. Both Late Developmental pit structures and Pueblo III Mesa Verde kivas are best interpreted as domestic spaces used by households. In the Rio Grande, the typical Late Developmental residence consisted of a pit structure in association with 5 to 10 surface rooms (Bussey 1968a, 1968b; Fowles 2004; Lakatos 2007; McNutt 1969; Wiseman 1995). The same pattern occurs in the Pueblo III Mesa Verde region, where a small kiva with approximately 12 m^2 of floor area was typically associated with a surface room block of 2 to 10 surface rooms (Bradley 1993:26; Lipe 1989:56; Ortman 1998:172). Many of these kivas also contain mealing bins, cooking pots, sleeping mat impressions, charred food remains, and the only substantial hearth in the entire house (Bradley 1993:28; Cater and Chenault 1988; Lekson 1988; Ortman 1998; Varien 1999a).

In contrast, many Coalition period kivas do not appear to have been elements of domestic architecture. The floor areas of these kivas are similar to those of earlier examples in both regions (Schmidt 2006, 2008; Van Zandt 1999:381), but the ratio of surface rooms to kivas in Pajarito room block sites is more variable. For example, Van Zandt (1999:381) estimated from Bandelier Archaeological Survey data that room to kiva ratios in Coalition period sites range between 8 and 28, and this range is borne out by excavated sites (see Tables 4.3 and 4.7; also Figure 13.4). In addition, subterranean or semi-subterranean kivas are absent from many Coalition period habitations (Carlson and Kohler 1990:18–20; Steen 1977, 1982; Kohler and Root 2004a:150–161; Vierra et al. 2008), suggesting that a kiva was not a standard component of domestic architecture in these sites. Thus, it appears that at least some Coalition period kivas functioned at a larger social scale than Late Developmental pit structures or Mesa Verde kivas.

Given the functional disanalogy between Coalition period kivas and earlier kivas and pit structures in both regions, it is important to ask whether other elements of Coalition period domestic architecture provided functional analogs to these structures, and whether the characteristics of these analogs derive from

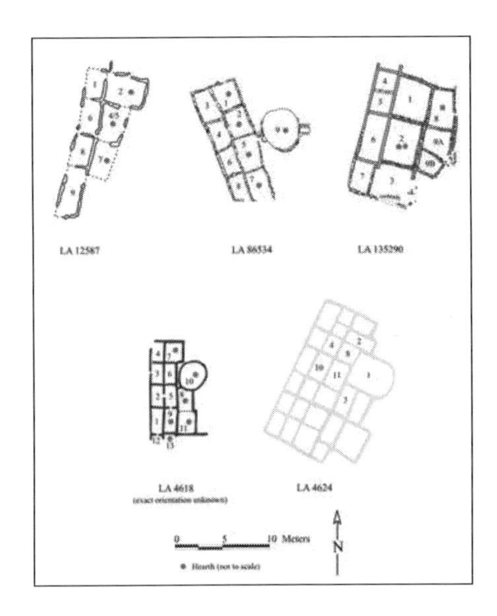

FIGURE 13.4. Coalition period room-block sites of the Pajarito Plateau (Vierra et al. 2008: Fig. 86.6, LA-UR-07-6205).

one or both sources. Early Coalition architecture consists primarily of above-ground room blocks of 1 to 25 rooms (Figure 13.4). These room blocks are often rectangular, with their long axis oriented north-south, and usually contain two or three rows of rooms. Rooms with hearths usually occur in the eastern, or front, row, with storage rooms in the western, or back, rows. If there is a kiva associated with a room block, it will occur east of the room block, and thus room-block sites "face" east.

In most room blocks, one or two rooms along the front row are larger than the others, have a square or D-shape as opposed to a rectangular shape, and contain a hearth, deflector, and vent tunnel (Kohler and Root 2004a:150–161; Steen 1977:11; Vierra 2008). There is no evidence for a doorway in these structures, so ingress and egress must have been by ladder through a hatch in the roof (Steen 1977:11). Also, if one includes these rooms along with kivas in a single category, the ratios of other rooms to "ceremonial" rooms in excavated Coalition room blocks become comparable to those of earlier unit pueblos in the Tewa Basin and Mesa Verde region, varying between 4 and 12 (see Table 4.7). So there is a range of evidence suggesting that these oversized rooms, which have been labeled "southeastern corner kivas" (Wendorf and Reed 1955:145–146) or "ceremonial rooms" (Steen 1977:11), represent a functional analog of both Late Developmental pit structures and Mesa Verde kivas. Where did ceremonial rooms come from? As in the case of kivas, many formal traits of these rooms have antecedents in Late Developmental architecture. For example, the adobe-rimmed hearth and eastern orientation of ceremonial rooms clearly reflect the floor features and orientation of Late Developmental pit structures. In addition, square and D-shaped ceremonial rooms with adobe-rimmed hearths, deflectors and vent tunnels have been reported from Late Developmental sites (Lakatos 2007: 37; McNutt 1969:5).[4]

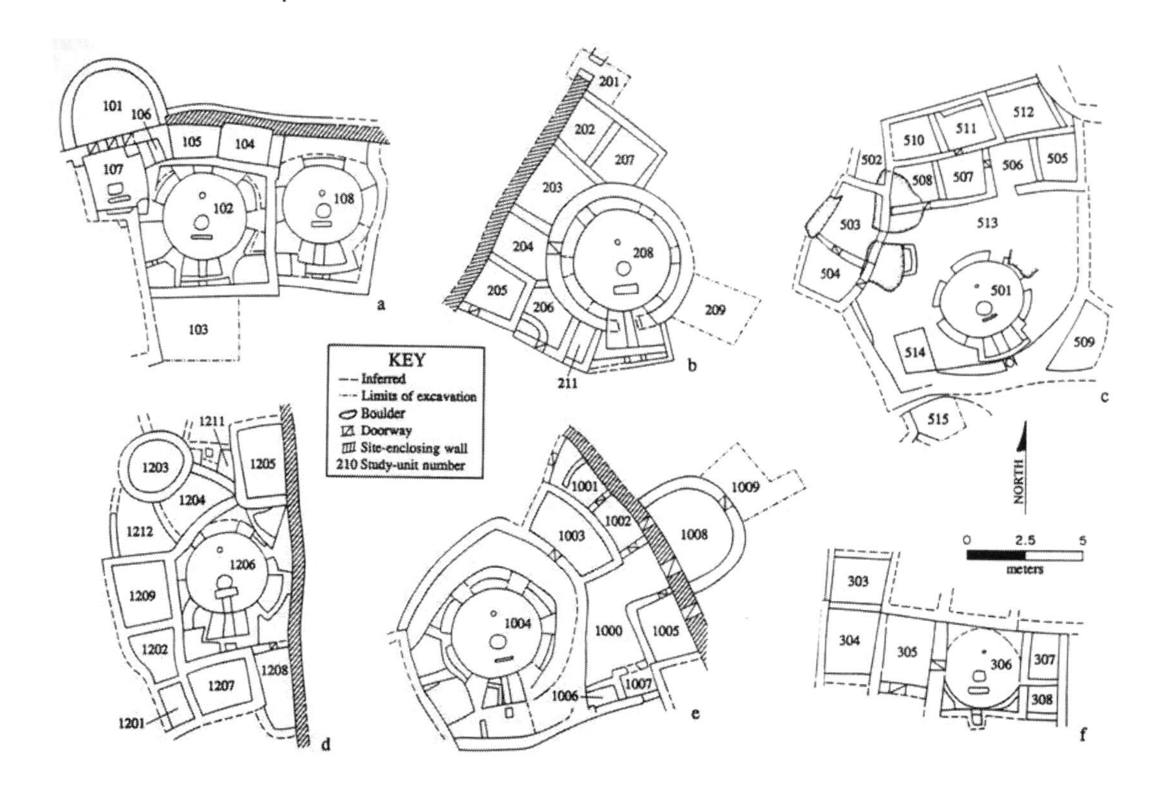

FIGURE 13.5. Unit pueblo architecture at Sand Canyon Pueblo in southwest Colorado: *a*, Block 100; *b*, Block 200; *c*, Block 500; *d*, Block 1200; *e*, Block 1000; *f*, Block 300. (© Crow Canyon Archaeological Center.)

It is important, however, to emphasize that several characteristics of ceremonial rooms also have analogs in mid-AD 1200s Mesa Verde region architecture. For example, parallels can be seen with unit pueblo residences in canyon-rim villages (Figure 13.5). The kivas in these residences were constructed above ground within masonry enclosures that were contiguous with the other surface rooms. The area enclosed by the outer kiva wall in these residences is comparable to the floor area of Coalition period ceremonial rooms, and access to the kivas and most rooms remained via ladders through the roof (Bradley 1993; Morley 1908). It is also important to note that the south-facing orientation of earlier unit pueblos was not followed in canyon-rim villages, where many houses faced downslope rather than in a specific direction (see Lipe 2010; Ortman and Bradley 2002:75–76). If one removed the bench and pilasters from the kivas in these residences and replaced the cribbed roof with a flat one, one would be left with a house that looks fairly similar to a Coalition period room block site with a ceremonial room.

Finally, people who participated in the Mesa Verde cultural tradition but lived in the region's western periphery often created simpler kivas and habitation rooms that bear a closer resemblance to Coalition period Tewa Basin forms than the prototypical Mesa Verde unit pueblo. In the cliff-dwelling communities of Cedar Mesa, for example, jacal and unshaped-stone masonry continued to be used as wall construction methods in sites dating as late as the AD 1260s, and kiva/ceremonial rooms with hearths were often constructed with a rounded

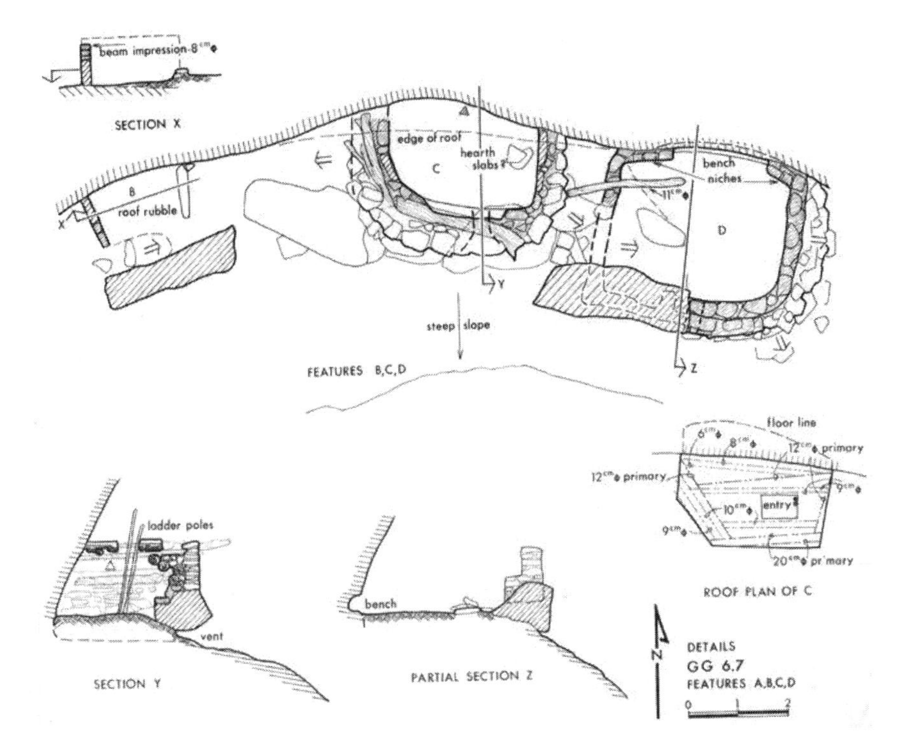

FIGURE 13.6. Aboveground kivas/ceremonial rooms from GG C6-7 (425A5112), Grand Gulch, Utah. Note the flat roof, roof entry, ladder poles, vent tunnel, interior hearth, and D-shape of Room C, a kiva constructed in AD 1258. (Architectural drawing by Ruby Buick, reproduced courtesy of Washington State University.)

wall against the flat face of a ledge or alcove, thus producing a D-shape (Figure 13.6). The roofs of such structures were either provided by the roof of the alcove or were flat, and when a roof was present, entrance was through a hatch in the roof. Finally, a vent opening, or doorway, occurred on the apex of the rounded wall, depending on the roofing method. The point is that people who lived in the Mesa Verde region maintained knowledge of a wider-range of building methods and architectural forms than those expressed in the highly formalized unit pueblo residences of the most densely populated areas. It is possible to view regional variation in Mesa Verde tradition architecture as resulting from application of this knowledge to local contexts. If Pajarito colonists were similarly flexible, the domestic architecture of Coalition room block sites can be viewed as functional equivalents of Mesa Verde region unit pueblos, with Tewa Basin forms being substituted for the more baroque elements of Mesa Verde architecture.[5]

In summary, the earliest sites on the Pajarito Plateau contain kivas that exhibit formal and functional characteristics of kivas found at that time throughout the San Juan drainage, including the Mesa Verde region, but by the Early Coalition period, Pajarito Plateau room block sites expressed local architectural forms and a domestic spatial organization that would have been at home in either area. The east-facing orientation of houses and kivas, and kiva architecture itself, clearly derive from Late Developmental antecedents; however, several additional elements, including ceremonial rooms with roof entry and the front-facing arrangement of storage and habitation rooms, could have derived from antecedents in either area or, more precisely, would have been familiar to migrants from the Mesa Verde region even if they had developed locally. So even though Coalition period architectural forms were less elaborate than Mesa Verde forms and likely had different symbolic associations, these forms were consistent with Mesa Verde region unit pueblo architecture in a functional sense. It would not have entailed a significant change in domestic spatial organization for Mesa Verde migrants to have adopted them. Thus, domestic architecture can be construed as supporting either territorial expansion of the Late Developmental Rio Grande population or long-distance colonization from the Mesa Verde region. It does not support immigration models, in which more Mesa Verde style architecture would be expected.

Community Organization

A range of evidence suggests that Early Coalition Pajarito Plateau society was practical and flexible. For example, a range of building styles — including adobe, adobe with stone, rough block masonry, and cut stone masonry with chinking — were used to build these sites (Steen 1982:37–38). Certain of these techniques have precursors in both the Rio Grande and Mesa Verde regions, but the variation from site to site suggests that there was more concern about adapting construction methods to available resources than a social preference for any specific method of wall construction. Also, Early Coalition Pajarito sites formed loose spatial clusters that reflect some form of regular interaction and cooperation among the residents of sites within each cluster (Ruscavage-Barz 2002). Nevertheless, public architecture such as enclosed plazas or great kivas are completely lacking from these clusters, despite being present in both Late Developmental (Wiseman 1995; McNutt 1969:4) and Mesa Verde region communities (Lipe and Ortman 2000; Lipe 2002; Ortman and Bradley 2002). Finally, the overriding characteristic of room-block sites is variability in the number and arrangement of rooms (Kohler and Root 2004a:118–119). These patterns suggest that Early Coalition populations of the Pajarito maintained fluid social networks, noninstitutionalized forms of cooperation, and flexible architectural templates. This pattern is not characteristic of a society experiencing immigration or territorial expansion, but is typical of pioneer communities on an agricultural frontier.[6] Thus, the emphasis on practicality and flexibility is consistent with the hypothesis that early communities of the Pajarito Plateau formed through long-distance colonization.

Artifact Assemblages

Several elements of Classic period Tewa Basin artifact assemblages first appeared as a group in Early Coalition sites. The list of items includes carbon-painted pottery (which replaced mineral-painted pottery), slab metates (which replaced trough metates), full-grooved axes (added to notched axes), side-notched projectile points (which replaced corner-notched varieties), the raising of turkeys for food, and bird bone artifacts (McNutt 1969:82; Wendorf and Reed 1955:143–145). All of these items are characteristic of Mesa Verde region assemblages dating prior to AD 1200, but none are characteristic of Late Developmental assemblages. It is not difficult to imagine an in situ society adopting each of these items individually through contacts with areas from which each specific innovation originated. This was, in fact, the pattern of change in the Mesa Verde region, where each item was added to the local material culture complex one at a time, in sites that were occupied across the period of adoption. In the Tewa Basin, in contrast, these items replaced earlier forms as a package, in new sites, and during a period of rapid population growth — a pattern of change consistent with long-distance colonization.

It is also important to highlight characteristics of Late Developmental assemblages that continued into the AD 1200s in the Taos Valley, northeast of the Tewa Basin, but not in Coalition period assemblages within the Tewa Basin.[7] Several characteristics of pottery assemblages follow this pattern. For example, a variety of culinary pottery known as Taos Incised occurs in Late Developmental sites in the Tewa Basin (Mera 1935:6; McNutt 1969:15–16) as well as Valdez phase (AD 950–1200) sites in the Taos Valley (Fowles 2004:222–225). This distinctive type continued to be produced in AD 1200s sites in the Taos Valley (Fowles 2004: 332; Jeançon 1929; Smiley et al. 1953:38), but occurs only in trace amounts in Coalition period Tewa Basin assemblages (Kohler and Root 2004a; Wilson 2008b).

In addition, mineral-painted pottery continued to be produced in the Taos Valley well after it had been replaced by carbon-painted pottery in the Tewa Basin. Mera (1935:6) viewed the decorated pottery of the AD 1050–1200 Tewa Basin and Taos Valley as regional variants of a single earlier, mineral-painted type known as Chaco 2 or Red Mesa Black-on-white. The Tewa Basin descendant of this type, Kwahe'e Black-on-white, was replaced by carbon-painted Santa Fe Black-on-white early in the Coalition period. The other descendant, Taos Black-on-white, continued to be produced throughout the AD 1200s in the Taos Valley (Fowles 2004: Fig. 6.3). Mera suggested Taos Black-on-white could be distinguished from Kwahe'e Black-on-white on the basis of higher-quality slipping, but recent studies have suggested that this difference is minor, and have taken to lumping mineral-painted pottery of the Taos Valley with Kwahe'e Black-on-white (Fowles 2004:220–221; Fowles et al. 2007:128–130). This implies that the Late Developmental Tewa Basin and the Valdez phase Taos Valley shared a single decorated pottery tradition that continued into the AD 1200s in the Taos Valley, but was replaced by a new, carbon-painted tradition in the Tewa Basin.

Finally, a third characteristic of Late Developmental pottery that continued in the AD 1200s Taos Valley but not in the Tewa Basin was the production of painted jars. Mineral-painted bowls and jars occur in Late Developmental Tewa Basin assemblages (Kohler and Root 2004:140; McNutt 1969:12) and in AD 1200s Taos Valley assemblages (Jeancon 1929:22), but Santa Fe Black-on-white occurs almost exclusively as bowls in Coalition period Tewa Basin assemblages (Kohler and Root 2004b:164; Wilson 2008b:241). This restriction of decoration to bowls also contrasts with AD 1200s Mesa Verde region assemblages, in which significant numbers of decorated ollas, seed jars, ladles, mugs, and canteens also occur (Ortman 2000, 2002, 2003; Pierce et al. 1999; Till and Ortman 2007). Thus, Early Coalition inhabitants of the Pajarito Plateau produced simpler pottery assemblages than Late Developmental inhabitants of the Tewa Basin, contemporary inhabitants of the Mesa Verde region, and contemporary inhabitants of the Taos Valley. This pattern of cultural simplification is also mirrored in domestic architecture, and is more characteristic of a pioneer society than an expanding local society or a society experiencing immigration and ethnic coresidence.

Several additional elements of material culture follow the same pattern seen in pottery assemblages. For example, trough metates open at one or both ends are characteristic of Late Developmental sites (McNutt 1969:23–24) and continue to occur in AD 1200s Taos Valley sites (Jeançon 1929: Plate 6), but are absent from Coalition period Tewa Basin sites where only slab metates occur (McNutt 1969:58; Vierra and Dilley 2008:381). Also, turkey bone artifacts occur in neither Late Developmental sites nor AD 1200s Taos Valley sites, but they do occur in Coalition period Tewa Basin sites, as detailed earlier. So this pattern of change, distributed across pottery, stone, and faunal remains, suggests that Late Developmental Tewa Basin assemblages are overall more similar to subsequent assemblages of the Taos Valley than they are to Coalition assemblages of the Tewa Basin. This pattern is consistent with a model of displacement or absorption of the Late Developmental Tewa Basin population, but cultural continuity in the Taos Valley.[8]

Smeared-Indented-Corrugated Utility Ware

An element of Coalition pottery assemblages that was innovative relative to both Mesa Verde and Tewa Basin pottery traditions is smeared-indented-corrugated utility ware. Between AD 1050 and 1200, cooking pottery in both the Mesa Verde region and the Tewa Basin had a distinctive surface treatment formed by indenting a spiraling coil of clay on the outside of the vessel with a tool or finger. This surface treatment, known as "corrugated" in the Mesa Verde region and "indented corrugated" in the Rio Grande region, was also produced in Early Coalition sites. But during the middle AD 1200s, a new surface treatment that involved smearing the exterior surface of indented corrugated vessels replaced all other treatments (Kohler and Root 2004a:161, 197; Orcutt 1999a:111).

Because the smeared-indented-corrugated surface treatment was new, researchers have tended to overlook this innovation when discussing the sources of the ancestral Tewa population, yet several factors suggest that it may be significant. First, in Chapter 10 I argued that in the Mesa Verde region, corrugated pottery expressed a metaphoric conceptualization of pottery vessels as baskets. This conceptualization is also enshrined in one of the words for pottery in the Tewa

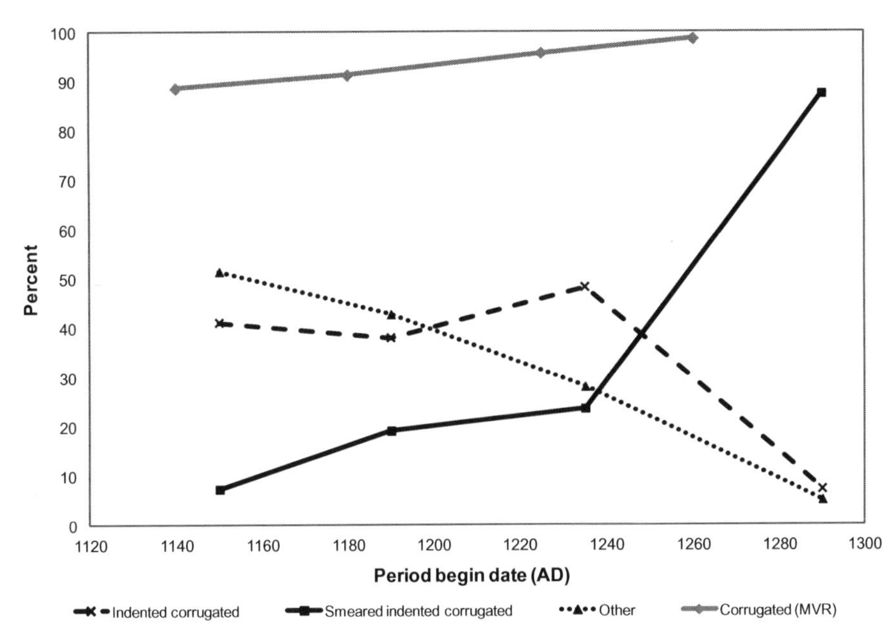

FIGURE 13.7. Utility ware assemblage change, Pajarito Plateau and Mesa Verde region. Sources: Pajarito Plateau, Orcutt 1999a: Table 3.5 (Periods 2–3 and 4–5 averaged); Mesa Verde region, Village Ecodynamics Project calibration data set (Ortman et al. 2007).

language. This suggests that among Mesa Verde people the corrugated surface treatment had symbolic connotations. Second, smeared-indented-corrugated surfaces replaced indented-corrugated surfaces remarkably fast: the smeared-indented-corrugated surface treatment only occurs on about 19 percent of utility wares deposited prior to AD 1235, but on 88 percent of utility wares deposited after AD 1290 (Figure 13.7). This implies that the people who constructed new villages and towns during the Late Coalition period adopted the practice of smearing indented-corrugated vessel surfaces at the same time. To the extent that these people were also migrants, it would imply that the practice of smearing was adopted as these migrants moved into the Tewa Basin.

Third, although indented-corrugated pottery was produced in the Tewa Basin during the Late Developmental period, it occurs mixed with plain-surfaced and neckbanded utility wares in sites dating between AD 1050 and 1250, whereas in the Mesa Verde region nearly all utility wares were corrugated during this period (Figure 13.7). Thus, even though the smearing technique was new, the pattern of change in the Tewa Basin, from a diversity of surface treatments to a single treatment, resulted in utility ware assemblages that exhibited comparable homogeneity to Mesa Verde region assemblages.

Finally, the advent of smeared-indented-corrugated pottery is difficult to explain on a functional basis. Why did potters bother to create indented-corrugated surfaces, only to partly obliterate them as soon as they were finished? And if smooth-surfaced cooking pots worked better than textured ones, why did production of smooth-surfaced pots decline over time, and why did potters bother to make indented-corrugated surfaces before smoothing them? It is difficult to account for these changes using materialist arguments, but it is not difficult to imagine a social motivation for Mesa Verde migrants to have begun smearing the surfaces of their cooking pots.

During the Pueblo Revolt (AD 1680–1692), Pueblo people consciously obliterated material symbols of Christianity and attempted to reinvent their society according to recollections of the prehispanic period (Hackett and Shelby 1942, I:ii–iii; Liebmann et al. 2005; Preucel 2000, 2002). It is not difficult to imagine a similar dynamic taking shape among Mesa Verde migrants, who would have recently chosen to leave their homeland behind. In this case, the smearing of indented-corrugated surfaces could have been invented by migrants to symbolize their break with the past and their embrace of a new society. On the other hand, it would be difficult to imagine a similar social dynamic taking shape if the Coalition period archaeological record reflected territorial expansion of a successful local society, and one would not expect smearing to have been adopted so uniformly if Late Coalition society were a product of immigration and ethnic coresidence.

If obliteration was socially motivated, however, why didn't Mesa Verde migrants just make cooking pots differently? Perhaps the reason had to do with the functional advantages of the earlier, indented-corrugated style. Studies of indented-corrugated cooking pottery show that, among other things, the increased exterior surface area created by this treatment improved cooking effectiveness by reducing the incidence of boilovers (Pierce 2005a:137–138). Thus, if a group of migrants were interested in "erasing" symbols of the society they had left behind, but wanted to maintain the functionality of the indented-corrugated surface, one solution would be to smear away the details of that surface. This would have lessened the visual correspondence of the vessel exterior to earlier cooking pots and baskets, but would have retained the increased exterior surface area and its functional benefits. Also, by smearing an indented-corrugated surface, potters would have not only expressed a break with the past, but also created subtle reminders of that past.[9] Viewers of smeared-indented-corrugated vessels would have been simultaneously reminded of their new society and the society they had left behind. Other explanations are certainly possible, but it is clear that changes in utility ware assemblages can at least be accommodated to the population movement hypothesis.

Santa Fe Black-on-White

The final element of Coalition period material culture I discuss here is Santa Fe Black-on-white pottery. In a recent study, Wilson (2008b) showed that several characteristic elements of the Mesa Verde design style, including thick-and-thin framing patterns and rim ticking, are practically nonexistent in Pajarito Plateau assemblages that would have been created by Mesa Verde migrants or their direct descendants under the population movement hypothesis. Wilson interprets these patterns, along with continuities in resource use (other than paint) between Kwahe'e and Santa Fe Black-on-white, as evidence that the latter type represents the continuation of a local tradition.

To make sense of the patterns identified by Wilson, it is necessary to first examine the spread of carbon paint technology in the Rio Grande region. The decorated pottery of Late Developmental Tewa Basin sites, known as Kwahe'e Black-on-white, is a thin-slipped or unslipped ware with poorly executed hatched and solid designs in mineral paint (McNutt 1969:11–12; Mera 1935: 5–6; Lang 1982:175–176; Wendorf and Reed 1955:141). Some researchers (e.g., Mera 1935:34; Wendorf and Reed 1955:141) have viewed the designs on Kwahe'e Black-on-white as poorly made local cognates of contemporary Chacoan wares, but pottery design styles and technologies were broadly distributed throughout the San Juan drainage during the Chacoan era, so Kwahe'e Black-on-white need not have derived from Chaco Canyon in particular. In fact, several researchers (Gladwin 1945:146; Kidder and Shepard 1936:597; Lang 1982:175; McNutt 1969: 104) have argued that Kwahe'e Black-on-white is more similar to Northern San Juan wares. Regardless, it is reasonable to view this type as having derived from pottery traditions somewhere in the San Juan drainage.[10]

Starting around AD 1200, a new type known as Santa Fe Black-on-white rapidly replaced Kwahe'e Black-on-white in the Tewa Basin (but not in the Taos Valley). Early Santa Fe Black-on-white retains the hard and thin blue-gray paste, sand temper, washy or absent slip, and general design style of Kwahe'e Black-on-white (Stubbs and Stallings 1953:48; Wendorf and Reed 1955:145; Wilson 2008b), but it is painted with a carbon-based rather than a mineral-based paint. Wilson (2008b) suggests that Santa Fe Black-on-white is a result of local potters changing their paint preference, and Mera (1935:11) and Lang (1982:176-177) view it as the product of interactions among adjacent local peoples outside the Northern Rio Grande.[11] As a result, most researchers have invoked diffusion as the mechanism behind its spread.[12]

Given its widespread distribution, diffusion must have been involved in the spread of Santa Fe Black-on-white to some extent (see Habicht-Mauche 1993: 19–20); however, two lines of evidence suggest migration was also involved in the spread of carbon-painted pottery to the Tewa Basin in particular. First, Table 13.1 tabulates the number of Tewa Basin sites at which the characteristic pottery type of each phase has been noted. The table also includes the number of sites for which the characteristic type of the previous phase is also noted. These data show that at more than 85 percent of the sites on which Santa Fe Black-on-white occurs, it is not mixed with Kwahe'e Black-on-white.[13] Thus, the shift from mineral-painted to carbon-painted pottery occurred simultaneously with the establishment of hundreds of new sites. In other words, most sites inhabited during the Early Coalition period were new sites established by people who had already adopted carbon paint, and there are very few sites at which the switch, reflected in a mixture of mineral-painted and carbon-painted sherds in associated trash, took place during the site occupation.

TABLE 13.1. Association of pottery types and settlement change in recorded sites

Phase	Begin Date (AD)	End Date (AD)	Index Type	Sites with Period Index Type	Sites with Previous Period Index Type	Proportion
Early Developmental	900	1050	Red Mesa B/W	23		
Late Developmental	1050	1200	Kwahe'e B/W	60	20	.333
Early Coalition	1200	1275	Santa Fe B/W	340	42	.124
Late Coalition	1275	1350	Wiyo B/W	182	153	.841
Early Classic	1350	1400	Biscuit A	134	88	.657
Middle Classic	1400	1450	Biscuit B	101	70	.693
Late Classic	1450	1500	Potsuwi'i Incised	38	29	.763

Second, Figure 13.8 graphs the proportion of carbon-painted sherds in well-dated assemblages of the Pajarito Plateau (from Orcutt 1999a: Table 3.5). I have also graphed the data presented in Table 13.1 on the same axes, labeling the proportion of sites occupied in each phase at which the index type of the previous phase is also present as an index of continuity in settlement. These data show that carbon-painted pottery rapidly replaced mineral-painted pottery in trash assemblages during the same period that hundreds of new settlements at which only carbon-painted pottery occurs were founded. To provide a point of contrast, Figure 13.8 also graphs the proportion of carbon-painted sherds in well-dated assemblages of bowl-rim sherds from central Mesa Verde region sites (from Ortman 2003: Table 13). The shift in technology from mineral- to carbon-based paints occurred much more gradually in the Mesa Verde region, is apparent in mixed assemblages from numerous sites, and was not complete by the time of the final depopulation. This marked difference in the pace of carbon-paint adoption in the two regions suggests that the change occurred among an in situ population in the Mesa Verde region, and coincident with population movement in the Tewa Basin (also see McNutt 1969:106–107).

These data suggest that Early Coalition colonists adopted the carbon-painted pottery technology of the western Jemez Mountains area as they moved onto the Pajarito Plateau. Does this mean the initial colonists themselves came from the Gallina or Jemez districts? Possibly, but for a number of reasons this is not a necessary conclusion. First, resources suitable for pottery making were similar on all sides of the Jemez Mountains and differed from resources traditionally used in the San Juan drainage, so one might expect colonists to have adopted a local pottery technology regardless of where they came from. Second, if these colonists came from the northwest, they would have come into contact with potters who made carbon-painted wares on the west side of the Jemez Mountains as well as potters who made mineral-painted wares in the Rio Grande Valley and

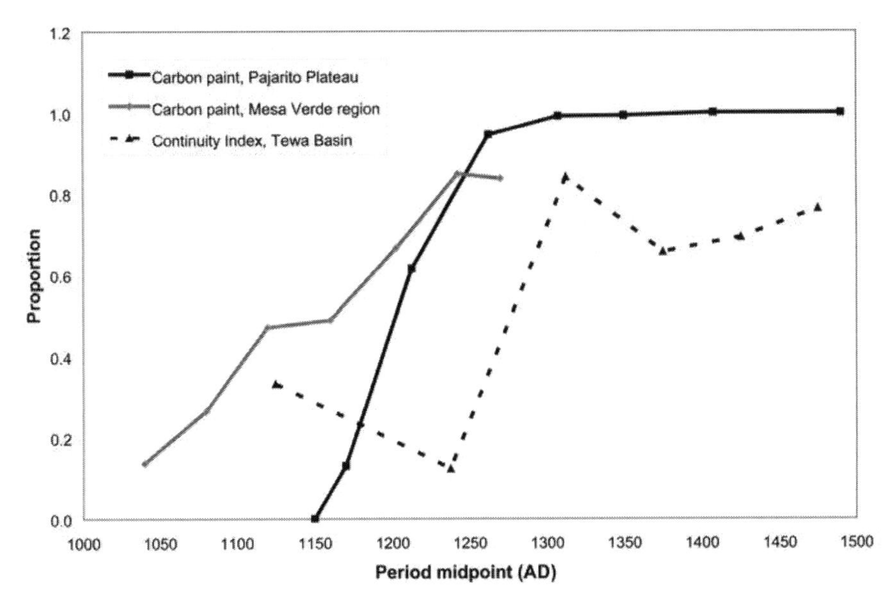

FIGURE 13.8. Carbon paint adoption in the Tewa Basin and Mesa Verde region. Sources: Pajarito Plateau, Orcutt 1999a: Table 3.5; Mesa Verde region, Ortman 2003: Table 13; continuity index is taken from Table 12.5.

its eastern tributaries. Third, by the early AD 1200s, most potters in the central Mesa Verde region had largely completed the shift to carbon paint, and thus carbon-paint technology would have been more familiar to them.

Finally, researchers have perceived some influence of Mesa Verde Black-on-white on the design style of both Gallina and Santa Fe Black-on-white, as evidenced by statements to this effect by Mera (1935:12) and Lang (1982:177).[14] These indications of Mesa Verde influence in early carbon-painted wares of the Jemez Mountains region are consistent with a scenario wherein local populations on the west side of the Jemez Mountains and early Mesa Verde migrants both contributed to the development of the relatively simple and perhaps anachronistic design style of Early Coalition Pajarito Plateau pottery known as Santa Fe Black-on-white. Then, the technology and design style created by this charter group was adopted by subsequent migrants from the Mesa Verde region.

As to why this might have occurred, Kohler and others (2004) demonstrate that Santa Fe Black-on-white designs from the Late Coalition Pajarito Plateau are surprisingly homogeneous and suggest social pressures favoring conformity are partly responsible. This finding raises the possibility that absence of the characteristic elaborations of the Mesa Verde design style may be due to potters adopting a relatively uniform, simple, and perhaps anachronistic design style as an emblem of social solidarity, and/or as a reaction against the society they had left behind. Oaxacan migrants to Teotihuacan continued to produce the characteristic pottery of their homeland centuries after it was no longer produced in Oaxaca as a positive commentary on their homeland identity (Spence 1992). In a mirror image, Mesa Verde migrants may have adopted a simpler and anachronistic design style as a negative commentary on the society they had recently chosen to leave behind.

A number of attributes of Coalition period material culture — including ceremonial rooms, wall construction techniques, smeared-indented-corrugated pottery, and Santa Fe Black-on-white design style — differ from Mesa Verde region practices in the direction of less elaboration or, perhaps more accurately, the disappearance, obliteration, or masking of elaborations that were characteristic of AD 1200s Mesa Verde material culture. Thus, the absence of continuity in design style between Mesa Verde Black-on-white and Santa Fe Black-on-white need not imply the absence of population movement. Rather, the degree to which the homeland style was expressed may have been influenced by migrants' perspectives on the society they had left behind, and by the degree to which they encountered alternatives in the destination area. I examine this possibility in greater detail in the final section of this chapter.

Summary

Many aspects of Early Coalition material culture — including ceremonial room architecture, community organization, and painted pottery assemblages — are less elaborate than both Pueblo III Mesa Verde region and Late Developmental Rio Grande material culture. In addition, Early Coalition sites exhibit patterns of domestic spatial organization that are found in both regions and exhibit evidence of continuity in cuisine and technological styles from the Mesa Verde region. Finally, Early Coalition society presents a mixture of Mesa Verde, Developmental Rio Grande, and totally new traits. The appearance of a complex of Mesa Verde traits in new sites established during the Early Coalition period, combined with a pattern of cultural simplification and hybridity in these sites, is consistent with a society formed through long-distance migration. In addition, the punctuated pattern of change is inconsistent with the model of in situ growth and territorial expansion, and the absence of site-unit intrusions is inconsistent with the model of immigration followed by ethnic coresidence.

Late Coalition Migration and Group Size

The fourth expectation for the destination area of a population movement is an accelerating pace and scale of in-migration over time. Because the Tewa Basin population increased geometrically during the Coalition period, and regional populations can increase in this manner as a result of intrinsic growth, it is difficult to distinguish increasing migration rates from in situ growth on the basis of population reconstructions alone. One would, however, expect an increasing pace of migration to be correlated with an increase in the scale of migrating groups in the case of population movement, and this should be reflected in increases in the sizes of new settlements across the period of in-migration.

Several lines of evidence suggest that the size of migrant groups did in fact increase during the Late Coalition period. First, Figure 12.7, discussed in the previous chapter, illustrates the distributions of initial populations for sites founded during the AD 1050–1200, 1200–1275, and 1275–1350 periods. These distributions show that settlements founded in the Tewa Basin prior to AD 1200 were almost entirely hamlet-sized and smaller; that many new settlements were village-sized in the Early Coalition period; and this trend intensified in the Late Coalition period, when some new settlements were town-sized. Figure 13.2 also illustrates the distribution of settlements inhabited in each of these periods. These maps show that during the Late Coalition many new villages and towns were founded in areas where Early Coalition populations were limited or nonexistent, including areas north of the Rio Grande–Rio Chama confluence and the foothills of the Sangre de Cristos, east of the Rio Grande. There is no evidence of population decline elsewhere in the Tewa Basin during this period, so there were no local small-site populations from which to derive these new large-site populations. It therefore appears that large groups of migrants either founded many Late Coalition villages and towns, or moved into them immediately upon arrival.

Second, it is clear that the scale of site planning, if not the actual scale of construction, increased over the course of the Coalition period. During the late AD 1200s a new class of village-sized settlement known as the plaza pueblo began to be constructed on the Pajarito Plateau and elsewhere (Kohler and Root 2004b:175–176; Snead 2008b; Steen 1977:13). These sites consist of a rectilinear arrangement of four surface room blocks surrounding a central plaza containing a kiva. In many such sites the western room block appears to have been taller than the others, and a second kiva is present to the east of the enclosed plaza area. The presence of continuous walls along one or more sides of the plaza at a few sites (Kohler and Root 2004b:211; Vierra et al. 2003:139–140) suggests that the scale of construction at plaza pueblos was at least at the room block level. Stratigraphic observations and construction sequence information also suggest that these sites were built within a short period of time. Finally, the 50 to 100 rooms in these sites suggest their populations were about 3 to 10 times larger than those of Early Coalition room-block sites. These data suggest that plaza pueblos, at minimum, reflect the aggregation of existing populations into larger settlements, and may also indicate an increase in the size of Late Coalition in-migrating groups.

Plaza pueblos have no antecedents in Late Developmental architecture, but they do exhibit formal parallels with great houses that were constructed in the Mesa Verde region between AD 1060 and 1140, and used well into the AD 1200s (see Ryan 2008; Figure 13.9). Snead (2008b:166) notes that plaza pueblos and great houses were constructed in similar settings: on ridge tops that would have commanded the local area and provided clear views of the horizon; however, Mesa Verde region great houses appear to have been the homes of community leaders and their families, whereas Late Coalition plaza pueblos were villages or community houses. Thus, just as Early Coalition period kivas functioned at a larger social scale than earlier pithouses and kivas, Late Coalition plaza pueblos may represent great houses for an entire community. Under this interpretation,

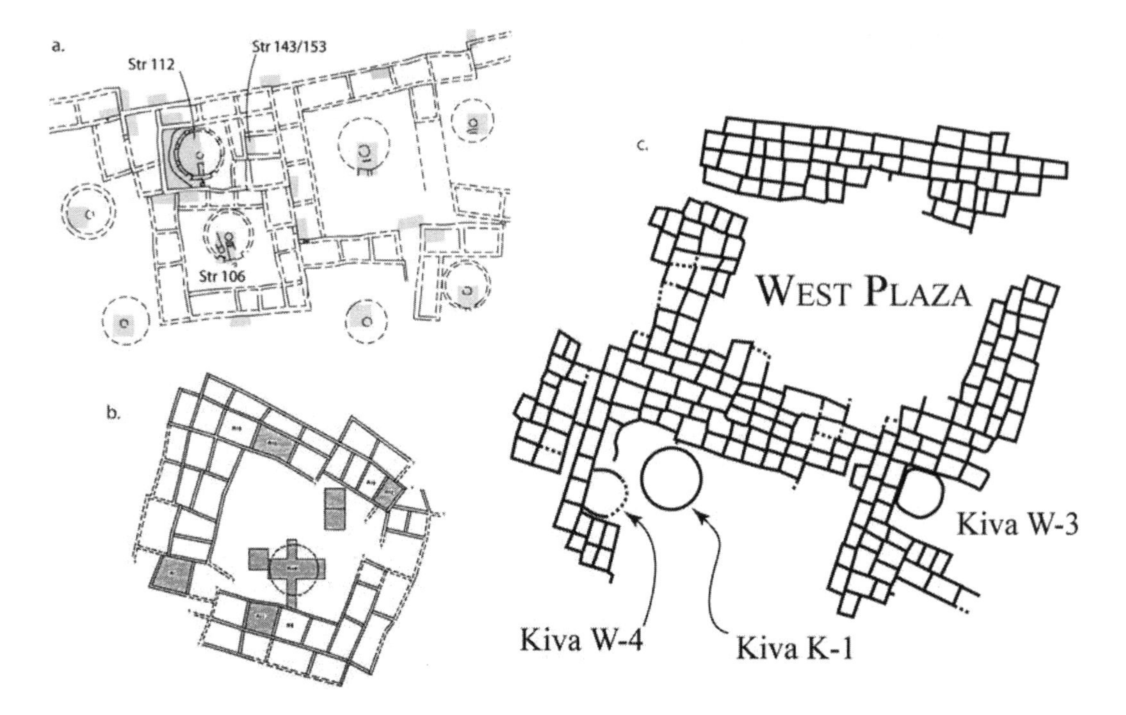

FIGURE 13.9. Mesa Verde great houses and Tewa Basin plaza pueblos: *a*, central portion of Block 100, Albert Porter Pueblo (© Crow Canyon Archaeological Center); *b*, Burnt Mesa Pueblo, Area 1 (courtesy of Washington State University); *c*, Tsama Pueblo, West Plaza (courtesy of Tom Windes). Sites are depicted at approximately the same scale (the Burnt Mesa kiva and Tsama Kiva W-4 are ca. 4.6 m in diameter, and Albert Porter Structure 112 is 4 m in diameter at the floor). North is up.

plaza pueblos represent a hybrid of locally developed and imported forms that were mapped onto social units in innovative ways. Notice also that, under this interpretation, continuities from the Mesa Verde region are more apparent in Late Coalition architecture than in Early Coalition architecture. This is not unexpected for the destination area of a population movement, for reasons discussed in the final section of this chapter.

Elsewhere in the Tewa Basin, villages constructed during the Late Coalition period appear to have been created by even larger groups than those who built the Pajarito plaza pueblos. For example, at Tsama, in the Chama District, a village of approximately 120 rooms was built surrounding one enclosed and one open plaza shortly after AD 1250 (Figure 13.9; also see below). Wall abutments suggest small suites of 4 to 6 rooms were the modal unit of construction, but most of the excavated rooms rested on sterile soil, indicating the village grew rapidly (Windes and McKenna 2006:236). During the same period, Pindi Pueblo, in the vicinity of Santa Fe, grew from an Early Coalition room-block site of some 40 rooms into a village of 175 rooms, also with one enclosed and one open plaza. Finally, Arroyo Hondo Pueblo grew even more explosively, from nothing to a town of more than 1,000 rooms in a span of only 15 years, AD 1315–1330

TABLE 13.2. Total momentary populations of sites by size class and phase

Phase	Dates (AD)	Houses and Hamlets (1–49)	Villages (50–499)	Towns (500+)	Total
Early Developmental	900–1050	1,644	105	0	1,749
Late Developmental	1050–1200	2,696	644	0	3,340
Early Coalition	1200–1275	3,173	4,045	473	7,691
Late Coalition	1275–1350	2,828	8,782	5,489	17,099

Notes: Data extracted from Table 4.8. Numbers in parentheses are population ranges of sites in size class.

(Creamer 1993:152–153). Wall abutment patterns indicate construction events on the order of 50 to 100 rooms were common at Arroyo Hondo during this period (Creamer 1993:140–147). Surface evidence from many other sites suggests that numerous villages and towns developed in a similar fashion throughout the Tewa Basin during the Late Coalition period (e.g., Beal 1987; Marshall and Walt 2007; Snead 1995). At minimum, these data suggest that Late Coalition villages and towns were planned as residences for hundreds of people. It is difficult to reconcile this scale of design and construction with a purely household-scale of movement. It rather appears that larger groups moved together into sites that had either been prepared for their arrival by existing residents or were constructed by the group upon arrival.

Finally, the third line of evidence which suggests the pace and scale of in-migration increased over time is that the small-site population of the Tewa Basin did not increase during the Late Coalition period. Table 13.2 extracts the total momentary population estimates for sites of each size class from the population history developed in Chapter 4. These data show that population growth during the Late Coalition period is reflected primarily in dramatic increases in the number of people residing in villages and towns, with a relatively constant small-site population. It appears that, by and large, early migrants moved into houses and hamlets, whereas later migrants moved directly into villages and towns. Thus, the larger scale and faster pace of construction at new sites, combined with the lack of evidence for increases in small-site populations, implies an accelerating pace and scale of in-migration over the course of the Coalition period—a pattern consistent with expectations for the destination area of a population movement.

Homeland Continuities and Destination Context

The final expectation for the destination area of a population movement is that expressions of homeland material culture should vary in accordance with conditions experienced by migrants in the destination area, and over the course of the movement. I have already discussed aspects of the social context experienced by early colonists on the Pajarito Plateau and argued that the material culture of Early Coalition sites derives from this context. The social contexts experienced by subsequent, Late Coalition migrants can be characterized as falling into one of two configurations. When Late Coalition migrants moved to areas that had already been settled, such as the Pajarito Plateau or the Santa Fe District, they would have encountered charter groups that had already established local ways of doing things. Because later migrants came from the same homeland as many of the people in these charter groups, and the desire of later migrants to join these groups was probably involved in their decision to migrate, one would expect later arrivals in these areas to have adopted material practices established by the charter groups.

In contrast, when Late Coalition migrants moved to areas that had not been settled previously, the migrants would not have had as much contact with charter groups. In such cases, one might expect stronger expressions of homeland material culture for two reasons. First, later arrivals probably came in larger groups and thus would have formed communities where a higher proportion of residents already knew each other, and where pressures to assimilate to local material traditions would have been correspondingly reduced. Second, in the same way one would expect early migrants to have had little to lose by leaving the homeland, one might also expect later migrants to have had a more positive opinion of the society they had left behind. Thus, one might expect stronger traces of homeland material culture in areas settled relatively late in the migration process.

The best portions of the Tewa Basin in which to look for such traces are the Chama and the Santa Cruz districts. The Chama District appears to have been uninhabited prior to the Late Coalition period (Beal 1987), and although the Santa Cruz District was inhabited during the Developmental period, it did not experience significant in-migration during the Early Coalition period (Marshall and Walt 2007). Thus, Late Coalition migrants to these areas would have experienced very different conditions than those who joined existing communities on the Pajarito Plateau or in the Santa Fe District. In the following pages I discuss two areas where material emblems of late AD 1200s Mesa Verde society were expressed more strongly in Late Coalition communities of the Chama and Santa Cruz districts than they were in the Pajarito or Santa Fe districts.

Place-Making Practices

The first line of evidence comes from place-making practices. Contemporary Tewa landscape concepts and practices are well known due to Alfonso Ortiz's (1969:18–25) thorough description of the cultural landscape surrounding Ohkay Owingeh. In this model, the village lies in the center of the world and is surrounded by a series of shrines, low hills, and finally mountains that radiate out toward cardinal points on the horizon (also see Anschuetz et al. 2002: Chap. 3; Fowles 2004: Chap. 8; Ortman 2008a). The cardinal mountains are adorned with keyhole-shaped arrangements of stones with openings facing inward and downhill, toward one or more Tewa villages (Curtis 1926; Douglass 1915). These directional shrines are spiritual power conduits that gather blessings from that world region and channel them through the opening toward the village. In the past, similar shrines were also constructed on cardinal hills surrounding villages, with their openings also facing inward (Ortiz n.d.:8). The best-documented example of such a system is the group of four directional shrines surrounding Poshuouinge, a Classic period village in the Chama district (Jeançon 1923:70–73).

In present-day Tewa communities the actual center of the world, known as the "earth-mother earth-navel middle place," is represented by an upright stone in the center of one of the plazas (Ortiz 1969:21). In prehispanic times the world center was represented by a "world-quarter" or "earth-navel" (*nan-si-pu* 'earth-belly base') shrine that was larger than directional shrines and had an opening facing east rather than toward the pueblo per se (Hewett 1938:55; Jeançon 1923: 70–72; Nelson 1914:70–471; Wendorf 1953:53). I have visited world-quarter shrines adjacent to the Classic period Tewa pueblos of Tsiping, Te'ewi, Ku, Tsama, Poshuouinge, Howiri, Hupobi, and Posiouinge. In all cases, the earth-navel is located on the top of a hill or low rise within a kilometer or two of the pueblo. And unlike directional shrines, which are located on the side of the landform facing a village, earth-navel shrines are located on the very top of the landform, and thus address all directions equally. There are many other types of shrines surrounding ancestral Tewa villages, including grinding slicks, cupule boulders, stone piles, and single upright stones (Anschuetz 1998: Chap. 8, 2005; Fowles 2004b: Chap. 8; Ortiz 1969:18–25; Snead 2008a: Chap. 4), but for reasons that will become apparent, the discussion here will focus on directional shrines and world-quarter shrines.[15]

According to Spanish accounts, both directional and world-quarter shrines were constructed and used within villages during the Pueblo Revolt period.[16] Both types of shrines were also clearly constructed in association with earlier, Classic period villages and towns; in fact, an earth-navel shrine is present at nearly every Classic period ancestral Tewa pueblo. It is difficult, however, to tell whether such features were constructed in association with Coalition period villages. Shrines are rarely associated with artifacts, so in order to date them, one must rely on the periods of occupation of the pueblo they relate to. A shrine could have been constructed at any time during the occupation of its associated pueblo, so the only way to determine when directional and world-quarter shrines first appeared in the Tewa Basin is to identify the longest-abandoned pueblos around which such shrines occur. Another issue is that researchers have only recently begun to pay attention to shrines, and thus it is unknown whether directional and/or world-quarter shrines occur around many ancestral villages and towns. The patchwork of land ownership around many ancestral sites also makes it difficult for researchers to survey the surrounding hinterlands, and shrines are relatively easy to destroy, so it is possible that many are no longer identifiable.

With these caveats in mind, a number of examples suggest that directional and world-quarter shrines were first constructed in association with Late Coalition villages. The most compelling case was recently documented surrounding LA158, also known as Wiyo Pueblo.[17] A 12 m diameter cobblestone ring with an opening facing east occurs about 500 m southeast of this pueblo, a clear example of a world-quarter shrine (Marshall and Walt 2007:C-2). A directional shrine consisting of two stone rings, the larger of which is 2 m in diameter, also occurs on the north slope of a knoll about 1.5 km south of the world-quarter shrine. These stone rings face north, toward the world-quarter shrine and Wiyo Pueblo. The knoll also lies on a cardinal east-west line running between Tsímáyôp'in ('Superior flaking stone mountain' [Chimayo]), the eastern cardinal hill of several present-day Tewa pueblos, and K'usänp'in ('Stone man mountain' [North Truchas Peak]), the eastern cardinal mountain (Harrington 1916:341–342; Ortiz 1969:19; Marshall and Walt 2007:V-12-15).

The settlement that these shrines relate to is remembered in Tewa oral tradition (*Wiyoˀówînkeyi* 'Great gap pueblo village ruin') and is the largest ancestral Tewa settlement in the Santa Cruz watershed, with an estimated 1,000 rooms in three major architectural blocks (Marshall and Walt 2007:A-33-34).[18] The pottery assemblage of all three blocks is dominated by smeared-indented-corrugated utility ware, transitional Santa Fe–Wiyo Black-on-white, Wiyo Black-on-white, and transitional Wiyo–Biscuit A sherds (Marshall and Walt 2007: A-36). The assemblage suggests that the settlement was founded after AD 1250 and abandoned prior to 1375. In addition, the absence of significant Early Coalition populations in the Santa Cruz watershed (Marshall and Walt 2007) suggests that this site complex was founded by large social groups from beyond the local area. The evidence from this locality thus provides strong evidence that world-quarter and directional shrines were constructed around at least one Late Coalition community that was occupied by Tewa speakers, and was founded by migrants who brought these place-making practices with them.

A second example of a possible world-quarter shrine was identified by Anschuetz (1998: Fig. 7.13, App. I) surrounding Maestas Pueblo, a Late Coalition village in the Rio del Oso, a western tributary of the lower Rio Chama (Figure 13.10). The surface pottery assemblage from this site consists primarily of Santa Fe Black-on-white and transitional Santa Fe–Wiyo Black-on-white, with some Wiyo Black-on-white and traces of Biscuit A (Anschuetz 1998: App. E). Thus, the site appears to have had an occupational history similar to Wiyo Pueblo's. The shrine itself consists of two concentric rock circles, the larger of which is 7 m in diameter, located approximately 25 m northeast of the house mound, on a projection of the mesa on which the site occurs. This example is not as clear as Wiyo's but may represent an early version of a world-quarter shrine. Anschuetz (1998) dates the earliest phase of occupation in the Rio del Oso to the mid to late AD 1200s, and suggests the "Santa Fe phase" settlement was created

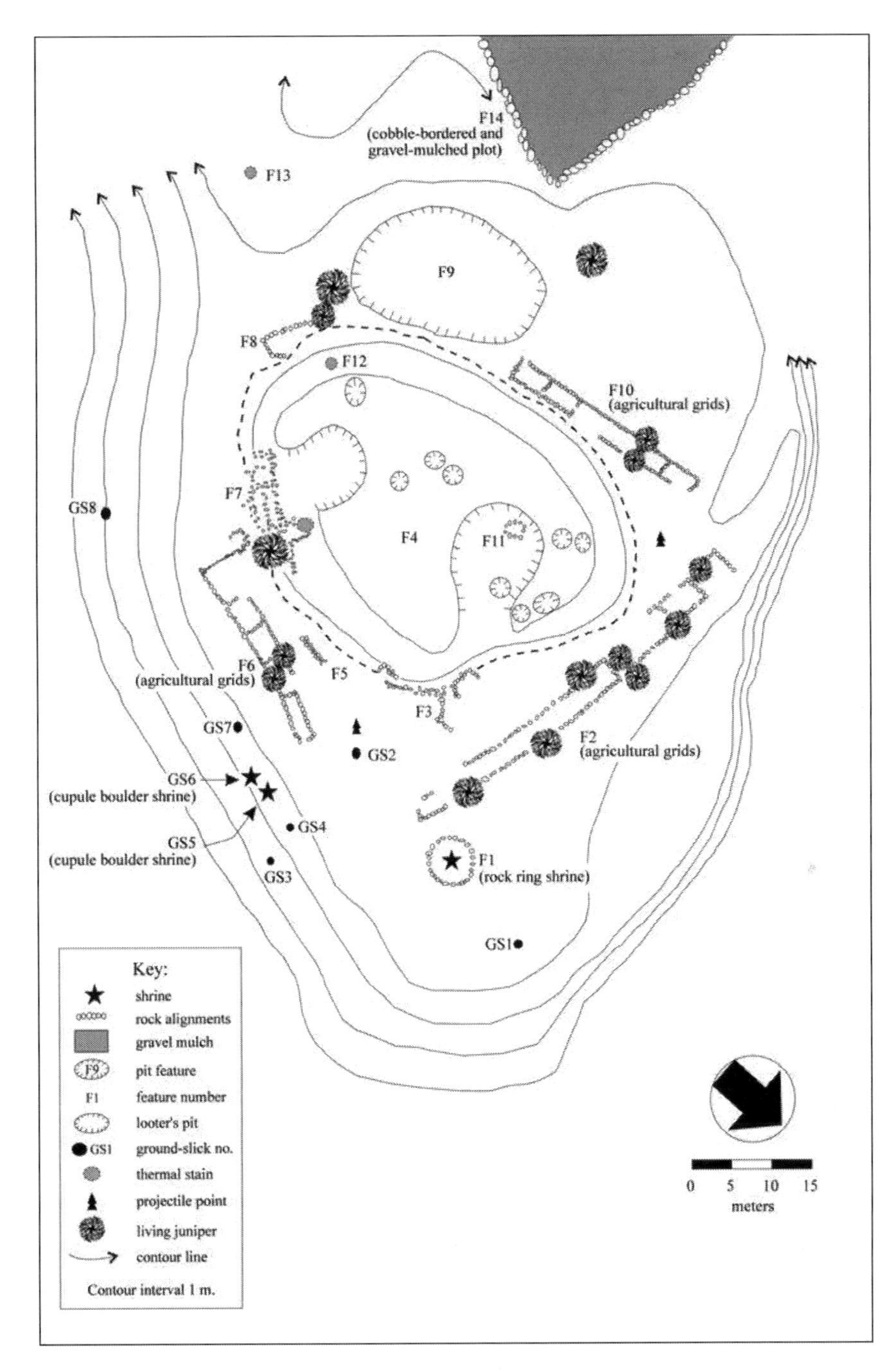

FIGURE 13.10. Maestas Pueblo, a Late Coalition village in the Rio del Oso drainage. Note the rock ring shrine (F1) northeast of the house mound (F4). After Anschuetz 1998: Figure 7.13, courtesy of Kurt Anschuetz.

by migrants. It therefore appears the Maestas Pueblo shrine was constructed adjacent to one of the first settlements constructed in the Rio del Oso, and thus the practice and its associated landscape conceptions must have come with the initial colonists.

A third example is from the Burnt Corn community in the Galisteo Basin. This area lies outside the Tewa Basin but was inhabited by Southern Tewa speakers in the early historic period and appears to have been settled during the

Coalition period by same biological population that colonized the Tewa Basin (see Chapter 5). Snead (2008a:95) reports a 12 m diameter circle of piled stone with an opening to the east, on top of a low summit 300 m north of Burnt Corn Pueblo. Tree-ring dates from excavations at the pueblo indicate the site was constructed between AD 1290 and 1302, and the associated pottery indicates it was abandoned prior to AD 1320 (Snead 2004). Thus, a clear earth-navel shrine was constructed in association with one of the first-constructed and first-abandoned settlements in the Galisteo Basin.

There are a few additional examples of world-quarter shrines that could date from the Late Coalition period, but their dating is less secure because they occur in association with sites occupied during the Classic period as well. One example lies on a hill about a kilometer southeast of Arroyo Hondo Pueblo (Creamer 1993: 103, 109). The shrine consists of a doughnut-shaped, low mound of medium to large unshaped boulders about 30 cm high at its highest point and 5 to 7 m in diameter on the inside. Since Arroyo Hondo was occupied between AD 1315 and 1410 (Creamer 1993:134, 152–153), the shrine could date to any point in this span. A second example is a damaged, partly buried, and partly eroded ring of cobbles on top of a low rise 150 m east of the East Plaza at Tsama (Duwe 2008). This shrine could have been constructed at any time between AD 1250 and 1600 based on pottery and tree-ring dates from the pueblo (see below). A third is a well-preserved world-quarter shrine adjacent to Tsiping, a Late Coalition and Early Classic village.

Finally, it is important to note cases where features that exhibit some characteristics of directional or world-quarter shrines have been documented in association with ancestral sites of non-Tewa peoples. If one considers only the general characteristics of these features, one could argue that stone circles occur around ancestral villages of many different Pueblo peoples and thus have no bearing on Tewa origins; however, the details of these cases suggest the shrines either expressed different landscape concepts or reflect the presence of a Tewa group in the community.

In one case, Snead (2008a:101) describes a system of four "community shrines" on a north-south alignment that passes through the fifteenth-century ancestral Keres site of Los Aguayes. This site was likely inhabited by Keres speakers because: (1) Tetilla Peak, about 4 km south-southeast of Los Aguayes, figures prominently in Cochiti oral tradition and is the location of a major Cochiti shrine (Snead 2008a:100); (2) the dual plaza layout of this site is very similar to that of Kotyiti, a Cochiti village constructed during the Pueblo Revolt (Snead and Preucel 1999); and (3) Harrington (1916:459) did not record a Tewa name for Los Aguayes, and interpreted the Tewa name for Tetilla Peak (*Wawagip'in* 'Breastlike Mountain') as a calque from Spanish. Several of the shrines at Los Aguayes are C-shaped and open toward the east, but their arrangement along a precise north-south line suggests a strict cardinal orientation rather than an attempt to define and gather blessings from cardinal landforms and regions, as Tewa directional shrines do. Snead and Preucel (1999:183) also indicate that an ancient trail follows this alignment north of the village. This association of roads and shrines with the cardinal directions is reflected in the Keres worldview (White 1942:80–94, 1960, 1962:110–115) but is not emphasized in Tewa worldview (Ortiz 1969: 18–25).

In a second case, Fowles (2004b:522–527) identifies two "large bermed circle shrine[s]" approximately 1.5 km north-northwest and 1.1 km south-southeast of Pot Creek Pueblo, an ancestral Northern Tiwa village in the Taos District. The southern shrine appears to have an opening facing toward Pot Creek Pueblo, and the northern example consists of two stone circles, one complete and the other C-shaped with an opening to the east. A variety of additional shrine types, many of which are commonly found around ancestral Tewa villages (especially grinding slicks, cupule boulders, and upright stones), also occur around Pot Creek Pueblo but have not been identified at other sites in the Taos District (Fowles 2004b:519–550). Tree-ring dates, construction sequences, and pottery from Pot Creek Pueblo suggest that it was constructed and occupied between AD 1260 and 1320 (Fowles 2004b:429). Thus, the shrines surrounding Pot Creek Pueblo likely date from the same period as the examples from Wiyo, Maestas, and Burnt Corn pueblos. Fowles (2004b:547) interprets these patterns as evidence that a group of Tewa migrants lived with local Tiwa people at Pot Creek Pueblo. This interpretation is reflected in Taos and Picuris oral tradition (Fowles 2004b:407–409) and is consistent with the analysis of shared phonetic innovations in Chapter 6 which suggests a period of contact-induced change between the Northern Tewa and Northern Tiwa dialects following a period of isolation. Fowles's interpretation also implies that the place-making practices associated with Classic period Tewa pueblos were already present by the Late Coalition period.

To summarize, current evidence suggests that shrines with the characteristics of Tewa directional and world-quarter shrines were constructed around at least some Late Coalition ancestral Tewa sites. The clearest cases, from the Chama and Santa Cruz districts and the Galisteo Basin, occur in areas that were not home to significant Early Coalition populations, and thus occur around settlements founded by groups of Late Coalition migrants to these areas. This suggests that the founders of these communities brought these place-making practices and associated concepts with them, which in turn raises the question of whether precursors of world-quarter shrines and directional shrines occur around thirteenth-century Mesa Verde region villages. It turns out that they do.

Circular, stacked-rock features are common at thirteenth-century Mesa Verde region villages (Fetterman and Honeycutt 1987:107; Rohn 1977:113), and several examples adjacent to canyon-rim villages appear to be precursors of world-quarter shrines. At Yellow Jacket Pueblo, for example, a C-shaped shrine 5 m in diameter and with an east opening occurs on the east edge of the mesa on which the village lies (Ferguson and Rohn 1986:129). An identical feature occurs in an identical setting at Coalbed Village, in Montezuma Canyon. At the Hedley

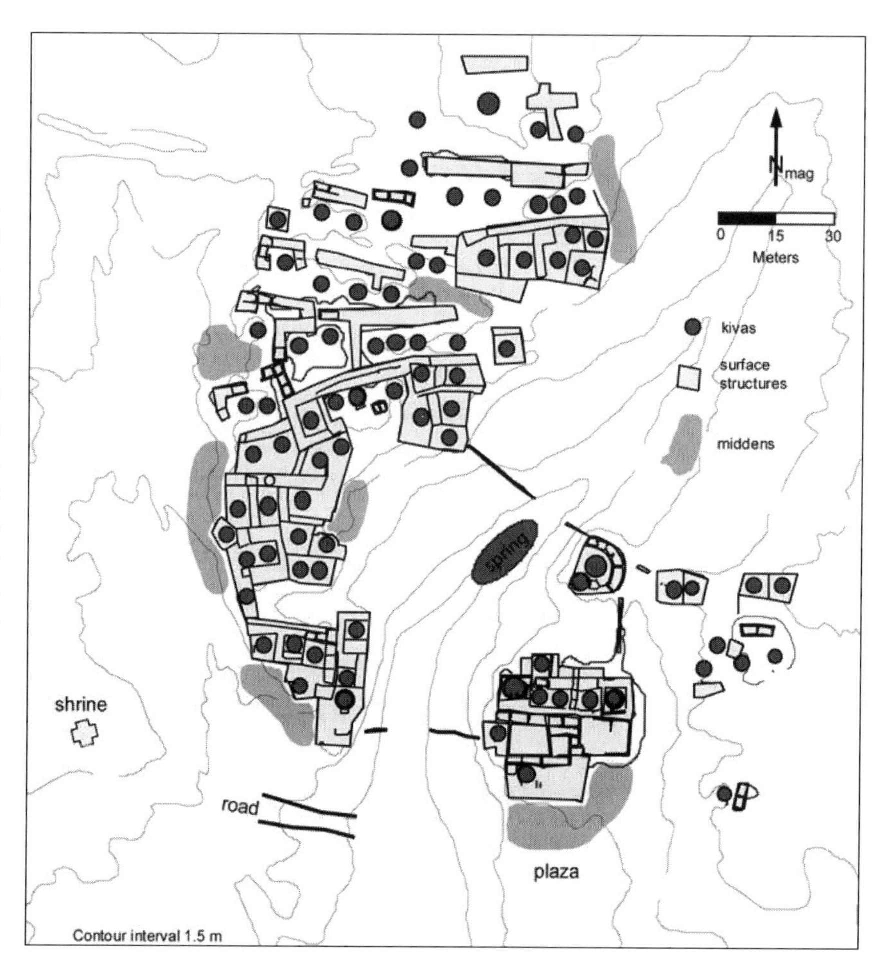

FIGURE 13.11. Hedley Main Ruin (42SA22760), a canyon-rim village in southeast Utah. Note the McElmo style great house embedded within the southeastern room block, and the alignment between the bedrock plaza south of the great house, a road segment, and a cross-shaped shrine on an adjacent knoll. Also note the D-shaped building on the east side of the drainage, and the roundish plaza on the west side, with the spring in between.

Main Ruin there is a 6 m diameter, cross-shaped enclosure with the arms oriented toward the cardinal directions on a knoll west of the village (Figure 13.11). Finally, at Sand Canyon Pueblo there is a 5 m diameter, circular shrine on the crest of a hill aligned with Ute Mountain to the south of the village, from which location one has a panoramic view of distant landforms in all directions.[19]

In addition, I have identified a complete directional shrine system surrounding Castle Rock Pueblo, a thirteenth-century village in the Mesa Verde region (Ortman 2008a). Each of the four C-shaped directional shrines in this system is approximately 5 m in diameter and is situated in a significant location that relates Castle Rock Pueblo to the surrounding landscape and prominent topographic features. All four features are located on the slopes of low ridges or hills that face Castle Rock Pueblo and also offer views of distant landforms behind topographic breaks on the near horizon. Three have openings that face Castle Rock Pueblo with a line-of-sight view, one has a due east orientation with it, and three have cardinal orientations with respect to distant landforms. This system is nearly identical to the more recent directional shrine systems at Poshuouinge and Wiyo.

It is therefore clear that shrines relating villages to the cardinal directions and to distant landforms were common around thirteenth-century villages in the Mesa Verde region. This is not to suggest that the more recent Tewa Basin shrines are exact replicas of the earlier Mesa Verde examples. The Mesa Verde region precursors of earth-navel shrines, for example, are generally smaller than Tewa Basin examples, vary more in their form and arrangement, and have not been identified adjacent to sites abandoned prior to the late AD 1200s. In addition, I have only identified a complete directional shrine system surrounding a single village thus far, and searches around other sites suggest directional shrine systems do not exist around all thirteenth-century villages. These bits of evidence suggest that the practices, beliefs, and discourses associated with thirteenth-century Mesa Verde shrines were relatively new and not yet standardized (see Ortman 2008a for an extended discussion). Nevertheless, the obvious continuity in shrine systems surrounding thirteenth-century Mesa Verde region villages, fourteenth-century ancestral Tewa villages, and modern Tewa pueblos makes a strong case that the place-making practices and discourses maintained by present-day Tewas have direct antecedents in the Mesa Verde region. The place-making practices of ancestral Tewa communities thus exhibit greater continuity with Mesa Verde region precursors than is apparent in domestic architecture and pottery assemblages. The fact that these continuities are most apparent in areas that were settled relatively late in the Coalition period is also consistent with the expectation that material emblems of the homeland society should be expressed most clearly in these areas.

Pottery Style

Earlier in this chapter I noted that elements of pottery decoration most emblematic of Mesa Verde Black-on-white are not characteristic of Coalition period assemblages from the Pajarito Plateau. I also suggested a possible reason for this may be that Early Coalition potters consciously adopted a simpler and perhaps anachronistic design style as a form of negative commentary on the society they had left behind, and subsequent migrants to the Pajarito Plateau followed the lead of these charter groups. Under this scenario one might expect the Mesa Verde design style to have been expressed more strongly in areas that were settled by larger migrant groups during the Late Coalition period, because in these situations groups of potters would have arrived together and would not have entered communities where there was pressure to conform to an established local style. In addition, these potters might have had a less negative view of the homeland society than earlier migrants who established charter groups elsewhere. In the final analysis of this chapter I present new pottery assemblage and design attribute data from Tsama Pueblo to evaluate this expectation.

Tsama (see Figure 10.5) is a major ancestral Tewa settlement on a terrace above the north bank of the lower Rio Chama. First recorded by Harrington (1916:147) as Tsámaˀówînkeyi ('Wrestling pueblo village ruin'), the site consists of three plaza areas that were constructed and occupied in sequence. The West

Plaza consists of low, single-story mounds of melted adobe arranged to form one enclosed and one open plaza; the Middle Plaza, two detached but taller adobe mounds with some embedded cobbles; and the East Plaza, a massive quadrangle of melted, multistory adobe architecture enclosing a plaza larger than a football field, with outlines of cobble wall foundations still visible on top of the mound. Based on surface pottery, Mera (1934) suggested that the Middle Plaza and East Plaza were occupied from the beginning of the fourteenth century to the beginning of the sixteenth. Greenlee (1933) also excavated several rooms in the East Plaza and confirmed that it was occupied during the Late Classic period.

In 1970 Florence Hawley Ellis directed field school excavations at Tsama (see Windes and McKenna 2006). Her work revealed that the West Plaza was a village of approximately 120 rooms surrounding one enclosed and one open plaza. Its layout was similar to that of other villages constructed in the Northern Rio Grande during the AD 1200s, including Pindi in the Santa Fe area (Stubbs and Stallings 1953) and Forked Lightning in the Pecos District (Kidder 1958:5–46). Wall abutments in the shovel-stripped West Plaza suggest small suites of 4 to 6 rooms were the modal unit of construction. Most of the excavated rooms rest on sterile soil, suggesting that the village grew rapidly (Windes and McKenna 2006: 236).

The most exciting discovery of the 1970 field school was Kiva W-4, a burned and trash-filled, D-shaped ceremonial room in the southwestern corner of the West Plaza (Figure 13.12). This room was constructed using a combination of coursed adobe and refuse supported by a jacal framework covered with plaster. It was also oriented east and contained a subrectangular adobe-rimmed fire pit, deflector, and ash-pit complex on the floor, with a vent tunnel opening to the east (Windes and McKenna 2006:247–249). Overall, the architecture of Kiva W-4 is identical to other D-shaped, aboveground ceremonial rooms in Coalition period sites, such as Kivas E and F at Pindi (Stubbs and Stallings 1953:39–45) and Corner Kivas 3, 4 and 5 at Forked Lightning (Kidder 1958:35–42). A cutting date of 1231r and a noncutting date of 1249vv suggest Kiva W-4 was constructed during the middle decades of the AD 1200s (Windes and McKenna 2006: Table 2). This dating is consistent with noncutting dates of 1269 and 1270 from a D-shaped ceremonial room at Pindi (Kiva E) (Smiley et al. 1953:14). The next earliest tree-ring-dated Chama District sites are Palisade Ruin (AD 1313–1314) and Riana Ruin (AD 1335–1350), both of which postdate AD 1300 (Peckham 1981; Smiley et al. 1953:36–37). Thus Kiva W-4 and the associated West Plaza appear to represent the earliest tree-ring-dated occupation currently known for the Chama District.

Windes and McKenna (2006: Table 3) present field school pottery tabulations that suggest Wiyo Black-on-white and Biscuit A were the dominant pottery types in the West Plaza rooms and kivas. These types suggest a more recent period of occupation than is suggested by the architecture and tree-ring dates. To better understand the West Plaza pottery assemblage, and especially the

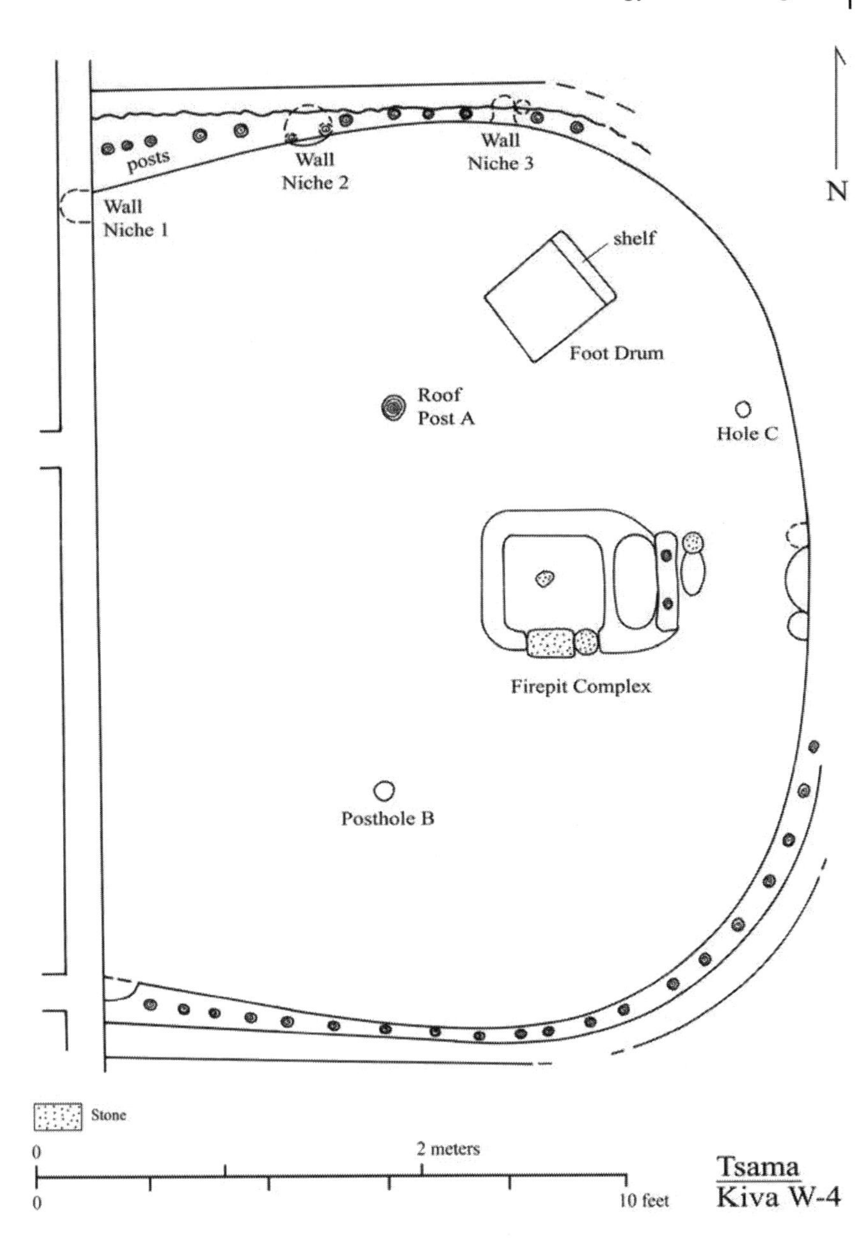

FIGURE 13.12. Kiva W-4, a Coalition period ceremonial room from the West Plaza at Tsama (Windes and McKenna 2006: Fig. 10). (Courtesy of Tom Windes.)

trash that filled Kiva W-4 after it burned, the Crow Canyon Archaeological Center laboratory cataloged and reanalyzed the field school surface collections from each plaza area and the assemblage from Kiva W-4 in the fall of 2008.[20] The results, presented in Table 13.3, greatly clarify the pueblo's occupational history.

Two aspects of these results are noteworthy. First, surface assemblages clearly suggest an occupational sequence from west to east that corresponds with patterns in surface architecture. The West Plaza appears earliest based on high frequencies of smeared-indented-corrugated utility wares and a mixture of Santa Fe Black-on-white, Wiyo Black-on-white, and Biscuit ware. This assemblage appears to date to the Late Coalition and Early Classic periods. The

TABLE 13.3. Pottery analysis results, Tsama Pueblo (LA908/909)

	Kiva W-4 (AD 1231r–1249vv)		West Plaza (AD 1250–1400)		Middle Plaza (AD 1350–1500)		East Plaza (AD 1400–1600)	
Type	n	%	n	%	n	%	n	%
Utility Ware								
Rio Grande Plain Gray	24	1.4	133	12.8	10	10.4	148	21.1
Clapboard Corrugated	95	5.5	37	3.6	2	2.1	8	1.1
Incised Gray, not further specified	—	—	—	—	—	—	1	.1
Plain Corrugated	15	.9	8	.8	7	7.3	—	—
Indented Corrugated	67	3.9	62	6.0	3	3.1	7	1.0
Smeared-indented-corrugated	1,500	86.6	741	71.2	11	11.5	90	12.8
Washboard Corrugated	10	.6	12	1.2	—	—	11	1.6
Sapawe Micaceous Washboard	3	.2	4	.4	6	6.3	47	6.7
Cordova Micaceous Ribbed	5	.3	—	—	—	—	1	.1
Cundiyo Micaceous Slipped	10	.6	1	.1	5	5.2	10	1.4
Micaceous Slipped	—	—	2	.2	5	5.2	75	10.7
Micaceous Tempered	3	.2	25	2.4	23	24.0	86	12.3
Potsuwi'i Incised	—	—	16	1.5	24	25.0	217	31.0
Subtotal	1,732	100	1,041	100	96	100	701	100
Matte Paint Ware								
Kwahe'e Black-on-white	—	—	—	—	—	—	1	.0
Santa Fe Black-on-white	597	63.5	433	19.2	167	9.5	84	3.0
Pindi Black-on-white	62	6.6	109	4.8	4	.2	6	.2
Santa Fe / Wiyo Black-on-white	81	8.6	89	3.9	47	2.7	53	1.9
Wiyo Black-on-white	102	10.9	357	15.8	148	8.4	96	3.4
Galisteo Black-on-white	5	.5	4	.2	—	—	1	.0
Poge Black-on-white	—	—	—	—	1	.1	—	—
Biscuit A	34	3.6	632	28.0	519	29.5	293	10.5
Biscuit B	3	.3	331	14.7	549	31.2	1569	56.4
Biscuit C	—	—	1	.0	1	.1	6	.2
Biscuit ware, not further specified	6	.6	216	9.6	157	8.9	389	14.0
Tsankawi Black-on-Cream	3	.3	47	2.1	156	8.9	184	6.6
Rio Grande White ware, not Biscuit	22	2.3	40	1.8	8	.5	52	1.9

TABLE 13.3. (cont'd.) Pottery analysis results, Tsama Pueblo (LA908/909)

	KIVA W-4 (AD 1231R–1249VV)		WEST PLAZA (AD 1250–1400)		MIDDLE PLAZA (AD 1350–1500)		EAST PLAZA (AD 1400–1600)	
TYPE	n	%	n	%	n	%	n	%
Rio Grande White ware	23	2.4	—	—	3	.2	44	1.6
Vadito Black-on-white	—	—	—	—	—	—	1	.0
Vallecitos Black-on-white	2	.2	—	—	—	—	3	.1
Chupadero Black-on-white	—	—	—	—	—	—	1	.0
Subtotal	940	100	2,259	100	1,760	100	2,783	100
Glaze Ware								
Glaze A, undifferentiated	—	—	—	—	—	—	5	4.1
Glaze C, undifferentiated	—	—	1	20.0	—	—	4	3.3
Glaze D, undifferentiated	—	—	—	—	—	—	1	.8
Glaze E, undifferentiated	—	—	—	—	—	—	3	2.4
Glaze-on-red	1	100.0	1	20.0	31	86.1	83	67.5
Glaze-on-yellow	—	—	2	40.0	4	11.1	8	6.5
Glaze Polychrome	—	—	—	—	—	—	14	11.4
Glaze ware, undifferentiated	—	—	1	20.0	1	2.8	5	4.1
Subtotal	1	100	5	100	36	100	123	100
Total	2,673		3,305		1,892		3,607	

Middle Plaza assemblage is somewhat later. It contains much more micaceous utility ware and Potsuwi'i Incised, equal amounts of Biscuit A and B, and some Tsankawi Black-on-cream, thus suggesting occupation from the Early Classic into the Late Classic period. Finally, the East Plaza assemblage is dominated by Potsuwi'i Incised, Biscuit B, and Tsankawi Black-on-cream, and also includes sherds of Glaze A through E. This suggests that the East Plaza was occupied from the Middle Classic into the Contact period.[21]

Second, the assemblage from Kiva W-4 appears to reflect the early years of occupation in the West Plaza. It consists primarily of smeared-indented-corrugated and Santa Fe Black-on-white, with lesser amounts of transitional Santa Fe/Wiyo and Wiyo Black-on-white, and traces of Biscuit A. Also notable is the occurrence of Pindi Black-on-white, a variety of Santa Fe Black-on-white distinguished on the basis of coarse, pumiceous ash temper that dates to AD 1300–1350 (Stubbs and Stallings 1953:50). The Kiva W-4 assemblage thus appears to represent a pure Late Coalition occupation dating to the late AD 1200s and early AD 1300s, consistent with the tree-ring dates from this structure. The relatively short time span reflected in this assemblage also suggests that the West Plaza surface collection reflects both a longer overall occupation of this area and contamination from the later Middle Plaza occupation.

In sum, the West Plaza at Tsama represents a village of 120 rooms that was constructed rapidly around AD 1250–1275 in an area that had not been previously inhabited. The architecture and layout of this village are very similar to other villages constructed during this same period elsewhere in the Northern Rio Grande. Also, Kiva W-4, which was constructed early in the pueblo's history, burned and was filled with trash from the early West Plaza occupation. The pottery assemblage from Kiva W-4 thus represents the earliest well-dated assemblage currently available from the Chama District.

If the doubling of population in the Late Coalition Tewa Basin was due to accelerating in-migration from the Mesa Verde region, one would expect the initial West Plaza population to have consisted primarily of migrants from that region, and for most of the broken vessels deposited in Kiva W-4 to have been made by them. The typological profile of this assemblage — which focuses on paste, temper, and surface treatment in distinguishing types — clearly indicates that these early inhabitants made vessels using local techniques and raw materials; however, elements of the Mesa Verde design style are much more common in this assemblage than they are in contemporaneous Pajarito Plateau assemblages (Figure 13.13). To document this pattern, an assistant and I subjected the bowl rim sherds from Kiva W-4 and the surface collections from each plaza to an analysis that I developed to record Mesa Verde pottery designs (see Ortman 2000b). This system focuses on features of painted pottery designs that derive from details of woven objects from Mesa Verde sites. As discussed in Chapter 10, Mesa Verde region potters imagined pottery vessels as woven objects and expressed this conceptualization in numerous features of painted decoration. So if the founding population of Tsama consisted of Mesa Verde migrants who established a village in which the influence of charter groups was low, one might expect the earliest painted pottery produced in this village to have expressed the same weaving-inspired imagery.

Table 13.4 presents the results of this analysis and compares them with Mesa Verde region sites dating between AD 1180 and 1280.[22] Each column represents bowl rim sherds of all types from a group of sites dating to the given time period or from a specific provenience at Tsama. Each row represents a design attribute numbered according to its analogous feature number in my previous study of Mesa Verde pottery designs (Ortman 2000b: Table 3). I have slightly modified the attribute names in this table to make them easier to interpret without going into detail on the source imagery of each.[23] Finally, the percentages reflect the number of vessels in each group on which the given attribute is present, divided by the number of vessels in each group on which the given attribute is definitely present or absent.

These results suggest several points. First, these data confirm that the percentages of vessels on which thick and thin framing lines and/or rim ticks occur

FIGURE 13.13. Bowl rims from the floor of Kiva W-4, Tsama Pueblo. Nine of the 34 rims in this image exhibit thick and thin framing lines.

are much higher in the Kiva W-4 and West Plaza assemblages than they are on contemporary assemblages from the Pajarito Plateau. Figure 13.14 illustrates this finding by comparing the frequencies of these attributes from the AD 1260–1280 Mesa Verde region and Tsama Kiva W-4 with Coalition period Pajarito Plateau sites studied by Wilson (2008b) and Ruscavage-Barz (1999).[24] It is obvious that by these two measures Late Coalition potters at Tsama painted emblematic features of the Mesa Verde design style much more frequently than did Pajarito Plateau potters.

Second, it is clear that a wide range of design attributes on bowls from Kiva W-4 and the West Plaza occur in similar proportions on bowls from AD 1200s Mesa Verde region sites. These attributes include exterior banded designs, rim ticking, Xs and zigzags painted on the rim, thick and thin framing lines, ticks between framing lines, plain-weave (squared) tapestry band designs, twill-weave (diagonal) tapestry band designs, colored twill-plaited basket designs, and twill-weave textures (background hachure). In short, the weaving imagery that appears most often on AD 1200s Mesa Verde region pottery appears in similar frequencies on Late Coalition pottery at Tsama. These findings are consistent with the expectation that material emblems of the Mesa Verde homeland should be most apparent in areas of the Tewa Basin settled late in the process by larger groups of migrants. This evidence, in turn, makes what is perhaps the strongest

TABLE 13.4. Design attribute data for the Mesa Verde region and Tsama Pueblo

Attribute[a]	Mesa Verde Region (AD) 1180–1225[b]	1225–1260[c]	1260–1280[d]	Tsama Pueblo (LA908/909) Kiva W-4	West Plaza	Middle Plaza	East Plaza
Exterior							
Corrugation or basket impression (13)	.4	.7	.3	.5	.0	.0	.0
Exterior band design (17)	2.0	8.1	11.1	3.0	10.6	34.9	61.8
Rim decoration							
Line painted along rim (1)	2.9	2.0	.1	.6	1.9	.8	.0
Rim ticks (2)	46.5	46.1	42.3	31.8	36.5	54.8	57.0
Patterned ticks (3)	10.3	9.9	8.2	.6	1.1	.4	.9
Xs, zig-zags on rim (4)	4.2	4.4	8.0	1.2	6.8	10.7	23.4
Ticks and zig-zags on rim (2 & 4)	.0	.0	.0	.0	2.6	5.4	14.8
Other rim decoration (26)	.4	.5	.7	.0	.0	3.4	5.7
Framing patterns							
Thin framing lines (5)	3.7	5.6	6.1	20.1	19.5	12.6	9.8
Multiple thick framing lines (6)	13.0	6.9	7.0	1.5	2.0	.9	.4
Thick and thin framing lines (7)	21.5	34.4	34.2	24.7	24.8	21.7	5.7
Ticks between framing lines (8)	5.4	4.3	4.2	4.6	.8	3.0	.8
Other framing pattern (27)	2.3	1.7	2.1	.0	.0	.0	.0
Interior designs							
Checkerboard (14)	3.8	2.1	2.1	8.0	3.3	1.6	.0
Coiled basketry design (9)	9.1	8.3	5.5	21.2	11.7	3.3	5.5
Framing band design (10)	6.3	9.8	9.0	3.5	1.7	4.9	.0
Narrow loom design (18)	.8	.9	1.4	18.6	10.0	9.8	5.5
Plain-weave band (19)	8.3	7.3	5.8	8.8	8.3	1.6	5.5
Twill-weave band (22)	22.6	24.6	26.5	28.3	16.7	9.8	.0
Twill-plaited texture design (15)	1.5	3.4	1.1	.9	6.7	3.3	.0
Twill-plaited color pattern (16)	10.5	10.2	8.7	4.4	6.7	3.3	3.6
Twill-weave texture (21)	18.1	14.5	18.1	19.5	16.7	4.9	.0
Angled twill-weave design (23)	2.3	3.5	2.8	.0	.0	.0	.0
Nonweaving pattern (28)	2.6	2.8	4.3	6.2	10.0	21.3	36.4
Number of vessels scored[e]	266	623	1,671	214	302	289	401

Notes: Data are percentages calculated by dividing the number of sherds on which attribute is present by the number of sherds on which the attribute is absent. Indeterminate cases are not included.

[a] Numbers in parentheses refer to the analogous feature number in Ortman 2000a: Table 3. Feature names have been modified to make them more self-explanatory.

[b] Phase 5 (AD 1180–1230) in Ortman 2000a: Table 6.

[c] Average of Phase 6 (AD 1230–1250) and Phase 7 (AD 1250–1260) in Ortman 2000a: Table 6.

[d] Phase 8 (AD 1260–1280) in Ortman 2000a: Table 6.

[e] Sample sizes control for conjoining sherds and sherds from the same vessel.

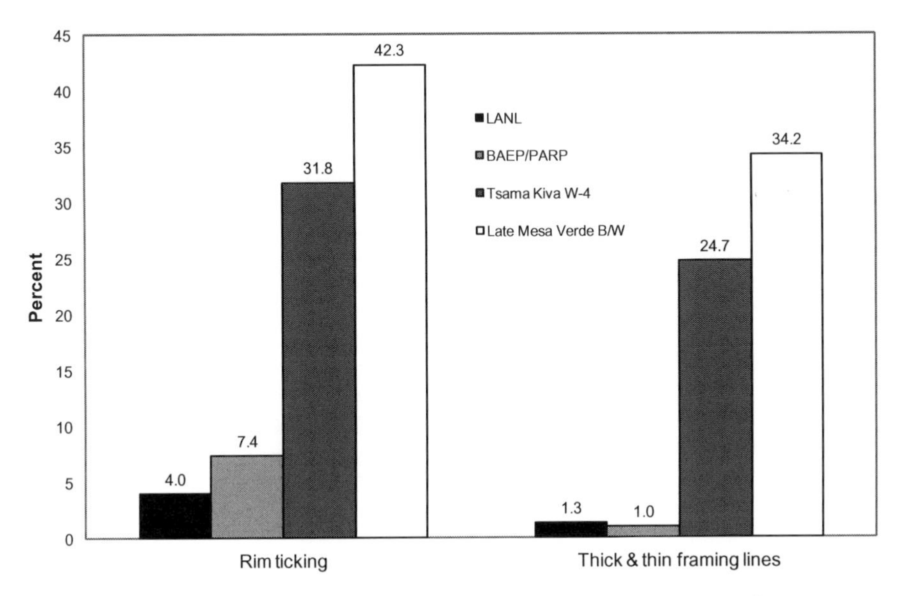

FIGURE 13.14. Attribute percentages for the Pajarito Plateau, Tsama, and Mesa Verde region. Sources: Los Alamos National Laboratory (LANL), Wilson 2008: Tables 58.18, 58.19; Bandelier Archaeological Excavation Project/Pajarito Archaeological Research Project (BAEP/PARP), Ruscavage-Barz 1999; Tsama Kiva W-4, Table 13.4; Late Mesa Verde Black-on-white, Table 13.4, AD 1260–1280.

possible case on the basis of material culture continuities that ancestral Tewa culture was created primarily by Mesa Verde migrants.

Third, expressions of weaving imagery changed in various ways over the history of occupation at Tsama. Figures 13.15 and 13.16 illustrate these trends by tracing attribute frequencies across the six samples in Table 13.4. These data show, for example, that rim ticking and zigzag designs on the rim increased in popularity over the history of occupation at Tsama. In fact, on many Biscuit ware rims both ticking and zigzag designs occur — the former on the rim itself, and the latter on the interior surface of the fillet. Also, the frequency of thick and thin framing patterns on the inside surface of bowls declined over time, but this was offset by dramatic increases in their presence on bowl exteriors, as reflected in rising frequencies of exterior band designs. Finally, interior designs that expressed weaving imagery declined over time and were replaced by patterns that either combine elements from different weaving methods in incoherent ways or do not use weaving imagery at all.

Another aspect of this change is not captured by these data but is obvious to one who has studied thousands of Mesa Verde black-on-white vessels: rim decorations and framing patterns appear to have been executed in an increasingly stereotyped way over time (Figure 13.17). In late Mesa Verde region sites such as Sand Canyon Pueblo, rim ticks occur as dots, dashes, and slashes in a wide range of patterns, and framing patterns involving thick lines, thin lines, and tick marks exhibit a huge range of variation. At Tsama, in contrast, a few relatively simple

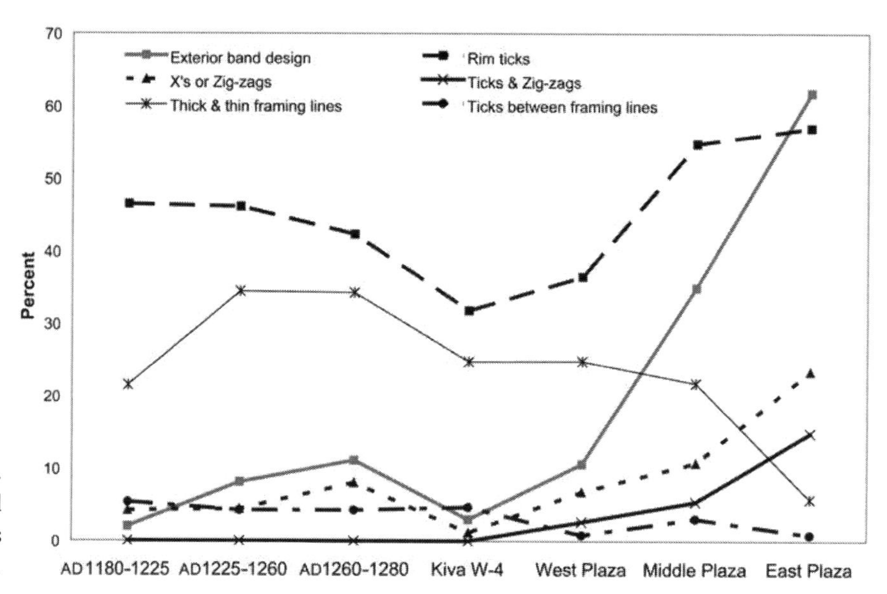

FIGURE 13.15. Exterior, rim, and framing attributes through time.

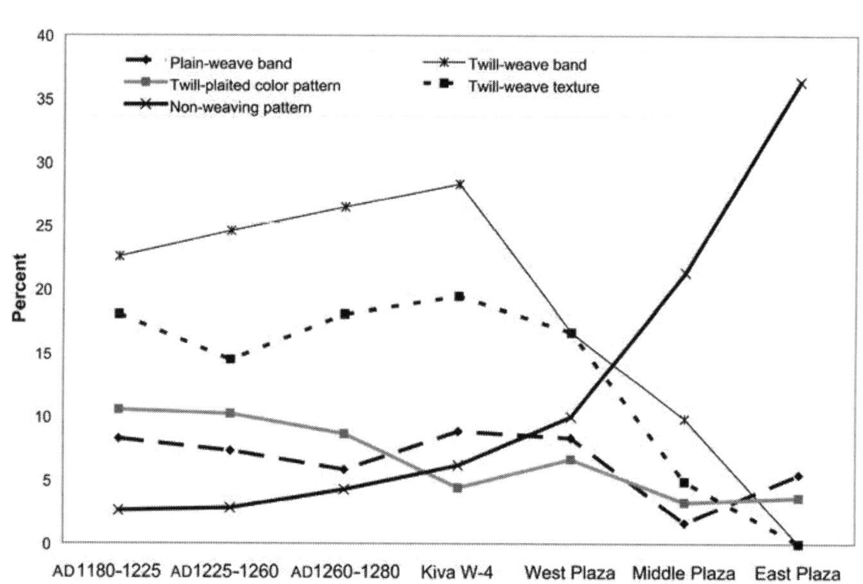

FIGURE 13.16. Interior design attributes through time.

rim decorations and framing patterns were painted very routinely over a long period of time. This suggests that unlike Mesa Verde potters who creatively manipulated weaving imagery to create a variety of rim decorations and framing patterns, Tsama potters painted these embellishments as a matter of convention. This in turn suggests the retention of certain iconic forms of the older decorative tradition, but a loss of the original conceptual basis for these forms. Tsama potters never stopped painting elements of the Mesa Verde style, but over time these elements appear to have become emblems of Tewa identity and heritage, and were no longer involved in creative expression. Thus, rim decorations and framing patterns became fossilized expressions of a dead metaphor, parallel to

FIGURE 13.17. Mesa Verde Black-on-white (*top*) and Biscuit B (*bottom*). Note consistent weaving imagery and creative rim decoration in the earlier vessel, and fragmented weaving imagery with stereotyped rim decoration and framing on the later vessel. (Top photo by David Grimes © Crow Canyon Archaeological Center; bottom photo MIAC Cat. # 21445/11 Bandelier Black-on-Cream (Biscuit B) ca. 1400–1550 Museum of Indian Arts and Culture/ Laboratory of Anthropology, Department of Cultural Affairs, www.miaclab.org. Photography by David McNeece.)

the continued unreflective use of *natˀú* (lit. "clay-baskets") to refer to pottery in the Tewa language.

Forging Tewa Culture

In this chapter I have examined the archaeological record of the Coalition period Tewa Basin to evaluate whether it is most consistent with population movement from the Mesa Verde region, expansion of the local population, or immigration followed by ethnic coresidence. A recapitulation of the major findings of this analysis follows.

Early Coalition population growth in the Tewa Basin was due almost exclusively to settlement of the Pajarito Plateau, and the period of initial colonization of this area corresponds in time with the development of strong material push factors in the Mesa Verde region, the most likely homeland of the colonists. These early settlers pursued a direct precipitation farming strategy and raised turkeys for meat. Both practices were well established in the Mesa Verde region prior to AD 1200, but were not characteristic of the Late Developmental Tewa Basin.

A few pioneers who settled the southern Pajarito Plateau constructed kivas that combine architectural traits of both the San Juan and Northern Rio Grande architectural traditions. Subsequent Pajarito colonists adopted architectural forms that were largely local in derivation. These architectural forms were less elaborate than Mesa Verde forms, but they reflect patterns of domestic spatial organization that were common to both regions. Early Pajarito communities consisted of loose clusters of farmsteads situated so as to facilitate communal agricultural labor, but with no central villages or public architecture. These characteristics are common in pioneer societies created through long-distance colonization.

Several material culture innovations including carbon-painted pottery, slab metates, full-grooved axes, the raising of turkeys for food, and birdbone artifacts were all introduced simultaneously with the construction of hundreds of new sites in the Early Coalition period. All of these innovations are characteristic of pre-AD 1200 Mesa Verde material culture, but none are characteristic of Developmental Rio Grande material culture. Whereas these innovations appeared one at a time during the occupations of sites in the Mesa Verde region, they appeared all at once, and largely in new sites, in the Tewa Basin. Also, Late Developmental material culture bears a closer resemblance to AD 1200s Taos Valley material culture than it does to Tewa Basin material culture of the same period. This is apparent in the continued production of incised utility ware, mineral-painted pottery, decorated jars, trough metates, and the absence of turkey husbandry in the Taos Valley.

Changes in utility ware assemblages during the Coalition period involved the addition of smearing to indented-corrugated surfaces and the loss of other surface treatments. These changes resulted in utility ware assemblages that were comparably homogeneous to earlier, Mesa Verde region assemblages. One possible explanation for the rapid replacement of all other surface treatments by smeared-indented-corrugated treatments during the mid-AD 1200s is that migrants obliterated the characteristic appearance of homeland cooking pots as a negative commentary on their homeland society, even as they maintained the differential surface area of the traditional treatment.

Carbon-painted pottery was adopted simultaneously with the establishment of hundreds of new sites in the Tewa Basin during the Early Coalition period. The relative scarcity of sites at which the transition from mineral to carbon paint is observable in the form of mixed assemblages suggests that in many areas the spread of Santa Fe Black-on-white was due to the movement of people who had already adopted a carbon-paint technology elsewhere.

Over the course of the Coalition period the distribution of initial site sizes changed from one dominated by small sites to one where most new sites rapidly grew to village or town size. The scale of construction events also increased, suggesting that most Late Coalition settlements were planned and built to house larger migrating groups. In addition, stability in the number of people residing in small sites combined with robust growth in large-site populations suggests an increasing pace and scale of in-migration over the course of the Coalition period.

Late Coalition plaza pueblos were constructed to house larger social groups than Early Coalition room-block sites. This new settlement form does not have antecedents in earlier Tewa Basin architecture, but it may have antecedents in Mesa Verde region great house architecture. If so, it may be appropriate to view plaza pueblo architecture as resulting from a mapping of earlier great house architecture onto the community writ large.

The place-making practices of Classic period ancestral Tewa communities, especially the construction of world-quarter and directional shrines, are first evident around Late Coalition villages and towns in the Tewa Basin. Both practices have clear and direct antecedents in the thirteenth-century Mesa Verde region. Finally, characteristic rim decorations and framing patterns of the Mesa Verde style of pottery decoration do not occur in Coalition period assemblages of the Pajarito Plateau, but the Mesa Verde style is thoroughly expressed on locally made vessels from Tsama Pueblo, the earliest well-dated occupation in the Chama District.

These findings are all consistent with expectations for the destination area of a population movement. First, the timing of initial colonization of the Pajarito Plateau by people who brought a complex of intrusive traits corresponds to the development of strong material push factors in the central Mesa Verde region. Second, the subsistence economy of these initial colonists was more similar to the Mesa Verde region subsistence economy than it was to the Developmental Rio Grande subsistence economy. Third, several new material culture traits arrived as a package in hundreds of new settlements established during the Early Coalition period. Early Coalition material culture is also simplified with respect to Mesa Verde material culture; exhibits continuity with Mesa Verde practices in cuisine, domestic spatial organization and technological style; and mixes Late Developmental, Mesa Verde, and totally new traits. In addition, it appears that the pattern of change — characterized by the conspicuous absence, inversion, or obliteration of many characteristic Mesa Verde traits — suggests an overt negative commentary on the homeland society on the part of migrant groups. Fourth, there is evidence for an increasing pace of in-migration and an increasing size of migrating groups over time. Finally, material emblems of Mesa Verde society were expressed most strongly in areas settled later in the migration process by larger social groups.[25]

These findings define a pattern of change in the Coalition period archaeological record that is characteristic of other well-known cases of population movement (e.g., Rouse 1986) but is inconsistent on several counts with expected patterns for an expanding local society or a society experiencing immigration followed by ethnic coresidence. Thus, the archaeological record appears most consistent with the hypothesis that is also most strongly supported by studies of population, biological variation, phonetic innovations, reconstructed vocabulary, place-names and place-lore, oral tradition, conceptual metaphors in language and material culture, and the archaeological record of depopulation in the Mesa Verde region.

Notes

1. For example, only two small clusters of sites with Kwahe'e Black-on-white, and lacking Santa Fe Black-on-white, occur on lands administered by Los Alamos National Laboratory (Vierra et al. 2006:190); no ancestral Pueblo habitations with assemblages lacking Santa Fe Black-on-white are known for Bandelier National Monument; and only a single cluster of five small habitations is known for the AD 1150–1190 period within the monument (Ruscavage-Barz 1999:95). In addition, Anschuetz (1998) found no evidence for Late Developmental occupation of the Rio del Oso, a western tributary of the Rio Chama at the northeastern edge of the Jemez Mountains.
2. As argued in Chapter 4, the fact that Early Coalition settlement of the Pajarito represents a new population center, as opposed to an overflow of population from areas settled during the preceeding Developmental period, also argues against alternative interpretations of these patterns.
3. One aspect of the Early Coalition subsistence economy that does not exhibit continuity with that of the Mesa Verde region is the hunting and consumption of artiodactyls. Deer and antelope bones are common in Late Developmental (Jelinek 1969) and Early Coalition sites (Kohler and Root 2004a:122–123; Schmidt 2007; Trierweiler 1990), but are in fact quite rare in AD 1200s Mesa Verde region sites (Driver 2002:154). This suggests that early inhabitants of the Pajarito Plateau hunted deer and ate deer meat much more often than contemporaneous populations of the Mesa Verde region. Although this difference is real, the rare occurrence of artiodactyl remains in Mesa Verde region sites is likely a result of overhunting rather than a cultural proscription (Badenhorst and Driver 2009; Kohler et al. 2007:100), and indeed the availability of large game may have been an additional attractive feature of the Pajarito Plateau for people who could no longer easily obtain such game.
4. Interestingly, the early example at Tesuque By-Pass is paired with an oversized kiva instead of a small residential pit structure, and thus the site overall may presage later Tewa Basin architectural patterns.
5. The point of this discussion is not to suggest that Coalition period architectural forms originated in the Mesa Verde region, but to suggest that these elements would not have seemed especially foreign to Mesa Verde migrants.
6. For example, Ruscavage-Barz (1999:170–172) notes parallels between early Pajarito Plateau communities and Kofyar farming communities studied by Glenn Davis Stone (1996). The Kofyar communities were created by the initial settlers of an agricultural frontier several days' walk from their homeland. The settlement pattern consisted of loose clusters of small farmsteads separated by areas of unsettled territory, so as to facilitate communal agricultural work. Early Coalition Pajarito Plateau communities mirror this pattern precisely.
7. The following paragraphs follow the line of reasoning developed by Matson and Magne (2007:6–7) for their study of Athapaskan migrations in British Columbia, which they label "the parallel direct historical approach." The idea is that population movement is indicated when there is a marked change in the material culture of one region while continuity from the previous period prevails in an adjacent region.
8. This pattern conforms to the model of Rio Grande prehistory suggested by the linguistic evidence presented in Chapters 6 and 7; namely, that the earliest inhabitants of the

Northern Rio Grande region, including the Taos District and Tewa Basin, spoke Tiwa, and this dialect continuum was later broken into northern and southern groups by in-migrating Tewa speakers who absorbed the original, Tiwa-speaking population of the Tewa Basin during the Coalition period.

9. This scenario could also account for the change in coil application method from outside to inside, noted by Hensler and Blinman (2002) on some smeared-indented-corrugated sherds.
10. Derivation of Kwahe'e Black-on-white from the Upper San Juan would be most consistent with the linguistic evidence reviewed in Chapters 6–10, which suggests that the Kiowa-Tanoan homeland was in the Northern San Juan; that the early Kiowa-Tanoan dialect chain included dialects ancestral to Kiowa, Jemez, Tewa, and Tiwa, in that order across the landscape; and that Developmental inhabitants of the Rio Grande spoke Tiwa.

    Lakatos (2007) suggests that initial settlement of the Tewa Basin was from the south rather than the north. There are sites that predate AD 900 along the Rio Grande south of the Tewa Basin, but earlier sites also occur in the San Juan drainage to the north and west. In addition, Fowles (2004a:208–234) argues that occupation of the Taos Plateau began in the north and spread southward over time. Finally, recent excavations suggest that the Middle to Upper San Juan is a plausible source for at least a portion of early Northern Rio Grande populations. For example, excavations at Piedra phase sites such as LA78533 (Sesler 2002) and LA82977 (Hovezak 2002), in the Cedar Hill area north of Aztec, have uncovered round, east-facing pit structures with four-post roofing systems and circular, adobe-rimmed hearths and ash pits that would seem to provide plausible prototypes for Developmental Tewa Basin pit structures. The artifact assemblages at these sites are characterized by mixtures of Piedra and Red Mesa style vessels decorated using mineral paint, neckbanded and plain utility wares, trough metates, and the near absence of turkey bones, and thus appear consistent with this possibility. These sites are well dated to AD 885–910 and thus immediately predate the earliest occupations of the Tewa Basin and Taos Valley (McNutt 1969:70). In addition, these sites were part of substantial communities that burned shortly after AD 900, with subsequent depopulation of the area, and thus represent populations that plausibly made long-distance moves at that time (Wilshusen and Wilson 1995). Finally, as discussed in Chapter 5, I found that the most closely related population to the Late Developmental Tewa Basin population is from the Piedra District, and that ancestral Tiwa populations appear to be affiliated with the Totah population. For all these reasons, it may prove productive to invest more research effort into connections between Piedra phase communities of the Upper San Juan and Developmental communities of the Northern Rio Grande.
11. For example, Mera (1935:11) and Lang (1982:176–177) suggest that Santa Fe Black-on-white originated from the fusion of Kwahe'e Black-on-white and Gallina Black-on-white along the Rio Puerco of the East and the southwestern slopes of the Jemez Mountains. According to their model, the new carbon-painted ware spread rapidly from this area across the southern slopes of the Jemez Mountains to the southeastern Pajarito Plateau, and then to the remainder of the Tewa and Galisteo basins.
12. For example, Wendorf and Reed (1955:145) argued: "It seems unlikely that this [the spread of Santa Fe Black-on-white] was caused by the movement to this area of any significant numbers of new migrants, since there are no evident accompanying changes in other aspects of the Rio Grande Anasazi culture which could be attributed to a western source." And for Lang (1982:177): "Major probable factors in the

acceptance of carbon paint and its rapid spread, through the Jemez, Pajarito, Santa Fe, and Española Districts between 1200 and 1250, were the presence of a carbon vehicle in indigenous mineral paint and the scarcity of iron paint raw material in the region, as well as the energy demands of processing some forms of mineral paint. I believe it was simply more efficient to switch fully to carbon when the technology became available." Finally, Hensler and Blinman (2002) argue that it would have been advantageous for Northern Rio Grande potters to adopt carbon paint once they became aware of it, because carbon paint will fuse to the clay body at a lower temperature than mineral paint, and the ash-derived clays of the Northern Rio Grande tend to overfire at the temperatures needed to fuse mineral paint. Thus, adoption of carbon paint would have resulted in fewer overfired and poorly decorated pots. It would have also paved the way for development of carbon-painted Biscuit wares during the Classic period.

13. It is possible to construct a table similar to Table 13.1 using data from all sites in the Rio Tesuque drainage compiled by Lang (1995:28–30). See Ortman (2009:522–523, n. 118) for a discussion of these data.
14. Mera (1935:12) noted that a factor in the development of Santa Fe Black-on-white was "an influence, first noticed in late Gallina times, that was derived, either directly or indirectly, from a Mesa Verde source. Coincidentally with the move down the Rio Puerco, this influence may be seen to be gaining in intensity but it is principally confined to the matter of design though there appear to be but few atempts actually to copy." Lang also noted this influence on both types. With regard to Gallina Black-on-white Lang (1982:177) noted: "The design system is primarily rooted in types that directly precede Gallina, i.e., Piedra, Arboles, and Bancos. However, strong design ties to Mancos and McElmo Black-on-white of the Mesa Verde are obvious in rim bands of parallel horizontal lines, some with ticked rims, broad line chevrons, hourglass figures, dot fillers, and hatching and cross-hatching, as well as general line work." With regard to Santa Fe Black-on-white Lang (1982:178) noted: "The McElmo and Mesa Verde designs appearing in both Santa Fe and Vallecitos Black-on-white prior to 1250 are associated with the gradual abandonment of the Mesa Verde area and the resulting movement into the Chaco Basin and Rio Puerco of the east between about AD 1200 and 1220."
15. Grinding slicks and pecked cupule boulders are commonly found in association with Late Coalition and Classic period sites in the Tewa Basin (see Anshuetz 1998, 2005). These features have not been noted in association with Developmental sites, but I have observed both grinding slicks and pecked cupules on boulders at the front of thirteenth-century alcove sites at Mesa Verde, and also on Cedar Mesa in southeastern Utah. Thus, it appears reasonable to hypothesize that these shrine types originated in the Mesa Verde region. However, the overall distribution of these features is unknown, so I do not emphasize them in the following discussion.
16. "For their churches, they placed on the four sides and in the center of the plaza some small circular enclosures of stone where they went to offer flour, feathers, and the seed of maguey, maize and tobacco, and performed other superstitious rites, giving the children to understand that they must do all this in the future" (Hackett and Shelby 1942, II:240)
17. See Appendix C, note 11, for an explanation of the various site names attached to LA158.
18. According to Harrington (1916:357), "this pueblo plays an important role in one version of the Tewa migration legend. It was built, so it is related, by the united summer

and winter people after they had wandered separated for generations. It was here that the two cacique government was first instituted."

19. I have previously argued (Ortman 2008a:146) that a shrine above Jackson's Hovenweep Castle is a directional shrine, but I now believe this example is another world-quarter shrine like the one on the crest of the hill south of Sand Canyon Pueblo. However, there may be a directional shrine system surrounding Nancy Patterson Village, a late, canyon-oriented village in Montezuma Canyon (Winston Hurst, personal communication, 2008), and a possible directional shrine has also been recorded to the east of Sand Canyon Pueblo.
20. This work was supported by the National Science Foundation (DDIG # 0753828). I am indebted to Tom Windes for alerting me to the significance and location of the Tsama collection; to the Maxwell Museum of Anthropology for allowing Crow Canyon to receive the collection on loan; to Dean Wilson for training the Crow Canyon laboratory staff in Northern Rio Grande pottery identification; and to the laboratory staff, interns, and participants at Crow Canyon who accomplished this work.
21. Ellis (1975:20) reports that "a metal piece that once may have been the clasp from an old Spanish book was found deep in one of the Tsama rooms" as evidence that occupation continued into the Contact period. Barrett (2002:47) also suggests that Tsama was occupied in the Contact period based on documentary evidence: Oñate included "Tzooma" in his list of pueblos to which he assigned a priest in 1598, and "Sama" appears on the Enrico Martinez map of New Mexico, which was based on information provided by one of Oñate's soldiers in 1602 (Barrett 2002:7).
22. I am grateful to Fumi Arakawa for assisting with this analysis.
23. For further explanation, see Ortman 2000b and Chapter 10.
24. I am grateful to Samantha Ruscavage-Barz for sharing her raw dissertation data.
25. The notion that later migrants should be expected to express material practices of the homeland more thoroughly than earlier migrants during a population movement is echoed in a remarkable way by Edward Curtis in his study of early-twentieth-century Ohkay Owingeh. He noted, as many others have done since, that among the Tewa Pueblos, Ohkay Owingeh is often viewed as supreme in ceremonial matters. According to Curtis, "The probable interpretation of this idea of supremacy is that in the southerly migration of the Tewa the more conservative element, which of course would include the priesthood, lingered in the rear and founded San Juan at the northern limit of Tewa territory. The more adventurous, footloose groups were the ones that pushed boldly forward, seeking better homes, and when they finally became sedentary in their present habitat they were compelled to look to the nucleus of the tribe for their ceremonial institutions" (Curtis 1926:12). In other words, during a population movement one might expect more progressive factions to move first and more conservative factions to follow later. The greater degree of continuity between Mesa Verde and ancestral Tewa material practices noted for areas of the Tewa Basin that were first settled during the Late Coalition period is consistent with Curtis' view, and with the continued correlation of ceremonial prestige with latitude among the Tewa pueblos.

Population Movement, Social Movements, and Ethnogenesis

He said that what they had done had been because of a Teguas Indian named El Popé, who had made them all crazy and was like a whirlwind. He had told them and given them to understand that the father of all the Indians, their great captain, who had been such since the world had been inundated, had ordered the said Popé to tell all the Pueblos to rebel and to swear that they would do so; that no religious and no Spanish person must remain; and that after this they would live as in ancient times.

Declaration of Diego López, December 22, 1681
(Hackett and Shelby 1942, II:295)

In this book I have examined the genetic, linguistic, and cultural backgrounds of the Tewa people of northern New Mexico in an attempt to determine whether this group originated through in situ development, immigration and incorporation of small groups, or a large-scale population movement. I was originally drawn to this particular case of ethnic group formation because it potentially represents an example of unpackaged evolution in genes, language, and culture for which sufficient information is available to examine how and why such disjunctions in population history, language history, and culture history come about. I have emphasized methods that connect human biology and language directly to the archaeological record because such methods allow the genes, language, and culture of ethnic groups to derive from different sources without forcing this result. Following this approach, I have tied down genetic, linguistic, and cultural reconstructions to specific times and places without assuming that they have followed parallel patterns of descent. As a result, it has been possible to evaluate whether Tewa origins are best characterized as a process of local continuity, phylogenesis, or ethnogenesis.

In the process of investigating Tewa origins, I have ranged widely, from studies of paleodemography and population history to phonetic innovations, reconstructed vocabulary and metaphor, and to place-names, oral tradition, and material culture. In this final chapter I summarize the major results and evaluate the three hypotheses developed in Chapter 2. I then present a new model of Tewa origins that attempts to account for the full range of evidence brought to bear in this work. I will suggest that the only realistic way to account for the dramatic cultural disjunction characteristic of Tewa origins is to posit a significant sociopolitical movement that forced the extinction of several Mesa Verde material traditions and the adoption of indigenous Rio Grande traditions. I will also suggest that memories of this movement provided a template for dramatic social action in subsequent phases of Tewa history. Finally, I consider the implications of this study for historical anthropology in the U.S. Southwest and beyond.

Summary of Results

Conducting and interpreting the various analyses presented in this book has required a background in a number of distinct areas of research, including paleodemography, biodistance analysis, the comparative method in linguistics, linguistic paleontology, conceptual metaphor theory, and archaeological approaches to migration. To ease the burden on readers, I introduced these distinct bodies of method and theory at various points throughout this work, immediately preceding applications to specific data, and summarized the results of each analysis at the end of each chapter. Here I provide a condensed, conceptually focused summary of these major findings. Readers who wish to refresh their memories on the details can do so by consulting the final pages of specific chapters.

The three models of Tewa origins that I investigated in this study are: (1) in situ development, in which the Tewa emerged from the initial settlers of the Tewa Basin; (2) immigration, in which the Tewa resulted from the assimilation of thirteenth-century migrants into an existing society; and (3) population movement, in which the Tewa resulted from a mass migration from the Mesa Verde region in the AD 1200s. Evaluation of these hypotheses began in Chapter 4, where I applied insights from recent archaeological perspectives on population and previous studies of Northern Rio Grande population to a new study of Tewa Basin population history. The results suggest that intrinsic growth at an unusually high rate over a period of four to six generations could have produced the Classic period Tewa Basin population from the Late Developmental population; however, the spatial pattern of growth is inconsistent with this model because nearly all population growth during the Early Coalition period was on the Pajarito Plateau, and not in areas that had been settled during the Developmental period. In addition, the population history of the most densely settled portion of the Mesa Verde region, the most likely source area under migration scenarios, is complementary in timing, magnitude, and shape to that of the Tewa Basin. Finally, estimates of intrinsic growth obtained from age-at-death distributions of human skeletal remains suggest that intrinsic growth during the AD 1200s was more robust in the San Juan drainage than it was in the Rio Grande. Collectively, these data suggest that in-migration was the primary cause of Coalition period population growth in the Tewa Basin.

In Chapter 5, I examined metric phenotypic traits of human skeletal remains from sites across the late prehispanic Eastern Pueblo area to assess the ancestry of the ancestral Tewa population. I conducted four analyses. The first was a principal coordinates analysis of the minimum genetic distance matrix estimated from craniometric data. This analysis suggests that post-1275 ancestral Tewa populations of the Pajarito Plateau, Chama Valley, and Galisteo Basin had not descended from early populations of the Rio Grande, but were lineal descendants of pre-1275 populations of the Mesa Verde region. The second analysis examined gene flow; results suggest that Mesa Verde migrants mingled with local populations in the previously settled Santa Fe District when they began to arrive, but also colonized previously unsettled areas throughout the Tewa Basin. The third analysis addressed genetic drift and shows that it is highly unlikely that early Rio Grande populations drifted to match the post-1275 Tewa Basin and Galisteo Basin populations. Finally, the fourth analysis was an admixture analysis which suggests that Late Developmental populations contributed in proportion to their numbers to the ancestral Tewa population. The biological evidence thus suggests that nearly all the migrants who entered the Tewa Basin during the Coalition period came from the Mesa Verde region.

In Chapter 6 I examined the history of the Tewa speech community through an analysis of shared phonetic innovations in Kiowa-Tanoan languages. The results of this analysis indicate that several branches of Kiowa-Tanoan developed early in the history of this language family. The initial stage, which may have been driven by demic expansion following the adoption of agriculture (see Bellwood 2005; Matson 2002), involved the development of a lectal linkage in which dialects ancestral to Kiowa, Towa, and Tiwa-Tewa were arranged in that order on the landscape. At some point after the ancestral Kiowa and Towa dialects separated from this linkage, and Tiwa-Tewa developed into a second lectal linkage, the Tiwa-Tewa linkage fissioned into two isolated speech communities, probably due to migration of the Proto-Tiwa speech community away from the Proto-Tewa speech community. The third stage involved the differentiation of Proto-Tiwa into a third lectal linkage, and the final stage, a rejoining of the Northern Tewa dialect with the Northern Tiwa dialects to create a fourth lectal linkage.

In Chapter 7 I employed three tools of linguistic paleontology to relate this sequence of speech community events to the archaeological record. First, application of linguistic migration theory to the present-day distribution of Kiowa-Tanoan languages suggests either: (1) that Tewa diversified from Proto-Tiwa in the Tewa Basin, and a group of Tiwa-speakers later migrated northward, around the Tewa speech community and into the Taos District northeast of the Tewa Basin; or (2) that the Tiwa-Tewa split involved the migration of Proto-Tiwa speakers to the Rio Grande, and the resultant Tiwa lectal linkage was subsequently broken into northern and southern groups by in-migrating Tewa and

Keres speakers at a later time. Second, reconstructed terms for specific plant and animal species suggest that the Proto-Kiowa-Tanoan speech community was located adjacent to the high mountains of southern Colorado and/or northern New Mexico, but was not likely located exclusively to the south of the Tewa Basin in the Rio Grande drainage. Third, the archaeological record of material culture items for which terms are reconstructible to various Kiowa-Tanoan subgroups suggests that Proto-Kiowa-Tanoan was spoken in Eastern Basketmaker II communities (1500 BC–AD 450), Proto-Tanoan was spoken between AD 450 and 725 (Basketmaker III), Proto-Tiwa-Tewa was spoken between 725 and 920 (Pueblo I), and Proto-Tiwa between 980 and 1100 (Pueblo II and Developmental). This analysis indicates that the Tewa language became distinct around AD 920–980, well before the onset of the Rio Grande Coalition period.

In Chapter 8 I presented three analyses of Tewa place-names and place-lore. In the first analysis I examined Taos Tiwa and San Juan Tewa place-names for geographic features of the northern Rio Grande landscape and found no definite evidence that speakers of these two languages have inherited a common stock of place-names from Proto-Tiwa-Tewa. I did, however, identify several cases in which it appears that the Tewa place-name is a loan or loan-translation from Tiwa. This suggests that Tiwa has been spoken in the Northern Rio Grande for a longer period of time than Tewa. I also found that the Taos name for Ute Mountain, a landform in southwestern Colorado, appears to be a loan-translation from Tewa. In the second analysis I examined the occupation dates of archaeological sites associated with Tewa names. I found that several of these sites had been abandoned by the end of the Coalition period, but that no village-sized Tewa Basin settlements abandoned prior to AD 1275 are associated with Tewa names. In contrast, I did identify a Taos Valley site associated with a Taos Tiwa name that was abandoned around 1190, and a Mesa Verde region site associated with a Tewa name that was abandoned around 1280. The existence of Tewa names for an ancestral village and associated landforms in southwestern Colorado provides direct testimonial evidence that at least some Tewa ancestors lived in the Mesa Verde region. In the third analysis I found evidence that social memories of former Mesa Verde region occupancy were widespread among Tewa people in seventeenth-century New Mexico. All three studies thus suggest that Tewa ancestors lived in the Mesa Verde region and migrated to the northern Rio Grande during the 1200s, either bringing the Tewa language with them or translating place-names and place-lore into Tewa upon arrival.

In Chapter 9 I suggested that in order to determine whether the Tewa language originated in the Mesa Verde region, the most diagnostic evidence should come from traces of Mesa Verde culture that did not continue in Rio Grande Tewa culture but are nevertheless enshrined in the Tewa language. I then made the case that conceptual metaphors involving material culture are a useful currency for this purpose. Metaphors of past speakers remain enshrined in languages long after they have ceased to function, and these fossilized metaphors can be identified through etymology, polysemy, and semantic change in a language family. In addition, material metaphors can be identified in the archaeological record by establishing that their expressions are consistent with patterns in figurative speech behavior. Thus, it is possible to link languages to archaeological complexes created by past speakers by identifying material metaphors in the archaeological complex that have fossilized reflexes in the language. In Chapter 10 I applied this method to the archaeological records of the Mesa Verde region and Tewa Basin, and to the Kiowa-Tanoan languages, especially Tewa. This analysis identified a complex of material metaphors involving pots and baskets that are expressed in Mesa Verde material culture, and also enshrined in the Tewa language. Furthermore, I found that several of these metaphors were never routinely expressed in Tewa Basin material culture and are also absent from contemporary Tewa discourse. These patterns thus constitute the strongest evidence available that the Tewa language was in fact spoken in the Mesa Verde region prior to AD 1280 and, by implication, that it came to be spoken in the Tewa Basin as a result of population movement.[1]

In Chapter 11 I turned to the question of why Coalition period material culture exhibits so little overt continuity with Mesa Verde region material culture. I suggested that most of the models used by archaeologists to study migration have focused on episodes of immigration, where migrants join an existing society and neither the migrants nor the locals are immediately absorbed or replaced by the other. In contrast, many ancient migrations, including the one identified in this study, were population-scale movements in which the migrants either incorporated or displaced the indigenous population. I also suggested that population movements encourage rapid material culture change because the migrants' identity as a distinct people does not become linked to the continued performance of homeland practices. In short, immigration can encourage material culture continuity due to the dynamics of ethnic group interaction, and population movement can encourage material culture change due to the dynamics of population movement as a social process.

I applied this framework to the archaeological record of the Mesa Verde region in Chapter 12 and found that this record exhibits five characteristics one would expect to observe in the source area of a population movement. First, land pressure in this region reached the highest level of the entire ancestral Pueblo sequence during the same period that the Pajarito Plateau began to be colonized. Second, population decline in the Mesa Verde region took place over a period of decades, during which time the remaining population clustered into the core area before it too declined. Third, there was increasing interaction between the Mesa Verde region and the Tewa Basin, and especially the Pajarito Plateau, during the period of population decline. Specifically, the flow of Jemez obsidian, primarily in the form of finished arrows, arrow points, and arrow point blanks, increased during the period of population decline and is consistent with return migration as a primary underlying mechanism. Fourth, the pace and scale of long-distance movement increased over the final century of occupation. This trend is reflected in kiva abandonment modes, the construction dates of kivas that were burned at abandonment, and changes in the size distributions of abandoned sites through time. Fifth, there is abundant evidence for escalating violence during the period of population decline in the form of defensive architecture, healed fractures, and actual warfare events, and there is also evidence of attempts by political leaders to shore up Mesa Verde society during its final decades. Despite the increased incidence of violent death, however, there is no evidence to suggest that intrinsic population decline was responsible for the disappearance of Mesa Verde society. Instead, all indications suggest that an initial trickle of out-migration became a flood in the 1270s as the entire population either left the region, was killed, or died. Thus, the Mesa Verde archaeological record appears most consistent with the population movement hypothesis of Tewa origins, and could be accommodated to the immigration hypothesis, but is inconsistent with the in situ development hypothesis.

Finally, in Chapter 13 I applied the population movement framework to the archaeological record of the Tewa Basin and once again identified a range of patterns that are consistent with the population movement hypothesis. First, the subsistence economy of early migrants to the Pajarito Plateau exhibits greater continuity with that of the Mesa Verde region than with the Late Developmental Tewa Basin. Specifically, the pioneers chose to settle areas that were well suited to direct precipitation agriculture, and introduced the raising of turkeys as a source of meat. Second, the society and culture of the Early Coalition Pajarito Plateau were consistent with that of a pioneer group. This evidence includes the appearance of a package of new artifact types and techno-functional traits in new sites; a simpler material culture and community organization than both the Pueblo III Mesa Verde region and the Developmental Rio Grande; continuities with Mesa Verde domestic spatial organization, cuisine, and technological styles; and a mixture of Mesa Verde, Developmental Rio Grande, and totally new traits. I also suggested that several aspects of Coalition period material culture reflect deliberate attempts on the part of migrants to erase symbols of the homeland, perhaps as a negative commentary on the society they had left behind. Third, the social scale of migrating units increased over time, as indicated by the size distributions of new sites, the scale of site planning, and a relatively stable small-site population despite rapid overall population growth. In short, it appears that in many cases Late Coalition villages were not constructed by aggregating local groups, but by village-sized migrant groups. Finally, material culture continuities from the Mesa Verde region, especially as seen in shrines and pottery designs, are clearest in areas that were initially settled during the Late Coalition period by larger social groups. These results suggest that the archaeological record of the Tewa Basin can be accommodated to the population movement hypothesis just as readily as it has been accommodated to immigration and in situ development scenarios by previous researchers.

Evaluation of Hypotheses

In Chapter 2 I laid out a series of expectations for the various lines of evidence considered in this study for each of the three hypotheses that dominate the literature on Tewa origins. I am now in a position to provide a final evaluation of these hypotheses. Table 14.1 presents a condensed version of the major results of this study and the hypotheses that are supported by each line of evidence. The first general point to make about these results is that even though various lines of evidence can be construed as supporting each of the three hypotheses, none of the evidence considered in this study directly contradicts the population movement hypothesis. Indeed, I found that population movement is the only realistic explanation for several lines of evidence, and that the remaining lines of evidence can at least be accommodated to this view. In contrast, several expectations of the other two hypotheses are directly contradicted by the data. Specifically, the patterns of population and settlement growth, biological affinity, and language history identified in this study are not readily accommodated to either of these models. The number and size of new settlements is too great, the biological affinities too strong, and the evidence of language continuity too extensive to suggest that population movement from the Mesa Verde region was not involved in Tewa origins.

A second and perhaps more important point is that social processes associated with all three hypotheses were involved in Tewa origins to some extent. For example, even though the biological evidence suggests that nearly the entire population of the Pajarito Plateau and Chama Valley descended from Mesa Verde migrants, it also suggests that these migrants blended with locals in the Santa Fe District in a manner consistent with immigration models. Also, even though many lines of evidence suggest that a mass migration of many thousands of people took place between AD 1260 and 1280, the fact that the initial migrants settled the Pajarito Plateau in small groups suggests that these early migrants experienced the dynamics of ethnic group interaction upon arrival, also as expected under the immigration model. Finally, despite the fact that the pattern of change in the Coalition period archaeological record is consistent with population movement, it is clear that many aspects of ancestral Tewa material culture were not inherited from the Mesa Verde region, but were instead inherited from Developmental communities of the Tewa Basin, as proposed by in situ development. This result is not surprising. The three models of Tewa origins evaluated in this study have dominated previous discussions because various lines of evidence provide support for each of them. This study suggests that, in fact, all three were all involved to some extent.

The third general point is that although I have developed a framework for investigating the archaeology of population movement in this study and have shown that the archaeological records of the Mesa Verde region and Tewa Basin are both consistent with this hypothesis, it is by no means the case that Late Coalition Tewa Basin material culture exhibits descent with modification from Late

TABLE 14.1. Evaluation of hypotheses

CATEGORY OF EVIDENCE	RESULTS	SUPPORTED HYPOTHESES	CONTRADICTED HYPOTHESES
Population history	Growth at the limit of natural increase; development of a new population center on the Pajarito Plateau early in the migration period.	Population movement	In situ, Immigration
Pace and duration of movement	Accelerating pace and geographic scale of in-migration during the Late Coalition period; establishment of villages in previously unoccupied areas.	Population movement	In situ, Immigration
Biological affinity of ancestral Tewa population	With the Mesa Verde region, not the Developmental Rio Grande.	Population movement, Immigration	In situ
Pattern of genetic admixture	Proportional to size of immigrant and indigenous populations in various districts.	Population movement, Immigration	In situ
Period of Tewa language divergence	AD 920–980	Population movement, Immigration, In situ	None
Antiquity of Tewa language in Rio Grande	Shallower time depth than Tiwa, definite from the Coalition period.	Population movement	In situ, Immigration
Homeland of the Tewa language	Mesa Verde region	Population movement	In situ, Immigration
Oral tradition, Spanish documents	Social memory of Mesa Verde homeland widespread in the seventeenth century.	Population movement	In situ, Immigration
Source area archaeological record	Scouting correlated with strong material push factors, accelerating population decline and long-distance moves, increasing contact with Tewa Basin, increasing conflict, and cultural retrenchment.	Population movement, Immigration	In situ
Destination area archaeological record	Colonization correlated with strong material push factors in homeland; continuity in pioneer subsistence economy, domestic spatial organization, cuisine, and technological styles; appearance of new artifact types and techno-functional traits as a package in new sites; increasing pace and scale of in-migration; continuities most apparent in areas initially settled by larger groups later in the process.	Population movement	In situ, Immigration

Pueblo III Mesa Verde material culture. Indeed, continuities from Mesa Verde material culture are conspicuously absent in the areas that archaeologists have traditionally paid the most attention to. This contrasts strongly with substantial evidence that the Tewa language and most ancestral Tewa genes derived from the Mesa Verde region. Together these findings make a strong case that the Tewa Pueblos originated through an episode of unpackaged evolution in which an incoming population imposed their genes and language on the Tewa Basin, but chose to leave many aspects of their homeland material culture behind in favor of simpler forms, forms that obscured or obliterated homeland attributes, and forms developed by earlier inhabitants of the Rio Grande.

A Model of Tewa Ethnogenesis

It is one thing to suggest that during the Early Coalition period colonists on the Pajarito Plateau developed a hybrid frontier society that provided the social charter for subsequent migrants. It is quite another to claim that during the Late Coalition period 10,000 people entered the Tewa Basin from the Mesa Verde region, in village-sized groups, and overwhelmed the indigenous population and earlier migrants but strictly avoided reproducing their homeland material culture. Even if this scenario is the most plausible one to emerge from the full range of evidence, it is still a remarkable one — and one that requires an equally remarkable social process to be explained. Indeed, despite the wide range of evidence supporting the population movement model of Tewa origins, this conclusion still does not account for the remarkable cultural transformation associated with it.

Given the evidence for biological and linguistic continuity adduced in this study, it is difficult to imagine how processes of everyday social reproduction could have produced the dramatic cultural changes associated with Tewa origins, or what it is now appropriate to call Tewa ethnogenesis. Indeed, the strict discontinuities between the architecture and pottery of source area and destination area villages could only have come to pass through the operation of strong cultural selection against source area forms on the part of the in-migrating population. In addition, horizontal transmission from the indigenous Rio Grande population cannot account for the wholesale dismissal of Mesa Verde material traditions, because in this case the migrants were in the majority, and as Shennan (Table 1.1) notes, horizontal transmission tends to increase cultural variation, whereas the Mesa Verde migration appears to have been associated with reduced variation. Finally, if most Late Coalition Tewa Basin people were, in fact, recent migrants from the Mesa Verde region, it is difficult to imagine how free decision making by individual migrants could have resulted in such a conspicuous absence of cultural continuity in so many areas. In short, the pattern of cultural change associated with Tewa ethnogenesis does not appear to reflect the processes of everyday social reproduction. Instead, it appears to reflect the processes involved in social transformation, including discourse, ideology, power, resistance, and revolution. In the following pages I draw upon these concepts to build a new model of Tewa ethnogenesis that accounts for the dramatic social transformation that took place as a large segment of the Mesa Verde region population moved to the Tewa Basin.

Material Culture Discourses

All human action is symbolic in the sense that it communicates something as well as does something. Most often these actions are acts of reference with respect to existing cultural models and schemas that inflect their meanings in accordance with the interests of the actors (Sewell 2005:203). As a result, the products of human action, including material culture, constitute a form of running commentary on the social context in which action takes place. From this perspective, patterns in material culture can be viewed as reflections of the dominant construals of the social context, discourses by actors concerning the manner in which the present should be framed or conceptualized relative to existing cultural models. I adopt this perspective in the following pages and suggest that the changes in material culture associated with Tewa ethnogenesis are expressions of discourses on the relationship between the new society that was forming and the old society that was being left behind.

To better understand these discourses, it is useful to compare Pueblo III Mesa Verde material culture with Coalition period Tewa Basin material culture under the assumption that the latter was, in fact, produced by Mesa Verde migrants. Table 14.2 summarizes the changes in material culture implied by the population movement hypothesis and the interpretation I offered for each in Chapter 13. This summary shows that there were no significant changes in the basic household economy associated with the initial stages of movement, as reflected by continuities in subsistence, toolkits, and domestic spatial organization. Changes in wall construction techniques and pottery technology at this time can also be explained as resulting from the adoption of established local patterns of resource use, and changes in Early Coalition community organization can be viewed as simplifications resulting from the social context of pioneer life.

Other changes cannot be explained as a product of frontier life or resource distributions, but there is a pattern to these changes. For example, several changes in pottery assemblages appear to reflect the re-adoption of practices that were characteristic of earlier periods in the Mesa Verde region but were still being practiced in the Tewa Basin when Mesa Verde migrants began arriving. Neck-banded surface treatments on cooking pots, for example, fell out of use in the Mesa Verde region around AD 1000 but continued to be produced in the Late Developmental Tewa Basin (Figure 13.7) and appear to have been re-adopted by early Mesa Verde migrants as well. In addition, the early Santa Fe style of pottery decoration, which lacked complex framing patterns and rim decoration, was more similar to the Mancos and McElmo styles that preceded the Mesa Verde style in the Mesa Verde region.

TABLE 14.2. Changes in cultural practices associated with population movement, AD 1200–1350

TRAIT	MESA VERDE REGION	TEWA BASIN	INTERPRETATION
Subsistence economy (early)	Upland direct precipitation farming, turkey husbandry	Upland direct precipitation farming, turkey husbandry	Continuity
Toolkit	Slab metates, full-grooved axes, side-notched projectile points, bird-bone artifacts	Slab metates, full-grooved axes, side-notched projectile points, bird-bone artifacts	Continuity
Domestic spatial organization	Front row of living rooms, back row of storage rooms	Front row of living rooms, back row of storage rooms	Continuity
Wall construction	Pecked-block masonry with chinking in core area, jacal and adobe with stone in hinterlands	Adobe, adobe with stone, rough block masonry, cut-stone masonry with chinking	Expediency
Primary domestic structure	Kiva	Ceremonial room (a stripped-down, aboveground kiva)	Aboveground kiva in style of destination area
Room to kiva ratio	2 to 10 rooms per kiva	8 to 28 rooms per kiva early, 25–50 rooms per kiva late	Increased social scalc of kivas
Kiva architecture	Subterranean to aboveground, south-facing, keyhole-shape, benches, southern recess, pilasters, cribbed roof, roof entry, pit-hearth, deflector, vent tunnel	Semi-subterranean, east-facing; circular; no benches, recess, or pilasters; flat roof; roof entry; adobe-lined hearth, ash pit, deflector, vent tunnel	Adoption of destination area style and symbols
Community organization (early)	Villages with great houses, great kivas, linear room blocks of 1–3 unit pueblos each	Clusters of room-block sites (1–3 households each), no public architecture	Simplification
Community organization (late)	Canyon-rim villages, multi-walled structures, plazas, towers, feasting	Plaza pueblos	Increased social scale of traditional architectural forms
Pottery technology	Geologic shale clays; sherd, sand, or rock temper; carbon and mineral paint	Alluvial volcanic clays; sand or tuff temper; carbon paint only	Adaptation to local resources
Pottery forms (early)	Corrugated jars; painted bowls, jars, mugs, ladles, seed-jars, canteens	Indented-corrugated jars, neck-banded jars, painted bowls	Simplification, anachronism
Pottery design (early)	Weaving-inspired patterns, complex framing patterns and rim decorations	Geometric patterns, no framing patterns or rim decorations	Simplification, anachronism

TABLE 14.2. (cont'd.) Changes in cultural practices associated with population movement, AD 1200–1350

TRAIT	MESA VERDE REGION	TEWA BASIN	INTERPRETATION
Pottery forms (late)	Corrugated jars; painted bowls, jars, mugs, ladles, seed-jars, canteens	Smeared-indented-corrugated jars, painted bowls	Simplification, anachronism conformity, negative commentary
Pottery design (late)	Weaving-inspired patterns, complex framing patterns and rim decorations, exterior designs	Continuity in villages established by large groups in previously unsettled areas; adoption of local style in previously settled areas	Continuity or charter group influence
Place-making practices	Earth-navel, directional shrines	Earth-navel, directional shrines	Continuity

Note: early = Early Coalition (AD 1200–1275); late = Late Coalition (AD 1275–1350).

The same pattern is apparent in architecture. The most prominent architectural change involved the replacement of the forms and symbols of the Mesa Verde kiva by the forms and symbols of Rio Grande pit structures. Some of these changes, such as the change in orientation from south to east, represent symbolic replacements, but others — such as the disappearance of pilasters, cribbed roofs, benches, and southern recesses — involve the removal of elaborations that developed during the AD 1100s in the Mesa Verde region. The resulting kiva form was in fact more similar to Mesa Verde kivas of the 1000s than to Mesa Verde kivas of the 1200s.

The results of this study indicate that when early Mesa Verde migrants encountered indigenous Tewa Basin populations, they found a people who spoke a vaguely familiar language and who behaved in ways that were more characteristic of their ancestors than of the people currently living in their homeland. For example, the indigenous population of the Rio Grande still made neck-banded cooking pots that would have appeared anachronistic to contemporary Mesa Verde migrants. In addition, the Tiwa-speaking peoples of the Northern Rio Grande had not participated in the Chacoan regional system, whereas Tewa-speaking peoples from the Mesa Verde region were involved in some way (Figure 14.1) (see Lipe 2006; Varien et al. 2008). Thus, Mesa Verde migrants had ample reason to view the locals as people who were living in the present as their ancestors had done in the past. In Tewa worldview, traveling great distances from home is equivalent to traveling back in time, so when early Mesa Verde migrants traveled southeast, toward the sunrise at the beginning of the year, and to the other side of the mountains that defined the edge of their current world, and they encountered a people whose practices reflected those of their ancestors, the migrants may well have interpreted the experience as one of stepping back in time

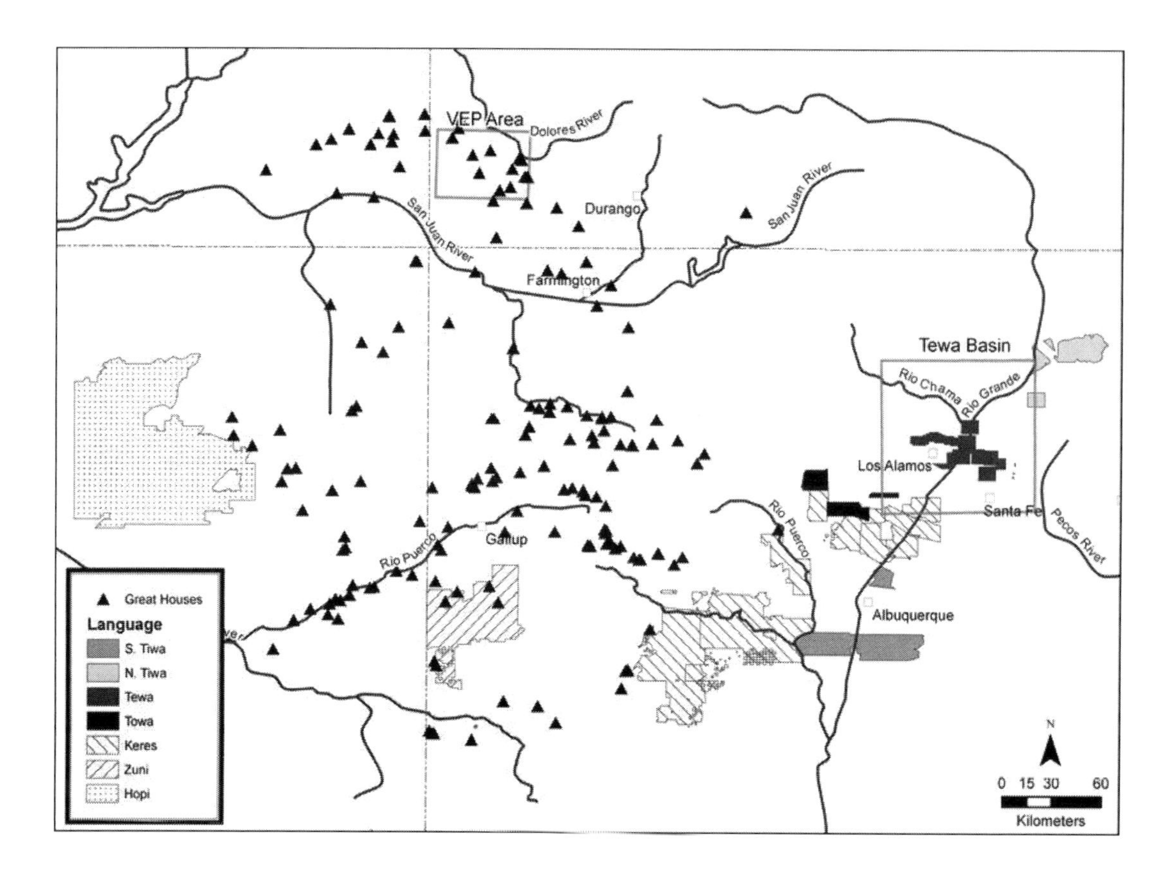

FIGURE 14.1. Distribution of Chaco style great houses and contemporary Pueblo lands.

to an earlier age. In embracing local architectural forms and pottery styles, then, the migrants would have reconnected with images of an ancestral way of life.

If one of the discourses suggested by the adoption of indigenous Rio Grande architecture and pottery traditions is one of return to an earlier age, the other appears to have been an overt, negative commentary on the recent past. This is most clearly seen in the rapid spread of smeared-indented-corrugated cooking pottery during the middle decades of the 1200s, as migration from the Mesa Verde region accelerated. These vessels were made by first constructing a Mesa Verde style indented-corrugated vessel and then smearing the surface treatment. Indented-corrugated vessels were commonly made in Late Developmental and Early Coalition communities, so there is no reason to suspect that the raw materials available to Tewa Basin potters encouraged them to change how they constructed cooking pots. In fact, indented-corrugated vessels may have functioned better than smooth-surfaced vessels when cooking cornmeal, because the increased exterior surface area would have moderated the temperature inside the vessel, thus encouraging a slow simmer as opposed to boilovers (see Chapter 13). The smearing technique may therefore signal a conscious attempt to obliterate the appearance of Mesa Verde style cooking pots without compromising their functionality. This appears to have been a material metonym for what Mesa Verde migrants were doing overall as they moved to the Tewa Basin.

FIGURE 14.2. Cannonball Ruin, a canyon-rim village in Canyons of the Ancients National Monument, Colorado.

Additional expressions of this discourse of erasing, or undoing, the recent past may be seen in changes in community architecture associated with the Late Coalition period. During the 1200s the prototypical form of community architecture in the Mesa Verde region was the canyon-rim pueblo, a bowl-shaped, inward-facing settlement constructed around the head of a canyon and enclosing a spring (Figure 14.2; also see Chapter 9). These villages also contained multiwalled structures that appear to have been the homes of community political and/or religious leaders, public food storage structures, and also a small number of houses that lacked the normal complement of storage rooms, as though their inhabitants were not required to provision themselves (Lipe and Ortman 2000).[2] These indications of high-status residences, pooling of surpluses, and bowl-shaped village plans are completely lacking in Late Coalition villages, despite the fact that many of these settlements must have been constructed by groups of people who only months before had lived in canyon-rim villages. Instead, Late Coalition villages took the form of plaza pueblos, an innovative form that has no precursors in the Tewa Basin or the Mesa Verde region, but appears to reflect a remapping of the architecture of great houses, which preceded multiwalled structures as the homes of community leaders, onto the community writ large (see Figures 8.3, 13.9). So here again, changes in material culture associated with the Mesa Verde migration appear to reflect the twin discourses of "wiping out" emblematic features of the recent past and of returning to a previous way of life — in this case an earlier period of Mesa Verde culture history.[3]

These two discourses were expressed with striking uniformity in the Late Coalition Tewa Basin despite the rapid arrival of approximately 10,000 people from the Mesa Verde region. Indeed, the pace at which the final depopulation of the Mesa Verde region took place, the rate at which smeared-indented-corrugated pottery replaced a variety of earlier forms, the synchronized way in which plaza pueblos replaced earlier community patterns in the Tewa Basin, the complete absence of 1200s Mesa Verde architectural forms, and the almost total disappearance of many 1200s Mesa Verde vessel forms all suggest that these changes did not take place as a result of everyday processes of social reproduction among indigenous people, charter groups, and recent arrivals. Instead, it appears that the migration itself was connected to discourses that had the power to convince most of the migrants, and to coerce the rest, to leave their homeland, move to the Tewa Basin, and replace many current material practices with new practices modeled after indigenous Rio Grande practices and earlier Mesa Verde practices. The only discourses that could have wielded such power over so many people are religious discourses. To provide a satisfactory account of Tewa ethnogenesis, then, it would appear that one needs to delve into religious movements and the profound ways in which they influence culture and practice.

Religion and Revolution

The notion that religion was somehow involved in the transformation of material culture and social life observed across the Pueblo world in the late 1200s is not new (see, for example, Adams 1991; Bradley 1996; Crown 1994; Lipe 1995; VanPool et al. 2006). In most cases, however, previous researchers have focused on the development of communal ritual and shared iconography as a means of integrating migrant groups into rapidly developing hybrid communities in destination areas.[4] In other words, these studies have adopted a view of religion that emphasizes its role in maintaining and integrating society, following Durkheim (1968), Malinowski (1954), Radcliffe-Brown (1965), and Eliade (1959). Such views appear inadequate to account for Tewa ethnogenesis because, in this case, one needs to account not only for the ways in which the new society was maintained after migration, but also for complete depopulation in the homeland, mass migration to the Tewa Basin, and the pattern of material culture change that resulted. In other words, one needs to consider the role of religion and religious movements in social conflict and transformation, not just social reproduction.

The work of comparative religion scholar Bruce Lincoln is especially helpful for this purpose. Lincoln (2003:5–7) defines a religion as having four components: (1) a discourse whose concerns transcend the human, temporal, and contingent, and that claims for itself a similarly transcendent status; (2) a set of practices whose goal is to produce a proper world and/or proper human subjects as defined by a religious discourse to which these practices are connected; (3) a community whose members construct their identity with reference to a religious discourse and its attendant practices; and (4) an institution that regulates religious discourse, practices, and community, reproducing them over time and modifying them as necessary while asserting their eternal validity and transcendent value.

With this definition in mind, the most useful aspect of Lincoln's work for present purposes is his treatment of the role of religion in social and cultural transformation.[5] Lincoln (2003:79) notes that within any society there is a religion associated with the social fraction that controls the bulk of material resources and prestige, and occupies most positions of authority. These "religions of the status quo" tend to promote ideological hegemony as a means of maintaining the society—and thus the position of the dominant or privileged fraction within it. In practice, however, total hegemony is rarely achieved, because the religion of the status quo "meets strong resistance among various sectors of the population, particularly those which have most reason to be dissatisfied with the givens of the status quo and are most alienated from the dominant fraction" (Lincoln 2003:82). Within such groups, "religions of resistance"—ideologies that run counter to that promoted by the religion of the status quo and institutional structures for their preservation—often come into being. Initially these religions of resistance create cohesive, insular, and defensive communities because their greatest challenge is mere survival. Their rituals focus on group solidarity and ritual healing, their members tend to come from the disadvantaged fractions of society, and their leaders tend to be discontents who derive their authority from claims of direct experience of transcendent reality (Lincoln 2003: 82–86).

When peace and prosperity prevail, it is easy for the religion of the status quo to maintain the position of the dominant fraction. As a result, religions of resistance come and go, and have little opportunity to spread beyond the small communities that maintain them for a time. When material conditions worsen, however, the task of the religion of the status quo becomes more difficult, even as it becomes more essential to the continued authority of the dominant fraction. Under these circumstances, a religion of resistance can be transformed into "a religion of revolution" by articulating a new theory of political legitimacy and by beginning to recruit adherents from a broader cross section of society. In this way, a religion that was initially defined in opposition to the religion of the status quo and its ideological domination becomes a religion that defines itself in opposition to the privileged fraction and its control over society.

So long as the religion of the status quo is able to persuade the bulk of society that the authority of the dominant fraction is legitimate, it will be difficult to dislodge the privileged fraction, even in a crisis situation. But when the religion of the status quo fails to do so, the door is opened for religions of resistance to become "more militant in their ideology, more strident in their rhetoric, and more active throughout society at large" (Lincoln 2003:87). In their struggles to displace the dominant authority, religions of resistance often promote a millenarian doctrine in which "the world of the present is condemned as decadent or senescent, while a radically different mode of being is expected in the immediate future in the wake of an apocalyptic struggle" (Lincoln 2003:87); however, for a religion of revolution to succeed, it must also forge bonds of solidarity and commitment among those who have recently been recruited. These often take the form of iconoclastic public rituals through which the ideological constructs that were used by the dominant fraction to maintain its authority in the past are dismantled and their material trappings are disrespectfully destroyed. "Such spectacular gestures irrevocably bind witnesses and participants together in an enterprise from which there can be no turning back" (Lincoln 2003:89–90). If the revolution is then successful, the religion of revolution rapidly becomes the new religion of the status quo in service of the new privileged fraction, whereas the religion of the defeated fraction becomes the nostalgic religion of counter-revolution seeking to restore the defeated fraction to its former place.

Lincoln's account of the role of religion in social transformation provides a ready explanation for the archaeological record of Tewa ethnogenesis. Material conditions in the Mesa Verde region were clearly difficult during the 1200s due to climate fluctuations, land pressure, and in-migration. Given these conditions, it is reasonable to view the development of canyon-rim villages as a response of the dominant fraction, and the initial colonization of the Pajarito Plateau as a response of more disadvantaged fractions. In addition, accounts by return migrants of the "ancestral" society they had encountered in the Tewa Basin would have introduced an alternative to the status quo, and as conditions worsened, this alternative would have been incorporated into the ideology of a religion of resistance whose purpose was to return the entire society to this ancestral way of life by moving to the Tewa Basin. The fact that most of the population resided in villages by the 1260s would have made it easier for the revolutionary ideology to spread, and the ritual destructions and actual massacres associated with the collapse of Mesa Verde society would have created a situation where remaining was no longer an option.

After arriving in the Tewa Basin, the strict avoidance of material reminders of the old society would appear to reflect the adherence or acquiescence of the migrants to the ideology of the revolution, which dictated the avoidance of recent practices and a "re-adoption" of "ancestral" practices by clothing these changes in authoritative discourse and transcendent moral principles. Settling migrant groups directly in plaza pueblos would have also facilitated continued oblique transmission of the revolutionary ideology from leaders to followers, and encouraged surveillance by community members to enforce compliance. In addition, the notion that no religion ever achieves complete ideological hegemony helps to explain why recently invented place-making practices and the

Mesa Verde pottery style did continue in some Late Coalition communities established in previously unsettled areas toward the end of the population movement. These may have been communities in which a disproportionate number had acquiesced to the revolution but had a more positive and nostalgic view of Mesa Verde society.[6] Also, the fact that discourses and practices can shift in their association with social fractions over time helps to explain why these elements of Mesa Verde culture, which were maintained only in certain Late Coalition communities, spread to communities throughout the Tewa Basin during the Classic period. Perhaps expressions of Mesa Verde heritage became more appealing as the people who participated in the revolution passed away and direct experience was replaced by social memory.

Finally, the upheavals of revolution — including the breaking and burning of kivas and possessions, violence against opposing fractions, the abandonment of villages, migration to the Tewa Basin, the construction of a new society, and public surveillance to ensure compliance with the new norms of behavior — would have encouraged the formation of strong bonds of solidarity and common commitment among the migrants. In short, these shared experiences, and memories of having lived through them, would have provided ample material for the development of a new Tewa identity, and would have bound the culture and practices associated with the movement to the Tewa speech community and its associated mating network. In this way Tewa ethnogenesis would have taken place.

Digression on an Analogous Case

The model of Tewa ethnogenesis proposed here is essentially parallel to the process by which the Cheyenne Nation formed in the northern Great Plains during the late eighteenth century. James Mooney (1907:361) identified the Cheyenne as being "of special interest to the ethnologist as a rare instance of a sedentary and agricultural people... transformed by pressure of circumstance within the historic period into a race of nomad and predatory hunters, with such entire change of habit and ceremony that the old life is remembered only in sacred tradition and would seem impossible... but for the connected documentary proof of the fact." Cheyenne origins are well understood because the culture formed relatively recently, it is reflected in historic documents and oral traditions recorded shortly after the events they describe, and recent analyses of both data sets by John Moore (1987, 1996) have worked through historiographic issues surrounding interpretation of these sources. Thus, a brief digression on Cheyenne origins is helpful because it illustrates that the model of Tewa ethnogenesis proposed above has been documented for other tribal groups.

In the middle decades of the eighteenth century a number of Proto-Cheyenne bands lived in farming villages along the rivers of North and South Dakota. William Duncan Strong (1940) excavated one such village known as the Sheyenne-Cheyenne or Biesterfeldt site and found earth lodges and fortifications, cord-marked and incised pottery, evidence of maize cultivation, the presence of horses, evidence of buffalo hunting, and European trade goods. Wood (1971) reexamined this material and concluded that the site's material culture is indistinguishable from that of historic Arikara, Mandan, and Hidatsa farming villages of the Middle Missouri area.[7]

By 1800 these same Proto-Cheyenne bands had abandoned these ancestral farming villages and adopted the fully nomadic, equestrian, tipi-dwelling and buffalo-hunting adaptation of nineteenth-century High Plains cultures (Moore 1987:68–125, 1996:30–32; Moore et al. 2001:863; Oliver 1962:29–31). In his description of a well-used, nineteenth-century Cheyenne campsite, Strong (1940: 376) noted the striking archaeological discontinuity that resulted: "The contrast with the Sheyenne-Cheyenne village was tremendous. There were no fortifications, no earth lodges, and but faintly marked tipi circles, no pottery, no evidence of agriculture, abundant glass beads and trade materials on the surface, and little else."

Strong's observations suggest that it would be nearly impossible to demonstrate the connection between Proto-Cheyenne farming villages and nineteenth-century Cheyenne camps using archaeological material culture, yet it is clear from historic documentation that these two archaeological complexes were created by the same bio-linguistic lineage. Once the connection is known, the archaeological record provides a faithful register of the social transformation that took place, but in the absence of documentary evidence, one could only show that these complexes are related using the alternative lines of evidence emphasized in this book, including biology, place-names, and oral tradition.

Moore's (1987) analysis of historical documents and oral traditions also provides insight into the social process by which Proto-Cheyenne agricultural groups were transformed into the Cheyenne Nation. According to Moore, the Cheyenne Nation arose through the unification of several distinct bands, each of which had its own name and only some of which spoke Cheyenne at the time. The agent of this unification was Mutsiev, or "Sweet Medicine," a prophet figure who made a pilgrimage to a cave inside Bear Butte in the Black Hills of South Dakota and returned with four arrows: two for the buffalo, and two for their enemies. He also brought back the necessary concepts and ceremonies for their use, and established a number of military societies, thus facilitating the integration of Proto-Cheyenne bands into a tribal nation. Thus, Cheyenne ethnogenesis resulted from a social movement led by a charismatic religious and political leader that resulted in rapid social change, population movement, and the formation of a new social identity. Based on the range of evidence adduced in this study, I suggest that Tewa ethnogenesis resulted from a similar process.

Historical Metaphors and Revolutionary Action

If something as momentous as a religious revolution was the social process that led to Tewa ethnogenesis, it would be very surprising indeed if social memories of this experience were not maintained in oral tradition for generations after the actual events had taken place. I believe such memories were maintained, but in order to perceive them, one must first consider how the leaders of resistance movements motivate their communities to revolutionary action. A common rhetorical device used by such leaders is framing the present moment in such a way that it becomes a reinstantiation of paradigmatic historical or mythical events that are well known in that community. This is accomplished through discourses that map the image-schematic structure of past events, point for point, onto the current situation, the required actions, and their intended outcomes. Marshall Sahlins (1985:11) refers to such constructions as "historical metaphors of mythical realities."[8]

It appears that the Tewa leaders of the Pueblo Revolt used this hermeneutic technique to inspire seventeenth-century Tewa people, and perhaps other Pueblo peoples as well, to rise up against the Spanish. In Chapter 8 I presented an analysis of Spanish documents from the Pueblo Revolt period which suggests that the lake of Copala referred to in several of the Otermín captive accounts is a synonym for Tewayó, the ancient Tewa homeland in the northwest that Escalante associated with the Mesa Verde region. With this association in mind, Pedro Naranjo's statement that, through the revolt, the Pueblos "thereby returned to the state of their antiquity, as when they came out of the lake of Copala" (Hackett and Shelby 1942, II:248) can be read as an indication that the Tewa people believed they had turned back the clock before, when they returned "to the state of their antiquity" by leaving the lake of Copala, meaning Tewayó, or the Mesa Verde region. Thus, through their references to Copala, Po'pay and other leaders of the revolt appropriated a paradigmatic event in Tewa history, which was widely known in the Pueblo world, as the template for a new religious revolution.[9] In other words, the planned rebellion was to be a reinstantiation of the Mesa Verde migration. In the following pages I explore several implications of this remarkable connection for the religious revolution hypothesis of Tewa ethnogenesis.

The Mesa Verde Migration as an Episode of Emergence

The notion that leaving a primordial home is a reflection of spiritual preparedness is deeply embedded in Tewa philosophy. In the Tewa origin narrative, for example, the people had to return to the lake four times when they were trying to come out because they were not yet complete, meaning they had not yet established all the institutions that were needed for a smoothly functioning society (Ortiz 1969:15). Also, according to Hopi-Tewa tradition, their ancestors would not agree to leave Ts'ą̨wa̱di until Hopi representatives had come to ask for help four times, thus completing a ritual circuit (Yava 1979:27–28). And when Tewa religious leaders hold a ceremony, they enter the kiva through the *p'o:kwik^{h}oyi* ('lake roof-hatch') and do not come out until the ceremony has been completed and they are fully prepared to emerge. These examples illustrate that in Tewa philosophy spiritual preparedness is indicated by the act of departure. Tewa people were not created perfect, but they approached perfection when they were able to come out of the lake and not go back again.[10] In other words, the act of leaving *p'o:kwin*, a kiva, or an ancestral home is the outcome of spiritual preparation as well as a return to a primordial state.

It is clear from the Otermín documents that Po'pay and other leaders of the Pueblo Revolt modeled it in accordance with this schema. For example, the rebellion was planned from a kiva in Taos, the northernmost Pueblo village, where according to Pedro Naranjo, "there appeared to the said Popé three figures of Indians who never came out of the estufa. They gave the said Popé to understand that they were going underground to the Lake of Copala" (Hackett and Shelby 1942, II:246). In addition, Po'pay and other leaders were said to have remained in the kiva until the Spanish had fled and the world had been prepared for their emergence. At this point, according to a Tewa named Juan:

> the said Indian, Pope, came down in person with all the war captains and many other Indians, proclaiming through the pueblos that the devil was very strong and much better than God, and that they should burn all the images and temples, rosaries and crosses, and that all the people should discard the names given them in holy baptism and call themselves whatever they liked. They should leave the wives whom they had taken in holy matrimony and take any one whom they might wish, and they were not to mention in any manner the name of God, of the most holy Virgin, or of the Saints, on pain of severe punishment, particularly that of lashing, saying that the commands of the devil were better than that which they taught them of the law of God. They were ordered likewise not to teach the Castilian language in any pueblo and to burn the seeds which the Spaniards sowed and to plant only maize and beans, which were the crops of their ancestors. (Hackett and Shelby 1942, II:235)

This procession of religious leaders from the *p'o:kwin* in the north to all the pueblos after the people had been prepared for their emergence via the removal of the Spaniards would have resonated with Tewa people as an instance of the most fundamental ritual script in their culture. In addition, by framing the situation this way, leaders of the revolt presented the social transformation they demanded, which involved "leaving behind" all things related to the Spanish and Christianity, as a return to the spiritually and morally complete way of life associated with the original emergence from *p'o:kwin*.

If leaders of the Pueblo Revolt framed it as an episode of emergence, then the fact that they so often alluded to Copala/Tewayó in their discourse suggests that seventeenth-century Tewas also viewed this legendary episode in which they "came out of the Lake of Copala" as a quintessential example of emergence. In fact, it may not be too much of a stretch to suggest that the historical event enshrined in this legend — namely, the Mesa Verde migration — provided the framework upon which present-day Tewa notions of emergence were constructed. This conclusion has two important implications for the present discussion. First, it implies that leaders of the Pueblo Revolt not only drew upon the schema of emergence in their discourse promoting rebellion, but also appealed to memories of the emergence par excellence—namely, the Mesa Verde migration and the return to an earlier way of life that it accomplished—in their efforts to motivate the Pueblos to collective action. Second, it implies that the Mesa Verde migration was the foundational event that created the Tewa people. This is consistent with the range of evidence presented throughout this study.

Tewayó and P'oseyemu

The Spanish documents examined in Chapter 8 indicate that at the time of the Pueblo Revolt, it was widely believed that a person referred to as "the lieutenant of P'oseyemu" had come from the distant north bearing orders to revolt. Given my argument that the ancestral Tewa homeland in the distant north should be equated with Copala, Tewayó, and the Mesa Verde region, these passages raise the possibility that P'oseyemu was somehow associated with past events in this homeland. This, in turn, suggests that legends surrounding P'oseyemu derive from "a culture hero, the deification of an outstanding leader who had actual, historical existence" (Curtis 1926:46), who was involved in the Mesa Verde migration itself. Several lines of evidence support this inference, thus reinforcing the hypothesis that Tewa ethnogenesis was the result of a religious revolution.

Stories about P'oseyemu occur in many pueblos and are often syncretized with Christian, Spanish, or Anglo elements (Parmentier 1979); however, the actual person who inspired these stories probably lived during prehispanic times, because the earliest documentary references to P'oseyemu associate him with legendary places of the past, and recent oral traditions indicate his birth and early deeds took place during a time when "there were only Indians, no White people, no Mexicans" (Parsons 1994 [1926]:112).

P'oseyemu almost certainly lived in a Tewa-speaking community, because his name has a transparent morphological analysis in Tewa, whereas his names in other Pueblo languages do not. Parmentier (1979:611) suggests that his name refers to mist or fog that spreads over the ground, as can be seen rising from a lake in the morning; Ortiz (2005 [1980]:88) translates *P'ose-yemu* as "mist-scattering" or "he who scatters mist before him." These translations suggest a benevolent person, but it is important to note that due to their rain-making properties, *p'ose* can also refer to scalps taken in war (Parsons 1929:138). Thus, P'oseyemu may simultaneously refer to a powerful, "scalp-scattering" leader, someone who brings blessings by killing and scattering his enemies. This connotative reading is more consistent with the Otermín documents, which indicate that the lieutenant of P'oseyemu "ordered all the Indians to take part in this treason and rebellion, saying that they would kill immediately anyone who refused to agree to it" (Hackett and Shelby 1942, I:15–16).

Several lines of evidence in addition to the Otermín documents associate P'oseyemu with Tewa origins and the Mesa Verde migration. For example, in the early twentieth century, Edward Curtis (1926:10) was told by a Tewa elder that, among other deeds, P'oseyemu founded the K'ósa society. Curtis (1926:18) was also told that "the *K'ósa* 'come from the north,' that is, the society was instituted in the ancient home of the Tewa." This is significant because, as mentioned in Chapter 8, Harrington (1916:564) independently recorded a statement to the effect that "the *K'ósa*, a mythic person who founded the *K'ósa* society," first appeared to the Tewa when their ancestors lived in the Montezuma Valley. If the K'ósa society was established when Tewa ancestors lived in the Mesa Verde region, and P'oseyemu founded this society, then P'oseyemu must have lived in the Mesa Verde region as well.[11]

A song composed for the Ohkay Owingeh Turtle Dance in 1974 also connects P'oseyemu with the ancestral Tewa homeland. This particular song was recorded for New World Records, and the lyrics translated in liner notes by Alfonso Ortiz (1979b).

> Here at Dewy Water Structure, sacred village
> Here at Misty Corn Structure, sacred village
> Poseyemu's sons
> Poseyemu's daughters
> Gracefully they are shaking their rattles!
> Beautifully there is heard the sound of rattles!
>
> Here at Dewy Water Structure, sacred village
> Here at Misty Corn Structure, sacred village
> Poseyemu's sons
> Poseyemu's daughters
> Gracefully they are moving about as turtles!
> Beautifully they are dancing as turtles!
>
> Poseyemu youths have here come to look in on us,
> Bringing blessings of all kinds, rain!
> Poseyemu maidens have here been accepted!

This song connects P'oseyemu with Tewa origins via the context and meaning of the dance itself. The Turtle Dance is held annually just after the winter solstice and is named for the first animal to emerge from hibernation in the spring. For each performance the singers compose four songs that emphasize traditional themes of origins, fertility, renewal, regeneration, and the continuing process of creation. Present-day singers also indicate that during the Turtle Dance they sing to ancestors who dwell on the high, flat-topped mountain northwest of Ohkay Owingeh known as Tsip'in, or Cerro Pedernal (Richard Ford, personal communication, 2011). This is important because Tsip'in lies along a natural route of travel between the Tewa Basin and the San Juan drainage. Thus, in sending their songs toward Tsip'in, the singers also send them toward the place from which the Tewa originated. And by referring to the people of the pueblo as Poseyemu's sons and daughters, the composer of the song presents P'oseyemu as the father of the Tewa and associates him with the ancestral Tewa homeland.

The attributes and actions of P'oseyemu in Tewa oral tradition suggest that this person was in fact the leader of a religious movement. Lincoln (2003:84–85) notes that the leaders of religions of resistance tend to possess certain characteristics. First, they tend to be discontents from outside the dominant fraction of society — people of sufficient talent to take on positions of authority, who have been excluded for various reasons. By coming to prominence from outside the entrenched power structures of the dominant fraction, leaders of religions of resistance are counter-structural symbols, embodiments of the injustices of the dominant fraction, and a contradiction to their hegemonic discourses. Second, the leaders of such movements are also often referred to as "charismatic," which Lincoln (2003:84) suggests is "not so much a gift of individual personality as it is the following called forth by one who is able to catalyze latent discontents and extend the hope of overcoming them." Third, these leaders draw their authority from direct revelation or experience of transcendent reality, sources that come to be viewed among followers as superior to the indicators of legitimate authority associated with the dominant fraction.

Early-twentieth-century traditions from Ohkay Owingeh concerning the birth and deeds of P'oseyemu present him as a person who possessed all these qualities.[12] In the tradition recorded by Parsons (1994 [1926]:108–113), for example, P'oseyemu was conceived when the Sun, or "World Man," placed a pinyon nut in the mouth of a poor girl who was out gathering. As a child he had no name and was scorned by the villagers, but he was a precocious hunter who provisioned his family with rats, then rabbits, and eventually deer. When the time for initiation came, he was told to move on, but he refused, and spoke to the "made" people using "hard" or "ripe" words. The moiety chiefs wondered where he had learned to speak so well since he had no father or grandfather, and told the people to respect him. But the people refused, throwing trash outside the door of his house.

Later, while hunting in the mountains, the young man met his father, who named him P'oseyemu and gave him buckskin clothing and a fine bow and quiver of arrows. The Sun then told him, "You are going to rule all the Indians. When you grow up to be a man you are going to be the father to them all" (Parsons 1994 [1926]:111).[13] P'oseyemu subsequently spoke with the elders a second time, saying, "You do not know from whom you are getting along well. You do not think anything good about who is working for the people to live well." These passages show that in Tewa oral tradition, P'oseyemu came from beyond the privileged fraction of society, he embodied and was able to articulate the injustices of his time, and he drew his authority from direct experience of the spirit world. In short, P'oseyemu possessed all the characteristics of the leader of a religion of resistance.

Subsequent passages in the same legend suggest that P'oseyemu not only had the characteristics of a revolutionary leader, but also actually led a revolutionary movement. After preaching to the moiety chiefs in the episode mentioned above, the moiety chiefs responded, "You are talking the truth," and ordered all the people of the town to sweep up the trash they had thrown outside the homes of the poor people. When the sweepers came to P'oseyemu's house, however, they debated whether or not to sweep it. "Some of them said, 'We have to sweep, because he is a good man.' But some of them were angry with him and wanted to treat him badly. Some said, 'this boy wants to rule this place, this people. If we sweep in front of his house, he will do what he pleases with us. We don't know who his father is'" (Parsons 1994 [1926]:111). Some of the people then swept in front of P'oseyemu's house, signaling their allegiance with his message, whereas others disobeyed the moiety chiefs and did not.[14]

P'oseyemu appears to have preached against the inequalities in lineage, status, and wealth that were characteristic of his day, and promoted movement to a new place as a means of correcting these inequalities. For example, the K'ósa society that P'oseyemu is believed to have established consists of clowns who make fun of authority and enforce communal norms. As such, they provide an antidote to overt hierarchy and grandiosity, and would have supported the transformation in values, essentially the opposite of the old, that are reflected in the pattern of material culture change between the Mesa Verde and Tewa Basin archaeological records.

Also, according to Parsons's account, the following events took place following the conflict related to sweeping around P'oseyemu's house.

> [Poseyemu] said "Yes. Now I am going to talk to you boys here. I am going to talk about what is good, what is needed. I have no grandfather, no father, I just grew up; but I am going to talk." He talked. He just talked hard words, good words. *How they could move from that place, what they were to do, how they could live.* He talked well, so nobody should hurt him. Those old men said, "Harąhi'! this boy talks well. Wonder who gave him so good a head, he talks so well." The old men said, "What do you think about this boy? This boy knows everything." They said, "We must give all the things to him. He has to be Mother and Father and rule us." They said to him, "You rule us, all this place." He said, "No, I do not want to." But everybody wanted him. (Parsons 1994 [1926]:112, emphasis added)

Finally, according to an account recorded by Harrington,

> The Tewa built themselves a village.... They had not been many years at this place when Poseyemu appeared to them and told them that they were not at the middle place; he said "You must cross the river," and he gave the

> people instructions as to where they would find the middle place.... Obeying...the people built a village. [The middle] point was found by the water bug stretching her legs to the north, west, south, and east, the central point found directly under her heart. (Harrington n.d., cited in Swentzell 1990:26)

This passage suggests that P'oseyemu promoted movement to a place that lay across a river from their current home, where the watercourses formed a pattern corresponding to the legs of a water bug. It is not difficult to envision the river to be crossed as the San Juan, and the destination as the Tewa Basin. The central, low spot of this basin is in the vicinity of present-day Española, and from this vantage point the Rio Chama and Rio Grande north of Ohkay Owingeh would correspond to the front legs, Santa Clara Creek and the Rio Santa Cruz to the middle legs, and the Rio Grande and Rio Tesuque to the hind legs (see Figure 13.1).

In light of this evidence and the association of P'oseyemu with Tewayó in seventeenth-century Spanish documents, there is ample basis for hypothesizing that P'oseyemu legends refer to the leader of a religious revolution that resulted in the depopulation of the Mesa Verde region and the creation of a new society in the Tewa Basin. Given this, it is easy to see why, some four centuries later, Po'pay and other leaders of the Pueblo Revolt appealed to his memory when the Pueblos found themselves in a situation of oppression similar to what P'oseyemu had endured in Tewayó. In doing so, the present moment was transformed into the first act of a prophetic spiritual drama that, if allowed to play out, would result in a new age of freedom and abundance for the Pueblo people.

The Original Pueblo Revolt

The suggestion that Tewa leaders of the Pueblo Revolt promoted it as a reenactment of the Mesa Verde migration leads to a third line of evidence supporting the religious revolution model of Tewa ethnogenesis. If this historical metaphor was a template for the Pueblo Revolt, the discourses and actions of the revolt should correspond to seventeenth-century oral traditions surrounding the Mesa Verde migration. Furthermore, the elements of these seventeenth-century oral traditions should bear some relationship to the actual discourses and actions of the original thirteenth-century events. In other words, it should be possible to perform a sort of reverse structural analysis to identify correspondences in the schematic structure of the Pueblo Revolt and the Mesa Verde migration.

There are, in fact, several parallels between the discourses and actions associated with the Pueblo Revolt, and those reflected in the archaeological record of Tewa ethnogenesis. The discourses and actions of Po'pay during the revolt clearly conformed to the ritual schema of emergence and also encouraged the destruction of current symbols and a return to an earlier way of life (Figure 14.3). This is documented by passages presented earlier in this chapter, and also by the following statement by Pedro Naranjo.

FIGURE 14.3. Statue of Po'pay in the National Statuary Hall, U.S. Capitol. Marble, by Cliff Fragua, Jemez Pueblo.

Asked for what reason they so blindly burned the images, temples, crosses, and other things of divine worship, he stated that the said Indian, Popé, came down in person, and with him El Saca and El Chato from the pueblo of Los Taos, and other captains and leaders and many people who were in his train, and he ordered in all the pueblos through which he passed that they instantly break up and burn the images of the holy Christ, the Virgin Mary and the other saints, the crosses, and everything pertaining to Christianity, and that they burn the temples, break up the bells, and separate from the wives whom God had given them in marriage.... They did this, and also many other things which he does not recall, given to understand that this mandate had come from the Caydi and the other two who emitted fire from their extremities in the said estufa of Taos, and that they thereby returned to the state of their antiquity, as when they came from the lake of Copala; that this was the better life and the one they desired. (Hackett and Shelby 1942, II:247–248)

These discourses are repeated in several of the captive testimonies in the Otermín documents (Hackett and Shelby 1942, II:235, 239–240, 244), and the fact that the Pueblos actually carried out these directives is attested to in eyewitness accounts of destroyed mission pueblos: "He entered it and found the church and convent entirely burned and everything else demolished. The pueblo was inspected and there were found two broken bells, in five pieces, a silver salter, a wine vessel, a censer for incense, and a small broken crown" (Hackett and Shelby 1942, II:230–231).

Po'pay also emphasized the material benefits that would come to his people if they followed the script to its conclusion: "he said likewise that the devil had given them to understand that living thus in accordance with the law of their ancestors, they would harvest a great deal of maize, many beans, a great abundance of cotton, calabashes, and very large watermelons and cantaloupes; and that they could erect their houses and enjoy abundant health and leisure" (Hackett and Shelby 1942, II:248). This detail is significant because religious discourse gains its power not only by constituting certain human preferences as revealed truths, ancestral traditions, or divine commandments, but also by connecting these preferences to basic notions of what is good and pleasing (Lincoln 2003: 55). In other words, successful religious discourses connect transcendent ideological constructs to bodily experience and emotional life.[15]

The ideology of the Pueblo Revolt can thus be characterized as one of a return to a state of bodily satisfaction through the overthrow of the dominant fraction, destruction of items related to the religion of that fraction, the abandonment of villages in which the religion of the dominant fraction had been practiced, and the re-adoption of the way of life of an earlier period. In addition, the revolt was presented as an episode of emergence through the procession of Po'pay and other leaders southward from the kiva at Taos after the Spanish had been expelled.

All of these discourses and actions correspond to discourses and actions associated with the Mesa Verde migration itself (Table 14.3). For example, in addition to ordering the churches destroyed, Po'pay ordered the rebuilding of kivas, the characteristic religious structures of the prehispanic era (Hackett and Shelby 1942,II:248). This sequence of actions corresponds to the destruction of Mesa Verde style kivas and their replacement by Rio Grande style kivas, which I have argued symbolized the "re-adoption" of religious forms and concepts of a previous era by ancestral Tewa people. In addition, the breaking and burning of crosses, bells, and Christian images correspond to the breaking and burning of kiva jars and mugs prior to leaving the Mesa Verde region, and the near-total absence of these forms in Tewa Basin pottery assemblages. The procession of Po'pay and other leaders southward from the Taos kiva in the far north corresponds to population movement from the Mesa Verde region to the Tewa Basin, and the abandonment of mission villages during the revolt in favor of newly constructed villages where the architecture reasserted traditional worldview concepts (Liebmann et al. 2005; Preucel 2000, 2002, 2006: Chap. 9) echoes the abandonment

TABLE 14.3. Correspondences between the Pueblo Revolt and Mesa Verde migration

Attribute	Pueblo Revolt	Mesa Verde Migration
Recently imposed authority	Spanish	Leaders of canyon-rim villages
Leader of religious revolution	Po'pay	P'oseyemu
Dominant discourse	Removal of Spanish authority and return to a previous way of life, as occurred when the people left Tewayó.	Elimination of hierarchy based on lineage, wealth, and status, and return to image of an ancestral way of life.
Treatment of religious structures	Churches burned, kivas rebuilt.	Ritual destruction of Mesa Verde kivas, adoption of Rio Grande kiva architecture.
Treatment of religious paraphernalia	Bells and Christian images broken and burned.	Kiva jars, mugs broken and burned; corrugations on cooking pots smeared.
Pattern of movement	Procession of leaders southward from the kiva at Taos.	Depopulation of the Mesa Verde region, movement south to the Tewa Basin.
Architectural changes	Abandonment of mission villages; new villages constructed in the mountains in the image of prehispanic cosmology.	Abandonment of canyon-rim pueblos; new villages constructed in the image of older great house architecture.
Treatment of opposing factions	Execution.	Massacres of opposing factions/villages.
Enforcement of compliance	Threat of punishment.	Increased surveillance in plaza pueblos; increased visibility of food preparation.

of canyon-rim villages in favor of plaza pueblos, or what Snead (2008b) calls "community houses," and which I have argued mapped the symbols of civic architecture from the great house era onto the community writ large.

Finally, the commandment by P'oseyemu and Po'pay that people who did not revolt would be killed appears to correspond to the evidence of factional conflict associated with the final depopulation of the Mesa Verde region (see Chapter 12). Their threats to punish individuals who did not behave in accordance with their dictates also appear to be reflected in changes in the built environment and daily practice following the Mesa Verde migration. The adoption of plaza pueblo architecture, for example, would have increased the public visibility of daily practices during the Late Coalition period, thus encouraging surveillance of individual behavior by community members to enforce compliance. Also, the movement of corn grinding from private rooms within Mesa Verde unit pueblos to plazas and rooftops in plaza pueblos would have increased the public visibility of household food preparation, discouraging individual households from hoarding private surpluses (Ortman 1998). Thus a surprising number of structural correspondences between the Mesa Verde migration and the Pueblo Revolt can be identified. This pattern reinforces the suggestion that the former was enshrined in social memory and used as a model for the latter in the seventeenth century.

Summary

I have suggested that it is productive to view the changes in material culture associated with Tewa ethnogenesis as reflections of discourses concerning the relationship between the new society that was forming in the Tewa Basin and the old society that was falling apart in the Mesa Verde region. When viewed from this perspective, the pattern of change suggests two discourses: one of a return to an ancestral mode of life represented by indigenous Rio Grande and earlier Mesa Verde practices, and a second of erasing the characteristic symbols of recent Mesa Verde society. I have also suggested that the only way practices reflecting these discourses could have been adopted so thoroughly and rapidly as a portion of the Mesa Verde population moved to the Tewa Basin is if they were connected to the sort of authoritative, transcendent, and moral discourses that are characteristic of religious movements. In short, I suggest that the depopulation of the Mesa Verde region, the mass migration to the Tewa Basin, and the construction of a new society in the Tewa Basin were all products of a religious revolution. Four findings support this model: (1) the discourses and actions reflected in the archaeological record of Tewa ethnogenesis are typical of those that accompany episodes of religious revolution; 2) seventeenth-century Tewas viewed their social memories of the Mesa Verde migration as a prototypical example of emergence; (3) the Tewa culture hero P'oseyemu appears to be a reflection in oral tradition of the leader of a successful religious revolution connected with Tewa ethnogenesis; and (4) the Pueblo Revolt was viewed by those who participated in it as a reenactment of the Mesa Verde migration, and as a result, the discourses and actions of the revolt exhibit a number of correspondences with the archaeological record of Tewa ethnogenesis itself.

The religious revolution model of Tewa ethnogenesis sheds considerable new light on the depopulation of the Mesa Verde region. If, in fact, the archaeological record of the Coalition period Tewa Basin was created by the same people who created the archaeological record of the Pueblo III Mesa Verde region, the differences between these two records provide a rich source of information on the social conditions that led to the collapse of Mesa Verde society in the late thirteenth century. In light of this model, the archaeological record of the final decades of occupation in the Mesa Verde region would appear to present a record of the losing side in an epic struggle over the path this society was to follow when it came to a critical juncture. The Coalition period record in the Tewa Basin would then reflect the preferences of the side that prevailed. Future comparisons of the relationship between these two records should shed considerable light on both.

The hypothesis regarding Tewa ethnogenesis developed here focuses on the movement of Mesa Verde populations to the Tewa Basin, but in the course of this study I have discussed a range of evidence suggesting that speakers of additional languages, especially Keres and Towa, also entered the Rio Grande region between AD 1200 and 1350. It is beyond the scope of this study to examine whether the proposed religious revolution affected these other groups, whether the movements of these groups were influenced by analogous social or religious movements, or whether other, unrelated but contemporaneous social processes were involved. It may be useful, however, to once again turn to the Great Plains for models. Over a fairly short period in the late eighteenth and early nineteenth centuries, several distinct ethnolinguistic groups—some of whom had been hunter-foragers, and others farmers—gave up their former way of life and adopted the nomadic, equestrian, hunting, raiding, and trading way of life characteristic of the historic High Plains culture area. Although traces of their former ways of life remained embedded in their social organizations (Oliver 1962), this process of mixing, borrowing, and transposing existing cultural elements in a context of intensive cross-cultural interaction resulted in a homogeneous material culture across the entire culture area that belies the diverse historical backgrounds of the peoples involved. The rapid and widespread adoption of new ceremonial practices such as the Sun Dance indicates that the formation of the Plains culture area was driven in part by a new and rapidly diffusing ideology (Archambault 2001; Young 2001), but studies of the histories of specific Plains tribes such as the Cheyenne show that internal political processes also contributed to the adoption of the historic Plains lifeway.

I suggest that the formation of the Rio Grande Pueblos in the thirteenth century is profitably viewed as a more modest example of culture area formation. During this period a number of bio-linguistically distinct peoples, some of whom already lived in the Rio Grande region, and some of whom lived in various portions of the San Juan drainage, moved to the Rio Grande and adopted a relatively homogeneous material culture created through the rearrangement and transposition of the bits and pieces of several preexisting cultures, including the ancestral Pueblo cultures of the San Juan drainage and the indigenous cultures of the Rio Grande drainage. Traces of the distinct cultural background of each group remained, but overall the process resulted in a new and relatively homogenous culture area. In this book I have traced the pathway followed by one such group from their homeland in the Mesa Verde region to the Tewa Basin in the Northern Rio Grande. The pathways by which other bio-linguistic lineages came to reside in the Rio Grande culture area is an important topic for future research.

Tewa Origins and Historical Anthropology

The studies presented in this book lead to a number of conclusions regarding the origins of the Tewa as a definable ethnic group. First, most of the ancestral Tewa population derived from the thirteenth-century population of the Mesa Verde region. Second, the Tewa language also originated in the Mesa Verde region and was brought to the Tewa Basin by migrants from there. Third, ancestral Tewa culture did not descend in a straightforward way from Mesa Verde culture, but instead appears to represent a hybrid of indigenous Rio Grande, earlier Mesa Verde, and newly invented models and practices. Fourth, I have argued in this chapter that the pattern of social change associated with this movement, discourses concerning the Pueblo Revolt some four centuries later, and oral traditions concerning the Tewa culture hero all suggest that a religious revolution was the mechanism that created the new identity that bound the Mesa Verde biolinguistic lineage to an emerging, hybrid culture, resulting in the formation of a new Tewa identity and associated ethnic group.

These conclusions have several implications for the practice of historical anthropology. One implication for archaeologists in the United States is the suggestion that historical anthropology should be viewed as distinct from cultural affiliation research. The Native American Graves Protection and Repatriation Act defines *cultural affiliation* as “a relationship of shared group identity which can be reasonably traced historically or prehistorically between a present day Indian Tribe or Native Hawaiian organization and an identifiable earlier group” (cited in Ferguson 2004:32–33). This law also stipulates that cultural affiliation is established based on the preponderance of 10 lines of evidence, including “geographical, kinship, biological, archaeological, anthropological, linguistic, folkloric, oral traditional, historical, and other relevant information or expert opinion.”

This study has presented a wealth of evidence supporting the claim that the Tewa language and the ancestral Tewa population originated in the Mesa Verde region, and on this basis it would appear reasonable to conclude that the Tewa Pueblos are affiliated with ancestral Pueblo archaeological sites of that region; however, I have also presented a range of evidence suggesting that the Tewa people as we know them today emerged as a self-conscious ethnic group only in the thirteenth century as a portion of the Mesa Verde population relocated to the Tewa Basin. In other words, even though the Tewa language originated in the Mesa Verde region, and Tewa ancestry can be traced to the Mesa Verde region, it does not seem appropriate to label the relationship between Mesa Verde people and Tewa people as one of shared group identity that can be traced into the past from the present. This is because, as argued in Chapter 2, ethnic groups are nothing more than material correlates of ethnic identities defined on the basis of whatever objective characteristics the members of such groups view as important at a given moment.

Also, it is important to not take the results of this study as indicating a straightforward, one-to-one relationship between ancestral Pueblo people of the Mesa Verde region and present-day Tewa people, because it is obvious from the evidence I have amassed that certain fractions of Mesa Verde society chose not to become a part of the emerging Tewa people. Instead, many chose to move elsewhere and incorporate with other groups, and some chose to resist movement altogether at the cost of their lives. There are almost certainly biological descendants of Mesa Verde people in a large number of present-day American Indian tribes, not to mention other fractions of contemporary U.S. society. In addition, early peoples of the Northern Rio Grande also contributed in substantive ways to Tewa ethnogenesis, so it would seem appropriate to suggest that Tewa people also have an affiliation with Developmental sites in the Northern Rio Grande, even though the Tewa language does not appear to have been spoken by the people who lived in them.

The issue, it would seem, is that it is possible to establish the nature of the relationship between present-day groups and ancient groups using multiple lines of evidence, but relationships of shared group identity — or, in other words, enduring ethnic groups — are never defined in this way by the members of the groups themselves. Rather, each of the objective characteristics associated with ethnic groups, the criteria for defining these groups, and the repertoire of identities that individuals ascribe to all evolve over time, and not necessarily as a package. Thus, in the same way that one can use the preponderance of evidence to show that present-day Tewa people do not have an exclusive relationship of shared group identity with all ancient Mesa Verde people, one can also imagine situations where a relationship of shared group identity might exist between a modern and ancient group without being reflected in the preponderance of evidence because the ethnic identity has endured, but the objective characteristics that define it have changed over time.

These are complex issues that cannot be resolved here, and it is important to recognize that, in the end, *cultural affiliation* is a legal concept and not a scientific one. For now, the key insight raised by this study is that shared group identity is not necessarily reflected in the preponderance of evidence that anthropologists have at their disposal to reconstruct human history. As a result, researchers should not delegitimize claims of cultural affiliation when various lines of evidence do not converge, nor presume affiliations are necessarily straightforward when they do.

A second implication of this study for the practice of historical anthropology is that it suggests new directions for the archaeology of migration. The recent literature on migration focuses on specifying the material culture attributes that are most reliable for tracking it. Based on Clark's (2001, 2004) work, the most useful attributes are those that result from childhood learning and that tend not to send social messages due to their low contextual visibility. As a result, practices that produce low-visibility attributes are likely to continue being performed by migrants in the destination area, at least initially. In this study I have applied these insights to the case of Tewa origins and found that the aspects of material culture that travel most reliably with migrants do exhibit continuity between the Pueblo III Mesa Verde region and the Early Coalition Tewa Basin. Nonetheless, these continuities would not likely convince a skeptic because the specific attributes involved also exhibit continuity with Developmental Tewa Basin material culture.

Thus, a basic problem with identifying migration on the basis of material culture continuities is that low-visibility attributes are often too general to distinguish the specific groups one would like to trace, whereas more-visible attributes, which are also often more specific and detailed, will only be expressed in the destination area when the migrants choose to do so—and the locals either allow it or are unable to stop it. It is also important to recognize that low-visibility attributes are not close analogues of neutral genetic variation because, in the latter case, genetic traces of population history remain for generations after migration, whereas traces of this history in low-visibility attributes often fade within a generation.[16]

I have used a variety of alternative methods in this study to identify migration between regions, including population studies, biodistance analysis, linguistic paleontology, long-distance exchange patterns, and the patterns of change within and between archaeological complexes. All of these studies paint a consistent picture of significant population movement over the course of the AD 1200s, but material culture only follows suit for certain traits and in certain areas, and by no means provides a signal of comparable strength. This cannot be taken as evidence against population movement because the wide range of patterns related to biology and language that have been identified in this study cannot be explained any other way. Instead, the issue may lie in the assumption that material culture should necessarily travel to the destination area when migrants outnumber the locals.[17]

I suggest that the recurrent difficulties archaeologists have had in tracing ancient migrations using material culture, even when other lines of evidence agree that a migration has occurred, indicate that *material culture continuities of any particular type are not a necessary correlate of migration*. Biology does bear a necessary relationship to population history due to the mechanisms of inheritance, gene flow, drift, and admixture, and language also preserves a signal of speech community events that include various forms of movement. Culture, on the other hand, bears a weak relationship to population history due to its role in adaptation to the environment, the relative ease with which cultural models are transmitted between individuals, the ability of humans to manipulate cultural models, and the nature of cultural selection. I therefore suggest that it may be more productive to view the material cultures of migrants as expressions of discourse, politics, power, and resistance than as reflections of inheritance or as functions of social kinetics. The notion that material culture reflects these processes is not new (e.g., Hodder 1991; Preucel 2006; Shanks and Tilley 1987), but the notion that migrants also use material culture to express their history and identity as a distinct people, to express how their new society relates to the old one, or to express their desire to incorporate into the destination area society is often overlooked. Material culture will only betray that movement has taken place when migrants choose the first strategy, whereas a number of alternative methods may be used to identify movement regardless of the migrants' choices.

This is not to say that cultural phylogenies do not exist. Rather, this is simply to say that the long-term relationship of cultural phylogenies to population history is generally weak. Cultural practices readily diffuse across social boundaries, but they are still transmitted between individuals and take the form of traditions exhibiting descent with modification, regardless of who practices them. Cultural traditions are therefore amenable to phylogenetic analysis but bear no necessary relationship to population history or to speech community history over the long term, and one is likely to badly misrepresent these aspects of human history when one attempts to use material culture as a proxy for genes or language.

A third general conclusion of this study for historical anthropology is the suggestion that religious movements, and especially those tied to population movements, represent one mechanism through which culture can become decoupled from a bio-linguistic lineage, and new social identities that bind this lineage to a transformed culture can emerge. Religious movements tied to population movement appear to be especially effective instruments of cultural transformation because culture change is always encouraged by movement, the oblique transmission characteristic of religious movements encourages reduced variation and rapid change, the discourses associated with such movements connect transcendent ideological constructs to the bodily experience of individuals, and the authority accorded to leaders of such movements enable them to impose their values and preferences upon the whole of society through persuasion or coercion. Thus, religious movements appear to be an important mechanism through which ethnogenesis took place in the prehispanic past as well as the period of European colonialism.

An important direction for future research should be an investigation of how often religious movements have been involved in motivating and supporting population movements. It would be premature to generalize at this point, but it is clear that population movements have been associated with religious or para-religious movements in several well-known cases, including the movement of Israelites from Egypt to Palestine, the movement of Cheyenne people from the Missouri River to the Black Hills, the movement of Latter-Day Saints from Illinois to Utah, and the movement of Euro-Americans across the North American frontier. A better understanding of how often such movements are associated with religious movements would be an important step in developing generalizations on the social processes responsible for unpackaged evolution in genes, language, and culture.

Finally, the most general conclusion of this study for the practice of historical anthropology, and for our understanding of ourselves, is that using the methods employed here, it is possible to trace the prehistory of "peoples without history," even when phylogenesis is an inappropriate model for characterizing their development. Utilizing methods that focus on areas where human biology and language intersect the archaeological record, I have shown that it is possible to trace the process of ethnic group formation without assuming the underlying process. The particular case of ethnic group formation examined here turned out to be an episode of ethnogenesis in which culture did not follow the path of genes and language, but if Tewa origins had involved phylogenetic descent, the methods used in this study would have identified it equally readily.

I believe the methods and conclusions of this study are important because they make a strong case that ethnogenesis has not been limited to recent human history. The time depth of most previous studies of ethnogenesis has been limited to the period covered by documentary history (e.g., Hill 1996). Because the onset of written history in many areas of the world coincides with European contact, ethnogenesis is at present best understood in the context of political, social, and economic disruptions that native cultures experienced as a result of European conquest and colonialism (Ferguson 2004). Consequently, some historical anthropologists have questioned whether ethnogenesis was as common in earlier periods of human history as it has been in recent centuries.

In this study, I have argued that ethnogenesis did occur in the prehispanic U.S. Southwest, and if the sorts of socioreligious movements that enable ethnogenesis could develop among groups of subsistence farmers living on a relatively high, dry, and isolated plateau, it would seem reasonable to propose that similar processes have been going on for much of our history as a species. Thus, ethnogenesis may lay behind many of the curious disjunctions in genes, language, and culture that anthropologists have noted among the world's peoples, and may also lie behind the recurrent difficulty that archaeologists have had linking archaeological sequences of adjacent regions. In this study I have utilized methods through which one can examine the formation of ethnic groups in prehistory regardless of the underlying process. The ability to trace ethnogenesis as well as phylogenesis in prehistory is essential if historical anthropology is to come to understand how the rich tapestry of contemporary human diversity has been woven. My hope is that this study will contribute to that end.

Notes

1. For a discussion of correlations between Kiowa-Tanoan speech communities and archaeological complexes, see Appendix D.
2. Bradley (1993) and Lipe and Ortman (2000) refer to these houses as "kiva-dominated units."
3. The changes in material practices highlighted in this section can also be characterized as "transpositions of schemas" (after Sewell 2005). If one considers historical events such as Tewa ethnogenesis as events that transform cultural structures, then "the structures that emerge from an event are always transformations of preexisting structures" (Sewell 2005:102). As a result, the new structures are recognizable as transformations of the old. The transposition of architectural and social models that took place as great house architecture was transformed into plaza pueblo architecture is a clear example of this process.
4. Notable exceptions are the suggestions of Bradley (1996) and Glowacki (2009) that the Pueblo III Mesa Verde region archaeological record reflects a religious

revitalization movement that developed following the collapse of the Chacoan regional system.

5. Lincoln's work is truly global in scope and incorporates the findings of several classic studies of American Indian revitalization movements, including the Ghost Dance religion (Mooney 1965), the Sun Dance religion (Jorgensen 1972), and the peyote cult (Aberle 1966), as well as studies of the French, American, and Iranian revolutions, the Reformation and Counter-Reformation, ancient Chinese rebellions, and so forth.
6. Liebmann (2002) shows that leaders of the Pueblo Revolt were not able to achieve total ideological hegemony either, as illustrated by Christian images in revolt period rock art.
7. However, Moore (1996:28) notes that numerous crescent-shaped mussel shell fragments found at Biesterfeldt are still used in present-day Cheyenne medicine bundles. These objects are known as *máthöhevo* 'the claw' and symbolize claws, the crescent moon, and protection from death. This semantic chain is based on the Cheyenne idea that the dark, negative forces in the world are counteracted by the light of the moon, and especially the waxing crescent moon due to its correspondence in shape with the claws of predators. Thus, the crescent shape is viewed as providing protection from death and darkness. In addition, the upward-facing tips of the waxing crescent moon at midsummer are likened to buffalo horns, and it is at this time that the major summer ceremonials begin (Moore 1996:207). Thus, there are material expressions of Cheyenne metaphors in the Biesterfeldt assemblage, and this reinforces Cheyenne and Dakota oral traditions that identify this site as an ancestral Cheyenne settlement.
8. Several excellent studies of this process are available. Sahlins (1985) illustrates that Hawaiian nobles appropriated an important myth and its associated rituals to interpret Captain Cook, the first European to visit the islands, as a god associated with temporary inversion of the political order. As a result, he was honored on his first visit, but killed during his second. In another example, Lincoln (2003:8–18) provides an analysis of the instructions given to Mohamed Atta, the leader of the Al-Qaeda cell that carried out the 9/11 attacks, concerning the way he and his associates were to spend their last day on earth. These instructions mapped elements of the present-day political situation onto paradigmatic events in the early history of Islam, thus converting their actions into equally momentous reinstantiations of these transcendent events. Gossen (2004) likewise argues that one of the main reasons that the Zapatista movement has received such widespread support among Maya people is that it has proceeded in accordance with ritual forms and a calendrical script that resonate deeply in Maya consciousness. Finally, Whiteley (1988:254–263) summarizes Hopi perspectives on the Oraibi split which suggest that it was encouraged to happen by village leaders, who promoted a construal of the situation in 1906 as an instantiation of a traditional Hopi schema connected to the demise of many ancestral villages, including Awatovi.
9. Po'pay (Popé) was the Tewa man from Ohkay Owingeh who is credited as the primary leader of the Pueblo Revolt. Alfonso Ortiz (2005 [1980]:84) translates *Po'pay* as 'ripe cultigens' and suggests that this potent name was earned through religious service as an adult. Ortiz also contends that Po'pay was a ceremonial leader of the summer people at Ohkay Owingeh, due to the associations of his name with the agricultural season. According to Spanish documents (Hackett and Shelby 1942, I:xxii), Po'pay was one of 47 Pueblo leaders who were arrested in 1675 in an attempt to stamp out traditional religious practices. Three of them were hanged, one committed suicide,

and the rest, including Po'pay, were publicly flogged and imprisoned in Santa Fe. A group of Tewas subsequently secured the release of Po'pay and the other survivors, and shortly after Po'pay moved to Taos and began to plot the revolt in the kiva there.

10. This is in exact opposition to Judeo-Christian tradition, in which humans were created perfect but fell from grace and were thus forced to leave the Garden of Eden.
11. Curtis (1926:18) suggests on etymological grounds that both of the major Pueblo clown societies (K'ósa and Kwi:raná among the Tewa) originated among Tewa-speaking people, but Curtis's Tewa consultants indicated that the Kwi:raná "came from the south, that is, from the Keres." Fortunately, the resolution of this contradiction has no bearing on the argument presented here.
12. In Parsons's (1994 [1926]:108) account, P'oseyemu was born at P'osíˀówînkeyi ('moss-greenness ruin'), the site adjacent to Ojo Caliente hot springs (P'osíp'o:), in the northern Tewa Basin. Harrington (1916:165) also recorded that P'oseyemu dwelled at P'osíˀówînkeyi and at the paired villages of Howídíˀówîngeyi and Hųųpóviˀówînkeyi, a short distance upstream and to the north. Finally, according to Harrington (1916: 164), P'oseyemu's grandmother lived, and still lives, in the pool at Ojo Caliente.

    A literal reading of these traditions would suggest that the person who inspired the P'oseyemu legends lived in the Tewa Basin as opposed to the Mesa Verde region. However, an argument can be made that P'oseyemu is associated with this locality due to the way these sites correspond to elements of the Tewa origin narrative. In addition to being the birthplace of P'oseyemu, P'osíˀówînkeyi is viewed as the place where the summer and winter people came together after migrating southward, on opposite sides of the Rio Grande, from their emergence place in the north (Ortiz 1969: 15–16). This episode could not have literally taken place in this way because many earlier ancestral Tewa villages are known, and the three sites under discussion here were all occupied contemporaneously (see Table 8.2 and Appendix B). However, the arrangement of ancestral sites in this locality mirrors the image-schematic structure of this narrative. The paired villages Hųųpóviˀówînkeyi and Howídíˀówîngeyi lie a few kilometers north and upstream of P'osíˀówînkeyi, on opposite banks of the Rio Ojo Caliente. These two sites were described as companion pueblos to Harrington (1916:161) and represent the northernmost ancestral Tewa villages in the Tewa Basin. In addition, the hot springs adjacent to P'osíˀówînkeyi are viewed as an emergence place "closer to home" than the primordial lake of emergence in the distant north (Richard Ford, personal communication, 2007). The local landscape thus presents the image of two pueblos straddling a watercourse, upstream and to the north of a single pueblo and hot spring representing a Tewa emergence place. Thus, P'oseyemu may be associated with this locality because it presents a potent, on-the-ground representation of the Tewa origin narrative, and P'oseyemu was involved in the ancient migration from the north and in Tewa ethnogenesis. For a similar approach to the interpretation of contradictions between the archaeological record and oral tradition, see Schmidt 2006.
13. This passage is especially important because, in Tewa origin narratives (e.g., Ortiz 1969:13–15), the first person to emerge from *p'o:kwin* was initiated by the carnivores, raptors, and carrion birds, who dressed him in buckskin and gave him a bow and quiver of arrows. This person then descended back into *p'o:kwin* as the hunt chief, the first "made" person, and subsequently gave "blue corn mother close to summer" to the summer chief, and "white corn mother close to winter" to the winter chief, thus installing the moiety chiefs that govern Tewa villages today. The hunt chief, as the supreme religious authority, also initiates the moiety chiefs and other "made" people.

14. Ortiz (1969:17) notes that two of the names for the common Tewa people who serve in no official capacity in the political or ritual system are "trash people" and "dust-dragging people," after an old practice whereby the common people swept the village prior to ceremonies or festivals.
15. For an extended and persuasive treatment of the relationship between meaning and human biology, see Slingerland 2008.
16. Technological traits of perishable material culture, which is rarely preserved in Tewa Basin sites, may be our best hope of finding additional, non-trivial material culture continuities between the Mesa Verde region and Tewa Basin. One study that could be done to assess this is an analysis of impressions left by coiled baskets on the exteriors of Santa Fe Black-on-white bowls. Basket-impressed sherds are also found in Mesa Verde region collections dating to the AD 1100s, and large numbers of baskets have been preserved in cliff dwellings throughout the San Juan drainage. Recent studies have also shown that it is possible to identify the foundation, stitch type, stitch direction, and stitch density of the baskets that made the impressions on the pottery vessels (Till et al., in prep.).
17. Researchers have no problem accepting unpackaged evolution when examining synchronic variation within a region. For example, during the Classic period (AD 1350–1540), Tewa Basin potters made black-on-white pottery, whereas Galisteo Basin potters, who also spoke Tewa, made glaze-painted red wares and polychromes (Cameron 1998; Creamer 2000; Spielmann 1998). Researchers have not viewed the replacement of black-on-white ware by glaze ware in the Galisteo Basin as indicating population replacement because this change took place during the occupations of established sites. Rather, the change is generally viewed as resulting from the adoption of foreign material culture traits via diffusion, or, in other words, unpackaged evolution. Yet, if this same change had taken place as Southern Tewa people moved to new sites, or to another area, some archaeologists might have difficulty accepting that the same population was involved.

Appendix A:
Kiowa-Tanoan Reconstructions

APPENDIX A: Kiowa-Tanoan Reconstructions

RECONSTRUCTION	TAOS (N. TIWA)[a]	ISLETA (S. TIWA)[b]	SAN JUAN (TEWA)[c]	JEMEZ (TOWA)[d]	KIOWA[e]	REFERENCE[f]
1. KT **tu* 'house'	*tu-ła* 'big-house'	*tú-łá* 'old house, pithouse, kiva'	*te:* 'house, hole, burrow'	*tɨ́:* 'shelter, corral'	*tó:~tò:-* 'house, tipi'	KH107
2. KT *t^{h}*ɨ* 'dwell'	*t^{h}ɨ-* 'house, building, room, to live, dwell'	*t^{h}ɨ* 'dwelling' (n.)	*t^{h}a:* 'to dwell, live'	*ṣ̌ô* 'live, dwell'	*t^{h}ol-* 'cohabit'	KH116, D31
3. KT *'*į̨ęt^{h}u-* 'ladder' (3a. KT *'*į̨ęn-* 'foot')	*'į̨ę-t^{h}u-* 'ladder' ('*į̨ęn-* 'foot')	*'ę-t^{h}u* 'stepladder' (*èn* 'foot')	*še'é* 'ladder' (*ân* 'foot')	*t^{y}â:kyę̀ n'į̨* 'ladder' *ę̀ hèlè* 'rung of a ladder' (*ǫ̂:t'ǣ~ǫ́:nǭ-* 'foot')	*ɔ̀n-t^{h}ót-à:dɔ̀* 'ladder' (*ɔ̀n* + *t^{h}ót* 'to rise, climb' + *á:dɔ̀* 'pole') (*ɔ̀n-* 'foot')	KH84
4. KT **pį̨ę* 'sleeping mat'	*pį̨ę-* 'bed'	*na-pę* 'bed'	*w^{h}ǫh-pą'* 'mattress' *nangeh-pą'* 'floor mat'	*hį́-pǫ̂* 'sleeping mat'	*pal* 'bed'	
5. KT **si* 'stone point'				*t^{y}í* 'arrowhead'	*sesegɔ* 'arrowhead'	KH8
6. KT **cǿ* 'hammer'			*k'u-c ǿ:'i'* (stone-hammer)	*sǫ́:nį́* 'hammer'	*t^{h}ǫ́:* 'club'	
7. KT **k^{h}æy* 'skin, hide'	*xóy-* 'skin, hide'	*k^{h}ay* 'skin'	*k^{h}owa* 'skin, bark, leaf-sheath, corn-husk'	*wǽ-hæ* 'skin, hide' *hǽ̂:* 'cornhusk'	*k^{h}ɔ́y* 'skin, hide, cloth, mat'	KH167, D44
8. KT **bų* 'bag'	*môn-mú* 'glove' (hand-bag)	*tąmų'u* 'seed bag'	*mú:* 'sack'	*fį́-mą* 'bag' (*fî-* 'buckskin')	*sɔ́:-bį́* 'quiver' (arrow-bag)	KH12
9. KT **cę* 'sinew'	*cę́-* 'ligament, sinew'			*zį̂* 'sinew, bowstring'	*tę-gɔ:'t* 'sinew, thread, cord'	
10. KT **to* 'shoe, moccasin' (10a. PTi **kɨob* 'moccasin')	(*kɨob-* 'moccasin, shoe')	*ta-* 'shoe' (*kɨab* 'shoe, moccasin')	*an-to* 'shoe' *púyeh anto* 'moccasin' (buckskin-shoe)	*į̂:* 'shoe'	*tò:-hį̂:* 'moccasins' (shoes-real) *kɔ^{h}-'ɔn* 'moccasin' (skin-foot)	

11. KT **pʰu* ‘snare’	*pɨo-pʰo-ne* ‘horsehair rope’ (*pʰɨo* ‘horsehair’ + *pʰo* ‘rope’)	*na-fɨa-fa* ‘rope’	*pʰe:* ‘trap’	*fó:* ‘rope, snare’	*pʰò-* ‘trap, snare’	KH171
12. KT **pǫ́* ‘to sound’	*pų̂* ‘noise’	*pua-hʷiad* ‘drum’ (*pua* + *hʷiad* ‘hit’)	*pų̂:* ‘sound’ *tanbay* ‘drum’	*pǫ́:* ‘drum’	*pǫ́:-y* ‘to sound’ *pɔ́l-kʰɔ̀-* drum’ (*pɔ́l* ‘musically rousing’ + *kʰɔ̀* ‘skin, hide’)	D4
13. KT **tup-* ‘flute, whistle’	*tub-* ‘flute’	*tup* ‘flute’	*tę́ŋ* ‘tube, flute’	*tų́* ‘flute, whistle’	*tǫ́:-bá~-bɔ́t* ‘flute, wind instrument’	KH82
14. KT **sa* ‘tobacco’	*łá-ne*	*łe*	*sa:*	*tʸu-ne*	*sɔ́:-tóp* ‘pipe’	KH192, D83
15. KT **pʰe* ‘to smoke’	*pʰi-wi* ‘to smoke’		*pʰih-pa:* ‘cigarette’	*fî:* ‘smoke a cigarette’	*há:b* ‘to smoke’	KH170, D11
16. KT **p’ɨo* ‘ripe corn’	*p’ɨo-’óna* ‘fresh corn on the cob, green corn’	*p’ɨ* ‘green corn, corn on the cob’ *p’ɨa* ‘ripe corn’ *p’ɨam* ‘ripe’	*p’e:* ‘fresh corn, ripeness’	*p’ô:* ‘green ear of corn’ *p’ó* ‘ripe’	*p’ɔ́:gyá* ‘green, fresh’ *é:-p’ɔ́:gyá* ‘fresh ear of corn’	KH45, D17, JH9
17. KT **’ɨa* ‘(pop)corn’	*’ɨa-ˀáne* ‘ripe corn’	*’ɨya* ‘dried corn on the cob’			*é:-tʰáttɔ̀* ‘corn kernel’ (plural: *é:-tʰâl*) *é:-gɔ́* ‘seed, fruit’ *é:-góp* ‘corn plant’ *é:-tʰâl-kʰɔ̨̀y* ‘corn husk’	D99, JH3
18. KT **cʰą* ‘squash, gourd’	*kʷœ-póne* ‘water-melon’ (Mexican-squash)		*sąndía* ‘watermelon’ *po’wiyeh* ‘gourd rattle’	*tʸį́:* ‘gourd, dipper, spoon’	*tʰɔ̨̀:-gɔ̀* ‘cultivated gourd, gourd rattle’ *ta:ˀhe-pį-gɔ* ‘water-melon’	
19. KT **sį-* ‘to boil’	*łɨya* ‘to boil’	*łąr* ‘to boil’	*sæ-nbé:* ‘cooking pot’	*tʸǫ́:* ‘to boil’	*sɔ́n* ‘to boil’	KH25, WT77

RECONSTRUCTION	TAOS (N. TIWA)[a]	ISLETA (S. TIWA)[b]	SAN JUAN (TEWA)[c]	JEMEZ (TOWA)[d]	KIOWA[e]	REFERENCE[f]
20. KT **k'uo* 'to lay down'	*k'úo* 'put, place, lay'	*k'ua* 'to lay down'	*k'û*ˀ 'lay down'		*é:-k'ú:* 'planted field' *k'óp~ k'ú:~ k'úl* 'lay down plural object, plant seeds'	KH115
21. KT *'*eya* 'willow'	*'ía-ło* (willow-tree)	*'iya-ła* (willow-tree)	*yán*		*á:-hį̀:* 'cottonwood' (tree-real) *àyp'í-gɔ̀* 'willow'	
22. KT **sę* 'prickly pear'	*łę́-* 'cactus, thorn'	*łį-feura* 'prickly-pear'	*sǽ̨:* 'prickly pear'	*tʸǽ̨:* 'prickly pear, cactus'	*sę́:* 'cactus, stickers, peyote'	KH36
23. KT **siw-* 'wild onion'	*łiw-* 'wild onion, onion'	*łiw* 'onion'	*si* 'wild onion, onion'	*tʸíwé* 'onion'	*sôl* 'wild onion'	KT136, JH28
24. KT **kʷę* 'oak'	*kʷę* 'hard, iron metal'		*kʷǽ̨:* 'oak' *kʷǽ̨:-k'ų* 'iron'	*gį̂:* 'scrub oak' *gį́* 'metal, steel'	*gų́* 'animal horn' *tok'ft-a:'dɔ* 'oak tree'	KH135, D54, WT22, JH25
25. KT **tu* 'cotton-wood, tree'	*tu-ło-*	*tu-ła*	*te:*	*tɨ-dabɨ* 'in the forest'	*to-p* 'stick, stake' *á:-hį̀:* 'cottonwood (tree-real)'	D25, WT91, KH195
26. KT **k'uo* 'spruce'	*k'úwo-* 'spruce, fir'	*k'uawa* 'large cedar'	*ka-'ąyǽ̨:* 'white pine' ("leaf-smoothness")	*k'ʸó* 'spruce, evergreen tree'	*k'ol* 'cedar'	WT69
27. KT **kʷæl* 'coyote, wolf'	*kol-éna*	*kar*	*kʰų:-yó*	*kʸǽ̨nį̄* 'dog' *tî̧-kǽ̨̀į̄* (coyote? fox? wolf?)	*kûy, kúyɔ̀l* 'wolf, coyote'	WT23
28. KT **kiu* 'prairie dog'		*ki'u*	*kée*		*cá:*	
29. KT **k'ʷuo* 'jack-rabbit'	*k'óna*	*k'ią*	*k'ʷán*	*bɨ́dǽ̂:*	*k'ómsɔ̀*	
30. KT **t'o* 'antelope'	*t'ó-* 'deer, antelope'	*t'a*	*t'on*	*t'â:~t'âpē*	*t'ɔ̀:-* 'antelope, deer' *t'áp* 'deer'	KH4, WT94, JH42

31. KT **pę* 'deer'	*pę́-*		*pǽ̨:*	*pǽ̨:*	*pį* 'food'	KH50, D6, JH45
32. KT **kol-* 'bison'	*kon-*		*kǫ̂'*	*tôtʸā*	*kɔ́l* 'buffalo (cow), cattle'	KH34, D43, JH56
33. KT **kodo* 'crow' (?)	*kókì-*	*kara*	*odo*	*kʸá:*	*kɔ̀ɔ́:*	
34. KT **kʰæwi* 'grasshopper' (?)		*kʰawrų*	*kʰowi'*	*hédá*	*k'ɔ̀:lɔ́-kʰɔ̂:yí*	
35. PT **suo* 'arrow'	*łuo-* 'arrow'	*łua* 'arrow'	*sú* 'arrow'	*tʸá:* 'arrow'	*sɔ́:-bį:* 'quiver'	KH7, D95
36. PT **tukʰʷa* 'pit-house'	*tuła* 'big-house'	*túłá* 'old house, pit-house, kiva'	*te:whá* 'house' (*te:* 'house, hole, burrow' + *whá* 'home, room block')	*tɨ́:hæ̂:* 'house' (*tɨ́:* 'shelter, corral')		
37. PT **t'ų́-* '(coiled) basket'	*tˀęną*	*łicha*	*t'ún*	*t'ɨ̨́:-pove* 'basket-flowers'	*són-k' ɔ'at-dɔ* 'grass-dish'	
38. PT **búlu* 'pottery (bowl), round'	*mulu-* 'pottery'	*búru* 'pottery bowl'	*be:* 'pottery bowl, vessel, fruit' *be:-gi'* 'small and round' *bu:* 'encircle' *bú:'ú* 'town, plaza'	*bɨ́-dó* 'round, fat, chubby' *tʸa:-bɨ* 'sacred (pottery) bowl'	*cęn-ď'ɔ'at-dɔ* 'clay dish'	
39. PT **ɨ* 'bow' (39a. TT **xʷíd* 'string')	(*xʷíl-* 'bow')	(*hʷír* 'bow')	*á* (*kʰʷi* 'vegetal fiber')	*ó*	*'al-ia-dɔ* 'bowstring' (*'al* 'to force' + *ya* 'string, rope, cord')	KH27, JH49
40. PT **kʰia* 'axe'	*kʷǫ́* 'axe'	*šia-kʰoa* 'axe'	*k'ù:-wí:* 'axe' *k'u:-pʰé* 'tomahawk'	*hé:* 'axe' *hé:-sǫ́:nį́* 'tomahawk'	*hǫ́:-tʰǫ́:* 'axe, tomahawk' (metal-club)	
41. PT **pį* 'thread' (41a. PTi **pʰɨ* 'thread')	(*pʰɨ-* 'thread')	(*pʰɨ* 'wire, thread')	*pą'*	*pį́:-nį́*	*ya-e-bɔ* 'string, rope'	

RECONSTRUCTION	TAOS (N. TIWA)[a]	ISLETA (S. TIWA)[b]	SAN JUAN (TEWA)[c]	JEMEZ (TOWA)[d]	KIOWA[e]	REFERENCE[f]
42. PT **pęd-* 'sew'	*pę́lą* 'sew'	*pɨ̨r* 'sew'	*pæn* 'sew'	*pùnų* 'sew'	*so* 'sew, mend'	
43. PT **p'ę̨* 'road, trail'	*p'įęna*	*p'ę*	*p'ô:*	*p'ǫ́:* 'path, road'	*hǫ́ɔ̀n* 'road, way'	KH148, D15
44. PT **kų* 'ceremony, dance' (44a. PTi **p^hɨl* 'dance')	*kųɬi-* 'ceremonial dance' (*p^hɨl-* 'dancers')	(*p^hɨ́ar* 'dance')	*šaḏeh*	*kɨ̨́:* 'dance, dancer' (cf. *vɨ́:tè* 'jump')	*kún-gyà* 'dance' (*kún-* 'jump')	
45. PT **'æ* 'metate'	*óna* 'grinding stone, metate'		*ó* 'metate'	*ǽ:* 'metate'	*é:-sǫ̂:-bɔ̀* (*é:-* 'grain, corn'; *sóm* 'grind, sharpen')	
46. PT **t'á:* 'to grind'	*tîl-* 'to grind'	*tiar* 'to grind'	*t'á:* 'to grind'	*t'ǽ:* 'to grind'	*sóm* 'to grind, sharpen, brush hair'	KH95, WT52
47. PT **kæ* 'to plant'	*kó* 'to plant, plough' *ko-ˀóne* 'planting, cultivating'	*ka* 'to plant' *na-ka* 'planted field' (earth-planted)	*ko:* 'to plant'	*kê:* 'to plant' *kê:-p'ô:* 'planting corn'	*k'óp~ k'ú:~ k'úl* 'lay down plural object, plant seeds'	KH143, WT17
48. PT **k^hų* '(flour) corn'	*k'ǫˀóne* 'corn cob'		*k^hų:* 'corn cob, corn plant' *k^hų́:-k^hæn* 'cornmeal' (*k^hæn* 'flour')	*hɨ̨́* 'cornmeal'		D47, WT21, JH6a
49. PT **k^hɨ* 'kernel'	*xɨ-* 'seed'	*k^hɨ* 'corn kernels'	*k^he* 'corn grains'	*k^{hy}ínɨ̨́-hɨ* 'corn kernels'		D47, WT21, JH6b
50. PT **tą* 'bean'	*tą-* 'bean' *tǫ* 'seed'	*tą* 'seed, bean'	*tą́* 'seed' *tû:* 'beans'	*tǫ* 'bean'	*dǫ̂:-gɔ́t* 'seed' (*dǫ́:-* 'down, inside')	
51. PT **nąpa* 'field'	*nąpá-* 'field'	*napé* 'field, garden' *naka* 'planted field'	*nava* 'field'	*nǫ́:pæ̀* 'field; plot of land for planting'	*é:- k' ú:* 'planted field'	

52. PT *'ɨo 'sunflower plant'	p'o-'ɨow-	'ɨa 'sunflower-plant' 'ɨa-nąpap 'sunflower-flower'	e:į' 'sunflower plant' e:į-cí-póvi 'sunflower-flower'	ošt^{y}-poh	ho-sɔm'a:'dɔ t'ep-sɔy-a:'dɔ		
53. PT *p^{h}uol- 'yucca'	p^{h}uol-	fórɫa	p^{h}a:	f^{w}â:lā fâ: 'banana'	ɔ́l-p'ɔ́$^{?}$ɔ̨́: 'yucca root, soap' ("hair-wash")	KH210	
54. PT *t'o 'pinyon nut'	t'ow- 'pinyon'	t'au-ɫa 'pinyon tree'	t'o	t'â:		KH134, D35, WT50, JH22	
55. PT *g^{w}ę 'ponderosa'	wę- 'pine'	wį 'big tall pine'	wæn 'ponderosa'	wą-k^{w}ǽ̨ 'pine' k^{w}ǽ̨ 'ponderosa' k^{w}ǽ̨-nį́ 'pine tree'	zǫ́:~zón 'pine tree'	KH142, D58, WT11	
56. PT *nǫ- 'aspen'	nął-		nana	nǫnį́ 'cottonwood'		KH11	
57. PT *hų 'juniper'	hú- 'cedar' hų́-p'oha- 'juniper'	hų- 'cedar'	hų́: 'cedar, juniper'	ħɨ̨́ 'juniper'	ɔ̀:-hį́ 'cedar' (?-real)	D91, WT14, JH52	
58. PT *tɨ 'elk'	tɨ-	tɨ	ta:	tôt^{y}ā 'buffalo'	k'o-gɔ-e	KH63, D22, WT47, JH39	
59. PT *k'uo 'bighorn sheep'	k'ua- 'wool, sheep'	k'oa 'sheep'	k'úwá 'sheep' p'in-k'úwá 'mountain sheep'	k'^{y}ǽ: 'sheep'	ká:bòlì: 'domestic sheep'	KH159	
60. PT *sǫ 'skunk'	kuylulú-	kuchuru	są́:	t^{y}į́:	tal tal-to'eknɔt		
61. PT *delu 'turkey'	p'ian-lîl- 'turkey' "mountain-chicken" lilú- 'chicken'	tu-diru (cf. diru 'chicken')	p' in-di: 'turkey' (mountain-chicken) di: 'chicken, turkey' šą̈ ´ą̈ 'grouse'	dél'ī 'chicken, fowl' p'é:lì--dèl'ī "mountain-chicken"	pę'	KH85, D38, WT8	
62. PT *ce 'eagle'	cíw-	šiw	ce:	sé:	kuto-hį	KH59	
63. PT *pɨ 'fish'	pɨ-	pɨ	pa:	pô	ɔ̀:-pį́:	KH78	

RECONSTRUCTION	TAOS (N. TIWA)[a]	ISLETA (S. TIWA)[b]	SAN JUAN (TEWA)[c]	JEMEZ (TOWA)[d]	KIOWA[e]	REFERENCE[f]
64. TT **k'ɨo-ti* 'roof-top'	*ik'ɨo-to* 'ceiling, roof' *k'ɨo* 'on top'	*k'ɨa-chu* 'roof' *k'ɨa-tit* 'on top of'	wha'-k'e:-d̲i 'room-top, roof' *k'é-wé* 'on top of'			
65. TT **sį-bulu* 'cooking pot'	*łol-múlu* 'pot'		*sæ-nbé:* 'cooking pot'	*gídá* 'pot'		
66. TT **p'o-bulu* 'olla'		*p'a-búru* 'water-jar'	*p'o-nbe:* 'olla'	*gíbǽ* 'olla'		
67. TT **k'ulu* 'dipper'		*k'uru*	*k'éd̲éh*	t^{y}*į́:nį́* 'dipper' t^{y}*į́:čile* 'spoon, dipper' *zį́:* 'handle of dipper'	t^{h}*ǫ'o-p* 'dipper'	
68. TT **kɨn* 'cradle-board'	*kɨn-* 'cradleboard'	*na-kuna* 'cradle'	*kan* 'cradle'	*kį́-dàbǽ* 'child-board'	p^{h}*ą:'top* 'cradle'	
69. TT **cia* 'knife'	*cia*	*šia*	*ci-yó* 'flint-big'	*gį́*t^{y}*ī* 'knife'	*k'a*	D68, WT68
70. TT *k^{hw}*ę́d-* 'pick, hoe' (70a. PTi k^{hw}*iad* 'hoe')	x^{w}*ę́l-* 'pick, digger' (x^{w}*iad-* 'hoe')	(*nąpe-hwíena* 'hoe', 'field-hitter')	*nan-whę́d̲i* 'hoe'	*hę́* 'inter' *tâ* 'hoe'	*dɔmku'* 'digging stick' ("earth-hitter")	WT59, JH16
71. TT **po* 'squash'	*pó-*	*pa*	*po:* 'squash, pumpkin' *po:yo* 'pumpkin'	*wę́hę́:* 'pumpkin, squash'		KH174
72. TT **t'ó* 'sage-brush'	*t'ówlu-*		*t'ó:*	k'^{y}*ǽláfō* ('Navajo weed')	t^{h}*a'gɔ't* t^{h}*á:gyá* 'blue sage'	
73. TT **kɨo* 'bear'	*kɨo-*	*kɨa*	*ke:*	*fǽlá*	*'ɔn-ha:'de*	KH15
74. TT **piw-* 'cotton-tail' (?)	*piw-*	*piwú*	*pu:*	*ɦî̜:*	p^{h}* òlą́:-hį:* '?-real'	

75. TT **cu* 'dog'	*culo-*	*kwinide* 'dog'	*céh*		*cę̂:* 'horse' *cę̂:-hį̀:* 'dog-real' *cádô:* 'small, long-haired native dog'	KH54, D63
76. TT **k*^{h}*ęm* 'mountain lion'	*xęm-*	*k*^{h}*im*	*k*^{h}*æn*	*šǽ̨:t*^{y}*ā* 'cougar' *šǽ̨mɨ̨́* 'bobcat' *ǽ̨yɨ̨́* 'mountain lion'	*k'ɔ̨́-p*^{h}*òp* 'bobcat' (lion-spotted)	
77. PTi **łuo-mų́* 'quiver'	*łuo-mų́* 'quiver'	*łua-mų́* 'arrow-bag'	*sú-d̠eh*	*sa-d̠e*	*sɔ́:-bį́:*	
78. PTi *t'įęn-* 'dish'	*t'įęn-* 'dish'	*t'ę* 'tub'	*są̈ʔą̈wéh* 'dishes'	***tâsæ̀*** 'dish, bowl, cup'	*són-k'ɔ'at-dɔ* 'grass-dish'	
79. PTi **cial* 'gourd rattle'	*cial-* 'gourd, gourd rattle'	*šiar* 'gourd rattle'	*po'wiyeh* 'gourd rattle'	*t*^{y}*į́:* 'gourd, dipper, spoon'		
80. PTi **łowo* 'viga'	*t*^{h}*ɨ-łówǫ-* (house + *ło-wo* 'pole', *ło* 'wood')	*łą́wa* 'viga'	*te-p*^{h}*éh* ("house timber")	*ǽ̨t*^{y}*ā* 'viga' (*t*^{y}*ê* 'stick, wood')	*guɔ-n* 'tipi pole'	
81. PTi **ną-k*^{h}*ų́* 'adobe'	*ną-xú-* 'earth-stone' *kuyúna* 'stone'	*ną-k*^{h}*ų́* (*k*^{h}*iaw* 'stone')	*na-p'o-k*^{h}*ų:* 'mud-stone' *k'u:* 'rock, stone'	*k'*^{y}*â:-pæya* 'adobe, rock-make' *k'*^{y}*â:* 'stone, rock'	*cęįn-to* 'mud house'	
82. PTi **kwiawi-p'įę* 'race-road'	*kwiawi-p'įę-* 'race-track'	*hwiawi-p'ę* cf. *hwiat-hum* 'to chase'	*ǿ̨:-p'ô:* 'run-road'	*mį́:n'į̄-p'ǫ́:* 'race-road'		
83. PTi **cud-* 'shirt'	*cud-* 'shirt, garment' (*c'un-* 'deerhide')	*šud* 'shirt'	*to* 'shirt, dress'	*té:-dè* 'shirt'	*t'ǫ-gya* 'shirt, article of clothing' (*t'ǫ-* 'to scrape')	
84. PTi **cɨlmųyu* 'turquoise'	*cą̀lmųyų́*	*šį̀rmųyu*	*k'ų:yœ:*	*sįgi*	*tso-sɔhye*	

Reconstruction	Taos (N. Tiwa)[a]	Isleta (S. Tiwa)[b]	San Juan (Tewa)[c]	Jemez (Towa)[d]	Kiowa[e]	Reference[f]
85. PTi **t'ok*^{h}*ę* 'cotton'	*t'oxę-* 'cotton'	*t'ak*^{h}*į* 'cotton, cotton plant'	*sek*^{h}*œ* 'cotton'	*pį́:* 'thread, cotton'	*t'œ̨-k*^{h}*ɔ'-dɔ* 'white cotton cloth' *pal-p*^{h}*ɔt'-dɔ* 'filament of cotton' (quilt-fuzz) *pal-p'ɔl-gop* 'cotton plant'	
86. PTi **pisólo* 'blanket'	*pisólo*	*pisára*	*pesânda*	*pœ́hœ̄l'è*	*k'ɔ'-dɔ*	
87. PTi **p'okú* 'tortilla'	*p'okú-* 'bread' (any kind)	*p'ak*^{h}*u-łįta* 'tortilla (*łįta* 'wheat') *p'akú-šįr* 'bread-blue, paper-bread'	*buwá-t*^{h}*ít*^{h}*í* 'corn tortilla (made w/ dough)' *buwá* 'paper bread'	*t*^{y}*į́:-bèlà* 'tortilla' *šílá-bèlà* 'round-bread, blue-corn tortilla'		
88. PTi **kolno* 'badger'	*kolno-*	*karna*	*k'ę́yá*	*sǫ*	*k*^{h}*ɔ'ku*	
89. PTi **tolí* 'macaw'	*tolú-* 'parrot'	ter-íðe	*tanį́'* 'macaw'	*mą́:pē* 'parrot'	*tǫ-kuto* (talk-bird)	
90. KT **sęgo* 'wild potato'	*łí-phíana* 'root, carrot, beet, turnip'	*na-łí*^{ʔ}*u* 'vegetables'	*sœ̨go-be* 'wild potato-fruit'	*nœ̨́-t*^{y}*œ̨̀* 'potato' ('earth' + *t*^{y}*œ̨̀*)	*sęgɔ* 'sweet potato'	JH32
91. PTi **łowa* 'ritual officer'	łowa'ána 'officer' (cf. *łowa'áne* 'speech') *p'i* 'head' *p'iwási* 'boss' (head-one-is) *t*^{h}*i-p' iyana* 'councilor' (house head-of-house)	*wiłáwide* 'member of ritual society' *p'i* 'head' *ką́beh*^{w}*íride* 'chief-bow' (assistant to town chief) *ch'umide* 'chief, first-person' (cf. *ch'up* 'first')	*p'ôn* 'head' *tų:yón* 'chief' (*tų:* 'sound, word') *con:in* tribal officers	*t'i* 'head' *fí:* 'chief'	*t*^{h}*aum* 'head' *t*^{h}*aum-dók'i* 'head-society leader'	

92. KT **mąhų* 'owl' (92a. PTi **kǫw-* 'owl')	(*kǫ̀wéna* 'owl')	(*kįwíde* 'owl') *łųk'ų́de* 'owl'	*mąhų̂:* 'owl' *ciso'yo* 'owl' (eyes-big) *ké:-mąhų̂:* 'burrowing owl' (prairie-dog owl)	*hį́:nì̜:* 'owl'	*mǫ'hį* horned owl' *sǫn-mǫ'hį* 'grass owl' *belkitgya* 'screech owl' (*bel-* 'mouth') *t*^{h}*ǫp*^{h}*ɔhol* 'large owl, no horns' ('leg' + 'downy') *c'ǫgu* 'horned owl' *sɔp*^{h}*ol* 'large owl' (*k'op-sɔp*^{h}*ol* 'mountain-ghost')
93. PT **kįn* 'corn stalk' (93a. PTi **koptu-* 'corn tassel')	*koptúne* 'corn tassel'	*kaptu* 'corn tassel' (*kaptu'ɨju* 'mythic being', lit. 'corn tassel-growing')	*kąn* 'tassel' *kątęn* 'tassel stalk' *kątu* 'pollen'	*kį́n'ī̜* 'corn plant; corn stalk' *ɦô:lī* 'corn pollen'	*'a't*^{h}*ąn* 'corn tassel' (*'a'* 'stick, plant') *é:-góp, é:-t*^{h}*âl-góp* 'corn plant, corn stalk'

Notes: Noncognate terms for a given reconstruction are printed in gray-shaded text.
[a] George L. Trager Papers, University of California, Irvine; Trager 1946.
[b] Brandt p.c.; C. T. Harrington 1920; Frantz and Gardner 1995.
[c] Harrington 1916; Henderson and Harrington 1914; Martinez 1982; Robbins et al. 1916.
[d] Hale 1962; Harper 1929; Watkins p.c.; Yumitani 1998.
[e] Hale 1962; Harrington 1928; Trager and Trager 1959; Meadows 2010; Watkins, p.c.
[f] References with a 'KH' prefix are represented in Hale's (n.d.) cognate sets; notes with a 'D' prefix are represented in Davis's 1989 cognate sets; notes with a 'WT' prefix are represented in Whorf and Trager's 1937 cognate sets; and notes with a 'JH' prefix are examples given in Hill 2008.

Notes for specific reconstructions:
3. May be a transparent compound, but I have not identified a Tiwa verb corresponding to Kiowa *tʰót* 'to rise, climb' and thus infer that the Tiwa forms for 'ladder' are cognates that no longer have a clear morphological analysis.
5. The proto-meaning of this form is inferred to be 'stone point' because the Jemez and Kiowa cognates refer to a flaked-stone projectile point as opposed to an arrow per se.
6. The initial Kiowa correspondence is incorrect, but the vowels are regular. This reconstruction may be suspect, but it plays no role in the arguments presented in Chapter 7.
9. The Jemez correspondence should be /s/ instead of /z/, but the vowels are regular.
12. The Isleta and Kiowa forms for 'drum' are not cognate because the Kiowa form incorporates the root for 'skin, hide,' whereas the Isleta form incorporates the root for 'hit.'
15. The Kiowa consonant is irregular (should be /pʰ/ instead of /h/), but the vowel is regular.
18. The Taos word for 'watermelon' (Robbins et al. 1916:111) demonstrates that this cultigen was introduced by the Spanish, and that Pueblo people viewed watermelons as being similar to squash. Note also that the Kiowa word for 'watermelon' is not cognate with the Tewa or Taos forms. Thus, the meaning of the Tewa cognate must have shifted to 'watermelon' from an older meaning. The original meaning was probably 'squash' or 'gourd,' based on the Kiowa cognate.
27. This reconstruction assumes that the labial component of the initial KT consonant was lost in Tiwa and descended as /uy/ in Kiowa (Hale 1967:116, 118).
28. The Kiowa form is likely cognate palatalization of *k > c.
33. Onomatopoeic?
34. The second part of the Kiowa form is inferred to be cognate, but the compound is unanalyzed.
35. The initial vowel in the Kiowa form does not correspond.
37. The initial vowel in the Taos form does not correspond, but the Tewa and Jemez forms confirm a Proto-Tanoan reconstruction.
39. Kiowa term for "bowstring," which Hale took as cognate, requires too much semantic latitude to be so.
43. The vowel in the Tewa form is irregular.
44. The Kiowa form is not cognate because the initial vowel does not correspond, and the word derives from the Kiowa reflexive verb *gún* 'to jump, dance' (Laurel Watkins, personal communication, 2008).
47. The Kiowa meaning 'to plant seeds' is probably a semantic extension that developed after Kiowa became distinct from Tanoan.
52. The initial vowels exhibit regular correspondence.
56. The Jemez form has been applied to a different species in the same plant family.

57. The Kiowa vowel is irregular.
59. The Kiowa form is a loan from Spanish.
65 and 66. The Tiwa and Tewa forms are identical transparent compounds, but are more likely to be cognate because they are from closely related dialects that were adjacent during their period of divergence.
70. The Jemez form is cognate, but due to the wide semantic and functional difference, it is not considered to reflect a Proto-Tanoan age for picks or hoes.
74. The Tewa vowel is irregular. It is assumed that the Tewa form is a contraction.
75. The Kiowa forms resemble but do not correspond with the Taos and Tewa cognates. Campbell (1997:272, 418–419) views the phonetically similar forms for 'dog' in many American Indian language families as an example of pan-Americanism: a word that is widespread due to borrowing and sound symbolism more so than genealogy. This would seem to provide a better explanation for the Kiowa form than cognacy.
77. The Tewa and Jemez forms are not cognate, but the Tewa form does contain the Tewa word for 'arrow.' Thus, the Jemez form is probably a Tewa loan. The Kiowa and Proto-Tiwa forms appear to be independently coined compounds involving cognates for 'bag.'
81. The Tiwa and Tewa forms are transparent compounds, but are not identical.
84. The Tiwa forms are probably from Keres **šúwimu* (Miller and Davis 1963:326, no. 313).
85. The Tewa and Tiwa terms are probably loans from Uto-Aztecan Hopi *tusqeni* 'cleaned cotton' (Hill 1998:676), Tohono O'odham *tokih* 'raw or absorbent cotton, cotton string, any material made of cotton' (Saxton et al. 1983)
86. The Tewa and Tiwa terms are probably loans from Hopi *pösaala* 'blanket' (woven, cotton), which was probably also loaned into Zuni *pisa:li* 'rug.'
89. The Tewa form may be evidence of subsequent contact with Tiwa.
90. Hill (2008:171) suggests that the Tewa form refers to sego lily. This is incorrect because a full cognate set with meanings referring to potatoes, vegetables, and roots is available. Furthermore, Robbins et al. (1916:73) associate this term with the wild potato species *Solanum jamesii*, "a white-flowered plant, native to this region, which bears small edible tubers similar to potatoes."

Appendix B: Archaeological Dating of Kiowa-Tanoan Terms

Proto-Kiowa-Tanoan Reconstructions

The following reconstructions are based on cognates in Kiowa and at least one Tanoan language.

1. **tu* 'house.' The earliest houses in the northern U.S. Southwest are found in Archaic period sites of the Gunnison Basin (Stiger 2001), the upper San Juan drainage (Sesler and Hovezak 2002:122–123), and near Abiquiu, New Mexico (Stiger 2001: App. F). Houses also occur in Eastern and Western Basketmaker II sites (Charles and Cole 2006; Charles et al. 2006; Smiley 1993, 1994). These structures are often called pithouses, but are better described as basin houses (Matson 1991).

2. **tʰɨ* 'to dwell.' The earliest year-round habitation sites in the northern U.S. Southwest date to the Basketmaker II period. These sites contain roofed, circular houses with internal fire pits and entryways, as well as slab-lined pits for the storage of agricultural produce (Charles and Cole 2006).

3. **´įętʰu-* 'ladder.' The earliest ladder of which I am aware is a fragmentary specimen from Broken Flute Cave dating to the Basketmaker III period. Ladders would not have been needed to enter the basin houses of the Basketmaker II period, but logs may have been used for scaling ledges in canyon environments. Such artifacts, however, would not likely be preserved.

4. **pįę* 'sleeping mat.' Mats of twined bulrush (*Scirpus* spp.) large enough to sleep on have been found in Eastern Basketmaker II sites, including the Falls Creek rockshelters (Morris and Burgh 1954:66), Tabeguache Cave (Hurst 1942: 15), and Dolores Cave (Hurst 1947:11). Twined mats dating from 5300–1250 BC have also been recovered from Hogup Cave, near Salt Lake City (Adovasio 1970: 137), but none have been found in Western Basketmaker II sites (Guernsey and Kidder 1921; Kidder and Guernsey 1919:205). Twilled rush matting is commonly found in cliff dwellings throughout the ancestral Pueblo area, and mats of sewn, split-willow rods are common at Mesa Verde (Osborne 2004:356–367). Twined and split-willow rod mats have also been recovered from Antelope House in Canyon de Chelly (Adovasio and Gunn 1986:313–315).

5. *si* 'stone point.' Although the Jemez and Kiowa cognates on which this reconstruction is based have the meaning 'arrowhead,' I believe 'stone point' is a better gloss because: (1) both forms refer to the stone point at the tip of an arrow; (2) terms for 'bow' and 'arrow' are only reconstructible to Proto-Tanoan; and (3) stone points were hafted on the tips of atlatl darts prior to the introduction of the bow and arrow. Chipped stone dart points are characteristic of Archaic and Basketmaker II sites throughout the northern U.S. Southwest (Morris and Burgh 1954; Kidder and Guernsey 1919; Guernsey and Kidder 1921; Lindsay et al. 1968: 64–67; Matson 1991: Chap. 2). Bow and arrow technology appears to have diffused southward over time. Specifically, chipped stone arrow points and reed arrow foreshafts occur in contexts dating as early as AD 100–250 at Cowboy Cave and other sites north of the Colorado River in Utah, but are absent from Western Basketmaker II sites (Geib 1996:65). Arrow points may also occur in terminal Eastern Basketmaker II sites in the Durango area, but, in general, arrow points were rare in the San Juan drainage prior to Basketmaker III (Holmer 1986:106; Morris 1980:124–126).

6. *cę̨* 'hammer.' This form appears to refer to hand-held hammerstones, which were used from the Archaic period into historic times for making chipped stone tools.

7. *kʰæy* 'skin, hide.' A variety of artifacts of animal hide have been recovered from Archaic and Basketmaker II sites throughout the northern U.S. Southwest.

8. *bų* 'bag.' Twined *Apocynum* bags are common in Western and Eastern Basketmaker II contexts (Kidder and Guernsey 1919:172–173; Guernsey and Kidder 1921:65–74; Morris and Burgh 1954:67). Animal skin bags and pouches are also found in Basketmaker II sites of both regions (Kidder and Guernsey 1919:175–177; Guernsey and Kidder 1921:108–109; Hurst 1941:18) and at Cowboy Cave (Hull 1980). Twined bags do not occur in the assemblages of Hogup and Danger caves, but hide bags are present (Aikens 1970:112). Sacks of animal skin also occur in Prayer Rock District Basketmaker III sites (Morris 1980:91).

9. *cę* 'sinew.' The achilles tendon of deer and/or mountain sheep were used for fletching atlatl darts, hafting projectile points, making brushes, and serving as a substitute for string in Western Basketmaker II sites (Kidder and Guernsey 1919: 177–178), Eastern Basketmaker II sites (Hurst 1940:12), and Archaic cave sites (Aikens 1970:112). Bundles of sinew and sinew cordage have also been recovered from the Prayer Rock District Basketmaker III sites (Morris 1980:93).

10. ***ta-* 'shoe.'** Although cognates of this form refer generically to shoes at present, prehispanic shoes would have been woven sandals or hide moccasins. Woven sandals are common in Archaic sites of the Glen Canyon area (Ambler 1996:50), Eastern Basketmaker II sites (Morris and Burgh 1954:64; Hurst 1942: 14–15), Western Basketmaker II sites (Kidder and Guernsey 1919:157–160; Lindsay et al. 1968:90–97), and the Prayer Rock Basketmaker III sites (Morris 1980: 115–121). Moccasins have been found in Fremont sites in Utah (Jennings 1978: 61) and in Western Basketmaker II sites (Guernsey 1931:66–68; Lindsay et al. 1968:74–77). Moccasins also occur in more recent sites, including the Aztec Ruin, several thirteenth-century cliff dwellings at Mesa Verde, and the Alvey site in Kane County, Utah (Obsorne 2004:74–80). Finally, hide sandals have been recovered from Western and Eastern Basketmaker II sites (Kidder and Guernsey 1919:169; Morris and Burgh 1954:65; Osborne 2004:80–81), and from the Prayer Rock District Basketmaker III sites (Morris 1980:93).

11. ***phu* 'snare.'** Snares of yucca fiber cordage occur in Western and Eastern Basketmaker II sites (Guernsey and Kidder 1921:79; Morris and Burgh 1954:69), at Cowboy Cave (Janetski 1980:80–81), and at Hogup Cave in contexts dating as early as 5300 BC (Aikens 1970:125).

12. ***pǫ́* 'to sound.'** Magers (1986a:281) classified four slender sticks that were bent into a loop at one end as drumsticks. These objects were found in Pueblo III contexts at Antelope House, in Canyon de Chelly, Arizona, and appear to have been identified on the basis of ethnographic accounts of such items (Brown 2005:321–348). No other clearly identifiable, hand-held drums or drumsticks have been reported from ancestral Pueblo sites. However, elongate floor pits covered with wooden planks, which are often interpreted as foot drums, do occur in Pueblo I pit structures (Wilshusen 1989) and in more recent sites. The Southern Tiwa and Kiowa words for 'drum' are not cognate, but reconstruction of the verb 'to sound' is secure, and may indicate that the making of rhythmic, percussive sounds took place in the Kiowa-Tanoan speech community.

13. ***tup-* 'flute, whistle.'** Bird-bone whistles occur in Western and Eastern Basketmaker II sites (Kidder and Guernsey 1919:189; Morris and Burgh 1954:63), in contexts dated 4450–4010 BC at Hogup Cave (Aikens 1970:90), and in Prayer Rock District Basketmaker III sites (Morris 1980:85). In addition, reed whistles occur in Western Basketmaker II sites (Kidder and Guernsey 1919:186), and wooden flutes occur in the Prayer Rock Basketmaker III sites (Morris 1980:134).

14. ***sa* 'tobacco.'** A charred residue, presumably of tobacco, is occasionally found inside the bowls of stone and clay pipes (see below). Morris (1980:77) reports chemical analyses of these residues which confirm that tobacco was smoked in the pipes.

15. *p^he 'to smoke.' Bowl-shaped pipes of stone or clay to which wooden mouthpieces were attached occur in Western and Eastern Basketmaker II sites (Kidder and Guernsey 1919:187–188; Morris and Burgh 1954:59), and in Basketmaker III (Morris 1980:77) sites. Stone or clay pipes are not reported from Danger or Hogup caves.

16. *p’ɨo 'ripe corn.' Hill (2008:162–163) believes this term derives from the loan of Northern-Uto-Aztecan *pa´ca* 'corn kernel, hominy' into Proto-Kiowa-Tanoan. Maize is characteristic of Basketmaker II sites in the northern U.S. Southwest (Matson 2002, 2006) and appears to have been a dietary staple for Western and Eastern Basketmaker II people (Coltrain et al. 2006; Matson and Chisholm 1991).

17. *´ia '(pop)corn.' This term is associated with popcorn for several reasons: (1) a second term for 'corn' which clearly refers to a variety that was ground into flour is reconstructible for Proto-Tanoan; (2) terms for 'cornmeal' and 'to grind' are also reconstructible for Proto-Tanoan, but not Proto-Kiowa-Tanoan; (3) Kiowa cognates for this term refer to hard seeds in addition to corn; and (4) the archaeological record suggests that the earliest maize in the Southwest was likely a small popcorn (Benz and Iltis 1990; Huckell 2006:105). Hill (2008:159–160) believes this term derives from the loan of Northern Uto-Aztecan **ɨya* 'to plant' into Proto-Kiowa-Tanoan. Remains of maize are characteristic of Basketmaker II sites (Matson 1991: Chap. 2, 2006).

18. *c^hą 'squash, gourd.' Cultivated squash/pumpkin remains are present in all Basketmaker II sites. A gourd vessel, apparently of *Cucurbita pepo*, was recovered from White Dog Cave, a Western Basketmaker II site (Guernsey and Kidder 1921:42). *Cucurbita pepo* has also been identified in Eastern Basketmaker II sites (Cutler and Whitaker 1961:471; Jones and Fonner 1954:105). Remains of *Lagenaria siceraria*, or bottle gourd, occur for the first time in the Prayer Rock Caves (Morris 1980:141) and in Step House on Mesa Verde (Cutler and Whitaker 1961:473), both of which date to Basketmaker III. However, *Cucurbita* rinds were also used as containers at Mesa Verde (Osborne 2004:349–351), and Cutler and Meyer (1965:152) note that that *Lagenaria* was not likely grown at Mesa Verde because no seeds or peduncles occur along with rind fragments, and Mesa Verde represents the northern limit of *Lagenaria* finds. Today, Tewa people make the rattles referred to in the Kiowa cognate for this set from *Cucurbita* (Robbins et al. 1916:100). It therefore appears that the Proto-Kiowa-Tanoan reconstruction either refers to *Cucurbita pepo* or to containers of either species, both of which appear for the first time in Basketmaker II sites.

19. *sɨ̨- 'to boil.' The earliest evidence of boiling as a method of cooking consists of fire-cracked rock, which results from the dropping of heated stones into pitch-lined baskets filled with water, mush, gruel, or soup. Fire-cracked rock is found at Late Archaic and Basketmaker II sites throughout the northern U.S. Southwest (Sesler and Hovezak 2002:125, 149; Stiger 2001).

20. **k'uo* 'to lay down.' The meanings associated with cognates of this form include 'to place', 'to lay down', and 'to plant.' Because the agricultural meaning is restricted to Kiowa, and there are separate, Proto-Tanoan forms for 'to plant' and 'field' (47 and 51, below), Proto-Kiowa-Tanoan-speakers may have had a mixed horticultural and foraging economy that did not develop into an intensive agricultural economy until Proto-Tanoan times. A range of archaeological evidence — including house styles, botanical evidence, lithic assemblages, basketry techniques, and human biology — all suggest that the Western Basketmakers were migrants from the south who introduced an agricultural lifeway to the northern U.S. Southwest, whereas the Eastern Basketmakers were indigenous foragers who gradually adopted an agricultural lifeway (Coltrain et al. 2006:282–284; LeBlanc 2008; LeBlanc et al. 2007; Matson 1991, 2002, 2006; Matson and Chisholm 1991; Sesler and Hovezak 2002). Hill (2008) also presents linguistic data that suggest an association of the Western Basketmakers with Proto-Northern Uto-Aztecan, and the Eastern Basketmakers with Proto-Kiowa-Tanoan. The fact that terms for cultigens reconstruct to Proto-Kiowa-Tanoan, but terms associated with intensive agriculture reconstruct only to Proto-Tanoan, appears consistent with this view.

Proto-Tanoan Reconstructions

The following reconstructions are based on the presence of cognates in Towa and at least one other Tanoan dialect, and the absence of a cognate in Kiowa.

35. **suo* 'arrow.' This form refers specifically to arrows in all cognates. Arrow points and reed arrow foreshafts have been recovered from layers dating ca. AD 100–250 at Cowboy Cave north of the Colorado River in Utah (Geib 1996; Holmer 1980; Janetski 1980), but these are completely absent from Western Basketmaker II sites in the San Juan drainage (Kidder and Guernsey 1919; Guernsey and Kidder 1921; Matson 1991: Chap. 2). Arrow technology may have reached the Eastern Basketmaker area near the end of Basketmaker II (Geib 1996), but none were found at the Falls Creek rockshelters or at Talus Village (Morris and Burgh 1954). Thus, arrow technology only became widespread in the San Juan drainage during Basketmaker III.

36. **tu-k^{hw}a* 'pithouse.' Circular and subrectangular houses constructed inside pits first appeared during the Basketmaker III period in the northern U.S. Southwest (e.g., Morris 1980:21–23).

37. **t'ú-* '(coiled) basket.' Coiled basketry represents a technology much older than the earliest ancestral Pueblo cultures. It is represented in contexts dating as early as 7000 BC at Hogup and Cowboy caves (Adovasio 1970; Geib and

Jolie 2008) and is present in both Eastern and Western Basketmaker II sites (Morris and Burgh 1954:67–68; Kidder and Guernsey 1919:168; Guernsey and Kidder 1921:59–63). The absence of a Kiowa cognate for this form is almost certainly due to vocabulary replacement. In this vein, it is important to note that nineteenth-century Kiowas are known to have played a dice game using coiled baskets, but they do not appear to have maintained a tradition of making these or any other coiled baskets by that time (Jolie 2006; Merrill et al. 1997).

38. **búlu* 'pottery (bowl), round.' The addition of pottery is one of the diagnostic material culture traits that distinguish the Basketmaker III period from the preceding Basketmaker II period, and well-fired and decorated pottery bowls are common throughout the northern U.S. Southwest, including at the Prayer Rock District Basketmaker III sites (Morris 1980:63–64). It is important to note that Proto-Tiwa-Tewa terms for specific vessel forms incorporate reflexes of this Proto-Tanoan form (see Nos. 67–68, below). That a term which originally referred to a bowl was later compounded to form words for other vessel forms indicates that the bowl was the prototypical vessel form in early ancestral Pueblo societies. The prototypical member of a material culture category such as "pottery" often reflects the first member of the category that appeared historically. In this light, it may be significant that the earliest, hardened clay containers in the northern U.S. Southwest are unfired, fiber-tempered bowls molded in coiled basketry trays. These vessels occur in the Prayer Rock District Basketmaker III sites (Morris 1980:65). Bowls are also the most common vessel form in Basketmaker III sites excavated by the Dolores Archaeological Program (Blinman 1988:471).

39. **ɨ* 'bow.' Chipped stone projectile points of appropriate size and weight for use as arrow points largely replaced the earlier and larger dart points during the Basketmaker III period in the San Juan drainage (Holmer 1986). Remains of bows and arrows are present in the Prayer Rock District Basketmaker III sites (Morris 1980:124) but do not occur in earlier Basketmaker II sites (Kidder and Guernsey 1919:205; Morris and Burgh 1954:76). As discussed for related terms (Nos. 5 and 35, above), bow and arrow technology appears to have diffused from north to south during the first few centuries AD, but did not reach the San Juan drainage until the end of the Basketmaker II period.

40. **kʰia* 'axe.' Hafted stone axes are not found in Eastern Basketmaker II sites dating prior to AD 400 (Morris and Burgh 1954:74) but are present in Los Pinos (AD 400–550) phase sites in the Navajo Reservoir District (Eddy 1966:414), the Basketmaker III Prayer Rock District sites, and more recent sites (e.g., Etzkorn 1993:170).

41. **pɨ̨* 'thread.' In English, "thread" refers to a thin cord used for sewing or weaving. Both sewing and weaving of fine cordage are known for Basketmaker

II sites, the former from hide working (see No. 42, below) and the latter from twined bags (see No. 8, above). Thus the absence of a Kiowa cognate for this form is probably due to vocabulary replacement.

42. **pę̨d-* 'to sew.' Sewing involves piercing a hide or fabric with a threaded needle to stitch two pieces together. Two eyed needles of bone were recovered from Hogup Cave, one from a stratum dated as early as 4450 BC (Aikens 1970: 88). The hide moccasins found at this site were sewn together with sinew, presumably using such needles. Morris and Burgh (1954:70) describe pieces of hide that had been mended using sinew or yucca cordage from the Falls Creek rockshelters, and Kidder and Guernsey (1919:176) also report finding bags made by sewing together two prairie dog pelts. It appears that knowledge of hide sewing predates the Basketmaker II period. Thus, the absence of a Kiowa cognate for this form is probably due to vocabulary replacement.

43. **p'æ̨* 'road, trail.' Formal constructed roads, worn-in footpaths, and hand- and toehold trails over slickrock expanses occur throughout the northern U.S. Southwest. The use of informal, worn-in trails and footpaths, including game trails, presumably dates from the Archaic period, at least. Constructed roads are not known to predate the Chaco Phenomenon, but there are depictions of formal processions along roads or trails in rock art panels dating from the late Basketmaker III period (Robins and Hays-Gilpin 2000:241–242). The absence of a Kiowa cognate for this form may be due to vocabulary replacement, or the term may refer to the more formally constructed or defined routes of travel that are first evidenced during the late Basketmaker III period.

44. **kų* 'ceremony, dance.' This word refers not to the act of dancing but to a social event. Its cognates refer to ceremonial dances, which today involve coordinated movements of groups of people. Human figures in San Juan Anthropomorphic style rock art, which dates to the Basketmaker II period, are depicted in static and standardized positions. When multiple anthropomorphs appear together, they form noninteracting collections as opposed to interacting compositions (Robins 1997:76–77). In contrast, human figures in the subsequent Chinle Representational style, which dates from Basketmaker III, are often depicted in dynamic compositions, including processions leading toward circular enclosures containing ritual objects (Robins and Hays-Gilpin 2000:241–242). Dance circles defined by upright sandstone slabs actually occur in Basketmaker III sites (Martin 1939:356; Morris 1980:12–15), as do the ritual objects depicted in these procession panels (Morris 1980:133). It would therefore appear that the earliest indications of public ceremonial dances date to the Basketmaker III period.

45. **'æ* 'metate.' The cognates of this word refer to milling stones on which maize kernels are ground into flour. This grinding was done using a mano held in both hands while kneeling over the metate, and involved a back-and-forth rocking motion. The earliest milling stones that were used in this way are the trough metates with openings at one end that first appear in Basketmaker III sites (Morris 1980:71). Basketmaker II grinding stones, in contrast, were basin-shaped and used in combination with a hand stone and a rotary, or horseshoe-shaped, motion (Morris and Burgh 1954:58–59).

46. **t’á:* ‘to grind.’ This word refers to the action of grinding maize kernels into flour using a mano and metate as described above. This action is first evidenced in the archaeological record during the Basketmaker III period, as described above.

47. **kæ* ‘to plant.’ Maize must be planted in the ground in order to germinate, and cognates of this form all refer to the act of planting seeds in agricultural fields. Although maize agriculture dates from the Basketmaker II period (1000 BC–AD 450) in the northern U.S. Southwest, an argument can be made that the practice referenced by this term was not widespread in the Eastern Basketmaker area prior to Basketmaker III. As mentioned above, the Western Basketmakers appeared around 1000 BC as a fully agricultural people, as reflected in subsistence data, site locations (Matson 1991), and the presence of planting sticks in Western Basketmaker II sites (Kidder and Guernsey 1919:184; Guernsey and Kidder 1921:89–90). The Eastern Basketmakers, in contrast, developed from local, Late Archaic foragers and adopted agriculture gradually (Coltrain et al. 2006; Sesler and Hovezak 2002). It may therefore be significant that planting sticks have not been recovered from Eastern Basketmaker II sites (Hurst 1940, 1941, 1942; Morris and Burgh 1954:76) but only appear in this area during the Basketmaker III period (Morris 1980:134–136). In addition, land-extensive, direct precipitation agriculture expanded dramatically in the U.S. Southwest during the Basketmaker III period, and this would have required a more labor intensive planting process. Specifically, maize kernels would have needed to be planted deep enough to utilize stored soil moisture as opposed to surface water. I suggest that this term dates from this period of agricultural intensification (also see No. 50, below).

48. **k*^{h}*ų* ‘(flour) corn.’ Cognates of this word indicate that it refers to a starchy variety of maize that was ground into flour. Starchy varieties of maize occur in the northern U.S. Southwest from the Basketmaker III period onward (Cutler and Meyer 1965; Manglesdorf 1980:151–155). The appearance of starchy maize varieties is also correlated with the appearance of trough metates and two-hand manos, as mentioned above. Hill (2008:160–162) suggests that cognates of this reconstruction, and of **k*^{h}*ɨ* ‘kernel’ (see below), relate to a single Proto-Kiowa-Tanoan form that was loaned from Northern-Uto-Aztecan *kuma* ‘corn.’ The data in Appendix A show that this is incorrect on two counts. First, these reconstructions lack Kiowa cognates and are therefore only secure to Proto-Tanoan. Second, the data in Appendix A show that these two forms are distinct.

49. ***kʰɨ* 'kernel.'** This form refers to the starchy kernels of flour corn, which first appeared in the northern U.S. Southwest during the Basketmaker III period (see above).

50. ***tą* 'bean.'** Beans are absent from Basketmaker II sites but have been found in the Prayer Rock District sites dating to the Basketmaker III period (Morris 1980:151). They are absent from Eastern and Western Basketmaker II sites (Morris and Burgh 1954:75; Kidder and Guernsey 1919:205), and from Archaic deposits in Great Basin cave sites (Aikens 1970; Jennings 1957).

51. ***nąpa* 'field.'** Cognates of this form refer to plots of land developed specifically for agricultural use. The earliest indications of land clearance for agricultural fields are associated with Late Basketmaker II (AD 200–450) sites on Cedar Mesa, in the Western Basketmaker area, where site locations imply an emphasis on upland, direct precipitation agriculture on land that would have otherwise been covered by dense pinyon-juniper woodland (Matson 1991:73–101). The earliest Eastern Basketmaker sites in comparable settings date from AD 400–550 and straddle the boundary between the Basketmaker II and Basketmaker III periods (Charles et al. 2006; Sesler and Hovezak 2002). The reconstruction of a Proto-Tanoan word for "axe" (see No. 40, above) and the initial appearance of hafted axes in Basketmaker III period sites are consistent with the view that intensive agriculture replaced a mixed horticultural and foraging economy around AD 450 in the Eastern Basketmaker area.

52. ***'ɨo* 'sunflower plant.'** Sunflower seeds occur in flotation samples from Late Archaic and Basketmaker II sites in the Upper San Juan region of New Mexico (Brandt 2002:322) and from Basketmaker II sites near Durango, Colorado (Adams and Murray 2008:196; Matthews 1988:402). Sunflower seeds also occur in Late Archaic coprolites and macrofossils at Cowboy Cave north of the Colorado River in Utah (Jennings 1980). Thus, the absence of a Kiowa cognate for this form is probably due to vocabulary replacement.

61. ***delu* 'turkey.'** The cognates of this form refer primarily to "chicken" today. With respect to the Tewa form, Henderson and Harrington (1914:34–35) state: "The unaccompanied *di:* is now applied mostly to the introduced domestic fowl or chicken and not to turkey as it doubtlessly was formerly. *P´in* 'mountain' is usually prejoined to distinguish turkeys from chickens. . . . There is no doubt that they were formerly much more abundant than now and probably constituted an important article of food of the ancient inhabitants. The Indians long ago domesticated this bird, or, at any rate, kept many of them in inclosures [*sic*]." Based on this account, it would appear that the Proto-Tanoan form refers to tame or domestic fowl, which in prehispanic times would have been turkeys, and in the historic period, chickens.

Turkey bones are completely absent from Late Archaic sites in central Utah, western Colorado, and northern New Mexico (Hovezak and Schniebs 2002:420; Lucius 1980; Stiger 2001:48). In the Eastern Basketmaker area, isolated turkey bones have been reported from the Durango rockshelters (Rodeck 1954:121), but no turkey feathers were identified in the assemblage (Morris and Burgh 1954: 66), and turkey remains are completely absent in more recently examined Basketmaker II assemblages from nearby Ridges Basin (Potter and Edwards 2008: 283) and the Fruitland Project area (Hovezak and Schniebs 2002:420). In the Western Basketmaker area, no turkey bones or feathers were found in the Marsh Pass sites (Kidder and Guernsey 1919:156; Guernsey and Kidder 1921:44), but turkey droppings and eggshells have been identified from Basketmaker II contexts at Turkey Pen Ruin in Grand Gulch, Utah (Lipe, personal communication, 2009). Morris (1939:18) claimed that Basketmaker II turkey feather blankets are known from Grand Gulch, Durango, and Canyon del Muerto, but the published data do not support this. Turkey feathers are present in the Prayer Rock District Basketmaker III sites (Morris 1980:89–91), and turkey burials are regularly found in sites of this age (McKusick 1980:227–228). Overall, it appears that turkeys are not native to the northern U.S. Southwest, but were introduced by the Western Basketmakers, who appear to represent a migrant population from the south (Matson 2002; LeBlanc 2008). Turkeys are not clearly present in Eastern Basketmaker sites prior to the Basketmaker III period.

93. **kɨ̨n* 'corn stalk.' This term implies not only knowledge of edible maize, but also of specific parts of the maize plant; as such, it suggests knowledge of maize agriculture. Maize agriculture spread to the northern U.S. Southwest during the Basketmaker II period, and many terms related to maize reconstruct to Proto-Kiowa-Tanoan. Thus, the absence of a Kiowa cognate for this term is likely due to vocabulary replacement.

Proto-Tiwa-Tewa Reconstructions

The following reconstructions are based on the presence of cognates in Tewa and at least one Tiwa dialect, and the absence of cognates in Towa and Kiowa.

39a. **xʷíd* 'string.' Chronological interpretation of this term is problematic. Twisted fiber cordage is an ancient technology that is evidenced in Archaic Great Basin cave sites dating as early as 6400 BC (Aikens 1970:121). The Tiwa cognates for this form refer to bows, which were strung with sinew or yucca cordage (Magers 1986b:285; Osborne 2004:233–238); the Tewa cognate refers to vegetal fiber. Despite a few isolated finds, cotton thread is not widespread in the northern U.S. Southwest prior to AD 1100 (Kent 1957:639–640). Due to its unclear semantic history, and the reconstruction of a Proto-Tanoan word for "thread" (see No. 40, above), this form is probably the result of vocabulary replacement and is of little value for dating.

64. **k'ɨo-ti* 'rooftop.' Cognates of this form refer not only to the covering over an architectural space, but also a surface that can be walked on. The earliest roofs matching this description are the roofs of Pueblo I period pit structures, which were excavated much more deeply than their predecessors and were entered through a rooftop hatch using a ladder (Wilshusen 1988:620). Earlier basin houses and shallow pit structures were typically entered from the side and had gabled roofs (Wilshusen 1988:616–619).

65. **sį-bulu* 'cooking pot.' In Basketmaker III sites, exterior soot indicative of repeated cooking occurs on vessels of a variety of shapes and sizes (Morris 1980: 56–65; Morris 1939:144–145; Blinman 1988:471). Pottery vessels were used for cooking, but there does not appear to have been a category of vessel designed specifically for cooking. In Pueblo I period sites, in contrast, sooting is restricted to a narrower range of vessel forms, and neck-banded surface treatments occur primarily on vessels used for cooking (Morris 1939:157–160). During this period, potters also developed distinct pastes and surface treatments for culinary versus nonculinary vessels (Breternitz et al. 1974; Ortman et al. 2005: Chap. 5). Thus, it appears that a distinct category of pottery vessel designed specifically for cooking developed during the Pueblo I period. The cognates on which this reconstruction is based are transparent compounds that could have been coined independently in Tiwa and Tewa; however, the fact that cognates for three functionally specialized vessel forms reconstruct to the same subgroup of Kiowa-Tanoan, and that the word for "dipper" at least is not a transparent compound, suggests that all three terms date from the period of time during which functionally specialized pottery vessels developed.

66. **p'o-bulu* 'olla.' The vessel form to which this word refers is a large jar suitable for transporting water from a source back to the house. Large, narrow-necked jars with lug handles and painted decoration, suitable for transporting water with the vessel balanced on top of the head, first become common in Pueblo I sites (Etzkorn et al. 1993:140; Morris 1939:170–172; Blinman 1988: 471). The cognates upon which this reconstruction is based are transparent compounds that could have been coined independently in Tiwa and Tewa; however, based on the discussion under **sį-bulu* 'cooking pot' (No. 65, above), it appears that cognates of this form do reflect a Proto-Tiwa-Tewa compound that was coined as functionally specialized pottery vessels developed.

67. ***k'ulu*** **'dipper.'** This form first appears in pottery assemblages as half-gourd-shaped pottery vessels dating to the Pueblo I period (Etzkorn et al. 1993; Morris 1939:151; Blinman 1988:471). The closest analogs to such vessels from Basketmaker III sites are undecorated globular jars with lateral spouts. These vessels have two openings, one on top of the vessel and the other at the end of the spout/handle (Morris 1980: Fig. 28; Morris 1939:147). It is clear that these vessels were not used as dippers.

68. ***kɨn*** **'cradleboard.'** Several types of cradles are known from ancestral Pueblo sites. The dominant type of cradle from Western Basketmaker II sites is flexible and consists of woven juniper bark (Kidder and Guernsey 1919:165–166). A few examples of rigid frame-and-rod cradles have also been recovered from Basketmaker II contexts (Kidder and Guernsey 1919:164–165; Morris 1980: 131; Morris and Burgh 1954:69; Osborne 2004:261–266). The bed materials for these specimens are described as reeds, "peeled narrow rods," or "sticks." The third type of cradle, which occurs in Mesa Verde cliff dwellings and at Antelope House in Canyon de Chelly, consists of a wooden board with or without side boards (Osborne 2004:266–273; Magers 1986a: Fig. 77).

The Northern Tiwa cognate and noncognate Jemez word for this item suggest that the reconstruction refers to the wooden, "board" type. Cradleboards do not occur in Basketmaker II or Basketmaker III sites. Perishable material culture dating to the Pueblo I period is poorly known, but it is likely that cradleboards were first used during this period because artificial cranial deformation — which is caused by binding an infant's head to a hard, flat surface — is rare in skeletal remains dating prior to Pueblo I (Kidder and Guernsey 1919:205; Morris and Burgh 1954:75), but common on remains dating from Pueblo I onward (Brew 1946:67–73).

69. ***cia*** **'knife.'** This word refers to a chipped stone knife that was hafted to a wooden handle. Hafted knives have been recovered from Hogup Cave in a context dating prior to 1250 BC (Aikens 1970:172), from Western Basketmaker II sites (Guernsey and Kidder 1921:95–96), and from Prayer Rock District Basketmaker III sites (Morris 1980:134), in addition to the Mesa Verde cliff dwellings (Osborne 2004:395–400). This word was either newly coined in Proto-Tiwa-Tewa, used to replace an older word in this subgroup, or dates to an older subgroup for which the evidence has been lost through vocabulary replacement. In either case, it is of little value for dating.

70. ***k^{hw}ę́d-*** **'pick, hoe.'** Digging sticks and wooden scoops apparently used for digging storage cists have been recovered from Western Basketmaker II sites (Guernsey and Kidder 1921:89–91) and from the Prayer Rock District Basketmaker III sites (Morris 1980:134–136); however, the earliest stone artifacts that were hafted and used as picks or hoes appear to come from Rosa phase sites in the Upper San Juan dating to the late Pueblo I period (AD 800–920) (Eddy 1966: 415; Hovezak and Sesler 2002:104, 116; Roberts 1930:149).

71. ***po* 'squash.'** The discussion for Proto-Kiowa-Tanoan **c^{h}ą* 'squash, gourd' (No. 18, above) suggests that the latter form refers to *Cucurbita pepo*, which is known from Basketmaker II contexts. If so, this form may refer to *Cucurbita mixta*, another species of cultivated squash found in northern U.S. Southwest sites dating after approximately AD 900 (Cutler and Whitaker 1961:472; Cutler and Meyer 1965:151).

Proto-Tiwa Reconstructions

The following reconstructions are based on the presence of cognates in Northern and Southern Tiwa, and the absence of cognates in Tewa, Towa, and Kiowa.

10a. ***kɨob* 'moccasin.'** This form represents a neologism for "moccasin" or "shoe" that was coined by Proto-Tiwa speakers, and thus is not useful for estimating the age of this subgroup.

41a. ***p^{h}ɨ* 'thread.'** This form represents a replacement of Proto-Tanoan ** pį* 'thread' in Proto-Tiwa (see No. 41, above). Thus, it is not helpful for estimating the age of this subgroup.

70a. ***k^{hw}iad* 'hoe.'** This form represents a replacement of Proto-Tiwa-Tewa **k^{hw}ę́d-* 'pick, hoe.' Thus, it is not helpful for estimating the age of this subgroup.

77. ***łuo-mų́* 'quiver.'** Quivers made of animal hide have been found at several Pueblo III sites in the northern U.S. Southwest (Osborne 2004:250), but were presumably introduced with bows and arrows during Basketmaker III. The Jemez word for "quiver" appears to have been a loan from Tewa that took place after the period of Keres influence on Towa; otherwise, the Towa form would begin with /t^{y}/. Due to the fact that terms for "bow" and "arrow" are both reconstructible to Proto-Tanoan, the Tewa form and Towa loan likely replaced an older word that was cognate with the Tiwa forms. Thus, this form is of little value for dating.

78. **t'įęn- 'dish.'** This form refers to pottery vessels as a generic category. It was likely coined well after the development of pottery, and thus is of little value for dating in light of the reconstructions related to pottery for older subgroups of Kiowa-Tanoan.

79. ***cial* 'gourd rattle.'** This form refers specifically to rattles made from a dried gourd and used in ceremonies. The earliest depictions of such objects in the Southwest come from Classic Mimbres (AD 1050–1150) pottery vessels. An additional depiction occurs on a pottery vessel from Long House, a Pueblo III cliff dwelling at Mesa Verde (Brown 2005:396–398). Actual gourd rattles have been recovered from Canyon de Chelly and Aztec Ruin (Brown 2005:401–403), and more recent depictions are fairly common in Classic period Rio Grande rock art and kiva murals. It appears that gourd rattles first began to be made and used in the mid-AD 1000s, during Pueblo II.

80. _*łowo_ ‘viga.’ Vigas are primary load-bearing beams that span the distance between two load-bearing walls of an aboveground room. The earliest such roofs occur in early great houses in Chaco Canyon dating from the late AD 800s (Windes 2007); however, their earliest appearance in small house construction dates from the mid-AD 1000s (Truell 1986:298). Vigas are common features of surface rooms in the northern U.S. Southwest from the mid-AD 1000s onward (e.g., Bradley 1988; Martin 1936).

81. _*ną-k_^{h}_ų́_ ‘adobe.’ The earliest documented uses of puddled adobe for wall construction occur in early twelfth-century sites of the Bis sa’ni community near Chaco Canyon (Marshall 1982:178–185, 348–349) and in mid-AD 1000s sites in the Rio Grande (McNutt 1969). Adobe is also the characteristic construction material of Coalition and Classic period pueblos throughout much of the Tewa Basin (Creamer 1993; Jeançon 1923; Stubbs and Stallings 1953; Wendorf 1953).

82. _*kwiawi-p’įę_ ‘racetrack.’ The advent of racetracks is unfortunately difficult to date, and thus this form is of little use for dating. Linear racetracks have been found in association with several historic pueblos, including the Tewa pueblos of Ohkay Owinge, Santa Clara, and San Ildefonso (Parsons 1974 [1929]), and the Tiwa pueblos of Taos (Parsons 1936:Map) and Isleta (Parsons 1932:200). I have also observed a racetrack at San Lazaro, a protohistoric Southern Tewa pueblo in the Galisteo Basin, and the linear feature running north-south between the great house and plaza at Yellow Jacket Pueblo in southwest Colorado (Fig. 9.3, center) has been interpreted as a racetrack by Tewa visitors to the site. These observations suggest that racetracks could have originated during the occupation of Yellow Jacket, AD 1060–1280 (Kuckelman and Ortman 2003; Ortman 2003; Varien and Ortman 2005; Varien et al. 2008).

83. _*cud-_ ‘shirt.’ Although many pieces of leather were recovered from the Durango rockshelters, these sites yielded no examples of tailored clothing (Morris and Burgh 1954:70). Tailored clothing is also absent from Marsh Pass Basketmaker II sites (Kidder and Guernsey 1919:156; Guernsey and Kidder 1921:45–46) and from Prayer Rock District Basketmaker III sites (Morris 1980). A buckskin shirt dating no later than AD 1200 was found at Mesa Verde, as were two cotton shirts that likely date to the AD 1200s (Osborne 2004:37–43). Kent (1957:607–608) also describes several cotton shirts and ponchos that date from the Pueblo III period onward. Finally, Smith (2008:560) reports on the remarkable find of an intact cotton shirt from a cavate dwelling in White Rock Canyon, on the Pajarito Plateau, dating AD 1400–1500.

84. **cɨlmųyu* 'turquoise.' This term is probably a loan from Keres (Proto-Keres **šúwimu* 'turquoise' [Miller and Davis 1963:326]). Evidence for widespread manufacture of turquoise ornaments is associated with the development of the Chacoan regional system in the late AD 900s (Harbottle and Weigand 1992; Windes 1992).

85. **t'ok*^{h}*ę* 'cotton.' This term is probably a loan from Uto-Aztecan (e.g., Tohono O'odham *tokih* 'raw or absorbent cotton, cotton string, any material made of cotton' [Saxton et al. 1983]). The comparable Tewa term (*sek*^{h}*ǽ̜* 'cotton') may also derive from Uto-Aztecan (Hopi *tusqeni* 'cleaned cotton' [Hill 1998:676]), but the Towa term (*pį́:* 'cotton, thread') derives from a native term (cf. *pį́:-nį́* 'thread'). The cultivation and weaving of cotton became widespread in the San Juan region only after AD 1000 (Kent 1957:639–640). The earliest evidence for cotton in the Rio Grande region consists of loom anchors in the floors of Late Developmental period pit structures at the North Bank site (LA6462), located along the Rio Grande floodplain near Cochiti Pueblo (Bussey 1968; Webster 1997:741).

86. **pisólo* 'blanket.' This term probably refers to a loom-woven cotton blanket as opposed to tanned hides or robes of fur- or feather-cloth. This Proto-Tiwa word and the noncognate Tewa word for "blanket" are also likely loans from Uto-Aztecan (Hopi *pösaala* 'blanket, rug, wrap, especially a man's' [Hill 1998:441]). Loom-woven cotton blankets were common in the northern U.S. Southwest during Pueblo III (Kent 1957:605–607) but also occur in Late Pueblo II contexts at Chaco Canyon (Judd 1954). Fragments of plain-weave cotton cloth, presumably of blankets, are also reported from numerous Classic period sites throughout the Rio Grande region (Webster 1997: App. G).

87. **p'okú* 'tortilla.' The most direct archaeological correlate of tortillas is the griddle stones on which they were cooked. The earliest griddle stones come from thirteenth-century sites, including the Llano site in the Taos District (Jeançon 1929:17; Smiley et al. 1953:38) and Eagle House in Mancos Canyon south of Mesa Verde (Morris 1919). Griddle stones are also commonly found in Late Coalition and Classic period sites of the Rio Grande region (e.g., Fallon and Wening 1987: 74; Stubbs and Stallings 1953:124).

89. **tolí* 'macaw.' The source of this term is unknown, but phonetic similarities between the Proto-Tiwa and Tewa terms suggest that these noncognate forms derive from the same source. Macaw bones and breeding pens have not been found in sites predating the development of the Chacoan regional system in the late AD 900s (Hargrave 1970:54).

Appendix C: Correlation of Site Numbers with Tewa Names

APPENDIX C: Correlation of Site Numbers with Tewa Names

LA Number	ARMS Site Name	Tewa Name[1]	English Gloss	Begin Date (AD)	End Date (AD)	Earliest Phase	Latest Phase	Latest Pottery Type	Harrington Reference	Notes
17	Nambe Pueblo	Nambáyˀówînge	Roundish earth pueblo	1300	Present	Late Coalition	Present	Tewa Black, Red	[23:5]:358	2
18	Sahkeowinge/ Yohe kwaiye ouinge	Yoheˀkw'áyeˀ ówînkeyi	? pueblo ruin	1350	1425	Early Classic	Middle Classic	Biscuit A	n/a	2, 3
23	Black Mesa	Tʰų̨nyókw'áye tewhákeyi	Tunyo height old houses	1680	1695	Revolt	Revolt	Tewa Poly	[18:24]:297	4
31	Cundiyo	Kų̨diyóˀówînkeyi	Kundiyó pueblo ruin	1300	1375	Late Coalition	Early Classic	Wiyo	[25:8]:378	2
36	Tsawari/ San Cristóbal de la Puebla/ Montez Site	Ts'ą̈wad̲iˀówînkeyi	Wide white gap pueblo ruin	1100	1696	Late Developmental	Revolt	Tewa Poly	[15:24]:253	5
38	Cuyamungue	K'uyemugeˀ ówînkeyi	Stones thrown down pueblo ruin	1300	1680	Late Coalition	Colonial	Tewa Poly	[21:24]:332	2
41	Perage	Ped̲ageˀówînkeyi	Kangaroo rat place pueblo ruin	1300	1450	Late Coalition	Late Classic	Biscuit B	[16:36]:263	2
47	Puye	Puujéˀówînkeji	Rabbit assembly pueblo ruin	1200	1625	Early Coalition	Colonial	Tewa Poly	[14:46]:236	2
59	Yunge Oweenge	Yûngeˀówînkeyi	Mockingbird place ruin	1275	1610	Late Coalition	Contact	Sankawi	[13:27]:227	2
61	Pojoaque Pueblo	P'osų̨wäge ˀówînkeyi	Water-drink place pueblo ruin	1350	Present	Early Classic	Present	Tewa Black, Red	[21:31](2):337	2

63	Jaconita	Sakǫnąˀe, Sakǫnąkwąk'ųˀiˀe	Little tobacco barranca Mexican place	1300	1450	Late Coalition	Middle Classic	Biscuit A	[21:7]:330	2
68	Po'wakwaiye ouinge	Punwąkw'áye ˀówînkeyi	Buttocks thorn height pueblo ruin	1000	1450	Late Develop-mental	Middle Classic	Biscuit A	[23:36]:365	6
71	Howiri	Howíd̲íˀówîngeyi	Gray Point Ruin	1400	1525	Middle Classic	Terminal Classic	Potsuwi	[6:21]:161	2
82	Tyuonyi	Puqwigeˀówînkeyi	Where the bot-toms of the pottery vessels were wiped thin pueblo ruin	1350	1650	Early Classic	Colonial	Tewa Poly	[28:12]:411	7
122	San Ildefonso	P'oqwógeˀówînge	Water cuts down through pueblo	1300	Present	Late Coalition	Present	Tewa Black, Red	[19:22]:303	2
126	Cochiti Pueblo	K'uutáyˀayˀówînge	Stone kiva pueblo	1250	Present	Early Coalition	Present	Tewa Black, Red	[28:77]:438	8
144	Pioge	Phíˀôegeˀówînkeyi	Flicker pueblo ruin	1300	1696	Late Coalition	Revolt	Tewa Poly	[9:43]:203	9
153	Chimayo	Tsímáyôe, Tsímáyôbúˀú	Chimayo, Chimayo town	1350	1680	Early Classic	Colonial	Tewa Poly	[22:18]:341	10
158	Pueblo Quemado	Wiyoˀówînkeyi	Great gap pueblo ruin	1300	1400	Late Coalition	Middle Classic	Biscuit A	[22:unloc.]:357	11
169	Otowi	P'otsuwiˀówînkeyi	Water sinks gap pueblo ruin	1325	1625	Early Classic	Colonial	Tewa Poly	[16:105]:271	2
170	Tsirege	Tsid̲egeˀówînkeyi	Bird-place pueblo ruin	1275	1608	Late Coalition	Colonial	Tewa Poly	[17:34]:282	2

LA Number	ARMS Site Name	Tewa Name[1]	English Gloss	Begin Date (AD)	End Date (AD)	Earliest Phase	Latest Phase	Latest Pottery Type	Harrington Reference	Notes
180		Pʰinikʰą̈wiˀówînkeji	Dwarf cornmeal gap pueblo ruin	1250	1325	Early Coalition	Late Coalition	Santa Fe/ Wiyo	[14:93]:245	12
211	Tsankawi	Są̈k'ewiˀówînkeyi, Są̈kewikwáje ˀówînkeyi	Sharp round cactus gap pueblo ruin	1325	1625	Late Coalition	Colonial	Tewa Poly	[16:114]:274	2
234	Pueblo de las Estrellas	K'upʰųbukw'ájeˀ ówînkeji	Rabbit-brush corner height pueblo ruin	1250	1400	Late Coalition	Early Classic	Wiyo	[14:35]:235	13
245	K'ate ong-winkeji	K'aatayˀówînkeyi	Cottonwood grove pueblo ruin	1275	1350	Late Coalition	Late Coalition	Santa Fe/ Wiyo	[25:23]:380	14
250	Yapashi	Kʰändaˀą̈ndiwe ˀówînkeyi	Where the two mountain lions crouch pueblo ruin	1325	1500	Early Classic	Late Classic	Biscuit B	[28:26]:417	8
252	Te'ewi	Tayˀâyˀówînkeyi	Little cottonwood gap ruin	1275	1600	Late Coalition	Contact	Sankawi	[5:43]:153	2
253	Ku	K'uuˀówînkeyi	Stone ruin	1400	1540	Middle Classic	Terminal Classic	Potsuwi	[5:42]:153	2
254	Tabipange Pueblo	Nambáyˀówînkeyi	Roundish earth pueblo ruin	1300	1400	Late Coalition	Middle Classic	Biscuit A	[25:30]:381	15
257	Navawi II	Navawiˀówînkeyi	Pitfall gap pueblo ruin	1375	1450	Early Classic	Middle Classic	Biscuit A	[17:16]:280	2
264	Pueblo Sarco	P'ibiḏiˀówînkeyi	Little red mound pueblo ruin	1275	1350	Late Coalition	Late Coalition	Santa Fe/ Wiyo	[25:18]:380	16
271		Tekʰeˀówînkeyi	Cottonwood bud pueblo ruin	1200	1350	Early Coalition	Late Coalition	Santa Fe/ Wiyo	[21:31](1):336	17

274	Poshuouinge	Poshúˀúk'âyd̲i ˀowînkeyi	Squash projection height pueblo ruin	1370	1540	Early Classic	Terminal Classic	Potsuwi	[3:9]:130	2
275	Abiquiu Ruin	Ábéshúˀúˀówînkeyi, Ábekyuˀówînkeyi	Abiquiu ruin	1325	1600	Late Coalition	Contact	Sankawi	[3:38](2):138	2
297	Ponsipa-akeri	Poyįpaˀak'âyd̲iˀ ówînkeyi, Poyįpaˀak'âyd̲i kw'áyeˀówînkeyi	Plumed arroyo shrub heights ruin	1275	1680	Late Coalition	Colonial	Tewa Poly	[7:14]:170	2
298	Nuté	Nų́ųteˀówînkeyi	Oven ash ruin	1400	1540	Middle Classic	Terminal Classic	Potsuwi	[7:2]:168	2
299	Pesedeuinge	Phésé̲d̲éˀówînkeyi	Slender stick ruin	1300	1600	Late Coalition	Contact	Sankawi	[5:37]:152	2
300	Kapo/Leaf Water	Kaap'oeˀówînkeyi	Leaf water ruin	1250	1350	Early Coalition	Late Coalition	Santa Fe/ Wiyo	[5:23]:150	8
301	Tsiping	Tsip'inˀowînkeyi	Flaking-stone mountain pueblo ruin	1275	1400	Late Coalition	Early Classic	Wiyo	[2:7]:121	2
306	Sapawe	Są̈ p'ą̈́ą̈weˀówînkeyi	? Village ruin	1400	1600	Middle Classic	Contact	Sankawi	[4:8]:144	2
380	Hupobi/ Homayo	Hų́ųpóviˀówînkeyi	Juniper flower ruin	1400	1515	Middle Classic	Terminal Classic	Potsuwi	[6:18]:161	2
547	Sahiu	Są̈́ˀą̈ shûˀówînkeyi	Corn-silk pueblo ruin	1350	1540	Early Classic	Terminal Classic	Potsuwi	[9:22]:200	2
632	Pose	P'osíˀówînkeyi	Moss-greenness ruin	1375	1600	Early Classic	Contact	Sankawi	[6:24]:165	2
795	Shufinne	Shupʰinną̈ ˀówînkeji	Point-narrow pueblo ruin	1325	1450	Late Coalition	Middle Classic	Biscuit A	[14:33]:235	2

LA Number	ARMS Site Name	Tewa Name[1]	English Gloss	Begin Date (AD)	End Date (AD)	Earliest Phase	Latest Phase	Latest Pottery Type	Harrington Reference	Notes
874	San Juan Pueblo	Ohkayˀówînge	Ohkay pueblo	1350	Present	Early Classic	Present	Tewa Black, Red	[11:21]:211	2
908	Tsama (Central and East)	Tsámaˀówînkeyi	Wrestling pueblo ruin	1350	1600	Early Classic	Contact	Sankawi	[5:7]:147	2, 18
917	Old Casita	Tewhákeyi, Tewhábúˀúkeyi	Little house town ruin	1350	1760	Early Classic	Re-conquest	Tewa Black, Red	[4:10](2):145	8
918		Shų̨p'ód̲éˀówînkeyi	Cicada head ruin	1275	1350	Late Coalition	Late Coalition	Santa Fe/ Wiyo	[5:19]:150	19
925	Santa Clara/ Kapo	Kʰaap'ôˀówînge		1350	Present	Early Classic	Present	Tewa Black, Red	[14:71]:240	2
930	Ogapoge	Tʰanugeˀówînkeyi	Down-country place pueblo ruin	1275	1680	Late Coalition	Revolt	Tewa Poly	[29:39](1):483	20
1064	Tesuque Pueblo	T'atʰų̨geˀówînge	Dry spotted place pueblo	1350	Present	Early Classic	Present	Tewa Black, Red	[26:8]:387	2
1065	Jacona	Sakǫną̨ ˀówînkeyi	Tobacco barranca pueblo ruin	1600	1680	Colonial	Colonial	Tewa Poly	[21:9]:330	2
3641	Agawi ouinge	Kʰa̧ˀą̧́wiˀówînkeyi	Bird (sp.?) pueblo ruin	1350	1400	Early Classic	Early Classic	Wiyo	[22:42]:345	21
3642	Agawano ouinge	Agawonuˀówînkeyi	Olivella hanging down pueblo ruin	1350	1400	Early Classic	Early Classic	Wiyo	[22:41]:345	22
12655	Nake'muu	Nakeˀmuu	Land-point village	1250	1325	Early Coalition	Late Coalition	Santa Fe/ Wiyo	n/a	23

21422		Tsipiwiˀówînkeji	Flaking-stone issuing gap pueblo ruin	1250	1350	Early Coalition	Late Coalition	Santa Fe/ Wiyo	[14:39]:236	24
21427		Navahuˀówînkeji	Cultivable field arroyo pueblo ruin	1250	1325	Late Coalition	Late Coalition	Santa Fe/ Wiyo	[14:90]:244	25
51858	Kekwaiye ouinge	K'ekw'áyeˀówînkeyi	Sharply-pointed height pueblo ruin	1350	1540	Early Classic	Terminal Classic	Potsuwi	[22:40]:344	26
102746	Oyawidi	Oyáˀwid̲iˀówînkeyi	? pueblo ruin	1275	1400	Late Coalition	Early Classic	Wiyo	n/a	27
900020	Okeh Ruin/ Sunflower Corner Pueblo	Okeˀówînkeyi	Okeh pueblo ruin	1700	1760	Re-conquest	Re-conquest	Tewa Black, Red	[10:26]:207	28

Notes:

1. The Tewa forms are written using the practical orthography developed by the Ohkay Owingeh (San Juan) Bilingual Program (Martinez 1982; San Juan Pueblo 2000) as opposed to the technical orthography used in comparative analyses of Tewa language data.
2. The correlation between this LA number and the Tewa name was established by Mera (1934) and has been corroborated by subsequent investigators (Anschuetz 2005; Ellis 1964; Fowles 2004a; Marshall and Walt 2007; Snead 1995; Snead et al. 2004).
3. Ellis (1964, 1974) established the correlation of LA18 with this name.
4. LA23 is associated with the site of Black Mesa and this Tewa name in the current New Mexico ARMS database.
5. Marshall and Walt (2007, II:45) discuss the evidence associating this Tewa name with this LA36. This correlation is also reflected in the current New Mexico ARMS database.
6. Ellis (1964:39) incorrectly listed this site as Harrington [25:36], and suggested that it dates to the Late Developmental period. Subsequent fieldwork at the site by Ellis (1974:8) corrected the Harrington site number and showed that the primary occupation of this site dates from the Early to Middle Classic period.
7. Bandelier (1892a:145) claims that *tyuonyi* is "a word having a signification akin to that of treaty or contract. It was so called because of a treaty made there at some remote period, by which certain of the Pueblo tribes, probably the Queres, Tehuas and perhaps the Jemez, agreed that certain ranges loosely defined should belong in the future to each of them exclusively." Harrington could not corrobrate the story or the etymology. This site is claimed to be the earliest home of the Cochiti people in the Rio Grande region.
8. The correlation between this LA number and the Tewa name is reflected in the current New Mexico ARMS database.
9. The New Mexico ARMS data suggest that LA144 is Pioge or Popobi. Harrington's map is inconclusive, but Richard Ford and Steven Townsend confirm that this site is Pioge.
10. Marshall and Walt (2007: F-14) established that there is an Early Classic village beneath the modern town of Chimayo, based on the presence of a kiva beneath the Santuario, and the presence of agricultural features associated with Biscuit A pottery surrounding the present town.
11. The site with this name was not located by Harrington. Mera (1934) associated this name with LA158, and Snead (1995) agreed, but Marshall and Walt (2007) consider Wiyo to be unlocated and call LA158 "Pueblo Quemado." I follow Mera and Snead because it is unlikely that additional significant village sites exist "at or near Wiyo" (Harrington 1916:357), and the presence of a historic shrine on top of the ruined mounds at this site (Marshall and Walt 2007: C-9) suggests that it was remembered in the recent past.
12. This name is associated with Hewett (1906) Site 5. The correspondence with LA180 is inferred from site location and Hewett's description.
13. The site number associated with this name is inferred from the correlation of ARMS site locations and Harrington's description and mapping of the site location.
14. Ellis (1964, 1974) associates this name with LA264, but Snead (1993) and Marshall and Walt (2007) associate it with LA245, and call LA264 "Pueblo Sarco." Harrington located but did not obtain a Tewa name for this site; thus the Tewa form is retranscribed from Ellis (1964, 1974).
15. Ellis (1964, 1974) obtained the name "Nambe Bugge" for this ruin. It is also known as "Tabipange."
16. I infer that this Tewa name is associated with LA264, Pueblo Sarco, because: (1) this is the first major ruin south of Cundiyo; (2) the name and site number of the second and

third ruins in this sequence have been established; and (3) the Marshall and Walt (2007) location for LA264 matches Harrington's location for the site with this name.
17. The site number associated with this name is inferred from the correlation of ARMS site locations and Harrington's description and mapping of the site location.
18. LA909 represents the early component at this site.
19. The site number associated with this name is inferred from the correlation of ARMS site locations and Harrington's description and mapping of the site location, and also from Peckham's (1981:132) listing of LA918 as an early Tewa site in the Chama Valley near LA300.
20. This is the name of Pueblo Galisteo, which was transferred to the village constructed on the ruins of the Palace of the Governors in Santa Fe during the Pueblo Revolt.
21. The site with this Tewa name was identified, mapped, and dated by Ellis (1964, 1974). The associated LA number is inferred from ARMS site locations vis-à-vis Ellis's maps.
22. The site with this Tewa name was identified, mapped, and dated by Ellis (1964, 1974). The associated LA number is inferred from ARMS site locations vis-à-vis Ellis's maps.
23. This site is also Hewett (1906) Site 18. The Tewa name, LA number, and occupation span of this site are from Vierra and others (2003). Note that the second part of this name is likely a variant of *ˀbúˀú* 'town, village.' Harrington (1916:39) described the Tewa phoneme */b/* as a "voiced inflative *b*, preplosively nasal." In other words, a more phonetically precise way to write early-twentieth-century Tewa */b/* is */ᵐb/*. Recall also the sound change Proto-Kiowa-Tanoan *b > Tewa *mVµ*, *bV*, and that the Northern Tiwa reflex of Proto-Kiowa-Tanoan *b is *m*.
24. This correlation was established by Trierweiler (1990:50), following Harrington (1916) and Hewett (1906).
25. This correlation was established by Trierweiler (1990:50), following Harrington (1916) and Hewett (1906).
26. The site with this Tewa name was identified, mapped, and dated by Ellis (1964, 1974). The associated LA number is inferred from ARMS site locations vis-à-vis Ellis's maps.
27. The site with this Tewa name was identified, mapped, and dated by Ellis (1964, 1974). The associated LA number is inferred from ARMS site locations vis-à-vis Ellis's maps.
28. The New Mexico ARMS data associate this Tewa name with LA233, but based on the location recorded by Harrington, this name belongs to an unrecorded site. I have estimated its location based on Harrington's location description and the information in Marshall and Walt 2007, II:32. I have numbered sites in my database that do not yet have Laboratory of Anthropology site numbers with an arbitrary number, starting from 900001.

Appendix D: Correlation of Kiowa-Tanoan Speech Communities with Archaeological Complexes

Much of this study has focused on the history of the Tewa language, and in the process of delineating that history, I have been forced to consider the history of the Kiowa-Tanoan language family overall. Several studies presented in this work — including the biodistance analysis, the study of shared phonetic innovations, the applications of linguistic paleontology, the studies of place-names, and the examination of conceptual metaphors in archaeology and language — provide sufficient evidence for a trial correlation of Kiowa-Tanoan speech communities with archaeological complexes. It is important to take advantage of this opportunity, despite the fact that it lies beyond the focus of this work, because establishing the languages that were spoken in archaeological sites has led to a quantum leap in understanding the cultures of the people who created those sites in other parts of the world (e.g., Anthony 2007; Kirch and Green 2001). In addition, Kiowa-Tanoan is the only reconstructed language that can be reasonably associated with the beginnings of Pueblo culture in the San Juan drainage. Thus, the Kiowa-Tanoan languages present a unique reservoir of information about the development of Pueblo culture from the Basketmaker II period to the present, and a secure correlation of Kiowa-Tanoan speech communities with archaeological complexes should create new opportunities for research that integrates the precise spatial, chronological, environmental, and behavioral data of archaeology with the rich conceptual data embedded in language.

Elements of the model presented here have been discussed along with supporting evidence at various points throughout this work. Here I bring these various threads together, along with ancillary data necessary for tracing the history of the Kiowa speech community beyond the San Juan drainage. Readers interested in the data that support elements of this proposal should consult the summaries at the end of specific chapters. It is also important to emphasize that the correlation offered here concerns the reflection of speech community history in the bioarchaeological and archaeological records, but this is not the same thing as population history or culture history. I hope this study has shown that although the three do interweave, they are not identical, and we should not expect them to be. Thus, this proposal should be viewed as a hypothesis that accommodates the linguistic evidence to bioarchaeological and archaeological data, rather than a narrative of the past movements of bounded ethnic groups.

The cultural inventory of Proto-Kiowa-Tanoan suggests that this language was a Late Archaic hunter-gatherer language of the Colorado Plateau that began to differentiate following the addition of maize and squash cultivation to the foraging economy of ancestral speakers in the San Juan drainage. Demic expansion and increased sedentism following the adoption of maize horticulture led to the formation of a lectal linkage that encompassed much of the area in which Eastern Basketmaker II material culture is found, including the Upper San Juan region in southwestern Colorado and northwestern New Mexico, the Uncompahgre Plateau in western Colorado, and the La Sal Mountains region surrounding Moab, Utah (Charles and Cole 2006; Matson 2002; Hill 2008). Patterns in shared phonetic innovations (Chapter 6) suggest that, in its initial stages, the Kiowa-Tanoan dialect chain consisted of the Proto-Kiowa, Proto-Towa, and Proto-Tiwa-Tewa dialects, in that order on the landscape. It would appear most reasonable to place the Proto-Tiwa-Tewa dialect at the southeastern end of this distribution, in the Upper San Juan, based on the association of later, Proto-Tiwa speakers with Developmental Rio Grande sites (see below). This would then place the Proto-Towa dialect in the middle of the Proto-Kiowa-Tanoan dialect chain, and Proto-Kiowa at the northwestern end.

Proto-Kiowa appears to have become isolated from Proto-Towa, and thus also from Proto-Tiwa-Tewa, by AD 450. I suggest that Kiowa was subsequently spoken by: (1) the inhabitants of Eastern Fremont sites in the Green River drainage, Uinta Basin, and Great Salt Lake areas; (2) the inhabitants of late prehistoric Northwest Plains sites in western Wyoming and southwest Montana; and (3) the historic Kiowa people. The evidence on which this proposal is based is outlined below (also see Ortman 2010).

The association of Proto-Kiowa with Eastern Fremont archaeology is based on several lines of evidence. First, Eastern Basketmaker II sites predate and overlap spatially with Fremont sites, and archaeologists have long noted that several elements of Fremont culture — including cultigens, pithouses, and pottery — spread into the Fremont area from the Basketmaker area. In contrast, bow and arrow technology appears to have diffused southward from the Fremont area north of the Colorado River to the Basketmaker area south of that river during the first few centuries AD (Geib 1996). This bidirectional diffusion pattern indicates some form of interaction between the two areas at an early date and is consistent with a model in which early agricultural peoples moved northward from the San Juan and Colorado drainages into the Green River drainage by AD 400.

Basketry and rock art suggest even more detailed continuities between Eastern Basketmaker and Fremont peoples. Fremont coiled basketry — which emphasizes either a half rod and bundle foundation with noninterlocking stitches, or a whole rod foundation with interlocking stitches — exhibits continuities with both Late Archaic and Eastern Basketmaker II coiled basketry (Adovasio et al.

2002; Geib and Jolie 2008; Hurst 1940, 1941, 1942, 1944, 1945, 1947; Morris and Burgh 1954; Simms 2008:199–205). Several researchers have also suggested that Eastern Fremont rock art has antecedents in the Basketmaker II San Juan Anthropomorphic style, and the latter has antecedents in the Late Archaic Barrier Canyon style (Cole 2009:243–244; Schaafsma 1971). Finally, mitochondrial DNA evidence suggests that ancient Fremont populations and present-day Jemez people derive from the same maternal lineage (Carlyle et al. 2000). Importantly, the Towa language spoken at Jemez Pueblo is also the most closely related dialect to Kiowa. Thus, several lines of evidence are consistent with the suggestion that the Eastern Basketmakers were indigenous foragers of the Colorado Plateau who adopted agriculture and spoke Proto-Kiowa-Tanoan, and that the Fremont derived, at least in part, from Eastern Basketmakers who drifted northward and ended up speaking Proto-Kiowa.

I suggest that some Proto-Kiowa-speaking Fremont people later moved northward, beyond the headwaters of the Green River, by around AD 1300. Many have commented on possible relationships between the Fremont and the Northwest Plains (Aikens 1966, 1967; Gebhard 1966; Janetski 1994; Schaafsma 1971; Wormington 1955), but only recently have the nature and direction of influence become clear. Specifically, Francis and Loendorf's (2002) work on rock art dating shows that the direction of influence was from south to north, and the period of influence corresponds with the decline of Fremont society.

The first line of evidence for a Fremont movement to the Northwest Plains is a shift in the direction of interaction networks in the thirteenth-century Utah Valley. At this time the sources of obsidian found in Utah Valley sites shifted from an emphasis on southern Utah to an emphasis on more northerly sources in southern Idaho, Montana, and Wyoming, including Obsidian Cliff in Yellowstone National Park (Janetski 1994, 2002). To the extent that long-distance exchange maps onto kinship ties created through migration (Anthony 1990; Arakawa et al., in press; Duff 1998), this northward shift in the direction of obsidian importation suggests a strengthened relationship with the Northwest Plains. Second, Fremont style basketry has been found in sites in southern Idaho and Wyoming that postdate the decline of the Fremont (Adovasio et al. 2002). This is the only area outside the Fremont range where Fremont style basketry has been found. Third, gray ware pottery decorated using the same techniques used on Fremont pottery appeared on the Northwest Plains for the first time during the late prehistoric period (Aikens 1966:80), and rock rings identified as tipi rings occur at and around Fremont sites and Northwest Plains sites dating to the same period (Aikens 1967:201).

Finally, there are striking continuities between Eastern Fremont and Northwest Plains rock art styles. Shield-bearing warriors, horned headdresses, scalps displayed on poles, and weeping eyes are commonly depicted in Eastern Fremont rock art. Although some of the shields appear to be made of basketry, others depict what appear to be decorated hide shields, examples of which have been found in the Fremont area (Loendorf and Conner 1993). This symbol complex subsequently appears in Castle Gardens Shield style rock art of the Wind River and Bighorn basins in Wyoming and Montana (Aikens 1967:201; Francis and Loendorf 2002:136–144; Schaafsma 1971:142–145; Wormington 1955:162). The Castle Gardens Shield style has been radiocarbon dated to as early as AD 1250 and clearly continued into the historic period based on depictions of firearms with some figures (Francis and Loendorf 2002:141–142). This style also shares the unusual combination of abrading, incising and painting seen in Eastern Fremont rock art.[1] These various lines of evidence thus suggest that the Proto-Kiowa speech community drifted northward, from the Colorado Plateau to the Northwest Plains, during the thirteenth century.

The final link in this proposed chain of Proto-Kiowa speech communities is the historic Kiowa people. Kiowa place-names, oral traditions, and historic documents all indicate that the present-day Kiowa tribe, as distinct from the Kiowa language, took shape around 1700 in the area of Yellowstone National Park in northwest Wyoming and southwest Montana. Several Kiowa place-names refer to geographic features of this region, including the Kiowa Mountains in southwest Montana, Yellowstone Park, the Yellowstone River, Devil's Tower, and the Black Hills (Harrington 1939; Meadows 2008:114–117; Mooney 1898:153–157). Kiowa people also retain social memories of having once lived in these areas, and of having left the Yellowstone area prior to acquiring horses (Boyd 1981: 7–21; Meadows 2008:115–121; Mooney 1898:153; Nabokov and Loendorf 2004: 67–75). Finally, historic documents mention the Kiowa people as having lived around the Black Hills in the eighteenth century (Mooney 1898:156–157).

An association of the historic Kiowa with the late prehistoric Northwest Plains is reinforced by detailed correspondences between Castle Gardens Shield style imagery and historic Kiowa material culture, as known from nineteenth-century ethnographic notes, collections, and artwork. Specifically, the entire complex of shield-bearing warrior imagery — including horned headdresses, scalps mounted on poles, weeping eyes, and shields with heraldic symbols — is ubiquitous in historic Kiowa material and visual culture (see Greene 2001; Merrill et al. 1997). These correspondences provide the final link in the chain connecting the historic Kiowa people back to Proto-Kiowa-Tanoan.

Returning now to the Pueblo area, the dialect ancestral to Towa originally formed between the Kiowa and Tiwa-Tewa dialects and appears to have become distinct by AD 725. On the basis of these findings and Jemez oral tradition, it appears reasonable to suggest that Proto-Towa was spoken in Early Pueblo I villages of southeastern Utah, in the area where San Juan Red ware was produced (Hegmon et al. 1997). Around this same time, Proto-Tiwa-Tewa developed into a second lectal linkage consisting of the Proto-Tewa dialect in the central Mesa Verde region and the Proto-Tiwa dialect in the Totah and Upper San Juan regions. The locations of these two speech communities appear to correlate with the distributions of Piedra Black-on-white and Rosa Black-on-white, respectively

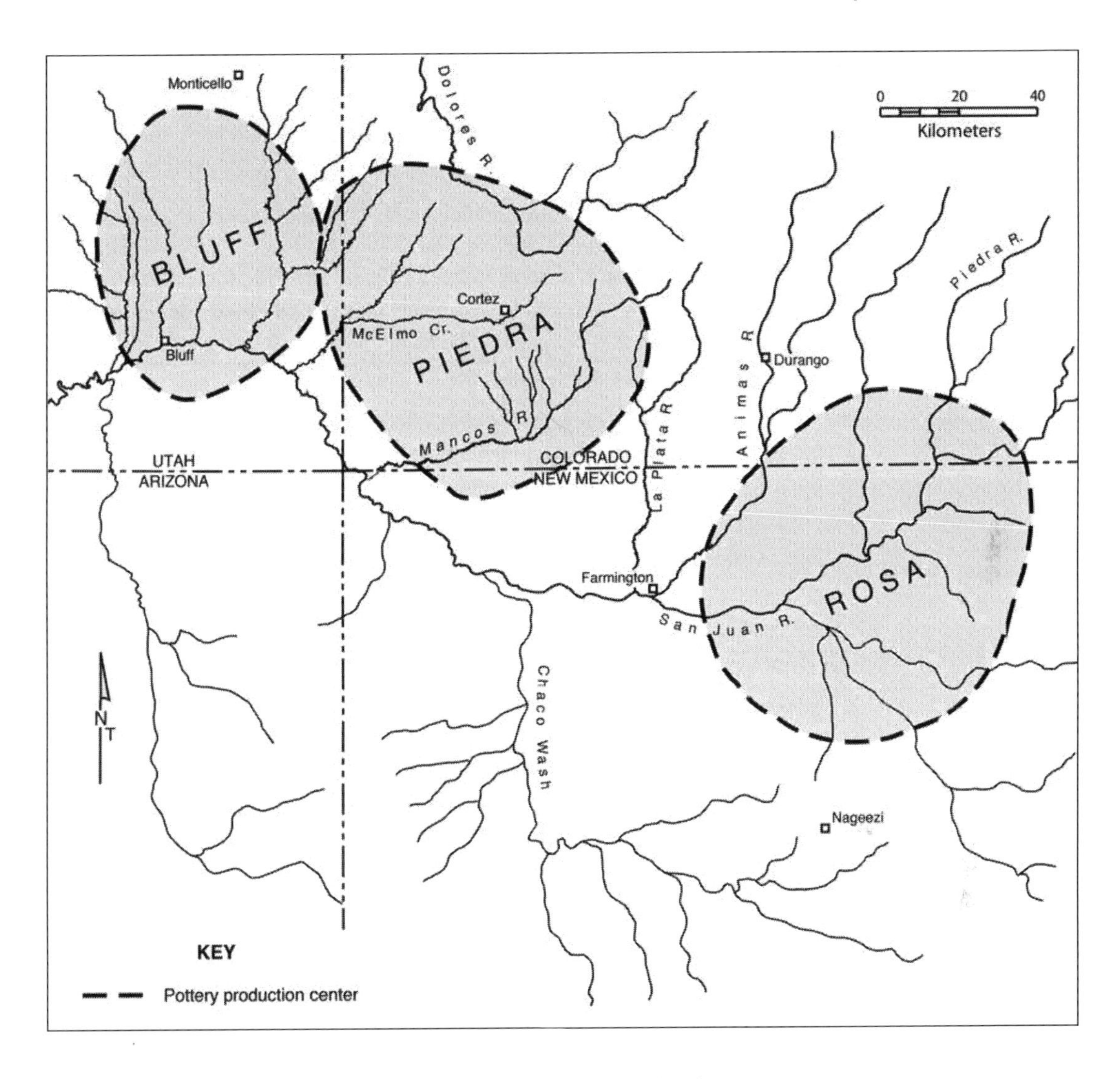

FIGURE D.1. Decorated pottery types in the San Juan drainage, AD 840 (Lipe et al. 1999: Fig. 7.4. Courtesy of Crow Canyon Archaeological Center).

(Figure D.1). Population decline in the Upper San Juan shortly after AD 900 may then reflect the movement of Proto-Tiwa speakers into the Northern Rio Grande drainage, thus isolating them from Proto-Tewa speakers in the Mesa Verde region, and perhaps other Tiwa-speakers in the Totah (the local population as opposed to the intrusive, Chaco-affiliated population of Salmon and Aztec [Reed 2008]). Given that the Rio Grande drainage south of the Tewa Basin was already occupied at the time of this movement (Akins et al. 2003; Lakatos 2007), one would have to suggest that earlier inhabitants shifted to Tiwa or were displaced as these northern migrants spread southward. In this model, Rio Grande sites bearing Red Mesa Black-on-white would derive from the southward spread of Tiwa-speaking peoples, and sites bearing Lino Black-on-white and San Marcial Black-on-white would represent earlier, non-Tiwa-speaking inhabitants.[2]

By AD 1200 Towa speakers had moved from southeastern Utah into the Rio Puerco of the East (Roney 1995, 1996), probably via the San Juan Basin, where they would have been in contact with Keres speakers.[3] By this time Proto-Tewa speakers had also expanded from the central Mesa Verde region into the previous area of Proto-Towa speech in southeastern Utah and had begun colonizing the Pajarito Plateau. Then, between AD 1260 and 1280, the Gallina population dispersed, the San Juan drainage emptied, and additional Proto-Tewa-speakers from the Mesa Verde region moved into the Tewa and Galisteo basins, splitting the Tiwa dialect chain into northern and southern groups. This movement also appears to have brought Northern Tewa and Northern Tiwa dialects back into contact in the Tewa Basin.[4] Based on biological evidence and Cochiti oral tradition (Preucel 2005), I suggest that Keres-speaking peoples then entered the Northern Rio Grande from the Cibola area to the west, along with the spread of glaze-painted red wares and perhaps following depopulation of the El Morro Valley villages during the early decades of the AD 1300s. As a result, Proto-Tewa was split into a southern group in the Galisteo Basin whose dialect is preserved as Santa Clara Tewa, and a northern group in the Tewa Basin whose dialect is preserved as San Juan Tewa. Finally, in AD 1696, a mixed group of Northern and Southern Tewas moved to Hopi First Mesa. The northern dialect became the language of this group, and was subsequently influenced by Hopi to produce Arizona Tewa.

Notes

1. Depictions of shields and shield-bearing warriors also spread from the Fremont area southward into the ancestral Pueblo area during the thirteenth century, and this is the probable route by which this imagery reached the Rio Grande (Crotty 2001:67–69).
2. The fact that Southern Tiwa exhibits a number of phonetic innovations from Proto-Tiwa that did not occur in Northern Tiwa is consistent with this scenario, although more recent contact between Southern Tiwa and Spanish speakers might also explain these changes. An important follow-up study would be an examination of these Southern Tiwa innovations in light of Spanish phonology.
3. As far as the linguistic affiliation of the Gallina complex is concerned, it would seem reasonable to suggest that these people spoke a Tanoan language, but the evidence concerning Jemez ancestry presented throughout this study does not support the association of Towa speech with the Upper San Juan to Gallina to Jemez sequence. There appears to be a basis for associating the Gallina complex with subgroups of Proto-Tiwa speakers, Proto-Tewa speakers, or Towa speakers, but regardless, it appears erroneous to treat the Gallina complex as a direct or singular ancestor of any modern ethnic group or speech community.
4. Presumably some Proto-Tewa speakers also migrated to the Hopi mesas and to the Zuni, Upper Little Colorado, and Mogollon Rim areas as well, but these migrants would have been incorporated into the communities they joined and would have eventually shifted from Proto-Tewa to the local language.

References Cited

Abbott, D. R. (editor)

2003 *Centuries of Decline during the Hohokam Classic Period at Pueblo Grande*. University of Arizona Press, Tucson.

Aberle, D. F.

1966 *The Peyote Cult among the Navaho*. Viking Fund Publications in Anthropology, Chicago.

Adams, E. C.

1991 *The Origin and Development of the Pueblo Katsina Cult*. University of Arizona Press, Tucson.

Adams, E. C., and A. I. Duff (editors)

2004 *The Protohistoric Pueblo World, AD 1275–1600*. University of Arizona Press, Tucson.

Adams, K. A., and S. Murray

2008 Archaeobotanical Results. In *Anima — La Plata Project Volume 10: Environmental Studies*, ed. J. M. Potter, pp. 193–234. SWCA Environmental Consultants, Phoenix.

Adams, K. R., and V. E. Bowyer

2002 Sustainable Landscape: Thirteenth-century Food and Fuel use in the Sand Canyon Locality. In *Seeking the Center Place: Archaeology and Ancient Communities in the Mesa Verde Region*, ed. M. D. Varien and R. H. Wilshusen, pp. 123–142. University of Utah Press, Salt Lake City.

Adams, W. Y., D. P. van Gerven, and R. S. Levy

1978 The Retreat from Migrationism. *Annual Review of Anthropology* 7:483–532.

Adler, M. A.

1992 The Upland Survey. In *The Sand Canyon Archaeological Project: A Progress Report*, ed. W. D. Lipe, pp. 11–23. Occasional Papers No. 2. Crow Canyon Archaeological Center, Cortez, CO.

1994 Population Aggregation and the Anasazi Social Landscape: A View from the Four Corners. In *The Ancient Southwestern Community: Models and Methods for the Study of Prehistoric Social Organization*, ed. W. H. Wills and R. D. Leonard, pp. 85–101. University of New Mexico Press, Albuquerque.

1996 *The Prehistoric Pueblo World, AD 1150–1350*. University of Arizona Press, Tucson.

Adler, M. [A.], and A. Johnson

1996 Appendix: Mapping the Puebloan Southwest. In *The Prehistoric Pueblo World, AD 1150–1350*, ed. M. A. Adler, pp. 255–272. University of Arizona Press, Tucson.

Adler, M. A., and M. D. Varien

1994 The Changing Face of the Community in the Mesa Verde Region AD 1000–1300. In *Proceedings of the Anasazi Symposium, 1991*, ed. A. Hutchinson and J. E. Smith, pp. 83–97. Mesa Verde Museum Association, Mesa Verde, CO.

Adovasio, J. M.
1970 Textiles. In *Hogup Cave*, ed. C. M. Aikens, pp. 133–152. Anthropological Papers No. 93. University of Utah Press, Salt Lake City.
Adovasio, J. M., and J. D. Gunn
1986 The Antelope House Basketry Industry. In *Archeological Investigations at Antelope House*, ed. D. P. Morris, pp. 306–397. National Park Service, Department of the Interior, Washington, DC.
Adovasio, J. M., D. R. Pedler, and J. S. Illingsworth
2002 Fremont Basketry. *Utah Archaeology* 15(1):5–26.
Aikens, C. M.
1966 *Fremont-Promontory-Plains Relationships in Northern Utah*. Anthropological Papers No. 82. University of Utah Press, Salt Lake City.
1967 Plains Relationships of the Fremont Culture: A Hypothesis. *American Antiquity* 32(2):198–209.
1970 *Hogup Cave*. Anthropological Papers 93. University of Utah Press, Salt Lake City.
Akins, N. J.
1986 *A Biocultural Approach to Human Burials from Chaco Canyon, New Mexico*. Reports of the Chaco Center 9. Branch of Cultural Research, Department of the Interior, National Park Service, Santa Fe, NM.
Akins, N. J., S. S. Post, and C. D. Wilson
2003 Life at the Edge: Early Developmental Period Mobility and Seasonality in the Northern Middle Rio Grande Valley. In *Anasazi Archaeology at the Millennium: Proceedings of the Sixth Occasional Anasazi Symposium*, ed. P. F. Reed, pp. 145–154. Center For Desert Archaeology, Tucson.
Allison, P. D.
2001 *Missing Data*. Quantitative applications in the social sciences 07-136. Sage Publications, Thousand Oaks, CA.
Ambler, J. R.
1996 Dust Devil Cave and Archaic Complexes of the Glen Canyon Area. In *Glen Canyon Revisited*, ed. P. R. Geib, pp. 40–52. University of Utah Anthropological Papers No. 119. University of Utah Press, Salt Lake City.
Ammerman, A. J., and L. L. Cavalli-Sforza
1984 *The neolithic transition and the genetics of populations in Europe*. Princeton University Press, Princeton, N.J.
Anschuetz, K. F.
1998 *Not Waiting for the Rain: Integrated Systems of Water Management by Pre-Columbian Pueblo Farmers in North-Central New Mexico*. Ph.D. Dissertation, Department of Anthropology, University of Michigan, Ann Arbor.
1999 National Register of Historic Places Registration Form for Rowe Pueblo, New Mexico. Nomination on File, Rio Grande Foundation for Communities and Cultural Landscapes, Santa Fe, NM.
2005 Landscapes as Memory: Archaeological History to Learn From and to Live By. In *Engaged Anthropology: Essays in Honor of Richard I. Ford*, ed. M. Hegmon and S. Eiselt. Museum of Anthropology, University of Michigan, Ann Arbor.
Anschuetz, K. F., T. J. Ferguson, H. Francis, K. B. Kelley, and C. L. Scheick
2002 *"That Place People Talk About": The Petroglyph National Monument Ethnographic Landscape Report*. Community and Cultural Landscape Contribution 8. Rio Grande Foundation for Communities and Cultural Landscapes, Santa Fe, NM.

Anthony, D. W.
1990 Migration in Archaeology: The Baby and the Bathwater. *American Anthropologist* 92(4):895–914.
2007 *The Horse, the Wheel, and Language: How Bronze-Age Riders from the Eurasian Steppes Shaped the Modern World.* Princeton University Press, Princeton.

Arakawa, F.
2006 *Lithic Raw Material Procurement and the Social Landscape in the Central Mesa Verde Region, AD 600–1300.* Ph.D. Dissertation, Washington State University.

Arakawa, F., S. G. Ortman, A. I. Duff, and M. S. Shackley
in press Obsidian Evidence of Interaction and Migration from the Mesa Verde Region, Southwest Colorado. Accepted for publication, *American Antiquity.*

Archambault, J.
2001 Sun Dance. In *Handbook of North American Indians*, Vol. 13, Pt. 2: *Plains*, ed. R. J. Demallie, pp. 983–995. Smithsonian Institution, Washington, DC.

Badenhorst, S.
2008 The Zooarchaeology of Great House Sites in the San Juan Basin of the American Southwest. Ph.D. dissertation, Simon Fraser University.

Badenhorst, S., and J. C. Driver
2009 Faunal Changes in Farming Communities from Basketmaker II to Pueblo III (AD 1–1300) in the San Juan Basin of the American Southwest. *Journal of Archaeological Science* 36: 1832–1841.

Bamberg, J., A. del Rio, Z. Huaman, S. Vega, M. Martin, A. Salas, J. Pavek, S. Kiru, C. Fernandez, and D. Spooner
2003 A Decade of Collecting and Research on Wild Potatoes of the Southwest USA. *American Journal of Potato Research* 80:159–172.

Bamforth, D. B.
2008 Climate, Chronology and the Course of War in the Middle Missouri Region of the North American Great Plains. In *The Archaeology of Warfare: Prehistories of Raiding and Conquest*, ed. E. N. Arkush and M. W. Allen, pp. 66–100. University Press of Florida, Tallahassee.

Bandelier, A. F.
1892a *Final Report of Investigations Among the Indians of the Southwestern United States, Carried on Mainly from the Years 1880–1885, Part II.* Papers of the Archaeological Institute of America, American Series. John Wilson and Son, Cambridge.
1892b The "Montezuma" of the Pueblo Indians. *American Anthropologist* 5(4):319–326.

Barkow, J. H., L. Cosmides, and J. Tooby (editors)
1992 *The Adapted Mind: Evolutionary Psychology and the Generation of Culture.* Oxford University Press, New York.

Barnes, E.
1994 *Developmental Defects of the Axial Skeleton in Paleopathology.* University Press of Colorado, Niwot.

Barnett, K. E.
2000 Human Skeletal Analysis: Towaoc Canal Reach I Project. In *Archaeological Excavations on Reach I of the Towaoc Canal*, ed. N. S. Hammack. Four Corners Archaeological Project, Vol. 19. Complete Archaeological Service Associates. Cultural Resource Program, Bureau of Reclamation, Upper Colorado Region, Salt Lake City.

Barrett, E. M.

2002 *Conquest and Catastrophe: Changing Rio Grande Pueblo Settlement Patterns in the Sixteenth and Seventeenth Centuries*. University of New Mexico Press, Albuquerque.

Barth, F.

1969 Introduction. In *Ethnic Groups and Boundaries: The Social Organization of Culture Difference*, ed. F. Barth, pp. 9–38. Waveland Press, Prospect Heights, IL.

Beal, J. D.

1987 *Foundations of the Rio Grande Classic: The Lower Chama River AD 1300–1500*. Research Series 137. Southwest Archaeological Consultants, Santa Fe, NM.

Bedell, M. L.

2000 Late Pueblo II and Pueblo III Cliff Dwellings and Community Patterns in Grand Gulch, Southeastern Utah. M.A. thesis, Washington State University.

Bellwood, P. S.

2005 *First Farmers: The Origins of Agricultural Societies*. Blackwell, Oxford.

Bellwood, P. [S.], and C. Renfrew (editors)

2003 *Examining the Farming/Language Dispersal Hypothesis*. McDonald Institute for Archaeological Research, University of Cambridge. Distributed by Oxbow Books, Oxford.

Beninato, S.

1990 Popé, Pose-yemu, and Naranjo: A New Look at Leadersip in the Pueblo Revolt of 1680. *New Mexico Historical Review* 65(4):417–435.

Bennett, K. A.

1966 Analysis of Prehistoric Human Skeletal Remains from the Navajo Reservoir District. In *Prehistory in the Navajo Reservoir District, Northwestern New Mexico*, Vol. 15, ed. F. W. Eddy, Part 2, pp. 523–546. Museum of New Mexico, Santa Fe.

1975 *Skeletal Remains from Mesa Verde National Park, Colorado*. Publications in Archaeology 7F. Department of the Interior, National Park Service, Washington, DC.

Benz, B. F., and H. H. Iltis

1990 Studies in Archaeological Maize I: The "Wild" Maize from San Marcos Cave Reexamined. *American Antiquity* 55(3):500–511.

Bernardini, W.

2005 *Hopi Oral Tradition and the Archaeology of Identity*. University of Arizona Press, Tucson.

Billman, B. R., P. M. Lambert, and B. L. Leonard

2000 Cannibalism, Warfare, and Drought in the Mesa Verde Region During the Twelfth Century AD. *American Antiquity* 65:145–178.

Binford, L. R.

1962 Archaeology as Anthropology. *American Antiquity* 28:217–225.

1968 Post-Pleistocene Adaptations. In *New Perspectives in Archaeology*, ed. S. Binford and L. Binford, pp. 313–341. Aldine, Chicago.

1981 Behavioral Archaeology and the "Pompeii Premise." *Journal of Anthropological Research* 37:195–208.

Bird-David, N.

1990 The Giving Environment: Another Perspective on the Economic System of Hunter-Gatherers. *Current Anthropology* 31:189–196.

Black, M. E.

1984 Maidens and Mothers: An Analysis of Hopi Corn Metaphors. *Ethnology* 23:279–288.

Blinman, E.

1988 Ceramic Vessels and Vessel Assemblages in Dolores Archaeological Program Collections. In *Dolores Archaeological Program: Supporting Studies: Additive and Reductive Technologies*, ed. E. Blinman, C. J. Phagan, and R. H. Wilshusen, pp. 449–482. Bureau of Reclamation, Engineering and Research Center, Denver.

Bloom, L. B.

1934 Note on the Peñalosa Map. *New Mexico Historical Review* 9(2):228–230.

Bloomer, W. W.

1989 Moon House: A Pueblo III Period Cliff Dwelling Complex in Southeastern Utah. Unpublished master's thesis, Washington State University, Pullman.

Boas, F.

1912 Changes in the Bodily Form of Descendants of Immigrants. *American Anthropologist* 14:530–562.

Boquet-Appel, J.-P., and C. Masset

1982 Farewell to Paleodemography. *Journal of Human Evolution* 11:321–333.

Boquet-Appel, J.-P., and S. Naji

2006 Testing the Hypothesis of a Worldwide Neolithic Demographic Transition: Corroboration from American Cemeteries. *Current Anthropology* 47(2):341–365.

Boroditsky, L.

2000 Metaphoric Structuring: Understanding Time Through Spatial Metaphors. *Cognition* 75:1–28.

Boserup, E.

1965 *The Conditions of Agricultural Growth: The Economics of Agrarian Change Under Population Pressure*. Aldine, Chicago.

Bourdieu, P.

1973 The Berber House. In *Rules and Meaning*, ed. M. Douglas, pp. 98–110. Penguin, Middlesex, England.

1990 *The Logic of Practice*. Stanford University Press, Palo Alto, CA.

Bowser, B. J.

2000 From Pottery to Politics: An Ethnoarchaeological Case Study of Political Factionalism, Ethnicity, and Domestic Pottery Style in the Ecuadorian Amazon. *Journal of Archaeological Method and Theory* 7(3):219–248.

Boyd, M.

1981 *Kiowa Voices*. Vol. 1, *Ceremonial Dance, Ritual and Song*. Texas Christian University Press, Fort Worth.

Boyd, R., and P. J. Richerson

1985 *Culture and the Evolutionary Process*. University of Chicago Press, Chicago.

Boyer, J. L., J. L. Moore, S. A. Lakatos, N. J. Akins, C. D. Wilson, and E. Blinman

2010 Remodeling Immigration: A Northern Rio Grande Perspective on Depopulation, Migration, and Donation-Side Models. In *Leaving Mesa Verde: Peril and Change in the Thirteenth-Century Southwest*, ed. T. A. Kohler, M. D. Varien, and A. Wright, pp. 285–323. University of Arizona Press, Tucson.

Bradley, B. A.

1988 Wallace Ruin Interim Report. *Southwestern Lore* 54(2):8–33.

1992 Excavations at Sand Canyon Pueblo. In *The Sand Canyon Archaeological Project: A Progress Report*, ed. W. D. Lipe, pp. 79–97. Occasional Papers No. 2. Crow Canyon Archaeological Center, Cortez, CO.

1993 Planning, Growth, and Functional Differentiation at a Prehistoric Pueblo: A Case Study from SW Colorado. *Journal of Field Archaeology* 20:23–42.

1996 Pitchers to Mugs: Chacoan Revival at Sand Canyon Pueblo. *Kiva* 61:241–255.

Brandt, C. B.

2002 Macrobotanical Remains. In *Archaeological Investigaitons in the Fruitland Project Area: Late Archaic, Basketmaker, Pueblo I, and Navajo Sites in Northwestern New Mexico.* Vol. 5, *Material Culture, Bioarchaeological and Special Studies*, ed. T. D. Hovezak and L. M. Sesler, pp. 307–336. Research Papers No. 4. La Plata Archaeological Consultants, Dolores, CO.

Breternitz, D. A., A. H. Rohn Jr., and E. A. Morris

1974 *Prehistoric Ceramics of the Mesa Verde Region.* Museum of Northern Arizona, Flagstaff.

Brettel, C. B., and J. F. Hollifield (editors)

2008 *Migration Theory: Talking Across Disciplines.* Routledge, New York.

Brew, J. O.

1946 *Archaeology of Alkali Ridge, Southeastern Utah.* Papers of the Peabody Museum of American Archaeology and Ethnology Vol. 21. Harvard University, Cambridge, MA.

Brown, B. M.

1987 Population Estimation from Floor Area: A Restudy of "Naroll's Constant." *Behavior Science Research* 22(1–4):1–49.

Brown, C. H.

2006 Glottochronology and the Chronology of Maize in the Americas. In *Histories of Maize: Multidisciplinary Approaches to the Prehistory, Linguistics, Biogeography, Domestication and Evolution of Maize*, ed. J. E. Staller, R. H. Tykot, and B. F. Benz, pp. 648–664. Academic Press, Burlington, MA.

Brown, E. J.

2005 Instruments of Power: Musical Performance in Rituals of the Ancestral Puebloans of the American Southwest. Ph.D. dissertation, Columbia University.

Brues, A.

1946 Appendix A: Alkali Ridge Skeletal Material, Measurements, Indices, and Observations. In *The Archaeology of Alkali Ridge, Southeastern Utah.* Papers of the Peabody Museum of American Archaeology and Ethnology Vol. 21. Harvard University, Cambridge, MA.

Bugé, D. E.

1978 *Preliminary Report: 1978 Excavations at NM-01-1407, Ojo Caliente, New Mexico.* Manuscript on file, Laboratory of Anthropology. Museum of New Mexico, Santa Fe.

1984 Prehistoric Subsistence Strategies in the Ojo Caliente Valley New Mexico. In *Prehistoric Agricultural Strategies in the Southwest*, ed. S. K. Fish and P. R. Fish, pp. 27–34. Anthropological Research Papers No. 33. Arizona State University, Tempe.

Buikstra, J.

1977 Biocultural Dimensions of Archaeological Study: A Regional Perspective. In *Biocultural Adaptation in Prehistoric America*, ed. R. L. Blakely, pp. 67–84. Proceedings of the Southern Anthropological Society Vol. 11. University of Georgia Press, Athens.

Buikstra, J. E., and D. H. Ubelaker (editors)

1994 *Standards for Data Collection from Human Skeletal Remains.* Arkansas Archaeological Survey Research Series 44, Fayetteville.

Bussey, S. D.

1968a Excavations at LA6461, the Red Snake Hill Site. In *The Cochiti Dam Archaeological*

Salvage Project, Part 1: *Report on the 1963 Season,* ed. C. H. Lange, pp. 5–12. Research Records No. 6. Museum of New Mexico, Santa Fe.

1968b Excavations at LA6462, the North Bank Site. In *The Cochiti Dam Archaeological Salvage Project,* Part 1: *Report on the 1963 Season,* ed. C. H. Lange, pp. 13–72. Research Records No. 6. Museum of New Mexico, Santa Fe.

Cabana, G., K. Hunley, and F. Kaestle

2008 Population Continuity or Replacement: A Novel Computer Simulation Approach and Its Application to the Numic Expansion (Western Great Basin, USA). *American Journal of Physical Anthropology* 135:438–477.

Cadien, J. D., E. F. Harris, W. P. Jones, and L. J. Mandarino

1974 Biological Lineages, Skeletal Populations, and Microevolution. *Yearbook of Physical Anthropology* 18:194–201.

Cameron, C. [M.]

1990 Pit Structure Abandonment in the Four Corners Region of the American Southwest: Late Basketmaker III and Pueblo I Periods. *Journal of Field Archaeology* 17: 27–37.

1998 Coursed Adobe Architecture, Style, and Social Boundaries in the American Southwest. In *The Archaeology of Social Boundaries,* ed. M. T. Stark, pp. 183–207. Smithsonian Institution Press, Washington, DC.

Campbell, L.

1997 *American Indian Languages: The Historical Linguistics of Native America.* Oxford Studies in Anthropological Linguistics 4. Oxford University Press, Oxford.

1998 *Historical Linguistics: An Introduction.* MIT Press, Cambridge, MA.

2002 What Drives Linguistic Diversification and Language Spread? In *Examining the Farming/Language Dispersal Hypothesis,* ed. P. Bellwood and C. Renfrew, pp. 49–64. McDonald Institute for Archaeological Research, Cambridge.

Campbell, L., and T. Kaufman

1976 A Linguistic Look at the Olmecs. *American Antiquity* 41(1):80–89.

Carlsen, R. S.

1997 *The War for the Heart and Soul of a Maya Town.* University of Texas Press, Austin.

Carlson, I. K., and T. A. Kohler

1990 Prolegomenon to the Study of Habitation Site Architecture During the Coalition Period on the Pajarito Plateau. In *Bandelier Archaeological Excavation Project: Summer 1989 Excavations at Burnt Mesa Pueblo,* ed. T. A. Kohler, pp. 7–26. Department of Anthropology Reports of Investigations 62. Washington State University, Pullman.

Carlyle, S. W., R. L. Parr, G. Hayes, and D. H. O'Rourke

2000 Context of Maternal Lineages in the Greater Southwest. *American Journal of Physical Anthropology* 113:85–101.

Carneiro, R. L.

1967 On the Relationship Between Size of Population and Complexity of Social Organization. *Southwestern Journal of Anthropology* 23:234–243.

Carr, C.

1995 A Unified Middle-range Theory of Artifact Design. In *Style, Society, and Person: Archaeological and Ethnological Perspectives,* ed. C. Carr and J. E. Neitzel, pp. 171–258. Plenum Press, New York.

Carr, C., and J. Neitzel (editors)

1995 *Style, Society, and Person: Archaeological and Ethnological Perspectives.* Plenum Press, New York.

Carson, E. A.
2006 Maximum Likelikood Estimation of Human Craniometric Heritabilities. *American Journal of Physical Anthropology* 131:169–180.
Cater, J. D., and M. L. Chenault
1988 Kiva Use Reinterpreted. *Southwestern Lore* 54(3):19–32.
Cattanach, G. S., Jr.
1980 *Long House, Mesa Verde National Park, Colorado.* National Park Service, Washington, DC.
Cavalli-Sforza, L. L., and W. F. Bodmer
1971 *The Genetics of Human Populations.* W. H. Freeman, San Francisco.
Cavalli-Sforza, L. L., and M. W. Feldman
1981 *Cultural Transmission and Evolution: A Quantitative Approach.* Princeton University Press, Princeton, NJ.
Cavalli-Sforza, L. L., P. Menozzi, and A. Piazza
1994 *The History and Geography of Human Genes.* Princeton University Press, Princeton, NJ.
Chambelain, A.
2006 *Demography in Archaeology.* Cambridge University Press, Cambridge.
Charles, M. C., and S. J. Cole
2006 Chronology and Cultural Variation in Basketmaker II. *Kiva* 72(2):167–216.
Charles, M. C., L. M. Sesler, and T. D. Hovezak
2006 Understanding Eastern Basketmaker II Chronology and Migrations. *Kiva* 72(2): 217–238.
Chavez, F. A.
1967 Pohe-yemo's Representative and the Pueblo Revolt of 1680. *New Mexico Historical Review* 42(2):85–126.
Cheverud, J. M.
1988 A Comparison of Genetic and Phenotypic Correlations. *Evolution* 42(5):958–968.
Church, T.
2000 Distribution and Sources of Obsidian in the Rio Grande Gravels of New Mexico. *Geoarchaeology* 15:649–678.
Churchill, M. J.
2002 The Archaeology of Woods Canyon Pueblo: A Canyon-rim Village in Southwestern Colorado [html title]. http://www.crowcanyon.org/woodscanyon.
Churchill, M. J., and S. G. Ortman
2002 Chronology. In The Archaeology of Woods Canyon Pueblo: A Canyon-Rim Village in Southwestern Colorado [html title], ed. M. J. Churchill. http://www.crowcanyon.org/woodscanyon.
Clark, J. J.
2001 *Tracking Prehistoric Migrations: Pueblo Settlers among the Tonto Basin Hohokam.* Anthropological Papers of the University of Arizona No. 65. University of Arizona Press, Tucson.
2004 Tracking Cultural Affiliation: Enculturation and Ethnicity. In *Identity, Feasting, and the Archaeology of the Greater Southwest*, ed. B. J. Mills, pp. 42–73. Proceedings of the 2002 Southwest Symposium. University Press of Colorado, Boulder.
Cobos, R.
2003 *A Dictionary of New Mexico and Southern Colorado Spanish, Revised and Expanded Edition.* Museum of New Mexico Press, Santa Fe.

Cole, S. J.

2009 *Legacy on Stone: Rock Art of the Colorado Plateau and Four Corners Region*. Johnson Books, Boulder, CO.

Collins, S. M.

1975 Prehistoric Rio Grande Settlement Patterns and the Inference of Demographic Change. Ph.D. dissertation, University of Colorado, Boulder.

Coltrain, J. B., J. C. Janetski, and S. W. Carlyle

2006 The Stable and Radio-Isotope Chemistry of Eastern Basketmaker and Pueblo Groups in the Four Corners Region of the American Southwest: Implications for Anasazi Diets, Origins, and Abandonments in Southwestern Colorado. In *Histories of Maize: Multidisciplinary Approaches to the Prehistory, Linguistics, Biogeography, Domestication, and Evolution of Maize*, ed. J. E. Staller, R. H. Tykot, and B. F. Benz, pp. 276–289. Elsevier, New York.

Comaroff, J. L., and J. Comaroff

1997 *Of Revelation and Revolution*. Vol. 2, *The Dialectics of Modernity on a South African Frontier.* University of Chicago Press, Chicago.

Conkey, M. W., and C. A. Hastorf (editors)

1990 *Uses of Style in Archaeology*. Cambridge University Press, Cambridge.

Cordell, L. S.

1979 Prehistory: Eastern Anasazi. In *Handbook of North American Indians*, vol. 9: *Southwest*, ed. A. Ortiz, pp. 131–151. Smithsonian Institution, Washington, DC.

1995 Tracing Migration Pathways from the Receiving End. *Journal of Anthropological Archaeology* 14:203–211.

Cordell, L. S., C. R. Van West, J. S. Dean, and D. A. Muenchrath

2007 Mesa Verde Settlement History and Relocation: Climate Change, Social Networks, and Ancestral Pueblo Migration. *Kiva* 72:379–405.

Cordero, R. M.

2005 The Faunal Remains from a Coalition Period Structure. Chap. 9 of *Coalition Period Remains Under the West Alcove, U.S. Federal Courthouse, Santa Fe, New Mexico*, ed. C. L. Scheick, pp. 185–210. Report 477C, NMCRIS 87632. Southwest Archaeological Consultants, Santa Fe, NM.

Corruccini, R. S.

1983 Pathologies Relative to Subsistence and Settlement at Casas Grandes. *American Antiquity* 48(3):609–610.

Creamer, W.

1993 *The Architecture of Arroyo Hondo Pueblo, New Mexico*. Arroyo Hondo Archaeological Series 7. School of American Research Press, Santa Fe, NM.

2000 Regional Interactions and Regional Systems in the Protohistoric Rio Grande. In *The Archaeology of Regional Interaction: Religion, Warfare, and Exchange Across the American Southwest and Beyond*, ed. M. Hegman, pp. 99–118. University Press of Colorado, Boulder.

Crotty, H. K.

1999 Kiva Murals and Iconography at Picuris Pueblo. In *Picuris Pueblo Through Time: Eight Centuries of Change at a Northern Rio Grande Pueblo*, ed. M. A. Adler, pp. 149–188. William P. Clements Center for Southwest Studies, Southern Methodist University, Dallas.

2001 Shields, Shield Bearers, and Warfare Imagery in Anasazi Art, 1200–1500. In *Deadly Landscapes: Case Studies in Prehistoric Southwestern Warfare*, ed. G. E. Rice and S. LeBlanc, pp. 65–84. University of Utah Press, Salt Lake City.

2007 Western Pueblo Influences and Integration in the Pottery Mound Painted Kivas. In *New Perspectives on Pottery Mound Pueblo*, ed. P. Schaafsma, pp. 85–108. University of New Mexico Press, Albuquerque.

Crown, P. L.

1991 Evaluating the Construction Sequence and Population of Pot Creek Pueblo, Northern New Mexico. *American Antiquity* 56(2):291–314.

1994 *Ceramics and Ideology: Salado Polychrome Pottery.* University of New Mexico Press, Albuquerque.

2000 Women's Role in Changing Cuisine. In *Women and Men in the Prehispanic Southwest*, ed. P. L. Crown, pp. 221–266. School of American Research Press, Santa Fe, NM.

Crown, P. L., J. D. Orcutt, and T. A. Kohler

1996 Pueblo Cultures in Transition: The Northern Rio Grande. In *The Prehistoric Pueblo World, AD 1150–1350*, ed. M. A. Adler, pp. 188–204. University of Arizona Press, Tucson.

Cutler, H. C., and W. Meyer

1965 Corn and Cucurbits from Wetherill Mesa. In *Contributions of the Wetherill Mesa Archeological Project*, ed. B. S. Katz. Memoirs of the Society for American Archaeology Vol. 19. Salt Lake City.

Cutler, H. C., and T. W. Whitaker

1961 History and Distribution of the Cultivated Cucurbits in the Americas. *American Antiquity* 26:469–485.

Damasio, A.

1994 *Descartes' Error: Emotion, Reason, and the Human Brain.* G. P. Putnam, New York.

1999 *The Feeling of What Happens: Body and Emotion in the Making of Consciousness.* Harcourt Brace, New York.

Davis, E. L.

1965 Small Pressures and Cultural Drift as Explanations for Abandonment of the San Juan Area, New Mexico and Arizona. *American Antiquity* 30:353–355.

Davis, I.

1959 Linguistic Clues to Northern Rio Grande Prehistory. *El Palacio* 66 (June): 73–84.

1964 The Language of Santa Ana Pueblo. In *Bureau of American Ethnology Bulletin* 191, pp. 59–190. Government Printing Office, Washington, DC.

1989 A New Look at Aztec-Tanoan. In *General and Amerindian Ethnolinguistics: In Remembrance of Stanley Newman*, ed. M. R. Key and H. M. Hoenigswald, pp. 365–379. Mouton de Gruyter, Berlin and New York.

Dawkins, R.

1986 *The Blind Watchmaker: Why the Evidence of Evolution Reveals a Universe Without Design.* Norton, New York.

De Marco, B.

2000 Voices from the Archives, Part 1: Testimony of the Pueblo Indians in the 1680 Pueblo Revolt. *Romance Philology* 53(2):375–448.

Dean, J. S.

1988 A Model of Anasazi Behavioral Adaptation. In *The Anasazi in a Changing Environment*, ed. G. J. Gumerman, pp. 25–44. Cambridge University Press, Cambridge.

Dean, J. S., W. H. Doelle, and J. D. Orcutt

1994 Environment and Demography. In *Themes in Southwest Prehistory*, ed. G. Gumerman, pp. 53–86. School of American Research Press, Santa Fe, NM.

Devor, E. J.

1987 Transmission of Human Craniofacial Dimensions. *Journal of Craniofacial Genetics and Developmental Biology* 7:95–106.

Di Peso, C. C.

1958 *The Reeve Ruin of Southeastern Arizona: A Study of Prehistoric Western Pueblo Migration into the Middle San Pedro Valley.* Amerind Foundation 8. Amerind Foundation, Dragoon, AZ.

Dice, M. H.

1993 Formal Burial Analysis. In *Archaeological Investigations on Prehistoric Sites, Reach III of the Towaoc Canal*, pp. 651–674. Four Corners Archaeological Project Vol. 21. Complete Archaeological Service Associates. Cultural Resource Program, Bureau of Reclamation, Upper Colorado Region, Salt Lake City.

Dickson, D. B., Jr.

1979 *Prehistoric Pueblo Settlement Patterns: The Arroyo Hondo, New Mexico, Site Survey.* School of American Research, Santa Fe, NM.

Dixon, R. M. W.

1997 *The Rise and Fall of Languages.* Cambridge University Press, Cambridge.

Dobyns, H. F.

1993 Disease Transfer at Contact. *Annual Review of Anthropology* 22:273–291.

Douglass, W. B.

1915 Notes on the Shrines of the Tewa and Other Pueblo Indians of New Mexico. In *Proceedings of the 19th International Congress of Americanists*, pp. 344–378.

Dozier, E. P.

1954 *The Hopi-Tewa of Arizona.* University of California Publications in American Archaeology and Ethnology 44(4): 259–376. University of California Press, Berkeley and Los Angeles.

Driver, J. C.

1996 Social Complexity and Hunting Systems in Southwestern Colorado. In *Debating Complexity: Proceedings of the Twenty-Sixth Annual Chacmool Conference*, ed. D. A. Meyer, P. C. Dawson, and D. T. Hanna, pp. 364–374. Archaeological Association of the University of Calgary, Calgary, Alberta.

2002 Faunal Variation and Change in the Northern San Juan Region. In *Seeking the Center Place: Archaeology and Ancient Communities in the Mesa Verde Region*, ed. M. D. Varien and R. H. Wilshusen, pp. 143–160. University of Utah Press, Salt Lake City.

Droessler, J.

1981 *Craniometry and Biological Distance: Biocultural Continuity and Change at the Late-Woodland-Mississippian Interface.* Center for American Archaeology at Northwestern University, Evanston, IL.

Duff, A. I.

1998 The Process of Migration in the Late Prehistoric Southwest. In *Migration and Reorganization: The Pueblo IV Period in the American Southwest*, ed. K. A. Spielmann, pp. 31–52. Anthropological Research Papers No. 51. Arizona State University, Tempe.

Duff, A. I., K. R. Adams, and S. C. Ryan

2010 The Impact of Long-term Residential Occupation of Community Centers on Local Plant and Animal Resources. In *Leaving Mesa Verde: Peril and Change in the Collapse and Migration in the Thirteenth-Century Southwest*, ed. T. A. Kohler, M. D. Varien, and A. Wright, pp. 156–179. University of Arizona Press, Tucson.

Duff, A. I., and R. H. Wilshusen

2000 Prehistoric Population Dynamics in the Northern San Juan region, AD 950–1300. *Kiva* 66(1):167–90.

Durham, W. H.

1991 *Coevolution: Genes, Culture, and Human Diversity.* Stanford University Press, Stanford, CA.

Durkheim, E.

1968 *The Elementary Forms of the Religious Life.* Free Press, New York. Originally published 1915, George Allen and Unwin.

Dutton, B. [P.]

1963 *Sun Fathers Way: The Kiva Murals of Kuaua.* University of New Mexico Press, Albuquerque.

1964 Las Madres in the Light of Anasazi Migrations. *American Antiquity* 29:449–454.

Duwe, S.

2008 *Report on Archaeological Mapping Surveys Conducted at Leafwater-Kap (LA300) and Tsama (LA908-909).* Report on file, The Archaeological Conservancy, Albuquerque.

Eddy, F. W.

1966 *Prehistory in the Navajo Reservoir District, Northwestern New Mexico.* Museum of New Mexico, Santa Fe.

Edmonson, M. S.

1993 The Mayan Faith. In *South and Meso-American Native Spirituality: From the Cult of the Feathered Serpent to the Theology of Liberation*, ed. G. H. Gossen and M. León-Portilla, pp. 65–85. Crossroads, New York.

Eighmy, J. L.

1979 Logistic Trends in Southwest Population Growth. In *Transformations: Mathematical Approaches to Culture*, ed. C. Renfrew and K. L. Cooke, pp. 205–220. Academic Press, New York.

Eliade, M.

1959 *The Sacred and the Profane.* Harcourt Brace Jovanovich, New York.

Elliott, M. L.

1998 Coalition Period Adaptations in the Jemez Region: Origins of the Jemez Phenomenon. Paper presented at the Annual Meeting of the Society for American Archaeology, Seattle, WA.

Ellis, F. H.

1964a Archaeological History of Nambe Pueblo, 14th Century to the Present. *American Antiquity* 30(1):34–42.

1964b *A Reconstruction of the Basic Jemez Pattern of Social Organization, with Comparisons to Other Tanoan Social Structures.* University of New Mexico Publications in Anthropology 11. University of New Mexico Press, Albuquerque.

1967 Where Did the Pueblo People Come From? *El Palacio* 74(3):35–43.

1974 *Nambe: Their Past Agricultural Use of Territory.* Prepared for the USDI Bureau of Indian Affairs. Manuscript on file, New Mexico State Engineer Office, Santa Fe.

1975 Highways to the Past. *New Mexico Magazine* 53:18–40.

El-Najjar, M. Y.

1986 The Biology and Health of the Prehistoric Inhabitants of Canyon de Chelly. In *Archaeological Investigations at Antelope House*, ed. D. P. Morris, pp. 206–220. Department of the Interior, National Park Service, Washington, DC.

Emberling, G.

1997 Ethnicity in Complex Societies: Archaeological Perspectives. *Journal of Archaeological Research* 5(4):295–344.

Errickson, M. P., and C. D. Wilson

1988 Ceramic Evidence of Post-Anasazi Occupation in the Dolores Project Area. In *Dolores Archaeological Program: Aceramic and Late Occupations at Dolores*, ed. G. T. Gross and A. E. Kane, pp. 403–411. Bureau of Reclamation, Engineering and Research Center, Denver.

Etzkorn, M. C.

1993 Stone and Mineral Artifacts. In *The Duckfoot Site*, Vol. 1: *Descriptive Archaeology*, ed. R. R. Lightfoot and M. C. Etzkorn, pp. 157–182. Occasional Papers No. 3. Crow Canyon Archaeological Center, Cortez, CO.

Fauconnier, G.

1997 *Mappings in Thought and Language*. Cambridge University Press, Cambridge.

Fauconnier, G., and M. Turner

1994 *Conceptual Projection and Middle Spaces*. Report 9401. University of California, San Diego, Department of Cognitive Science, La Jolla.

Fenn, F.

2004 *The Secrets of San Lazaro Pueblo*. One Horse Land and Cattle Company, Santa Fe, NM.

Ferguson, T. J.

2004 Academic, Legal, and Political Contexts of Social Identity and Cultural Affiliation Research in the Southwest. In *Identity, Feasting, and the Archaeology of the Greater Southwest*, ed. B. J. Mills, pp. 27–41. University Press of Colorado, Boulder.

Ferguson, W. M., and A. H. Rohn

1986 *Anasazi Ruins of the Southwest in Color*. University of New Mexico Press, Albuquerque.

Fetterman, J., and L. Honeycutt

1987 *The Mockingbird Mesa Survey, Southwestern Colorado*. Bureau of Land Management, Denver.

Fewkes, J. W.

1919 *Prehistoric Villages, Castles, and Towers of Southwestern Colorado*. Smithsonian Institution, Washington, DC.

1923 *Archeological Field-Work on the Mesa Verde National Park: Explorations and Field-Work for 1922*. Smithsonian Institution, Washington, DC.

Flannery, K. V. (editor)

1976 *The Early Mesoamerican Village*. Academic Press, New York.

Flannery, K. V., and J. Marcus (editors)

1983 *The Cloud People: Divergent Evolution of the Zapotec and Mixtec Civilizations*. Academic Press, New York.

Ford, R. I., A. H. Schroeder, and S. L. Peckham

1972 Three Perspectives on Puebloan Prehistory. In *New Perspectives on the Pueblos*, ed. A. Ortiz, pp. 19–39. University of New Mexico Press, Albuquerque.

Forster, P. S., and C. Renfrew (editors)

2006 *Phylogenetic Methods and the Prehistory of Languages*. McDonald Institute for Archaeological Research, Cambridge.

Fowler, C. S.

1972 Some Ecological Clues to Proto-Numic Homelands. In *Great Basin Culture*

Ecology: A Symposium, ed. D. D. Fowler, pp. 105–121. Desert Research Institute Publications in the Social Sciences Vol. 8. University of Nevada, Reno.

1983 Some Lexical Clues to Uto-Aztecan Prehistory. *International Journal of American Linguistics* 49(3):224–257.

1994 Corn, Beans and Squash: Some Linguistic Perspectives from Uto-Aztecan. In *Corn and Culture in the Prehistoric New World*, ed. S. Johannessen and C. A. Hastorf, pp. 445–467. Westview Press, Boulder.

Fowles, S. M.

2004a Tewa versus Tiwa: Northern Rio Grande Settlement Patterns and Social History, AD 1275 to 1540. In *The Protohistoric Pueblo World, AD 1275–1600*, ed. E. C. Adams and A. I. Duff, pp. 17–25. University of Arizona Press, Tucson.

2004b The Making of Made People: The Prehistoric Evolution of Hierocracy Among the Northern Tiwa of New Mexico. Ph.D. dissertation, University of Michigan.

Fowles, S. M., L. Minc, S. Duwe, and D. V. Hill

2007 Clay, Conflict, and Village Aggregation: Compositional Analyses of Pre-Classic Pottery from Taos, New Mexico. *American Antiquity* 72(1):125–152.

Francis, J. E., and L. L. Loendorf

2002 *Ancient Visions: Petroglyphs and Pictographs of the Wind River and Bighorn Country, Wyoming and Montana*. University of Utah Press, Salt Lake City.

Frantz, D., and D. Gardner

1995 Southern Tiwa Lexicon: Isleta. Manuscript in possession of the author.

Gabler, B. M.

2008 Settlement Change and Demography on the Pajarito Plateau. In *The Land Conveyance and Transfer Data Recovery Project: 7000 Years of Land Use on the Pajarito Plateau*, Vol. 4: *Research Design*, ed. B. J. Vierra and K. M. Schmidt. Ecology and Air Quality Group, Los Alamos National Laboratory, NM.

Gebhard, D.

1966 The Shield Motif in Plains Rock Art. *American Antiquity* 31(5):721–732.

Geib, P. R.

1996 The Early Agricultural Period: Transition to Farming. In *Glen Canyon Revisited*, ed. P. R. Geib, pp. 53–77. University of Utah Anthropological Papers Vol. 98. University of Utah Press, Salt Lake City.

Geib, P. R., and E. A. Jolie

2008 The Role of Basketry in Early Holocene Small Seed Exploitation: Implications of a Ca. 9,000 Year-Old Basket from Cowboy Cave, Utah. *American Antiquity* 73(1): 83–102.

Gibbs, R. W., Jr.

1994 *The Poetics of Mind: Figurative Language, Thought, and Understanding*. Cambridge University Press, Cambridge.

Gilman, P. A.

1987 Architecture as Artifact: Pit Structures and Pueblos in the American Southwest. *American Antiquity* 52:538–564.

Gladwin, H. S.

1945 *The Chaco Branch: Excavations at White Mound and in the Red Mesa Valley*. Gila Pueblo, Globe, AZ.

Glowacki, D. M.

2001 *Yucca House (5MT5006) Mapping Project Report*. Unpublished report on file, Crow Canyon Archaeological Center and Mesa Verde National Park, CO.

2006 *The Social Landscape of Depopulation: The Northern San Juan, AD 1150–1300*. Ph.D. dissertation, Arizona State University, Tempe.

2009 Religion and the Mesa Verde Migrations. Paper presented at the Advanced Seminar: Religious Ideologies in the Pueblo Southwest, AD 1250–1540, The Amerind Foundation, Dragoon, AZ.

2010 The Social and Cultural Contexts of the Thirteenth-century Migrations from the Mesa Verde Region. In *Leaving Mesa Verde: Peril and Change in the Thirteenth-Century Southwest*, ed. T. A. Kohler, M. D. Varien, and A. Wright, pp. 200–221. University of Arizona Press, Tucson.

Goss, J. A.

1972 Ute Lexical and Phonological Patterns. Ph.D. dissertation, University of Chicago.

Gossen, G. H.

2004 "Everything Has Begun to Change": Appraisals of the Mexican State in Chiapas Maya Discourse, 1980–2000. In *Pluralizing Maya Ethnography: Comparison and Representation in Maya Cultures, Histories, and Identities*, ed. J. M. Watanabe and E. F. Fischer, pp. 127–162. School of American Research Press, Santa Fe, NM.

Gould, S. J.

1989 *Wonderful Life: The Burgess Shale and the Nature of History*. W. W. Norton, New York.

Graves, M. W.

1983 Growth and Aggregation at Canyon Creek Ruin: Implications for Evolutionary Change in East-Central Arizona. *American Antiquity* 48(2):290–315.

Gravlee, C. C., H. R. Bernard, and W. R. Leonard

2003 Heredity, Environment, and Cranial Form: A Reanalysis of Boas' Immigrant Data. *American Anthropologist* 105(1):125–138.

Greene, C. S.

2001 *Silver Horn: Master Illustrator of the Kiowas*. University of Oklahoma Press, Norman.

Greenlee, R.

1933 *Archaeological Sites in the Chama Valley, and Report on Excavations at Tsama, 1929–1933.* Manuscript on file (P651), Laboratory of Anthropology, Museum of New Mexico, Santa Fe.

Guernsey, S. J.

1931 *Explorations in Northeastern Arizona*. Harvard University, Cambridge, MA.

Guernsey, S. J., and A. V. Kidder

1921 *Basket-Maker Caves of Northern Arizona: Report on the Explorations, 1916–1917.* Harvard University, Cambridge, MA.

Habicht-Mauche, J. A.

1993 *The Pottery from Arroyo Hondo Pueblo, New Mexico: Tribalization and Trade in the Northern Rio Grande*. Arroyo Hondo Archaeological Series 8. School of American Research Press, Santa Fe, NM.

Hackett, C. W., and C. C. Shelby

1942 *Revolt of the Pueblo Indians of New Mexico and Otermin's Attempted Reconquest, 1680–1682*. University of New Mexico Press, Albuquerque.

Hale, K. L.

1962 Jemez and Kiowa Correspondences in Reference to Kiowa-Tanoan. *International Journal of American Linguistics* 28(1):1–5.

1967 Toward a Reconstruction of Kiowa-Tanoan Phonology. *International Journal of American Linguistics* 33(2):112–120.

n.d. Kiowa-Tanoan Cognate List (with annotations by Laurel Watkins). Manuscript in possession of the author.

Hale, K. [L.], and D. Harris

1979 Historical Linguistics and Archeology. In *Handbook of North American Indians,*

Vol. 9: *Southwest*, ed. A. Ortiz, pp. 170–177. Smithsonian Institution, Washington, DC.

Hanihara, T., and H. Ishida

2005 Metric Dental Variation of Major Human Populations. *American Journal of Physical Anthropology* 128:287–298.

Harbottle, G., and P. C. Weigand

1992 Turquoise in Pre-Columbian America. *Scientific American* (February): 78–85.

Hargrave, L. L.

1970 *Mexican Macaws: Comparative Osteology and Survey of Remains from the Southwest*. Anthropological Papers of the University of Arizona 20. University of Arizona Press, Tucson.

Harlow, F. H.

1965 Tewa Indian Ceremonial Pottery. *El Palacio* (Winter): 13–23.

1973 *Matte-Paint Pottery of the Tewa, Keres, and Zuni Pueblos*. Museum of New Mexico Press, Santa Fe.

Harper, B. W.

1929 Notes on the Documentary History, the Language, and the Rituals and Customs of Jemez Pueblo. MA thesis, University of New Mexico.

Harper, D.

2001 Online Etymology Dictionary. http://www.etymonline.com/. Accessed November 1, 2008.

Harrington, C. T.

1920 Isleta Language: Texts and Analytical Vocabulary. In *Harrington Papers*, microfilm edition, *Part 4: Southwest*. Reel 36, Frame 399-516. Kraus International, New York.

Harrington, J. P.

1909 Notes on the Piro Language. *American Anthropologist* 11(4):563–594.

1910a A Brief Description of the Tewa Language. *American Anthropologist* 12(4):497–504.

1910b An Introductory Paper on the Tiwa Language, Dialect of Taos, New Mexico. *American Anthropologist* 12(1):11–49.

1916 The Ethnogeography of the Tewa Indians. In *29th Annual Report of the Bureau of American Ethnology*, pp. 29–618. Government Printing Office, Washington, DC.

1928 *Vocabulary of the Kiowa Language*. Bureau of American Ethnology Bulletin 84. Government Printing Office, Washington, DC.

1939 Kiowa Memories of the Northland. In *So Live the Works of Men*, ed. D. D. Brand and F. E. Harvey, pp. 162–176. University of New Mexico Press, Albuquerque.

1947 Three Tewa Texts. *International Journal of American Linguistics* 13(2):112–116.

Haury, E. W.

1994 [1958] Evidence at Point of Pines for a Prehistoric Migration from Northern Arizona. In *Emil W. Haury's Prehistory of the American Southwest*, ed. J. J. Reid and D. E. Doyel, pp. 414–421. University of Arizona Press, Tucson.

Hayes, A. C., J. N. Young, and A. H. Warren

1981 *Excavation of Mound 7, Gran Quivira National Monument, New Mexico*. Publications in Archeology 16. Department of the Interior, National Park Service, Washington, DC.

Hays-Gilpin, K. A.

2008 Life's Pathways: Geographic Metaphors in Ancestral Puebloan Material Culture. In *Archaeology Without Borders: Contact, Commerce and Change in the U.S. South-*

west and Northwestern Mexico, ed. L. Webster and M. McBrinn, pp. 257–270. University Press of Colorado, Boulder.

Hegmon, M.

1998 Technology, Style, and Social Practices: Archaeological Approaches. In *The Archaeology of Social Boundaries*, ed. M. T. Stark, pp. 264–280. Smithsonian Institution Press, Washington, DC.

Hegmon, M., J. R. Allison, H. Neff, and M. D. Glascock

1997 Production of San Juan Red Ware in the Northern Southwest: Insights into Regional Interaction in Early Puebloan Prehistory. *American Antiquity* 62:449–463.

Henderson, J., and J. P. Harrington

1914 *Ethnozoology of the Tewa Indians*. Government Printing Office, Washington, DC.

Henrich, J.

2001 Cultural Transmission and the Diffusion of Innovations: Adoption Dynamics Indicate That Biased Cultural Transmission Is the Predominate Force in Behavioral Change. *American Anthropologist* 103:992–1013.

2004 Demography and Cultural Evolution: How Adaptive Cultural Processes Can Produce Maladaptive Losses: The Tasmanian Case. *American Antiquity* 69(2): 197–214.

Hensler, K. N., and E. Blinman

2002 Experimental Ceramic Technology — Or, the Road to Ruin(s) Is Paved With Crack(ed) Pots. In *Traditions, Transitions, and Technologies: Themes in Southwestern Archaeology*, ed. S. H. Schlanger, pp. 366–385. University Press of Colorado, Boulder.

Herr, S. A.

2002 *Beyond Chaco: Great Kiva Communities on the Mogollon Rim Frontier.* Anthropological Papers of the University of Arizona No. 66. University of Arizona Press, Tucson.

Hewett, E. L.

1906 *Antiquities of the Jemez Plateau, New Mexico.* Bureau of American Ethnology Bulletin 32. Smithsonian Institution, Washington, DC.

1938 *Pajarito Plateau and Its Ancient People.* University of New Mexico Press and School of American Research Press, Albuquerque and Santa Fe.

Hibben, F. C.

1937 *Excavation of the Riana Ruin and Chama Valley Survey.* University of New Mexico Anthropological Series 2. University of New Mexico Press, Albuquerque.

Hill, J. B., J. J. Clark, and W. H. Doelle

2010 Depopulation of the Northern Southwest: A Macro-regional Perspective with Insights from the Hohokam. In *Leaving Mesa Verde: Peril and Change in the Thirteenth-Century Southwest*, ed. T. A. Kohler, M. D. Varien, and A. Wright, pp. 34–52. University of Arizona Press, Tucson.

Hill, J. B., J. J. Clark, W. H. Doelle, and P. D. Lyons

2004 Prehistoric Demography in the Southwest: Migration, Coalescence, and Hohokam Population Decline. *American Antiquity* 69(4):689–716.

Hill, J. D.

1996 Introduction: Ethnogenesis in the Americas, 1492–1992. In *History, Power, and Identity: Ethnogenesis in the Americas, 1492–1992*, ed. J. D. Hill, pp. 1–19. University of Iowa Press, Iowa City.

Hill, J. D. (editor)

1996 *History, Power, and Identity: Ethnogenesis in the Americas, 1492–1992.* University of Iowa Press, Iowa City.

Hill, J. H.

2006 The Historical Linguistics of Maize Cultivation in Mesoamerica and North America. In *Histories of Maize*, ed. J. E. Staller, R. H. Tykot, and B. F. Benz, pp. 631–647. Elsevier, New York.

2008 Northern Uto-Aztecan and Kiowa-Tanoan: Evidence of Contact Between the Proto-Languages? *International Journal of American Linguistics* 74(2):155–188.

Hill, K. C. (editor)

1998 *Hopi Dictionary*. University of Arizona Press, Tucson.

Hodder, I.

1982 *Symbols in Action*. Cambridge University Press, Cambridge.

1991 *Reading the Past*. 2nd ed. Cambridge University Press, Cambridge.

Hodge, F. W.

1912 *Handbook of American Indians North of Mexico*. Bureau of American Ethnology Bulletin 30. Smithsonian Institution, Washington, DC.

Hoijer, H., and E. P. Dozier

1949 The Phonemes of Tewa, Santa Clara Dialect. *International Journal of American Linguistics* 15(3):139–144.

Holmer, R. N.

1980 Chipped Stone Projectile Points. In *Cowboy Cave*, pp. 31–38. Anthropological Papers 104. University of Utah Press, Salt Lake City.

1986 Common Projectile Points of the Intermountain West. In *Anthropology of the Desert West: Essays in Honor of Jesse D. Jennings*, ed. C. J. Condie and D. D. Fowler, pp. 89–115. Anthropological Papers No. 110. University of Utah Press, Salt Lake City.

Holmes, W. H.

1878 Report on the Ancient Ruins of Southwestern Colorado, Examined During the Summers of 1875 and 1876. In *Tenth Annual Report of the U.S. Geological and Geographical Survey of the Territories for 1876*, pp. 382–408. Geological Survey, Washington, DC.

1886 A Study of the Textile Art in Relation to the Development of Form and Ornament. In *Bureau of Ethnology, 4th Annual Report*, pp. 189–252. Smithsonian Institution, Washington, DC.

Honea, K. H.

1968 Material Culture: Ceramics. In *The Cochiti Dam Archaeological Salvage Project, Part 1: Report on the 1963 Season*, ed. C. H. Lange, pp. 111–169. Research Records No. 6. Museum of New Mexico, Santa Fe.

Hooton, E. A.

1930 *The Indians of Pecos Pueblo: A Study of Their Skeletal Remains*. Yale University Press, New Haven.

Hovezak, T. D.

2002 Site LA82977. In *Archaeological Investigations in the Fruitland Project Area: Late Archaic, Basketmaker, Pueblo I, and Navajo Sites in Northwestern New Mexico*, Vol. 3: *The Basketmaker and Pueblo I Sites*, ed. T. D. Hovezak and L. M. Sesler, pp. 371–456. La Plata Archaeological Consultants, Dolores, CO.

Hovezak, T. D., and L. Schniebs

2002 Vertebrate Faunal Remains. In *Archaeological Investigations in the Fruitland Project Area: Late Archaic, Basketmaker, Pueblo I, and Navajo Sites in Northwestern New Mexico*. Vol. 5: *Material Culture, Bioarchaeological, and Special Studies*, ed. T. D. Hovezak and L. M. Sesler. Research Papers No. 4. La Plata Archaeological Consultants, Dolores, CO.

Hovezak, T. D., and L. M. Sesler
2002 Prehistoric and Protohistoric Lithic Technologies in the Fruitland Study Area. In *Archaeological Investigations in the Fruitland Project Area: Late Archaic, Basketmaker, Pueblo I, and Navajo Sites in Northwestern New Mexico.* Vol. 5: *Material Culture, Bioarchaeological, and Special Studies*, ed. T. D. Hovezak and L. M. Sesler, pp. 51–186. Research Papers No. 4. La Plata Archaeological Consultants, Dolores, CO.

Howells, W. W.
1973 *Cranial Variation in Man: A Study by Multivariate Analysis of Patterns of Differences Among Recent Human Populations*. Papers of the Peabody Museum of Archaeology and Ethnology 67. Harvard University, Cambridge, MA.

Hrdliçka, A.
1931 Catalogue of Human Crania in the United State National Museum Collections. *Proceedings of the U.S. National Museum* 78(2):1–95.

Huckell, L. W.
2006 Ancient Maize in the American Southwest: What Does It Look Like and What Can It Tell Us? In *Histories of Maize*, ed. J. E. Staller, R. H. Tykot, and B. F. Benz, pp. 97–108. Elsevier, New York.

Huntley, D. L., and K. W. Kintigh
2004 Archaeological Patterning and Organizational Scale of Late Prehistoric Settlement Clusters in the Zuni Region of New Mexico. In *The Protohistoric Pueblo World, AD 1275–1600*, ed. E. C. Adams and A. I. Duff, pp. 62–74. University of Arizona Press, Tucson.

Hurst, C. T.
1940 Preliminary Work in Tabeguache Cave — 1939. *Southwestern Lore* 6(1):4–18.
1941 The Second Season in Tabeguache Cave. *Southwestern Lore* 7(1):4–19.
1942 Completion of Work in Tabeguache Cave. *Southwestern Lore* 8(1):7–16.
1944 1943 Excavation in Cave II, Tabeguache Canyon, Montrose County, Colorado. *Southwestern Lore* 10(1):2–14.
1945 Completion of Excavation of Tabeguache Cave II. *Southwestern Lore* 11(1):8–12.
1947 Excavation of Dolores Cave — 1946. *Southwestern Lore* 13(1):8–17.

Jackson, W. H.
1876 Ancient Ruins in Southwestern Colorado. In *Annual Report of the United States Geological and Geographical Survey of the Territories, Embracing Colorado and Parts of Adjacent Territories; Being a Report of Progress of the Exploration for the Year 1874*, ed. F. V. Hayden, pp. 367–381. Government Printing Office, Washington, DC.

Janetski, J. C.
1980 Wood and Reed Artifacts. In *Cowboy Cave*, pp. 75–95. Anthropological Papers 104. University of Utah Press, Salt Lake City.
1994 Recent Transitions in Eastern Great Basin Prehistory: The Archaeological Record. In *Across the West: Human Population Movement and the Expansion of the Numa*, ed. D. B. Madsen and D. Rhode, pp. 157–178. University of Utah Press, Salt Lake City.
2002 Trade in Fremont Society: Contexts and Contrasts. *Journal of Anthropological Archaeology* 21:344–370.

Jeançon, J. A.
1923 *Excavations in the Chama Valley, New Mexico.* Bureau of American Ethnology Bulletin 81. Government Printing Office, Washington, DC.
1925 Primitive Coloradoans. *Colorado Magazine* 2(1):35–40.

1929 Archaeological Investigation in the Taos Valley, New Mexico, During 1920. *Smithsonian Miscellaneous Collections* 81(12):1–29.

1930 Taos Notes. *El Palacio* 18(1–4):3–11.

Jelinek, A. J.

1969 Appendix: Identification of Mammalian Fauna. In *Early Puebloan Occupations at Tesuque By-Pass and in the Upper Rio Grande Valley*, ed. C. H. McNutt, pp. 127–133. Anthropological Papers No. 40. Museum of Anthropology, University of Michigan, Ann Arbor.

Jennings, J. D.

1957 *Danger Cave*. Anthropological Papers 27. University of Utah Press, Salt Lake City.

1980 *Cowboy Cave*. Anthropological Papers 104. University of Utah Press, Salt Lake City.

Johnson, M.

1987 *The Body in the Mind: The Bodily Basis of Meaning, Imagination, and Reason*. University of Chicago Press, Chicago.

Johnson, M., and G. Lakoff

2002 Why Cognitive Linguistics Requires Embodied Realism. *Cognitive Linguistics* 13(3):245–263.

Jolie, E. A.

2006 The Technomechanics of Plains Indian Coiled Gaming Baskets. *Plains Anthropologist* 51(197):17–49.

Jones, S.

1997 *The Archaeology of Ethnicity: Constructing Identities in the Past and Present*. Routledge, London.

Jones, V. H., and R. L. Fonner

1954 Plant Materials from Sites in the Durango and La Plata Areas, Colorado. In *Basketmaker II Sites Near Durango, Colorado*, ed. E. H. Morris and R. F. Burgh, pp. 93–116. Publication 604. Carnegie Institute, Washington, DC.

Jorgensen, J.

1972 *The Sun Dance Religion*. University of Chicago Press, Chicago.

1980 *Western Indians: Comparative Environments, Languages, and Cultures of 172 Western American Indian Tribes*. W. H. Freeman and Company, San Francisco.

Judd, N. M.

1954 *The Material Culture of Pueblo Bonito*. Smithsonian Institution, Washington, DC.

Karhu, S.

2000 *Mortuary Practices and Population Health at Two Yellow Jacket Hamlets, 5MT1 and 5MT3*. University of Colorado Museum, Boulder.

Kayser, J.

1965 Phantoms in the Pinyon: An Investigation of Ute-Pueblo Contacts. In *Contributions of the Wetherill Mesa Archeological Project*, ed. D. Osborne, pp. 82–91. Memoirs 19. Society for American Archaeology, Salt Lake City.

Kendrick, J. W., and W. J. Judge

2000 Household Economic Autonomy and Great House Development in the Lowry Area. In *Great House Communities Across the Chacoan Landscape*, ed. J. Kantner and N. M. Mahoney, pp. 113–129. Anthropological Papers of the University of Arizona No. 64. University of Arizona Press, Tucson.

Kent, K. P.

1957 *The Cultivation and Weaving of Cotton in the Prehistoric Southwestern United States*. Transactions of the American Philosophical Society 47, Part 3. Philadelphia.

1983 *Prehistoric Textiles of the Southwest.* School of American Research Press, Santa Fe, NM.

Kenzle, S. C.

1997 Enclosing Walls in the Northern San Juan: Sociophysical Boundaries and Defensive Fortifications in the American Southwest. *Journal of Field Archaeology* 24: 195–210.

Kessell, J. L.

1987 *Kiva, Cross, and Crown: The Pecos Indians of New Mexico, 1540–1840.* Southwest Parks and Monuments Association, Tucson, AZ.

Kidder, A. V.

1924 *An Introduction to the Study of Southwestern Archaeology with a Preliminary Account of the Excavations at Pecos.* Yale University Press, New Haven.

1958 *Pecos, New Mexico: Archaeological Notes.* Papers of the Robert S. Peabody Foundation for Archaeology 5. Phillips Academy, Andover, MA.

Kidder, A. V., and S. J. Guernsey

1919 *Archaeological Investigations in Northeastern Arizona.* Smithsonian Institution, Washington, DC.

Kidder, A. V., and A. O. Shepard

1936 *The Pottery of Pecos.* Yale University Press, New Haven.

Kintigh, K. W., D. M. Glowacki, and D. L. Huntley

2004 Long-term Settlement History and the Emergence of Towns in the Zuni Area. *American Antiquity* 69(3):432–456.

Kirch, P. V.

2010 *How Chiefs Became Kings: Divine Kingship and the Rise of Archaic States in Ancient Hawai'i.* University of California Press, Berkeley and Los Angeles.

Kirch, P. V., and R. C. Green

2001 *Hawaiki, Ancestral Polynesia: An Essay in Historical Anthropology.* Cambridge University Press, Cambridge.

Kirch, P. V., and M. D. Sahlins

1992 *Anahulu: The Anthropology of History in the Kingdom of Hawaii.* 2 vols. University of Chicago Press, Chicago.

Knab, T. J.

2004 *The Dialogue of Earth and Sky: Dreams, Souls, Curing, and the Modern Aztec Underworld.* University of Arizona Press, Tucson.

Kohler, T. A. (editor)

2004 *Archaeology of Bandelier National Monument: Village Formation on the Pajarito Plateau, New Mexico.* University of New Mexico Press, Albuquerque.

Kohler, T. A., and E. Blinman

1987 Solving Mixture Problems in Archaeology: Analysis of Ceramic Materials for Dating and Demographic Reconstruction. *Journal of Anthropological Archaeology* 6:1–28.

Kohler, T. A., S. Cole, and S. Ciupe

2009 Population and Warfare: A Test of the Turchin Model in Pueblo Societies. In *Pattern and Process in Cultural Evolution*, ed. S. J. Shennan, pp. 277–296. University of California Press, Berkeley.

Kohler, T. A., M. P. Glaude, J.-P. Boquet-Appel, and B. M. Kemp

2008 The Neolithic Demographic Transition in the U.S. Southwest. *American Antiquity* 73(4):645–669.

Kohler, T. A., S. A. Herr, and M. J. Root

2004 The Rise and Fall of Towns on the Pajarito (AD 1375–1600). In *Archaeology of Bandelier National Monument: Village Formation on the Pajarito Plateau, New Mexico*, ed. T. A. Kohler, pp. 215–264. University of New Mexico Press, Albuquerque.

Kohler, T. A., C. D. Johnson, M. D. Varien, S. G. Ortman, R. Reynolds, Z. Kobti, J. Cowan, K. Kolm, S. Smith, and L. Yap

2007 Settlement Ecodynamics in the Prehispanic Central Mesa Verde Region. In *The Model-Based Archaeology of Socionatural Systems*, ed. T. A. Kohler and S. van der Leeuw, pp. 61–104. School for Advanced Research Press, Santa Fe, NM.

Kohler, T. A., R. P. Powers, and J. D. Orcutt

2004 Bandelier from Hamlets to Towns. In *Archaeology of Bandelier National Monument: Village Formation on the Pajarito Plateau*, ed. T. A. Kohler, pp. 293–304. University of New Mexico Press, Albuquerque.

Kohler, T. A., and M. J. Root

2004a The First Hunter/Farmers on the Pajarito Plateau (AD 1150–1250). In *Archaeology of Bandelier National Monument: Village Formation on the Pajarito Plateau, New Mexico*, ed. T. A. Kohler, pp. 117–172. University of New Mexico Press, Albuquerque.

2004b The Late Coalition and Earliest Classic on the Pajarito Plateau (AD 1250–1375). In *Archaeology of Bandelier National Monument: Village Formation on the Pajarito Plateau, New Mexico*, ed. T. A. Kohler, pp. 173–214. University of New Mexico Press, Albuquerque.

Kohler, T. A., S. VanBuskirk, and S. Ruscavage-Barz

2004 Vessels and Villages: Evidence for Conformist Transmission in Early Village Aggregations on the Pajarito Plateau, New Mexico. *Journal of Anthropological Archaeology* 23:100–118.

Kohn, L. A. P., S. R. L. Leigh, and J. M. Cheverud

1995 Asymmetric Vault Modification in Hopi Crania. *American Journal of Physical Anthropology* 98:173–195.

Konigsberg, L. W.

2006 A Post-Neumann History of Biological and Genetic Distance Studies in Bioarchaeology. In *Bioarchaeology: The Contextual Analysis of Human Remains*, ed. J. Buikstra and L. Beck, pp. 263–279. Elsevier, New York.

Konigsberg, L. W., and S. D. Ousley

1995 Multivariate Quantitative Genetics of Anthropometric Traits from the Boas Data. *Human Biology* 67(3):481–498.

Kopytoff, I.

1987 The Internal African Frontier: The Making of African Political Culture. In *The African Frontier: The Reproduction of Traditional African Societies*, ed. I. Kopytoff, pp. 3–86. Indiana University Press, Bloomington.

Kövecses, Z.

2002 *Metaphor: A Practical Introduction*. Oxford University Press, New York.

Kroskrity, P. V.

1993 *Language, History, and Identity: Ethnolinguistic Studies of the Arizona Tewa*. University of Arizona Press, Tucson.

Kuckelman, K. A.

2000 The Archaeology of Castle Rock Pueblo: A Thirteenth-century Village in Southwestern Colorado [html title]. http://www.crowcanyon.org/castlerock.

2003 Architecture. In *The Archaeology of Yellow Jacket Pueblo: Excavations at a Large*

Community Center in Southwestern Colorado [html title], ed. K. A. Kuckelman, Available: http://www.crowcanyon.org/yellowjacket.

2008 An Agent-Centered Case Study of the Depopulation of Sand Canyon Pueblo. In *The Social Construction of Communities: Agency, Structure and Identity in the Prehispanic Southwest*, ed. M. D. Varien and J. M. Potter, pp. 109–121. Altamira Press, Lanham, MD.

2010 The Depopulation of Sand Canyon Pueblo, a Large Ancestral Pueblo Village in Southwestern Colorado. *American Antiquity* 75(3):496–526.

Kuckelman, K. A., G. D. Coffey, and S. R. Copeland

2009 *Interim Descriptive Report of Research at Goodman Point Pueblo (Site 5MT604), Montezuma County, Colorado, 2005–2008* [PDF title]. http://www.crowcanyon.org/goodmanpoint2005_2008.

Kuckelman, K. A., R. R. Lightfoot, and D. L. Martin

2000 Changing Patterns of Violence in the Northern San Juan Region. *Kiva* 66:147–165.

2002 The Bioarchaeology and Taphonomy of Violence at Castle Rock and Sand Canyon Pueblos, Southwestern Colorado. *American Antiquity* 67(3):486–513.

Kuckelman, K. A., and D. L. Martin

2007 Human Skeletal Remains. In *The Archaeology of Sand Canyon Pueblo: Intensive Excavations at a Late-Thirteenth Century Village in Southwestern Colorado* [html title], ed. K. A. Kuckelman. http://www.crowcanyon.org/sandcanyon.

Kuckelman, K. A., and S. G. Ortman

2003 Chronology. In *The Archaeology of Yellow Jacket Pueblo (Site 5MT5): Excavations at a Large Community Center in Southwestern Colorado* [html title], ed. K. A. Kuckelman. http://www.crowcanyon.org/yellowjacket.

Kulisheck, J.

2005 The Archaeology of Pueblo Population Change on the Jemez Plateau, AD 1200 to 1700: The Effects of Spanish Contact and Conquest. Ph.D. dissertation, Southern Methodist University, Dallas.

Kulisheck, J., and M. L. Elliott

2005 A Proposed Late Prehistoric and Early Historic Phase Sequence for the Jemez Plateau, North-Central New Mexico, USA. Paper presented at the 70th Annual Meeting of the Society for American Archaeology, Salt Lake City.

Kurath, G. P., and A. Garcia

1970 *Music and Dance of the Tewa Pueblos*. Research Records No. 8. Museum of New Mexico, Santa Fe.

Labov, W.

1972 *Sociolinguistic Patterns*. University of Pennsylvania Press, Philadelphia.

2001 *Principles of Linguistic Change*. Vol. 2, *Social Factors*. Language in Society 23. Blackwell, Oxford.

Lakatos, S.

2007 Cultural Continuity and the Development of Integrative Architecture in the Northern Rio Grande Valley of New Mexico, AD 600–1200. *Kiva* 73(1):31–66.

Lakoff, G.

1987 *Women, Fire, and Dangerous Things: What Categories Reveal About the Mind*. University of Chicago Press, Chicago.

1993 The Contemporary Theory of Metaphor. In *Metaphor and Thought*, ed. A. Ortony, pp. 202–251. 2nd ed. Cambridge University Press, Cambridge.

Lakoff, G., and M. Johnson
1980 *Metaphors We Live By*. University of Chicago Press, Chicago.
1999 *Philosophy in the Flesh: The Embodied Mind and Its Challenge to Western Thought*. Basic Books, New York.
Lakoff, G., and Z. Kövecses
1987 The Cognitive Model of Anger Inherent in American English. In *Cultural Models in Language and Thought*, ed. D. Holland and N. Quinn, pp. 195–211. Cambridge University Press, Cambridge.
Lakoff, G., and R. Núñez
2000 *Where Mathematics Comes From*. Basic Books, New York.
Lakoff, G., and M. Turner
1989 *More Than Cool Reason: A Field Guide to Poetic Metaphor*. University of Chicago Press, Chicago.
Lande, R.
1977 Statistical Tests for Natural Selection of Quantitative Characters. *Evolution* 31(2): 442–444.
Lang, R. W.
1982 Transformation in White Ware Pottery of the Northern Rio Grande. In *Southwestern Ceramics: A Comparative Review*, ed. A. H. Schroeder, pp. 152–200. Arizona Archaeologist No. 15. Arizona Archaeological Society.
1984 Artifacts of Hide, Fur, and Feathers from Arroyo Hondo Pueblo. In *The Faunal Remains from Arroyo Hondo Pueblo, New Mexico*, pp. 255–286. School of American Research Press, Santa Fe, NM.
1995 A Cultural Overview of the Rio Tesuque Drainage. In *Flint Procurement and Other Limited Activity Sites of the Upper Tesuque Valley, New Mexico: A Sampling from the Bishop's Lodge Locality*, ed. R. W. Lang, pp. 19–34. Research Series 284b. Southwest Archaeological Consultants, Santa Fe, NM.
Lang, R. W., and A. H. Harris
1984 *The Faunal Remains from Arroyo Hondo Pueblo, New Mexico*. Arroyo Hondo Archaeological Series 5. School of American Research Press, Santa Fe, NM.
Lang, R. W., and C. L. Scheick
1991 A Second Look at LA 2, the Agua Fria Schoolhouse Site: Recognition of a Coalition Phase Occupation. In *Puebloan Past and Present: Papers in Honor of Stewart Peckham*, ed. M. S. Duran and D. T. Kirkpatrick, pp. 87–111. Papers of the Archaeological Society of New Mexico Vol. 17. Albuquerque.
Lange, C. H.
1968 *The Cochiti Dam Archaeological Salvage Project: Part 1: Report on the 1963 Season*. Museum of New Mexico Research Records 6. Santa Fe.
Larsen, C. S.
1997 Historical Dimensions of Skeletal Variation: Tracing Genetic Relationships. In *Bioarchaeology: Interpreting Behavior from the Human Skeleton*, pp. 302–332. Cambridge University Press, Cambridge.
Laski, V.
1959 *Seeking Life*. American Folklore Society, Philadelphia.
Leap, W. L.
1971 Who Were the Piro? *Anthropological Linguistics* 13(7):321–330.
LeBlanc, S.
2008 The Case for an Early Farmer Migration into the Greater American Southwest. In

Archaeology without Borders: Contact, Commerce and Chance in the U.S. Southwest and Northwestern Mexico, ed. L. Webster and M. McBrinn, pp. 227–256. University Press of Colorado, Boulder.

LeBlanc, S. A., L. S. C. Kreisman, B. M. Kemp, F. E. Smiley, A. N. Dhody, and T. Benjamin

2007 Quids and Aprons: Ancient DNA from Artifacts from the American Southwest. *Journal of Field Archaeology* 32(2):161–175.

Lechtman, H.

1977 Style in Technology — Some Early Thoughts. In *Material Culture: Styles, Organization, and Dynamics of Technology*, ed. H. Lechtman and R. S. Merrill, pp. 3–20. West Publishing, St. Paul, MN.

Lefferts, H. L., Jr.

1977 Frontier Demography: An Introduction. In *The Frontier: Comparative Studies*, ed. D. H. Miller and J. O. Steffen, pp. 33–56. University of Oklahoma Press, Norman.

Leh, L. L.

1942 A Preliminary Report on the Monument Ruins in San Juan County, Utah. *University of Colorado Studies in the Social Sciences* 1(3):261–295.

Lekson, S. H.

1988 The Idea of the Kiva in Anasazi Archaeology. *The Kiva* 53:213–234.

2006 *The Archaeology of Chaco Canyon, an Eleventh-Century Pueblo Regional Center.* School of American Research Press, Santa Fe, NM.

Lekson, S. H., M. Bletzer, and A. C. MacWilliams

2004 Pueblo IV in the Chihuahuan Desert. In *The Protohistoric Pueblo World, AD 1275–1600*, ed. E. C. Adams and A. I. Duff, pp. 53–61. University of Arizona Press, Tucson.

Lekson, S. H., C. P. Nepstadt-Thornberry, B. E. Yunker, T. S. Laumbach, D. P. Cain, and K. W. Laumbach

2002 Migrations in the Southwest: Pinnacle Ruin, Southwestern New Mexico. *Kiva* 68(2):73–102.

Liebmann, M. J.

2002 Signs of Power and Resistance: The (Re)Creation of Christian Imagery and Identities in the Pueblo Revolt Era. In *Archaeologies of the Pueblo Revolt*, ed. R. W. Preucel, pp. 132–146. University of New Mexico Press, Albuquerque.

Liebmann, M. J., T. J. Ferguson, and R. W. Preucel

2005 Pueblo Settlement, Architecture, and Social Change in the Pueblo Revolt Era, AD 1680–1696. *Journal of Field Archaeology* 30:1–16.

Lightfoot, R. R.

1988 Roofing an Early Anasazi Great Kiva: Analysis of an Architectural Model. *The Kiva* 53:253–272.

1993 Abandonment Processes in Prehistoric Pueblos. In *Abandonment of Settlements and Regions: Ethnoarchaeological and Archaeological Approaches*, ed. C. M. Cameron and S. A. Tomka, pp. 165–177. Cambridge University Press, Cambridge.

1994 *The Duckfoot Site.* Vol. 2, *Archaeology of the House and Household.* Crow Canyon Archaeological Center, Cortez, CO.

Lightfoot, R. R., and K. A. Kuckelman

2001 A Case of Warfare in the Mesa Verde Region. In *Deadly Landscapes: Case Studies in Prehistoric Southwestern Warfare*, ed. G. E. Rice and S. A. LeBlanc, pp. 51–64. University of Utah Press, Salt Lake City.

Lincoln, B.

2003 *Holy Terrors: Thinking about Religion after September 11*. University of Chicago Press, Chicago.

Lindsay, A. J., Jr., J. R. Ambler, M. A. Stein, and P. M. Hobler

1968 *Survey and Excavations North and East of Navajo Mountain, Utah, 1959–1962*. Museum of Northern Arizona, Flagstaff.

Linford, L. D.

2000 *Navajo Places: History, Legend, Landscape*. University of Utah Press, Salt Lake City.

Lipe, W. D.

1989 Social Scale of Mesa Verde Anasazi Kivas. In *The Architecture of Social Integration in Prehistoric Pueblos*, ed. W. D. Lipe and M. Hegmon, pp. 53–71. Occasional Papers No. 1. Crow Canyon Archaeological Center, Cortez, CO.

1995 The Depopulation of the Northern San Juan: Conditions in the Turbulent 1200s. *Journal of Anthropological Archaeology* 14(2):143–169.

2002 Social Power in the Central Mesa Verde Region, AD 1150–1290. In *Seeking the Center Place: Archaeology and Ancient Communities in the Mesa Verde Region*, ed. M. D. Varien and R. H. Wilshusen, pp. 203–232. University of Utah Press, Salt Lake City.

2010 Lost in Transit: The Central Mesa Verde Archaeological Complex. In *Leaving Mesa Verde: Peril and Change in the Thirteenth-Century Southwest*, ed. T. A. Kohler, M. D. Varien, and A. Wright, pp. 262–284. University of Arizona Press, Tucson.

Lipe, W. D., and S. G. Ortman

2000 Spatial Patterning in Northern San Juan Villages, AD 1050–1300. *Kiva* 66(1):91–122.

Lipe, W. D., M. D. Varien, and R. H. Wilshusen (editors)

1999 *Colorado Prehistory: A Context for the Southern Colorado River Basin*. Colorado Council of Professional Archaeologists, Denver.

Little, A. L., Jr.

1971–1978 *Atlas of United States Trees*. 5 vols. U.S. Department of Agriculture, Washington, DC.

Loendorf, L. L., and S. W. Conner

1993 The Pectol Shields and the Shield-Bearing Warrior Rock Art Motif. *Journal of California and Great Basin Anthropology* 15(2):216–224.

Lowell, J. C.

2007 Women and Men in Warfare and Migration: Implications of Gender Imbalance in the Grasshopper Region of Arizona. *American Antiquity* 72(1):95–124.

Lucius, W. A.

1980 Bone and Shell Material. In *Cowboy Cave*, pp. 97–108. Anthropological Papers 104. University of Utah Press, Salt Lake City.

Luebben, R. A.

1953 Leaf Water Site. In *Salvage Archaeology in the Chama Valley, New Mexico*, ed. F. Wendorf, pp. 9–33. Monographs No. 17. School of American Research, Santa Fe, NM.

MacEachern, S.

1998 Scale, Style, and Cultural Variation: Technological Traditions in the Northern Mandara Mountains. In *The Archaeology of Social Boundaries*, ed. M. T. Stark, pp. 107–131. Smithsonian Institution Press, Washington, DC.

MacKenzie, M.

1991 *Androgynous Objects: String Bags and Gender in Central New Guinea*. Harwood Academic Press, Melbourne.

Mackey, J.
1977 A Multivariate, Osteological Approach to Towa Culture History. *American Journal of Physical Anthropology* 44:477–482.
1980 Arroyo Hondo Population Affinities. In *Pueblo Population and Society: The Arroyo Hondo Skeletal and Mortuary Remains*, ed. Ann M. Palkovich, pp. 171–181. Arroyo Hondo Archaeological Series Vol. 3. School of American Research Press, Santa Fe, NM.
Madsen, D. B., and D. Rhode
1994 *Across the West: Human Population Movement and the Expansion of the Numa*. University of Utah Press, Salt Lake City.
Magers, P. C.
1986a Miscellaneous Wooden and Vegetal Artifacts. In *Archeological Investigations at Antelope House*, ed. D. P. Morris, pp. 277–305. National Park Service, Department of the Interior, Washington, DC.
1986b Weaving at Antelope House. In *Archeological Investigations at Antelope House*, ed. D. P. Morris, pp. 224–276. National Park Service, Department of the Interior, Washington, DC.
Malinowski, B.
1954 *Magic, Science and Religion and Other Essays*. Doubleday, Garden City, NJ.
Mallory, J. P.
1989 *In Search of the Indo-Europeans*. Thames and Hudson, London.
Malville, N. J.
1997 Enamel Hypoplasia in Ancestral Puebloan Populations from Southwestern Colorado, Part 1: Permanent Dentition. *American Journal of Physical Anthropology* 102:351–367.
Manglesdorf, P. C.
1980 Report on the Maize Specimens in the Morris Collection. In *Basketmaker Caves in the Prayer Rock District, Northeastern Arizona*, ed. A. A. Morris, pp. 151–154. Anthropological Papers Number 35. University of Arizona Press, Tucson.
Manica, A., W. Amos, F. Balloux, and T. Hanihara
2007 The Effect of Ancient Population Bottlenecks on Human Phenotypic Variation. *Nature* 448:346–349.
Marshall, M. P.
1982 Bis Sa'ani Pueblo: An Example of Late Bonito-Phase, Great House Architecture. In *Bis Sa'ani: A Late Bonito Phase Community on Escavada Wash, Northwest New Mexico,* Vol. 2, Pt. 1, ed. C. D. Breternitz, D. E. Doyel, and M. P. Marshall, pp. 169–358. Navajo Nation Papers in Archaeology 14, Window Rock, AZ.
Marshall, M. P., J. R. Stein, R. W. Loose, and J. E. Novotny
1979 *Anasazi Communities of the San Juan Basin*. Public Service Company of New Mexico and Historic Preservation Bureau, Planning Division, Department of Finance and Administration of the State of New Mexico, Santa Fe.
Marshall, M. P., and H. Walt
2007 *The Eastern Homeland of San Juan Pueblo: Tewa Land and Water Use in the Santa Cruz and Truchas Watersheds: An Archaeological and Ethnogeographic Study*. Prepared for Ohkay Owingeh (San Juan) Pueblo. Report No. 432. Cibola Research Consultants, Corrales, NM.
Martin, P. S.
1936 *Lowry Ruin in Southwestern Colorado*. Field Museum of Natural History, Chicago.
1939 *Modified Basket Maker Sites: Ackmen-Lowry Area, Southwestern Colorado, 1938*. Field Museum of Natural History, Chicago.

Martinez, E.
1982 *San Juan Pueblo Tewa Dictionary*. Bilingual Program, San Juan Pueblo, NM.
Matson, R. G.
1991 *The Origins of Southwestern Agriculture*. University of Arizona Press, Tucson.
2002 The Spread of Maize Agriculture into the U.S. Southwest. In *Examining the Farming/Language Dispersal Hypothesis*, ed. P. Bellwood and C. Renfrew. McDonald Institute for Archaeological Research, University of Cambridge. Distributed by Oxbow Books, Oxford.
2006 What IS Basketmaker II? *Kiva* 72(2):149–166.
Matson, R. G., and B. Chisholm
1991 Basketmaker II Subsistence: Carbon Isotopes and Other Dietary Indicators from Cedar Mesa, Utah. *American Antiquity* 56:444–459.
Matson, R. G., and M. P. R. Magne
2007 *Athapaskan Migrations: The Archaeology of Eagle Lake, British Columbia*. University of Arizona Press, Tucson.
Matthews, M. H.
1988 Macrobotanical Remains. In *Archaeological Investigations in the Bodo Canyon Area, La Plata County, Colorado*, ed. S. L. Fuller, pp. 397–420. UMTRA Archaeological Report 25. Complete Archaeological Service Associates, Cortez, CO.
Maxwell, T. D.
1994 Prehistoric Population Change in the Lower Rio Chama Valley, Northwestern New Mexico. Paper presented at the 59th Annual Meeting of the Society for American Archaeology, Anaheim, CA.
Maxwell, T. D., and K. F. Anschuetz
1992 The Southwestern Ethnographic Record and Prehistoric Agricultural Diversity. In *Gardens in Prehistory: The Archaeology of Settlement Agriculture in Greater Mesoamerica*, ed. T. W. Killion, pp. 35–68. University of Alabama Press, Tuscaloosa.
McKusick, C. R.
1980 Three Groups of Turkeys from Southwestern Archaeological Sites. *Contributions to Science* 330:225–235.
McNutt, C. H.
1969 *Early Puebloan Occupations at Tesuque By-Pass and in the Upper Rio Grande Valley*. Anthropological Papers No. 40. Museum of Anthropology, University of Michigan, Ann Arbor.
Meadows, W. C.
2008 *Kiowa Ethnogeography*. University of Texas Press, Austin.
Mera, H. P.
1934 *A Survey of the Biscuit Ware Area in Northern New Mexico*. Technical Series Bulletin No. 6. Laboratory of Anthropology, Santa Fe, NM.
1935 *Ceramic Clues to the Prehistory of North Central New Mexico*. Technical Series Bulletin No. 8. Laboratory of Anthropology, Santa Fe, NM.
Merrill, W. L.
1988 *Rarámuri Souls: Knowledge and Social Process in Northern Mexico*. Smithsonian Institution Press, Washington, DC.
Merrill, W. L., M. K. Hansson, C. S. Greene, and F. J. Reuss
1997 *A Guide to Kiowa Collections at the Smithsonian Institution*. Smithsonian Contributions to Anthropology 40. Smithsonian Institution Press, Washington, DC.
Miller, D.
1985 *Artefacts as Categories*. Cambridge University Press, Cambridge.

Miller, W. R.
1959 A Note of Kiowa Linguistic Affiliations. *American Anthropologist* 61(1):102–105.
1965 *Acoma Grammar and Texts*. University of California Publications in Linguistics 40. University of California Press, Berkeley and Los Angeles.
Miller, W. R., and I. Davis
1963 Proto-Keresan Phonology. *International Journal of American Linguistics* 29(4): 310–330.
Mills, B. J.
1998 Migration and Pueblo IV Community Reorganization in the Silver Creek Area, East-Central Arizona. In *Migration and Reorganization: The Pueblo IV Period in the American Southwest*, ed. K. A. Spielmann, pp. 65–80. Anthropological Research Papers No. 51. Arizona State University, Tempe.
2002 Recent Research on Chaco: Changing Views on Economy, Ritual, and Society. *Journal of Archaeological Research* 10:65–117.
2007 Performing the Feast: Visual Display and Suprahousehold Commensalism in the Puebloan Southwest. *American Antiquity* 72(2):210–241.
Mills, E. L., and A. J. Brickfield (editors)
1981 *The Papers of John Peabody Harrington in the Smithsonian Institution, 1907–1957.* Vol. 4, *A Guide to the Field Notes: Native American History, Language, and Culture of the Southwest*. Kraus International, White Plains, NY.
Monaghan, J.
1995 *The Covenants with Earth and Rain: Exchange, Sacrifice, and Revelation in Mixtec Sociality*. University of Oklahoma Press, Norman.
Montgomery, B. K.
1993 Ceramic Analysis as a Tool for Discovering Processes of Pueblo Abandonment. In *Abandonment of Settlements and Regions: Ethnoarchaeological and Archaeological Approaches*, ed. C. M. Cameron and S. A. Tomka, pp. 157–164. Cambridge University Press, Cambridge.
Mooney, J.
1898 *Calendar History of the Kiowa Indians*. 17th Annual Report of the Bureau of American Ethnology. Government Printing Office, Washington, DC.
1907 *The Cheyenne Indians*. Memoirs of the American Anthropological Association, Vol. 1, Pt. 6. New Era Printing, Lancaster, PA.
1965 *The Ghost Dance Religion and the Sioux Outbreak of 1890.* University of Chicago Press, Chicago.
Moore, J. H., M. P. Liberty, and A. T. Strauss
2001 Cheyenne. In *Handbook of North American Indians,* Vol. 13, Pt. 2: *Plains*, ed. R. J. Demallie, pp. 863–885. Smithsonian Institution, Washington, DC.
Moore, J. H.
1987 *The Cheyenne Nation: A Social and Demographic History*. University of Nebraska Press, Lincoln.
1994 Putting Anthropology Back Together Again: The Ethnogenetic Critique of Cladistic Theory. *American Anthropologist* 96(4):925–948.
1996 *The Cheyenne*. Blackwell, Malden, MA.
2001 Ethnogenetic Patterns in Native North America. In *Archaeology, Language, and History: Essays on Culture and Ethnicity*, ed. J. E. Terrell, pp. 31–56. Bergin and Garvey, Westport, CT.
Morley, S. G.
1908 The Excavation of the Cannonball Ruins in Southwestern Colorado. *American Anthropologist* 10:596–610.

Morris, D. P.

1986 *Archaeological Investigations at Antelope House*. National Park Service, Washington, DC.

Morris, E. A.

1980 *Basketmaker Caves in the Prayer Rock District, Northeastern Arizona*. University of Arizona Press, Tucson.

Morris, E. H.

1919 Preliminary Account of the Antiquities of the Region Between the Mancos and La Plata Rivers in Southwestern Colorado. In *Thirty-Third Annual Report of the Bureau of American Ethnology, 1911–1912*, pp. 155–205. Smithsonian Institution, Washington, DC.

1928 *Notes on Excavations in the Aztec Ruin*. Anthropological Papers 26, Pt. 5. American Museum of Natural History, New York.

1939 *Archaeological Studies in the La Plata District, Southwestern Colorado and Northwestern New Mexico*. Carnegie Institution of Washington, Washington, DC.

Morris, E. H., and R. F. Burgh

1941 *Anasazi Basketry, Basketmaker II through Pueblo III*. Publication 533. Carnegie Institution of Washington, Washington, DC.

1954 *Basket Maker II Sites Near Durango, Colorado*. Carnegie Institution of Washington, Washington, DC.

Morris, J. N.

1991 *Archaeological Excavations on the Hovenweep Laterals*. Complete Archaeological Service Associates, Cortez, CO.

Morss, N.

2009 [1931] *The Ancient Culture of the Fremont River in Utah*. University of Utah Press, Salt Lake City.

Muir, R. J.

1999 Zooarchaeology of Sand Canyon Pueblo, Colorado. Ph.D.dissertation, Simon Fraser University, Burnaby, BC.

Muir, R. J., and J. C. Driver

2002 Scale of Analysis and Zooarchaeological Interpretation: Pueblo III Faunal Variation in the Northern San Juan Region. *Journal of Anthropological Archaeology* 21(2):165–199.

Nabokov, P., and L. L. Loendorf

2004 *Restoring a Presence: American Indians and Yellowstone National Park*. University of Oklahoma Press, Norman.

Naranjo, T.

2006 We Came from the South, We Came from the North: Some Tewa Origin Stories. In *The Mesa Verde World*, ed. D. G. Noble, pp. 49–57. School of American Research Press, Santa Fe, NM.

Naroll, R.

1962 Floor Area and Settlement Population. *American Antiquity* 27:587–589.

Neiman, F. D.

1995 Stylistic Variation in Evolutionary Perspective: Inferences from Decorative Diversity and Inter-assemblage Distance in Illinois Woodland Ceramic Assemblages. *American Antiquity* 60(1):7–36.

Nelson, B. A., T. A. Kohler, and K. W. Kintigh

1994 Demographic Alternatives: Consequences for Current Models of Southwestern

Prehistory. In *Understanding Complexity in the Prehistoric Southwest*, ed. G. J. Gumerman and M. Gell-Mann, pp. 113–146. Santa Fe Institute Studies in the Sciences of Complexity, Proceedings Vol. 16. Addison-Wesley, Reading, MA.

Nelson, N. C.

1914 *Pueblo Ruins of the Galisteo Basin, New Mexico*. Anthropological Papers of the American Museum of Natural History, Vol. 15, Pt. 1. New York.

Neusius, S. W.

1986 The Dolores Archaeological Program Faunal Data Base: Resource Availability and Resource Mix. In *Dolores Archaeological Program: Final Synthetic Report*, ed. D. A. Breternitz, C. K. Robinson, and G. T. Gross, pp. 199–303. Bureau of Reclamation, Engineering and Research Center, Denver.

Newsome, E.

2005 Weaving the Sky: The Cliff Palace Painted Tower. *Plateau* 2(2):28–41.

Niskanen, M.

1990 Human Remains from 2 × 2 m Unit 144S 136E, Area 2. In *Bandelier Archaeological Excavation Project: Summer 1989 Excavations at Burnt Mesa Pueblo*, ed. T. A. Kohler, pp. 155–157. Reports of Investigations 62. Washington State University Department of Anthropology, Pullman.

Noble, A. G.

1992 Migration to North America: Before, During, and After the Nineteenth Century. In *To Build in a New Land: Ethnic Landscapes in North America*, ed. A. G. Noble, pp. 3–28. Johns Hopkins University Press, Baltimore.

Nordenskiöld, G.

1979 [1893] *The Cliff Dwellers of the Mesa Verde, Southwestern Colorado: Their Pottery and Implements*. Originally published 1893, P A Norstedt and Söner, Stockholm. Rio Grande Press, Glorieta, NM.

O'Crouley, S. D. P.

1972 *A Description of the Kingdom of New Spain*. Translated by S. Galvin. John Howell Books, San Francisco.

Oliver, S. C.

1962 *Ecology and Cultural Continuity as Contributing Factors in the Social Organization of the Plains Indians*. University of California Publications in American Archaeology and Ethnology 48(1). University of California Press, Berkeley and Los Angeles.

Orcutt, J. D.

1991 Environmental Variability and Settlement Changes on the Pajarito Plateau, New Mexico. *American Antiquity* 56(2):315–332.

1999a Chronology. In *The Bandelier Archaeological Survey*, vol. 1, ed. R. P. Powers and J. D. Orcutt, pp. 85–116. Professional Papers 57. Intermountain Cultural Resource Management, Santa Fe, NM.

1999b Demography, Settlement, and Agriculture. In *The Bandelier Archaeological Survey*, vol. 1, ed. R. P. Powers and J. D. Orcutt, pp. 219–308. Professional Papers 57. Intermountain Cultural Resource Management, Santa Fe, NM.

Ortiz, A.

1969 *The Tewa World: Space, Time, Being and Becoming in a Pueblo Society*. University of Chicago Press, Chicago.

1972 Ritual Drama and the Pueblo World View. In *New Perspectives on the Pueblos*, ed. A. Ortiz, pp. 135–161. University of New Mexico Press, Albuquerque.

1979a San Juan Pueblo. In *Handbook of North American Indians,* Vol. 9: *Southwest,* ed. A. Ortiz, pp. 278–295. W. C. Sturtevant, general editor. Smithsonian Institution, Washington, DC.

1979b The San Juan Turtle Dance. In *Oku Shareh: Turtle Dance Songs of the San Juan Pueblo.* New World Records 80301-2, New York.

2005 [1980] Po'pay's Leadership: A Pueblo Perspective. In *Po'pay: Leader of the First American Revolution,* ed. J. S. Sando and H. Agoyo, pp. 82–92. Clear Light Publishing, Santa Fe, NM.

n.d. A Sacred Symbol Through the Ages. Ms. in possession of the author.

Ortman, S. G.

1998 Corn Grinding and Community Organization in the Pueblo Southwest, AD 1150–1550. In *Migration and Reorganization: The Pueblo IV Period in the American Southwest,* ed. K. A. Spielmann, pp. 165–192. Anthropological Research Papers No. 51. Arizona State University, Tempe.

2000a Artifacts. In *The Archaeology of Castle Rock Pueblo: A Thirteenth-century Village in Southwestern Colorado* [html title], ed. K. A. Kuckelman. http://www.crowcanyon.org/castlerock.

2000b Conceptual Metaphor in the Archaeological Record: Methods and an Example from the American Southwest. *American Antiquity* 65(4):613–645.

2002 Artifacts. In *The Archaeology of Woods Canyon Pueblo: A Canyon-Rim Village in Southwestern Colorado* [html title], ed. M. J. Churchill. http://www.crowcanyon.org/woodscanyon.

2003 Artifacts. In *The Archaeology of Yellow Jacket Pueblo: Excavations at a Large Community Center in Southwestern Colorado* [html title], ed. K. A. Kuckelman. http://www.crowcanyon.org/yellowjacket.

2006 Ancient Pottery of the Mesa Verde Country: How Ancestral Pueblo People Made It, Used It, and Thought About It. In *The Mesa Verde World,* ed. D. G. Noble, pp. 101–110. School of American Research Press, Santa Fe, NM.

2008a Action, Place and Space in the Castle Rock Community. In *The Social Construction of Communities: Studies of Agency, Structure and Identity in the Southwestern U. S.,* ed. M. D. Varien and J. M. Potter, pp. 125–154. Altamira Press, Lanham, MD.

2008b Architectural Metaphor and Chacoan Influence in the Northern San Juan. In *Archaeology Without Borders: Contact, Commerce, and Change in the U.S. Southwest and Northwestern Mexico,* ed. L. Webster and M. McBrinn, pp. 227–255. Proceedings of the 2004 Southwest Symposium. University Press of Colorado, Boulder.

2009 Genes, Language and Culture in Tewa Ethnogenesis, AD 1150–1400. Ph.D. dissertation, Arizona State University, Tempe.

2010 Kiowa Odyssey: Evidence of a Colorado Plateau Origin of the Kiowa Speech Community. Paper presented at the 32nd Great Basin Anthropological Conference, Layton, UT.

Ortman, S. G., E. L. Baxter, C. L. Graham, G. R. Lyle, L. W. Matis, J. A. Merewether, R. D. Satterwhite, and J. D. Till

2005 *Crow Canyon Archaeological Center Laboratory Manual,* Version 1. *http://www.crowcanyon.org/researchreports/labmanual/laboratorymanual.pdf.* Crow Canyon Archaeological Center, Cortez, CO.

Ortman, S. G., and B. A. Bradley

2002 Sand Canyon Pueblo: The Container in the Center. In *Seeking the Center Place: Archaeology and Ancient Communities in the Mesa Verde Region,* ed. M. D. Varien and R. H. Wilshusen, pp. 41–78. University of Utah Press, Salt Lake City.

Ortman, S. G., D. M. Glowacki, M. J. Churchill, and K. A. Kuckelman
2000 Pattern and Variation in Northern San Juan Village Histories. *Kiva* 66(1):123–146.
Ortman, S. G., and M. D. Varien
2007 Settlement Patterns in the McElmo Dome Study Area. In *The Archaeology of Sand Canyon Pueblo: Intensive Excavations at a Late-Thirteenth-Century Village in Southwestern Colorado* [html title], ed. K. A. Kuckelman. http://www.crowcanyon.org/sandcanyon.
Ortman, S. G., M. [D.] Varien, and T. L. Gripp
2007 Empirical Bayesian Methods for Archaeological Survey Data: An Example from the Mesa Verde Region. *American Antiquity* 72(1):241–272.
Ortman, S. G., and R. H. Wilshusen
1996 Letter Report of Salvage-Based Research by Crow Canyon Archaeological Center at Hedley Ruins (42SA22760), San Juan County, Utah, with Recommendations for Site Management and Protection. Manuscript on file, Crow Canyon Archaeological Center, Cortez, CO.
Osborne, C. M.
2004 *The Wetherill Collections and Perishable Items from Mesa Verde*. www.Lulu.com. Los Alamitos, CA.
Palkovich, A. M.
1980 *Pueblo Population and Society: The Arroyo Hondo Skeletal and Mortuary Remains*. Arroyo Hondo Archaeological Series 3. School of American Research Press, Santa Fe, NM.
Parmentier, R. J.
1979 The Mythological Triangle: Poseyemu, Montezuma, and Jesus in the Pueblos. In *Handbook of North American Indians*, Vol. 9: *Southwest*, ed. A. Ortiz, pp. 609–622. Smithsonian Institution, Washington, DC.
Parsons, E. C.
1925 *The Pueblo of Jemez*. Yale University Press, New Haven, CT.
1932 Isleta, New Mexico. In *47th Annual Report of the Bureau of American Ethnology*, pp. 193–466. Government Printing Office, Washington, DC.
1936 *Taos Pueblo*. General Series in Anthropology No. 2. George Banta, Menasha, WI.
1974 [1929] *The Social Organization of the Tewa of New Mexico*. Memoirs of the American Anthropological Association No. 36. Kraus Reprint, Millwood, NY.
1994 [1926] *Tewa Tales*. University of Arizona Press, Tucson.
Pauketat, T. R.
2008 The Grounds for Agency in Southwest Archaeology. In *The Social Construction of Communities: Agency, Structure and Identity in the Prehispanic Southwest*, ed. M. D. Varien and J. M. Potter, pp. 233–250. Altamira Press, Lanham, MD.
Peckham, S. L.
1981 Pueblo IV Murals at Mound 7. In *Contributions to Gran Quivira Archaeology, Gran Quivira National Monument, New Mexico*, ed. A. C. Hayes, pp. 15–38. Publications in Archaeology No. 17. National Park Service, Washington, DC.
1996 The South House at Puye Reexamined. In *La Jornada: Papers in Honor of William F. Turney*, ed. M. S. Duran and D. T. Kirkpatrick, pp. 153–169. Papers of the Archaeological Society of New Mexico Vol. 22. Albuquerque.
Peckham, S. L., and B. Olinger
1990 Postulated Movements of the Tano or Southern Tewa, AD 1300–1700. In *Clues to the Past: Papers in Honor of William M. Sundt*, ed. M. S. Duran and D. T. Kirkpatrick, pp. 203–216. Papers of the Archaeological Society of New Mexico No. 16. Albuquerque.

Pierce, C.

2005a The Development of Corrugated Pottery in Southwestern Colorado. *Kiva* 71(1): 79–100.

2005b Reverse Engineering the Ceramic Cooking Pot: Cost and Performance Properties of Plain and Textured Vessels. *Journal of Archaeological Method and Theory* 12(2): 117–157.

Pierce, C., D. M. Glowacki, and M. M. Thurs

2002 Measuring Community Interaction: Pueblo III Pottery Production and Distribution in the Central Mesa Verde Region. In *Seeking the Center Place: Archaeology and Ancient Communities in the Mesa Verde Region*, ed. M. D. Varien and R. H. Wilshusen, pp. 185–202. University of Utah Press, Salt Lake City.

Pierce, C., M. D. Varien, J. C. Driver, G. T. Gross, and J. W. Keleher

1999 Artifacts. In *The Sand Canyon Archaeological Project: Site Testing* [html title], ed. M. D. Varien. http://www.crowcanyon.org/sitetesting.

Pietrusewsky, M.

2000 Metric Analysis of Skeletal Remains: Methods and Applications. In *Biological Anthropology of the Human Skeleton*, ed. M. A. Katzenberg and S. R. Saunders, pp. 375–415. Wiley-Liss, New York.

Pinker, S.

1994 *The Language Instinct: How the Mind Creates Language*. William Morrow, New York.

2007 *The Stuff of Thought: Language as a Window into Human Nature*. Penguin, New York.

Potter, J. M.

1997 Communal Ritual and Faunal Remains: An Example from the Dolores Anasazi. *Journal of Field Archaeology* 24(3):353–364.

2002 Community, Metaphor, and Gender: Technological Changes Across the Pueblo III to Pueblo IV Transition in the El Morro Valley, New Mexico. In *Traditions, Transitions, and Technologies: Themes in Southwestern Archaeology*, ed. S. H. Schlanger, pp. 332–349. University Press of Colorado, Boulder.

2004 The Creation of Person, the Creation of Place: Hunting Landscapes in the American Southwest. *American Antiquity* 69(2):322–338.

Potter, J. M., and J. S. Edwards

2008 Vertebrate Faunal Studies. Chapter 12 of *Animas-La Plata Project*, Vol. 10: *Environmental Studies*, ed. J. M. Potter, pp. 243–286. SWCA, Phoenix.

Potter, J. M., and S. G. Ortman

2004 Community and Cuisine in the Prehispanic American Southwest. In *Identity, Feasting, and the Archaeology of the Greater Southwest*, ed. B. J. Mills, pp. 173–191. University Press of Colorado, Boulder.

Powell, J. W.

1891 Indian Linguistic Families of America North of Mexico. In *7th Annual Report of the Bureau of American Ethnology for the Years 1885–1886*, pp. 1–142. Smithsonian Institution, Washington, DC.

Powers, R. P., W. B. Gillespie, and S. H. Lekson

1983 *The Outlier Survey: A Regional View of Settlement in the San Juan Basin*. National Park Service, Albuquerque.

Preston Blier, S.

1987 *The Anatomy of Architecture: Ontology and Metaphor in Batammaliba Architectural Expression*. University of Chicago Press, Chicago.

Preucel, R. W.

2000 Making Pueblo Identities: Architectural Discourse at Kotyiti, New Mexico. In *The Archaeology of Communities*, ed. J. Yaeger and M. A. Canuto, pp. 58–77. Routledge, London.

2002 Writing the Pueblo Revolt. In *Archaeologies of the Pueblo Revolt: Identity, Meaning and Renewal in the Pueblo World*, ed. R. W. Preucel, pp. 3–29. University of New Mexico Press, Albuquerque.

2005 The Journey from Shipap. In *The Peopling of Bandelier: New Insights from the Archaeology of the Pajarito Plateau*, ed. R. P. Powers, pp. 95–102. School of American Research Press, Santa Fe, NM.

2006 *Archaeological Semiotics*. Blackwell, Oxford.

Prudden, T. M.

1918 *A Further Study of Prehistoric Small House Ruins in the San Juan Watershed*. American Anthropological Association, Lancaster, PA.

Radcliffe-Brown, A. R.

1965 *Structure and Function in Primitive Society*. Free Press, New York.

Ramenofsky, A. F., and J. K. Feathers

2002 Documents, Ceramics, Tree Rings, and Thermoluminescence: Estimating Final Native Abandonment of the Lower Rio Chama. *Journal of Anthropological Research* 58(1):121–159.

Rawlings, T. A.

2007 Faunal Analysis and Meat Procurement: Reconstructing the Sexual Division of Labor at Shields Pueblo, Colorado. Ph.D. dissertation, Simon Frazer University.

Read, B. M.

1926 The Last Word on "Montezuma." *New Mexico Historical Review* 1(3):350–358.

Reed, E. K.

1949 Sources of Rio Grande Culture and Population. *El Palacio* 56:163–184.

1953 Human Skeletal Remains from Te'ewi. In *Salvage Archaeology in the Chama Valley, New Mexico*, ed. F. Wendorf, pp. 104–118. Monographs of the School of American Research Vol. 17. Santa Fe, NM.

1956 Human Skeletal Remains from Archaeological Surveys of New Mexico and Colorado. In *Pipeline Archaeology*, ed. F. Wendorf, pp. 393–399. Laboratory of Anthropology and Museum of Northern Arizona, Santa Fe, NM.

1957 Human Skeletal Remains from Some Highway Salvage Excavations in New Mexico. In *Highway Salvage Archaeology*, Vol. 3, ed. S. L. Peckham. New Mexico State Highway Department and Museum of New Mexico, Santa Fe.

1962 Human Skeletal Material from Site 59, Chaco Canyon National Monument. *El Palacio* 69:240–247.

1963a Human Skeletal Material. In *1961 Excavations, Glen Canyon Area*, ed. F. W. Sharrock, K. C. Day, and D. S. Dibble, pp. 307–346. Anthropological Papers Vol. 63. University of Utah, Salt Lake City.

1963b The Skeletal Material from LA 3643. In *Highway Salvage Archaeology*, Vol. 4, ed. S. L. Peckham. New Mexico State Highway Department and Museum of New Mexico, Santa Fe.

1964a Burials from a Kwahe'e Horizon. Manuscript 91EKR.087. Laboratory of Anthropology, Santa Fe, NM.

1964b Human Skeletal Material from Kin Kletso. In *Kin Kletso: A Pueblo III Community in Chaco Canyon, New Mexico*, ed. G. Vivian and T. W. Matthews. Southwestern Monuments Association, Globe, AZ.

1966 Human Skeletal Remains from LA4131 and 4198. In *Prehistory in the Navajo Reservoir District, Northwestern New Mexico*, Vol. 15, Pt. 2, ed. F. W. Eddy, pp. 607–617. Museum of New Mexico, Santa Fe.

1981 Human Skeletal Material from the Gran Quivira District. In *Contributions to Gran Quivira Archaeology*, ed. A. C. Hayes, pp. 75–118. Publications in Archeology Vol. 17. Department of the Interior, National Park Service, Washington, DC.

Reed, P. F.

2008 *Chaco's Northern Prodigies: Salmon, Aztec, and the Ascendancy of the Middle San Juan Region After AD 1100*. University of Utah Press, Salt Lake City.

Regier, T.

1996 *The Human Semantic Potential: Spatial Language and Constrained Connectionism*. MIT Press, Cambridge, MA.

Relethford, J. H.

1994 Craniometric Variation Among Modern Human Populations. *American Journal of Physical Anthropology* 95:53–62.

2002 Apportionment of Global Human Genetic Diversity Based on Craniometrics and Skin Color. *American Journal of Physical Anthropology* 118:393–398.

2003 Anthropometric Data and Population History. In *Human Biologists in the Archives: Demography, Health, Nutrition, and Genetics in Historical Populations*, ed. D. A. Herring and A. C. Swedlund, pp. 32–52. Cambridge University Press, Cambridge.

2004a Boas and Beyond: Migration and Craniometric Variation. *American Journal of Human Biology* 16(4):379–386.

2004b Global Patterns of Isolation by Distance Based on Genetic and Morphological Data. *Human Biology* 76(4):499–513.

Relethford, J. H., and J. Blangero

1990 Detection of Differential Gene Flow from Patterns of Quantitative Variation. *Human Biology* 62:5–25.

Relethford, J. H., M. H. Crawford, and J. Blangero

1997 Genetic Drift and Gene Flow in Post-Famine Ireland. *Human Biology* 69(4):443–465.

Relethford, J. H., and H. C. Harpending

1994 Craniometric Variation, Genetic Theory, and Modern Human Origins. *American Journal of Physical Anthropology* 95:249–270.

Relethford, J. H., and F. C. Lees

1982 The Use of Quantitative Traits in the Study of Human Population Structure. *Yearbook of Physical Anthropology* 25:113–132.

Renfrew, C.

1987 *Archaeology and Language: The Puzzle of Indo-European Origins*. J. Cape, London.

Renfrew, C., A. McMahon, and L. Trask (editors)

2000 *Time Depth in Historical Linguistics*. MacDonald Institute for Archaeological Research, Cambridge.

Robbins, W. W., J. P. Harrington, and B. Freire-Marreco

1916 *Ethnobotany of the Tewa Indians*. Bureau of American Ethnology Bulletin No. 55. Smithsonian Institution, Washington, DC.

Roberts, F. H. H., Jr.

1930 *Early Pueblo Ruins in the Piedra District, Southwestern Colorado*. Smithsonian Institution, Washington, DC.

Robins, M. R.

1997 Modeling the San Juan Basketmaker Socio-Economic Organization: A Preliminary Study in Rock Art and Social Dynamics. In *Early Farmers in the Northern*

Southwest: Papers on Chronometry, Social Dynamics, and Ecology, ed. F. E. Smiley and M. R. Robins. U.S. Department of the Interior, Bureau of Reclamation.

Robins, M. R., and K. A. Hays-Gilpin

2000 The Bird in the Basket: Gender and Social Change in Basketmaker Iconography. In *Foundations of Anasazi Culture: The Basketmaker-Pueblo Transition*, ed. P. F. Reed, pp. 231–250. University of Utah Press, Salt Lake City.

Rodeck, H. G.

1954 Animal and Bird Bones from the Durango Sites. In *Basketmaker II Sites Near Durango, Colorado*, ed. E. H. Morris and R. F. Burgh, pp. 117–122. Publication 604. Carnegie Institute of Washington, Washington, DC.

Rogers, S. L.

1954 Part IV: The Physical Type of the Paa-ko Population. In *Paa-ko, Archaeological Chronicle of an Indian Village in North Central New Mexico*, ed. M. F. Lambert. School of American Research Press, Santa Fe, NM.

Rogerson, P. A.

1984 New Directions in the Modeling of Interregional Migration. *Economic Geography* 60(2):111–121.

Rohn, A. H.

1971 *Mug House, Mesa Verde National Park, Colorado*. National Park Service, Washington, DC.

1977 *Cultural Change and Continuity on Chapin Mesa*. Regents Press of Kansas, Lawrence.

1989 Northern San Juan Prehistory. In *Dynamics of Southwest Prehistory*, ed. L. S. Cordell and G. J. Gumerman, pp. 149–177. Smithsonian Institution Press, Washington, DC.

Roney, J. R.

1995 Mesa Verdean Manifestations South of the San Juan River. *Journal of Anthropological Archaeology* 14(2):170–183.

1996 The Pueblo III Period in the Eastern San Juan Basin and Acoma-Laguna Areas. In *The Prehistoric Pueblo World, AD 1150–1350.*, ed. M. A. Adler, pp. 145–169. University of Arizona Press, Tucson.

Ross, M.

1997 Social Networks and Kinds of Speech-Community Event. In *Archaeology and Language*, Vol. 1: *Theoretical and Methodological Orientations*, ed. R. Blench and M. Spriggs, pp. 209–261. Routledge, London and New York.

1998 Sequencing and Dating Linguistic Events in Oceania: The Linguistics/Archaeology Interface. In *Archaeology and Language*, Vol. 2: *Correlating Archaeological and Linguistic Hypotheses*, ed. R. Blench and M. Spriggs, pp. 141–173. Routledge, London and New York.

Rouse, I.

1986 *Migrations in Prehistory: Inferring Population Movement from Cultural Remains*. Yale University Press, New Haven.

Ruscavage-Barz, S.

1999 Knowing Your Neighbor: Coalition Period Community Dynamics on the Pajarito Plateau, New Mexico. Ph.D. dissertation, Washington State University.

2002 Understanding Santa Fe Black-on-white Style and Technology: An Example from the Pajarito Plateau, New Mexico. *Kiva* 67(3):249–268.

Ryan, S. C.

2008 Constructing Community and Transforming Identity at Albert Porter Pueblo. In *The Social Construction of Communities: Agency, Structure and Identity in the*

Prehispanic Southwest, ed. M. D. Varien and J. M. Potter, pp. 69–88. Altamira Press, Lanham, MD.

2010 Environmental Change, Population Movement, and the Post-Chaco Transition at Albert Porter Pueblo. *Kiva* 75(3):303–325.

Sackett, J. R.

1990 Style and Ethnicity in Archaeology: The Case for Isochrestism. In *Uses of Style in Archaeology*, ed. M. W. Conkey and C. A. Hastorf, pp. 32–43. Cambridge University Press, Cambridge.

Sahlins, M. D.

1985 *Historical Metaphors and Mythical Realities: Structure in the Early History of the Sandwich Islands Kingdom*. Association for Social Anthropology in Oceania Special Publications No. 1. University of Michigan Press, Ann Arbor.

San Juan Pueblo

2000 John P. Harrington Archive. In *San Juan Pueblo Tewa Language Project*, CD-ROM 3. University of Washington and San Juan Pueblo.

Sanchez, J. P.

2006 The Franciscan Search for Mythical Teguayo: New Mexico and Utah between 1678–1778. In *They Came to El Llano Estacado*, ed. J. Felix D. Almaraz, pp. 91–109. University of Texas, San Antonio.

Sanders, W. T., J. Parsons, and R. S. Santley

1979 *The Basin of Mexico: Ecological Processes in the Evolution of a Civilization*. Academic Press, New York.

Sandstrom, A. R.

1991 *Corn Is Our Blood: Culture and Ethnic Identity in a Contemporary Aztec Indian Village*. University of Oklahoma Press, Norman.

Sapir, E.

1936 Internal Linguistic Evidence Suggestive of the Northern Origin of the Navaho. *American Anthropologist* 38(2):224–235.

1949 [1916] Time Perspective in Aboriginal American Culture: A Study in Method. In *Selected Writings of Edward Sapir in Language, Culture and Personality*, ed. D. G. Mandelbaum, pp. 389–462. University of California Press, Berkeley.

1949 [1926] Central and North American Languages. In *Selected Writings of Edward Sapir in Language, Culture and Personality*, ed. D. G. Mandelbaum, pp. 169–178. University of California Press, Berkeley.

Saxton, D., L. Saxton, and S. Enos

1983 *Dictionary: Tohono O'odham/Pima to English, English to Tohono O'odham/Pima*. 2nd ed., revised and expanded. Ed. R. L. Cherry. University of Arizona Press, Tucson.

Schaafsma, P.

1971 *The Rock Art of Utah: A Study from the Donald Scott Collection, Peabody Museum, Harvard University*. Peabody Museum of Archaeology and Ethnology, Harvard University, Cambridge, MA.

Schachner, G.

2007 Population Circulation and the Transformation of Ancient Cibola Communities. Ph.D. dissertation, Arizona State University, Tempe.

Schacht, R. M.

1980 Two Models of Population Growth. *American Anthropologist* 82(4):782–798.

Schaefer, S. B.

1996 The Cosmos Contained: The Temple Where Sun and Moon Meet. In *People of the*

Peyote: Huichol Indian History, Religion, and Survival, ed. S. B. Schaefer and P. T. Furst, pp. 332–371. University of New Mexico Press, Albuquerque.

Schiffer, M. B.

1987 *Formation Processes of the Archaeological Record*. University of New Mexico Press, Albuquerque.

Schillaci, M. A.

2003 The Development of Population Diversity at Chaco Canyon. *Kiva* 68(3):221–245.

Schillaci, M. A., E. G. Ozolins, and T. C. Windes

2001 Multivariate Assessment of Biological Relationships Among Prehistoric Southwest Amerindian Populations. In *Following Through: Papers in Honor of Phyllis S. Davis*, ed. R. N. Wiseman, T. C. O'Laughlin, and C. T. Snow, pp. 133–149. Papers of the Archaeological Society of New Mexico Vol. 27. Archaeological Society of New Mexico, Albuquerque.

Schillaci, M. A., and C. M. Stojanowski

2005 Craniometric Variation and Population History of the Prehistoric Tewa. *American Journal of Physical Anthropology* 126:404–412.

Schlanger, S. H., and R. H. Wilshusen

1993 Local Abandonments and Regional Conditions in the North American Southwest. In *Abandonment of Settlements and Regions: Ethnoarchaeological and Archaeological Approaches*, ed. C. M. Cameron and S. A. Tomka, pp. 85–98. Cambridge University Press, Cambridge.

Schmidt, K. M.

2006 *Excavations at a Coalition Period Pueblo (LA 4618) on Mesita del Buey, Los Alamos National Laboratory*. LA-UR-06-6621. Cultural Resources Report No. 260, Survey No. 289. U.S. Department of Energy, National Nuclear Security Administration, Los Alamos Site Office.

2007 Coalition Period Subsistence on the Pajarito Plateau: Faunal Remains from Five Room Block Sites. *Kiva* 73(2):155–172.

2008 Airport-East Tract (A-3): LA86534. In *The Land Conveyance and Transfer Data Recovery Project: 7000 Years of Land Use on the Pajarito Plateau*, Vol. 2: *Site Excavations*, ed. B. J. Vierra, K. M. Schmidt, and B. C. Harmon. Ecology and Air Quality Group, Los Alamos National Laboratory, NM.

Schmidt, P. R.

2006 *Historical Archaeology in Africa: Representation, Social Memory, and Oral Traditions*. Altamira Press, Lanham, MD.

Schroeder, A. H.

1979 Pueblos Abandoned in Historic Times. In *Handbook of North American Indians*, Vol. 9: *Southwest*, ed. A. Ortiz, pp. 236–254. Smithsonian Institution, Washington, DC.

Sciulli, P. W., and M. C. Mahaney

1991 Phenotypic Evolution in Prehistoric Ohio Amerindians: Natural Selection versus Random Genetic Drift in Tooth Size Reduction. *Human Biology* 63(4):499–511.

Sekaquaptewa, E., and D. Washburn

2004 They Go Along Singing: Reconstructing the Past from Ritual Metaphors in Song and Image. *American Antiquity* 69(3):457–486.

Sesler, L. M.

2002 Site LA78533. In *Archaeological Investigations in the Fruitland Project Area: Late Archaic, Basketmaker, Pueblo I, and Navajo Sites in Northwestern New Mexico*.

Vol. 3: *The Basketmaker and Pueblo I Sites*, ed. T. D. Hovezak and L. M. Sesler, pp. 253–292. La Plata Archaeological Consultants, Dolores, CO.

Sesler, L. M., and T. D. Hovezak

2002 Synthesis: Cultural and Adaptational Diversity in the Fruitland Study Area. In *Archaeological Investigations in the Fruitland Project Area: Late Archaic, Basketmaker, Pueblo I, and Navajo Sites in Northwestern New Mexico*. Vol. 1: *Introductory Chapters and Synthesis*, ed. T. D. Hovezak, L. M. Sesler, and S. L. Fuller, pp. 109–240. Research Papers No. 4. La Plata Archaeological Consultants, Dolores, CO.

Sewell, W. H.

2005 *Logics of History: Social Theory and Social Transformation*. University of Chicago Press, Chicago.

Shackley, M. S.

1988 Sources of Archaeological Obsidian in the Southwest: An Archaeological, Petrological, and Geochemical Study. *American Antiquity* 53:752–772.

1995 Sources of Archaeological Obsidian in the Greater American Southwest: An Update and Quantitative Analysis. *American Antiquity* 60:531–551.

2005a *Obsidian: Geology and Archaeology in the North American Southwest*. University of Arizona Press, Tucson.

2005b Source Provenance of Obsidian Artifacts from Mesa Verde, Sand Canyon, Duckfoot, and Dolores Project Sites, Southwestern Colorado. Manuscript on file, Crow Canyon Archaeological Center, Cortez, CO.

2008 Source Provenance of Obsidian Artifacts from Archaeological Sites from the Dolores Archaeological Project, Southwestern Colorado. Manuscript on file, Crow Canyon Archaeological Center, Cortez, CO.

Shanks, M., and C. Tilley

1987 *Social Theory and Archaeology*. Polity Press, England.

Shaul, D. L.

1985 Azteco-Tanoan ***-l/r-. *International Journal of American Linguistics* 51(4):584–586.

Shaul, D. L., and J. H. Hill

1998 Tepimans, Yumans, and Other Hohokam. *American Antiquity* 63(3):375–396.

Shelton, A. A.

1996 The Girl Who Ground Herself: Huichol Attitudes toward Maize. In *People of the Peyote: Huichol Indian History, Religion, and Survival*, ed. S. B. Schaefer and P. T. Furst, pp. 451–467. University of New Mexico Press, Albuquerque.

Shennan, S.

2002 *Genes, Memes and Human History: Darwinian Archaeology and Cultural Evolution*. Thames and Hudson, London.

Shennan, S. J., and M. Collard

2005 Investigating Processes of Cultural Evolution on the North Coast of New Guinea with Multivariate and Cladistic Analyses. In *The Evolution of Cultural Diversity: A Phylogenetic Approach*, ed. R. Mace, C. J. Holden, and S. J. Shennan, pp. 133–164. Left Coast Press, Walnut Creek, CA.

Shennan, S. J., and J. R. Wilkinson

2001 Ceramic Style Change and Neutral Evolution: A Case Study from Neolithic Europe. *American Antiquity* 66(4):577–593.

Shore, B.

1996 *Culture in Mind: Cognition, Culture, and the Problem of Meaning*. Oxford University Press, Oxford.

Sillar, B.
1996 The Dead and the Drying. *Journal of Material Culture* 1:259–289.

Silver, S., and W. R. Miller
1997 *American Indian Languages: Cultural and Social Contexts*. University of Arizona Press, Tucson.

Simms, S. R.
2008 *Ancient Peoples of the Great Basin and Colorado Plateau*. Left Coast Press, Walnut Creek, CA.

Slingerland, E.
2004 Conceptual Metaphor Theory as Methodology for Comparative Religion. *Journal of the American Academy of Religion* 72(1):1–31.
2008 *What Science Offers the Humanities: Integrating Body and Culture*. Cambridge University Press, Cambridge.

Smiley, F. E.
1993 Early Farmers in the Northern Southwest: A View from Marsh Pass. In *Anasazi Basketmaker: Papers from the 1990 Wetherill-Grand Gulch Symposium*, ed. V. M. Atkins. Cultural Resource Series No. 24. U.S. Department of the Interior, Bureau of Land Management, Salt Lake City.
1994 The Agricultural Transition in the Northern Southwest: Patterns in the Current Chronometric Data. *Kiva* 60(2):165–190.

Smiley, T. L., S. A. Stubbs, and B. Bannister
1953 *A Foundation for the Dating of Some Late Archaeological Sites in the Rio Grande Area, New Mexico: Based on Studies in Tree-Ring Methods and Pottery Analyses*. University of Arizona, Tucson.

Snead, J. E.
1995 Beyond Pueblo Walls: Community and Competition in the Northern Rio Grande, AD 1300–1400. Ph.D. dissertation, University of California, Los Angeles.
2004 Ancestral Pueblo Settlement Dynamics: Landscape, Scale and Context in the Burnt Corn Community. *Kiva* 69(3):243–269.
2008a *Ancestral Landscapes of the Pueblo World*. University of Arizona Press, Tucson.
2008b History, Place, and Social Power in the Galisteo Basin, AD 1250–1325. In *The Social Construction of Communities: Agency, Structure and Identity in the Prehispanic Southwest*, ed. M. D. Varien and J. M. Potter, pp. 155–170. Altamira Press, Lanham, MD.

Snead, J. E., W. Creamer, and T. Van Zandt
2004 "Ruins of Our Forefathers": Large Sites and Site Clusters in the Northern Rio Grande. In *The Protohistoric Pueblo World, AD 1275–1600*, ed. E. C. Adams and A. I. Duff, pp. 26–34. University of Arizona Press, Tucson.

Snead, J. E., and R. W. Preucel
1999 The Ideology of Settlement: Ancestral Keres Landscapes in the Northern Rio Grande. In *Archaeologies of Landscape: Contemporary Perspectives*, ed. W. Ashmore and A. B. Knapp, pp. 169–197. Blackwell, Oxford.

Snow, D. H.
1963 A Preliminary Report on Excavations at Sapawe New Mexico. Manuscript on file. Laboratory of Anthropology, Santa Fe, NM.
1974 *The Excavation of Saltbush Pueblo, Bandelier National Monument, New Mexico 1971*. Note No. 97. Laboratory of Anthropology, Santa Fe, NM.
1979 *Archaeological Excavations at Pueblo del Encierro, LA70, Cochiti Dam Salvage Project, Cochiti, New Mexico, Final Report: 1964–1965 Field Season*. Laboratory of Anthropology Notes No. 78. Museum of New Mexico, Santa Fe.

Sokal, R. R., and P. H. Sneath

1963 *Principles of Numerical Taxonomy*. W. H. Freeman, San Francisco.

Sparks, C. S., and R. L. Jantz

2002 A Reassessment of Cranial Plasticity: Boas Revisited. *Proceedings of the National Academy of Sciences* 99(23):14636–14639.

Speirs, A.

1974 Classificatory Verb Stems in Tewa. *Studies in Linguistics* 24:45–64.

Speirs, R. H.

1966 Some Aspects of the Structure of Rio Grande Tewa. Ph.D. dissertation, State University of New York, Buffalo.

Speller, C. F., B. M. Kemp, S. D. Wyatt, C. Monroe, W. D. Lipe, U. M. Arndt, and D. Y. Yang

2010 Ancient Mitochondrial DNA Analysis Reveals Complexity of Indigenous North American Turkey Domestication. *Proceedings of the National Academy of Science of the U.S.A.* 107(7):2807–2812.

Spence, M. W.

1992 Tlailotlacan, a Zapotec Enclave in Teotihuacan. In *Art, Ideology, and the City of Teotihuacan*, ed. J. C. Berlo, pp. 59–88. Dumbarton Oaks, Washington, DC.

1994 Human Skeletal Material from Teotihuacan. In *Mortuary Practices and Skeletal Remains at Teotihuacan*, ed. M. L. Sempowski and M. W. Spence. University of Utah Press, Salt Lake City.

Spielmann, K. A.

1996 Impressions of Pueblo III Settlement Trends Among the Rio Abajo and Eastern Border Pueblos. In *The Prehistoric Pueblo World, AD 1150–1350*, ed. M. A. Adler, pp. 177–187. University of Arizona Press, Tucson.

1998 Ritual Influences on the Development of Rio Grande Glaze A Ceramics. In *Migration and Reorganization: The Pueblo IV Period in the American Southwest*, ed. K. A. Spielmann, pp. 253–261. Anthropological Research Papers No. 51. Arizona State University, Tempe.

Spinden, H.

1993 *Songs of the Tewa*. Sunstone Press, Santa Fe, NM.

Stark, M. T.

1998 Technical Choices and Social Boundaries in Material Culture Patterning: An Introduction. In *The Archaeology of Social Boundaries*, ed. M. T. Stark, pp. 1–11. Smithsonian Institution Press, Washington, DC.

Stark, M. T., M. D. Elson, and J. J. Clark

1995 Causes and Consequences of Migration in the 13th Century Tonto Basin. *Journal of Anthropological Archaeology* 14(2):212–246.

Steen, C. R.

1977 *Pajarito Plateau Archaeological Survey and Excavations*. Los Alamos Scientific Laboratory Report 77-4. Los Alamos, NM.

1982 *Pajarito Plateau Archaeological Surveys and Excavations*. Vol. 2. Los Alamos National Laboratory, Los Alamos, NM.

Stevenson, M. G.

1982 Toward an Understanding of Site Abandonment Behavior: Evidence from Historic Mining Camps in the Southwest Yukon. *Journal of Anthropological Archaeology* 1:237–265.

Stewart, T. D.

1940 Skeletal Remains from the Whitewater District, Eastern Arizona. In *Archaeological Remains in the Whitewater District, Eastern Arizona*, ed. F. H. H. Roberts, Jr., pp. 153–166. Bureau of American Ethnology Bulletin Vol. 126. Government Printing Office, Washington, DC.

Stiger, M. A.

2001 *Hunter-Gatherer Archaeology of the Colorado High Country.* University Press of Colorado, Boulder.

Stojanowski, C. M., and M. A. Schillaci

2006 Phenotypic Approaches for Understanding Patterns of Intracemetery Biological Variation. *Yearbook of Physical Anthropology* 49:49–88.

Stone, G. D.

1993 Agricultural Abandonment: A Comparative Study in Historical Ecology. In *Abandonment of Settlements and Regions: Ethnoarchaeological and Archaeological Approaches*, ed. C. M. Cameron and S. A. Tomka, pp. 74–84. Cambridge University Press, Cambridge.

1996 *Settlement Ecology: The Social and Spatial Organization of Kofyar Agriculture.* University of Arizona Press, Tucson.

Stone, T.

2003 Social Identity and Ethnic Interaction in the Western Pueblos of the American Southwest. *Journal of Archaeological Method and Theory* 10(1):31–67.

Strong, W. D.

1940 From History to Prehistory in the Northern Great Plains. In *Essays in the Historical Anthropology of North American in Honor of John R. Swanton*, pp. 353–394. Smithsonian Miscellaneous Collections 100. Washington, DC.

Stubbs, S. A.

1954 Summary Report on an Early Pueblo Site in the Tesuque Valley, New Mexico. *El Palacio* (February):43–45.

Stubbs, S. A., and W. S. Stallings, Jr.

1953 *The Excavation of Pindi Pueblo, New Mexico.* Monographs of the School for American Research and the Laboratory of Anthropology No. 18. Santa Fe, NM.

Sturtevant, W. C.

1971 Creek into Seminole: North American Indians. In *Historical Perspective*, ed. E. Leacock and N. Lurie, pp. 92–128. Random House, New York.

Sutton, L.

2010 Noun Class and Number in Kiowa-Tanoan: Comparative-historical Research and Respecting Speakers' Rights in Fieldwork. In *Fieldwork and Linguistic Analysis in Indigenous Languages of the Americas*, ed. A. L. Berez, J. Mulder, and D. Rosenblum, pp. 57–89. Language Documentation and Conservation Special Publication 2. University of Hawai'i Press, Honolulu.

Swadesh, M.

1955 Towards Greater Accuracy in Lexicostatistical Dating. *International Journal of American Linguistics* 21:121–137.

Sweetser, E.

1990 *From Etymology to Pragmatics: Metaphorical and Cultural Aspects of Semantic Structure.* Cambridge University Press, Cambridge.

Swentzell, R.

1990 Pueblo Space, Form and Mythology. In *Pueblo Style and Regional Architecture*, ed. N. C. Markovich, W. F. E. Preiser, and F. G. Sturm, pp. 23–30. Van Nostrand Reinhold, New York.

1993 *Pottery in Santa Clara.* Cultural Preservation Program, Santa Clara Pueblo, NM.

Terrell, J. E.

2001 The Uncommon Sense of Race, Language, and Culture. In *Archaeology, Language, and History: Essays on Culture and Ethnicity*, ed. J. E. Terrell, pp. 11–30. Bergen and Garvey, Westport, CT.

Terrell, J. E., T. L. Hunt, and C. Gosden

1997 Dimensions of Social Life in the Pacific: Human Diversity and the Myth of the Primitive Isolate. *Current Anthropology* 38(2):155–195.

Thomas, N.

1991 *Entangled Objects*. Harvard University Press, Cambridge, MA.

Thomason, S. G., and T. Kaufmann

1988 *Language Contact, Creolisation, and Genetic Linguistics*. University of California Press, Berkeley and Los Angeles.

Tichy, M. F.

1947 A Painted Ceremonial Room at Otowi. *El Palacio* 54(3):59–69.

Till, J. D.

in prep. Stone Artifacts. In The Archaeology of Shields Pueblo, ed. A. I. Duff. Manuscript on file, Crow Canyon Archaeological Center, Cortez, CO.

Till, J. D., J. A. Merewether, G. R. Lyle, and S. G. Ortman

in prep. Pottery. In The Archaeology of Shields Pueblo, ed. A. I. Duff. Manuscript on file, Crow Canyon Archaeological Center, Cortez, CO.

Till, J. D., and S. G. Ortman

2007 Artifacts. In *The Archaeology of Sand Canyon Pueblo: Intensive Excavations at a Late-Thirteenth Century Village in Southwestern Colorado* [html title], ed. K. A. Kuckelman. http://www.crowcanyon.org/sandcanyon.

Tilley, C.

1999 *Metaphor and Material Culture*. Blackwell, Oxford and London.

Toll, H. W.

1995 *An Analysis of Variability and Condition of Cavate Structures in Bandelier National Monument*. Intermountain Cultural Resources Center Professional Paper No. 53. National Park Service, Santa Fe, NM.

Trager, G. L.

1942 The Historical Phonology of the Tiwa Languages. *Studies in Linguistics* 1(5):1–10.

1944 Spanish and English Loanwords in Taos. *International Journal of American Linguistics* 10(4):144–158.

1946 An Outline of Taos Grammar. In *Linguistic Structures of Native America*, pp. 184–221. Viking Fund Publications in Anthropology No. 6. New York.

1967 The Tanoan Settlement of the Rio Grande Area: A Possible Chronology. In *Studies in Southwestern Ethnolinguistics*, ed. D. H. Hymes and W. E. Bittle, pp. 335–350. Mouton, The Hague.

1969 Taos and Picuris: How Long Separated? *International Journal of American Linguistics* 35(2):180–182.

Trager, G. L., and E. C. Trager

1959 Kiowa and Tanoan. *American Anthropologist* 61(6):1078–1083.

Traugott, E. C.

1989 On the Rise of Epistemic Meanings in English: An Example of Subjectification in Semantic Change. *Language* 65(1):31–55.

Trierweiler, W. N.

1990a Faunal Resources and Their Caloric Yields. In *Bandelier Archaeological Excavation Project: Summer 1989 Excavations at Burnt Mesa Pueblo*, ed. T. A. Kohler, pp. 103–128. Department of Anthropology Reports of Investigations 62. Washington State University, Pullman.

1990b *Prehistoric Tewa Economy: Modeling Subsistence Production on the Pajarito Plateau.* Garland, New York and London.

1992 Faunal Analysis. In *Bandelier Archaeological Excavation Project: Summer 1990 Excavations at Burnt Mesa Pueblo and Casa del Rito*, ed. T. A. Kohler and M. J. Root, pp. 135–147. Department of Anthropology Reports of Investigations 64. Washington State University, Pullman.

Trigg, H. B., and D. L. Gold

2005 Mestizaje and Migration: Modeling Population Dynamics in Seventeenth-Century New Mexico's Spanish Society. In *Engaged Anthropology: Research Essays on North American Archaeology, Ethnobotany, and Museology*, ed. M. Hegmon and B. S. Eiselt, pp. 73–88. Anthropological Papers 94. Museum of Anthropology, University of Michigan, Ann Arbor.

Truell, M. L.

1986 A Summary of Small Site Architecture in Chaco Canyon, New Mexico. In *Small Site Architecture of Chaco Canyon, New Mexico*, ed. P. J. McKenna and M. L. Truell, pp. 115–502. Publications in Archeology No. 18D. National Park Service, Santa Fe, NM.

Turner, C. G., II

1961 Human Skeletal Material. In *1960 Excavations, Glen Canyon Area*, ed. F. W. Sharrock, K. M. Anderson, D. D. Fowler, and D. S. Dibble, pp. 338–359. Anthropological Papers Vol. 52. University of Utah, Salt Lake City.

1993 Southwest Indian Teeth. *National Geographic Research and Exploration* 9(1): 32–53.

Turner, T.

1991 "We are Parrots," "Twins are Birds": Play of Tropes as Operational Structure. In *Beyond Metaphor: The Theory of Tropes in Anthropology*, ed. J. W. Fernandez, pp. 121–158. Stanford University Press, Palo Alto, CA.

Twitchell, R. E.

1914 *The Spanish Archives of New Mexico.* Vol. 2. Torch Press, Cedar Rapids.

Tyler, S. L.

1952 The Myth of The Lake of Copala and Land of Teguayo. *Utah Historical Quarterly* 20(4):313–329.

Ucko, P. J.

1969 *Penis Sheaths: A Comparative Study.* Proceedings of the Royal Anthropological Institute of Great Britain and Ireland 24A-67.

Van Zandt, T.

1999 Architecture and Site Structure. In *The Bandelier Archaeological Survey*, ed. R. P. Powers and J. D. Orcutt, pp. 309–388. Intermountain Cultural Resources Management Professional Paper No. 57. National Park Service, Santa Fe, NM.

VanPool, C. S., T. L. VanPool, and D. A. Phillips Jr. (editors)

2006 *Religion in the Prehispanic Southwest.* Altamira Press, Lanham, MD.

Varien, M. D.

1999a Regional Context: Architecture, Settlement Patterns, and Abandonment. Chap. 21 of *The Sand Canyon Archaeological Project: Site Testing* [html title], ed. M. D. Varien. http://www.crowcanyon.org/sitetesting.

1999b *Sedentism and Mobility in a Social Landscape: Mesa Verde and Beyond.* University of Arizona Press, Tucson.

2010 The Depopulation of the Northern San Juan Region: A Historical Perspective. In *Leaving Mesa Verde: Peril and Change in the Thirteenth-Century Southwest*, ed. T. A. Kohler, M. D. Varien, and A. Wright, pp. 1–33. University of Arizona Press, Tucson.

Varien, M. D., and S. G. Ortman

2005 Accumulations Research in the Southwest United States: Middle-range Theory for Big-picture Problems. *World Archaeology* 37(1):132–155.

Varien, M. D., S. G. Ortman, T. A. Kohler, D. M. Glowacki, and C. D. Johnson

2007 Historical Ecology in the Mesa Verde Region: Results from the Village Project. *American Antiquity* 72(2):273–299.

Varien, M. D., S. G. Ortman, S. C. Ryan, and K. A. Kuckelman

2008 Population Dynamics Among Salmon's Northern Neighbors in the Central Mesa Verde Region. In *Chaco's Northern Prodigies: Salmon, Aztec, and the Ascendancy of the Middle San Juan Region After* AD *1100*, ed. P. F. Reed, pp. 351–365. University of Utah Press, Salt Lake City.

Varien, M. D., C. R. Van West, and G. S. Patterson

2000 Competition, Cooperation, and Conflict: Agricultural Production and Community Catchments in the Central Mesa Verde region. *Kiva* 66(1):45–65.

Vierra, B. J.

2008 Research Questions and Conclusions. In *The Land Conveyance and Transfer Data Recovery Project: 7000 Years of Land Use on the Pajarito Plateau,* Vol. 4: *Research Design*, ed. B. J. Vierra and K. M. Schmidt, pp. 313–353. Ecology and Air Quality Group, Los Alamos National Laboratory, NM.

Vierra, B. J., and M. J. Dilley

2008 Coping with Change: Stone Tool Technology on the Pajarito Plateau. In *The Land Conveyance and Transfer Data Recovery Project: 7000 Years of Land Use on the Pajarito Plateau,* Vol. 3: *Artifact and Sample Analyses*, ed. B. J. Vierra, K. M. Schmidt and B. C. Harmon. Ecology and Air Quality Group, Los Alamos National Laboratory, NM.

Vierra, B. J., and R. I. Ford

2006 Early Maize Agriculture in the Northern Rio Grande Valley, New Mexico. In *Histories of Maize*, ed. J. E. Staller, R. H. Tykot, and B. F. Benz, pp. 497–510. Elsevier, New York.

Vierra, B. J., S. R. Hoagland, and W. B. Masse

2006 Culture History of the Pajarito Plateau. In *Archaeological Significance Standards at Los Alamos National Laboratory*, ed. B. J. Vierra and K. M. Schmidt, pp. 67–78. Los Alamos National Laboratory, Los Alamos, NM.

Vierra, B. J., J. E. Nisengard, B. C. Harmon, B. M. Larson, D. C. Curewitz, K. M. Schmidt, P. J. McBride, S. J. Smith, and T. L. Binzen

2002 *Excavations at a Coalition Period Pueblo (LA 4624) on Mesita del Buey, Los Alamos National Laboratory.* NMCRIS No. 80127. Department of Energy. Copies available from LA-UR-02-5929.

Vierra, B. J., L. Nordby, and G. Martinez

2003 Nake'muu: Village on the Edge. In *Anasazi Archaeology at the Millennium*, ed. P. F. Reed, pp. 137–144. Proceedings of the Sixth Occasional Anasazi Symposium. Center for Desert Archaeology, Tucson.

Vitzthum, V. J.

2003 A Number No Greater Than the Sum of Its Parts: The Use and Abuse of Heritability. *Human Biology* 75(4):539–558.

Vogt, E.

1976 *Tortillas for the Gods: A Symbolic Analysis of Zinacanteco Rituals*. University of Oklahoma Press, Norman.

Walens, S.

1981 *Feasting with Cannibals: An Essay in Kwakiutl Cosmology*. Princeton University Press, Princeton, NJ.

Wallace, A. F. C.

1956 Revitalization Movements. *American Anthropologist* 58(2):264–281.

Warner, T. J.

1995 *The Dominguez-Escalante Journal: Their Expedition Through Colorado, Utah, Arizona, and New Mexico in 1776*. Trans. F. A. Chavez. University of Utah Press, Salt Lake City.

Watkins, L.

1984 *A Grammar of Kiowa*. Studies in the Anthropology of North American Indians. University of Nebraska Press, Lincoln.

Weaver, D. S.

1976 Analysis of Skeletal Remains from Tijeras Pueblo. Report submitted to the Maxwell Museum and the University of New Mexico Archaeological Field School.

Webster, L. D.

1997 Effects of European Contact on Textile Production and Exchange in the North American Southwest: A Pueblo Case Study. Ph.D. dissertation, University of Arizona, Tucson.

Weissner, P.

1983 Style and Social Information in Kalahari San Projectile Points. *American Antiquity* 48:253–276.

Welsch, R. L., and J. E. Terrell

1992 Language and Culture on the North Coast of New Guinea. *American Anthropologist* 94(3):568–600.

Wendorf, F.

1953 Excavations at Te'ewi. In *Salvage Archaeology in the Chama Valley, New Mexico*, ed. F. Wendorf, pp. 34–93. Monographs No. 17. School of American Research, Santa Fe, NM.

1954 A Reconstruction of Northern Rio Grande Prehistory. *American Anthropologist* 56(2):200–227.

Wendorf, F., and E. K. Reed

1955 An Alternative Reconstruction of Northern Rio Grande Prehistory. *El Palacio* 62(5–6):131–173.

White, L. A.

1942 *The Pueblo of Santa Ana*. Memoirs No. 60. American Anthropological Association, Washington, DC.

1960 The World of the Keresan Pueblo Indians. In *Culture in History: Essays in Honor of Paul Radin*, ed. S. Diamond, pp. 53–64. Columbia University Press, New York.

1962 *The Pueblo of Sia, New Mexico*. Smithsonian Institution, Washington, DC.

White, T. D.

1992 *Prehistoric Cannibalism at Mancos 5MTUMR-2346*. Princeton University Press, Princeton, NJ.

Whiteley, P. M.

1988 *Deliberate Acts: Changing Hopi Culture Through the Oraibi Split*. University of Arizona Press, Tucson.

Whitley, D. S.

2008 Archaeological Evidence for Conceptual Metaphors as Enduring Knowledge Structures. *Time & Mind* 1(1):7–30.

Whittlesey, S. M.
2009 Mountains, Mounds and Meaning: Metaphor in the Hohokam Cultural Landscape. In *The Archaeology of Meaningful Places*, ed. B. J. Bowser and M. N. Zedeno, pp. 73–89. University of Utah Press, Salt Lake City.

Whorf, B. L., and G. L. Trager
1937 The Relationship of Uto-Aztecan and Tanoan. *American Anthropologist* 39:609–624.

Wilcox, D. R., D. A. Gregory, and J. B. Hill
2007 Zuni in the Puebloan and Southwestern Worlds. In *Zuni Origins: Toward a New Synthesis of Southwestern Archaeology*, ed. D. A. Gregory and D. R. Wilcox, pp. 165–209. University of Arizona Press, Tucson.

Wilhelm, H. G. H.
1992 Germans in Ohio. In *To Build in a New Land: Ethnic Landscapes in North America*, ed. A. G. Noble, pp. 60–78. Johns Hopkins University Press, Baltimore.

Wilshusen, R. H.
1986 The Relationship Between Abandonment Mode and Ritual Use in Pueblo I Anasazi Protokivas. *Journal of Field Archaeology* 13:245–254.
1988 Architectural Trends in Prehistoric Anasazi Sites During AD 600 to 1200. In *Dolores Archaeological Program: Supporting Studies: Additive and Reductive Technologies*, ed. E. Blinman, C. J. Phagan, and R. H. Wilshusen, pp. 599–633. Bureau of Reclamation, Engineering and Research Center, Denver.
1989 Unstuffing the Estufa: Ritual Floor Features in Anasazi Pit Structures and Pueblo Kivas. In *The Architecture of Social Integration in Prehistoric Pueblos*, ed. W. D. Lipe and M. Hegmon, pp. 89–111. Occasional Papers No. 1. Crow Canyon Archaeological Center, Cortez, CO.

Wilshusen, R. H., and S. G. Ortman
1999 Rethinking the Pueblo I Period in the San Juan Drainage: Aggregation, Migration, and Cultural Diversity. *Kiva* 64(3):369–399.

Wilshusen, R. H., and C. D. Wilson
1995 Reformatting the Social Landscape in the Late Pueblo I–Early Pueblo II Period: The Cedar Hill Data in Regional Context. In *The Cedar Hill Special Treatment Project: Late Pueblo I, Early Navajo, and Historic Occupations in Northwestern New Mexico*, ed. R. H. Wilshusen, pp. 43–80. La Plata Archaeological Consultants, Dolores, CO.

Wilson, C. D.
2008a Examination of Trends for Galisteo Black-on-white. In *Chasing Chaco and the Southwest: Papers in Honor of Frances Joan Mathien*, ed. R. N. Wiseman, T. C. O'Laughlin, C. T. Snow, and C. Travis, pp. 207–215. Archaeological Society of New Mexico No. 34. Albuquerque.
2008b Ceramic Analysis for the Land Conveyance and Transfer Project, Los Alamos National Laboratory. In *The Land Conveyance and Transfer Data Recovery Project: 7000 Years of Land Use on the Pajarito Plateau*, Vol. 3: *Artifact and Sample Analyses*, ed. B. J. Vierra and K. M. Schmidt. Ecology and Air Quality Group, Los Alamos National Laboratory, Los Alamos, NM.

Wilson, G. P.
2006 *Guide to Ceramic Identification: Northern Rio Grande and Galisteo Basin to AD 1700.* 2nd ed. Technical Series Bulletin 12. Laboratory of Anthropology, Santa Fe, NM.

Windes, T. C.
1992 Blue Notes: The Chacoan Turquoise Industry in the San Juan Basin. In *Anasazi Regional Organization and the Chaco System*, ed. D. E. Doyel, pp. 159–168. Anthropological Papers No. 5. Maxwell Museum of Anthropology, Albuquerque.
2007 Gearing Up and Piling On: Early Great Houses in the Interior San Juan Basin. In *The Architecture of Chaco Canyon, New Mexico*, ed. S. H. Lekson, pp. 45–92. University of Utah Press, Salt Lake City.
Windes, T. C., and P. J. McKenna
2006 The Kivas of Tsama (LA 908). In *Southwestern Interludes: Papers in Honor of Charlotte J., and Theodore R. Frisbie*, ed. R. N. Wiseman, T. C. O'Laughlin, and C. T. Snow, pp. 233–253. Vol. 32. Archaeological Society of New Mexico, Albuquerque.
Wiseman, R. N.
1995 Reassessment of the Dating of the Pojoaque Grant Site (LA 835), a Key Site of the Rio Grande Developmental Period. In *Of Pots and Rocks: Papers in Honor of A. Helene Warren*, ed. M. S. Duran and D. T. Kirkpatrick, pp. 237–248. Papers of the Archaeological Society of New Mexico 21. Albuquerque.
Wiseman, R. N., and J. A. Darling
1986 The Bronze Trail Site Group: More Evidence for a Cerrillos-Chaco Turquoise Connection. In *Collected Papers in Honor of James G. Bain*, ed. A. V. Poore, pp. 115–143. Papers of the Archaeological Society of New Mexico 12. Ancient City Press, Santa Fe.
Wobst, H. M.
1977a Boundary Conditions for Paleolithic Social Systems: A Simulation Approach. *American Antiquity* 39:147–178.
1977b Stylistic Behavior and Information Exchange. In *Papers for the Director: Research Essays in Honor of James B. Griffin*, ed. C. E. Cleland, pp. 317–342. Anthropological Papers No. 67. Museum of Anthropology, University of Michigan, Ann Arbor.
Wood, J. W., G. R. Milner, H. C. Harpending, and K. M. Weiss
1992 The Osteological Paradox. *Current Anthropology* 33:343–370.
Wood, W. R.
1971 *Biesterfeldt: A Post-Contact Coalescent Site on the Northeastern Plains*. Smithsonian Contributions to Anthropology 15. Smithsonian Institution Press, Washington, DC.
Woolf, G.
1998 *Becoming Roman: The Origins of Provincial Civilization in Gaul*. Cambridge University Press, Cambridge.
Wormington, H. M.
1955 *A Reappraisal of the Fremont Culture*. Proceedings No. 1. Denver Museum of Natural History.
Wright, A. M.
2010 The Climate of the Depopulation of the Northern Southwest. In *Leaving Mesa Verde: Peril and Change in the Thirteenth-Century Southwest*, ed. T. A. Kohler, M. D. Varien, and A. M. Wright, pp. 75–101. University of Arizona Press, Tucson.
Wroth, W.
2000 Ute Civilization in Prehistory and the Spanish Colonial Period. In *Ute Indian Arts and Culture*, ed. W. Wroth, pp. 53–72. Colorado Springs Fine Art Center.

Yava, A.

1978 *Big Falling Snow: A Tewa-Hopi Indian's Life and Time, and the History and Traditions of His People*. University of New Mexico Press, Albuquerque.

Young, G. A.

2001 Intertribal Religious Movements. In *Handbook of North American Indians,* Vol. 13, Pt. 2: *Plains*, ed. R. J. Demallie, pp. 996–1010. Smithsonian Institution, Washington, DC.

Yumitani, Y.

1998 A Phonology and Morphology of Jemez Towa. Ph.D. dissertation, University of Kansas.

Zedeño, M. N.

1994b *Sourcing Prehistoric Ceramics at Chodistaas Pueblo, Arizona: The Circulation of People and Pots in the Grasshopper Region*. Anthropological Papers of the University of Arizona 58. University of Arizona Press, Tucson.

Index

Numbers in italics refer to tables.